POPULATION

An Introduction to Concepts and Issues
Fourth Edition

John R. Weeks
San Diego State University

Wadsworth Publishing Company
Belmont, California
A Division of Wadsworth, Inc.

To Deanna

Sociology Editor: Serina Beauparlant
Production: Greg Hubit Bookworks
Manuscript Editor: Deanna H. Weeks
Copy Editor: Patricia Talbot Harris
Technical Illustrations: Ayxa Art, Larry Jansen, Warner-Cotter Company
Print Buyer: Randy Hurst

© 1989 by Wadsworth, Inc. All rights reserved. No part of this
book may be reproduced, stored in a retrieval system, or
transcribed, in any form or by any means, electronic, mechanical,
photocopying, recording, or otherwise, without the prior written
permission of the publisher, Wadsworth Publishing Company,
Belmont, California 94002, a division of Wadsworth, Inc.

The cover illustration shows countries of the world in proportion
to population. Data from United Nations Monthly Bulletin of
Statistics 31 (6), June 1977, Table 1.

The quotation on page 288 is from "Sandra" by Barry Manilow
and Enoch Anderson, reprinted with permission, © 1974
Kamakazi Music Corp.

Printed in the United States of America
2 3 4 5 6 7 8 9 10—93 92 91 90 89

Library of Congress Cataloging in Publication Data

Weeks, John Robert, 1944–
    Population: an introduction to concepts and issues.

    Bibliography: p. 505
    Includes index.
    1. Population.   I. Title.
HB871.W43 1989   304.6   88-37833
ISBN 0-534-10122-4

BRIEF TABLE OF CONTENTS

DETAILED TABLE OF CONTENTS

PREFACE

Population growth in the 1950s and 1960s could have been likened to a run-away train without an engineer, veering perilously close to a collision course with shortages of food and resources. That specter was altered somewhat by the events of the 1970s, especially by a few hopeful signs of a downturn in the birth rates of several large developing nations. In the 1980s, and as we move into the 1990s the imagery has changed from the collision course to something equally terrifying. We are faced with a situation analogous to an immense locomotive hurtling down the track at a speed faster than the roadbed can tolerate. The engineer is groping for the brakes, but if and when those brakes are fully applied, the train will still cover a huge distance before it comes to a halt. How much havoc will the charging locomotive of population wreak before it stops, and what condition will we be in at that point? These are two of the most important questions that face the world.

Over the years I have found that most people are either blissfully unaware of the enormous impact that population growth and change have on their lives, or else they have heard so many horror stories about impending doom that they are nearly overwhelmed whenever they think of population growth. My purpose in this book is to shake you out of your lethargy (if you are one of those types), without necessarily scaring you in the process. I will introduce you to the basic concepts of population studies and help you develop your own demographic perspective, enabling you to understand some of the most important issues confronting the world. My intention is to sharpen your perception of population growth and change, to increase your awareness of what is happening and why, and to help prepare you to cope with (and help shape) a future that will be shared with billions more people than there are today.

I wrote this book with a wide audience in mind because I find that students in my classes come from a wide range of academic disciplines and bring with them an incredible variety of viewpoints and backgrounds. No matter who you are, demographic events are influencing your life, and the more you know about them, the better off you will be.

ORGANIZATION AND FEATURES OF THIS BOOK

The book is organized into five parts, each building on the previous one.

Part One "A Demographic Perspective" (Chapters 1–3) introduces you to some major sources of information about population studies and to some major facts and perspectives about population growth. Chapter 1 has been updated for this fourth edition; Chapter 2, "An Overview of the World's Population," has been relocated for the fourth edition (it was previously the third chapter) conforming to the way a majority of people prefer to read the book, and it has been updated to reflect the changing demography of the world. Chapter 3, "Demographic Perspectives," has traded places with Chapter 2 in this fourth edition.

Part Two "Population Processes" (Chapters 4–7) follows the introductory overview and discusses the three basic demographic processes: fertility, mortality, and migration. For this edition, each of these chapters has been updated to reflect current research. Knowledge of the three population processes provides you with the foundation you need to understand why changes occur and what might be done about them.

Part Three In "Population Structure and Characteristics" (Chapters 8 and 9), I discuss the interaction of the population processes and the number of people in a society according to demographic characteristics such as age, sex, race, ethnicity, socioeconomic level, and marital status. Chapters 8 and 9 have been revised and updated. The first nine chapters set the stage for the last seven.

Part Four In "Population and Contemporary Social Issues" (Chapters 10–14), I explore with you the demographic underpinnings of several major issues confronting the world—women and the family, aging, urbanization, economic development, and food and pollution. Each of these chapters has been updated for this edition.

Part Five I conclude with two chapters that make up the section on "Using Your Demographic Perspective." In Chapter 15 I discuss various ways to alter the course of demographic events, and this chapter has been brought up-to-date to reflect the latest changes in government attitudes and policies toward population growth. Chapter 16, "Demographics," is a new chapter in which I review the ways in which demographic information is used in business, social policy, and political planning.

To help increase your understanding of the basic concepts and issues of population studies, the book contains the following special features.

Short Essays   Each chapter contains a short essay on a particular population concept, designed to help the reader better understand current demographic issues.

Main Points   A list of main points appears at the end of each chapter, following the summary, to aid in your review of chapter highlights.

Suggested Readings   At the end of each chapter I have listed five of the most important and more readable references for additional review of the topics covered in that chapter.

Glossary   A glossary in the back of the book defines key population terms. These terms are in boldface type when introduced in the text to signal their appearance in the glossary.

PERSONAL ACKNOWLEDGMENTS

Like most authors, I have an intellectual lineage that I feel is worth tracing. In particular I would like to acknowledge Kingsley Davis, whose standards as a teacher and scholar will always keep me reaching, Judith Blake, Thomas Burch, Carlo Cipolla, Murray Gendell, Nathan Keyfitz, and Samuel Preston. In small and large ways, they have helped me to unravel the mysteries of how the world operates demographically. Thanks is due also to Steve Rutter at Wadsworth Publishing Company, whose idea this book was in the beginning. Sheryl Fullerton at Wadsworth provided key insights for the expansion and updating of this fourth edition. Greg Hubit is owed a large debt of gratitude for his expert work throughout the editing and production phases of both the third and fourth editions of this book. I would also like to thank the users of the earlier editions, including professors from various parts of the country and my own students, for their comments and suggestions. Special thanks go to John, Gregory, and Jennifer for teaching me the costs and benefits of children. They have instructed me, respectively, in the advantages of being first-born, in the coziness of the middle child, and in the joys that immigration can bring to a family. However, the one person who is directly responsible for the fact that the first, second, third, and now the fourth editions were written, and who deserves credit for the book's strengths, is my wife Deanna. Her creativity, good judgment, and hard work in editing the manuscript benefited virtually every page, and I have dedicated the book to her.

OTHER ACKNOWLEDGMENTS

I would like to acknowledge the contributions of Herbert Wong, who provided material for the essay in Chapter 7; and John Weeks, Jr., who did the programming for the population projections in Chapter 8. Portions of Chapter 8 were taken directly from John R. Weeks, *Aging: Introduction to Social Concepts and Issues* (Belmont, CA: Wadsworth), 1984. I express my gratitude to James Palmore and Robert Gardner, of the East-West Population Institute, for allowing me to use material from *Measuring Mortality, Fertility, and Natural Increase* (Honolulu: East-West Center), 1983, in the Appendix.

For their helpful comments and suggestions, I would also like to thank the following: John L. Anderson, University of Louisville; Phillips Cartright, Indiana University; Saad Gadalla, San Diego State University; Roberto Ham-Chande, El Colegio de la Frontera Norte (Mexico); Nan Johnson, Michigan State University; J. William Leasure, San Diego State University; Jerome McKibben, Indiana University; George Simmons, University of Michigan; Glenna Spitze, State University of New York, Albany; and Teresa Sullivan, University of Texas, Austin.

PART ONE
A Demographic Perspective

The study of population has had a changing profile in recent years. The "population explosion" that has occurred since the end of World War II gave rise to a host of doomsday prophecies proclaiming a calamitous end to human society. Although these messages may have been strident, they did hammer out a public consciousness about the quality of our physical and social environment. More recently, a fickle public has been swayed by headlines suggesting that the population explosion is over and that we can now feel free to move on to other matters. Unfortunately, we do not have the luxury of moving on just yet; concern over population pressures is not a fad, and complacency is several decades premature. The population of the world will continue to grow in historically unprecedented numbers for the remainder of our natural lifetimes. The only uncertainty is whether it will substantially slow its rate of increase.

Fortunately, prevailing attitudes in the eighties have demonstrated a distinctly pragmatic streak, and we have witnessed a substantial rise in the practical uses to which population information is put. There is a growing awareness that population change is not something that happens in the abstract; it is taking place all around us, and we each make our own contribution to it. Whether our concern with demography is personal or global, unraveling the "whys" of population growth and change will provide you with a better perspective on population issues and what can (or cannot) be done about them. For example, many people unfamiliar with the complexities of population growth and change are certain that Indians have larger families than Americans do because they do not know about, or cannot obtain, birth control services. Though that may be true for some women and men in India, research into the problem there indicates that many Indian couples actively desire large families. Other people have suggested that the birth rate in the United States is actually too low and that the government should encourage families to have more babies. But research indicates that when people want small families and have the means to achieve that goal, government persuasion is unlikely to bring about much of a rise in fertility in a country.

In order to understand the impact of population growth on your own life and on the future of the world, you must first know how populations are studied. In Chapter 1, I will introduce you to some of the basic terms and sources of data used in population studies. Then, in Chapter 2 I will review the major global trends in population growth so that you will have a clear mental image of the population explosion, which is an irresistible force for social change all over the world. We cannot go very far on that global journey, however, without a set of perspectives that organize population information into a meaningful framework. I try to do this for you in Chapter 3.

CHAPTER 1
Introduction

Six billion people will be sharing the world with us by the year 2000. This is a big jump from the 4 billion competing for space in 1980, which number, in turn, was up from 2.5 billion in only 1950. This phenomenon is unprecedented, and we are being forced to grapple with issues in heretofore uncharted territory. Primary among our concerns, for example, is the fact that coping with growth will consume an increasing amount of the world's resources. This massive increase in population density is a major contributor to concerns about energy sources, housing shortages, rampant hunger, pollution, inflation, and unemployment. In order to deal intelligently with a future that will be shared with billions more people than there are today, we have to understand why the populations of most countries are growing (and why some are not) and what happens to societies as their patterns of birth, death, or migration change. In recent years we have heard pessimists argue that population growth is a "bomb" about to explode with catastrophic consequences. On the other hand, optimists say that population growth is not really as threatening as it seems and that problems could be solved with more food, new technologies, or better distribution of resources. Either way, people are concerned about a future that they know will be altered by the consequences of population change—be it growth (as in most places) or decline (as in a few places). Understanding these and a wide range of related issues is the business of **demography**—the science of population.

Demography is concerned with virtually everything that influences, or can be influenced by, population size, distribution, processes, structure, or characteristics. Remember that worldwide issues are really the sum of millions, indeed billions, of individual decisions and personal events. For example, everyone experiences at least two of the basic demographic processes—they are born and they die. In between, most will have children of their own, and most are likely to migrate at least once. In addition, the lines at the supermarket, the price of gas at the pump, the chances that you will marry, have children, and divorce, the kind of housing you find, the choices that you might have for a mid-life career change, and the kind of social support you can expect in old age are only a few examples of the tremendously broad demographic foundation of our lives.

As you will see, population changes affect our lives in a variety of ways, many of which may seem unrelated to population at first glance. The diet of the average American, for example, has been influenced by the increase in the proportion of women who work and by the decline in the birth rate. These demographic trends have contributed to an increased demand for packaged and prepared foods and a decline in the consumption of eggs and milk (Rizek, 1982). Consider, too, that privacy and solitude are more difficult to find as population growth has combined with technology to shrink the world. For example, the number of visitors to the United States increased from 288,000 per year in 1950 to 8,405,400 in 1985 (a 2,819 percent increase) and the number of telephone calls to and from the United States grew from less than 1 million to more than 428 million per year in that same period (U.S. Department of Commerce, 1986; U.S. News and World Report, 1977). More than a century ago, Henry David Thoreau said, "I would rather sit on a pumpkin and have it all to myself than be crowded on a velvet cushion." By the 1960s, however, his Walden Pond had been gobbled up by the Boston Metropolitan Area (Cook, 1964), and, in all likelihood, Thoreau's ghost would now have to share his pumpkin, let alone a velvet cushion.

WHY STUDY DEMOGRAPHY?

One of the most compelling reasons to study demography is that population growth can compound and magnify, if not create, a wide variety of social, economic, and political problems. Lester Brown and his associates at the Worldwatch Institute in Washington, D.C. have identified some of the problems that in their opinion are associated with the growth of the world's population. I have summarized the more significant ones.

Food Security None of the basic resources required to expand food output—land, water, energy, fertilizer—can be considered abundant today. Third World countries with rapidly rising food demands and small oil reserves may have trouble continuing to feed their populations. Even now, in sub-Saharan Africa, food production is not keeping pace with population growth.

Pollution As the human population has increased, its potential for disrupting the earth's **ecosystem** has grown. The Mediterranean Sea now serves as a sewer for over 400 million people, and air pollution is a major source of environmental degradation as well as a direct threat to human health.

Inflation Inflation results when demand exceeds supply. As the population has grown, the result frequently has been scarcity-induced inflation, aggravated in third-world countries by governments borrowing money to meet the needs and demands of a growing population.

Housing As a result of the swelling demand for houses, the costs of land, lumber, cement, and fuel have risen beyond the financial means of many of the world's 5 billion people.

Income With the perceptible economic slowdown that has occurred in most of the world since the 1970s, population growth may offset all economic growth in some countries.

Energy Every person added to the world's population requires energy to prepare food, to provide clothing and shelter, and to fuel economic life. Each increment in demand is another claim on shrinking energy reserves, forcing further global adjustments in the use of energy.

Unemployment With current technologies, economists estimate that countries experiencing a 3 percent rate of population growth require a 9 percent rate of economic growth just to maintain employment at the current level. In many countries of the world population is skyrocketing while economic growth is stagnating, thus intensifying problems of unemployment.

Literacy In many countries of Asia, Africa, and Latin America, the number of illiterates is rising as population grows more rapidly than schools can be built and staffed with teachers. In parts of the Third World, a veritable tidal wave of youngsters has overwhelmed the schools.

Individual Freedom As more and more people require space and resources on this planet, more and more rules and regulations are required to supervise individual use of the earth's resources for the common good.

Source: Adapted from L. Brown et al., State of the World, 1988 (New York: W. W. Norton & Co., 1988) and L. R. Brown, P. L. McGrath, and B. Stoke, 1976. "The population problem in 22 dimensions," The Futurist, October, 238–45. Portions were reprinted by permission of The Futurist, published by the World Future Society, 4916 St. Elmo Avenue, Washington, D.C. 20014.

Most Americans are well aware of the substantial migration (legal and undocumented) from Mexico, and most can readily grasp the idea that people from a developing nation would prefer to earn the higher wages that prevail in the highly industrialized nations. Less obvious is the fact that demographic trends in both Mexico and the United States are contributing greatly to that migration stream. In Mexico, high rates of population growth have made it impossible for the economy to generate enough jobs for each year's crop of new workers. Thus, high unemployment in Mexico makes migration attractive—in effect, workers feel "pushed" out. Meanwhile, in the United States, low rates of population growth have left open many jobs at the low end of the economic ladder into which foreign laborers can fit, adding to the attractiveness of migration for people in a developing society where job prospects are minimal—they feel "pulled" to where the jobs are.

On another front, the population of the world in the 1980s is increasing by a quarter of a million people per day, and that rapid growth is reflected in the political instability of several regions of the world. Throughout the Middle East, for example, we can see with special clarity that demography has been crucial. It was, in part, pressure from population growth that encouraged oil-producing nations to think about raising prices in order to ensure a larger share of resources for their own nations. Also, the migration of poor rural peasants to the cities of Iran, especially Tehran, contributed to the political revolution in that country in 1978 (Kazemi, 1980). Further, one reason for the increased visibility of the Palestine Liberation Organization over time has been the very high birth rate among Palestinian refugees. Meanwhile, in Central America, population growth has created elbow-room problems for nearly all nations, and the result is conflict and political turbulence. Population growth is, of course, not the only source of trouble in the world, and its impact often is largely *incendiary*—igniting other dilemmas that face human society (Davis, 1984a). Increased scarcity of resources and economic inequality among nations are frequent sources of conflict, but these problems are fanned by and worsened by population growth (Choucri, 1984).

These are only some among many ways in which population influences people's lives, and as I explore with you the causes and consequences of population growth and the uses to which such knowledge can be applied, you will need to know about the sources of demographic data. What is the empirical base of our understanding of the relationship between population and society?

SOURCES OF DEMOGRAPHIC DATA

In order to analyze the demography of a particular society, we need to know how many people live there, how they are distributed geographically, how many are being born, how many are dying, how many are moving in, and how many are moving out. That, of course, is only the beginning. If we want to unravel the mysteries of why things are as they are and not just describe how they are, we have to know about the social, psychological, economic, and even physical characteristics of the people being studied. Let me begin the discussion, however, with the sources of basic information about the numbers of living people, births, deaths, and migrants.

The kind of information that we are looking for is often broken down into three categories: (1) population size and distribution, (2) population processes (fertility, mortality, and migration), and (3) population structure and characteristics. The primary source of data on size and distribution, as well as on structure and characteristics, is the **census of population.** The major source of information on the three population processes is the registration of **vital statistics.** In addition, these sources are often supplemented with data from **sample surveys** as well as historical sources.

Population Censuses

For centuries, governments have wanted to know how many people were under their rule. Rarely has their curiosity been piqued by scientific concern, but rather governments wanted to know who the taxpayers were, or they wanted to identify potential laborers and soldiers. Women and children were usually ignored. The most direct way to find out how many people there are is to count them, and when you do that you are conducting a population census. The United Nation defines a census of population more specifically as "the total process of collecting, compiling and publishing demographic, economic and social data pertaining, at a specified time or times, to all persons in a country or delimited territory" (United Nations, 1958:3). In practice, this does not mean that every person actually is seen and interviewed by a census taker. In most countries it means that one adult in a household answers questions about all the people living in that household. These answers may be written responses to a questionnaire sent by mail or verbal responses to questions asked in person by the census taker.

As far as we know, the earliest governments to undertake censuses of their populations were those in the ancient civilizations of Egypt, Babylonia, China, Palestine, and Rome (Shryock et al., 1973). For about 800 years, citizens of Rome were counted every 5 years for tax and military purposes, and this enumeration was extended to the entire Roman Empire in 5 B.C. The Bible records this event as follows: "In those days a decree went out from Caesar Augustus that all the world should be enrolled. This was the first enrollment, when Quirinius was governor of Syria. And all went to be enrolled, each to his own city" (Luke 2:1–3). You can, of course, imagine the deficiencies of a census that required people to show up at their birthplaces, rather than paying census takers to go out and do the counting.

The disintegration of the Roman Empire ended census-taking activity in the Western world for several centuries. Then in A.D. 1086, William the Conqueror of England ordered an enumeration of all the landed wealth in his newly conquered territory—as with many early censuses, William's major purpose was to determine how much revenue the landowners owed. Data were recorded in the Domesday Book, the term "domesday" being a corruption of the word doomsday, which is the day of final judgment. The census document was so named because once entered, the information was considered final and irrevocable. A few sporadic censuses were taken between the eleventh and seventeenth centuries, but it was not until the eighteenth century that censuses once again were conducted on a regular basis. Sweden began the practice of regular census taking in 1749, followed by Norway and Denmark in 1760 and the United States in 1790 (Kaplan and Van Valey, 1980).

By the latter part of the nineteenth century, the statistical approach to understanding business and government affairs had started to take root in the Western world (Cassedy, 1969). The population census began to be viewed as a potential tool for finding out more than just how many people there were and where they lived. Governments began to ask questions about age, marital status, whether people were employed and what their occupation was, literacy, and so forth.

Census data (in combination with other statistics) have become the "lenses through which we form images of our society." Frederick Jackson Turner announced this famous view on the significance of the closing of the frontier on the basis of data from the 1890 census. Our national self-image today is confirmed or challenged by numbers that tell of drastic changes in the family, the reversal of rural-to-urban migration, and many other trends. Winston Churchill observed that "first we shape our buildings and then they shape us. The same may be said of our statistics" (Alonso and Starr, 1982:30). The potential power behind the numbers that censuses produce can be gauged by public reaction to a census. In Germany, the enumeration of 1983 was postponed because of public concern that the census was prying unduly into private lives. Protests have occurred in England, Switzerland, and the Netherlands as well. In the latter case, the census was actually canceled following a survey indicating that the majority of the urban population would not cooperate (Robey, 1983).

In the decade 1855–64, it is estimated that only about 17 percent of the world's population had actually been counted (Shryock et al., 1973). Since the end of World War II, the United Nations has encouraged countries to enumerate their populations in a census, often providing financial as well as technical aid. As a result, between 1953 and 1964, 78 percent of the world's population (including that of mainland China) was enumerated by census. Based on data published by the United Nations, I have estimated that 55 percent of the world's population was enumerated between 1965 and 1974, and between 1975 and 1984, 96 percent of the world's population either was counted or was expected to be (United Nations, 1974; 1979). Throughout the world, there has been a fairly clear relationship between a country's level of economic advancement and the taking of censuses. Reasons for this relationship are numerous, but the most obvious is cost (the 1980 census in the United States had a $1 billion price tag, and the 1990 census is expected to cost more than $2.6 billion). In the less developed nations, there is less pressure on the government to conduct a census, because the benefits of the undertaking may not appear to outweigh the costs.

Nevertheless, in the early 1980s the world's two largest less developed nations (in fact, the two largest nations regardless of stage of development), China and India, each conducted a census. In July 1982 the Chinese government undertook the most ambitious census in world history when it counted its 1 billion inhabitants. The task itself involved nearly 5 million enumerators—nearly as many people as the entire population of Denmark. The Chinese were aided in their census by the United Nations Fund for Population Activities, and the project cost $200 million. The price tag included the purchase of 29 computers, 21 of them American-made IBM models; previously, census results in China had been tabulated using abacuses and manual methods. (The American census was so much more expensive than the Chinese, by the way, primarily because of the more thorough field checks and data-processing methods built into American census procedures.) One concern of Chinese demographers was that people might be reluctant to answer honestly about family size. Because of population control measures that had been imposed prior to the census, couples might withhold information about more than one child; and because of rationing based on household size, people might list as still alive a relative who had died but whose death had not been recorded, for fear that with fewer people the family would receive less food or be forced to move to a smaller home. However, a census pretest in 1980 had suggested that such fears were exaggerated (Ching, 1982).

1981 was the centennial year for census taking in India—the first census having been taken in 1881 under the supervision of the British. Using "only" 1.5 million enumerators, the 1981 census of India counted 12 million more people than the government had expected to find. These results called into question some of the optimism that Indian officials had expressed during the 1970s over the potential success of the nation's family planning program (Visaria and Visaria, 1981).

In contrast to India's regular census taking, Lebanon has not been enumerated since 1932, when the country was under French colonial rule (Domschke and Goyer, 1986). The most likely reason is that the nearly equal number of Christians and Moslems in the country and the political strife between those groups have combined to make a census a very sensitive political issue. Before the nation was literally torn apart by civil war in the 1980s, the Christians had held a slight majority with respect to political representation. But most people believe that the Moslems now hold the demographic majority. A census could either bolster or deny a group's claim to power and thus create the potential for further divisiveness. Nonetheless, following the Israeli takeover of the southern part of Lebanon in 1982, the Israeli army decided to conduct a census of that region of the country. Each village mayor was asked to complete a questionnaire describing the village population. Questions included the names of men between the ages of 13 and 65, the names of pregnant women, and the number of children and grandchildren per family (San Diego Union, 1983a). Since the majority of the population in that region is Moslem, the census was unlikely to resolve the nation's demographic controversy, but the primarily military purpose of the census was controversial in and of itself. We might also note that censuses historically have been unpopular in that part of the world. The Old Testament of the Bible tells us that in ancient times King David ordered a census of Israel, in which his enumerators counted "one million, one hundred thousand men who drew the sword. . . . But God was displeased with this thing [the census], and he smote Israel. . . . So the Lord sent a pestilence upon Israel; and there fell seventy thousand men of Israel" (1 Chronicles 21). Fortunately, in modern times the advantages of census taking seem more clearly to outweigh the disadvantages. This has been especially true in the United States, where records indicate that no census has been followed directly by a pestilence.

The Census of the United States

A census of population has been taken every 10 years since 1790 in the United States as a part of the constitutional mandate that seats in the House of Representatives be apportioned on the bases of population size and distribution. But even in 1790 the government used the census to find out more than just how many people there were. The census asked for the names of head of family, free white males aged 16 years and older, free white females, slaves, and other persons (Shryock et al., 1973:22). The census questions were reflections of the social importance of those categories.

For the first 100 years of census taking in the United States, the population was enumerated by U.S. marshals. In 1880 special census agents were hired for the first time, and by 1902 the Census Bureau had become a permanent part of the government bureaucracy (Francese, 1979). Beyond a core of demographic and housing information, the questions asked on the census have fluctuated according to the concerns of the time. Interest in international migration, for example, peaked in 1920 just before the passage of a restrictive immigration law (see Chapter 15), and the census in that year added a battery of questions about the foreign-born population. In 1970, as the number of disabled people in the country increased—especially young men disabled in the Vietnam War—questions about disabilities were asked for the first time since 1910. Questions are added and deleted by the Census Bureau by consultation with other government officials and census statistics users. For example, the Census Bureau considered deleting the questions on disability from the 1980 census, but there was overwhelming support for the question from people who had used the data from the 1970 census, so the item was retained in 1980 (U.S. Bureau of the Census, 1979a). Political motives have outweighed scientific ones with respect to the 1990 census as well. In 1987 the U.S. Office of Management and Budget proposed to eliminate several questions from the 1990 census form, even though they had been asked in previous population counts. Most of the threatened questions were ultimately retained, but only after supporters of each question were able to demonstrate the legislative mandates (regardless of the scientific uses) that required each piece of information to be asked in the census.

A tremendous amount of planning goes into every census. The 1990 census, for example, was kicked off by the U.S. Bureau of the Census on October 1, 1983—before most of the information from the 1980 census had yet been released—and by 1988 the final dress rehearsal had already been completed in part of St. Louis, Missouri and portions of rural Missouri. Other test censuses had been conducted in Jersey City, New Jersey and in Tampa, Florida in 1985; in several areas of Los Angeles, California in 1986; and in rural North Dakota in 1987.

The census is designed as a complete enumeration of the population, but only a few of the questions are actually asked of everyone. For reasons of economy, most items in the census questionnaire are administered to a sample of people. From 1790 through 1930, all questions were asked of all applicable persons, but as the American population grew, the savings involved in sampling grew. Fortunately, there has been no significant loss in accuracy (after all, a 20 percent sample of 220 million people in 1980 still resulted in responses from 44 million people).

The items of information obtained from everyone are often called the *100-*

percent items and include basic demographic and housing characteristics; the 100-percent (short-form) questionnaire from the 1990 census is reproduced as Figure 1.1. The first page asks that everyone in the household be listed by name, which allows the Census Bureau to check for duplicate listings of people (such as college students away from home). Then, information is requested for each person in the household regarding his or her relationship to the head of household (who is to be listed in column 1), sex, racial and ethnic identification, age, marital status, and Spanish/Hispanic origin. The remaining questions relate to characteristics of the housing unit. In 1980, about 79 percent of all households received only this short form to fill out, whereas in 1990 about 88 percent of households will receive the short form.

Approximately 12 percent of households will be asked to complete a longer, more detailed questionnaire. In addition to the 100-percent items, these long forms include questions on the following population and housing items:

Population	Housing
School enrollment	Type of unit
Educational attainment	Stories in building and presence of elevator
State or foreign country of birth	
Citizenship and year of immigration	Year built
Current language and English proficiency	Year moved into this house
Ancestry	Acreage and crop sales
Place of residence 5 years ago	Source of water
Activity 5 years ago	Sewage disposal
Veteran status and period of service	Heating equipment
Presence of disability or handicap	Fuels used for house heating, water heating, and cooking
Children ever born	
Employment status last week	Costs of utilities and fuels
Hours worked last week	Complete kitchen facilities
Place of work	Number of bedrooms
Travel time to work	Number of bathrooms
Means of transportation to work	Basement
Persons in carpool	Telephone
Year last worked	Air conditioning
Industry	Number of automobiles
Occupation	Number of light trucks and vans
Class of worker	Homeowner shelter costs for mortgage, real estate taxes, and hazard insurance
Work in 1989 and weeks looking for work in 1989	
Amount of income by source and total income in 1989	

Source: U.S. Bureau of the Census, Form D-2.

Figure 1.1   The 1990 U.S. Census Questionnaire

1990 Census of Population and Housing

A message from the Director Bureau of the Census

We are conducting the 21st decennial census of our Nation. Starting in 1790, when Thomas Jefferson directed the first decennial census, the census has monitored the vital signs of our great country. To preserve this legacy, I hope that we can count on you to participate by completing this form.

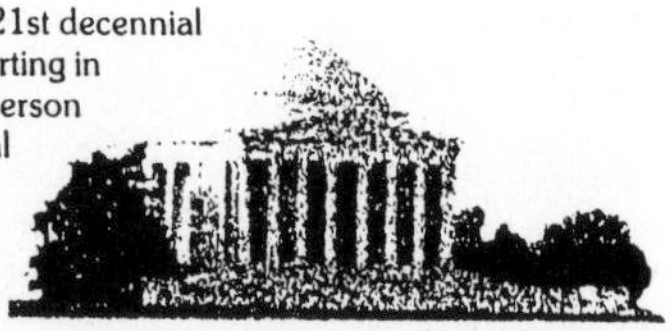

You may ask, "Why should I count myself in the census?" Although a law requires that you respond to the census, I hope that you choose to respond knowing that the results of the census are used to ensure fair representation in our government and to improve the quality of your life. For the sake of our Nation and your community, take this opportunity to put yourself in the picture by responding to the Bicentennial Census.

Perhaps you may be concerned that by participating, your name and information soon will be available to others. That is not the case. Federal law protects the confidentiality of your responses for the next 72 years, or until April 1, 2062. Until then, no one sees your completed form except Census Bureau workers, who are sworn to hold it in confidence and can be fined and/or imprisoned for disclosing information.

The census is vitally important, so stand right up for who you are. You do so by filling out this form accurately and completely. Kindly **return it by Census Day, April 1, 1990,** or as close to that date as possible. PLEASE DO MAIL IT BACK in the envelope provided. Doing so will save the expense and inconvenience of a personal visit from a census taker.

Your answers are confidential

By law (Title 13, U.S. Code), census employees are subject to fine and/or imprisonment for any disclosure of your answers. Only after 72 years can your individual census form become available to other government agencies or the public. The same law requires that you answer the questions to the best of your knowledge.

Para personas de habla hispana

(For Spanish-speaking persons): SI USTED DESEA UN CUESTIONARIO DEL CENSO EN ESPAÑOL llame a la oficina del censo. El número de teléfono se encuentra en el encasillado de la dirección.

U.S. DEPARTMENT OF COMMERCE
BUREAU OF THE CENSUS

FORM **D-2** (7-6-88)

OMB No. XXXX-XXXX
Approval Expires XX/XX/XX

This is a portion of the latest draft of the 1990 census questionnaire available to us as this book went to press. The final version will not differ much, if at all, from this.

Figure 1.1   (continued)

The 1990 census must count every person at his or her "usual residence." This means the place where the person lives and sleeps most of the time.

1a. List on the numbered lines below the name of each person living here on Sunday, April 1, including all persons staying here who have no other home. If EVERYONE at this address is staying here temporarily and usually lives somewhere else, follow the instructions given in question 1b below.

Include

- Everyone who usually lives here such as family members, housemates and roommates, foster children, roomers, boarders, and live-in employees
- Persons who are temporarily away on a business trip, on vacation, or in a general hospital
- College students who stay here while attending college
- Persons in the Armed Forces who live here
- Newborn babies still in the hospital
- Children in boarding schools below the college level
- Persons who stay here most of the week while working even if they have a home somewhere else
- Persons with no other home who are staying here on April 1

Do NOT include

- Persons who usually live somewhere else

- Persons who are away in an institution such as a prison, mental hospital, or a nursing home
- College students who live somewhere else while attending college
- Persons in the Armed Forces who live somewhere else

- Persons who stay somewhere else most of the week while working

Print last name, first name, and middle initial for each person. Begin on line 1 with the household member (or one of the household members) in whose name this house or apartment is owned, being bought, or rented. If there is no such person, start on line 1 with any adult household member.

	LAST	FIRST	INITIAL		LAST	FIRST	INITIAL
1				7			
2				8			
3				9			
4				10			
5				11			
6				12			

1b. If EVERYONE is staying here only temporarily and usually lives somewhere else, list the name of each person on the numbered lines above, fill this circle ⟶ ○ and print their usual address below. DO NOT PRINT THE ADDRESS LISTED ON THE FRONT COVER.

House number	Street or road/Rural route and box number	Apartment number
City	State	ZIP Code
County or foreign country	Names of nearest intersecting streets or roads	

NOW PLEASE OPEN THE FLAP TO PAGE 2 AND ANSWER ALL QUESTIONS FOR THE FIRST 7 PEOPLE LISTED.

Figure 1.1   (continued)

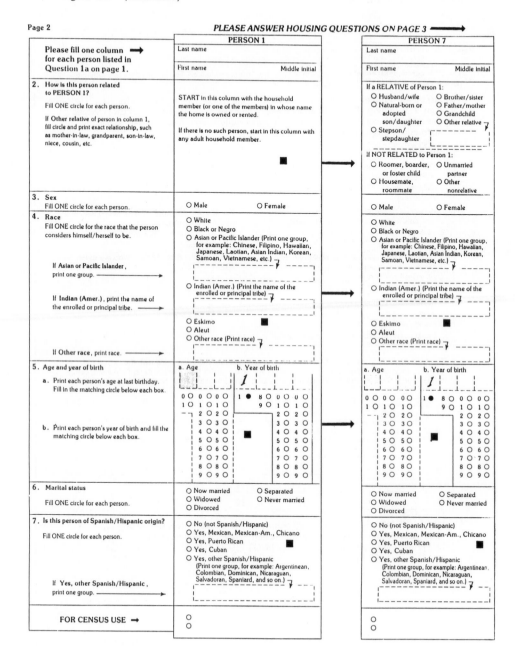

Figure 1.1   (continued)

NOW PLEASE ANSWER QUESTIONS H1a — H7a *FOR YOUR HOUSEHOLD*

H1a. Did you leave anyone out of your list of persons for Question 1a on page 1 because you were not sure if the person should be listed — for example, someone temporarily away on a business trip or vacation, a newborn baby still in the hospital, or a person who stays here once in a while and has no other home?

■   O Yes, please print the name(s) and reason(s). ⌐   O No

_____

b. Did you include anyone in your list of persons for Question 1a on page 1 even though you were not sure that the person should be listed — for example, a visitor who is staying here temporarily or a person who usually lives somewhere else?

O Yes, please print the name(s) and reason(s). ⌐   O No

_____

_____

H2. Which best describes this building? Include all apartments, flats, etc., even if vacant.

O A mobile home or trailer
O A one-family house detached from any other house
O A one-family house attached to one or more houses
O A building with 2 apartments
O A building with 3 or 4 apartments
O A building with 5 to 9 apartments
O A building with 10 to 19 apartments
O A building with 20 to 49 apartments
■ O A building with 50 or more apartments
O Other

H3. How many rooms do you have in this house or apartment? Do NOT count bathrooms, porches, balconies, foyers, halls, or half-rooms.

O 1 room   O 4 rooms   O 7 rooms
■ O 2 rooms   O 5 rooms   O 8 rooms
O 3 rooms   O 6 rooms   O 9 or more rooms

H4. Is this house or apartment —

O Owned by you or someone in this household with a mortgage or loan?
O Owned by you or someone in this household free and clear (without a mortgage)?
O Rented for cash rent?
O Occupied without payment of cash rent?

If this is a ONE-FAMILY HOUSE —

H5a. Is this house on ten or more acres?

O Yes   O No

b. Is there a business (such as a store or barber shop) or a medical office on this property?

O Yes   O No

Answer only if you or someone in this household OWNS OR IS BUYING this house or apartment —

H6. What is the value of this property; that is, how much do you think this house and lot or condominium unit would sell for if it were for sale?

O Less than $10,000   O $70,000 to $74,999
O $10,000 to $14,999   O $75,000 to $79,999
O $15,000 to $19,999   O $80,000 to $89,999
O $20,000 to $24,999   O $90,000 to $99,999
O $25,000 to $29,999   O $100,000 to $124,999
O $30,000 to $34,999   O $125,000 to $149,999
O $35,000 to $39,999   ■ O $150,000 to $174,999
O $40,000 to $44,999   O $175,000 to $199,999
O $45,000 to $49,999   O $200,000 to $249,999
O $50,000 to $54,999   O $250,000 to $299,999
O $55,000 to $59,999   O $300,000 to $399,999
O $60,000 to $64,999   O $400,000 to $499,999
O $65,000 to $69,999   O $500,000 or more

Answer only if you PAY RENT for this house or apartment —

H7a. What is the monthly rent?

O Less than $80   O $375 to $399
O $80 to $99   O $400 to $424
O $100 to $124   O $425 to $449
O $125 to $149   O $450 to $474
O $150 to $174   O $475 to $499
O $175 to $199   O $500 to $524
O $200 to $224   O $525 to $549
O $225 to $249   O $550 to $599
O $250 to $274   ■ O $600 to $649
O $275 to $299   O $650 to $699
O $300 to $324   O $700 to $749
O $325 to $349   O $750 to $999
O $350 to $374   O $1,000 or more

b. Does the monthly rent include any meals?

O Yes   O No

FOR CENSUS USE

A. DO   **ID**

0 0 0 0	0 0 0	0 0 0 0
1 1 1 1	1 1 1	1 1 1 1
2 2 2 2	2 2 2	2 2 2 2
3 3 3 3	3 3 3	3 3 3 3
4 4 4 4	4 4 4	4 4 4 4
5 5 5 5	5 5 5	5 5 5 5
6 6 6 6	6 6 6	6 6 6 6
7 7 7 7	7 7 7	7 7 7 7
8 8 8 8	8 8 8	8 8 8 8
9 9 9 9	9 9 9	9 9 9 9

B. Total persons

0 0
1 1
2 2
3
4
5
6
■ 7
8
9

C. Type of unit

Occupied   Vacant
O First form   1 O Regular
O Cont'n   2 O Usual home elsewhere

D1. Vacancy status
O For rent
O For sale only
O Rented or sold, not occupied
O For seas/rec/occ
O For mig workers
O Other vacant

D2. Is this unit boarded up?
O Yes
O No
■

E. Months vacant
O Less than 1
O 1 up to 2
O 2 up to 6
O 6 up to 12
O 12 up to 24
O 24 or more

F. Complete after
O ENUM   O IN/T
1 O LR   O C/O
O POP/F   O RE
O EDIT   O QA
O TC   O GP
O JIC 1   O JIC 2

G.Cov. O 1b   O 1a   O 7   O H1

Coverage Error   Although in theory the regular decennial (every 10 years) census counts everyone, in reality there are some people who are missed (this is called **coverage error**). In the 1970 census, for example, it is estimated that about 5 million people were missed (Siegel, 1974), representing a little more than 2 percent of the total. The 1980 census was even better, missing only an estimated 1.4 percent of the total population (Passel et al., 1983). Included in this total were more than 2 million undocumented migrants—a fact that has created continual controversy. Indeed, prior to the 1980 census date, a group called the Federation for American Immigration Reform (FAIR) filed suit to block the inclusion of any undocumented aliens in the count. FAIR contended that by including illegal aliens, the figures used for congressional representation and reapportionment would dilute the impact of citizens and give an undue number of seats in Congress to states like California and New York where there are considerable numbers of illegal aliens (Baskin, 1980). In rebuttal, the Census Bureau argued that Congress had clearly indicated that it wanted the census to reflect all people living in an area, regardless of their legal status, since illegal aliens are part of an area's population and burden.

Ultimately, that suit was turned aside by the courts and the 1980 census continued on schedule. The issue of which and how many people were being counted remained, however, especially in those areas with high concentrations of minority group members, since that segment of the population has a historically greater likelihood of being undercounted. In 1970 the Census Bureau estimated that nearly 8 percent of the black population as a whole was undercounted, and the underenumeration for black males aged 25–34 was nearly 20 percent (Siegel, 1974). It is curious to note, however, that in 1980 the greatest undercount was for black males aged 35–45—the same men who had reportedly been undercounted in 1970 when they were 10 years younger.

Undercounting has two components—not finding people in the first place and not motivating people to respond to the questionnaire. Although the Census Bureau was quite innovative in devising ways to reach as many people as possible in the 1980 census, it has been criticized for not paying enough attention to the motivation issue (National Research Council, 1978). Because motivation to respond to the census questionnaire appears to be lower among minority group members than among whites, the Census Bureau established a minority statistics program in conjunction with the 1980 census. Its purpose was to inform minority people about the usefulness of the census data to them and to their particular community, and to assist them in the use of such statistics.

Additionally, ethnic identity was expanded in the 1980 census to 15 categories, an increase from the 9 categories used in 1970. In 1980, the census classified each person according to whether he or she was white, black or Negro, Japanese, Chinese, Pilipino,[1] Korean, Vietnamese, American Indian, Asian Indian, Hawaiian, Guamanian, Samoan, Eskimo, Aleut, or other. A question was also asked about whether a person is of "Spanish/Hispanic origin or descent," with categories Mexican-American, Mexican or Chicano, Puerto Rican, Cuban, and other Spanish. For 1990, many of these categories have been replaced by write-in categories, as can be seen in Figure 1.1.

---

[1] Because there is no "F" sound in the languages of the Philippines, we will spell the name with a P.

How successful were these efforts by the Census Bureau? Estimates from the 1980 census suggest that about 6 percent of the black population was undercounted, compared with the 8 percent already noted for 1970 (Passel et al., 1982). It also appears that the Census Bureau did a better job of counting Hispanics in 1980 than in 1970 (Population Reference Bureau, 1985). There is still room for improvement, but substantial progress has been made, and plans have been made to improve coverage for the 1990 census.

Although it is now apparent that the 1980 census was quite accurate, it was not so obvious shortly after the count had been taken. In a process known as **postcensus local review**, the Census Bureau shared its preliminary population counts with major localities to allow local officials to comment on their accuracy and to ask for an investigation if the population of specific parts of a city or area seemed too low. The result was a highly politicized and publicized series of lawsuits filed by large cities with high percentages of minority group members, claiming that their cities had been undercounted. Detroit, New York City, Baltimore, Philadelphia, Chicago, Newark, and Chester (Pennsylvania) all sued the Census Bureau in federal court to force the bureau to revise its population estimates upward. At stake were millions of dollars of federal revenue that were, at that time, allocated on the basis of total population size.

Interestingly enough, the cases were finally settled not on the issue of accuracy but on the issue of confidentiality of the census data. In order to establish how accurate the census enumeration had been, the cities had wanted the Census Bureau to share the census returns with them so that local officials could match returns with local addresses to determine which households might have been missed. Lawyers for the Census Bureau argued that such a procedure would violate the confidentiality of the census, reduce public trust in the census, and hamper future census-taking efforts. The Supreme Court ultimately agreed, and the cities failed in their effort to have the census results changed. In the meantime, however, data from the 1980 census showed that most of the "missing" people from the large cities were showing up in the suburbs and were not really missing after all.

Let me add that the United States is far from being the only country in which politicians worry that their areas have not been adequately counted. The 1980 census of Brazil counted more than 2 million fewer people than government officials expected, and in a country that has traditionally had a pro-growth policy, the charge was heard that the census had been politically manipulated. To be sure, census takers in Brazil had been presented with some unusual circumstances. One enumerator in Rio de Janeiro swung open a wall icebox in a butcher shop to find a hidden street with houses lining each side. She managed to fill out forms for the residents, but she left without an explanation for why they lived concealed behind that refrigerator door (San Diego Union, 1980a).

Right now you are probably asking yourself how the Census Bureau could ever begin to estimate how many people are missed in the census. Two principal methods are used to evaluate the coverage of the census: The first involves actual case-by-case matching, whereas the second involves a more esoteric approach called *intercensal cohort analysis*. Case-by-case matching can involve either actual reinterviewing or matching records. A reinterview survey consists of selecting a probability sample of households included in the census and matching the people in the sample on a case-by-case basis with the persons enumerated in the census. The assumption is that the more intensive reinterview effort will be more likely than the actual census to get responses from each household and to include all the people within each household. Of course, a limitation is that if a household was missed entirely in the first count, it will also be missed in the reinterview sample. A second method of case-by-case matching consists of comparing lists of people counted in the census with lists obtained from other agencies and organizations.

Intercensal cohort analysis is based on the recognition that people of some ages (especially young adults and more especially young males) are more likely to be missed than people of other ages. Thus, by comparing the number of males aged 20–24 in 1980 with the number of males aged 10–14 in 1970, we can determine whether there are fewer males aged 20–24 in 1980 than we should have expected. By making similar calculations for all ages, we can arrive at an estimate of the possible undercount in certain age and sex categories.

Content Error   Although coverage error is a concern in any census, there can also be problems with the accuracy of the data obtained in the census (**content error**). How many errors are there of reporting, editing, or tabulating? In comparison with other censuses, the United Nations rates the American census as highly accurate, especially with respect to recording age—one of the most important demographic characteristics (United Nations, 1979). The U.S. Census Bureau conducts its own checks on accuracy by comparing the census results with the Current Population Survey (see page 23) and by selecting a sample of people for reinterview in order to see if they give the same answers they gave on the census questionnaire (U.S. Bureau of the Census, 1974; 1975a). By and large, content error is not a problem in the U.S. census, although the data are certainly not 100 percent accurate. In general, data from the United Nations suggest that the more highly developed a country is, the more accurate its census data will be. This fact is probably accounted for especially by the level of education of a population.

Finally, I should note that while the census is aimed at counting and characterizing the population of a given territory at a given time, there are at least two different estimates of population size that can result—the **de facto population** and the **de jure population**. The de facto population counts people who are in a given territory on the census day. The de jure population represents people who "belong" to a given area in some way or another, regardless of whether they were there on the day of the census (Shryock et al., 1973:92). For countries with few foreign workers and where working in another area is rare, the distinction makes little difference. But some countries, such as Switzerland or West Germany, with large numbers of alien workers, have a larger de facto than de jure population. On the other hand, a country such as Mexico, from which migrants regularly leave temporarily to go to the United States, the de jure population is actually greater than the de facto. In the United States, a slightly different concept is used to count people. Americans are enumerated on the basis of "usual residence," which is roughly defined as the place where a person usually sleeps. College students who live away from home, for example, are included at their college address rather than being counted in their parents' household. This is closer to the concept of de jure than de facto, as people with no usual residence (migratory workers, vagrants, and so on) are counted where they are found.

Throughout this text, and whenever you read or hear about reports based on census data, you should keep in mind that often people are categorized in rather arbitrary ways and that the data do not represent any absolute truth. Yet, let me also say that census data generally are of too high a quality to be debunked. A census of population, especially in the United States or another highly developed country, is an incredibly rich reservoir of information about human society, and frequent references will be made to census data throughout this book.

Registration of Vital Events

When you were born, a birth certificate was filled out for you, probably by a clerk in the hospital where you were born. When you die, someone (again, typically a hospital clerk) will fill out a death certificate on your behalf. Standard birth and death certificates used in the United States are shown in Figure 1.2. Births and deaths, as well as marriages, divorces, and abortions, are known as vital events, and when they are recorded by the government and compiled for use they become vital statistics. These statistics are the major source of data on births and deaths, and they are most useful when combined with census data, as I will discuss later in this chapter.

Registration of vital events first began in Europe as a chore of the church. Priests often recorded baptisms, marriages, and deaths, and in recent years historical demographers have used some of the surviving records to try to reconstruct the demographic history of part of Europe (see Wrigley, 1966). An early landmark in the registration of vital events for government purposes was the 1532 English ordinance that mandated parish priests to compile weekly "Bills of Mortality," giving the number and causes of deaths. The purpose of this regular reporting was to keep tabs on the plague epidemic (Shryock et al., 1973; Pollard et al., 1974).

More than 100 years later, in 1662, a Londoner named John Graunt, who is sometimes called the father of demography, analyzed the series of Bills of Mortality in the first known demographic analysis (Sutherland, 1963). Although he was a haberdasher by trade, Graunt used his spare moments to conduct studies that were truly remarkable for his time. He discovered that for every 100 people born in London, only 16 were still alive at age 36 and only 3 at age 66 (Dublin et al., 1949). With these data he uncovered the high incidence of infant mortality in London and found, somewhat to the amazement of people at the time, that there were regular patterns of death in different parts of London. Several years later, in 1693, Edmund Halley (of Halley's Comet fame) became the first scientist to elaborate on the probabilities of death. Although Halley, like Graunt, was a Londoner, he came across a list of births and deaths kept for the city of Breslau in Silesia (Poland). From these data, Halley used the life-table technique (discussed in Chapter 6) to determine that the expectation of life in Breslau between 1687 and 1691 was 33.5 years (Dublin et al., 1949). Yet despite the interest created by the work of Graunt and Halley, it was not until 1836 that registration of births and deaths became compulsory in England, and not until 1839 that an office of vital statistics was officially established in that country—the first in history.

Figure 1.2   Standard Birth and Death Certificates Used in the United States

TYPE OR PRINT IN PERMANENT INK FOR INSTRUCTIONS SEE HANDBOOK

CHILD
CERTIFIER
MOTHER
FATHER

Form Approved OMB No. 68R 1900

LOCAL FILE NUMBER

U.S. STANDARD
CERTIFICATE OF LIVE BIRTH

BIRTH NUMBER

CHILD–NAME   FIRST   MIDDLE   LAST   SEX   DATE OF BIRTH (Mo., Day, Yr.)   HOUR
1.   2.   3a.   3b.   M

HOSPITAL–NAME (If not in hospital, give street and number)   CITY, TOWN OR LOCATION OF BIRTH   COUNTY OF BIRTH
4a.   4b.   4c.

I certify that the stated information concerning this child is true to the best of my knowledge and belief.   DATE SIGNED (Mo., Day, Yr.)   NAME AND TITLE OF ATTENDANT AT BIRTH IF OTHER THAN CERTIFIER (Type or print)
5a. (Signature)   5b.   5c.
CERTIFIER–NAME AND TITLE (Type or print)   MAILING ADDRESS (Street or R.F.D. No., City or Town, State, Zip)
5d.   5e.

REGISTRAR   DATE RECEIVED BY REGISTRAR (Month, Day, Year)
6a. (Signature)   6b.

MOTHER–MAIDEN NAME   FIRST   MIDDLE   LAST   AGE (At time of this birth)   STATE OF BIRTH (If not in U.S.A., name country)
7a.   7b.   7c.
RESIDENCE–STATE   COUNTY   CITY, TOWN OR LOCATION   STREET AND NUMBER OF RESIDENCE   INSIDE CITY LIMITS (Specify yes or no)
8a.   8b.   8c.   8d.   8e.
MOTHER'S MAILING ADDRESS–If same as above, enter Zip Code only
9.

FATHER–NAME   FIRST   MIDDLE   LAST   AGE (At time of this birth)   STATE OF BIRTH (If not in U.S.A., name country)
10a.   10b.   10c.
I certify that the personal information provided on this certificate is correct to the best of my knowledge and belief.   RELATION TO CHILD
(Signature of Parent or other Informant)
11a.   11b.

INFORMATION FOR MEDICAL AND HEALTH USE ONLY

RACE–MOTHER (e.g., White, Black, American Indian, etc.) (Specify)   RACE–FATHER (e.g., White, Black, American Indian, etc.) (Specify)   BIRTH WEIGHT   THIS BIRTH–Single, twin, triplet, etc. (Specify)   IF NOT SINGLE BIRTH–Born first, second, third, etc. (Specify)   IS MOTHER MARRIED? (Specify yes or no)
12.   13.   14.   15a.   15b.   16.

PREGNANCY HISTORY (Complete each section)   EDUCATION–MOTHER (Specify only highest grade completed)   EDUCATION–FATHER (Specify only highest grade completed)

| | | Elementary or Secondary (0-12) | College (1-4 or 5+) | Elementary or Secondary (0-12) | College (1-4 or 5+) |

DEATH UNDER ONE YEAR OF AGE Enter State File Number of death certificate for this child

LIVE BIRTHS (Do not include this Child)   OTHER TERMINATIONS (Spontaneous and Induced)
18.   19.

17a. Now living   17b. Now dead   17d. Before 20 weeks   17e. After 20 weeks
Number   Number   Number   Number

DATE LAST NORMAL MENSES BEGAN (Month, Day, Year)   MONTH OF PREGNANCY PRENATAL CARE BEGAN First, second, etc. (Specify)   PRENATAL VISITS Total number (If none, so state)   APGAR SCORE 1 min.   5 min.
20.   21a.   21a.   22a.   22b.

MULTIPLE BIRTHS Enter State File Number for mate(s)

None ☐   None ☐   None ☐   None ☐

COMPLICATIONS OF PREGNANCY (Describe or write "none")
23.

LIVE BIRTH(S)

DATE OF LAST LIVE BIRTH (Month, Year)   DATE OF LAST OTHER TERMINATION (as indicated in d or e above) (Month, Year)   CONCURRENT ILLNESSES OR CONDITIONS AFFECTING THE PREGNANCY (Describe or write "none")
17c.   17f.   24.

FETAL DEATH(S)

COMPLICATIONS OF LABOR AND/OR DELIVERY (Describe or write "none")   CONGENITAL MALFORMATIONS OR ANOMALIES OF CHILD (Describe or write "none")
25.   26.

Note: Although each state may design its own birth and death certificates, these are the standard forms suggested by the U.S. National Center for Health Statistics.

Today we find the most complete vital registration system in countries that are most highly developed, and the least complete (often nonexistent) in the least developed. Such systems seem to be tied to literacy (there must be someone in each area to record events) and to adequate communication, both of which are associated with economic development. Among countries where systems of vital registration do exist, there is wide variation in the completeness with which events are recorded. Even in the United States the registration of births is not yet 100 percent complete.

Although most nations have separate systems of birth and death registration, there are at least 57 countries that maintain **population registers** (United Nations,

Figure 1.2   (continued)

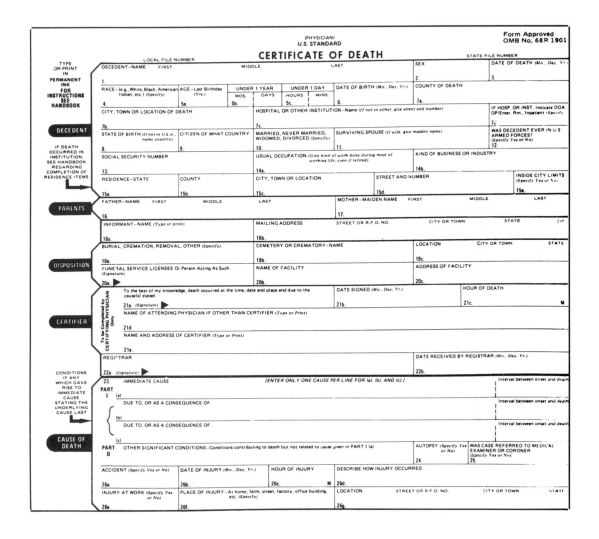

1970). These are lists of all people in the country. Alongside each name are recorded all vital events for that individual, typically birth, death, marriage, divorce, and change of residence. Such registers are kept primarily for administrative (that is, social control) purposes such as legal identification of people, an election roll, and a call for military service; but they are also extremely valuable for demographic purposes, since they provide a demographic life history for each individual. However, population registers vary widely in quality; the most complete and demographically usable ones are found in the Netherlands, Denmark, Norway, Sweden, Finland, and Japan (Spiegelman, 1968). Registers are expensive to maintain, but many countries that could afford them, such as the United States, avoid them because of the threat to personal freedom that can be inherent in a system that compiles and centralizes data.

International migration data are also collected regularly by many governments, largely "on the basis of the records of immigrants arriving at and emigrants departing from the official ports of entry and stations on land borders" (Shryock et al., 1973:33). You should be cautious, however, about the use and interpretation of such data, because migration is very difficult to control and even harder to record. Thus, most counts of migrants are incomplete. For example, in the United States there has been little information available on out-migration since 1957, and, of course, data on immigration of aliens are limited to legal immigrants, who may in fact be outnumbered by illegal aliens (see Chapter 7).

Combining the Census and Vital Statistics

Although the recording of vital events provides information about the number of births and deaths (along with other events) according to such characteristics as age and sex, we also need to know how many people there were at risk of these events. Thus, vital statistics data can be teamed up with census data, which do include that information. For example, you may know from the vital statistics that there were about 3.8 million births in the United States in 1987, but that figure tells you nothing about whether birth rates were high or low. In order to draw any conclusion you must relate those 3.8 million births to the nearly 244 million Americans who were alive in 1987, and only then do you discover a very low birth rate of 16 births per 1,000 population.

Since censuses are not conducted every year, you may wonder how an estimate of the population can be produced for the **intercensal years**. Again, the answer is that census data are combined with vital statistics data. For example, the population in any year following a census should be equal to the census population plus all the people who have been born since the census, minus the people who have died in the interim, plus the people who have migrated in, minus the people who have migrated out. Naturally, deficiencies in any of these data sources will lead to inaccuracies in the estimate of the number of people alive at any time.

Sample Surveys

There are two difficulties with using data collected in the census or by the vital statistics registration system: (1) they are collected for purposes other than demographic analysis and thus do not necessarily reflect the theoretical concerns of demography; and (2) they are collected by a lot of different people using many different methods and may be prone to numerous kinds of error. For these two reasons, in addition to the cost of big data-collection schemes, sample surveys have been used increasingly often to gather demographic data. Sample surveys may provide the social, psychological, economic, and even physical data that I referred to earlier as being necessary to an understanding of why things are as they are.

By using a carefully selected sample of even a few thousand people, demographers have been able to ask questions about births, deaths, migration, and other subjects that reveal aspects of the "why" of demographic events rather than just the "what." In some poor or remote areas of the world, sample surveys can provide reasonably accurate estimates of the levels of fertility, mortality, and migration in the absence of census or vital registration data.

In the United States, one of the most important sample surveys is the Current Population Survey conducted every month by the U.S. Bureau of the Census. Since 1943, thousands of households (currently over 50,000) have been queried each month about a variety of things, although a major thrust of the survey is to gather information on the labor force. Each year, detailed questions are also asked about fertility and migration, and these data are a major source of demographic information about the American population. In 1983, the Census Bureau launched the Survey on Income and Program Participation (SIPP), which is a companion to the Current Population Survey, collecting detailed data on sources of family income.

One of the largest social scientific projects ever undertaken was the World Fertility Survey, conducted under the auspices of the International Statistical Institute in Belgium. Between 1972 and 1982, a total of nearly 350,000 women of childbearing age were interviewed, encompassing 42 developing nations and 20 developed countries (Lightbourne et al., 1982). These data have contributed substantially to our knowledge of how and why people in different parts of the world control their fertility, as will be apparent in Chapter 5. Concurrent with the World Fertility Survey was a series of Contraceptive Prevalence Surveys, conducted in Latin America, Asia, and Africa with funding from the U.S. Agency for International Development. In 1984, the work of the World Fertility Survey and the Contraceptive Prevalence Surveys was combined into one large project called the Demographic and Health Surveys Program, jointly operated by a research organization within the Westinghouse Electric Corporation (which had conducted a majority of the Contraceptive Prevalence Surveys) and the Population Council (a nonprofit organization in New York that has played a major role in shaping population research throughout the world).

Historical Sources

I have already alluded to the lengthy history of demographic data gathering. The flip side is that our modern understanding of population processes is shaped not only by our perception of current trends but by historical events as well. Historical demography requires that we almost literally dig up information about the patterns of mortality, fertility, and migration in past generations—to reconstruct "the world we have lost," as Peter Laslett (1971) has called it. You may prefer to whistle past the graveyard, but researchers at England's Cambridge University Group for the History of Population and Social Structure have spent the past few decades pioneering ways in which to recreate history by reading dates on tombstones and organizing information contained in parish church registers and other local documents (Wrigley, 1974).

Historical sources of demographic information include censuses and vital statistics, but the general lack of good historical vital statistics is what typically necessitates special detective work to locate birth records in church registers and death records in the graveyards. Even in the absence of a census, a complete set of good local records for a small village may allow a researcher to reconstruct the demographic profile of families by matching entries of births, marriages, and deaths in the community over a period of several years. Yet another source of such information is family genealogies, the compilation of which has become somewhat more common in recent years.

The results of these labors can be of considerable importance in testing our notions about how the world used to work. For example, through historical demographic research we now know that the conjugal family (parents and their children) is not a product of industrialization and urbanization, as was once thought (Wrigley, 1974). In fact, such small family units were quite common throughout Europe for several centuries before the Industrial Revolution and may actually have contributed to the process of industrialization by allowing the family more flexibility to meet the needs of the changing economy.

By quantifying (and thereby clarifying) our knowledge of past patterns of demographic events, we are also better able to interpret historical events in a meaningful fashion. Wells (1985) has reminded us that the history of the struggle of American colonists to survive, to marry, and to bear children may tell us more about the determination to forge a union of states than would a detailed recounting of the actions of British officials.

WHO USES POPULATION DATA?

As the world has become more aware of its demographic underpinnings, population studies have been used in a wide range of planning strategies. In both government and business, people have discovered that demography has important implications for social, economic, and political planning. Several major government agencies in the United States are mandated to use census data, which, as I have said earlier, influences the kinds of questions asked on the census. At the state level, money is typically allocated to counties on the basis of population size for such purposes as maintaining schools, hospitals, libraries, prisons, fire departments, juvenile courts, and related services (U.S. Bureau of the Census, 1980). Local governments use demographic data for such purposes as anticipatory changes in municipal services, establishing voting district boundaries, estimating future tax revenue, and training public employees (such as police officers, paramedics, and social workers) about the characteristics of people living in the areas where they work. Politicians use population information to decide what their constituents are like and who will vote for them and to evaluate the issues likely to be important in the areas they represent. They also may use demographic data to provide insights into the forces producing social and economic change in their area, whether that area is a local region, a state, or a nation.

Demographic data are also crucial to business and social planners; just as legislators need to consider the future ratio of retirees to wage earners when determining the tax rate for old-age insurance, insurance companies need to know the probabilities of death before insuring a life. Building contractors need to know the age and economic status of prospective buyers before embarking on a residential construction project. Educators need to project the future number of students in an area before hiring (or firing) faculty and staff. A highway engineer needs to know how a proposed freeway interchange might change the population of a nearby village or town. Sales efforts are increasingly being based on demographic trends and characteristics; such data are used in picking sites for setting up new businesses, for targeting particular marketing strategies, and for forecasting long-term sales trends (see Chapter 16).

Most demographers use population data to improve the understanding of human society; that is my major focus in this book. Using data for this purpose, of course, also aids in the other uses of population data I have mentioned. People in business who can interpret population changes in human terms, rather than in mere statistical terms, are likely to use the data more effectively for profitable purposes. Similarly, a social understanding of the data used by government planners will lead to better decision making for the public welfare. For you as an individual, understanding the social, economic, and political causes and consequences of population growth will improve your ability to cope with a future that will, without any doubt, be significantly influenced by demographic events.

WHERE CAN YOU GO FOR PUBLISHED INFORMATION?

The most convenient and widely available source of international data is the *Demographic Yearbook,* published by the United Nations every year since 1948. The Population Reference Bureau regularly publishes information on the world's population in its *Population Bulletin*, and it also publishes an annual *World Population Data Sheet* that is a very handy reference for up-to-date estimates of basic demographic facts. The U.S. Bureau of the Census also publishes an annual compilation of data called *World Population.*

Data for the United States come primarily from the decennial censuses and from the Current Population Surveys. The census data are published in bound volumes, which are available in summary form for the entire country, separately for each state, and separately for each Standard Metropolitan Statistical Area (SMSA). SMSAs are the areas around each of the nation's larger cities. The Census Bureau also makes available to the public a series of computer tapes that contain data for specific geographic regions. These tapes are increasingly available at colleges and universities, state data centers, local government agencies, and private data-processing and consulting firms. There are also *Subject Reports* published on specific topics from the census data, such as ethnic groups, migration, fertility, marriage and living arrangements, and others. Results from the Current Population Surveys are reported regularly in several series of the *Current Population Reports* (especially Series P-20 and P-23) from the U.S. Bureau of the Census.

Birth and death data for the United States, along with information about marriages and divorces, are available in the *Monthly Vital Statistics Reports* published by the National Center for Health Statistics. For a quick overview of these data, you can consult the most recent *Statistical Abstract of the United States,* published annually by the Census Bureau. Another valuable source of data for the United States—also put out by the Census Bureau—is *Historical Statistics of the United States from Colonial Times.*

Finally, there is a wide range of periodicals that tend to concentrate on issues specific to population studies. At the more popular level is *American Demographics,* which is explicitly aimed at interpreting population statistics for applied users. Journals such as *Population and Development Review, Family Planning Perspectives,* and *International Family Planning Perspectives* are aimed especially at field practitioners and policy planners. The more technical journals include *Demography, Population Studies, Studies in Family Planning, European Journal of Population,* and *International Migration Review.* This list is by no means complete, but it is representative.

The preceding list captures the most readily available sources of demographic information. If you want to pursue data more intensively, there are at least two other good sources. One of them is the book referred to several times in this chapter—*The Methods and Materials of Demography* (in two volumes) by Henry Shryock, Jacob Siegel, and associates (Washington, D.C.: Government Printing Office, 1973). It is listed under U.S. Bureau of the Census in most library card catalogs. The second source is the regularly issued bibliography of published works in population studies called the *Population Index* (Princeton, N.J.: Princeton University, Office of Population and Research). These sources of information are normally available in college and university libraries.

SUMMARY AND CONCLUSION

Demography is a science concerned with analysis of the size, distribution, structure, characteristics, and processes of a population. While such analyses are of immense scientific interest, for most of you a greater value lies in understanding the consequences of population growth. In order to understand how to avoid undesirable consequences of population growth—indeed, even to know how to adjust to future change—you must understand the causes of population growth. The primary task of this book is to provide you with that kind of insight, to help you realize the important role that population issues will play in your future.

The working bases of any science are facts and theory. In this chapter I have discussed the major sources of demographic information, the wells from which population data are drawn. In the next chapter I will use the various sources of data to present an overview of the world's population situation.

MAIN POINTS

1. Pessimists argue that population growth is like a bomb ready to explode, whereas optimists hope for new technologies to take care of ever-increasing numbers.

2. Regardless of whether you are a pessimist or an optimist, you will be sharing a future with millions more people than there are today. Analyzing these changes is the business of demography—the science of population.

3. Demography is concerned with virtually everything that influences or can be influenced by population size, distribution, processes, structure, or characteristics.

4. The cornerstones of population studies are the processes of mortality (a deadly subject), fertility (a well-conceived topic), and migration (a moving experience).

5. In order to study population processes and change, you need to know how many people are alive, how many are being born, how many are dying, how many are moving in and out, and why these things are happening.

6. A basic source of demographic information is the population census, in which information is obtained about all people in a given area at a specific time.

7. Not all countries regularly conduct censuses. For example, between 1965 and 1974 only about 55 percent of the world's population was enumerated in a census, although 96 percent was enumerated between 1975 and 1984.

8. In the United States, censuses have been taken every 10 years since 1790.

9. In the 1970 census of the United States, ethnic minority groups were undercounted. The 1980 census attempted to correct that problem, and it is hoped that the 1990 census will continue the improvement.

10. Information about births and deaths usually comes from vital registration records—data typically recorded and compiled by government agencies. The most complete vital registration systems are found in the most highly developed nations, while they are often nonexistent in less developed areas.

11. Most of the estimates of the magnitude of population growth and change are derived by combining census data with vital registration data.

12. Sample surveys are sources of information for places in which census or vital registration data do not exist. Furthermore, most studies that explain why things happen as they do are based on sample surveys.

13. There is a wide range of users of population data, including people in business, government, and academics.

SUGGESTED READINGS

1. John A. Ross (ed.), 1985, International Encyclopedia of Population (New York: The Free Press).

   This is a resource book that will help you to define basic demographic concepts and issues, "from A to Z."

2. William Petersen and Renee Petersen, 1985, Dictionary of Demography (Westport, CT: Greenwood Press).

   This five-volume set includes biographies of population researchers from throughout the world; terms, concepts, and institutions; and a multilingual glossary. Think of this as the dictionary that complements the encyclopedia mentioned above.

3. Peter Francese, 1979, "The 1980 census: the counting of America," Population Bulletin 34(4).

   Although we are certainly closer to the 1990 census than to the 1980 census, the basic methods of gathering census data are the same, and this is an excellent summary.

4. Robert Lightbourne, Jr., Susheela Singh, and Cynthia Green, 1982, "The World Fertility Survey: charting global childbearing," Population Bulletin 37(1).

   The cost and vast coverage of the World Fertility Survey make it an important set of data you should know about, and this source provides a concise review.

5. Daedalus 97(2), 1968 (special issue on historical population studies).

   Roger Revelle organized this fascinating set of papers authored by some of the foremost researchers in the field of historical demography—providing glimpses of the "world we have lost."

CHAPTER 2
An Overview of the World's Population

"The increase of population is the most revolutionary phenomenon of our times." That is how the Spanish philosopher Ortega y Gasset summarized the situation, and it is difficult to quarrel with that assessment. After all, the population of the world is more than 5 billion and growing—rapidly. How long has this been going on? The world's two most populous countries (China and India) are growing at a phenomenal pace, but the third and fourth most populous countries (the Soviet Union and the United States) are growing much more slowly. What demographic factors make China and India different from the United States and the Soviet Union? These are the kinds of questions I will answer in this brief overview of the world's population.

I will begin the discussion with a look at growth in the premodern world and then work forward in time, examining both the size and the distribution of the population. Included in this historical review will be an examination of the history of population changes in the United States. I will conclude the chapter by observing the current demographics of selected countries, organizing that discussion around a grouping of countries as they fit into the broad phases of the demographic transition.

BRIEF HISTORY OF WORLD POPULATION

Human beings have been around for at least 1 million years. For almost all of that time, humans were hunter-gatherers living a primitive existence not marked by appreciable population growth, although clearly the size of the human race was increasing very slightly. Around 8000 B.C. it is estimated that the size of the world's population was about 8 million, as you can see in Figure 2.1; that number implies a **natural increase** (the excess of births over deaths) of about 15 people per million per year. Thus, during the first 990,000 years of human existence the population of the world had grown only to the size of New York City today. During the next 8,000 years the population grew to an estimated 300 million (these estimates are drawn from Cipolla, 1965 and Coale, 1974). The date 8000 B.C. is usually associated with the **Agricultural Revolution** and represents a time at which population growth began to accelerate slightly. From 8000 B.C. to A.D. 1, the population was growing at a rate that doubled population size every 1,530 years. From the Roman period (ca. A.D. 1) to the early beginnings of the Industrial Revolution (ca. 1750), the growth rate picked up somewhat and the world's population increased to a size of about 800 million. This represents a growth rate with a doubling time of about 1,240 years.

Since that time the size and rate of world population growth have increased dramatically, as I have shown graphically in Figure 2.1. In the relatively short span of time between 1750 and 1950, the population more than tripled from 800 million to 2.5 billion, a doubling time of 122 years. In the 35 years between 1950 and 1985, another 2.5 billion people were added, bringing the total to 5 billion, with a growth rate obviously associated with a doubling time of only 35 years. So, for nearly 1 million years the population of the world grew very slowly, then within little more

Figure 2.1   The World's Population Is Exploding in Size

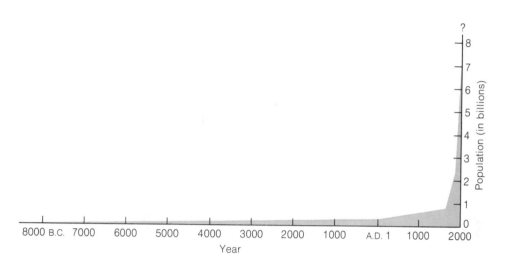

For thousands of years the world's population has been growing very slowly—that is, until about 200 years ago. The Industrial Revolution was accompanied by a decline in the death rate, which allowed population to grow much faster than ever before. Since World War II, the drop in the death rate has produced rapid population growth in less developed nations, which has led to an incredible increase in the size of the human population.

than 200 years the number of people mushroomed to more than 5 billion. There is no question that "population explosion" is an apt description of recent demographic events.

Before going any further, we should ask: How fast can a population actually grow?

How Fast Can Populations Grow?

Human populations, like all living things, have the potential to grow at an exponential rate. This is the same way that money "grows" in a savings account when interest is paid but not withdrawn. Imagine that the $100 you invested in a 25-year certificate at the beginning of the year really represented people, 50 men and 50 women. Imagine further that during the next 25 years each of the women had four children (two boys and two girls) and that each girl grew up and also had four children. Thus, the original 50 mothers had $4 \times 50 = 200$ children, of whom 100 became mothers bearing $4 \times 100 = 400$ children. So at the end of 25 years we have "saved" the original 100 people and added their 200 children and their 400 grandchildren, for a total of 700 people! In just 25 years, the population increased seven-fold, and that assumed mothers were having only four children each.

Children are actually spread out over a greater number of years than in my exaggerated example, but the point is that humans do have a tremendous *potential* for increase. A common way of measuring the growth potential of any combination of birth and death rates is to calculate the doubling time—the time required for a population to double if the current rate of growth continues. You can use the graph in Figure 2.2 to find the doubling time if you know the growth rate. For example, knowing that the world growth rate is about 2 percent per year, you can find that the doubling time is 35 years. If you do not want to carry this graph around with you, you can remember the "rule of 70." The doubling time is approximately equal to 70 divided by the growth rate (in percent per year). Using the same example, 70 divided by 2 (the world growth rate) equals 35.

Where does the 70 come from in the doubling formula? The answer is not so magical or mysterious as it might appear. It derives from the fact that populations grow **exponentially**; each generation builds on the preceding generation in a com-pound fashion. Mathematically, this exponential growth is expressed by natural **logarithms.** Thus, to find out how long it would take a population to double in size, we first must find the natural logarithm (ln or $\log_e$) of 2. This turns out to be 0.70, which we multiply by 100 to get rid of the decimal point. Then dividing the rate of growth into 70 tells us how many years would be required for a population to double. Similarly, if we wanted to know how long it would take a population to triple in size, we would first find the natural logarithm of 3, which is 1.10, or 110 when multiplied by 100. Dividing 110 by the rate of population growth then tells us how long it would take for the population to triple in size.

Once you realize how rapidly a population actually can grow, it is reasonable to wonder why early growth of the human population was so slow.

Figure 2.2   Population and Growth and Doubling Times

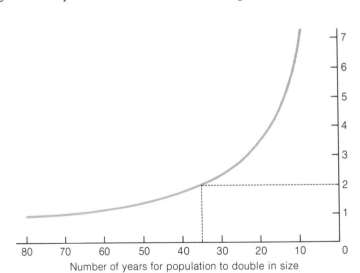

Number of years for population to double in size

Why Was Early Growth So Slow?

The reason the population grew so slowly during the first 99 percent of human history was that death rates were very high, and the risk of death was particularly high among infants and young children. Thus people were forced to have a large number of children if they wanted to have even two or three survive to adulthood. Premodern life expectancies were rarely more than 30 years (compared with 75 in the United States today), and under such conditions women had to bear an average of more than four children each just to ensure that two would survive to adulthood. In those areas where mortality was even higher (such as in India, where as recently as the beginning of this century life expectancy was less than 20 years) women had to bear more than six children on average just to ensure that two would live to adulthood. For most groups of people, the balance between this large number of births and an almost equally large number of deaths led over time to only slight increases in population size.

It was once believed that the Agricultural Revolution increased growth rates because when people settled down in stable farming communities, death rates were lowered. Sedentary life was thought to have improved living conditions, especially the supply of food. So the theory was that birth rates remained high but death rates declined slightly, and thus the population grew. However, recent archaeological evidence, combined with studies of an extant hunting-gathering group in Africa, have offered another explanation for growth during this period (Spooner, 1972). Possibly the sedentary life and the high-density living associated with farming actually raised death rates by creating sanitation problems and heightening the exposure to **communicable diseases.** Growth rates apparently went up because fertility rates rose as new diets improved the ability of women to conceive and bear children (see Chapter 4). Also, it became easier to wean children from the breast earlier due to the greater availability of soft foods, which are easily eaten by babies.

While this latter point may seem unrelated to fertility, it appears that a woman in a hunting-gathering society might have been motivated to space her children a few years apart to make it easier to nurse and to carry her youngest child, and to permit the mother to do her work (Dumond, 1975). She may have accomplished this by abstinence, abortion, or possibly even infanticide (Lee, 1972). In all events, the sedentary agricultural life probably eliminated the need for child spacing. This fact, combined with improved nutrition, enhanced reproductive capabilities and probably allowed fertility levels to rise enough to overcompensate slightly for high mortality (Howell, 1979).

It should be kept in mind, of course, that only a small difference between birth and death rates is required to account for the slow growth achieved after the Agricultural Revolution. Between 8000 B.C. and A.D. 1750, the world was adding an average of only 67,000 people each year to the population. By the 1980s, that many people were being added every seven hours.

How Fast Is the World's Population Growing Now?

It ought to be good news that the *rate* of population growth in the world has declined since hitting a peak in the 1960s, dropping from a high of 2.0 percent to the current rate of approximately 1.7 percent. Indeed, 1.7 percent may seem like a very slow rate of growth. If your bank offered to pay you interest on your money at that low rate, you might decide instead to keep your savings under your mattress. However, when you are dealing with 5 billion of *anything*, a growth rate of 1.7 percent adds a lot of something every year. At present, it translates into 83 million more humans next year than there are right now as you read these words. During the next 12 months, approximately 133 million babies will be born in the world while 50 million of all ages will die, resulting in the net addition of 83 million people. Back in 1950 the world's population was also growing at 1.7 percent per year and at that time, of course, the growth rate was on its way up, rather than on its way down from the peak. Yet, because the total population size was only 2.5 billion, we were adding 43 million new humans each year, as opposed to the current number that is virtually double that.

Many sanguine stories about the end of the population explosion have appeared in recent years, based primarily on a well-publicized study conducted by University of Chicago demographers Tsui and Bogue (1978). Their study suggested that "separate and independently prepared estimates show fertility declining at present. Although most are still at high fertility levels, a sizable number of these [high-fertility] countries have experienced at least some drop from their 1968 fertility levels" (1978:33). They attribute the decline especially to the impact of family planning programs and suggest that if the projected slowdown is to materialize, it will depend on a "strengthened role" for the family planning movement.

Tsui and Bogue's data provide a projection of the world's population in the year 2000 of about 5.8 billion people, slightly less than the 6 billion figure accepted by most demographers. They suggest that their projected slowdowns in population growth represent a "far more optimistic outlook than what demographers were forecasting a decade ago" (1978:39), but they have been taken to task for that interpretation by Paul Demeny, vice president and director of the Center for Population Studies at the Population Council in New York City.

Demeny (1979) says that Tsui and Bogue should actually feel gloomier, rather than more optimistic, if they compare their population projections for the year 2000 with those made in the mid-1960s—especially Bogue's own projections. In 1963 the United Nations' medium estimate of population size for 2000 was 6.13 billion. In 1973 the United Nations revised its estimate upward slightly to 6.254 billion, based on its assessment that fertility was not declining as rapidly as had been estimated in 1963. Thus, the United Nations had indeed become somewhat pessimistic in its projections between 1963 and 1973. On the other hand, in a 1967 article entitled "The End of the Population Explosion," Bogue had projected the world population in the year 2000 to be only 4.527 billion—a number that the world had already surpassed by 1980. Thus, Tsui and Bogue's projection of 5.84 billion for the year 2000 is, in fact, a considerable upward (thus, seemingly gloomier) revision of Bogue's own estimate of a decade earlier. Rather than seeing this as an optimistic picture, Demeny implies that Bogue has simply come into closer conformity with population analysts at the United Nations. Meanwhile, back at the United Nations, China's success in bringing the birth rate down caused the U.N. demographers to readjust their projections slightly downward in 1980—projecting a world total of 6.12 billion in 2000 (United Nations, 1981).

The point best kept in mind is that the developing nations are still growing rapidly in absolute population size. If the world's rate of growth remains at 1.7 percent per year, we will have a minimum of 6 billion people in the world by the year 2000. Even the most optimistic projections leave the developing nations swirling in demographic turbulence as the twenty-first century approaches, and "it is difficult not to conclude also that talk about the end of the population explosion is rather premature" (Demeny, 1979:157).

Why Are Recent Increases So Rapid?

The rapid acceleration in growth after 1750 was due almost entirely to the declines in the death rate that accompanied the **Industrial Revolution.** First in Europe and North America and more recently in less developed countries, death rates have decreased sooner and much more rapidly than have fertility rates. The result has been that many fewer people die than are born each year. In the industrialized countries, declines in mortality were due at first to the effects of economic development and a rising standard of living—people were eating better, wearing warmer clothes, living in better houses, bathing more often, drinking cleaner water, and so on (McKeown, 1976). These improvements in the human condition helped to lower the exposure to disease and also to build up resistance to disease. Later, after 1900, much of the decline in mortality was due to improvements in medical technology, especially vaccination against infectious diseases.

Declines in the death rates first occurred in only those countries experiencing economic development. In each of these areas, primarily Europe and North America, fertility also began to decline within at least one or two generations after the death rate began its decline. However, since World War II, medical and public health technology has been available to virtually all countries of the world regardless of their level of economic development. In the underdeveloped countries, although the risk of death has been lowered dramatically, as yet the birth rates have gone down less significantly and the result is rapid population growth, as you can see in Table 2.1.

As a population increases its size, the same rate of growth will produce a larger absolute increase in size from year to year. In fact, the age structure of the world is now so young (as I will detail in Chapter 8), and the population already so large, that more people will be added to the world's total between 1980 and 2000 than were added between 1960 and 1980, even though the average annual rate of growth was actually higher in the period 1960–80 than it is likely to be in 1980–2000. Figure 2.3 illustrates this for you.

The increase in size of the world's population is not the only important demographic change to occur in the past few hundred years. In addition, there has been a massive redistribution of population.

Table 2.1 Less Developed Regions Are the
Sites of Future Population Growth (to the Year 2000)

	Area		
	More Developed Nations	Less Developed Nations	World
Projection to year 2000 (in millions)	1,323	5,027	6,350
Population in 1980 (in millions)	1,170	3,300	4,469
Increase (1980–2000) (in millions)	153	1,727	1,881
Percent of increase attributable to each area	8%	92%	100%

Source: U.S. Bureau of the Census, 1979, "Illustrative Projections of World Populations to the 21st Century," Current Population Reports, Special Studies, Series P-23, No. 79. Data are from the medium-series projections.

Note: Projections made by the U.S. Census Bureau suggest that the world's population will exceed 6 billion by the year 2000. More than 90 percent of that growth will probably occur in the less developed nations.

Figure 2.3 More Than 2 Billion People Will Have Been Added to the World's Population Between 1975 and 2000

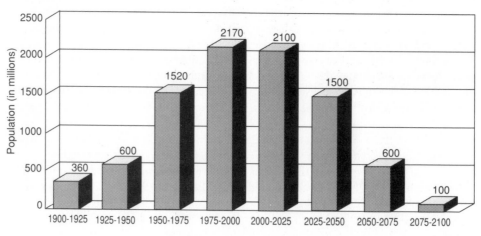

Source: United Nations, 1981, 1980 Report by the Executive Director of the United Nations Fund for Population Activities (New York: United Nations), Chart 1.

Note: The net additions to the world's population have skyrocketed during the twentieth century but should slow down during the next century.

Redistribution of the World's Population Through Migration

As populations have grown in different areas of the world, the pressures or desires to migrate have also grown. Migration generally has been from rapidly growing areas into less rapidly growing areas, for example, from Mexico to the United States. Also, when people move around within countries, it is usually from high-growth rural areas to urban areas.

In earlier decades, as population grew dense in a particular area, people were able to move to places that were not only growing less rapidly but also were less populated, much as high-pressure storm fronts move into low-pressure weather systems. The most notable illustration of this kind of migration is the expansion of European population into other parts of the world. It is especially notable because as Europeans moved around the world, they altered patterns of life, including their own, wherever they went. Indeed, European expansion has been such an important part of world history that it deserves additional comment.

European Expansion

Beginning in the fourteenth century, migration out of Europe started gaining momentum, and this expansion of the European population virtually revolutionized the entire human population. With their gun-laden sailboats, Europeans began to stake out the less developed areas of the world in the fifteenth and sixteenth centuries, and this was only the beginning. Migration of Europeans to other parts of the world on a massive scale waited until the nineteenth century, when the European nations began to industrialize and swell in numbers. As Kingsley Davis has put it:

> Although the continent was already crowded, the death rate began to drop and the population began to expand rapidly. Simultaneous urbanization, new occupations, financial panics, and unrestrained competition gave rise to status instability on a scale never known before. Many a bruised or disappointed European was ready to seek his fortune abroad, particularly since the new lands, tamed by the pioneers, no longer seemed wild and remote but rather like paradises where one could own land and start a new life. The invention of the steamship (the first one crossed the Atlantic in 1827) made the decision less irrevocable (1974:98).

Before the great expansion of European people and culture, Europeans represented about 18 percent of the world's population, and almost 90 percent of these people of European origin lived in Europe itself. By the 1930s, at the peak of European dominance in the world, people of European origin living in Europe, America, and Oceania accounted for 35 percent of the world's population. By the late 1980s, the percentage had declined to a bit more than 20 (Durand, 1967; Wrigley, 1969; United Nations, 1978c; Population Reference Bureau, 1988).

Since the 1930s, the outward expansion of Europeans has almost ceased. Until then, European populations had been growing more rapidly than the populations in Africa, Asia, and Latin America, but since World War II that trend has been reversed. The less developed areas now have the most rapidly growing populations.

Indeed, demographer Judith Blake has commented that "population growth used to be a reward for doing well; now it's a scourge for doing badly" (1979). This change in the pattern of population has resulted in a shift in the direction of migration. On balance, there is now more migration from less developed to developed areas than the reverse. Furthermore, since migrants from less developed areas generally have higher levels of fertility than natives of the developed regions, their migration makes a disproportionate contribution over time to the overall population increase in the developed area to which they migrated. As a result, the proportion of the population whose origin is one of the modern world's less developed nations tends to be on the rise in nearly every developed nation. Within the United States, for example, it is projected that the population of Hispanics and those of Asian origin in California could represent a majority of the total by early in the twenty-first century.

When Europeans migrated, they were generally filling up territory that had very few people. Those empty lands or frontiers have largely disappeared today, and as a consequence migration into a country now results in more noticeable increases in population density. Closely associated with this increasing population density in the modern world is another major form of population redistribution associated with migration, the urban revolution.

The Urban Revolution

Until very recently in world history, almost everyone lived in basically rural areas. Large cities were few and far between. For example, Rome's population of 650,000 in A.D. 100 was probably the largest in the ancient world (Chandler and Fox, 1974). It is estimated that as recently as 1800 less than 1 percent of the world's population lived in cities with populations of 100,000 or more. By the 1980s more than one third of all humans were living in cities of that size.

The redistribution of people from rural to urban areas is most marked in the industrialized nations. For example, in 1800 about 10 percent of the English population lived in urban areas, primarily London. By the 1980s, more than 75 percent of the British were in cities. Similar patterns of **urbanization** have been experienced in other European countries, the United States, Canada, and Japan as they have industrialized.

In the less developed areas of the world, urbanization was associated with a commercial response to industrialization in Europe, America, and Japan. In other words, in many areas where industrialization was not occurring, Europeans had established colonies or trade relationships. The principal economic activities in such areas were not industrial but commercial in nature, associated with buying and selling. The wealth acquired by people engaging in these activities naturally attracted attention, and urban centers sprang up all over the world as Europeans sought populations to whom they could sell their goods. Thus, urban populations began to grow in some countries even without industrialization.

Today urban populations are growing at a much more rapid rate in the less developed regions of the world than they ever did in the industrialized nations. Much of the current city growth is due less to people migrating from rural to urban areas, however, than to high birth rates and low death rates in the cities. This is in contrast to the early history of cities in Europe where birth rates were low and death rates were high.

In the United States the rise of cities was initially a response to commercial activity with England, which had begun to industrialize several decades earlier. It did not take long, though, for industry to develop and for American cities to attract people not only from rural areas in the United States but from other countries as well. Since the movement of people to and within the United States is one of the important elements of European expansion, let me briefly review American demographic history.

BRIEF HISTORY OF POPULATION IN THE UNITED STATES

It does not take a demographer to notice that the population of the United States has undergone a truly incredible transformation since Christopher Columbus mistook America for India. As was true throughout the New World, the European guns and diseases decimated the native American Indian population, making it easier to establish a new culture. In 1650 it is estimated that the population of North America consisted of about 50,000 European colonists and about 750,000 native American Indians—the Europeans were outnumbered 15 to 1. By 1850, disease and warfare had reduced the Indian population to 250,000, while the European population had increased to 23 million—they outnumbered the Indians 92 to 1.

Although early America was a model of rapid population growth, it was also a land of substantial demographic contrasts. Among the colonies existing in the seventeenth century, for example, those in New England seem to have been characterized by very high birth rates (women had an average of 7–9 children) yet relatively low mortality rates (infant mortality rates in Plymouth Colony may have been lower than in some of today's less developed nations, due apparently to the fairly good health of Americans even during that era) (Demos, 1965; Wells, 1982). Demos notes that "the popular impression today that colonial families were extremely large finds the strongest possible confirmation in the case of Plymouth. A sample of some ninety families, about whom there is fairly reliable information, suggests that there was an average of seven to eight children per family who actually grew to adulthood" (1965:270). In the southern colonies during the same time period, however, life was apparently much harsher, probably because the environment was more amenable to the spread of disease. In the Chesapeake Bay colony of Charles Parish, higher mortality meant that few parents had more than two or three living children at the time of their death (Smith, 1978).

Despite the regional diversity, the American population grew rather steadily during the seventeenth and eighteenth centuries, and while much of the increase in the number of Europeans in America was attributable to in-migration, the greater percentage was actually due to natural increase. Though the nation's first census, taken shortly after the American Revolution in 1790, counted 3.9 million Americans, and though the population was increasing by nearly 120,000 a year, only about 3 percent of the increase was a result of immigration.

With a **crude birth rate** of about 55 births per thousand population (comparable to the highest national birth rates in the world today) and a **crude death rate** of about 28 deaths per thousand, there were twice as many people being born each year as were dying. At this rate the population was doubling in size every 25 years. Although Americans may picture foreigners pouring in seeking freedom or fortune, it was not until the second third of the nineteenth century that migration became a substantial factor in American population growth. In fact, during the first half of the nineteenth century in-migrants accounted for less than 5 percent of the population increase in each decade, whereas in every decade from the 1850s through the 1920s in-migrants accounted for at least 20 percent of the growth of population (see Chapter 7 for more details).

Throughout this period of time, however, the birth rate in the United States was falling (there is evidence that fertility among American Quakers began to be limited at about the time of the American Revolution, but the rest of the nation was a few decades behind their pace—Wells, 1971). By the 1930s, fertility actually dropped below the level required to replace the next generation (as I will discuss more in Chapter 5). Furthermore, restrictions on immigration had all but halted the influx of foreigners, and Americans were facing the prospect of potential depopulation.

The early post–World War II era upset forecasts of population decline; they were replaced by the realities of a population explosion. The period from the mid-1940s to the early 1960s is generally known as the "Baby Boom era," a time when the United States experienced a rapid rate of increase in numbers, accomplished almost entirely by increases in fertility. The Baby Boom, in its turn, was followed in the late 1960s and early 1970s by a "Baby Bust," or "population implosion," as one pundit put it (Kilpatrick, 1978)—the renewed prospect of population decline. Despite the "baby boomlet" of the late 1970s and early 1980s fertility has remained below the replacement level. Nonetheless, population growth, rather than population decline, has continued to be the order of the day because in the 1960s a rewriting of the nation's immigration laws opened the nation's doors once more, and the result has been renewed high levels of migration into the United States.

By current world standards the United States is today one of the slower-growing countries. Specifically, the rate of growth in the United States is less than half that of the entire world. With a population of nearly 250 million people, about 5 percent of the world's total, the United States is the fourth most populous country, trailing only China, India, and the Soviet Union.

THE WORLD'S MOST POPULOUS COUNTRIES

It is questionable whether there is a direct relationship between population size and worldwide political clout. Yet there can be no question that population size is closely related to the impact a society has on the total world demographic picture. Let us consider then the demographic situation in today's largest (most populous) countries.

China

With a population of more than 1 billion people, the People's Republic of China is clearly the most populous country in the world. With more than one fifth of all human beings, China dominates the map of the world drawn to scale according to population size (see Figure 2.4). Many Westerners are surprised to learn that China's population is so large because for a long time the Chinese were rather close-mouthed about their demographics. For example, at the 1974 World Population Conference in Bucharest, Chinese officials asked the United Nations to delete all references to Chinese population from official documents (San Francisco Chronicle, 1974). The Chinese were perhaps fearful that outside reports of population size and growth rates would not take sufficient account of the fact that the Communist revolution inherited a very large problem.

In 1982 China took stock of the magnitude of its problem with its first national census since 1964. A total of 1,008,175,288 people were counted, and the results seemed to reinforce the government's belief that it was on the right track in vigorously pursuing a fairly coercive one-child policy to cut the birth rate (which I will discuss in detail in Chapter 15). It should be noted, however, that even before the government imposed these limits on childbearing, the birth rate had already begun to decline in China. The rate of population growth has been slowing since at least the 1960s (Goodstadt, 1982), and China's birth and death rates are now both below the world average, as is its overall rate of growth. Based on data summarized by the United Nations (1986; 1982d), we can guess that a female baby born in China has approximately a 98 percent chance of survival to age 1 and an 89 percent chance of survival to age 50. Women are now apparently bearing an average of scarcely more than two children each (the one-child norm has not yet taken root), which is an incredible drop from the average of six children as estimated from the 1953 census. These data, of course, disguise the demographic variability that exists from one part of the country to another. For example, both fertility and mortality are considerably lower in cities than in rural areas. Although the Chinese government claimed in 1980 that its goal was to limit the population to a maximum of 1.2 billion by the end of this century (Goodstadt, 1982), at its current rate of growth of 1.3 percent per year it is increasing by about 14 million people each year and could reach 1.2 billion several years before the year 2000 unless the growth rate continues to drop.

India

Second in population size in the world is India, with more than 800 million people. Mortality is somewhat higher in India than in China, and the birth rate is quite a bit higher than in China. Indian females have about a 90 percent chance at birth of still being alive at age 1 and close to a 75 percent chance of survival to age 50. Women are bearing children at a rate of more than four each, and nearly four (on average) of these are likely to live to adulthood. With an annual growth rate of 2.1 percent, the Indian population is adding nearly 17 million people to the world's total each year.

Figure 2.4 Map of Population Size

1. China	17. Philippines	35. Morocco	49. Venezuela
2. India	18. Thailand	36. Algeria	50. Malaysia
3. USSR	19. Turkey	37. German Democratic	51. Uganda
4. United States	20. Egypt	Republic	52. Iraq
5. Indonesia	21. Spain	38. China, Republic of	53. Hungary
6. Japan	22. Korea, Republic of	(Taiwan)	54. Chile
7. Brazil	23. Poland	39. Korea, Democratic	55. Ghana
8. Bangladesh	24. Iran	People's Republic	56. Belgium
9. Pakistan	25. Burma	40. Sudan	57. Cuba
10. Nigeria	26. Ethiopia	41. Peru	58. Portugal
11. Mexico	27. South Africa, Republic of	42. Tanzania, United	59. Bulgaria
12. Germany, Federal	28. Argentina	Republic of	60. Greece
Republic of	29. Zaire	43. Czechoslovakia	61. Mozambique
13. Italy	30. Colombia	44. Sri Lanka	62. Saudi Arabia
14. United Kingdom	31. Canada	45. Kenya	63. Austria
15. France	32. Yugoslavia	46. Netherlands	64. Kampuchea,
16. Vietnam, Socialist	33. Romania	47. Australia	Democratic Republic
Republic of	34. Afghanistan	48. Nepal	of (Cambodia)

In this map of the world, each country's size is proportional to its population. Thus, China dominates the map with its more than one billion people. The lists identify each country by number. The following map shows the size of each country by area.

Figure 2.4 (continued)

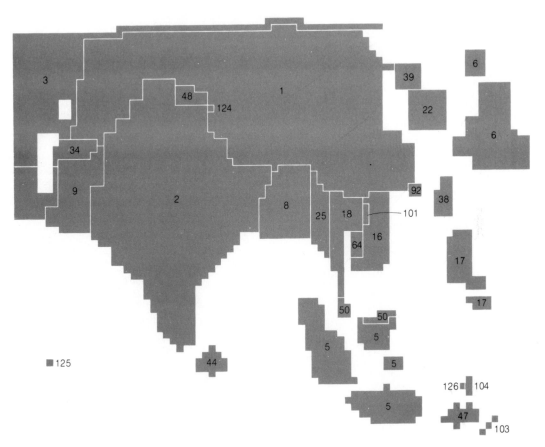

65. Madagascar	82. Guinea	100. Jordan	117. Botswana
66. Sweden	83. Haiti	101. Lao People's	118. Congo
67. Syrian Arab Republic	84. Ivory Coast	Democratic Republic	119. Gabon
68. Ecuador	85. Malawi	102. Lebanon	120. Gambia
69. Zimbabwe	86. Niger	103. New Zealand	121. Guyana
70. Switzerland	87. Senegal	104. Papua New Guinea	122. Kuwait
71. Cameroon, United	88. Zambia	105. Paraguay	123. Mauritania
Republic of	89. Burundi	106. Puerto Rico	124. Bhutan
72. Yemen	90. Chad	107. Sierra Leone	125. Mauritius
73. Angola	91. El Salvador	108. Somalia	126. Timor
74. Bolivia	92. Hong Kong	109. Uruguay	127. Iceland
75. Guatemala	93. Norway	110. Central African Empire	128. Greenland
76. Mali	94. Rwanda	111. Costa Rica	
77. Tunisia	95. Albania	112. Liberia	
78. Burkina Faso	96. Benin	113. Libyan Arab Republic	
79. Denmark	97. Honduras	114. Nicaragua	
80. Dominican Republic	98. Ireland	115. Panama	
81. Finland	99. Israel	116. Togo	

Figure 2.4　The World

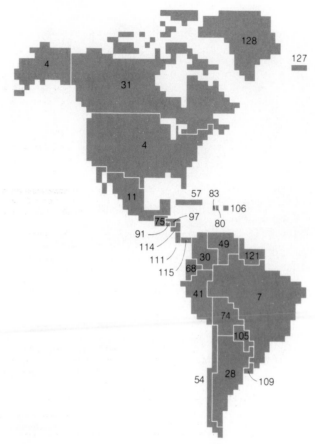

1. China	17. Philippines	35. Morocco	49. Venezuela
2. India	18. Thailand	36. Algeria	50. Malaysia
3. USSR	19. Turkey	37. German Democratic	51. Uganda
4. United States	20. Egypt	Republic	52. Iraq
5. Indonesia	21. Spain	38. China, Republic of	53. Hungary
6. Japan	22. Korea, Republic of	(Taiwan)	54. Chile
7. Brazil	23. Poland	39. Korea, Democratic	55. Ghana
8. Bangladesh	24. Iran	People's Republic	56. Belgium
9. Pakistan	25. Burma	40. Sudan	57. Cuba
10. Nigeria	26. Ethiopia	41. Peru	58. Portugal
11. Mexico	27. South Africa, Republic of	42. Tanzania, United	59. Bulgaria
12. Germany, Federal	28. Argentina	Republic of	60. Greece
Republic of	29. Zaire	43. Czechoslovakia	61. Mozambique
13. Italy	30. Colombia	44. Sri Lanka	62. Saudi Arabia
14. United Kingdom	31. Canada	45. Kenya	63. Austria
15. France	32. Yugoslavia	46. Netherlands	64. Kampuchea,
16. Vietnam, Socialist	33. Romania	47. Australia	Democratic Republic
Republic of	34. Afghanistan	48. Nepal	of (Cambodia)

A stylized representation of the political boundaries and land areas of countries. *Source:* Adapted from U.S. Bureau of the Census, International Statistics Programs Center, Map No. ISP-WGC-72.

Figure 2.4 (continued)

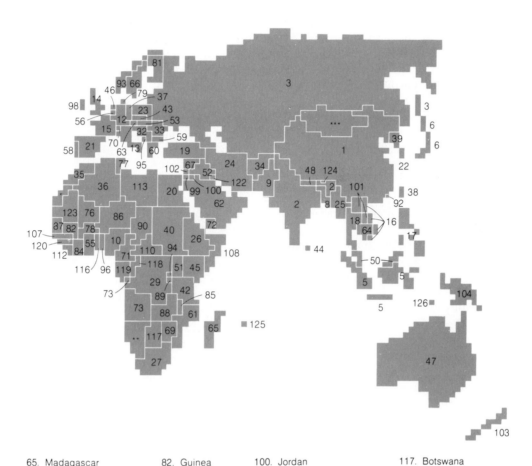

65. Madagascar	82. Guinea	100. Jordan	117. Botswana
66. Sweden	83. Haiti	101. Lao People's	118. Congo
67. Syrian Arab Republic	84. Ivory Coast	Democratic Republic	119. Gabon
68. Ecuador	85. Malawi	102. Lebanon	120. Gambia
69. Zimbabwe	86. Niger	103. New Zealand	121. Guyana
70. Switzerland	87. Senegal	104. Papua New Guinea	122. Kuwait
71. Cameroon, United	88. Zambia	105. Paraguay	123. Mauritania
Republic of	89. Burundi	106. Puerto Rico	124. Bhutan
72. Yemen	90. Chad	107. Sierra Leone	125. Mauritius
73. Angola	91. El Salvador	108. Somalia	126. Timor
74. Bolivia	92. Hong Kong	109. Uruguay	127. Iceland
75. Guatemala	93. Norway	110. Central African Empire	128. Greenland
76. Mali	94. Rwanda	111. Costa Rica	*Spanish Sahara
77. Tunisia	95. Albania	112. Liberia	**Nambia
78. Burkina Faso	96. Benin	113. Libyan Arab Republic	***Mongolia
79. Denmark	97. Honduras	114. Nicaragua	
80. Dominican Republic	98. Ireland	115. Panama	Note: Countries marked with asterisks include too few people for inclusion on the map of the world by population.
81. Finland	99. Israel	116. Togo	

The Indian government had been hopeful that family planning measures had helped to lower the rate of population growth during the 1970s, but, in fact, the 1981 census counted 12 million more Indians than the government had expected (Visaria and Visaria, 1981). To be sure, fertility has probably declined in recent years. I use the term "probably" because the data in India are not good enough to allow a more certain conclusion. It appears that "fertility prior to 1961 was high and remained virtually constant" (Jain and Adlakha, 1982:589); then, during the 1960s, fertility dropped by 7 to 11 percent; and during the 1970s fertility rates may have gone down by as much as 16 percent (Preston and Bhat, 1984). So, some progress is being made in retarding fertility, but these declines have been matched almost exactly by declining mortality, maintaining the rate of population growth in India at a higher level than the world's average.

Soviet Union and United States

The Soviet Union and the United States are the third and fourth most populous nations in the world. Despite their long-time political differences, the two countries were very similar in many demographic respects until quite recently. In the 1970s they nearly mirrored each other in terms of population and size and mortality and fertility rates, but things have changed. As of 1987, the 284 million people estimated for the Soviet Union was quite a few more than the 250 million in the United States, a result of the higher growth rate in the USSR—1.0 percent per year, compared with 0.7 percent in the United States. Fertility levels in the USSR suggest that Soviet women are bearing an average of 2.5 children, well above the 1.8-child average in the United States. On the other hand, while death rates have continued to decline in the United States to very low levels, they have stopped declining and may even be on the rise in the Soviet Union. The average American baby can now expect to live 6 years longer than the average Soviet baby.

The Soviet Union could reach a population of 314 million by the year 2000, whereas projections for the United States suggest a population of 268 million by that time. Remember that the below-replacement fertility levels in the United States do not translate into a declining population, because of the effects of immigration and because there are so many young women bearing 1.8 children that births continue to outnumber deaths in the United States.

GEOGRAPHIC DISTRIBUTION OF THE WORLD'S POPULATION

The four largest countries in the world account for virtually half the world's population but only 30 percent of the world's land surface. If we round out the world's top ten countries in terms of population size, we find that the list includes (in order of size) Indonesia, Brazil, Japan, Bangladesh, Pakistan, and Nigeria. Within these most populous ten nations reside two of every three humans. You would only have to visit ten countries, then, in order to shake hands with two thirds of all the people in the world. In doing so, you would travel across 43 percent of the earth's land surface. The rest of the population is spread out among more than 150 other countries accounting for the remaining 57 percent of the earth's terrain.

If it were your goal to be as efficient as possible in maximizing the number of people you could visit while minimizing the distance you would travel, your best bet would be to schedule a trip to China and the Indian subcontinent (which includes India, Pakistan, and Bangladesh). Forty-one percent of all the world's people live in those two contiguous regions of Asia, and you can see how these areas stand out in the map of the world drawn with country size proportionate to population (see Figure 2.4). Throughout this area, the average **population density** is a whopping 389 people per square mile, compared with the overall world average of 87 per square mile and the American average of 69 per square mile.

Population growth in Asia is not a new story. In Table 2.2 you can see that in 1650, as North America was first being settled by Europeans, there were already more people in Asia than there are even now in North America. In that year Asians accounted for 60 percent of all humans. More than three hundred years later, in 1985, Asians still accounted for 58 percent of all people. Africa, on the other hand, may have had as many as 100 million people in 1650, virtually the same number as in Europe. However, contact with Europeans tended to be deadly for Africans (as it was for Indians in America) because of disease, violence, and slavery. Only in this century has the African population rebounded in population size, composing 11 percent of the total world population in 1985, compared with 18 percent in 1650. Projections by the Population Reference Bureau suggest that between 1985 and 2020 Africa will have the most rapidly growing population of any region of the world, and by 2020 Africans could again represent 18 percent of the world's total.

Table 2.2 Geographic Distribution of the World's Population, 1650–1985 (Population in Millions)

Year	World	North America	Latin America	Africa	Europe[a]	Asia[b]	Oceania
1650	545	1	12	100	103	327	2
1750	728	1	11	95	144	475	2
1850	1,171	26	33	95	274	741	2
1930	2,008	134	110	155	530	1,069	10
1985	4,845	264	406	551	770	2,830	24
2020	8,053	327	711	1,497	853	4,629	36

Sources: Data for 1650 to 1930 from A. M. Carr-Saunders, 1935, World Population: Past Growth and Present Trends (Oxford: Oxford University Press); data for 1985 and 2020 from Population Reference Bureau, 1988, World Population Data Sheet, 1988.

[a] Including USSR.

[b] Excluding USSR.

Since differential rates of population growth help explain the shifting distribution of people around the globe, it is worth our while to examine them briefly.

CURRENT DIFFERENCES IN GROWTH RATES

The world's population, as I have discussed, is currently multiplying at a rate approximating 1.7 percent per year. At this rate (if it continues unchecked) the world's population will double in size in 41 years. Six of the ten largest countries in the world are growing even more rapidly than the world average, led by Nigeria, Pakistan, and Bangladesh, and followed by Brazil, India, and Indonesia. Nigeria is growing at a rate that doubles the population every 24 years, while in India the population will double in 35 years at the current rate.

Among the other four of the world's largest countries, Japan is growing most slowly, followed by the United States, the Soviet Union, and then by China. At the present rate, Japan's population will double in 133 years, compared with 99 years in the United States, 68 years in the USSR, and 49 years in China. In Figure 2.5 you can see that the most rapidly growing countries tend to be those that are least developed economically, and the slowest growing are the most advanced industrially. It has not always been that way, however.

Before the Great Depression of the 1930s, the populations of Europe and North America tended to be the most rapidly growing in the world. During the decade of the 1930s, growth rates declined in those two areas to match approximately the growth rates of most of the rest of the world. At that time the whole world's population was growing at a rate of 0.75 percent per year—a doubling time of 93 years. Since the end of World War II, the situation has changed again, and now Europe and North America rank among the more slowly growing populations. Rapid growth in the less developed countries of Asia, Latin America, and Africa is now responsible for most of the world's population increase.

You can see the dramatic difference between the less developed and the highly industrialized areas of the world in terms of population growth rates by examining Figure 2.5. Throughout the less developed regions of Africa, South America, and Asia, rates of increase are uniformly high. In Europe, the Soviet Union, and North America, they are uniformly low. The country with the single highest rate of total population growth is Kenya, the eastern African former colony of Great Britain, where birth rates have remained persistently high in the face of rapidly declining death rates. At its 1988 growth rate of 4.1 percent per year, the population of Kenya will double, from 23 to 46 million, in the short span of 17 years.

CHINA AND INDIA CONTRASTED WITH THE USSR AND THE UNITED STATES

Why are China and India growing faster than the Soviet Union and the United States? I raised this question at the beginning of the chapter, but the answer is not

Figure 2.5   Africa, Latin America, and Asia Have the Highest Rates of Population Growth

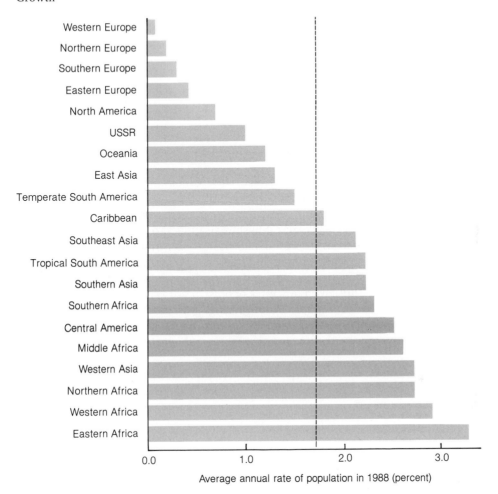

Average annual rate of population in 1988 (percent)

There are rather clear-cut differences in the rates of total population growth between the regions of Africa, Latin America, and Asia (except East Asia) and the regions of North America and Europe. The world's average rate of growth (dashed line) almost perfectly divides those slow-growing, economically advanced nations from the more rapidly growing, less developed areas of the world. *Source:* Data courtesy of Population Reference Bureau, Inc., Washington, D.C.

completely obvious. India is growing faster than any of the other "big four" because its high birth rate is paired with a slowly declining death rate. In China, the birth rate has declined substantially over the past few years and so, in 1988, the rate of natural increase of 1.4 percent was not dramatically higher than the Soviet Union's 1.0 percent. Yet, although the rates of growth for those two countries are not too dissimilar, the difference in population size means that each year China is still adding

14 million people to its population while the Soviet Union adds less than 3 million. At the slow-growth end of the group, the United States population is growing very slowly because of its very low level of fertility. Of course, even if China were growing only at the current American rate, that country would still be adding 7 million people each year to the world total, compared with the 1.7 million being added in the United States.

WORLD PATTERNS OF POPULATION GROWTH

The point has by now been well made that China and India have such large populations that they must be reckoned with. Still, they are only part of the world's demographic scene, and to comprehend that world demographic situation you have to look at the whole picture. To accomplish that, the rest of the chapter examines a few representative countries as they would fit into each stage of the demographic transition from high mortality and high fertility to low mortality and low fertility. I will begin the discussion with countries that still have high fertility and mortality rates and progress to those with low rates of both. Also, I have located each country and region discussed on a graph of the demographic transition (see Figure 2.6). Incidentally, the countries I have chosen to discuss were picked not for any esoteric reasons but only because they were countries for which reasonably complete data were available.

High Mortality and High Fertility

In recent decades, mortality has declined so much throughout the world that it is increasingly difficult to find countries with both high mortality and high fertility rates. Prior to World War II it was quite easy, because death rates in Africa were frequently as high as 40 deaths per 1,000 population—4.5 times the current U.S. rate. There is virtually no country with such high death rates any longer, although Africans still tend to have the highest risk of death in the world, as well as the highest levels of fertility. High mortality and high fertility are often closely associated with very low levels of economic development, and such countries rarely have the economic resources to keep records of births and deaths or to conduct more than an occasional census. Thus, the data for such countries are skimpy. If we rather arbitrarily define a high-mortality country as one in which the crude death rate is 20 or more deaths per 1,000 population, then we find that in 1988 there were at least 17 such countries in the world (the number depends somewhat on whose estimates of the death rate you use). All had accompanying high birth rates and all were located in either Africa (south of the Sahara) or Asia. In the past several years the tremendous suffering of people in countries in these regions—in Angola, Ethiopia, Chad, and Cambodia—has received worldwide attention.

Figure 2.6 Sweden's Demographic Transition Compared with the Current Situation in Several Other Countries

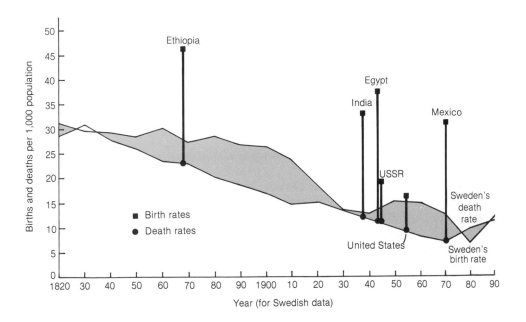

Sweden underwent a nearly "classic" demographic transition from high birth and death rates to low birth and death rates. However, most less developed nations today have much higher birth rates than Sweden did at comparable levels of mortality. For example, in 1988 the death rate in India was comparable to Sweden's death rate in about 1930. Yet India's birth rate was much higher in 1988 than was Sweden's in 1930. *Sources:* Adapted from data in Nathan Keyfitz and Wilhelm Flieger, 1971, Population: Facts and Methods of Demography (San Francisco: W. H. Freeman & Company); U.S. Bureau of the Census, 1978, World Population, 1977; United Nations, 1986, World Population Prospects as Assessed in 1984 (New York: United Nations); and Population Reference Bureau, 1988, World Population Data Sheet, 1988.

In the first edition of this book I suggested that the demographics of high-fertility, high-mortality countries could be illustrated by Cameroon, a middle-African country just north of the equator and facing the Atlantic Ocean. I further indicated that "countries like Cameroon all represent potentially explosive populations in terms of future growth if mortality conditions improve" (Weeks, 1978:49). By 1988 that was, in fact, happening. The death rate in Cameroon began to drop in the mid-1970s, and by 1988 the rate of population growth had jumped from 1.8 percent per year (a doubling in 39 years) to 2.6 percent per year (a doubling in 26 years).

Gambia is an even better example than Cameroon of a high-mortality, high-fertility nation. Estimates are somewhat speculative because data are incomplete, but it appears that over the last several decades mortality has declined only slightly, while fertility has remained virtually unchanged. Gambia is a nation of about 1 million people, situated south of the Sahara and bordering the Atlantic Ocean on the western side of the African continent. The high risk of death is exemplified by the fact that only 34 of 100 girls born will still be alive at age 55, compared with 93 of 100 in the United States. This is due especially to the very high death rates in infancy and early childhood in Gambia. For example, available evidence suggests that nearly two of every ten children die before reaching their first birthday, and almost three in ten die before age 10.

The high level of fertility in Gambia is illustrated by the fact that women bear an average of more than six children each, nearly four times the average level of childbearing in the United States. Because of the high mortality, however, only four of the six children are likely to survive to adulthood. Of course, having an average of four children still represents a rapid increase in numbers in each generation. Thus, despite having one of the (if not the) highest levels of mortality in the world, the Gambian population is growing at a rate of 2.1 percent per year. This implies a doubling time of only 34 years; indeed, its population more than doubled in the 34 years between 1954 and 1988.

Low Mortality and High Fertility

Of all the countries scattered over the globe, by far the largest number have achieved fairly low levels of mortality but retain high levels of fertility. These countries are experiencing the most rapid population growth, and among them the fastest growing are northern African and most Middle Eastern countries. Egypt provides a good example and will be discussed in the next section. Most Latin American countries also fall into this category, and I will examine Mexico as an illustration. Most Asian countries also have fairly low mortality and fairly high fertility, and I remind you that India is a very important country in that category.

Egypt   In 1988 there were 53 million Egyptians crowded into the narrow Nile Valley. With its rate of growth of 2.8 percent per year, Egypt's population could double in only 24 years, and this rapid growth constantly hampers even the most ambitious strategies for economic growth and development. This explosion in numbers is due, of course, to the dramatic drop in mortality since the end of World War II. In 1937, the life expectancy at birth in Egypt was less than 40 years (Omran, 1973), whereas by 1988 it had risen to 59. Even with such a drop, however, death rates are above the world average and there is considerable room for improvement.

As mortality declined, fertility remained almost intransigently high until very recently, save for brief dips during World War II and again during the wars with Israel in the late 1960s and early 1970s. For as long as statistics have been kept, Egyptian women had been bearing an average of six children until the late 1970s. Massive family planning efforts in the 1970s and 1980s may have begun to have an effect, however, and by 1988 the estimated fertility level translated into an average of 5.3 children per woman. With such high fertility, a very high proportion (40 percent) of the population is under age 15.

Mexico On the other side of the globe, in Mexico, the population is also growing very quickly as a result of a low death rate and a high, although quickly declining, birth rate. In Mexico, life expectancy (66 years) is higher than in Egypt, meaning that an even higher fraction of children survive to adulthood—Mexican women now have an average of four children each, and nearly all are likely to survive. As in Egypt, the population of Mexico is more than doubling every generation, and the age structure in Mexico is quite similar to that in northern African countries; children under 15 years of age make up 42 percent of the population.

Low Mortality and Low Fertility

The final stage in the demographic transition is the development of low risks of death accompanied by low levels of fertility, achieving a very slow rate of growth which could eventually lead to **zero population growth.** The United States in the late 1980s is an example of such a country. Other examples are Canada, Australia, Japan, the Soviet Union, and the entire European continent. I have already discussed the United States and the Soviet Union, but let me also briefly discuss Sweden, which has one of the lowest levels of mortality in the world, with a life expectancy at birth of 77 years.

Sweden's health (accompanied by its wealth) translates demographically into very high probabilities of survival to old age—indeed, nearly half of all Swedish babies will likely still be alive at age 80. This very low mortality is accompanied by very low fertility. Swedish women in 1988 were bearing an average of 1.8 children each, of whom virtually all will live to adulthood. This is a level well below that required to replace each generation (2.1), and Sweden is currently growing in numbers primarily because of immigration. Sweden's long experience with low mortality and low fertility has produced a population in which only 18 percent are under age 15, and more than 18 percent are 65 or older. The low birth rate in Sweden has been a source of genuine concern for at least some Swedes, and the Swedish Parliament has considered various means by which a rise in the birth rate could actually be encouraged (Gendell, 1979).

Throughout northern and western Europe, population growth would be almost zero or even declining were it not for the impact of in-migrants from other areas of the world. In fact, the World Bank (1984) projects that nearly all European countries will cease growing by the year 2000 and that West Germany's population will be declining by then.

SUMMARY AND CONCLUSION

High death rates kept the number of people in the world from growing rapidly until approximately the time of the Industrial Revolution. Then improved living conditions and medical advancements accelerated the pace of growth dramatically.

As populations have grown, the pressure or desire to migrate has also increased. The vast European expansion into the less developed areas of the world, which began in the fifteenth and sixteenth centuries, is the most notable illustration of massive migration and population redistribution. Today migration patterns have shifted and more people move from less developed areas to industrialized nations. Closely associated with migration and population density is the urban revolution—that is, the movement from rural to urban areas.

The current world situation finds China and India as the most populous countries, followed by the Soviet Union and the United States. The latter two countries are growing much more slowly than either China or India because their fertility is

HOW MANY HUMANS HAVE EVER LIVED?

In a burst of poetic license, not to mention perhaps unprecedented ethnocentricity, William Matthews wrote in the periodical *Vegetable Box* that "there are now more of us alive than ever have been dead" (San Diego Union, 1981b). It is certainly true that the population is increasing each year in numbers that strain credulity—could it be that today's 5 billion people exceed in number all the people who have ever been born and died over the entire history of human beings?

No, actually not. As a matter of fact, our contribution to history's total represents only a small fraction of all humans who have ever lived. Thus humbled, however, we can still hold our collective head high over the fact that more of us are alive today than lived and died during the whole of the Paleolithic Age, which spanned 86 percent of human experience (San Diego Union, 1981b). Not quite so impressive, I admit, but still a figure not to be dismissed lightly.

The question of how many humans have ever lived has intrigued scholars and been examined with some regularity over the decades. Calculations and conclusions have varied because of certain unresolved questions inherent in dealing with the unknowns of prehistorical times; nonetheless, taking into account possible flaws based on these uncertainties, it is interesting to consider the findings. In 1960, for example, William Deevey estimated that "a

cumulative total of about 110 billion individuals seem to have passed their days, and left their bones, if not their marks, on this crowded market" (1960:197). He based his figures on the assumption that human life began about 1 million years ago, that the average lifespan over history was 25 years, that the birth rate hovered just above the replacement level, and that population growth was accelerated twice in history: 10,000 years ago as a result of the Agricultural Revolution, and 300 years ago with the Industrial Revolution. In 1960 there was particular interest about how many had ever lived, since the world had just reached a total population of 3 billion, or approximately 3 percent of the total cumulative human population. According to his calculations, Deevey figured that on average "the patch of ground allotted to every person now alive may have been the lifetime habitat of 40 predecessors" (1960:197).

About the time Deevey's article was published, a similar piece of research was being prepared by Fletcher Wellemeyer and Frank Lorimer for the Population Reference Bureau (Desmond et al., 1962). Their estimate also divided history into roughly the same three periods (pre-Agricultural, Agricultural, and Industrial), each with slightly higher rates of growth than the previous one. The growth rates were influenced primarily by declines in the death much lower. In broad terms, that fact is associated with the higher standards of living in the United States and the Soviet Union, and a quick review of the demographic status of countries around the world confirms the suspicion that the slowest-growing nations tend to be the wealthier ones (although that is not universally true).

In this chapter and the preceding one, I have introduced you to population studies by discussing the sources of data and by reviewing where the world currently stands demographically. In the next chapter I will introduce you to a few of the major theories that attempt to explain how population growth is related to the social system.

---

rate: Implied in the first period was a life expectancy of only 16 years; in the second, 20 years; and in the third, 25. Wellemeyer and Lorimer started with one person (actually two) about 600,000 years ago and then calculated that from that time up to 1962 about 77 million babies had been born. "Thus, today's population of approximately three billion is about 4.0 percent of that number" (Desmond et al., 1962:1).

The most analytic of the estimates was made by Nathan Keyfitz in 1966. In a short, concise two-page article he produced a formula for estimating the number of people who have ever lived. He showed that this number was most sensitive to two assumptions: (1) the number of years we assume humans to have been around, and (2) the way in which one divides the time periods with assumed different rates of growth. Keyfitz discovered that the estimates are not very sensitive after all to assumed levels of life expectancy, at least within the 20–35-year range. He then proceeded to calculate his own estimate, assuming that human life began with two people a million years ago, with four different time periods in which growth rates differed, and with an average life expectancy of 25 years. The result was an estimated 69 billion people ever born as of 1960, of which the 3 billion then alive represented about 4 percent.

As the population of the world continues to increase, the fraction of all hu-mans who have ever lived is naturally bound to change. Thus, in 1981 Arthur Westing updated the estimate. However, he assumed a shorter span of human existence (300,000 years), and he also identified eight different periods of growth, ranging in assumed life expectancy from 20 to 50 years. As Keyfitz had suggested 15 years earlier, these changes in assumption significantly affected the overall estimates, and, sure enough, Westing calculated that as of 1980 "only" 50 billion people had ever lived. If we accept that number, then the 4.4 billion alive in 1980 accounted for 9 percent of all humans ever alive. On the other hand, if we carry Keyfitz's calculations forward from 1960 to 1980, we find that as of 1980 an estimated 71 billion people had ever been born, and the 4.4 billion people alive represented about 6 percent of the total.

It seems reasonable to conclude, then, that as of 1980 between 6 and 9 percent of all humans who had ever been born were still alive. That is a far cry from the idea that there are now more people alive than have ever previously been born and died, but it still gives us pause given the length of human history. Furthermore, the percentage increases daily—based on the projection of the world's population reaching 6 billion souls by the year 2000, the number of humans then alive will have grown to 8 to 11 percent of all humans ever born.

MAIN POINTS

1. During the first 990,000 years of some form of human existence, the population of the world had grown only to the size of New York City today.

2. Between 1750 and 1950 the world's population mushroomed from 800 million to 2.5 billion, and since 1950 it has expanded to more than 5 billion.

3. The doubling time is a convenient way to summarize the rate of population growth. It is found by dividing the average annual rate of population growth into 70.

4. Early growth of population was slow not because birth rates were low but because death rates were very high.

5. On the other hand, recent rapid increases are due to dramatic declines in mortality without a commensurate decline in fertility.

6. World population growth has been accompanied by migration from rapidly growing areas into less rapidly growing regions. Initially, that meant an outward expansion of the European population, but more recently it has meant migration from less developed to more developed nations.

7. Migration has also involved the shift of people from rural to urban areas, and urban regions on average are currently growing more rapidly than ever before in history.

8. Although many people think of migration when conjuring up images of population growth in the United States, the country has grown largely as a result of natural increase—the excess of births over deaths.

9. At the time of the American Revolution, fertility levels in the United States were among the highest in the world. Now they are among the lowest, even though there are still more babies born each year than there are people dying.

10. The world's ten most populous countries are the People's Republic of China, India, the USSR, the United States, Indonesia, Japan, Brazil, Pakistan, Bangladesh, and Nigeria. Together they account for about two thirds of the world's population.

11. At its present rate of growth the world's population could double in size in as few as 40 years. Six of the ten largest countries are growing even more rapidly than that due to their relatively low death rates combined with relatively high birth rates.

12. Countries of the world can fit roughly into each of the three stages of the demographic transition—high fertility and high mortality, high fertility and low mortality, and low fertility and low mortality.

SUGGESTED READINGS

1. Carlo Cipolla, 1965, The Economic History of World Population (Middlesex: Penguin Books).

   Professor Cipolla provides an excellent overview of the modern perspective on past population growth. This book is still timely despite its age.

2. United Nations, Demographic Yearbook (New York: United Nations), published annually.

   No matter how boring it first may seem, you will find yourself becoming absorbed by (and, in a way, *into*) this annual compilation of demographic data for nearly all of the countries on the globe.

3. Thomas McKeown, 1976, The Modern Rise of Population (London: Edward Arnold).

   This is probably the single most important study of why mortality began to decline in Europe, setting off the chain reaction around the world known as the population explosion.

4. H. Yuan Tien, 1983, "China: demographic billionaire," Population Bulletin 38(2).

   This is a summary of the overall demographic situation in China, including data from the most recent (1982) census of China.

5. Pravin Visaria and Leela Visaria, 1981, "India's population: second and growing," Population Bulletin 36(4).

   In combination with the above volume on China, you can read this and gain a background on four out of every ten human beings.

CHAPTER 3
Demographic Perspectives

In order to get a handle on population problems and issues, you have to put the facts of population together with the "whys" and "wherefores." In other words, you need a **demographic perspective**—a way of relating basic information to theories about how the world operates demographically. A demographic perspective will guide you through the sometimes tangled relationships between population factors (such as size, distribution, age structure, and growth) and the rest of what is going on in society. As you develop your own demographic perspective, you will acquire a new awareness about your community or your job, for example, or national and world political or social problems. You will be able to ask yourself about the influences that demographic changes have had (or might have had), and you will consider the demographic consequences of events.

In this chapter I will discuss several theories of how population processes are entwined with general social processes. Some of the world's most influential thinkers have analyzed the relationship between population and society, and their efforts have had important implications for government action (and inaction) in many parts of the world. The purpose of this review is to give you a start in developing your own demographic perspective by taking advantage of what others have learned and passed on to us.

There are two broad questions that have to be answered before you will be able to develop your own perspective: (1) what are the causes of population growth (or, at least, population change); and (2) what are the consequences of population growth or change? In this chapter I will discuss several perspectives that provide broad answers to these questions and that also introduce you to the major lines of demographic theory.

I begin the chapter with a brief review of premodern thinking on the subject of population. Most of these ideas are what we call **doctrine,** as opposed to **theory.** Early thinkers were certain they had the answers and certain that their proclamations represented the truth about population growth and its implications for society. By contrast, the essence of modern scientific thought is to assume that you do not have the answer and to acknowledge that you are willing to consider evidence regardless of the conclusion to which it points. In the process of sorting out the evidence, we develop tentative explanations (theories) that help to guide our thinking and our search for understanding.

PREMODERN POPULATION DOCTRINES

Ancient societies appear to have had a single consuming concern about population—they valued reproduction as a means of replacing people lost through the universally high mortality. Indeed, reproductive power was often deified, as in ancient Greece, where it was the job of a variety of goddesses to help mortals successfully bring children into the world and raise those children to adulthood. It is not until the classical Greek period, however, that we find a clearly stated population doctrine. Plato, writing in *The Laws*, emphasized that population stability was essential for the attainment of that human perfection he sought. Thus, Plato was an early exponent of the doctrine that quality in humans is more important than quantity. His views were not universally shared, however, as we note from the writings of an Indian, Kautilya, who in approximately the same century (300 B.C.) noted that although an area might contain either too many or too few people for its resources, the latter is the greater evil (see Keyfitz, 1972).

In the Roman Empire, the reigns of Julius and Augustus Caesar were marked by clearly **pronatalist** doctrines. Cicero noted that population growth was seen by emperors as a necessary means of replacing war casualties, of assuring enough people to help colonize the empire. Despite its pronatalist doctrines, however, the birth rate in the Roman Empire was declining near the end.

The Middle Ages, which followed the decline of Rome, tended to be dominated by an essentially **antinatalist** doctrine. For example, we know that Augustine (354–430) believed virginity to be the highest form of human existence. His doctrine of other-worldliness held that if all men would abstain from intercourse, then so much sooner would the City of God be filled and the end of the world hastened. This was an economically stagnant, fatalistic period of European history, and for centuries thinkers were content with the idea that population was a matter best regulated by God (Stangeland, 1904).

By the thirteenth century, following the rediscovery of Aristotle's writings, new murmurings began to be heard in Europe. Thomas Aquinas argued that marriage and family building were not inferior to celibacy. By the seventeenth century, with the rise of **mercantilism** (nations built on increasing trade and wealth), population growth (as opposed to mere replacement) was beginning to be seen as essential to an increase in public revenue. To writers such as Süssmilch in Germany, the wealth of a society was equal to the total production minus the wages paid to workers. Since the wage rate tended to decline as the labor force grew, it was clearly advantageous for a nation to have a growing population.

By the eighteenth century, it seemed that the pronatalist doctrine of the mercantilists had not succeeded in encouraging rapid population growth, but it *had* become associated with a rising level of poverty (Keyfitz, 1972). The reaction against mercantilist thought is generally labeled **physiocratic** philosophy, the essence of which is that land, not people, is the real source of wealth of a nation. Adam Smith is one of the most famous exponents of this line of reasoning, and he believed that there is a natural harmony between economic growth and population growth, with the latter depending always on the former. Thus, he felt that population size is determined by the demand for labor, which is determined by the productivity of the land.

Physiocratic thought was carried to its logical extreme by William Godwin. He was convinced that scientific progress would enable the food supply to grow far beyond the levels of his day (the late 1700s) and that such prosperity would not lead to overpopulation because people would deliberately limit their sexual expression and procreation. Furthermore, he believed that most of the problems of the poor were due not to overpopulation but to the inequities of the social institutions (United Nations, 1973b). Godwin had garnered many of his ideas from a writer of the French Revolution era, Marquis de Condorcet (Petersen, 1979), and together the ideas of these two men helped provoke the first major theory of population—that of Thomas Robert Malthus.

THE MALTHUSIAN PERSPECTIVE

The **Malthusian** perspective derives from the writings of Thomas Robert Malthus, an English clergyman and college professor. His first *Essay on the Principle of Population as it affects the future improvement of society; With remarks on the speculations of Mr. Godwin, M. Condorcet, and other writers* was published in 1798. It was followed by a substantially revised version in 1803, slightly retitled to read *An Essay on the Principle of Population; or a view of its past and present effects on human happiness; with an inquiry into our prospects respecting the future removal or mitigation of the evils which it occasions.* In all, seven editions of Malthus's *Essay* on population were published, and, as a whole, they have undoubtedly been the single most influential work relating population growth to its social consequences. Although Malthus drew heavily on earlier writers, he was the first to draw out in a systematic way a picture that links the consequences of growth to its causes.

Causes of Population Growth

Malthus believed that human beings, like plants and nonrational animals, are "impelled" to increase the population of the species by what he called a powerful "instinct"—the urge to reproduce. Further, if there were no checks on population growth, human beings would multiply to an "incalculable" number, filling "millions of worlds in a few thousand years" (Malthus, 1872:6). We humans, though, have not accomplished anything nearly that impressive. Why not? Because of the checks to growth that Malthus pointed out—factors that have kept population growth from reaching its biological potential for covering the earth with human bodies (see Table 3.1).

According to Malthus, the ultimate check to growth is lack of food (the "means of subsistence"). In turn, the means of subsistence are limited by the amount of land available, the "arts" or technology that could be applied to the land, and "social organization" or land ownership patterns. A cornerstone of his argument is that populations tend to grow more rapidly than does the food supply (a topic I return to in Chapter 14), since population has the potential for growing geometrically—two parents could have four children, sixteen grandchildren, and so on—while he believed that food production could be increased only arithmetically, by adding one acre at a time. In the natural order, then, population growth will outstrip the food supply, and the lack of food will ultimately put a stop to the increase of people.

Of course, Malthus was aware that starvation rarely operates directly to kill people, since something else usually intervenes to kill them before they actually die of starvation. This "something else" represents what Malthus calls **positive checks**, primarily those measures "whether of a moral or physical nature, which tend prematurely to weaken and destroy the human frame" (Malthus, 1872:12). Today we would call these the causes of mortality. There are also **preventive checks**—limits to birth. In theory, the preventive checks would include all possible means of birth control, including abstinence, contraception, and abortion. However, to Malthus

Table 3.1   Malthus's Frame of Reference

CAPACITY FOR POPULATION GROWTH	CHECKS TO POPULATION GROWTH											
	Preventive checks						Positive checks					
Instinct	Voluntary or rational limitations on births						All causes of mortality					
of	Moral restraint			Vice			Vice			Misery		
reproduction	Means of subsistence			Means of subsistence			Means of subsistence			Means of subsistence		
	Land	Arts	Social organization	Land	Arts	Social organization	Land	Arts	Social organization	Land	Arts	Social organization

Source: K. Davis, 1955, "Malthus and the theory of population," in P. Lazarsfeld and M. Rosenberg (eds.), The Language of Social Research (New York: The Free Press).

the only acceptable means of preventing a birth was to exercise **moral restraint**; that is, to postpone marriage, remaining chaste in the meantime, until a man feels "secure that, should he have a large family, his utmost exertions can save them from rags and squalid poverty, and their consequent degradation in the community" (1872:13). Any other means of birth control, including **contraception** (either before or after marriage), **abortion, infanticide,** or any "improper means," was viewed as a vice that would "lower, in a marked manner, the dignity of human nature." Moral restraint was a very important point with Malthus, because he believed that if people were allowed to prevent births by "improper means" (that is, prostitution, contraception, abortion, or **sterilization**), then they would expend their energies in ways that are, so to speak, not economically productive.

I should point out that as a scientific theory, the Malthusian perspective leaves much to be desired, since he constantly confuses moralistic and scientific thinking. Despite its shortcomings, however, which were evident even in his time, Malthus's reasoning led him to draw some important conclusions about the consequences of population growth.

Consequences of Population Growth

Malthus believed that a natural consequence of population growth was poverty. This is the logical end result of his arguments that (1) people have a natural urge to reproduce, and (2) the increase in the supply of food cannot keep up with population growth. In his analysis, Malthus turned the argument of Adam Smith and the physiocrats upside down. Instead of population growth being dependent on the demand for labor, as Smith argued, Malthus believed that the urge to reproduce always forces population pressure to precede the demand for labor. Thus, "overpopulation" (as measured by the level of unemployment) would force wages down to the point where people could not afford to marry and raise a family. At such low wages, with a surplus of labor and the need for each person to work harder just to earn a subsistence wage, cultivators could employ more labor, put more acres into production, and thus increase the means of subsistence. Malthus believed that this cycle of increased food resources leading to population growth leading to too many people for available resources leading then back to poverty was part of a natural law of population. Each increase in the food supply only meant that eventually more people could live in poverty.

As you can see, Malthus did not have an altogether high opinion of his fellow creatures. He figured that most of them were too "inert, sluggish, and averse from labor" (1798:363) to try to harness the urge to reproduce and avoid the increase in numbers that would lead back to poverty whenever more resources were available. In this way he essentially blamed poverty on the poor themselves. There remained only one improbable way to avoid this dreary situation.

Avoiding the Consequences

Malthus argued that "the endeavor to avoid pain rather than the pursuit of pleasure is the great stimulus to action in life" (1798:359). Pleasure will not stimulate activity until its absence is defined as being painful. Malthus suggested that the well-educated, rational person would perceive in advance the pain of having hungry children or being in debt, and would postpone marriage and sexual intercourse until he was sure that he could avoid that pain. If that motivation existed and the preventive check was operating, then the miserable consequences of population growth could be avoided. So, the only way to break the cycle is to change human nature. Malthus felt that if everyone shared middle-class values, the problem would solve itself. He saw that as impossible, though, since not everyone has the talent to be a virtuous, industrious, middle-class success story, but if most people at least tried, poverty would be reduced considerably.

To Malthus, material success is a consequence of human ability to plan rationally—to be educated about future consequences of current behavior—and he was a man who practiced what he preached. He planned his family rationally, waiting to marry and have children until he was 39—shortly after getting a secure job in 1805 as a college professor. Also, although his detractors later attributed 11 children to him, he and his wife, 11 years his junior, had only 3 children (Nickerson, 1975).

To summarize, the major consequence of population growth, according to Malthus, is poverty. Within that poverty, though, is the stimulus for action that can lift people out of misery. So, if people remain poor, it is their own fault for not trying to do something about it. For that reason, Malthus was opposed to the English Poor Laws (welfare benefits for the poor) because he felt they would actually serve to perpetuate misery. They permitted poor people to be supported by others and thus not feel that great pain, the avoidance of which might lead to birth prevention.

Malthus argued that if every man had to provide for his own children, he would be more prudent about getting married and raising a family.

Critique of Malthus

The single most obvious measure of Malthus's importance is the number of books and articles that have attacked him, and the attacks began virtually the moment his first *Essay* appeared in 1798. The three most strongly criticized aspects of his theory have been (1) the assertion that food production could not keep up with population growth, (2) the belief that moral restraint was the only acceptable preventive check, and (3) the conclusion that poverty was an inevitable result of population growth. Malthus was not a firm believer in progress; rather, he accepted the notion that each society had a fixed set of institutions that established a stationary level of living. He was aware, of course, of the Industrial Revolution, but he was skeptical of its long-run value. He was convinced that the increase in manufacturing wages that accompanied industrialization would promote population growth without increasing the agricultural production necessary to feed those additional mouths. Although it is clear that he was a voracious reader (Petersen, 1979), it is also clear that Malthus paid scant attention to the economic statistics that were available to him. "There is no sign that even at the end of his life he knew anything in detail about industrialization. His thesis was based on the life of an island agricultural nation, and so it remained long after the exports of manufacturers had begun to pay for the imports of large quantities of raw materials" (Eversley, 1959:256). Thus, Malthus either failed to see or refused to acknowledge that technological progress was possible, and that its end result was a higher standard of living, not a lower one.

Those who criticize Malthus's insistence on the value of moral restraint, while accepting many of his other conclusions, are typically known as **neo-Malthusians.** Specifically, neo-Malthusians favor contraception rather than simple reliance on moral restraint. During his lifetime, Malthus was constantly defending moral restraint against critics (many of whom were his friends) who encouraged him to deal more favorably with other means of birth control. In the fifth edition of his *Essay* he did discuss the concept of **prudential restraint,** which meant the delay of marriage until a family could be afforded without necessarily refraining from premarital sexual intercourse in the meantime. He never fully embraced the idea, however, nor did he ever bow to pressure to accept anything but moral restraint as a viable preventive check. Ironically, the open controversy actually helped to spread knowledge of birth control among people in nineteenth-century England. It was, in fact, the trial in 1877–79 of a neo-Malthusian, Charles Bradlaugh, for publishing a birth control handbook that enabled the English public to become more widely knowledgeable about those techniques (Himes, 1976).

Malthus's argument that poverty is an inevitable result of population growth is also open to scrutiny. For one thing, his writing reveals a certain circularity in logic. In Malthus's view, a laborer could achieve a higher standard of living only by being prudent and refraining from marriage until he could afford it, but Malthus also believed that you could not expect prudence from a laborer until he had attained a higher standard of living. Thus, our hypothetical laborer seems squarely enmeshed in a catch-22. Even if we were to ignore this logical inconsistency, there are problems with Malthus's belief that the Poor Laws contributed to the misery of the poor by discouraging them from exercising prudence. Historical evidence has revealed that between 1801 and 1835 those English parishes that administered Poor Law allowances did not have higher birth, marriage, or total population growth rates than those in which Poor Law assistance was not available (Huzel, 1969, 1980). Clearly, problems with the logic of Malthus's argument seemed to be compounded by his apparent inability to see the social world accurately. "The results of the 1831 Census were out before he died, yet he never came to interpret them. Statistics apart, the main charge against him must be that he was a bad observer of his fellow human beings" (Eversley, 1959:256).

Criticisms of Malthus do not, however, diminish the importance of his work:

> There are good reasons for using Malthus as a point of departure in the discussion of population theory. These are the reasons that made his work influential in his day and make it influential now. But they have little to do with whether his views are right or wrong. . . . Malthus' theories are not now and never were empirically valid, but they nevertheless were theoretically significant (Davis, 1955:541).

As I noted at the beginning of this section, part of Malthus's significance also lies in the storm of controversy his theories stimulated. Particularly vigorous in their attacks on Malthus were Karl Marx and Friedrich Engels.

THE MARXIST PERSPECTIVE

Karl Marx and Friedrich Engels were both teenagers in Germany when Malthus died in England in 1834, and by the time they had independently moved to England and met, Malthus's ideas already were politically influential in their native land. Several German states and Austria had responded to what they believed was overly rapid growth in the number of poor people by legislating against marriages in which the applicant could not guarantee that his family would not wind up on welfare (Glass, 1953). As it turned out, that scheme backfired on the German states, because people continued to have children, but out of wedlock. Thus, the welfare rolls grew as the illegitimate children had to be cared for by the state (Knodel, 1970). The laws were eventually repealed, but they had an impact on Marx and Engels, who saw the Malthusian point of view as an outrage against humanity. Their demographic perspective thus arose in reaction to Malthus.

Causes of Population Growth

Neither Marx nor Engels ever directly addressed the issue of why and how populations grew. They seem to have had little quarrel with Malthus on this point, although they were in favor of equal rights for men and women and saw no harm in preventing birth. Nonetheless, they were skeptical of the eternal or natural laws of nature as stated by Malthus (that population tends to outstrip resources), preferring instead to view human activity as the product of a particular social and economic environment. The basic **Marxist** perspective is that each society at each point in history has its own law of population that determines the consequences of population growth. For **capitalism**, the consequences are overpopulation and poverty, whereas for socialism, population growth is readily absorbed by the economy with no side effects. This line of reasoning led not to an open rejection of Malthusian theory of why populations grow, but rather to a rejection of his theory of the consequences of population growth.

Consequences of Population Growth

Marx and Engels flatly rejected the notion that poverty can be blamed on the poor. Instead, they said, poverty is the result of a poorly organized society, especially a **capitalist** society. Implicit in the writings of Marx and Engels is the idea that the normal consequence of population growth should be a significant increase in production. After all, each worker obviously was producing more than he or she required, or else how would all the dependents (including the wealthy manufacturers) survive? In a well-ordered society, if there were more people, there ought to be more wealth, not more poverty (Engels, 1844). Marx and Engels especially quarreled with the Malthusian idea that resources could not grow as rapidly as population, since they saw no reason to suspect that science and technology could not increase the availability of food and other goods at least as quickly as population grows.

Not only did Marx and Engels feel generally that poverty was not the end result of population growth, but they argued specifically that even in England at the time there was enough wealth to eliminate poverty. In England, more people had meant more wealth for the capitalists rather than for the workers because the capitalists were skimming off some of the workers' wages as profits for themselves. Marx argued that they did that by stripping the workers of their tools and then, in essence, charging the workers for being able to come to the factory to work. For example, if you don't have the tools to make a car but want a job making cars, you could get hired at the factory and work 8 hours a day. But, according to Marx, you might get paid for only 6 hours—the capitalist (owner of the factory) keeping part of your wages as payment for the tools you were using. The more the capitalist keeps, of course, the lower your wages and the poorer you will be.

Furthermore, Marx argued that capitalism worked by using the labor of the working classes to earn profits to buy machines that would replace the laborers, which, in turn, led to unemployment and poverty. Thus, the poor were not poor because they overran the food supply, but only because capitalists had first taken away part of their wages and then taken away their very jobs and replaced them with machines. Thus, the consequences of population growth that Malthus discussed were really the consequences of capitalist society, not of population growth per se. Overpopulation in a capitalist society was thought to be a result of the capitalists' desire for an industrial reserve army that would keep wages low through competition for jobs and, at the same time, would force workers to be more productive in order to keep their jobs. To Marx, however, the logical extension of this was that the growing population would bear the seeds of destruction for capitalism, because unemployment would lead to disaffection and revolution. If society could be reorganized in a more equitable (that is, **socialist**) way, then the population problems would disappear.

It is noteworthy that Marx, like Malthus, practiced what he preached. Marx was adamantly opposed to the notion of moral restraint, and his life repudiated that concept. He married at the relatively young age (compared with Malthus) of 25, proceeded to father eight children, including one illegitimate son, and was on intimate terms with poverty for much of his life.

In its original formulation, the Marxist (as well as the Malthusian) perspective was somewhat provincial, in the sense that its primary concern was England in the nineteenth century. Marx was an intense scholar who focused especially on the historical analysis of economics as applied to England, which he considered to be the classic example of capitalism. However, as his writings have found favor in other places and times, revisions have been forced upon the Marxist view of population.

Critique of Marx

Not all who have adopted a Marxist world view fully share the original Marx–Engels demographic perspective. Marxist countries have had trouble because of the lack of political direction offered by the Marxist notion that different stages of social development produce different relationships between population growth and economic development. Indeed, much of the so-called Marxist thought on population is in fact attributable to Lenin—one of the most prolific interpreters of Marx. For Marx, the Malthusian principle operated under capitalism only, whereas under pure socialism there would be no population problem. Unfortunately, he offered no guidelines for the transition period. At best, Marx implied that the socialist law of population should be the antithesis of the capitalist law. If the birth rate were high under capitalism, then the assumption was that it should be low under socialism; if abortion seemed bad for a capitalist society, it must be good for a socialistic society. Thus, it has been difficult for Soviet demographers to reconcile the fact that demographic trends in the Soviet Union have been remarkably similar to trends in other developed nations. Furthermore, Soviet socialism has been unable to alleviate one of the worst evils that Marx attributed to capitalism—higher death rates among people in the working class than those in the higher classes (Brackett, 1967).

Although Marx and Engels offered little guidance, their idea that population growth was not a problem has often been supported in official ideology. A typical official statement (typical, that is, until recently) is the following made by a Soviet official from the Republic of Ukraine at a meeting in Geneva in 1949: "I would consider as barbarous any suggestion, in this commission, of encouraging the limitation of marriages or the limitation of births in marriage. An adequate social system should be able to cope with any increases in population" (Sauvy, 1969:525).

Since the 1960s, however, Marxists have been less adamant. For example, in 1962 a Swedish proposal to the United Nations to provide birth control assistance to underdeveloped nations was met by silence on the part of the Soviet Union rather than by the usual indignation (Sauvy, 1969). In China, the empirical reality of having to deal with the world's largest national population has led to a departure from Marxist ideology. As early as 1953 the Chinese government organized efforts to control population by relaxing regulations concerning contraception and abortion. A good harvest in 1958 halted that move temporarily, however, and in 1960 a

WHO ARE THE NEO-MALTHUSIANS?

"Picture a tropical island with luscious breadfruits hanging from every branch, toasting in the sun. It is a small island, but there are only 400 of us on it so there are more breadfruits than we know what to do with. We're rich. Now picture 4,000 people on the same island, reaching for the same breadfruits: Number one, there are fewer to go around; number two, you've got to build ladders to reach most of them; number three, the island is becoming littered with breadfruit crumbs. Things get worse and worse as the population gradually expands to 40,000. Welcome to a poor, littered tropical paradise" (Tobias, 1979:49). This scenario would probably have drawn a nod of understanding from Malthus himself, and it is typical of the modern neo-Malthusian view of the world.

One of the most influential of recent neo-Malthusians is Garrett Hardin, a biologist at the University of California, Santa Barbara. In 1968, he published an article that raised the level of consciousness about population growth in the minds of professional scientists. Hardin's theme was simple and had been made in a previous article by Kingsley Davis (1963): Personal goals are not necessarily consistent with societal goals when it comes to population growth. Hardin's metaphor is "the tragedy of the commons." He asks us to imagine an open field, available as a common ground for herdsmen to graze their cattle. "As a rational being, each herdsman seeks to maximize his gain. Explicitly or implicitly, more or less consciously, he asks, "What is the utility *to me* of adding one more animal to my herd?" (Hardin, 1968:1244). The benefit, of course, is the net proceeds from the eventual sale of each additional animal, whereas the cost lies in the chance that an additional animal may result in overgrazing of the common ground. Since the ground is shared by many people, the cost is spread out over all, so for the individual herdsman, the benefit of another animal exceeds its cost. "But," notes Hardin, "this is the conclusion reached by each and every rational herdsman sharing a commons. Therein is the tragedy. Each man is locked into a system that compels him to increase his herd without limit—in a world that is limited" (1968:1244). The moral, as Hardin puts it, is that "ruin is the destination toward which all men rush, each pursuing his own best interest in a society that believes in the freedom of the commons. Freedom in a commons brings ruin to all" (1968:1244).

Hardin reminds us that most societies are committed to a social welfare ideal. Families are not completely on their own. We share numerous things in common: education, public health, and police protection, and in the United States we are guaranteed a minimum amount of food and income at the public expense. This leads to a moral dilemma that is at the heart of Hardin's message: "To couple the concept of freedom to breed with the belief that everyone born has an equal right to the commons is to lock the world into a tragic course of action" (Hardin, 1968:1246). He is referring, of course, to the ultimate Malthusian clash of population and resources, and Hardin is no more optimistic than Malthus about the likelihood of people voluntarily limiting their fertility before it is too late.

Meanwhile, the public was becoming keenly aware of the population crisis

Chinese official quoted Chairman Mao as having said, "A large population in China is a good thing. With a population increase of several fold we still have an adequate solution. The solution lies in production" (Ta-k'un, 1960:704). Yet by 1979 production no longer seemed to be a panacea, and the interpretation of Marx took an about-face as another Chinese official wrote that under Marxism the law of produc-

---

through the writings of another neo-Malthusian—Paul Ehrlich. Like Hardin, Ehrlich is a biologist (at Stanford University), not a professional demographer. In the second edition of his book, *The Population Bomb* (1971), Ehrlich phrased the situation in three parts: "too many people," "too little food," and, adding a wrinkle not foreseen directly by Malthus, environmental degradation (Ehrlich called Earth "a dying planet"). Of too many people, Ehrlich says: "Underdeveloped countries of the world face an inevitable population–food crisis. Each year food production in these countries falls a bit further behind burgeoning population growth, and people go to bed a little hungrier" (1971:3). At the same time, developed nations are overpopulated because they "show symptoms in the form of environmental deterioration and increased difficulty in obtaining resources to support their affluence" (1971:3). Ehrlich's point about too little food is summed up succinctly in the statement that "at least half of the people of the world are now undernourished (have too little food) or malnourished (have serious imbalances in their diet)" (1971:18). "There is not enough food today. How much there will be tomorrow is open to debate" (1971:24).

Ehrlich thus argues that Malthus was right—dead right. But the death struggle is more complicated than that foreseen by Malthus. To Ehrlich, the poor are dying of hunger, while rich and poor alike are dying from the by-products of affluence—pollution and ecological disaster. Indeed, this is part of the "commons" problem. A few benefit; all suffer. What does the future hold? Ehrlich suggests that there are only two solutions to the population problem: the birth-

rate solution (lowering the birth rate) and the death-rate solution (a rise in the death rate). He views the death-rate solution as being the most likely to happen because, like Malthus, he has little faith in the ability of humankind to pull its act together. The only way to avoid that scenario is to bring the birth rate under control—by force, if necessary.

Regardless of his theoretical tightness, regardless of his intellectual rigor, Ehrlich made his point. The population of the world was growing rapidly and somebody had to do something. A major part of his contribution was to encourage people to take some action themselves—to spread the word and practice what they preached. Like Hardin, Ehrlich feels that population growth is outstripping resources and ruining the environment. If we sit back and wait for people to react to this situation, disaster will likely strike. Therefore, we need to act swiftly to force people to limit their fertility by whatever means possible.

Neo-Malthusians thus differ from Malthus because they reject moral restraint as the only acceptable means of birth control and because they face a situation in which they see population growth as leading not simply to poverty but also to widespread calamity. For neo-Malthusians, the "evil arising from the redundancy of population" (Malthus, 1872: preface to the fifth edition) has broadened in scope and the remedies proposed are thus more dramatic.

Gloomy they may have been, but the messages of Ehrlich and Hardin were important and impressive and brought population issues to the attention of an entire generation of people in the developed world.

tion "demands not only a planned production of natural goods, but also the planned reproduction of human beings" (Muhua, 1979:724). Thus, despite Marx's denial of a population problem, the Marxist government in China is dealing with one.

This should not lead you to believe, of course, that Marxist writers have completely retooled their philosophy. In Pakistan, for example, where the government (non-Marxist) has officially recognized the need to slow population growth, there has been criticism by Marxists who continue to argue that the rampant poverty in that nation can only be alleviated by a redistribution of wealth (Ahmad, 1977). But there is subtle change. It is no longer stated that population growth can continue without deleterious consequences. Rather, many Marxists now suggest that only after a socialist revolution and reordering of society will people be motivated to lower the birth rate. "If . . . governments of developing countries move to socialize the labour and means of production so that everyone benefits equally, they will achieve a lower rate of growth. . . . When all enjoy the fruits of technological advancement people will reduce their family size" (Ahmad, 1977:27). In formulations such as this, Marxism is being revised in the light of new scientific evidence about how people behave, in the same way that Malthusian thought has been revised. Bear in mind that although the Marxist and Malthusian perspectives are often seen as antithetical, they both originated in nineteenth-century Europe in the midst of that milieu of economic, social, and demographic change.

The population-growth controversy, initiated by Malthus and fueled by Marx, emerged into a series of nineteenth-century and early twentieth-century reformulations that have led directly to prevailing theories in demography. In the next section I will briefly discuss three individuals who figured prominently in those reformulations—John Stuart Mill, Ludwig Brentano, and Emile Durkheim.

OTHER EARLY MODERN POPULATION THEORIES

Mill

An extremely influential writer of the nineteenth century was the English philosopher and economist John Stuart Mill. Mill was not so quarrelsome about Malthus as Marx and Engels had been; his scientific insights were greater than those of Malthus at the same time that his politics were less radical than those of Marx and Engels. Although Mill accepted the Malthusian calculations about the *potential* for population growth to outstrip food production as being axiomatic, a self-truth, he was more optimistic about human nature than was Malthus. Mill believed that, although a person's character is formed by circumstances, one's own desires can do much to shape circumstances and modify future habits (Mill, 1924).

Mill's basic thesis was that the standard of living is a major determinant of fertility levels. "In proportion as mankind rises above the condition of the beast, population is restrained by the fear of want, rather than by want itself. Even where there is no question of starvation, many are similarly acted upon by the apprehension of losing what have come to be regarded as the decencies of their situation in life" (1848:Book 1, Chap. 10). The belief that people could be and should be free to pursue their own goals in life led him to reject the idea that poverty is inevitable (as Malthus implied) or that it is the creation of capitalist society (as Marx argued).

Indeed, one of Mill's most famous comments is that "the niggardliness of nature, not the injustice of society, is the cause of the penalty attached to overpopulation" (1848:Book I, Chap. 13). In the event that population ever did overrun the food supply, however, Mill felt that it would likely be a temporary situation with at least two possible solutions—import food or export people.

The ideal state from Mill's point of view is that in which all members of a society are economically comfortable. At that point he felt (as Plato had centuries earlier) that the population should stabilize and people should try to progress culturally, morally, and socially instead of attempting continually to get ahead economically. It does sound good, but how do we get to that point? It was Mill's belief that, prior to reaching the point at which both population and production are stable, there is essentially a race between the two. What is required to settle the issue is a dramatic improvement in the living conditions of the poor. If social and economic development is to occur, there must be a sudden increase in income, which could give rise to a new standard of living for a whole generation, thus allowing productivity to outdistance population growth. According to Mill, this was the situation in France after the revolution:

> During the generation which the Revolution raised from the extremes of hopeless wretchedness to sudden abundance, a great increase of population took place. But a generation has grown up, which, having been born in improved circumstances, has not learnt to be miserable; and upon them the spirit of thrift operates most conspicuously, in keeping the increase of population within the increase of national wealth (1848:Book II, Chap. 7).

Mill was further convinced that an important ingredient in the transformation to a nongrowing population is that women do not want as many children as men do, and, if they are allowed to voice their opinions, the birth rate will decline. Mill, like Marx, was a champion of equal rights for both sexes, and one of Mill's more notable essays, "On Liberty," was co-authored with his wife. He reasoned further that a system of national education for poor children would provide them with the "common sense" (as Mill put it) to refrain from having too many children.

Overall, Mill's perspective on population growth was significant enough that we find his arguments surviving today in the writings of Kingsley Davis, Richard Easterlin, and Harvey Leibenstein, among other contemporary demographers whose names will appear in the pages that follow. However, before getting to those contemporary thinkers, it is important to acknowledge at least two other individuals whose thinking has an amazingly modern sound, even though many decades old—Brentano and Durkheim.

Brentano

Ludwig Brentano was a German-born economist who, like Marx, had moved to England to pursue his intellectual career. Brentano was a staunch critic of Malthus because Brentano believed, somewhat as Mill did, that one could not expect poor people to lower their fertility without some kind of motivation. Brentano suggested that prosperity is the cause of the decline in the birth rate (1910). How does this work? Brentano argued that "as prosperity increases, so do the pleasures which compete with marriage, while the feeling towards children takes on a new character of refinement and both tend to diminish the desire to beget and to bear children" (1910:384). For a woman, the motivation boils down to the desire not to spend her life being pregnant and the fact that child care may interrupt a career or other pleasurable pursuits. For a man, the motivation is seen as being largely economic, because the increased demand for his resources made by children can cut him off from other satisfactions. Further, limiting the number of children permits each child's welfare to be maximized. These thoughts presage the theories of alternative opportunities that dominate contemporary thinking, as you will see in subsequent chapters.

Durkheim

While Mill and Brentano were concerned with the causes of population growth, a late–nineteenth-century French sociologist, Emile Durkheim, was basing an entire social theory on the consequences of population growth. In discussing the increasing complexity of modern societies, characterized particularly by increasing divisions of labor, Durkheim proposed that "the division of labor varies in direct ratio with the volume and density of societies, and, if it progresses in a continuous manner in the course of social development, it is because societies become regularly denser and more voluminous" (1933:262). Durkheim proceeded to explain that population growth leads to greater societal specialization because the struggle for existence is more acute when there are more people.

If you compare a primitive society with an industrialized society, the primitive society is not very specialized. By contrast, in industrialized societies there is a lot of differentiation; that is, there is an increasingly long list of occupations and social classes. Why is this? The answer is in the volume and density of the population. Growth creates competition for society's resources, and in order to improve one's advantage in the struggle, each person specializes. This thesis of Durkheim that population growth leads to specialization was derived (he himself acknowledges) from Darwin's theory of evolution. In turn, Darwin acknowledged his own debt to Malthus.

The critical theorizing of the nineteenth and early twentieth centuries set the stage for more systematic collection of data to test aspects of those theories and to examine more carefully those that might be valid and those that should be discarded. As population studies became more quantitative, a phenomenon called the *demographic transition* took shape and took the attention of demographers.

THE THEORY OF THE DEMOGRAPHIC TRANSITION

Although it has dominated recent demographic thinking, the **demographic transition** theory actually began as only a description of the demographic changes that had taken place over time in the advanced nations. In particular, it described the transition from high birth and death rates to low birth and death rates. The idea emerged as early as 1929, when Warren Thompson gathered data from "certain countries" for the period 1908–27 and showed that the countries fell into three main groups, according to their patterns of population growth:

> Group A countries (northern and western Europe and the United States): From the latter part of the nineteenth century to 1927 they had moved from having very high rates of natural increase to having very low rates of increase "and will shortly become stationary and start to decline in numbers" (Thompson, 1929:968).

> Group B (Italy, Spain, and the "Slavic" peoples of central Europe): Thompson saw evidence of a decline in both birth rates and death rates, but suggested that "it appears probable that the death rate will decline as rapidly or even more rapidly than the birth rate for some time yet. The condition in these Group B countries is much the same as existed in the Group A countries thirty to fifty years ago" (Thompson, 1929:968–969).

> Group C (rest of the world): In the rest of the world Thompson saw little evidence of control over either births or deaths.

As a consequence of this relative lack of voluntary control over births and deaths, Thompson felt that the Group C countries (which included about 70 to 75 percent of the population of the world at the time) would continue to have their growth "determined largely by the opportunities they have to increase their means of subsistence. Malthus described their processes of growth quite accurately when he said 'that population does invariably increase, where there are means of subsistence. . . .'" (Thompson, 1929:971).

Thompson's work, however, came at a time when there was relatively little concern about overpopulation. Indeed, in 1936 birth rates in the United States and Europe were so low that Enid Charles published a widely read book called *The Twilight of Parenthood,* which was introduced with the comment that "in place of the Malthusian menace of overpopulation there is now real danger of underpopulation" (Charles, 1936:v). Furthermore, Thompson's labels for his categories had little charisma (it is difficult to build a theory around categories called A, B, and C).

Sixteen years after Thompson's work, in 1945, Frank Notestein picked up the threads of his thesis and provided labels for the three types of growth patterns that Thompson had simply called A, B, and C. Notestein called the Group A pattern **incipient decline,** the Group B pattern **transitional growth,** and the Group C pattern **high growth potential.** Thus was born the term *demographic transition.* It is that period of rapid growth when a country is moving from high birth and death rates to low birth and death rates—from high growth potential to incipient decline (see Figure 3.1). That same year, Kingsley Davis (1945) edited a volume of *The Annals of the American Academy of Political and Social Sciences* entitled *World Population in Transition,* and in the lead article he noted that "viewed in the long-run, earth's population has been like a long, thin powder fuse that burns slowly and haltingly until it finally reaches the charge and explodes" (Davis, 1945:1). At this point in the 1940s, however, the demographic transition was merely a picture of demographic change, not a theory. But each new country studied fit into the picture, and it seemed

Figure 3.1   The Demographic Transition

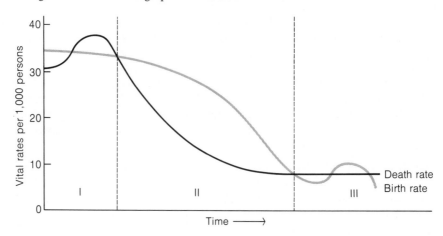

The demographic transition is divided roughly into three stages. In the first stage there is high growth potential because both birth and death rates are high. The second stage is the transition from high to low birth and death rates. During this stage the growth potential is realized as the death rate drops before the birth rate drops, resulting in rapid population growth. Finally, the last stage is a time when death rates are as low as they are likely to go, while fertility may continue to decline to the point that the population might eventually decline in numbers. In the developed countries, the full transition took place roughly as schematized. However, the less developed nations have not yet followed the full pattern of change.

as though some new universal law of population growth—an evolutionary scheme—was being developed. The apparent historical uniqueness of the demographic transition (all known cases have occurred within the last 200 years) has spawned a host of alternative names—the vital revolution and the demographic revolution, to give the more important. The term **population explosion,** for example, refers to what Notestein called *transitional growth*.

Between the mid-1940s and the late 1960s rapid population growth became a worldwide concern, and demographers devoted a great deal of time to the demographic transition perspective. By 1964, George Stolnitz was able to report that "demographic transitions rank among the most sweeping and best-documented trends of modern times . . . based upon hundreds of investigations, covering a host of specific places, periods and events" (1964:20). As the pattern of change took shape, explanations developed for why and how countries pass through the transition. These explanations tended to be cobbled together in a somewhat piecemeal fashion from the nineteenth- and early twentieth-century writers I discussed earlier in this chapter, but overall they were derived from the concept of **modernization.**

Thus, the demographic transition moved from a mere description of events to a demographic perspective. In its initial formulations this perspective was perhaps best expressed by the sentiments "take care of the people and population will take care of itself" or "development is the best contraceptive" (Teitelbaum, 1975). It drew on the available data for most countries that had gone through the transition. Death rates declined as the standard of living improved, and birth rates almost always declined a few decades later, eventually dropping to low levels, although rarely as low as the death rate. It was argued that the decline in the birth rate typically lagged behind the decline in the death rate because it takes time for a population to adjust to the fact that mortality really is lower, and because the social and economic institutions that favored high fertility require time to adjust to new norms of lower fertility that are more consistent with the lower levels of mortality. Since most people value the prolongation of life, it is not hard to lower mortality, but the reduction of fertility is contrary to the established norms of societies that have required high birth rates to keep pace with high death rates; such norms are not easily changed, even in the face of poverty.

Birth rates eventually declined, it was argued, as the importance of family life was weakened by industrial and urban life, thus weakening the pressure for large families. Large families are presumed to have been desired because they provided parents with a built-in labor pool, and because children provided old-age security for parents. The same **economic development** that lowered mortality is theorized to transform a society into an urban industrial state in which compulsory education lowers the value of children by removing them from the labor force, and people come to realize that lower **infant mortality** means that fewer children need to be born to achieve a certain number of live children. Finally, as a consequence of the many alterations in **social institutions**, "the pressure from high fertility weakens and the idea of conscious control of fertility gradually gains strength" (Teitelbaum, 1975:421).

Critique of the Demographic Transition Theory

In its original formulation, the demographic transition theory viewed high fertility as a reaction to high mortality. As mortality declines, the need for high fertility lessens and so birth rates go down. There is a spurt of growth in that transition period, but presumably the consequences will not be serious if the decline in mortality was produced by a rise in the standard of living, which, in its turn, produces a motivation for smaller families. But what will be the consequences if mortality declines and fertility does not? That situation presumably is precluded by the theory of demographic transition, but the demographic transition theory has not been capable of predicting levels of mortality or fertility or the timing of the fertility decline. This is because the initial explanation for the demographic behavior during the transition tended to be **ethnocentric.** It relied almost exclusively on the sentiment that "what is good for the goose is good for the gander." In other words, if this is what happened to the developed countries, why should it not also happen to other countries that are not so advanced? One reason might be that the preconditions for the demographic transition are considerably different now than they were when the industrialized countries began their transition.

For example, prior to undergoing the demographic transition, few of the currently industrialized countries had birth rates as high as those of most currently less developed countries, nor indeed were their levels of mortality so high. Yet, when mortality did decline, it did so as a consequence of internal economic development, not as a result of a foreign country bringing in sophisticated techniques of disease prevention, as is the case today. A second reason might be that the factors leading to the demographic transition were actually different from what for years had been accepted as true. These problems with the usual explanations of the demographic transition have led to new research and a reformulation of the perspective.

Reformulation of the Demographic Transition Theory

The long-held "classic" explanation for the demographic transition, which I have just outlined, was based essentially on **deductive logic.** Demographers had measured the changes in birth and death rates and had concluded unequivocally: "In traditional societies fertility and mortality are high. In modern societies fertility and mortality are low. In between, there is demographic transition" (Demeny, 1968:502). Though the explanations they offered for this state of affairs seemed reasonable enough, they have not always been supported by the facts emerging from more detailed research. One of the most important social scientific endeavors to cast doubt on the classic explanation was the European Fertility History Project, directed by Ansley Coale at Princeton University. In the early 1960s researchers working on this project began to reexamine the histories of all European provinces (cutting across virtually all European nations) in an attempt to establish exactly how and why the transition occurred. The focus was on the decline in fertility, because it is the most problematic aspect of the classic explanation. Based on these new findings, investigators have used **inductive logic** to revise the theory of the demographic transition.

One of the first clues that a revision was needed was the discovery that the decline of fertility in Europe occurred in the context of widely differing social, economic, and demographic conditions (van de Walle and Knodel, 1967). Economic development emerges, then, as a sufficient cause of fertility decline, though not a necessary one (Coale, 1973). For example, many provinces of Europe experienced a rapid drop in the birth rate even though they were not very urban, infant mortality rates were high, and a low percentage of the population was in industrial occupations. The data suggest that one of the more common similarities in those areas that have undergone fertility declines is the rapid spread of **secularization** (it has also been called *modernization,* although that term is broader and thus harder to pin down—Kelly and Cutright, 1980). Secularization is an attitude of autonomy from other-worldly powers and a sense of responsibility for one's own well-being (Lesthaeghe, 1977; Leasure, 1982). It is difficult to know exactly why such attitudes arise when and where they do, but we do know that industrialization and economic development are virtually always accompanied by secularization; secularization, however, can occur independently of industrialization. When it pops up, it often spreads quickly, being diffused through social networks as people imitate the behavior of others to whom they look for clues to proper and appropriate conduct.

Education has been identified as one potential stimulant to such altered attitudes, especially mass education that tends to emphasize modernization and secular concepts (Caldwell, 1980). Education facilitates the rapid spread of new ideas and information, which would perhaps help explain one of the more important findings from the European Fertility History Project—that the onset of long-term fertility decline tended to be concentrated in a relatively short period of time (van de Walle and Knodel, 1980). Thus, when the idea of family limitation was embraced in an area, the practice gained rapidly in popularity. However, it also was true that some areas of Europe that were similar with respect to socioeconomic development did not experience a fertility decline at the same time, whereas other provinces that were less similar socioeconomically experienced nearly identical drops in fertility. The data suggest that this riddle is solved by examining cultural factors rather than socioeconomic ones. Areas that share a similar culture (same language, common ethnic background, similar lifestyle) were more likely to share a decline in fertility than areas that were culturally less similar. The principal reason for this is that the idea of family planning seemed to spread quickly only until it ran into a barrier to its communication. Language is one such barrier (Leasure, 1962; Lesthaeghe, 1977), and social and economic inequality in a region is another (Lengyel-Cook and Repetto, 1982). Social distance between people turns out to be a very effective inhibitor of communication of new ideas and attitudes.

What kinds of ideas and attitudes might encourage people to rethink how many children they ought to have? The answer seems to be in the changing value that parents see in having children. Caldwell (1976; 1982) has suggested that "there is no ceiling in primitive and traditional societies to the number of children who would be economically beneficial" (1976:331). Children are a source of income and support for parents throughout life, and they produce far more than they cost in such societies. The **wealth flow**, as Caldwell calls it, is from children to parents. But the process of modernization eventually results in the tearing apart of large, extended family units into smaller, nuclear units that are economically and emotionally self-sufficient. As that happens, children begin to cost parents more (including the cost of educating them as demanded by a modernizing society) and the amount of support that parents get from children begins to decline (starting with the income lost because the children are in school rather than working). As the wealth flow reverses and parents begin to spend their income on children, rather than deriving income from them, the economic value of children declines and people no longer derive any economic advantage from children. Economic rationality would dictate having zero children, but in reality, of course, people continue having children for a variety of social reasons (which I will detail in Chapter 5).

I would be remiss if I did not also add that motivation to limit children needs to be linked to the means to do so. In the demographic transitions of the now developed societies, motivation to control children had to be particularly strong in order for fertility to drop, because the methods available to prevent conception or birth were not very sophisticated. In our modern world, safe, effective, and fairly easy to use methods of fertility control are available throughout the world (albeit unevenly so, as I will discuss in Chapter 15). Thus, fertility can be readily influenced with lower levels of motivation for family limitation than in the past or, more optimistically, birth rates can now decline much more rapidly as the motivation for fertility control grows. The existence of modern contraceptive methods has, of course, encouraged the development of programs designed to deliver those methods to couples wanting them and those programs have the potential to independently influence couples to limit fertility (World Bank, 1984).

A major strength of the reformulation of the demographic transition is that nearly all other perspectives can find a home here. Malthusians note with satisfaction that fertility first declined in Europe primarily as a result of a delay in marriage, much as Malthus would have preferred. Neo-Malthusians can take heart from the fact that rapid and sustained declines occurred simultaneously with the spread of knowledge about family planning practices. Marxists also find a place for themselves in the reformulated demographic transition perspective, because its basic tenet is that a change in the social structure is necessary to bring about a decline in fertility. This is only a short step away from agreeing with Marx that there is no universal law of population, but rather that each stage of development and social organization has its own law.

Marxists had shied away from embracing the classic explanation for the demographic transition because they considered it too simple and too amenable to a Malthusian interpretation. A. P. Sudoplatov, a demographer at the Center for Population Studies at Moscow State University, summarized the Soviet reaction to the original demographic transition by suggesting that "at first glance this posing of the problem gives grounds for counterposing it to the traditional Malthusian conceptions of overpopulation" (Sudoplatov, 1978:407). But Sudoplatov notes, on closer inspection, that the classic perspective on the demographic transition assumes that all nations face the same set of demographic conditions as they move through time. This led him to conclude that "adherents of the theory of 'demographic evolution' thus willy-nilly join forces with neo-Malthusian outlooks on the role and place of population in social development" (1978:407). The reformulation of the demographic transition is less deterministic than the classic explanation, and it provides more common ground on which non-Marxist demographers can meet their Marxist counterparts.

Another attempt to go beyond the usual explanation offered by the demographic transition theory is the theory of *demographic change and response*.

THE THEORY OF DEMOGRAPHIC CHANGE AND RESPONSE

The theory of **demographic change and response** was put forward by Kingsley Davis in 1963 as an adjunct, not really an alternative, to the demographic transition theory. Davis's concern is also with the causes of population growth, on the assumption that in order to do anything about the consequences, you have to know the causes. The basic problem Davis attempts to deal with is the central issue of the demographic transition theory: How (and under what conditions) can a mortality decline lead to a fertility decline?

To answer that question, Davis asked what happens to individuals when mortality declines. The answer is that more children survive through adulthood, putting greater pressure on family resources, and people have to reorganize their lives in an attempt to relieve that pressure—that is, people respond to the demographic change. But note that their response will be in terms of personal goals, not national goals. It rarely matters what a government wants. If individual members of a society do not stand to gain by behaving in a particular way, they probably will not behave that way. Indeed, that was a major argument made by the neo-Malthusians against moral restraint. Why advocate postponement of marriage and sexual gratification rather than contraception when you know that few people who postpone marriage are actually going to postpone sexual intercourse, too? In fact, Brentano (1910) quite forthrightly suggested that Malthus was insane to think that abstinence was the cure for the poor.

In all events, Davis argued that the response that individuals make to the population pressure created by more members joining their ranks is determined by the means available to them. A first response, nondemographic in nature, is to try to increase resources by working harder—longer hours perhaps, a second job, and so on. If that is not sufficient, then migration of some family members (typically unmarried sons or daughters) is the easiest demographic response. Davis (1963) has documented the response of rural people who have too many children and send them to the city to take advantage of whatever opportunities (that is, resources) might exist there. These are, of course, similar to the options laid out by Mill more than 100 years before Davis's writing.

But what will be the response of that second generation—the children who now have survived when previously they would not have, and who have thus put the pressure on resources? Davis argues that if (and this is a big if) there is in fact a chance for social or economic improvement, then people will try to take advantage of those opportunities by avoiding the large families that caused problems for their parents.

Davis suggests that the most powerful motive for family limitation is not fear of poverty or avoidance of pain as Malthus argued; rather it is the prospect of rising prosperity that will most often motivate people to find the means to limit the number of children they have (see Chapter 4 for a fuller discussion of these means). Davis echoes Brentano's theme here, but adds that at the very least, the desire to maintain one's relative status in society may lead to an active desire to prevent too many children from draining away one's resources. Of course, that assumes the individuals in question have already attained some status worth maintaining.

One of Davis's most important contributions to our demographic perspective is, as Cicourel put it, that he "seems to rely on an implicit model of the actor who makes everyday interpretations of perceived environmental changes" (1974:8). For example, people will respond to a decline in mortality only if they notice it, and then their response will be determined by the social situation in which they find themselves. Davis's analysis was one of the first to suggest the important link between the everyday lives of individuals and the kinds of population changes that take place in society.

Another contemporary demographer who has attempted this kind of analysis is Richard Easterlin, whose ideas have been called the *theory of relative income.*

THE THEORY OF RELATIVE INCOME

The **theory of relative income** is based on the idea that the birth rate does not necessarily respond to absolute levels of economic well-being but rather to levels that are relative to those to which one is accustomed (Easterlin, 1968; 1978). Easterlin assumes that the standard of living you experience in late childhood is the base from which you evaluate your chances as an adult. If you can easily improve your income as an adult relative to your late childhood level, then you will be more likely to marry early and have several children. On the other hand, if you perceive that it is going to be rough sledding as an adult even to match the level of living you were accustomed to as a child, that fear will probably lead you to postpone marriage or at least postpone childbearing.

So far the theory of relative income is strikingly similar to Mill's writing a hundred years earlier. But Easterlin goes on to ask what factors might cause you to be in relatively advantageous or disadvantageous position as you begin adulthood. He argues that the answer lies in the relationship between the business cycles and the demographic responses to those cycles. In a society unencumbered by government intervention, a long-term (say, 15-year) upswing in business will encourage immigration, and it may also make it easier for people to marry and have children. The *may* in this case depends on another demographic variable that has not yet entered the picture, the **age structure**—the number and proportion of people at each age in a society. If young people are relatively scarce in society and business is good, they will be in relatively high demand. In nearly classic Malthusian fashion, they will be able to command high wages and thus be more likely to feel comfortable about getting married and starting a family. Of course, how comfortable they are will depend on how much those wages can buy relative to what they are accustomed to. If young people are in relatively abundant supply, then even if business is good, the competition for jobs will be stiff and it will be difficult for people to maintain their accustomed level of living, much less marry and start a family.

You should be asking yourself why there might be a relative scarcity or abundance of young people in the age structure. Although I will discuss this in more detail in Chapters 5 and 8, suffice it here to note that it is due primarily to fluctuations in the birth rate, which are influenced by the pattern of people marrying and having children. Thus, Easterlin's thesis presents a model of society in which demographic change and economic change are closely interrelated. Economic changes produce demographic changes, which in turn produce economic changes, and so on. The model, however, has a certain middle-class bias. What about the people at the bottom end of the economic ladder, for whom relative deprivation does not necessarily apply because they already have so little? Are they caught in a constant Malthusian cycle of overpopulation and poverty? Mill suggested in 1848 that they were, unless one entire generation could be catapulted into the middle class.

When using data for entire societies the relationships that Easterlin predicts have generally been found—business cycles, cohort sizes, and birth rates do seem to work basically in tandem (Lee, 1976). Butz and Ward (1979), for example, have shown that fertility began to decline during the recent "Baby Bust" in the United States as two-earner families replaced the traditional one-earner family. In all likelihood, this happened because the economic circumstances brought about by the Baby Boom forced a recognition on the part of a growing proportion of young couples that two incomes were required to maintain the desired standard of living, and that two earners precluded a large family. The Easterlin effect would suggest that the children of the Baby Boomers, being fewer in number, will find it relatively easier to get a job, marry, and have children—leading to an expected rise in fertility in the United States in the late 1980s. "But since the 1960s a force has arisen that opposes this effect, which, for brevity's sake, can be called women's liberation. If women want to work, and have their importance in the world outside the confines of the family as men have always had, then they will have fewer children. The Easterlin effect is still there, but it is masked by the liberation effect. A few more years into the 1980s will tell us which of the two effects dominates" (Keyfitz, 1982:745).

It should be apparent to you by now that there is, at present, no overarching, all-encompassing theory that explains every aspect of demographic behavior. Population growth is no longer viewed as being caused by one set of factors, nor as having a simple prescribed set of consequences. We now know that the world is more complicated than that, and that population growth creates changes in society, which in turn stimulate further responses in demographic behavior. The remainder of this book is devoted to increasing your understanding of these interrelationships.

SUMMARY AND CONCLUSION

I have traced for you the progression of demographic thinking from ancient doctrines to contemporary systematic perspectives. Malthus was the first, and certainly the most influential, of the modern writers. Malthus believed that a biological urge to reproduce was the cause of population growth and that its natural consequence was poverty. Marx, on the other hand, did not openly argue with the Malthusian causes of growth, but he vehemently disagreed with the idea that poverty is the natural consequence of population growth. Marx denied that population growth was a problem per se—it only appeared that way in capitalist society. It may have seemed peculiar to you to discuss a person who denied the importance of a demographic perspective in a chapter dedicated to that very importance. However, the Marxist point of view is prevalent enough today among leaders in socialist countries that this attitude becomes in itself a demographic perspective of some significance.

The perspective of Mill, who seems very contemporary in many of his ideas, was somewhere between that of Malthus and Marx. He believed that increased productivity could lead to a motivation for having smaller families, especially if the influence of women was allowed to be felt and if people were educated about the possible consequences of having a large family. Brentano took these kinds of individual motivations a step further and suggested in greater detail the reasons why prosperity generally leads to a decline in the birth rate. Durkheim's perspective emphasized the consequences more than the causes of population growth. He was convinced that the complexity of modern societies is due almost entirely to the social responses to population growth—more people lead to higher levels of innovation and specialization.

More recently developed demographic perspectives have implicitly assumed that the consequences of population growth are serious and problematic, and they move directly to explanations of the causes of population growth. The theory of the demographic transition suggests that growth is an intermediate stage between the more stable conditions of high birth and death rates and low birth and death rates. If you accept this perspective, you view the world in an evolutionary way—a decline in mortality will almost necessarily be followed by a decline in fertility. The theory of demographic change and response considers the kind of individual decision making that has to take place before fertility will decline from previous high levels. The theory of relative income builds on the idea that reproductive behavior is not based solely on what is happening in the rest of society but also on one's relative status in society. It is a perspective that specifically ties together the interaction between the causes and consequences of demographic change.

With a bit of theory in hand (and hopefully in your head as well), we are now ready to probe more deeply into the analysis of population processes to come to an appreciation of why birth rates are high in some places and low in others, why death rates are low in some places and not in others, and why some people move and others do not.

MAIN POINTS

1. A demographic perspective is a way of relating basic population information to theories about how the world operates demographically.

2. Premodern population perspectives were more doctrinaire than theoretical in their orientation. They were also generally pronatalist.

3. The Malthusian perspective is based on the writings of Thomas Robert Malthus, whose first *Essay on Population* appeared in 1798 and has been one of the most influential works ever written on population growth and its societal consequences.

4. According to Malthus, population growth is generated by the urge to reproduce, although growth is checked ultimately by the means of subsistence.

5. The natural consequences of population growth according to Malthus are misery and poverty because of the tendency for populations to grow faster than the food supply. Nonetheless, he believed that misery could be avoided if people practiced moral restraint—a simple formula of chastity before marriage and a delay in marriage until you can afford all the children that God might provide.

6. Karl Marx and Friedrich Engels stenuously objected to the Malthusian population perspective because it blamed poverty on the poor rather than on the evils of social organization.

7. Marx and Engels believed that overpopulation was a product of capitalism and that in a socialist society either there would be enough resources per person or else people would be motivated to keep families small.

8. Not suprisingly, very few people have bought the Malthusian idea of moral restraint, although there are many who agree that population growth tends to

outstrip food production. Such people are usually called neo-Malthusians and believe in the use of birth control.

9. Revisions of Marxist ideology frequently include a more active government role in trying to influence birth limitation.

10. John Stuart Mill argued that the standard of living is a major determinant of fertility levels, but he also felt that people could influence their own demographic destinies.

11. Ludwig Brentano criticized Malthus because Brentano believed that poor women need to have positive motivation to encourage them to have fewer children.

12. Emile Durkheim built an entire theory of social structure on his conception of the consequences of population growth.

13. The theory of the demographic transition is a perspective that emphasizes the importance of economic and social development, which leads first to a decline in mortality and then, after some time lag, to a commensurate decline in fertility. It is based on the experience of the developed nations.

14. Reformulations of the demographic transition theory suggest that secularization, rather than socioeconomic development, may be an important key to declining fertility.

15. The theory of demographic change and response emphasizes that people must perceive a personal need to change behavior before a decline in fertility will take place, and that the kind of response they make will depend on what means are available to them.

16. The relative income perspective views changes in the birth rate as being a response to levels of economic well-being that are relative to those to which one is accustomed.

SUGGESTED READINGS

1. United Nations, 1973, The Determinants and Consequences of Population Trends (New York: United Nations).

   This volume was written by well-known and highly expert demographers and is the best single source for a comprehensive view of major demographic theories.

2. Thomas Malthus, 1798, An Essay on the Principles of Population, 1st Ed. (available from a variety of publishers).

   Despite the fact that numerous good summaries of Malthus have been written, you owe it to yourself to sample the real thing.

3. Kingsley Davis, 1955, "Malthus and the theory of population," in Paul Lazarsfeld and M. Rosenberg (eds.), The Language of Social Research (New York: The Free Press).

   After reading Malthus in the raw, you might wish to examine this famous, insightful essay. This work puts Malthus's theory into a format that makes it much easier to analyze the points he was trying to make.

4. Michael Teitelbaum, 1975, "Relevance of demographic transitions for developing countries," Science 188(May 2):420–25.

   This article succinctly summarizes the essence of the demographic transition theory.

5. John Caldwell, 1982, Theory of Fertility Decline (New York: Academic Press).

   Caldwell and his wife Pat are two of the most prolific researchers trying to establish the empirical underpinnings of the demographic transition theory. Their field work in Africa and Asia has combined some of the best methods of both demography and anthropology in an attempt to understand the human dimension of fertility change.

PART TWO
Population Processes

Fertility, mortality, and migration are the dynamic elements of demographic analysis. They are the **population processes** that lead to change in the demographic structure and often in the social, economic, and political structure of society as well. In the following four chapters that make up Part Two, I will analyze each of these population processes in turn. My purpose is to improve your understanding of how and why population change occurs. If you believe that a population is growing too rapidly and want to implement a remedy, you first have to understand why the population is growing to recognize what kinds of changes or policies are likely to work.

Population growth occurs as a result of the combination of fertility, mortality, and migration. Although I will discuss each process in some detail, I devote the greatest amount of time to fertility (Chapters 4 and 5), since the control of fertility is often viewed as a very high-priority item on the world agenda of contemporary issues. I will follow with mortality (Chapter 6). Bringing death under control has been one of the most significant achievements in human history, yet it has also been the cause of many problems. Specifically, lower rates of death are associated with resulting high rates of population growth.

Migration (Chapter 7) is not a factor at the global level, since interplanetary migration has never been documented. At national and international levels, however, migration is of considerable importance, since it relieves population pressure in some places while contributing to growth in other areas—sometimes with beneficial results, sometimes with negative consequences.

An important point for you to keep in mind as you read these four chapters is that there is incredible variety within the human experience, and the explanations for behavior in one society do not necessarily work in another. We must be constantly aware of the different social environments in which people live as we try to explain why they have as many children as they do, why some people are more likely to die younger than others, and why some people migrate when others do not.

CHAPTER 4
Fertility Concepts and Measurements

Whether or not lowering the birth rate would solve all the world's problems, many people seem to think it would. If countries are poor and their populations are growing, the popular answer to the dilemma is to lower their birth rates. If the welfare rolls are growing, the refrain is the same. A White House Domestic Council report joined the bandwagon in 1977 by concluding that a basic solution to the problem of illegal immigration would be to lower the birth rates in countries from which those migrants come.

Since this seeming panacea is so often talked about in relation to important national and international issues, it behooves you to know as much as possible about it. To lower the birth rate, of course, means to limit fertility. What is fertility? How and why does it vary from one area to another? In this chapter I will deal with these questions by discussing the concept of fertility and then analyzing the means by which fertility levels can be altered. I will conclude with a brief discussion of how fertility is measured. In the next chapter, I will discuss trends in fertility and offer explanations for differences in fertility levels.

WHAT IS FERTILITY?

Fertility refers to the number of children born to women. Note that though our concern lies primarily with the total impact of childbearing on a society, we have to recognize that the birth rate is the accumulation of thousands, even millions, of individual decisions to have or not have children. Thus, when we refer to a "high-fertility society," we are referring to a population in which most women have several children, whereas a "low-fertility society" is one in which most women have few children. Naturally, some women in high-fertility societies have few children, and vice versa.

Fertility is composed of two parts—one biological and one social. The biological component refers to the capacity to reproduce, and while obviously a necessary condition for parenthood, it is not sufficient alone. Whether children will actually be born and if so, how many—given the capacity to reproduce—is largely a result of the social environment in which people live.

The Biological Component

The physical ability to reproduce is usually called **fecundity** by demographers. A fecund person can produce children; an infecund (sterile) person cannot. The term *fertility* is typically reserved to describe reproductive performance, that is, the actual birth of children, rather than the mere capacity to do so. However, since most people are never tested in the laboratory to determine their level of fecundity, most estimates are based on levels of fertility. Couples who have tried unsuccessfully for a long time to have a child are generally considered to be infecund or **sterile**. Estimates of infecundity place the figure at about 10 percent for all American couples, ranging from a low of 2 percent among teenage couples to as high as 60 percent among couples in their early forties (Mosher, 1982; Menken et al., 1986). Couples who have been married for many years, have never used contraceptives, and still have only one or two children can be judged to have impaired fecundity though they are not considered sterile. Another 13 percent of American couples aged 25–34 may fall into that category (Mosher, 1988). In recent years it has been increasingly difficult to measure fecundity since so many women, especially in highly industrialized nations, routinely use contraceptives for long periods of time and thus do not put their biological capacity to the test.

For most people, fecundity is not an all-or-none proposition and varies according to age. For women, at least, it tends to increase from **menarche** (the onset of menstruation, which usually occurs in the early teens), peaks in the twenties, and then declines to **menopause** (the end of menstruation) (Henry, 1961). The fact that each year of a teenager's life may be associated with burgeoning fecundity has had some tragic consequences in the United States. As young women begin to enjoy sexual relations, fecundity is not often their primary concern, and the result is all too often an unexpected and unwanted pregnancy. The sad fact is that several studies have revealed that many teenage women engage in unprotected sexual intercourse on the mistaken belief that they are too young to get pregnant (Furstenberg, 1976; Akpom et al., 1976; Lowe and Radius, 1987).

Most of us (whether male or female) are fecund, at least during young adulthood, so the more interesting question of why there is so much variation in fertility is primarily a social one.

The Social Component

Opportunities and motivations for childbearing vary considerably from one social environment to another, and the result is great variability in the number of children women have. According to the *Guinness Book of World Records* (Russell and McWhirter, 1987), the individual record for fertility is held by a Russian woman of the eighteenth century who in 27 different pregnancies gave birth to 69 children, most of whom lived to adulthood. For a group, the highest childbearing record belongs to the Hutterites, an Anabaptist religious group, who live in communes in North and South Dakota and Canada. In the late nineteenth century about 400 Hutterites migrated to the United States from Switzerland, and in the span of about 100 years they have doubled their population five times to a current total of more than 15,000 (Westoff and Westoff, 1971). In the 1930s Hutterite women were averaging more than 12 children each. Their secret is a fairly early age at marriage, a good diet, good medical care, and a passion to follow the biblical prescription to "be fruitful and multiply." Also, of course, they engage regularly in sexual intercourse without using contraception or abortion, believing as they do that any form of birth control is a sin. By the 1950s, their fertility levels had declined to about 11 children each on average, apparently as a result of a slight increase in the age at which women marry (Eaton and Mayer, 1954).

Interestingly enough, despite their high rate of population growth, the Hutterites are today a very wealthy group of farmers. This is largely due to their self-sacrificing personal habits (they have a communal form of life) and their successful use of modern farming techniques. However, they represent only a tiny fraction of a larger industrial society on which they are partly dependent.

The Hutterites are a classic example of what French demographer Louis Henry (1961) has called **natural fertility**—that which exists in the absence of deliberate birth control. We know of no entire society that has ever approached the level of reproduction of the Hutterites, who are undoubtedly close to the biological maximum for a group (estimated to be about 15 births per woman) (Bongaarts, 1978). Kenya, for example, has one of the highest national fertility rates in the world, yet women there bear an average of "only" 8 children each. I have contrasted the age pattern of birth rates for the Hutterites with that of Kenya in Figure 4.1 and have also shown data for the United States—a startling contrast, since American women bear an average of fewer than 2 children each. Why the variation? There are two

Figure 4.1   The Hutterite Age Pattern of Natural Fertility Probably Represents the Biological Maximum for a Group

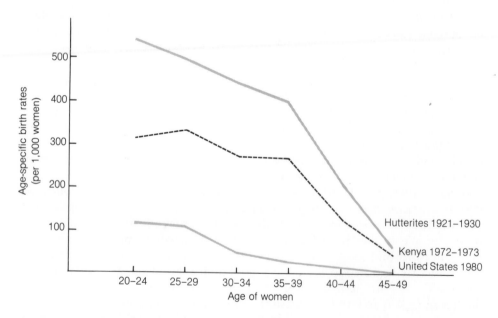

Sources: Louis Henry, 1961, "Some data on natural fertility," Eugenics Quarterly 8(2) :81–92, Table 1; U.S. Bureau of the Census, 1979, "A Compilation of Age-Specific Fertility Rates for Developing Countries," International Research Document No. 7, p. 24; U.S. Bureau of the Census, 1979, "Illustrative Projections of World Population to the 21st Century," Current Population Reports, Series P-23, No. 79, Table 6.

Note: Kenya's age-specific birth rates are well below the levels of the Hutterites, even though Kenya has one of the highest birth rates in the world, whereas birth rates for the United States are very low.

things that must be considered in answering that question. The first is *how* can variations in fertility be accomplished—what are the means available to limit births or encourage them? The second is **why** would people be motivated to use or not use the various means that exist to control fertility?

The means of fertility regulation (the *how*) in fact mediate the relationship between motivation (the *why*) and actual fertility behavior. Once we explore how it can be done in this chapter, we will proceed in the next chapter to try to understand why a couple decides for or against limiting fertility. For now, though, let's assume that you have already made your decision to keep your own family small. What means are available to help you do that? In the remainder of this chapter I will examine the array of means used in our society. Remember, though, that not all possible avenues of fertility control are open to all people. Abortion is a good example. Although it is a legal method of birth control in the United States, it is not "available" to people who object to it for religious or personal reasons.

HOW CAN FERTILITY BE CONTROLLED?

The means for regulating fertility have been popularly labeled (popular, at least, in population studies) the **intermediate variables** (Davis and Blake, 1956). These are the variables through which any social factors influencing the level of fertility must operate. Davis and Blake point out that there are actually three phases to fertility: intercourse, conception, and **gestation** (see Table 4.1). Intercourse is required if conception is to occur; if conception occurs, successful gestation is required if a baby is to be born alive. The process can be interrupted at any point, but let us begin at the beginning and consider first those variables that can affect a woman's exposure to sexual intercourse.

You will discover that as I discuss the conception and gestation variables, there is heavier emphasis on the behavior of women than of men. That is simply because if a woman never has intercourse, she will never have a child, whereas a man will never have a child no matter what he does. Of course, avoiding conception by sterilization or contraceptives can be done by either sex, but if conception occurs, it is only the woman who bears the burden of either pregnancy or abortion.

Intercourse Variables

Age at Entry into a Sexual Union   It is obvious that if a woman never engages in sexual intercourse, she will never bear a child. Although permanent virginity is rare, the longer past puberty a woman waits to begin engaging in sexual unions, the fewer children she will probably have. An average woman will be fecund approximately from age 12 through age 45, so the longer she waits (Variable 1 in Table 4.1), the shorter the time when she is at risk of bearing children. Cross-cultural data on age at menarche have revealed, however, that women with an earlier onset of

Table 4.1 Intermediate Variables Through Which Social Factors Influence Fertility

---

I. Factors affecting exposure to intercourse ("intercourse variables").

  A. Those governing the formation and dissolution of unions in the reproductive period.

    1. Age of entry into sexual unions (legitimate and illegitimate).

    2. Permanent celibacy: proportion of women never entering sexual unions.

    3. Amount of reproductive period spent after or between unions.

      a. When unions are broken by divorce, separation, or desertion.

      b. When unions are broken by death of husband.

  B. Those governing the exposure to intercourse within unions.

    4. Voluntary abstinence. (neg)

    5. Involuntary abstinence (from impotence, illness, unavoidable but temporary separations).

    6. Coital frequency (excluding periods of abstinence).

II. Factors affecting exposure to conception ("conception variables").

    7. Fecundity or infecundity, as affected by involuntary causes.

    8. Use or nonuse of contraception.

      a. By mechanical and chemical means.

      b. By other means.

    9. Fecundity or infecundity, as affected by voluntary causes (sterilization, medical treatment, and so on).

III. Factors affecting gestation and successful parturition ("gestation variables").

    10. Fetal mortality from involuntary causes.

    11. Fetal mortality from voluntary causes.

Source: Kingsley Davis and Judith Blake, 1956, "Social structure and fertility: An analytic framework," Economic Development and Cultural Change 4 (April): no. 3. Used by permission.

puberty tend to begin sexual activity and have their first child sooner than do women whose menarche occurs later (Udry and Cliquet, 1982). Thus, to a certain extent, age at entry into a sexual union is influenced by biological processes. In pre-1960 American society, the age at marriage and the age at entry into a sexual union were essentially the same. But times have changed, and now we recognize a distinction between the two events. During the 1970s, for example, the percentage of teenage women who had engaged in sexual intercourse rose substantially (Zelnick and Kantner, 1980), even though the average age at first birth was also rising in the United States during the same period (Bloom, 1982). Nonetheless, the fact remains that an effective way to postpone childbearing is to postpone engaging in sexual activity, particularly on the regular basis implied in marriage. In the United States there is clearly a relationship between age at marriage and family size, as you can see in Figure 4.2. Data for 1983 show that women who delay marriage have smaller families on average than those who marry young. One of the most important reasons for this is that within marriage a couple frequently encounters pressure from family and friends to have children (Veevers, 1973), and for this reason people who want no family, or only a small one, may avoid marriage for a while.

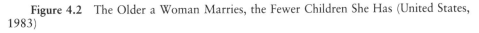

Figure 4.2 The Older a Woman Marries, the Fewer Children She Has (United States, 1983)

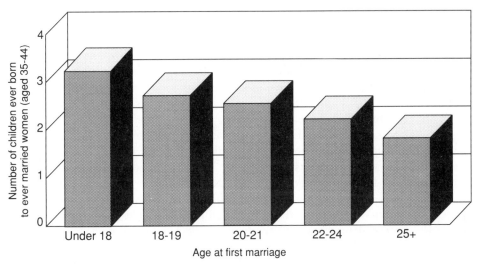

Source: U.S. Bureau of the Census, 1984, "Fertility of American Women: June 1983," Current Population Reports, Series P-20, No. 395, Table 11.

Note: Among women aged 35–44 in 1983, there was a clear relationship between the age at which they had first married and the number of children they had—the younger the bride, the more children she bore.

Permanent Celibacy   Permanent **celibacy** (Variable 2) refers to those women who never marry. It will not surprise you to learn that the greater the proportion of woman in a society who never marry, the lower the level of fertility tends to be. The idea of celibacy has not caught on, though, and the proportion of women who never marry is consistently low, never reaching even 10 percent outside of Europe (Dixon, 1971).

The highest level of permanent celibacy occurs in northwestern Europe, which has historically also had among the lowest levels of fertility in the world. In Ireland, for example, with the highest levels of nonmarriage in the world, in 1971, 18 percent of the women aged 40–44 had never married (Ireland Central Statistics Office, 1978).

Time Between Unions   Under normal circumstances, once a woman is involved in a sexual union such as marriage, sexual intercourse will be more or less regularly engaged in. However, not all sexual unions are permanent, since some are broken up by divorce, separation, or desertion (Variable 3a), while some are broken up by the death of a spouse (Variable 3b). During that fecund period of life when a woman has had a sexual union broken and has not entered into a new one, months or years of pregnancy risk are lost, never to be recouped. Data for the United States reveal that regardless of the age at which an American woman first married, if her marriage has broken up, her fertility will be lower than if she had remained continuously married.

While I sincerely doubt that people deliberately break up a marriage to keep from having children, the result is the same.

Voluntary Abstinence   Voluntary abstinence (Variable 4) will clearly eliminate the risk of pregnancy within a marriage, but this is not a popular option. It is uncommon in industrialized countries except shortly after the birth of a child, when abstinence does not have much effect on fertility anyway, since childbirth is normally followed by a period of 1 or 2 months of temporary sterility (called *postpartum amenorrhea,* and referring to the fact that a woman does not ovulate during this time). In preindustrial societies, **postpartum** (that is, after childbirth) taboos on intercourse occasionally extend to several months or even to a few years in societies in which intercourse is forbidden while a mother is nursing a child. The rationale is based generally on superstitions that intercourse will somehow be harmful to either mother or child (Davis and Blake, 1956:232) or on the generally correct notion that a pregnancy will be harmful to the nursing child because it will reduce the quantity of mother's milk. Voluntary abstinence after childbirth may help to keep birth rates below the potential maximum in many premodern societies by lengthening the intervals between childbearing.

In areas of the world where more sophisticated birth control techniques are either unheard of or at least not regularly available, abstinence may be a frequent means of fertility limitation for highly motivated people. For example, in 1970 Brandes (1975) studied a small Spanish peasant village in which there was considerable pressure to limit family size to two children. He relates the story of a 35-year-old man with five young children who "is constantly greeted with the refrain, '¡Atate al catre!'—Tie yourself to the bedpost!" Brandes goes on to explain:

> Through a combination of coitus interruptus and abstention, most villagers manage to keep births down. Though they openly complain about the frustrations which these methods entail, they are willing to make the sacrifice in order to assure their ability to provide their children the best possible opportunities. Those husbands who cannot exercise control are seen as somewhat animalistic (1975:43).

A similar story is related by Reining and her associates (1977) about behavior in a small Mexican village. In examining the life history of a 37-year-old woman with five children, it was discovered that the woman "doesn't want to have any more children, for the benefit of the children she already has, and in order not to deplete the economic resources of the family." But since her husband does not accept the use of contraceptives "she has refused to sleep with her husband" (Reining et al., 1977: 136).

Thus, if the motivation exists to limit family size, peasants will do so, turning to the time-honored methods of abstention and coitus interruptus (to be discussed later in the chapter). Even in the 1980s, an American woman wrote to "Dear Abby" explaining that "the most effective method yet found for birth control is a large dog sleeping in the middle of the bed on top of the covers. Try it. It works. That's what we've been doing for 17 years" (Universal Press Syndicate, 1982).

Involuntary Abstinence   Involuntary abstinence (Variable 5) could be a result of either impotence or involuntary separation. It is not easy to tell how important the role played by impotence is in involuntary birth control. On the other hand, we do know that temporary separations are fairly common in many occupations, such as sales and transportation, and for various other reasons—separate vacations, hospitalization, military duty, and so on. In underdeveloped countries, where migratory labor is more common than in the United States, we might also expect to find involuntary abstinence to be lowering fertility somewhat. Contrary to the typical pattern in the United States, in most parts of the world migratory labor involves the laborer only, not his or her family. The **bracero** program in the United States, which brought thousands of Mexican men into the United States in the 1950s and early 1960s to work on American farms, is a typical example. Many of the men were married and left their wives and children behind.

Coital Frequency   Within marriage (or any sexual union) the regularity of sexual intercourse (Variable 6) will influence the likelihood of a pregnancy, particularly if no contraception is used. In general, the more often a couple has intercourse, the more likely it is that the woman will get pregnant. It is, however, true that if a woman engages in sexual intercourse with the same man more than once a day, every day, the risk of pregnancy is lower than expected because the male's sperm does not have the opportunity to fully mature between ejaculations. This rarely appears to be a problem, however.

In a study done in Lebanon, Yaukey (1961) found that during the first year of marriage, among women who were not using contraceptives, the more frequently intercourse was engaged in, the less time it took for a woman to get pregnant. Studies in the United States have produced similar results. Further, Kinsey found that among stable married couples, coital frequency decreases steadily as age increases. He found that women aged 41–45 had sexual intercourse only half as often as women aged 21–25.

Conception Variables

Involuntary Infecundity   Even if a woman is regularly sexually active, she will not necessarily conceive a child because she may be involuntarily infecund (Variable 7). The principal control that a woman has over her fecundity is to provide herself with a good diet and physical care. Of course, the result of such good care tends to be higher, not lower, fertility. In some sub-Saharan African countries, for example, as many as 50 percent of the women are involuntarily sterile due largely to the effects of untreated diseases such as gonorrhea (Frank, 1983; McFalls and McFalls, 1984). In New Guinea, a massive penicillin campaign in 1975 designed to eradicate gonorrhea had the added effect of raising the birth rate (San Diego Union, 1977d). Studies of fertility rates of U.S. blacks also suggest that an increase in fertility among blacks during the 1940s and 1950s was due in part to improved health conditions, especially the eradication of venereal disease and tuberculosis (Farley, 1970; McFalls and McFalls, 1984).

Naturally, disease is not the only factor that can lower the level of fecundity in a population. Nutrition also plays a role. Rose Frisch, a Harvard demographer, suggested that a certain amount of fat must be stored as energy before menstruation and ovulation can occur on a regular basis (1978). Thus, if a woman's level of nutrition is too low to permit this level of fat accumulation she may experience **amenorrhea** and **anovulatory** cycles. For younger women, the onset of puberty may be delayed until an undernourished girl reaches a certain critical weight. However, Frisch's theory is still being tested and, at present, there is even some question as to whether ages at menarche are any lower now than they were hundreds of years ago. Women in Africa, in particular, seem traditionally to have experienced the onset of menstruation at later ages (around age 15 or even later), whereas European women may have typically experienced menarche between the ages of 12 and 14 (Bullough, 1981). A study in Bangladesh, however, suggested that girls who were better fed did, in fact, begin menstruating at an earlier age than their less fortunate counterparts (Haq, 1984).

Breast-feeding is also known to prolong the period of postpartum amenorrhea and suppress ovulation, thus producing in many women the effect of temporary **infecundity** or **subfecundity** (Hatcher et al., 1978). In fact, nature provides the average new mother with a brief respite from the risk of conception after the birth of a baby whether she breast-feeds or not; however, the period of infecundity is typically only about 2 months among women who do not nurse their babies, compared with 10 to 18 months among lactating mothers (Konner and Worthman, 1980). It appears that stimulation of the mother's nipples during nursing increases the secretion of plasma prolactin, which, in turn, seems to delay the return of ovulation and menstruation. On the other hand, the cessation of lactation signals a prompt return of menstruation and the concomitant risk of conception in most women (Prema and Ravindranath, 1982). Unfortunately, however, there has been concern that women in less developed nations are abandoning breast-feeding in favor of bottle-feeding (Knodel, 1977; Bader, 1976). The demographic impact will be twofold and possibly offsetting. On the one hand, less breast-feeding (in the absence of contraception) will tend to raise the birth rate. On the other hand, it is also likely to raise the infant death rate, since in the less developed nations bottle-feeding often is accompanied by watered-down formulas that are less nutritious than a mother's milk. Also, bacteria growing in unsterilized bottles and reused plastic liners are likely to lead to disease—especially diarrhea, which is often fatal to infants.

In response to these concerns, the World Health Organization approved a voluntary code in 1981 to regulate the advertising and marketing of infant formula. However, baby food companies lobbied strongly against the code, the United States opposed it, and a year later only 6 percent of the countries who voted for it had actually adopted it (Adelman, 1982). Yet, the publicity generated by the whole infant-formula controversy has at least created a greater awareness on the part of American women of the value of breast-feeding. Ironically, the women most likely to lead the movement back to breast-feeding in any given country are the better educated (Hirschman and Butler, 1981; Akin et al., 1981), the very same women whose fertility is apt to be kept low by deliberate use of contraception, rather than by the unintended influence of lactation.

Contraception   In the United States **contraception** (Variable 8) is usually the first thing we think of when we consider ways to lower fertility. There are so many different types of contraceptives, and so much new research currently being conducted on contraceptives, that it is useful to categorize methods before discussing them. In Table 4.2 I have divided contraceptive methods into three main categories, according to whether they are primarily female, male, or couple methods. Under each of those categories I have listed methods according to whether they are primarily barrier, chemical, or natural methods. Since individuals or couples often combine methods, this classification scheme is not mutually exclusive, but it is illustrative.

Female Methods   There are five major kinds of **birth control** methods that are typically called barrier methods: the **diaphragm; spermicidal** foams, jellies, or creams; a disposable **sponge**; the **douche**; and the **intrauterine device (IUD)**.

The diaphragm is a rubber disk that is inserted deep into the vagina and over the mouth of the uterus sometime before sexual intercourse. Used alone, it is a fairly ineffective physical barrier. It is normally used in conjunction with a spermicidal cream, jelly, or foam, which is spread in and around the diaphragm before insertion into the vagina. The **spermicide** acts to kill the sperm, and the diaphragm operates to keep the spermicide in place, preventing the passage of sperm into the uterus and on into the fallopian tubes where fertilization occurs. Since sperm can live in the vagina for up to 8 hours, it is necessary for a woman to leave the diaphragm in place for that long after intercourse. Used in this way, the diaphragm can be very effective, and until the 1960s when oral contraceptives were placed on the market, the diaphragm (invented in 1883) was a fairly common method of birth control for married women. Because it requires a great deal of forethought, it is obviously not useful for those occasions, especially outside of marriage, when intercourse occurs fairly spontaneously.

Table 4.2   Contraceptive Methods

Primary Characteristic	Primary User		
	Female	Male	Couple
Barrier	Diaphragm IUD Spermicides Sponge Douche	Condom	—
Chemical	Oral contraceptive (the pill) Morning-after pill Depo-Provera NORPLANT	—	—

Natural	—	Withdrawal	Rhythm
			Ovulation
			Basal body
			  temperature
			Symptothermal
			Oral-genital sex and
			  other forms of
			  incomplete
			  intercourse

New variations on the diaphragm theme have appeared in recent years. One of these is a vaginal sponge called "Today" that contains a spermicide and fits over the cervix. Tests have revealed that it is easier to use and is about equally effective as the diaphragm. Since it has been sold in the United States only since 1983, it is too soon to judge its long-run usefulness as a contraceptive. However, because it is an over-the-counter contraceptive (unlike the diaphragm, which requires a physician's approval) "Today" was received with tremendous enthusiasm when it hit the market. Cervical caps that are custom-made to fit over a woman's cervix and block sperm without requiring the use of a spermicide are also being developed. Such caps can be left in place for up to a year (Hull, 1983).

The douche—a postintercourse washing out of the vagina—is a nearly ineffective method of birth control, even though its use is widespread. If the douching substance contains a spermicide, then sperm still remaining in the vagina may be killed. However, since it takes only 10 –20 seconds after ejaculation for the sperm to go beyond the vagina and into the uterus and fallopian tubes, a woman would have to act quickly (to say the least) if there was to be any hope of preventing sperm from getting beyond the vagina.

The IUD is the contraceptive technique that many family planners believed would bring an end to the world's population explosion. Its success has been, however, much less spectacular than that. Although it is used by some 15 million women around the world (Hatcher et al., 1978), it has not enjoyed the wholesale acceptance that many had hoped. No one knows for certain how it works to prevent a birth, but it is generally believed that since it is a foreign object, it sets up a chemical reaction inside the uterus that may destroy the fertilized egg and/or prevent implantation of a fertilized egg from taking place. Although it comes in several different shapes and can be made of various materials, the IUD most commonly used in the United States is a nylon plastic coil.

About 2 or 3 percent of the women who have an IUD inserted expel it, but for the remainder the IUD theoretically will stay in place for long periods of time and is very effective in preventing pregnancy. A report to a 1976 meeting of experts arranged by the International Family Planning Research Association indicated that the IUD and the **vasectomy** (to be discussed later in this chapter) are the two methods of birth control that minimize cost while maximizing sexual spontaneity (San Francisco Chronicle, 1976). In the less developed areas of the world, however, high proportions of women (often as high as 50 percent) who have an IUD inserted choose to have it removed even if they do not want to get pregnant. The principal reasons are infections and excessive bleeding caused by the IUD, although fear and superstition may also be causes.

One brand of IUD, the Dalkon Shield, was responsible for the deaths of at least 13 women prior to its removal from the market in 1975. Most IUDs have a string attached to them to aid in removal and serve as a sign that the device is in place; the string of the Dalkon Shield turned out to be a "ladder for bacteria" (Roberts, 1978:406) and caused infection in some users. Lawsuits stemming from those cases caused all but one IUD manufacturer to withdraw the device from the U.S. market in 1986, although they continue to be available elsewhere in the world. Indeed, research continues on the IUD, and a new device is being sold in Finland, Mexico, and the United States that is copper-coated, smaller than the average IUD, and lasts for several years.

The oral contraceptive, or "the pill" as it is popularly known, has revolutionized birth prevention for many women, especially in the United States. The pill is a compound of synthetic hormones that suppress ovulation by keeping the estrogen level high in a female. This prevents the pituitary gland from sending a signal to the ovaries to release an egg. In addition, the progestin content of the pill makes the cervical mucus hostile to implantation of the egg if it is indeed released. There are three basic types of birth control pills, with varying effectiveness. The *combination* pill is virtually 100 percent effective when taken as directed. It has estrogen and progestin in each pill and is taken for 21 days, followed by 7 days when it is not taken and the woman has a menstrual flow. The *sequential* pill has 15–16 tablets that contain only estrogen, followed by 5 or 6 combination pills. This type of pill is about 98 percent effective in preventing ovulation, but does not have enough progestin to act as a contraceptive if ovulation occurs. The least effective oral contraceptive is the "mini-pill," which contains only progestin. It does not prevent ovulation, but rather works only on producing a hostile environment for sperm and egg. It is taken every day without stopping.

In the 1960s and 1970s the pill was the method of choice for women of all ages, and it continues to be the most popular method of birth control among younger married women in the United States (see Table 4.3). All things considered, the pill would be just about the perfect solution except for the problem of side effects. When first taking the pill, women often report nausea, breast tenderness, and spotting, although these problems do not usually persist. More important by far are the risks of death that might be associated with the pill. Although the evidence is far from conclusive, it appears that oral contraceptives can aggravate problems such as high blood pressure, blood clotting, diabetes, and migraine headaches. Women with histories of these problems are normally advised not to use the pill. Much of the

Table 4.3 Sterilization Is Now the Most Commonly Used Method of Fertility Control Among American Women

Method Currently Used	Ages (Married Women Only) (%)		
	15–44	15–29	30–44
Wife sterilized	25.6	11.0	35.0
Husband sterilized	15.4	6.4	21.2
Pill	19.8	40.5	6.4
IUD	7.1	7.2	7.0
Diaphragm	6.7	9.0	5.2
Condom	14.4	14.2	14.6
Other	11.1	11.8	10.6

Source: W. Mosher and C. Bachrach, 1986, "Contraceptive use: United States, 1982," Data from the National Survey of Family Growth, Series 23, No. 12 (Rockville, MD: National Center for Health Statistics), Table E.

Note: One third of all married women of reproductive age in the United States were using the pill in 1976. The proportion is much higher for younger than for older women. Indeed, among older couples, sterilization is clearly the most popular form of birth control.

early scare about increased risk of cancer, however, has subsided as researchers have learned that oral contraceptives do not, in fact, increase the risk of breast cancer, even after prolonged use (International Family Planning Perspectives, 1982; Ory et al., 1980).

The pill has been embroiled in a storm of controversy about its potentially harmful side effects ever since its introduction. It is, in fact, the most widely studied drug ever invented, and its principal inventor, Carl Djerassi of Stanford University, is understandably defensive. In 1981 he wrote:

> The point that these opponents of the Pill really miss is that the Pill as well as all other methods of fertility control should be available for any woman who is willing and able to use them given her particular circumstances. . . . The reality is that for many women throughout the world, the Pill is the best contraceptive method currently available (1981:47).

More recent research has, in fact, emphasized some of the more positive, non-contraceptive health benefits of the pill, including its ability to reduce the incidence of benign breast disease, ovarian cysts, iron-deficiency anemia, pelvic inflammatory disease, ectopic pregnancy, rheumatoid arthritis, and cancers of the reproductive tract (Ory, 1982). One study has even concluded that a woman who takes the pill for 5 years before the age of 30 can, in effect, add 4 days to her life expectancy (Fortney et al., 1986).

Another contraceptive, though one not widely used, is the *morning-after* pill. It is a massive dose of estrogen given to women who have had unprotected sexual intercourse at mid-cycle—in other words, women with a high risk of conception and a great desire not to wait for a pregnancy test. The morning-after pill, however, is made of DES (diethylstilbestrol), a synthetic estrogen, which is known to cause vaginal cancer in young women whose mothers took it during pregnancy. Thus, it is typically used only in emergency situations such as rape or incest.

Variations on the pill theme are constantly being developed by contraceptive researchers. Attention has focused especially on injections that would provide protection against pregnancy for a month or longer. Without doubt the most widely debated of these injectable contraceptives is Depo-Provera, a highly effective contraceptive that requires a woman to be injected with a massive dose of synthetic progestin every 3 months. Although it has been tested in the United States since 1968 and has been approved for contraceptive use in at least 90 countries, as of 1988 it still had not been approved for sale in the United States, because of questions about harmful side effects.

Another, perhaps even more promising, contraceptive is called NORPLANT, developed by the Population Council in New York. NORPLANT is a one-eighth-inch-long silicone rubber capsule containing a small amount of levonorgestrel, a synthetic progestin. The capsule is implanted just beneath the skin of a woman's upper arm and releases a tiny amount of progestin every day for up to 5 years before needing to be replaced (Sivin et al., 1982). The method has already been field tested by 14,000 women in 14 nations, including 800 women in the United States, and in 1985 a World Health Organization report endorsed its safety and effectiveness (San Diego Union, 1985a).

Still in the early testing stage is a substance known as RU486, which, when taken within 10 days after a missed period, appears effectively to terminate a pregnancy without major side effects. Although the compound has been called the "month-after" pill and sounds like a method to induce abortion, the French pharmaceutical firm that is developing it prefers to avoid controversy by calling it "contra-gestational" (Murphy, 1986).

Male Methods   Men have very few options available to them in contraceptives. In fact, they are basically rather severely limited to the **condom**. This is a rubber or latex sheath inserted over the erect penis just prior to intercourse. During ejaculation the sperm are trapped inside the condom, which is then removed immediately after intercourse while the penis is still erect, to avoid spillage. The condom is very effective, and when used properly in conjunction with a spermicidal foam, it is virtually 100 percent effective. The condom is also useful in preventing the spread of sexually transmitted diseases, including venereal disease and, more popularly, AIDS. Although use of the condom dropped off considerably during the 1960s and 1970s, by 1982 (the most recent year for which data are available) it had regained its place just after the pill in popularity among married American women (Mosher and Bachrach, 1986) (see Table 4.3).

Withdrawal is also an essentially (although not exclusively) male method of birth control. It has a long history (for example, it is referenced in the Bible), but its effectiveness is relatively limited. It is, in fact, a form of incomplete intercourse (thus its formal name "coitus interruptus") because it requires the male to withdraw his erect penis from his partner's vagina just prior to ejaculation. The method leaves little room for error, especially since there may be an emission of **semen** just prior to ejaculation (Hatcher et al., 1978).

Chinese scientists have reportedly developed a birth control pill for men derived from the cotton plant and called "gossypol." Unfortunately, testing in China since 1972 has revealed that its high degree of effectiveness may be coupled with a rare form of paralysis in a small but significant number of users (International Family Planning Perspectives, 1981). Research in the United States on male contraceptives has focused on the use of luteinizing hormone releasing hormone (LHRH), a substance that can suppress sperm production and reduce the level of the male hormone testosterone. However, studies of hormonal contraceptives have shown fairly consistently that these drugs adversely affect a wide range of sexuality measures, including frequency of orgasm and intensity of desire (Wiest, 1982).

Couple Methods   Until recently the principal method of contraception to require couple cooperation was rhythm. Users of this method, however, have been jokingly defined as parents. Recent developments have altered this view, as natural family planning has evolved into the considerably more effective **symptothermal method** of birth control. (This method is discussed in detail in this chapter's essay.)

Other methods of birth control that explicitly require cooperation between both partners are mutual masturbation and oral-genital sex. In Davis and Blake's 1956 article, these forms of incomplete intercourse were listed as "perversions," but in more recent years, with a significant change in openness about sex and with the introduction of best-selling "how-to" manuals, they have become more openly acceptable techniques for engaging in sexual activity. These methods are sometimes practiced in combination with coitus interruptus. Indeed, in France, data from the World Fertility Survey in 1978 indicate that withdrawal is the most popular form of contraception among couples aged 35 and older and is second to the pill among younger people (Leridon, 1979).

Traditional Methods   I would be remiss if I did not mention to you that modern science does not hold all the secrets to contraception. Premodern societies in many areas of the world have known for centuries of herbal methods to reduce the likelihood of conception. In the same vein, a research team working for the World Health Organization has discovered that a small green pea, which is a staple of the Tibetan diet, acts as a natural fertility suppressant (London Telegraph, 1979). It would be fascinating to learn whether Tibetan fertility reflects the presence of this natural contraceptive, but Tibet has been swallowed up by China and the data are unavailable. In the Amazon basin of Ecuador, primitive tribes use the root of the cyperus plant (a bog plant, not the same as the cypress) to induce temporary sterility, apparently with great success. Scientists believe that a microscopic fungus growing on the root is the organism that produces the contraceptive effect (Maxwell, 1977).

How Effective Are Different Contraceptive Techniques?   Contraceptive effectiveness refers to how well a contraceptive works to prevent a pregnancy. There are two ways to measure this effectiveness. The first is to look at **theoretical effectiveness,** meaning the percentage of the time that a method should prevent pregnancy after sexual intercourse if everything else is perfect. Thus, if we say that oral contraceptives are 100 percent effective, we mean that if a woman is in normal health and if she takes the pills exactly as directed, she will never get pregnant. Theoretical effectiveness is very difficult to measure and, in addition, it ignores the human failure that can occur with any method.

The more usual measure of a contraceptive's effectiveness is called **use effectiveness,** which measures the actual pregnancy performance associated with a particular method. There are several specific ways by which use effectiveness can be measured. The most common is called the Pearl method or the pregnancy-failure rate—the number of contraceptive failures per 100 woman-years of contraceptive exposure. For example, if 200 women used the pill for a year, they have had a combined total of 200 woman-years of exposure. If four of the women became pregnant while using the pill, then the pregnancy rate is two. In other words, there were two failures (accidental pregnancies) for every 100 woman-years of exposure. The lower the failure rate, the more effective the contraceptive.

Use effectiveness combines two kinds of failures: (1) method failure, such as when a woman gets pregnant even though she has an IUD in place, and (2) use failure, such as when a woman on the pill goes on a weekend trip and leaves her pills at home accidentally, or when a man is not sufficiently motivated to always use a condom.

The most precise way to measure use effectiveness is to study couples who are using a specific method of contraception for some period of time (such as a year) and see what proportion of the couples wind up with an accidental pregnancy. Such data are presented in Table 4.4. If a couple were to use no method at all and rely simply on chance to avoid a pregnancy, there is an 89 percent chance of a pregnancy during the year. The pill and implants improve on those odds considerably, with failure rates of 3 percent and 0.3 percent, respectively. The IUD is next most effective, followed by the condom, the diaphragm, and all methods of natural family planning. Data from the 1973 U.S. National Fertility Survey also have shown clearly that the more highly motivated couples (that is, those who do not want any more pregnancies, as opposed to those merely spacing their children) have higher use-effectiveness rates than the less motivated, regardless of the method chosen.

Voluntary Infecundity   The last of the conception variables that can be manipulated to achieve low fertility is voluntary infecundity or **sterilization** (Variable 9). For females, this procedure spans a spectrum from the removal of the ovaries (the most drastic) to a tubal ligation (the least drastic). Removal of the ovaries (called oophorectomy) not only removes all egg follicles and prevents further ovulation but also changes the hormonal balance of a woman. This operation is fairly serious and is generally done for medical reasons unrelated to a desire not to have children. The next most serious operation is a hysterectomy, the removal of the uterus. This too requires major surgery. Each year more than 400,000 American women have a hysterectomy, making it the fourth most frequently performed operation on women. Nevertheless, since most hysterectomies are performed on women over 35, its use as a birth control method is limited.

Table 4.4   Theoretical and Use Effectiveness for Selected Contraceptive Techniques

Method	Theoretical Effectiveness	Use Effectiveness (Percentage of Couples Experiencing an Accidental Pregnancy During the First Year of Use) Typical Findings[a]
None	Chance	89
Pill	Virtually no failures	3
Implants	Virtually no failures	0.3
IUD	Very few failures	6
Condom	Very few failures	12
Diaphragm	Very few failures	18
Natural family planning (all methods of periodic abstinence)	Some failures	20
Spermicidal foams and jellies	Some failures	21
Douche	Many failures	40

Sources: Adapted from Bernard Berelson, 1974, "World population: status report 1974," Reports on Population/Family Planning 15:39; and B. Vaughan, J. Trussell, J. Menken, E. Jones, and W. Grady, 1980, "Contraceptive efficacy among married women aged 15–44 years," Data from the National Survey of Family Growth, Series 23, No. 5 (Rockville, MD: National Center for Health Statistics), Table 3; and James Trussell and Kathryn Kost, 1987, "Contraceptive failure in the United States: a critical review of the literature," Studies in Family Planning 18(5):237 (Table 11).

[a] Based on a review of studies (see sources listed above).

The type of female sterilization most often recommended is tubal ligation, a tying off of the fallopian tubes, or tubectomy, partial removal of the tubes. In this way, an egg is released normally, but it is prevented from entering the uterus, and sperm are prevented from reaching the egg. This procedure generally does not

NATURAL FAMILY PLANNING: WHAT IS IT AND HOW EFFECTIVE IS IT?

In an era of highly sophisticated chemical technology, the search for alternative natural methods of doing things has been accelerating, and methods of fertility control have not been exempted from this search. Indeed, in the past few years natural family planning methods have emerged as extremely effective means for limiting births. No longer does Natural Family Planning (NFP) mean the rhythm method. It now refers to (1) the ovulation method, (2) the basal body temperature method, and (3) the combination of ovulation and temperature methods known as the symptothermal method of fertility control.

The ovulation method (OM) is based on the discovery that changing estrogen levels produce changes in the consistency of a woman's cervical mucus as ovulation approaches. With appropriate training most women can easily learn to identify these mucus changes and thus determine when ovulation is about to occur (Keefe, 1962). In a typical woman the vaginal area feels dry immediately after menstruation, followed in a few days by the secretion of a small amount of cervical mucus. As ovulation approaches, the mucus changes to a slippery, raw-egg-white–like consistency. This is an indication that ovulation is about to take place (McCarthy, 1977).

The basal body temperature method, on the other hand, gives evidence that ovulation has already occurred. Basal body temperature (BBT) is a person's resting temperature taken the same time daily under similar conditions (such as shortly after awakening in the morning). Prior to ovulation, the BBT is relatively low; however, it typically begins to shift upward as ovulation occurs and remains high until the next menses. Most experts feel that 3 days of a sustained upward shift in the BBT indicates that ovulation has occurred. Accurate recording of temperature is important in using this method, because the temperature shift that we're talking about is generally no more than 0.5 degree Fahrenheit.

The symptothermal (S-T) method is naturally more effective than either OM or BBT because S-T combines evidence about the timing of ovulation from both sources. OM tells you when ovulation is about to occur, while BBT tells you that it has occurred. Since the secret of success with NFP is abstaining from intercourse during the fertile (ovulatory) period, it is obvious that precise identification of the fertile period is crucial.

Since the mid-1970s an increasing number of studies have documented the effectiveness of the symptothermal method (Hermann et al., 1986). In a five-country study covering the United States, Canada, France, Mauritius, and Colombia, it was found that Pearl's index of contraceptive failure (discussed in this chapter) was 15 pregnancies per 100 woman-years of exposure for those women who wanted to delay a pregnancy, and only 4 for those who wanted to prevent any further pregnancies (Rice et al., 1977). For the delayers (those whose intent was only to space their children farther apart), the effectiveness rate was similar to that for users of the IUD. For the preventers (those who did not want a child), the method was virtually as effective as the pill. Rice and co-workers also demonstrated that the effectiveness rate was much better for those who used the S-T method than for those who used only OM or only BBT (1977). Those results have been require an overnight hospital stay. A new method developed simultaneously in China and the United States involves blocking the fallopian tubes by injecting into them a small amount of silicone rubber, which forms a plug. Neither this procedure nor a tubal ligation affects a female's hormonal secretions, and the menstrual cycle

echoed in a study in Los Angeles by Wade, who found that the failure rate for people who used only the OM method was 25, compared with 9 for users of the S-T method (Population Reference Bureau, 1979b).

In an evaluation of a natural family planning program in San Diego, I found in 1979 that among 100 clients followed, 5 became pregnant accidentally (a Pearl index of 11 pregnancies per 100 woman-years of exposure). But each of those pregnancies was to a woman who wanted only to delay a pregnancy, not to prevent one. Further, the pregnant women were younger, had fewer children, and had less previous experience with fertility control than those who were successful in preventing a pregnancy (Weeks, 1982). Similar results were found in a clinical study in Lancaster, Pennsylvania in 1978 (Kambic et al., 1981).

Overall, the picture that emerges is that a highly motivated couple can use natural family planning as a highly effective means of birth control. To be sure, the method makes certain demands if it is to be successful, such as the need regularly to observe and record mucus and temperature symptoms, and the forced abstinence from sexual intercourse during the fertile period. A couple could use a barrier method (such as foam, jellies, condom, or diaphragm) during the fertile period, but none of those methods is foolproof, and their use obviously carries with it at least some risk of conception if intercourse occurs during the fertile period. As yet, few studies exist to suggest how important these aspects of NFP may be for the eventual spread in popularity of this method of birth control. However, a study by Tolor and co-workers (1975) suggests that couples adjust fairly well to periodic abstinence. Their survey of American couples using the BBT method revealed that sexual abstinence had no demonstrable detrimental effects on either sexual satisfaction or marital happiness.

An important indicator of the potential importance of NFP is that technicians have devised and are marketing products that allow women to measure more accurately both cervical mucus symptoms and temperature. Researchers at Harvard and MIT have combined to develop an "ovutimer," which measures the fluidity of cervical mucus (San Diego Union, 1978b); a New York firm is producing the "ova-check," which, when inserted in a woman's ear, is able to record the subtle changes in temperature that occur with ovulation (Population Reference Bureau, 1979b); and a reproductive physiologist at the University of Florida has developed a bedside microprocessor that will automatically track a woman's temperature rise and will display a green light when the 3-day temperature rise has occurred (San Diego Union, 1981c).

Natural family planning, especially S-T, is thus emerging as an effective alternative to chemical and barrier methods of birth control. The U.S. Office of Population Affairs has estimated a tripling of natural family planning users between 1978 and 1980 (Arnett, 1981). NFP is potentially attractive not only to those couples who object to other methods on religious grounds but also to those who practice a natural or holistic approach to health and daily living.

continues as usual, except that the egg produced is absorbed into the body. Biologically there is no effect on a woman's sexual response, although psychologically the virtual absence of a reason to fear pregnancy may enhance a woman's sexuality.

As for females, there are drastic as well as simple means of sterilization for males. The drastic means is castration, which is removal or destruction of the testes. This generally eliminates sexual responsiveness in the male, causing him to be impotent (incapable of having an erection). However, a vasectomy does not alter a male's sexual response. A vasectomy involves cutting and tying off the vasa deferens, which are the tubes leading from each testicle to the penis. The male continues to generate sperm, but they are unable to leave the testicle and are absorbed into the body. Sterilization, especially vasectomy, has been a major focus of government-sponsored birth control in India, and in September 1976 the Health Ministry reported that a record 1.3 million persons had been sterilized in 1 month (San Francisco Chronicle, 1976b). Sterilization is also popular in the United States, as you can see in Table 4.3. In fact, by 1982 it had stolen the lead away from the pill as the most common method of fertility control among married women of reproductive age. More than half of all women aged 30–44 relied on sterilization in 1982, compared with only 17 percent in 1965.

Gestation Variables—Abortion

Assuming that conception has occurred, a live birth may still be prevented. This may happen as a result of involuntary fetal mortality (Variable 10), which is either a spontaneous abortion or a stillbirth. More important for our discussion, though, is voluntary fetal mortality or induced **abortion** (Variable 11). Abortions became legal in the United States in 1973 and they are now legal in all four of the world's most populous nations (China, India, the Soviet Union, and the United States) as well as in Japan, Scandinavia, and virtually all of Europe. Worldwide, the demand for abortion has been rising, and it has been estimated that one of three pregnancies in the world may end in abortion (Henshaw, 1987), with China and the Soviet Union leading the list. During the 1970s, abortion in many countries "changed from a largely disreputable practice into an accepted medical one, from a subject of gossip into an openly debated public issue" (Tietze and Lewit, 1977:21).

Abortion is undoubtedly the single most often used form of birth control in the world (Djerassi, 1978; Henshaw, 1987), and it is common even where it is illegal. "In Brazil, it is estimated that half of all pregnancies end in abortion, despite that country's highly restrictive abortion law. The largest maternity hospital in Bogota, Colombia, uses half its beds for women suffering the complications of illegal abortion" (Jaffe et al., 1981:3). Not surprisingly, then, abortions have played a major role in fertility declines around the world, and they are an important reason for the continued low birth rate in the United States.

The number of legally induced abortions reported in the United States has increased steadily from 1973 until 1980, at which time the number leveled off, as you can see in Figure 4.3. The abortion rate (abortions per 1,000 women of repro-

Figure 4.3   Legal Abortions Have Become More Common in the United States

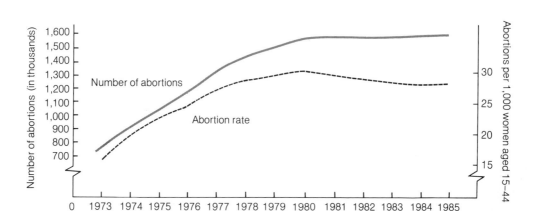

Source: Adapted from S. Henshaw, J. Forrest, E. Sullivan, and C. Tietze, 1982, "Abortion services in the United States, 1979 and 1980," Family Planning Perspectives 14(1):7; S. Henshaw, N. Binkin, E. Blaine, and J. Smith, 1985, "A portrait of American women who obtain abortions," Family Planning Perspectives 17(2):92; and S. Henshaw, J. Forrest, and J. Van Vort, 1987, "Abortion services in the United States, 1984 and 1985," Family Planning Perspectives 19(2):63.

Note: During the 1970s the number of legal abortions and the abortion rate went up steadily, then leveled off in the 1980s.

ductive age) has followed the same pattern over time. More than 80 percent of abortions are to unmarried women, 29 percent are to teenagers, and 70 percent are to white women (Henshaw et al., 1985)—a profile that has not changed much in recent years.

There are several different types of abortion techniques, varying primarily according to how far along the pregnancy is before an abortion is attempted. In the United States in 1985, the majority of reported induced legal abortions were performed during the first 12 weeks of pregnancy. Most of these abortions were done using vacuum aspiration (also known as suction curettage), in which gentle suction removes the contents of the uterus. The most common method of abortion between 13 and 15 weeks of pregnancy in the United States is D & E (dilatation and evacuation), involving a gentle scraping of the lining of the uterus with a long instrument. During the 16th to 19th weeks, a saline abortion is generally performed. In this technique, the amniotic fluid is replaced by a concentrated salt solution, which induces uterine contractions. After a few hours the fetus and placenta are expelled. This requires a 2- to 3-day hospital stay. After 20 weeks, or if the saline method fails, the typical abortion procedure is a hysterotomy, which is similar to a cesarean section, in which the fetus is removed through a small abdominal incision.

The Relative Importance of Each Intermediate Variable

Although each of the 11 intermediate variables plays a role in determining the overall level of fertility in a society, the relative importance of each varies considerably. In fact, an analysis by John Bongaarts (1982) has suggested that differences in fertility from one population to the next are largely accounted for by only four of those variables: proportion married, use of contraceptives, incidence of abortion, and involuntary infecundity (especially postpartum fecundity as affected by breast-feeding practices). Among countries with generally high birth rates, Bongaarts found that differences were due largely to lactation; countries where breast-feeding is common have somewhat lower levels of fertility than those in which breast-feeding is less common. Furthermore, the transition from high to low fertility is usually found to be accomplished with a combination of declines in breast-feeding, later marriage, increased use of contraception, and increased incidence of abortion.

➤ MEASURING FERTILITY

Having discussed the numerous means by which fertility can be controlled, we are almost ready to discuss and try to explain recent trends in fertility around the world. However, in that discussion I will, of necessity, use several different measures of fertility, and each of them deserves some comment ahead of time so that you can understand their various weaknesses and strengths. In some cases, the entire trend in fertility over time in a country will appear different just by using different measures of fertility. Since many of these measures regularly find their way into newspapers and popular magazines, familiarizing yourself with them will make you a better consumer of such information, in addition to the contribution it will make to your understanding of fertility trends and levels.

The basic goal in measuring fertility is to estimate the number of children that women are having. The data used for measuring fertility usually come from a combination of census and vital statistics sources, as I discussed in Chapter 1. In addition, detailed data are sometimes available from sample surveys or from special census tabulations. Nonetheless, measurement of fertility is often complicated by differences between one country (or state) and another in the amount and quality of data available. The less information available, the less sophisticated and accurate will be the estimates of fertility. Nowhere is this more apparent than in the contrast between period and cohort data.

Period Versus Cohort Data

Period data refer to a particular calendar year and represent a cross section of the population at one specific time. **Cohort** measures of fertility, on the other hand, "are designed to follow the fertility of groups of women as they proceed through the childbearing years of life. In other words, **period rates** focus on the experience of specific calendar years, but cohort rates focus on the experience of groups of women over a number of years" (Kiser et al., 1968:255). In the following discussion, we will look first at the usual period measures of fertility, since they require the least information. These include the simplest and most frequently used fertility measure—the crude birth rate—as well as the general fertility rate, the child-woman ratio, Coale's Index of Fertility, and age-specific fertility rates. Then, we will examine cohort methods, including the total fertility rate, gross reproduction rate, net reproduction rate, and fertility expectations.

Period Measures of Fertility

Crude Birth Rate   The **crude birth rate** (CBR) is the number of live births in a year divided by the midyear population. It is usually multiplied by 1,000 to eliminate the decimal point:

$$\text{CBR} = \frac{\text{Number of live births in year } x}{\text{Midyear population in year } x} \times 1,000$$

The CBR is "crude" because (1) it does not take into account which people in the population were actually at risk of having the births; and (2) it ignores the age structure of the population, which can greatly affect how many live births can be expected in a given year. Thus, the CBR can mask significant differences in actual reproductive behavior between two populations and, on the other hand, can indicate differences that do not really exist. For example, if a population of 1,000 people contained 300 women who were of childbearing age and one tenth of them (30) had a baby in a particular year, the crude birth rate would be (30 births/1,000 total people) = 30 births per 1,000 population. However, in another population, one tenth of all women may also have had a child that year. Yet, if out of 1,000 people there were only 150 women of childbearing age, then only 15 babies would be born, and the crude birth rate would be 15 per 1,000.

Despite this shortcoming, the crude birth rate is often used, because it requires only two pieces of information: the number of births in a year and the total population size. If, in addition, we have a distribution of the population by age and sex, usually obtained from a census, then we can be more sophisticated in our measurement of fertility and calculate the general fertility rate.

General Fertility Rate   The **general fertility rate** (GFR) uses information about the age and sex structure of a population to be more specific about who actually has been at risk of having the births that are recorded in a given year. The GFR is the total number of births in a year divided by the number of women in the childbearing ages:

$$\text{GFR} = \frac{\text{Total number of births in year } x}{\text{Women aged 15–44 in year } x} \times 1,000$$

Let me give you an example of the differences between CBR and GFR in measuring fertility. In 1935, during the Depression, fertility was low in the United States. The CBR was 19 births per 1,000 population. In 1967, in the middle of the fertility decline that followed the Baby Boom, the CBR was 18, suggesting that fertility was actually lower than during the Depression. However, the lower CBR in 1967 than in 1935 was a result of differences in the number of people at each age in the 2 years rather than lower levels of childbearing. In 1967 the total population was swelled by young Baby Boom children who were not of childbearing age but whose inclusion in the total population (the denominator of the CBR) lowered its value. This problem is corrected by calculating the GFR. In 1935 the GFR was 78 births per 1,000 women aged 15–44. In 1967 it was higher than that, 88 per 1,000. Thus, by relating the births more closely to the people having the babies, we get a more accurate sense of the actual level of reproduction.

Child-Woman Ratio   Thus far, the two measures we have discussed rely on vital statistics data for their information about births; however, even if such data are not available, all is not lost. The **child-woman ratio** (CWR) provides an index of fertility that is conceptually similar to the general fertility rate but relies solely on census data. The CWR is measured by the ratio of young children (aged 0–4) enumerated in the census to the number of women of childbearing ages (15–44):

$$\text{CWR} = \frac{\text{Total number of children aged 0–4}}{\text{Women aged 15–49}} \times 1,000$$

Notice that we use an older upper limit on the age of women than that used with the GFR, because some of the children aged 0–4 will have been born up to 5 years prior to the census date. The 1980 census of the United States counted 16,344,407 children aged 0–4 and 58,523,815 women aged 15–49; thus, the CWR was 279 children aged 0–4 per 1,000 women of childbearing age. By contrast, the child-woman ratio for Mexico in 1980 was a whopping 800.

The child-woman ratio can be affected by the underenumeration of infants, by infant and childhood mortality (some of the children born will have died before being counted), and by the age distribution of women within the childbearing years. The latter problem is usually considered to be the most serious, and it is taken into account with a technique called *age standardization* (see the Appendix). As an example, however, we can note that if the distribution of women by age in 1980 in Mexico had been identical to that in the United States, Mexico's CWR would have been 832—even higher than it actually was! The Baby Boom generation in the United States had so many women placed in the prime reproductive years that, had they been producing children at the same rate as Mexican women, they would have had even more children aged 0–4 in 1980 than did the Mexican women.

Coale's Index of Fertility   As part of the European Fertility History Project (first discussed in Chapter 3), Ansley Coale produced an index of fertility that has been useful in making historical comparisons of fertility levels. The overall index of fertility (I_f) is the product of the proportion of the female population that is married (I_m) times the index of marital fertility (I_g). Thus:

$$I_f = I_m \times I_g$$

Marital fertility (I_g) is calculated in an interesting way, however. It is the ratio of marital fertility (live births per 1,000 married women) in a particular population to the marital fertility rates of the Hutterites. Since they are known to have had the highest overall level of childbearing, any other group might come close to, but not likely exceed, that level (see Figure 4.1). Thus, the Hutterites represent a good benchmark for maximum fertility. An I_g of 1.0 would mean that a population's marital fertility was equal to that of the Hutterites, whereas an I_g of 0.5 would represent a level of childbearing only half that.

Calculating marital fertility as a proportion, rather than as a rate, allows the researcher to readily estimate how much of a change in fertility over time is due to the proportion of women who are married and how much is due to a shift in reproduction within marriage. Much of the work leading to the reformulation of the demographic transition (see Chapter 3) has been based on analyses of I_f, I_m, and I_g.

Age-Specific Fertility Rate   One of the most precise ways of measuring fertility is the **age-specific fertility rate**. These rates, like the other measures still to be discussed, require a rather complete set of data: births according to the age of the mother and a distribution of the total population by age and sex. An age-specific fertility rate (ASFR) is the number of births occurring annually per 1,000 women of a specific age (usually given in 5-year age groups):

$$\text{ASFR} = \frac{\text{Births in a year to women aged } x \text{ to } (x + 5)}{\text{Total women aged } x \text{ to } (x + 5)} \times 1,000$$

For example, in the United States in 1984 there were 107 births per 1,000 women aged 20–24. In 1955 in the United States, childbearing activity for women aged 20–24 was more than twice that, reflected in an ASFR of 242. In 1984 the ASFR for women aged 25–29 was 108, compared with 191 in 1955. Thus, we can conclude that between 1955 and 1984, fertility dropped more for women aged 20–24 than for women aged 25–29.

It is apparent that ASFRs require analysis of fertility on an age-by-age basis. For a quick comparison of an entire population, this can be a pain in the neck. Therefore, demographers have devised a method for combining ASFRs into a single fertility index covering all ages—the total fertility rate.

Cohort Measures of Fertility

Total Fertility Rate   The basic measure of cohort fertility is births to date, eventually resulting in a final measure of completed fertility, the **total fertility rate**

(TFR). For example, women born in 1915 began their childbearing during the Depression. By the time those women had reached age 25 in 1939, they had given birth to 890 babies per 1,000 women (Heuser, 1976). By age 44 in 1958 those women had finished their childbearing in the Baby Boom years with a total fertility rate of 2,429 births per 1,000 women. We can compare those women with another cohort of women who were raised during the Depression and began their childbearing right after World War II. The cohort of women born in 1930 had borne a total of 1,415 children per 1,000 women by the time they were age 25 in 1954. This level is 60 percent greater than the 1915 cohort. By age 44 in 1973 the 1930 cohort had borne 3,153 children per 1,000 women—30 percent higher than the 1915 cohort. Indeed, examining cohort data for the United States, we can see that the women born in 1933 were the most fertile of any group of American women since the cohort born in 1881.

Although such information is illuminating, we cannot always wait until women complete their childbearing to estimate their level of fertility; thus, although the TFR is technically a cohort measure, it is usually calculated from period data (age-specific fertility rates) as though they referred to a cohort. This is called a **synthetic cohort** approach and approximates being able to ask women how many children they have had when they are all through with childbearing by using the age-specific fertility rates at a particular date to project what *could* happen in the future if all women went through their lives bearing children at the same rate that women of different ages were bearing them at that date. For example, I have already mentioned that in 1984 American women aged 25–29 were bearing children at a rate of 108 births per 1,000 women per year. Thus, over a 5-year span (from ages 25 through 29), for every 1,000 women we could expect 540 births if everything else remained the same. By applying that logic to all ages, we can calculate the TFR as the sum (signified by the symbol Σ) of the ASFRs through all ages:

$$TFR = \Sigma(ASFR \times 5)$$

The ASFR for each age group is multiplied by 5 only if the ages are grouped into 5-year intervals. If we had data by a single year of age, we would not have to make that adjustment. The calculation of the TFR for period data is illustrated in Table 4.5.

The TFR can be readily compared from one population to another because it takes into account the differences in age structure, and, although the calculation of the TFR may seem slightly complicated, its interpretation is simple and straightforward. The total fertility rate is an estimate of the average number of children born to each woman, assuming that current birth rates remain constant. In 1984, the TFR in the United States was 1,806 children per 1,000 women, or 1.8 children per woman. This was half of the 1955 figure of 3.6 children per woman. The TFR calculated from period data was also substantially lower in 1984 than the completed fertility rate for women aged 40–44 in 1984. These women, who were wrapping up their childbearing by 1984, had given birth to an average of 2.5 children during their lifetimes.

Table 4.5   Calculation of Total Fertility Rate for the United States, 1984

Age	Women in Age Group	(1,000 ·000) Live Births to Women in Age Group	Age-Specific Fertility Rates (Live Births per 1,000 Women)	ASFR × 5
10–14	8,304,000	9,965	1.2	6.0
15–19	9,228,000	469,682	50.9	254.5
20–24	10,639,000	1,141,578	107.3	536.5
25–29	10,764,000	1,165,711	108.3	541.5
30–34	9,902,000	658,496	66.5	332.5
35–39	8,585,000	195,755	22.8	114.0
40–44	6,884,000	26,846	3.9	19.5
45–49	5,540,000	1,108	0.2	1.0
				1,805.5

$$\text{TFR} = \Sigma(\text{ASFR} \times 5) = 1,805.5$$

Gross Reproduction Rate   A further refinement of the total fertility rate is to look at female births only (since it is only the female babies who eventually bear children). Thus, if we multiply the TFR by the proportion of all births that are girls, we have the **gross reproduction rate** (GRR). Specifically,

$$\text{GRR} = \text{TFR} \times \frac{\text{Female births}}{\text{All births}}$$

In the United States in 1984, 48.7 percent of all births were girls. Since the TFR was 1.8, we multiply that figure by 0.487 (the percentage converted to a proportion) to obtain a GRR of 0.88.

The gross reproduction rate is generally interpreted as the number of female children that a female just born may expect to have during her lifetime, assuming that birth rates stay the same and ignoring her chances of survival through her reproductive years. Thus, the GRR is called "gross" because it *assumes* that a girl will survive through all her reproductive years. Actually, some women will die before reaching the oldest age at which they might bear children. To take account of mortality risks, we can calculate the net reproduction rate.

Net Reproduction Rate   The **net reproduction rate** (NRR), like the TFR and GRR, is a cohort measure that is frequently used with period data to construct a synthetic cohort. With a real cohort, the net reproduction rate is typically referred to as the *generational replacement* rate. Either way, the NRR represents the number of female children that a female child just born can expect to bear, taking into account her risk of dying before the end of her reproductive years. Thus, the NRR is always less than the GRR, since some people always die before the end of their reproductive periods. How much before, of course, depends on death rates. In a low-mortality society such as the United States, the NRR is only slightly less than the GRR (the ratio of the NRR of .86 to the GRR of .88 is .98). By contrast, in a high-mortality society such as Pakistan, the difference can be substantial (the ratio of the NRR of 2.24 to the GRR of 3.43 is .65). Since calculation of the NRR is somewhat complicated, I have spared you having to deal with it at this point, putting it instead in the Appendix. The most important point is that you understand how to interpret it, for it is a fairly often cited measure of fertility.

As an index of generational replacement, an NRR of 1 indicates that each generation of females has the potential to just replace itself. This indicates a population that will eventually stop growing if fertility and mortality do not change. A value less than 1 indicates a potential decline in numbers, and a value greater than 1 indicates the potential for growth unless fertility and mortality change. It must be emphasized that the NRR is *not* equivalent to the rate of population growth in most societies. For example, in the United States the NRR in 1984 was less than 1 (0.86, to be specific), yet the population was still increasing by 1.5 million people each year. The NRR represents the *future potential* for growth inherent in a population's fertility and mortality regimes. However, peculiarities in the age structure (such as large numbers of women in the childbearing ages), as well as migration, affect the actual rate of growth at any point in time.

Birth Expectations   It is useful to have estimates of what the women who are presently of childbearing age might do in the future, and period data cannot do that any better than the cohort births-to-date information, so demographers estimate future cohort fertility by asking women about the number of births they expect in the future. For example, in June 1971, the Current Population Survey asked women how many births they expected to have had by 1976. Women aged 18–24 (the birth cohorts of 1946 to 1953) responded with an average of 1.99 births. Overall, they expected to have 2.38 births on average during their lifetime. In 1976, when they were reinterviewed, it appeared that their expectations had exceeded reality; they were averaging only 1.76 births per woman, and it seemed unlikely that they would reach their lifetime expectations. But, by 1981, when interviewed a third time (now aged 28–34) their behavior had nearly caught up with their expectations of a decade earlier, and they were averaging 2.21 children each. What had happened? Women who were single in 1971 failed to anticipate their average delay in getting married and, with marriage, a postponement of children. Thus, their short-run expectations missed the mark (O'Connell and Rogers, 1983). Yet, ultimately, they made up for lost time, and by 1986 they had reached their expected number of lifetime births. Other, more systematic analyses have confirmed that, overall, fertility intentions are only a moderately good predictor of fertility. In recent years, as fertility declined, fertility intentions have consistently overestimated the future levels of fertility (Westoff and Ryder, 1977; Freedman et al., 1980). Nonetheless, research by George Masnick (1981) suggests that birth expectation data may be a useful guide to the future if such information is compared with the behavior of women in earlier cohorts who had similar levels of fertility.

SUMMARY AND CONCLUSION

Fertility has both a biological and a social component. The capacity to reproduce is biological (although it can be influenced to a certain extent by the environment), but we have to look to the social environment to find out why women are having a particular number of children. Fertility control can be accomplished by a variety of means. In general, they include ways by which intercourse can be prevented, conception can be prevented if intercourse takes place, and successful gestation can be prevented if conception occurs. An understanding of these intermediate variables is an important preliminary to a good analysis of fertility trends and levels, as is the knowledge of how fertility is measured. In this chapter I examined the measures of fertility most commonly used in demographic analysis. In the next chapter I will build on the concepts and measures of fertility as I examine and attempt to explain reproductive behavior in different parts of the world.

MAIN POINTS

1. Fertility refers to the number of children born to women (or fathered by men).

2. Fecundity, on the other hand, refers to the biological capacity to produce children.

3. The group of people who are always pointed out when high fertility is discussed is the Hutterites, who live in the northern plains of the United States and in Canada. In the 1930s each woman averaged 12 children.

4. Fertility can be controlled by manipulating exposure to intercourse, trying to prevent conception, or interrupting pregnancy.

5. Researchers have discovered that women who do not engage in sexual intercourse do not have babies. This may be the cheap and effective means of birth control that the world has been looking for.

6. The longer a woman delays marriage, the fewer children she will likely have.

7. Women whose marriages are interrupted by the death of a spouse, divorce, or separation tend to have fewer children than those who remain continuously in a marriage.

8. The pill is one of the most effective means of contraception, but the IUD is also effective, as is the condom, especially when used in conjunction with a spermicidal foam or jelly.

9. The douche is almost useless as a contraceptive, as is the rhythm method. However, the symptothermal method appears to be effective for highly motivated couples.

10. Sterilization is an increasingly popular method of avoiding conception and, furthermore, governments around the world are increasingly allowing abortion as a legal means to end unwanted pregnancies.

11. The principal measures of fertility used by demographers are the crude birth rate, general fertility rate, child-woman ratio, Coale's Index of Fertility, age-specific fertility rate, total fertility rate, gross reproduction rate, net reproduction rate, and birth expectations. Don't let people tell you what the birth rate is without finding out what rate they are referring to and whether the rate refers to period or cohort data.

SUGGESTED READINGS

1. Kingsley Davis and Judith Blake, 1956, "Social structure and fertility: an analytic framework," Economic Development and Cultural Change 4(4):211–35.

   The chapter that you have just finished reading has leaned heavily on this classic statement of the role of "intermediate variables" as determinants of fertility levels in human societies.

2. John Bongaarts, 1978, "A framework for analyzing the proximate determinants of fertility," Population and Development Review 4(1):105–32.

   This is a very important updating of the analysis of Davis and Blake's "intermediate variables," which Bongaarts has redefined as the "proximate determinants of fertility."

3. Robert Hatch and associates, Contraceptive Technology (New York: Irvington Publishers), published annually.

   This basic reference work provides updated information on the prevalence and effectiveness of various fertility control methods.

4. Norman E. Himes, 1976, The Medical History of Contraception (New York: Schocken Books).

   The numerous studies summarized in this important work put into historical perspective the fact that at least some human groups have known for centuries how to control fertility.

5. Stanley Henshaw, 1987, "Induced abortion: a worldwide perspective," International Family Planning Perspectives 13(1):12–16.

   This article is particularly good for getting into better focus the world picture of abortion patterns and levels.

CHAPTER 5
Fertility Trends, Levels, and Explanations

I am inclined to think that the most important of Western values is the habit of a low birth-rate. If this can be spread throughout the world, the rest of what is good in Western life can also be spread. There can be not only prosperity, but peace. But if the West continues to monopolize the benefits of low birth-rate(s), war, pestilence, and famine must continue, and our brief emergence from those ancient evils must be swallowed in a new flood of ignorance, destitution and war.

When Bertrand Russell, whose words these are (1951:49), died in 1970 at age 89, he had witnessed almost the entire demographic transition in the Western nations; birth rates in less developed areas, however, seemed stubbornly high.

Then, as now, it was widely believed that the fertility level would decline dramatically in those countries where it is now high if only women could be given the pill or fitted with an IUD, but that is a simplistic and erroneous view. What we face is, in fact, an extremely complex situation, and in this chapter I will discuss some of the important social, psychological, and economic factors that help to explain why some people have large families while others do not. The discussion is double-edged, giving you a background in fertility trends and levels while at the same time providing possible explanations for them. In so doing, I will examine the role of the intermediate variables discussed in the preceding chapter, along with the role of the social environments in which people live and reproduce.

Since high fertility is frequently cited as a problem (it is, for example, the single factor most responsible for the *continued* high rate of growth in the world today—the decline in mortality created the problem, but high fertility sustains it), and since virtually all low-fertility societies experienced high fertility at one time or another, I will begin the chapter with some explanations for this phenomenon. I will be using illustrations from areas where those high levels of reproduction currently prevail, especially India. Then I will take you through the transition from high to low fertility as the process occurred in England, Japan, and the United States, using these countries as case histories as I explain how and why low fertility is accomplished.

EXPLANATIONS FOR HIGH FERTILITY

A widely accepted explanation for high fertility is that in virtually every society individuals feel pressured to have children, although in some societies these pronatalist pressures are stronger than in others. Pronatalist pressures are usually a response to the need to replace the members of society, which shows up especially as a need for children for labor and old-age security and as a desire for sons.

Need to Replenish Society

A crucial aspect of high mortality is that a baby's chances of surviving to adulthood are not very good. Yet if a society is going to replace itself, an average of at least two children for every woman must survive long enough to be able to produce more children. So, under adverse conditions, any person who limited fertility might be threatening the very existence of society. In this light it is not surprising that societies have generally been unwilling to leave it strictly up to the individual or to chance to have the required number of children. Societies everywhere have developed **social institutions** to encourage childbearing and reward parenthood in various ways. For example, among the Kgatla people in southern Africa, mortality was very high during the 1930s when they were being studied by Schapera. He discovered that " to them it is inconceivable that a married couple should for economic or personal reasons deliberately seek to restrict the number of its offspring" (1966:213). Schapera found several social factors that encouraged the Kgatla to desire children:

> A woman with many children is honored. Married couples acquire new dignity after the birth of their first child. Since the Kgatla have a patrilineal descent system (inheritance passes through the sons), the birth of a son makes the father the founder of a line that will perpetuate his name and memory . . . [the mother's] kin are pleased because the birth saves them from shame (Nag, 1962:29).

In a 1973 study of another African society, the Yoruba people of western Nigeria, families of fewer than four children were looked upon with horror (Ware, 1975). Ware reports that "even if it could be guaranteed that two children would survive to adulthood, Yoruban parents would find such a family very lonely, for many of the features of the large family which have come to be negatively valued in the West, such as noise and bustle, are positively valued by them" (1975:284).

Social encouragements to fertility have been discussed in a more general form by Davis:

> We often find for example that the permissive enjoyment of sexual intercourse, the ownership of land, the admission to certain offices, the claim to respect, and the attainment of blessedness are made contingent upon marriage. Marriage accomplished, the more specific encouragements to fertility apply. In familistic societies where kinship forms the chief basis of social organization, reproduction is a necessary means to nearly every major goal in life. The salvation of the soul, the security of old age, the production of goods, the protection of the hearth, and the assurance of affection may depend upon the presence, help, and comfort of progeny. . . . [T]his articulation of the parental status with the rest of one's statuses is the supreme encouragement to fertility (1949:561).

You may notice from these examples that social pressures are not actually defined in terms of the need to replace society, and an individual would likely not recognize them for what they are. By and large the social institutions and **norms** that encourage high fertility are so taken for granted by the members of society that anyone who consciously said, "I am having a baby in order to continue the existence of my society" would be viewed as a bit eccentric. Further, if people really acted solely on the basis that they had to replace society, then high-fertility societies would actually have much lower levels of fertility, since in all such countries the birth rates exceed the death rates by a substantial margin. What is more likely to motivate people is the belief that they will please other family members and bring power and prestige to themselves and the family as a group. Sometimes those reasons can be made even more specific, as in the case of children as security and labor.

Children As Security and Labor

In a premodern society with high mortality and high fertility, human beings are the principal economic resource. Even as youngsters they can help in many tasks, and as they mature they provide the bulk of the labor force that supports those, such as the aged, who are no longer able to support themselves. Boserup (1981) reports, for example, that:

> In most of Africa, a large share of the agricultural work was and is done by women and the children, even very young ones, perform numerous tasks in rural areas. A man with many children can have his land cleared for long-fallow cultivation by young sons, and all, or nearly all, other agricultural work done by women and smaller children. He need not pay for hired labor or fear for lack of support in old age. A large family is an economic advantage—a provider of social security, and of prestige in the local community. Therefore, the large family is the universally agreed on ideal in most African communities (1981:180).

More broadly speaking, children can be viewed as a form of insurance that rural parents, in particular, have against a variety of risks, such as a drought or a poor harvest (Cain, 1981). Though at first blush it may seem as though children would be a burden under such adverse conditions, many parents view a large family as providing a safety net—at least one or two of the adult children may be able to bail them out of a bad situation.

Desire for Sons

Although it is clear in many countries today that the status of women is steadily improving, it is nonetheless true that in many societies around the world, desired social goals can be achieved only by the birth and survival of a son—indeed, most known societies throughout human history have been dominated by men. Since in most societies males have been valued more highly than females, it is easy to understand why many families would continue to have children until they have at least one son. Furthermore, if babies are likely to die, a family may have at least two sons in order to increase the likelihood that one of them will survive to adulthood. In a high-mortality society, then, the desire to have even one son survive may require the birth of almost four children on average (since nearly but not quite half of all births in any society are girls—see Chapter 8) (Heer and Smith, 1969). India is a good example of a country where the desire for a surviving son is relatively strong, since the Hindu religion requires that parents be buried by their son (Mandelbaum, 1974). Malthus was very aware of this stimulus to fertility in India and, in his *Essay on Population*, quoted an Indian legislator who wrote that under Hindu law a male heir is "an object of the first importance. 'By a son a man obtains victory over all people; by a son's son he enjoys immortality; and afterwards by the son of that grandson he reaches the solar abode'" (Malthus, 1872:116). Such beliefs, of course, also serve to ensure that society will be replaced in the face of high mortality.

Data from the World Fertility Survey (WFS) allow us to quantify the desire for sons and to see, as well, the differing importance of sons around the world. This was accomplished as follows: The WFS asked women if they wanted any more children than they already had; then, by correlating that answer with the number of sons already born, a sense of their desire for sons could be inferred. For example, among Korean women who already had two children, 77 percent of those with two sons said they wanted no more children, compared with only 36 percent of those with two daughters (Kent and Larson, 1982). Thus, a Korean woman is twice as likely to be satisfied with her current family size if she has two sons than if she has two daughters.

Though it is true that Korean women show a stronger son preference than do people in most other countries, Asian societies in general seem to have stronger desires for sons than do most Western nations. So strong, in fact, is the feeling toward having a son in China that the one-child policy there may have precipitated a spate of girl-baby infanticides and physical abuse of mothers who give birth to a girl (Haupt, 1983).

> While the birth of a son has always been a more important event than the arrival of a daughter, Peking's policy of one child per family has raised the stakes. For the peasantry birth has become a kind of Russian roulette: The arrival of a son heralds a relaxed and secure old age; the coming of a daughter portends poverty and slow starvation during one's declining years. . . . If the child isn't male, then the choice is a stark one: Either kill or abandon the newborn female infant, reserving your one-child quota for the birth of a boy, or face a harrowing old age (Mosher, 1983:13).

Moslem nations also exhibit a marked son preference. A study in Pakistan, for example, revealed that even among women who already had six children, if all six were daughters, there was a 46 percent chance that the mother wanted more children (obviously hoping for a son), whereas if all six were boys, there was only a 4 percent chance that she would want additional children (Khan and Sirageldin, 1977). Similarly, in rural Egypt, where the average woman bears seven children, 41 percent of the women with four or more sons were regular users of the pill in 1977, compared with only 11 percent of the women who had five or more children, none of whom were boys (Gadalla et al., 1985). We must recognize, of course, that the desire for sons cannot alone account for high birth rates. For example, despite Korea's strong son preference (as I mentioned in the previous chapter), the birth rate has declined dramatically in that country and is currently barely above replacement level. We must keep looking if we are to understand the full picture.

Ambivalence

As mortality has declined in India and many other less developed countries, the birth rate has not declined nearly as rapidly, if at all. Why not? To look for an answer to this question we have to ask why people would be motivated to change their reproductive behavior. In Chapter 3, I discussed the theories of the demographic transition and demographic change and response, which suggested that a decline in mortality would impinge on the lives of individuals as increasing numbers of family members remained alive to be fed and cared for. The theory goes that couples would eventually perceive it to be advantageous to have fewer children than their parents had, or fewer than their older siblings are having, and so forth. Remember, though, that I also noted that migration is a quick solution for a while, delaying the pinch of a large family. Furthermore, there is another pitfall, since a major tenet of those theories was that there had to be an incentive to get ahead materially—to take advantage of economic opportunities. If none exist, where will the motivation to improve your life by having a small family come from?

In the time that currently intervenes between a decline in mortality and the arousal of motivation for smaller families in less developed nations, high fertility may tend to persist because of **ambivalence.** A couple may be ambivalent when they do not necessarily want as many children as are now unexpectedly surviving, and yet they are still being socially rewarded. Childbearing is rarely an end in itself, but rather a means to achieve other goals; so if the attainment of the other goals is perceived as being more important than limiting fertility, a woman may continue to risk pregnancy even though she may be ambivalent about having a child.

Some of the factors that may enhance feelings of ambivalence at various points in a woman's life include the exclusive identification of a woman's role with reproduction (that is, males do not help with child rearing), lack of participation of women in work outside of the immediate family, low levels of education, lack of communication between husband and wife, lack of potential for social mobility, and an extended family system in which couples need not be economically independent to afford children. Most of these factors are related to the domination of women by men.

An interesting example of relative ambivalence toward childbearing is provided by Nag (1962) in discussing the rural Sinhalese people of Ceylon (now Sri Lanka) in the 1950s. Among these people it is believed that the number of children one has is a reflection of the merit achieved in a previous life, so this is a pleasant goal. However, the burden of large families, grown larger because of declining mortality, which permits more children to live longer, falls entirely on the mother, while more children make life easier and more prestigious for the father. Nag reports that "men sincerely want large families without any qualification, and they are vehemently against any form of birth control" (1962:47). The men question the use of birth control when they are legally married and entitled to have children. With respect to the women, however, Nag notes that "the women's attitude is ambivalent. Many women are in conflict between the societal ideal of a large family and a personal desire for fewer children. Their responses in the presence of other neighbors and relatives were different from their responses when interviewed alone" (1962:47). Keyfitz and Fleiger (1971) report further that these Sinhalese people compare their population size with that of a competitive **ethnic group,** the Tamils. Thus, the men may have reinforced positive motivation for enlarging families even though feelings of ambivalence may be growing among the women. Indeed, that very ambivalence among women may well have represented the leading edge of a fertility decline in Sri Lanka, where the total fertility rate fell from 5.9 in 1953 (at about the time Nag was interviewing women) to 2.8 in 1988.

Simmons (1974) found evidence of ambivalence toward family size among women in rural Mexico—another country in which fertility levels have only recently begun to come down. In Mexico, the total fertility rate in 1970–72 was about 6.5 births per woman (Seiver, 1975), but Simmons still found that only 7 percent of a sample of 2,009 women clearly favored large families. A large proportion was unsure about the personal advantages and disadvantages of either a large or small family. Other researchers in rural Mexico in 1975 discovered the same thing: "Significant proportions of high-parity women [that is, those with many children] perceive their large families with ambivalence or do not desire another pregnancy. However, ambivalence toward future childbearing is counterbalanced by ambivalence toward fertility regulation" (Shedlin and Hollerbach, 1981:294).

In the midst of such indecision, families tend to grow large. Again, however, ambivalence seemed to be a forerunner of a reduction in fertility. A 1978 fertility survey in Mexico suggested that the total fertility rate had declined from 6.8 in 1969–71 to 5.2 in 1978. This apparently was the result of a dramatic rise in the use of the pill and the IUD (Rowe, 1982). By 1986 the total fertility rate in Mexico had dropped to 3.8, as low fertility values and greater availability of fertility control methods had taken hold (Urbina, 1988). Especially noteworthy has been an increase in the use of condoms, signaling a rise in men's motivations for fertility control.

In sum, the encouragements to high fertility often persist even after mortality declines, because they are taken for granted as part of a person's life. An important point to remember is that high fertility is usually much easier to achieve than low fertility, regardless of the level of motivation. For the average person, a high level of desire is required to keep families small.

HIGH-FERTILITY COUNTRIES

Having analyzed why high fertility might persist even after mortality has declined, let me now turn to an analysis of three different countries where we find that very situation today: India, Ghana, and Kuwait (see Figure 5.1). India is especially interesting, since virtually every explanation I have discussed for high fertility applies to at least some area of India.

India

You will recall from Chapter 2 that India is a large, culturally diverse society, where the pattern of fertility has been one of consistently high levels. Davis (1951) has estimated that in 1881–91 the crude birth rate was about 49 per 1,000 population. After 1921 there is some evidence of a decline, such that by 1941 the birth rate was about 45 per 1,000. Data were not reliable enough to ensure that the decline was real, and if it was, there is no apparent explanation for it, since historically there has been little use of contraceptives in India. In fact, Davis reports that in a study

Figure 5.1   The Contrast Between High and Low Fertility

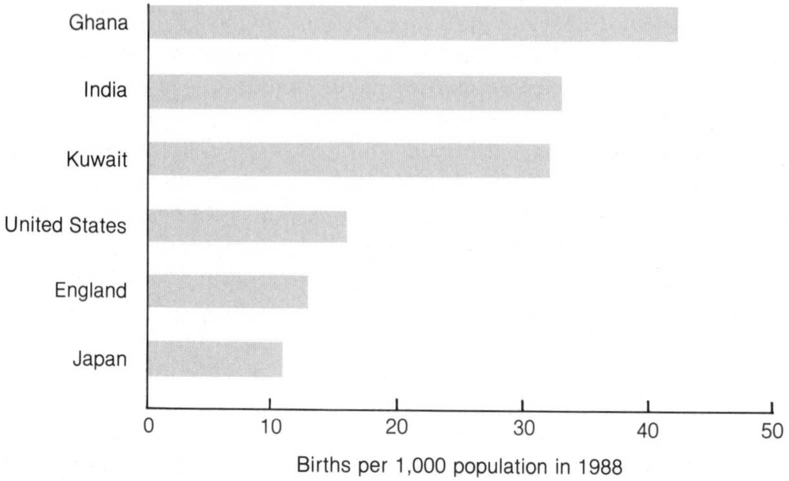

Births per 1,000 population in 1988

The difference between the high- and low-fertility countries discussed in this chapter is vividly portrayed in this graph. High-fertility countries like Ghana, Kuwait, and India have crude birth rates that are more than double those of low-fertility countries such as Japan, England, and the United States. *Source:* Data courtesy of Population Reference Bureau, Inc., Washington, D.C.

done in 1941 in Kolhapur City with a population of nearly 100,000 people, in a sample of 1,661 married women, only 3 practiced contraception (1951). In 1951, after an exhaustive analysis of the population of India and Pakistan, Davis reached "the melancholy conclusion that an early and substantial decline of fertility in India seems unlikely unless rapid changes not now known or envisaged are made in Indian life" (1951:82).

In 1958, Coale and Hoover concluded that low fertility had become established among only a negligible fraction of the Indian population—a very small group of urban, highly educated people. Between 1941 and 1961, estimates of the birth rate in India indicate that it remained at a level of about 45 per 1,000 population. However, estimates for the period 1961–71 indicate a small decline in the crude birth rate to 42 per 1,000. An analysis by Adlakha and Kirk (1974) suggests that this decline represented a real drop in marital fertility among Indian women, which may have been a result of the concerted government efforts to promote family planning techniques, especially sterilization. However, the decline in fertility was outweighed by declines in the death rate, and in the 1960s the population of India was growing faster than ever before. By 1988 the crude birth rate had dropped to 33 per 1,000, but the steady drop in the death rate has maintained the pace of Indian population growth.

As has been alluded to earlier in this chapter, India is a nation in which sons are often preferred to daughters, and this fact is reflected in the marriage patterns. A bride usually lives with her husband's family and brings a dowry with her, which means that a son's marriage will provide his family with a young woman, who often is expected to do much of the domestic work, along with money or goods from the girl's family. On the other hand, a family with several daughters faces a very expensive prospect as the girls reach puberty. One chilling facet of the bride dowry custom is that a girl whose dowry is not large enough may face abuse or even death at the hands of her in-laws (Norland, 1981).

In a review of studies on India, Mandelbaum reports that "typically a woman knows of no acceptable alternative for herself than that of wife-mother. . . . For all but a relative few, a woman's destiny lies mainly in her procreation; the mark of her success as a person is in her living, thriving children" (1974:16). Women know that husbands may die before they do and children, especially sons, may offer a source of economic security. "Parents look to sons for support in old age and, in keeping with tradition, maintain that it is only with sons that parents can share a home" (Mehta, 1975:134). Further, fathers often argue that they need the sons to help work the land, even if their farm is small (Mandelbaum, 1974). Above all, in a nation where there is little material wealth to which most people can aspire, children help fulfill aspiration for some status in society and for expressing their parents' creativity.

From 1954 through 1960 an intensive birth control program was conducted in the Indian state of Punjab. Known as the Khanna study, it was sponsored by the Harvard School of Public Health, and it cost well over $1 million. A follow-up study in 1969 showed that the program had been a failure. Why did it fail? In analyzing the data from the program, Mamdani concluded that "no program would have succeeded, because birth control contradicted the vital interests of the majority of the villagers. To practice contraception would have meant to willfully court economic disaster" (1972:21). The point is that if a person does not see a clear advantage to limiting family size, it is not likely to happen.

During the 1970s there were encouraging signs of a slowdown in the rate of growth. Between 1971 and 1978, the total fertility rate was estimated to have dropped from 5.6 to 4.7 (Preston and Bhat, 1984), and the rate of population growth is thought to have dropped to less than 2.0 percent per year in 1978. The decline was probably due to a trend among young women toward delaying marriage (the legal age at marriage for girls in India has been raised from 15 to 18) and to a slight increase in fertility control among older couples (Jain and Adlakha, 1982). Still, less than one fourth of all Indian couples of childbearing age use a contraceptive, with male sterilization being by far the most popular method.

It is of some importance to note that although fertility is high in India, with few signs of yielding, it is still well below what might be the biological maximum. In India the total fertility rate is about 4.3 births per woman, nearly one-third the Hutterite level. Why is fertility not any higher? The answer to this question is related to the social environment in which reproduction occurs. Childbearing is only one of the activities necessary for the ongoing conduct of society. There are many institutions, such as religion, government, and education, that are also important, and activities involving other aspects of social life often compete or conflict with sexual intercourse or childbearing. It is because of this fact that most premodern societies have been able to maintain a relative balance between resources and population (Lesthaeghe, 1980). Thus, virtually every known society has social barriers to maximizing fertility and India is no exception. In different societies, these barriers may involve late age at marriage, restrictions against marriage, special times when inter-course is taboo, or a host of other customs that keep fertility lower than it would otherwise be. Individuals may not be consciously motivated to limit family size, but social institutions prevent them from reaching their maximum potential.

These competing pressures operate through the intermediate variables. For ex-ample, in India it is believed (correctly so) that the health of an infant is endangered if the next child comes too quickly. Thus, in many regions there is a taboo on the mother having sexual intercourse for several months (sometimes longer) after the birth of a child. As a result, Indian children are spaced an average of 3 to 4 years apart (Mandelbaum, 1974). This of course lowers the overall number of children that a woman can have in her lifetime. Hutterite women space their children very close together (less than 2 years on the average—see Sheps, 1965), and that fact alone could help to explain why Indians have fewer children than Hutterites do.

It is also reported that there is a "pregnant grandmother complex" in India; that is, a woman is openly criticized and disgraced if she becomes pregnant after she is already a grandmother (for a review, see Mandelbaum, 1974). Further, once a couple's childbearing days are over, it is commonly accepted that intercourse will cease, to ensure that they remain over. (It is thus no surprise to learn that women who have already completed their family are among the first to avail themselves of birth control technology as soon as they hear of it.)

Indian couples, then, are able to control their fertility if they want to—steriliza-tion is widely available and, of course, abstinence is a common birth control tech-nique available to anyone; a majority of couples simply are not motivated to keep families small. As Davis has put it: "What is rational in the light of a couple's situation may be totally irrational from the standpoint of society's welfare" (1967:733).

The Indian government has become increasingly concerned about how the na-tion's welfare is being affected by population growth and has adopted several poli-cies to try to coerce people to be "voluntarily" sterilized after their third child. In Chapter 15 I will discuss their policies in more detail, but it will suffice here to note that government attempts to limit births were met by opposition leading to violence in 1976 and the subsequent ouster of the antinatalist government of Indira Gandhi. After she regained power, Gandhi carefully sidestepped the family limitation issue.

Ghana

Ghana is located in western tropical Africa and, like many African countries, is characterized by birth and death rates that are among the highest in the world. If death rates should continue to decline substantially on the African continent without a corresponding drop in fertility, this area of the world will be hit by a massive growth in numbers. Even now, birth rates in Africa are enough higher than death rates so that the population will, at its present rate, double in only 24 years.

In Ghana, the crude birth rate is estimated to be 42 births per 1,000 population, and the total fertility rate is approximately 5.8 (Population Reference Bureau, 1988)—numbers that have dropped only slightly in the past decade. These figures are incredibly high, of course, and substantial changes must occur before birth rates decline to levels comparable to those in industrialized countries. In the urban areas, the capital city of Accra especially, men and women alike are becoming educated and are adopting a Western style of life, including family limitation. Changes occur slowly, however, and in a 1966 survey in Accra, only 11 percent of all women knew of some method of birth control. However, among educated women (those with at least some high school), 28 percent knew of birth control techniques. Among the educated urban elite, the percentage was 65 (Pool, 1970).

In January 1970 a National Family Planning Program was instituted in Ghana, but by 1978 only 4 percent of married women were active users of a contraceptive method (U.S. Bureau of the Census, 1983f). Fertility remains high because in Ghana most couples want large families. In 1966 in Accra, 63 percent of males sampled wanted five or more children, and 49 percent of women wanted at least that many children. In rural areas, 78 percent of the women wanted five or more, and practically no one wanted families with fewer than four children. Among urban males in Ghana only 8 percent wanted a family that small, compared with 43 percent in Taiwan, 34 percent in Pakistan (Pool, 1970), and 83 percent in the United States (Blake, 1974). The few signs that exist for a potential decline in fertility are present among a relatively small elite located high in the occupational strata—professionals, administrators, and executives, among whom 60 percent wanted families with fewer than five children.

Although it is difficult to disentangle cause and effect, it appears that rapid population growth and political instability may go hand in hand in less developed countries like Ghana. Ghana was the first tropical African colony to gain independence. In 1951 the British allowed limited internal self-government and in 1957 granted independence, but after leading his country to independence, President Nkrumah established an authoritarian government. He was overthrown in 1966 while visiting Hanoi and was replaced by a military government, which ruled until 1969 when Dr. Busia became prime minister in a popular election. Under Busia, a population policy was enacted, calling for government encouragement of family planning, but an army coup overthrew Busia as he was visiting London in 1972. Civilian rule was restored in 1979 when President Hilla Limann was inaugurated, but he, in turn, was ousted by another military coup in 1981, and democracy has been "suspended" ever since. Such political instability provides a difficult milieu in which to develop economically, and the rapid population growth also contributes to problems such as unemployment. Indeed, the population doubled in size between 1950 and 1976, and the unemployment rate grew in tandem to an estimated 25 percent. The population will probably be double its 1976 size before the end of this century, and one can only imagine the impact on the economics and the politics of Ghana as that demographic force makes itself felt.

Kuwait

Kuwait is a small Middle Eastern, oil-producing nation that is one of the richest countries in the world. Since 1945 it has experienced "one of the most dramatic rises in income anywhere in the world" (Hill, 1975:537). It also has low levels of mortality and very high levels of fertility—fertility levels typical of Arab Moslem countries. Currently each woman is bearing about six children and almost all survive. This combination of high fertility and very low mortality produces one of the highest levels of natural increase anywhere in the world. The population of Kuwait is still small (2.0 million in 1988) but will double every 22 years unless fertility declines dramatically.

High fertility in Kuwait is not a result of ignorance or lack of accessibility to contraceptives. Hill reports that women who already have large families have been using the pill or IUD for years because they feel "saturated" by several pregnancies. A Kuwaiti has access to free medical service and can obtain contraceptives free of charge, but one must question what motivation for small families would exist in a strongly pronatalist society in which all education is free from first grade through college, all health care and drugs are free, parents receive a subsidy for primary school children, and, once educated, a Kuwaiti is practically guaranteed a job. It is a welfare state from birth to death, including a comprehensive social security system. Thus, parents have the opportunity to increase their own standard of living and have large families as well. Though data are not available on the use of contraception, it is obvious that Kuwaiti women, despite their very high fertility, do not maximize their reproduction. It appears that the higher rate of divorce, some polygamy, and a required waiting period between divorce and remarriage help to offset an early age at marriage and marital fertility rates that approach the level of Hutterites (Hill, 1978).

Pronatalist pressures are reinforced by the domination of males over females and the large age differential between husbands and wives, strengthened by limited opportunities for women outside the family. However compelling these pressures may be, they are nonetheless insufficient to explain continued high fertility, because we know that social customs can bow to changing social and economic circumstances. It appears that the rapid accumulation of wealth, generously distributed throughout society, does not provide much motivation to have small families, at least in the short run. Thus, Kuwait provides an important lesson in the explanation of high fertility—it is not only the poor who have children. Just what is it that motivates people to have small families or no families at all? This is one of the most important questions facing the world.

EXPLANATIONS FOR LOW FERTILITY

Most explanations for low fertility can be traced back to a Darwinian-type theory of the survival of the fittest (a theory, you may recall, that was derived by Darwin from the writings of Malthus—Smith, 1951). The explanation usually offered is that if a society has scarce resources that are considered desirable, and if people have to adjust their demographic behavior to obtain some of those scarcities, they will. This is the basic ingredient of the theory of demographic change and response discussed in Chapter 3. In some cases, the appropriate demographic response is to limit family size, and history suggests that the desire to acquire wealth and prestige is often a motivation for a demographic response that does indeed include keeping families small.

Wealth, Prestige, and Fertility

Historically the most persistent socioeconomic factors related to fertility are wealth and prestige (both of which are further related to power). A study of primitive societies has shown that population control was related to a competition for power and prestige (Douglas, 1966), which often led to an emphasis on high fertility (there may be power in numbers) rather than low fertility. However, as Benedict (1972) has noted, in urban industrial societies of the nineteenth and twentieth centuries, prestige and wealth tend to be linked with low fertility rather than high fertility. This reversal may seem puzzling at first glance. After all, it would seem on an a priori basis that as people acquired wealth and prestige they would acquire more children, since presumably they could afford more rather than fewer. Indeed, in Kuwait, high incomes are helping to maintain high birth rates. But Kuwait is an exception. The key seems to be the availability of resources. In most countries, wealth and prestige are scarce economic and social commodities, and it may require sacrifices of one kind or another if an individual is to beat the competition. One sacrifice is the large family. In 1938, an Englishman put it rather succinctly: ". . . in our existing economic system, apart from luck, there are two ways of rising in the economic system; one is by ability, and the other by infertility. It is clear that of two equally able men—the one with a single child, and the other with eight children—the one with a single child will be more likely to rise in the social scale" (quoted by Daly, 1971:33).

Thus, acquiring wealth may require that a family be kept small, whereas already having wealth may permit, and even encourage, the growth of families. Often people who have kept families small in order to acquire wealth and prestige are past their reproductive years when they reach their goal (if they reach it), or they may have grown comfortable with a small family and decide not to have more children even though finally they might be able to afford them. This difference in the timing of fertility and wealth is one important point to keep in mind in reviewing explanations for low fertility.

In study after study, demographic researchers have discovered that in industrially developed countries the middle classes especially have much lower fertility than the lower classes. In some, but not all, cases there is a consistent trend toward smaller families as you go higher up the wealth and prestige ladder. Let me examine recent fertility differentials in the United States to illustrate the point, using family income as a measure of wealth and occupational level as a measure of prestige.

Income and Fertility

In June of each year, the Current Population Survey of the U.S. Census Bureau asks American women about their reproductive behavior. I have reproduced some of the findings from the 1986 survey in Table 5.1. From these data we may infer that, for wives of any age, whether they are working or not, the more money the family has, the fewer children are likely to have been born to date. When the wife is working, the impact on fertility is greater. On average, each 1,000 working wives aged 30–34 had about 350 fewer children than each 1,000 nonworking wives of the same ages. The most extensive difference is between working wives with high incomes (1,449 births per 1,000 wives) and low-income, nonworking wives (2,621 births per 1,000 wives). Fertility among those poorer, nonworking women was 80 percent higher than among the high-income workers.

Occupation and Fertility

In industrialized nations, those people who hold the more prestigious occupations have fewer children than others with lower-prestige occupations. There are few exceptions to this generalization, and the United States is not one of them. As you can see in Table 5.2, the highest and lowest levels of fertility are found at the two occupational extremes, with wives of managerial and professional men in the United States having nearly one fewer child by ages 30–34 than farmers' wives of the same age. The younger ages also show a distinct difference between white- and blue-collar occupations, the latter having clearly higher levels of reproduction.

Table 5.1 Higher-Income Women Have Fewer Children (United States, 1986)

	Children Ever Born per 1,000 Wives		
Family Income	Ages 18–24	Ages 25–29	Ages 30–34
Wife in labor force			
Under $10,000	809	1,437	2,191
$10,000–$14,999	797	1,372	2,146
$15,000–$19,999	708	1,286	2,172
$20,000–$24,999	613	1,223	1,824
$25,000–$29,999	506	1,189	1,879
$30,000–$34,999	435	1,039	1,767
$35,000 and over	374	785	1,449
Wife not in labor force			
Under $10,000	1,340	2,141	2,621
$10,000–$14,999	1,248	2,041	2,284
$15,000–$19,999	1,340	1,811	2,343
$20,000–$24,999	1,432	1,764	2,266
$25,000–$29,999	[a]	1,815	2,499
$30,000–$34,999	[a]	1,790	2,061
$35,000 and over	[a]	1,456	2,023

Source: U.S. Bureau of the Census, 1987, "Fertility of American Women: June 1986," Current Population Reports, Series P-20, No. 421, Table 9.

[a] Sample too small for calculation.

Table 5.2 Occupational Level Is Related to Fertility Levels (United States, 1986)

Occupational Level of Employed Civilian Husband	Children Ever Born per 1,000 Wives		
	Ages 18–24	Ages 25–29	Ages 30–34
Managerial and professional	473	858	1,638
Technical, sales, and administrative support	726	1,157	1,697
Service	1,081	1,462	2,040
Precise production	883	1,488	2,025
Operators, fabricators, and laborers	974	1,602	2,163
Farm workers	767	1,534	2,309

Source: U.S. Bureau of the Census, 1987, "Fertility of American Women: June 1986," Current Population Reports, Series P-20, No. 421, Table 9.

If we examine the number of births expected instead of the births to date, an interesting twist appears in the data: Wives of professional husbands expect to have slightly more children than other white-collar wives. This suggests a pattern, noted by an increasing number of researchers, that fertility has a more complicated relation to income than appears at first glance. Bernhardt (1972), using data from Sweden, discovered that although there was a definite tendency for the smallest families to be in the middle classes, within each **social class,** the greater the income relative to others in the same class, the larger the family size (data were controlled for age and marriage duration).

In other words, it appeared that those at the top of the ladder in any social class were having larger families than those at the bottom. This could perhaps be explained in terms of those at the top being satisfied with their income level and thus deciding to yield to pronatalist pressures, whereas those at the bottom might still be struggling to improve their relative position and thus would be willing to limit family size. Data from the United States from 1900 to 1973 have been examined by Venieris (1979) with results that point to the same conclusion.

Although for many years the relationship between wealth and fertility dominated the search for the explanation of why people are motivated to have small families, the European Fertility History Project pointed the finger more toward the process of secularization, as you will recall from Chapter 3. The principal measure of secularization is education, which changes people's view of the world and, among parents of children being educated, may change the value of the children themselves (Caldwell, 1982). In nineteenth-century Switzerland, for example, "higher education became an important asset in the competition for employment, and parents recognized that their children would be at a substantial disadvantage unless their education met society's new norms" (van de Walle, 1980:471).

Nearly everywhere in the world, the better educated a woman (and/or her husband), the fewer children she is likely to have. Consider the case of a high-fertility society such as Egypt. Figure 5.2 showcases data from the 1980 World Fertility Survey in that country revealing that women with a university education delay childbearing and eventually have fewer than three children on average, whereas illiterate women have children rapidly and average more than six each. The reproductive behavior of women from other educational levels falls predictably between those two extremes. In Egypt, of course, so few women are well educated that their impact on the birth rate is negligible. If we turn to the United States, where women are far better educated on average than in Egypt, we see that education still influences fertility. In 1986, married American women aged 35–44 who had graduated from college had borne an average of 1.8 children each, compared with 3.0 children on average to women who never graduated from high school (U.S. Bureau of the Census, 1987b).

Compelling though the relationship between education and fertility may be, however, it is difficult to disentangle the effect of education from that of other

Figure 5.2   In Egypt, Educated Women Have the Smallest Families (1980)

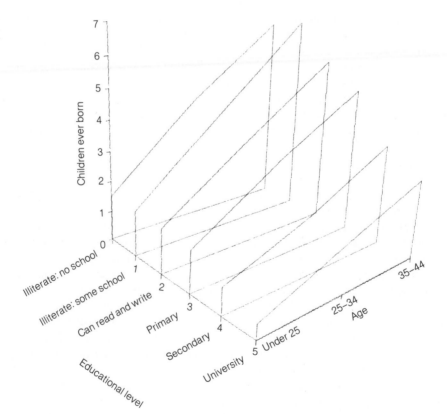

Source: A. Hallouda, S. Amin, and S. Farid, 1983, The Egyptian Fertility Survey 1980, Vol. II, Fertility and Family Planning (Cairo: Central Agency for Public Mobilisation and Statistics), Table 4.7

factors such as income and occupation. Since the three typically go together, we need a more general approach to explain why people are motivated to have small families. Researchers have used several different approaches to investigate this relationship and you should be familiar with the two most important of these—the economic and the sociological approaches.

The Economic Approach

In 1960 Gary Becker, an economist at the University of Chicago, introduced an economic analysis of fertility (sometimes called the "new home economics"). In his theory, he treated children as though they were consumer goods that required both time and money for parents to acquire. He further assumed that each couple exercised perfect economic rationality and also practiced perfect contraceptive effectiveness. Then he drew on classic microeconomic theory to argue that for each individual a utility function could be found that would express the relationship between a couple's desire for children and all other goods or activities that compete with children for time and money. It is important to note that time as well as money is being considered, for if money were the only criterion, then one would expect that (in a society where there are social pressures to have children) the more money a person had, the more children he or she would have, as I have already mentioned. Yet we know that in most societies, especially industrialized nations such as the United States, those who are less well-off financially tend to have more children than do the more well-off.

With the introduction of time into the calculations, along with an implicit recognition that social class determines a person's tastes and life-style, the economic theory turns into a trade-off between quantity and quality of children. For the less well-off, the expectations that exist for children are presumed to be low and thus the cost is at its minimum. In the higher economic strata the expectations for the children are presumed to be greater, possibly in terms of money and especially in terms of time spent on each child. The theory asserts that parents in the higher strata also are exposed to a greater number of opportunities to buy goods and engage in time-consuming activities. Thus, to produce the kind of child desired, the number must be limited.

The economic approach to fertility has a good deal of intuitive appeal, although its proponents sometimes make several untenable assumptions about human behavior. For example, not all people behave with the same kind of rationality, all couples are not perfect contraceptive users, and all couples do not share the same feelings about children. Nonetheless, it does seem reasonable to theorize that people are motivated to have small families because by having a large family they would have to give up things that are deemed too desirable. As Turchi has written in a review of microeconomic theories of fertility, "If one suspects, as I do, that the total opportunity cost of children is a major determinant of family size, then it is important to have theories available regarding the manner in which norms and preferences concerning the mode of childbearing affect the demand for children" (1975:113). Turchi is implicitly referring to the sociological factors that link an individual to the social and economic structure. They are those factors that determine how human decision making takes place using the information processed from the social and economic environments.

The Sociological Approach

The sociological approach emphasizes the fact that changes must occur in society to motivate people from high-fertility to low-fertility behavior. What kinds of changes might those be? Davis (1963; 1967) has suggested that people will be

---

INTELLIGENCE SEEMS TO BE RELATED TO FAMILY SIZE

The issue of quality versus quantity of children finds expression in the relationship between intelligence and family size. Specifically, with a larger family, the measured intelligence of an average child in the family will likely be lower. Within a family, the higher the birth order (that is, firstborn, second child, and so on), the lower will measured intelligence tend to be, at least according to recent research. We do not yet know whether there is a cause-and-effect relationship between family size (and birth order) and intelligence or whether what we see is due to some other as yet undiscovered factor, but the relationship is intriguing nonetheless.

Without question the largest and most impressive study is reported by Belmont and Marolla (1973). They were able to utilize data gathered for nearly 400,000 men in the Netherlands born in 1944–47 who were examined at age 19 to determine their fitness for military service. Intelligence was measured for the study using the Raven Progressive Matrices, which in this case was a 40-item written test. They found that the average IQ for men from families with two children was higher than the average for men from families of other sizes. The average IQ for men from large families was invariably lower than the average for men from small families. Belmont and Marolla also found that the average IQ of firstborn children was higher than the average for second children, and so forth. Curiously enough, however, they discovered that average intelligence was highest for firstborn men in a two-child family, followed by the

firstborn in a three-child family. "Only" children ranked sixth overall. As you might have guessed, the lowest average IQs were for the ninth child in families of nine (families of nine were the largest for which they reported data). Let me stress that these averages do not necessarily reflect what you, as an individual, might achieve in terms of measured intelligence. You may well be an only child and be "smarter" than the firstborn of a two-child family. The average reduces a lot of human variability into a single index, so don't take it personally one way or another.

Incidentally, the lower-than-expected measured intelligence for only children had shown up in earlier studies as well. Zajonc (1976) suggested that a plausible explanation might be that only children have fewer opportunities to be teachers. They are deprived of being an intellectual resource for younger siblings and they have to assume a more passive role in their at-home intellectual development.

Looking at the issue from yet another angle, more recent analyses have called those studies into question because they did not control for the fact that only children are more likely than others to come from a broken home, which fact is likely to lower test scores independently of family size. Studies that have taken broken or intact families into account suggest that only children actually do better than children of other birth orders on achievement tests (Blake, 1981).

Since it is often true that the larger families are found in the lower social motivated to delay marriage and limit births within marriage if economic opportunities make it advantageous for them to do so. He argues further that having children per se rarely satisfies an end in itself but is generally a means to some other end, such as expanding the ego, proving sex roles, continuing a descent group, continuing the inheritance of property, securing economic welfare in old age, securing future family

classes and vice versa, Belmont and Marolla looked at their data for each social class to see if that could explain the relationship they had found. It couldn't. The same facts were repeated for each social class.

One of the implications of the relationships among birth order, family size, and intelligence is that they might help to explain the decline in the average Scholastic Aptitude Test (SAT) score of high school seniors in the United States between 1962 and 1979. That drop in SAT scores caused considerable alarm and has been blamed on television, a desire to get away from disciplined learning, and the rising proportion of minority group students taking the test (Zajonc, 1976). But, as Zajonc has pointed out, there is no evidence to support any of those contentions. What was happening, though, was that the average birth order of children graduating from high school between 1964 and 1979 was going up. These were the children of the large families of the Baby Boom, and in each year that went by during that time, the average birth order of graduating seniors was higher. Since younger siblings tend to do less well on intelligence tests, it seems reasonable to infer that they would do less well on the SAT. The parallel changes between SAT scores and average birth order are striking, but Zajonc is careful to point out that we cannot yet jump to the conclusion that changes in family configuration are responsible for the drop in SAT scores. If there is, in fact, a relationship, then future analyses will show a rise in the SAT scores

as children from the smaller families of the 1960s and 1970s start graduating from high school. Indeed, if Zajonc is correct, we should discover that 1980 was the year that SAT scores bottomed out, because that was the year that the number of high school seniors who were firstborn reached a trough. Then the scores should have begun to rise in 1982, since in that year the number of seniors who were first children began to rise. What actually happened? "College entrance-test scores averaged the same in 1981 as they did in 1980" (Wall Street Journal, 1981a:1). In 1982 the report was that "nationwide scores by high school seniors on the Scholastic Aptitude Test inched upward this year, reversing a 19-year decline, testing officials announced. . . . A jubilant George H. Hanford, president of the College Board, said, 'This year's rise, however slight . . . is a welcome sign for educators, parents, and students that serious efforts by the nation's schools and their students to improve the quality of education are taking effect'" (Colvin, 1982). 1983 results were exactly the same as those of 1982, and then "average national scores on the Scholastic Aptitude Test rose a total of four points in 1984, the largest combined gain since 1963. . . . In Washington, Education Secretary Terrel Bell said that 'the gain in SAT scores reflects the movement toward excellence in our schools that is sweeping the nation'" (Mackey-Smith, 1984:60). But, you might well ask, did the quality of education improve or did the quality of the students improve through the birth-order effect?

labor, or satisfying the believed demand of a deity. If the goals that are important change, or if the means available to achieve those goals change (for example, money instead of children), then the desire to have children may change.

As an entire social structure changes or as a person's position within the social structure changes, the ends or goals that individuals have in mind change and their motivations to have children change. We know, for example, that as education increases, wealth and prestige tend to increase (see Chapter 9) and the number of children born in a family declines. Apparently, education leads to a greater ability to acquire wealth and prestige and this competes with having children, since children are for many years resource consumers rather than resource producers. This principle seems to work for individuals as they attempt to be **upwardly mobile** socially within a society, or as they try to prevent social slippage—a loss of social and economic status relative to others.

You must also recognize, of course, that motivations for low fertility do not appear magically just because one aspires to wealth, or has received a college education, or is an only child and also prefers a small family. Motivations for low fertility arise out of our communication with other people and other ideas. Fertility behavior, like all behavior, is in large part determined by the information we receive, process, and then act on. The people with whom, and the ideas with which, we interact in our everyday lives shape our existence as social creatures. Leon Tabah, director of the Population Division of the United Nations, has gone so far as to suggest that:

> Motivations for childbearing cannot in themselves explain behavior without reference to the social environment. Thus, American sociologists and demographers have for many years observed that changes in the social climate of the United States at the time of the Great Depression and equally during the postwar baby boom had more influence on fertility than the so-called personal variables (education, income, religion of the individual). Through this reasoning, one comes to appeal to the 'collective conscience,' that overriding force that operates on our lives at the same time that we believe we are controlling them ourselves (1980:364).

By and large, very little emphasis has actually been placed on these factors in attempts to account for low fertility. One of the first major exceptions to this is the reexamination of the demographic transition theory undertaken by Ansley Coale in 1973, in response to the findings from the European Fertility History Project. Coale tried to deduce how an individual would have to perceive the world on a daily basis if fertility were to be consciously limited. In this revised approach to the demographic transition, he states that there are three preconditions for a substantial fertility decline: (1) the acceptance of calculated choice as a valid element in marital fertility, (2) the perception of advantages from reduced fertility, and (3) knowledge and mastery of effective techniques of control (Coale, 1973). Although the societal changes that produced mortality declines may also induce fertility change, they will do so, Coale argues, only if the three preconditions exist. The preconditions, though, may exist even in the absence of mortality decline. The important causal factors determining whether these preconditions will exist include "unmeasured traditions and habits of mind" (Burch, 1975:132), especially secularization, as I discussed earlier.

Coale's preconditions implicitly incorporate both the economic and sociological approaches to explaining low fertility. His first and second preconditions relate to the way in which a person *perceives* the social environment, an essential sociological phenomenon. The acceptance of calculated choice (his first precondition) is exemplified even in modern America. In a study of lower-class women with large families in St. Louis in the late 1950s, Rainwater found that "lack of effective contraception so common in this group is not due simply to ignorance or misunderstanding; it is embodied in particular personalities, world views, and ways of life . . . which do not readily admit such foreign elements as conscious planning and emotion-laden contraceptive techniques" (1960:167–68). Coale's second precondition relating to the existence and perception of advantages of smaller families sums up the basic arguments of the sociological and economic approaches. His third precondition relates to the intermediate variables discussed in Chapter 4, the techniques by which fertility can be limited.

LOW-FERTILITY COUNTRIES

Let me now put these explanations of low fertility to work in describing and accounting for changes in fertility in three most impressive cases of long-run fertility declines accompanying improvements in the standard of living—England, Japan, and the United States. As a preface to that discussion, however, I should note that in England and other parts of Europe the beginnings of a potential fertility decline may well have existed before the Industrial Revolution touched off the dramatic rise in the standard of living. In English parishes there is evidence that withdrawal (coitus interruptus) was used to reduce marital fertility during the late seventeenth and early eighteenth centuries, and it was apparently also a major reason for a steady decline in marital fertility in France during the late eighteenth and early nineteenth centuries. Abortion was quite probably also fairly common (Wrigley, 1974). Furthermore, the fact that preindustrial birth rates were much higher in the European colonies of America than in Europe points to the fact that fertility limitation in Europe was widely accepted and practiced.

England

The enormous economic and social upheaval of industrialization took place earlier in England than anywhere else, and by the first part of the nineteenth century, England was well into the Machine Age. For the average worker, however, it was not until the latter half of the nineteenth century that sustained increases in real wages actually occurred. During the first part of the century the Napoleonic Wars were tripling the national debt in England, increasing prices by as much as 90 percent without an increase in production. Thus, during almost the entire professional life of Malthus, his country was experiencing substantial inflation and job insecurity. These relatively adverse conditions undoubtedly contributed to a general decline in the birth rate during the first half of the nineteenth century (see Figure 5.3). After about 1850, economic conditions improved considerably, and the first response was a rise in the birth rate, followed by a long-run decline, as can be seen in Figure 5.3.

This was a period in which all of Ansley Coale's preconditions for a fertility decline existed: (1) people had apparently accepted calculated choice as a valid element, (2) there were perceived advantages from lowered fertility, and (3) they were aware of effective means of birth control. As I mentioned earlier, the British were accustomed to thinking in terms of family limitation, and delayed marriage, abstinence, and coitus interruptus within marriage were known to be effective means to reduce fertility. In the second half of the nineteenth century, then, motivation to limit family size came in the form of larger numbers of surviving children combined with aspiration for higher standards of living.

As you can see in Figure 5.3, fertility actually went up in England before it went down. With fewer families broken by death and with increasing real income, which made earlier marriage more feasible, birth rates rose before people could adjust their reproductive behavior to meet the new demographic and economic situations. This is reflected in the net reproduction rate, which measures each woman's average

Figure 5.3   England's Demographic Transition

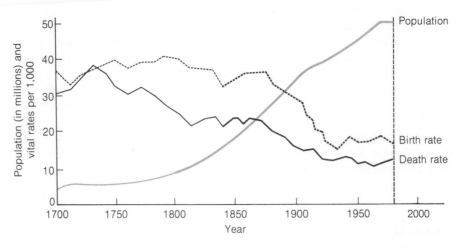

Between 1700 and 1980 England experienced all stages of the demographic transition. The death rate began to drop late in the eighteenth century during the preliminary period of the Industrial Revolution. Birth rates did not experience a sustained drop until almost 100 years later. Since the late nineteenth century, fertility has dropped fairly steadily to the point where both birth and death rates are currently low. *Source:* Derek Llewellyn-Jones, 1974, Human Reproduction and Society (New York: Pitman Publishing Corp.), Fig. 9/5. © 1974 by Pitman Publishing Corporation. Reprinted by permission of Fearon-Pitman Publishers, Inc., Belmont, California. Updated to 1980 from United Nations, 1980, Demographic Yearbook, 1980 (New York: United Nations).

number of female children who will survive to adulthood (a figure of 1 means exact generational replacement). In 1841, the net reproduction rate was 1.35, and it had increased to 1.51 by 1881. By 1911, however, it was down to 1.12 (Wrigley, 1974:195).

It is important to note that the restriction of fertility was in many ways a return to preindustrial patterns, in which an average of about two children survived to adulthood in each generation. Thus, as we discussed earlier in relation to the theories of low fertility, mortality declines produced changes in the lives of individuals to which they had to respond. The English reacted in ways that were consistent with the theory of demographic change and response. They responded to population growth by migrating, by delaying marriage, and then, only when those options were played out, did marital fertility clearly decline (Friedlander, 1983).

The best-known explanation of the fertility decline in England in the latter half of the nineteenth century is that offered by J. A. Banks (1954) in *Prosperity and Parenthood* and its sequel *Feminism and Family Planning in Victorian England* (Banks and Banks, 1964). Banks's thesis is by now a familiar one—that the rising standard of living in England, especially among the middle classes, gave rise to a declining fertility by (1) raising expectations of upward social mobility, (2) creating fears of social slippage (you had to "keep up with the Joneses"), and (3) redefining the roles of women from the housewife to a fragile luxury of a middle-class man.

While it is true that birth rates dropped more quickly in the upper social strata of English society than in the lower social strata, by at least 1876 all segments of English society were experiencing fertility declines. Fertility has continued on a slow downward trend since then, with the only interruptions occurring right after World War II and then again in the late 1950s and early 1960s. Since about 1964, however, birth rates have resumed their downward trend, and since 1973 England has been experiencing zero population growth.

Japan

During the nineteenth century, under the influence of the Tokugawa Shogunate, Japan developed an isolated, self-sufficient economy based on commerce rather than landholdings. The Japanese borrowed ideas and technology from China and Korea to produce a commercial economy similar to, but independent from, that which had developed in Europe. The real "take-off" period for Japan's economic development came, however, in 1878–1900 after the Meiji Restoration. Perhaps not coincidentally, this take-off came after Japan had reestablished relations with Europe. In 1920 both birth and death rates started to decline (Muramatsu, 1971). The decline in fertility was accomplished primarily through abortions and the use of condoms, which the Japanese were producing themselves. Nonetheless, mortality was decreasing more rapidly than fertility, and the population was experiencing fairly rapid growth as well as high rates of urbanization—the migration of people from the countryside to the city. Growth was fostered in the early twentieth century by the pronatalist, imperialistic policy of the Japanese government.

Japan, like England, has had a long history of demographic consciousness.

There is substantial evidence that mortality and fertility were both low in Japan by world standards as far back as the seventeenth century. Fertility was apparently kept low by a combination of delayed marriage and abortion (Hanley and Yamamura, 1977). But our demographic interest in Japan actually lies less in what happened before World War II than in the dramatic drop in fertility after the war. Between 1947 and 1957 the crude birth rate went down 50 percent, from 34.3 to 17.2 per 1,000 population. As measured by the total fertility rate (an approximation of the average number of children born), the drop was equally sensational. In 1947 the total fertility rate was estimated to have been 4.5 children per woman, and by 1957 it was down to 2.0, which was actually below the replacement level. Thus, in only a decade, reproductive performance was cut by more than half, principally by means of induced abortions. Previously, abortions had been illegal, but legal abortions were made possible by the Eugenics Protection Act of 1948. This law was not really aimed at reducing population growth but rather at protecting women's health by eliminating the need for illegal abortions, which had been increasing in number (see Table 5.3). During this time, the condom continued as a popular contraceptive, and the age at marriage for females also increased slightly (Kobayashi, 1969). Since 1955 the use of contraceptives has been increasing steadily and is currently the major source of maintaining low fertility (Aso, 1972). The condom and withdrawal methods, the so-called traditional techniques, predominate in Japan, and neither the pill nor the IUD has gained the acceptance characteristic of Europe and the United States.

Table 5.3 Abortion Played an Important Role in Japan's Fertility Decline

Year	Annual Totals (in Thousands)			Sum per 1,000 Population
	Births	Abortions	Sum	
1949	2,697	102	2,799	34.4
1950	2,338	320	2,658	32.1
1951	2,138	459	2,597	30.8
1952	2,005	798	2,803	32.8
1953	1,868	1,067	2,935	33.9
1954	1,770	1,143	2,913	33.1
1955	1,727	1,170	2,897	32.6
1956	1,665	1,159	2,825	31.4
1957	1,563	1,122	2,685	29.6
1958	1,653	1,128	2,781	30.4
1959	1,636	1,099	2,725	29.5

Source: K. Davis, 1963, "The theory of change and response in modern demographic history," Population Index 294:347, Table 1. Used by permission.

Note: Between the late 1940s and the late 1950s the birth rate fell dramatically in Japan, largely as a result of the rise in induced abortion. You can see that there was little variation from year to year in the number of conceptions (births plus abortions), with the number of abortions going up as the number of births went down. Note that due to rounding the births and abortions may not sum exactly.

An interesting sidelight is the incredible social impact of an ancient superstition on a modern, rational population. I refer to the Year of the Fiery Horse. In 1966 the birth rate made a sudden one-year dip—this was the Year of the Fiery Horse. According to a widely held Japanese superstition, girls born in the Year of the Fiery Horse (which occurs every 60 years) will have troublesome characters, such as a propensity to murder their husbands. Thus, girls born in that year are hard to marry off, and many couples avoided having children in 1966. Again, this was accomplished mainly by contraception rather than abortion. However, in 1906—another Fiery Horse year—fertility had also declined dramatically without the availability of modern contraception.

The United States

Around 1800, when Malthus was writing his *Essay on Population,* he found the growth rate in America to be remarkably high and commented on the large frontier families about which he had read. Indeed, it is estimated that the average number of children born per woman in colonial America was about eight. It is probably no exaggeration to say that early in the history of the United States, American fertility was higher than any European population had ever experienced. Early data are not very reliable, but in 1963 Ansley Coale and Melvin Zelnick made new estimates of crude birth rates in the United States going back as far as 1800; these indicate that the crude birth rate of nearly 55 per 1,000 population was higher than the rate in any less developed country today. Even in 1855, the crude birth rate in America was 42.8 per 1,000, comparable to India's rate in the early 1970s. However, the birth rate had clearly begun a rapid decline, and by 1870 the American birth rate had reached the lower levels of European countries. This decline continued virtually unabated until the Great Depression of the 1930s, during which time it bottomed out at a low level only recently reapproached. Why the precipitous drop?

As I discussed in Chapter 2, almost all voluntary migrants to the North American continent were Europeans. The people who made up the population of the early United States came from a social environment in which fertility limitation was known and practiced. Despite the frontier movement westward, America in the century after the Revolution was urbanizing and commercializing rapidly. For much the same reasons as in Europe, Americans apparently lowered fertility partly in response to declining mortality and partly in response to increasing opportunities to improve the condition of their lives. Lower fertility was accomplished by a rise in the average age at marriage and by various means of birth control within marriage. Abstinence and coitus interruptus (withdrawal) were undoubtedly important as a means by which family size could be kept lower than in the past, and it is very likely that induced abortion also played a significant role in reducing fertility levels (Sanderson, 1979). After World War I the use of condoms became widespread in the United States (and in Europe as well) and, along with withdrawal and abstinence, contributed to the very low levels of fertility during the Depression (Himes, 1976).

As you can see in Figure 5.4, douching was also popular in the United States in the 1930s, but you will recall from Chapter 4 that douching is relatively ineffective as a contraceptive technique. Nonetheless, its use indicates at least the motivation to control fertility, and that may lead to less risk taking (such as unprotected intercourse at mid-cycle, when the chance of conception is highest). Incidentally, estimates of the percentage of women who were using contraceptive methods at that time range from 42 to 95 percent (Himes, 1976:343). It is interesting to note that the condom method, like coitus interruptus and abstinence, requires the initiative or cooperation of the male, whereas most modern methods do not.

During the Depression, fertility fell to levels below generational replacement. The United States was not unique in this respect, but that bottoming out of fertility did cap the most sustained drop in fertility that the world has yet seen. It was undoubtedly a response to the economic insecurity of the period, especially since that insecurity had come about as a quick reversal of increasing prosperity. Fear of social slippage was thus a very likely motive for keeping families small. The American demographic response was for many couples to defer marriage and to postpone having children, hoping to marry later on and have a larger family. Gallup polls starting in 1936 indicate that the average ideal family size was three children, and that most people felt that somewhere between two and four was what they would

Figure 5.4 Withdrawal, Douche, and Condom Were Popular Contraceptive Methods in the United States (1933–34)

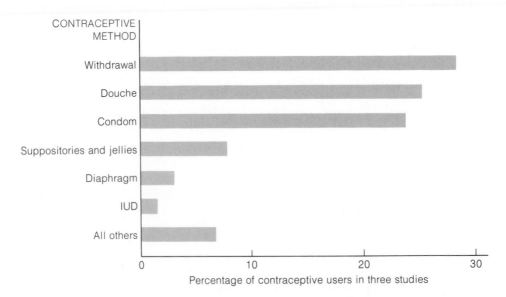

During the Depression, the low birth rate in the United States was achieved by a combination of contraceptive methods, especially withdrawal, douche, and condom. The role of abstinence was not ascertained, although it too was undoubtedly important. The IUD referred to was a forerunner of modern ones but was not identical. *Source:* N. E. Himes, 1976, *Medical History of Contraception* (New York: Schocken Books), p. 345, Table V. Used by permission.

like. Thus, people were apparently having fewer children than they would liked to have had under ideal circumstances.

In 1933, the birth rate hit rock bottom because women of all ages, regardless of how many children they already had, lowered their level of reproduction. But from 1934 on, the birth rates for first and second children rose steadily (reflecting people getting married and having small families), while birth rates for third and later children continued to decline (reflecting the postponement of larger families) until about 1940 (Grabill et al., 1958). Just as the United States was entering World War II in late 1941 and 1942, there was a momentary rise in the birth rate as husbands went off to war, followed by a lull during the war. However, the end of World War II signaled one of the most dramatic and least expected demographic phenomena in American history—the **Baby Boom.**

The Baby Boom   Most of you can probably appreciate that immediately after the end of a war, families and lovers are reunited and the birth rate will go up temporarily as people make up for lost time. This occurred in the United States as well as in almost every country actively involved in World War II. Surprisingly, however, the Baby Boom in America lasted not for 1 or 2 years but for 12 years after the war. Birth rates continued to rise through the 1950s, as the total fertility rate went from 2.19 in 1940 to 3.58 in 1957, an increase of nearly 1.5 children per woman.

An important contribution to the Baby Boom was the fact that after the war, women started marrying earlier and having their children sooner after marriage. For example, in 1940 the average first child was born when the mother was 23.2 years old. By 1960, the average age had dropped to 21.8. This had the effect of bunching up the births of babies, which in earlier times would have been more spread out. Further, not only were young women having children at younger ages, but older women were having babies at older than usual ages, due at least in part to their having postponed births during the Depression and war. After the war, many women stopped postponing and added to the crop of babies each year.

Why Did the Baby Boom Occur?   We do not have a definitive answer to this question, but a widely discussed explanation is offered by Easterlin (1968; 1978), which I mentioned in Chapter 3 as the relative income hypothesis. Easterlin begins his analysis by noting that the long-term decline in the birth rate in the United States was uneven, sometimes declining more rapidly than at other times. In particular, it declined less rapidly during times of greater economic growth. If a young man could easily find a well-paying job, he could get married and have children; if job hunting were more difficult, marriage (and children within marriage) would be postponed. Thus, it was natural that the postwar Baby Boom occurred, because the economy was growing rapidly during that time. What was unusual was that economic growth was more rapid than in previous decades, and the resultant demand for labor was less easily met by large numbers of immigrants, because in the 1920s the United States had passed very restrictive immigration laws (see Chapter 15). Furthermore, the number of young people looking for work was rather small because of the low birth rates in the 1920s and 1930s. Finally, the demand for labor was not easily met by females, since there was a distinct bias against married women working in the United States, particularly a woman who had any children. In some states legislation existed actually restricting married women from working in certain occupations. To be sure, women did work, particularly single women, but their opportunities were limited (see Chapter 10 for further discussion). Thus, economic expansion, restricted immigration, a small labor force, and discrimination against women in the labor force meant that young men looking for jobs could find relatively well-paying positions, marry early, and have children. Indeed, income was rising so rapidly in this country after the war and on into the 1950s that it was relatively easy for couples to achieve the life-style to which they were accustomed, or even to which they might moderately aspire, and still have enough money left over to have several children.

As Campbell (1969) has pointed out, Easterlin's thesis is consistent with Davis's theory of demographic change and response (see Chapter 3). Davis argued that fear of relative deprivation, rather than the threat of famine or absolute deprivation, is a subjective stimulus to limiting fertility. The other side of the coin is that when you feel more secure, the desire for children may resurface if pronatalist pressures still exist, as they did and still do.

In 1958 the crude birth rate and the general fertility rate in the United States registered clear declines—a downward change that carried into the late 1970s. At first the decline was due merely to the fact that the trend of earlier marriage and closer spacing of children had bottomed out. The number of women in the child-bearing ages had also declined as the relatively small number of babies born during the Depression reached childbearing age. At this point in the early 1960s there was no discernible trend toward smaller families. The ideal family size among Americans had remained quite stable between 1952 and 1966, ranging only between 3.3 and 3.6 children. But in 1967, Blake discovered in a national sample taken the year before that "young women (those under age 30) gave 'two' children as their ideal more frequently than they had in any surveys since the early nineteen-fifties" (1967:20). This was the first solid evidence that the desired family size might be on the way down.

There were social and economic factors that suggested fertility might continue to decline for awhile. The rate of economic growth had slackened off, and there was no longer a labor shortage. As Norman Ryder noted:

> In the United States today the cohorts entering adulthood are much larger than their predecessors. In consequence they were raised in crowded housing, crammed together in schools, and are now threatening to be a glut on the labor market. Perhaps they will have to delay marriage, because of too few jobs or houses, and have fewer children. It is not entirely coincidental that the American cohorts whose fertility levels appear to be the highest in this century were those with the smallest number (1960:845).

In fact, between the early 1960s and the mid-1970s the average age at marriage among American women went up slightly and the number of children ever born to women aged 20–24 went steadily down, declining by 27 percent between 1960 and 1971. The period 1967 to 1971 was especially dramatic. Between those two dates the total number of lifetime births expected by currently married American women aged 18–24 dropped from 2,852 to 2,375 per 1,000. By 1977 the birth rate had continued to drop at a slower pace to 2,137, and then the number rose in 1978 to 2,166 (U.S. Bureau of the Census, 1979d). Expectations for older women also dropped steeply between 1967 and 1977, but the decline came later than for the younger women. It was, of course, the younger couples who were most influenced by the cohort squeeze as outlined by Easterlin.

Almost all the fertility decline was due to a drop in marital fertility (Gibson, 1976; see Figure 5.5), mainly as a result of more efficient use of contraception, and to a rise in the use of abortion. As fertility has dropped, family size ideals have dropped as well. Gallup surveys reported by Blake (1974) indicate, for example, that the proportion of white women under age 30 saying that two children are an ideal number rose dramatically from a low of 16 percent in 1957 to 57 percent in 1971. By 1978, more than half of all Americans surveyed by the Gallup Poll felt that two children or fewer was the ideal family size (although most thought that two, not fewer, was ideal). Related to that shrinking ideal family size is an erosion of support for large families. In 1945, just as World War II ended, 47 percent of Americans polled felt that four or more children would be ideal; by 1978, such sentiment was expressed by only 17 percent of the public (Gallup, 1978). That figure was still

Figure 5.5   Recent Declines in American Fertility Are Due to a Drop in Marital Fertility

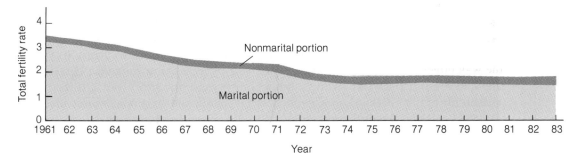

Since 1961 the dramatic post–Baby Boom fertility decline has been due almost entirely to a drop in the number of children that married women are having (marital fertility) rather than to delays in marriage or to declines in illegitimacy. In this graph the light portion shows the contribution of marital fertility to the decline in the fertility rate, and the dark portion shows the contribution of nonmarital factors. *Source:* Adapted from Campbell Gibson, 1976, "The U.S. fertility decline, 1961–1975: The contribution of changes in marital status and marital fertility," Family Planning Perspectives 8:249–52, Table 1. Used by permission. Updated to 1978 using data from National Center for Health Statistics, 1983, Vital Statistics of the United States, 1978, Vol. I, Natality (Hyattsville, MD: NCHS), Tables I-32–I-33; and National Center for Health Statistics, 1987, Vital Statistics of the United States, 1983, Vol. I, Natality (Hyattsville, MD: NCHS), Tables I-33, I-34.

higher than in Europe (10 percent), but lower than Gallup had found in the Far East (35 percent), Latin America (39 percent), or Africa (79 percent).

Since 1976 the crude birth rate has been slowly on the rise again, increasing from 14.6 births per 1,000 in 1976 to 15.5 per 1,000 in 1986. Most of the rise in the birth rate has been due to the increasing number of women in the childbearing ages—the youngest of the baby boomers entering adulthood. It is not expected that any dramatic rise in the level of fertility in the United States is in the offing. Of course, demographers have been wrong about such things before. . . .

SUMMARY AND CONCLUSION

High fertility is frequently explained in terms of the need to replace society, which, at the individual level, finds expression in a wide range of pronatalist pressures such as a desire for sons and a demand for children as a source of labor and old-age security. Furthermore, high fertility may persist even after mortality declines as a result of the ambivalence between the social rewards for having children and the burden they create. In India, Ghana, and Kuwait, high fertility can be explained by reference to pronatalist pressures that exist in the absence of motivation to change behavior.

People expect (and receive) pressures from others to have children, even in low-fertility countries such as the United States. This is why it is often difficult for fertility to decline when mortality declines, especially if no other economic or social changes have preceded the mortality decline. If marriage and childbearing are prestigious when mortality is high, why should it be any different when mortality is low? Social norms may change slowly in response to the new environment, because the link between mortality levels and fertility levels is not given conscious recognition.

Theories of low fertility emphasize the role of wealth and economic development in lowering levels of fertility, although it is clear that this is not a sufficient reason for fertility declines; in Kuwait, societal wealth and economic improvement have not yet yielded much of a decline in fertility. When there are desired and scarce resources, wealth, prestige, status, education, and other related factors often help to lower fertility because they change the way people perceive and think about the social world and their place in it. Human beings are amazingly adaptable when they want to be. When people believe that having no children or only a few children is in their best interest, they behave in that way. Sophisticated contraceptive techniques make it easier, but they are not necessary, as the history of fertility declines in England, Japan, and the United States illustrates.

Although over time many societies have proven that fertility rates can be lowered if people so desire, we have not been so fortunate until very recently in being able to control the forces of mortality. For the overwhelming part of human history, people have been at the mercy of the physical environment. Only within the last 100 years have humans really learned how to manipulate the probabilities of death. The next chapter analyzes mortality—theories and facts.

MAIN POINTS

1. High fertility is explained by some theorists as a response to the pressures to have children that are created in high-mortality societies by the need to replace members.

2. These and other pressures for children may be translated into a desire for children as security and labor and a desire for sons.

3. An explanation for the lag between a decline in mortality and a drop in fertility is that couples may be caught in a situation of ambivalence, in which they are still being pressured to have children even though greater percentages are surviving to adulthood.

4. India, Ghana, and Kuwait are good examples of high-fertility societies. In India there seem to be few motivations for having small families, so many are ambivalent about family size.

5. In Ghana many people seem actively to desire large families.

6. Kuwait is such a rich country that children are subsidized by the government from conception through school. Thus, you might suspect that there are few motivations to lower the traditionally large family size.

7. Low fertility is typically explained as one strategy by which people seek to acquire wealth and prestige.

8. In most low-fertility societies it is usually the middle classes (not necessarily the very wealthiest classes) in which fertility is lowest.

9. The economic explanation of low fertility rests on the thesis that higher-strata couples calculate more costs than benefits in having large families and thus decide to have fewer children than do people in the lower strata.

10. The sociological approach emphasizes the changing motivation for having children as a society develops economically and socially.

11. The decline in fertility from high to low levels is well illustrated by England, Japan, and the United States.

12. The Baby Boom is one of the most famous demographic events in U.S. history, but it was really a readily explainable detour on a long road of declining fertility.

13. In the world today, a woman gives birth to a child every 4 seconds. (We've got to find this woman and stop her!)

SUGGESTED READINGS

1. John Cleland and John Hobcraft (eds.), 1985, Reproductive Change in Developing Countries (London: Oxford University Press).

This volume of essays provides details about the world's largest social scientific undertaking—the World Fertility Survey. What did we learn? Was it worth the time and effort? Read all about it and try to decide for yourself.

2. Ansley Coale, 1973, "The demographic transition," Proceedings of the International Population Conference, Liège, Belgium, Vol. 1, pp. 53–72.

This paper, which outlines the preconditions for a fertility decline, summarizes much of the work of the European Fertility History Project and is written by the director of that project.

3. Charles Westoff, 1978, "Marriage and fertility in the developed countries," Scientific American 239(6):51–57.

This is a careful review of fertility trends in the developed nations.

4. Etienne van de Walle and John Knodel, 1980, "Europe's fertility transition: new evidence and lessons from today's developing world," Population Bulletin 34(6).

Two participants in the European Fertility History Project assess the importance of their findings for understanding fertility declines (or the relative lack thereof) in the now-developing nations.

5. Norman B. Ryder, "Observations on the history of cohort fertility in the United States," Population and Development Review 12(4):617–43.

Although this article may seem a bit technical, it is worth the effort to study the methods and findings of a demographer who helped to revolutionize the way in which demographers studied fertility by focusing on cohort fertility. This paper will also help you to appreciate the changes over time in American fertility levels.

CHAPTER 6
Mortality

Declining mortality, not rising fertility, is the root cause of current world population growth. It is not that people breed like rabbits; rather, they no longer die like
flies. Virtually within our lifetime, mortality has been brought under control to the
point that most of us now are able to take a long life pretty much for granted. In fact,
long life is enjoying widespread popularity all over the world, and we are surviving
in record numbers. Human triumph over disease and early death surely represents
one of the most significant improvements ever made in the condition of human life,
and we can rightly be proud of ourselves. Nevertheless, one by-product of our
triumph is current world growth and the problems that have grown along with
population size. Furthermore, the problems will continue to grow, for although
mortality is increasingly under control, there are still wide variations in life expectancy in different parts of the world as well as among different groups of people
within countries. These differences represent a potential reservoir of population
growth, since further declines in death rates will trigger even higher rates of growth
unless we are able to curtail fertility.

It was once widely believed that differences in death rates were genetic or
biological in nature and thus difficult to change, but we now know that most
variations are due to social, not biological, causes. I will pursue this point by beginning the chapter with a discussion of the differences between the biological and
social components of mortality. Then I will explore with you why people die—what
are the specific causes of death? Next, after a brief explanation of how to measure
mortality, I will turn to an examination of who dies. How are different ages, sexes,
and social categories differentially affected by the causes of death? After laying this
groundwork for understanding mortality as a basic demographic process, I will
examine its impact on population growth by looking at mortality trends and levels in
Europe, the United States, and the less developed nations of the world.

COMPONENTS OF MORTALITY

There are two biological aspects of mortality. The first is **lifespan,** and refers to
the oldest age to which human beings can survive. The second is **longevity** and refers
to the ability to remain alive from one year to the next—the ability to resist death.
Lifespan is almost entirely a biological phenomenon, whereas longevity has both
biological and social components.

Lifespan

Lifespan, remember, refers to how long a person can possibly live. Since it is, of
course, impossible accurately to predict how long a person *could* live, we must be
content to assume that the oldest age to which a human actually *has* lived (a figure
that may change from day to day) is the oldest age to which it is possible to live.
Claims of long human lifespan are widespread, but confirmation of those claims is
more difficult to find. The oldest authenticated age to which a human has ever lived

is 120 years, an age achieved by Shigechiyo Izumi of Japan, who died in 1986, four months shy of his 121st birthday (Russell and McWhirter, 1987). You probably have heard reports of people who claim to have lived longer than that, but none of those reports has ever been verified, principally because birth records were not scrupulously kept in the mid-nineteenth century, or else they have been destroyed (by fire or flood) or just plain lost. One such example is the case of an ex-slave named Charlie Smith who claimed to have been born in Liberia in 1842 and brought to the United States in 1854 and who died at a reported age of 137. The usual way to check on the reported age of an older person for whom no birth certificate exists is to look back through the census returns for information about those individuals when they were younger (these data are available on microfilm at the National Archives in Washington, D.C.). Unfortunately, Charlie Smith is such a common name, and he had moved so often, that he was impossible to trace (Meyers, 1978). However, a marriage record in Florida that appears to refer to him has led investigators to believe that his age was exaggerated by at least 33 years, and that he may not even have been quite 100 years old when he died (McWhirter, 1983).

Age exaggeration is often suspected among very old people. In a piece of fascinating detective work, Meyers was able to dig through old census data and show that a Pennsylvania man who died at a reported age of 112 in 1866 had, in fact, "aged" 27 years in the 10-year period between the 1850 and 1860 censuses and had "aged" 8 years in the 6-year period from the 1860 census to his death. Clearly, there was some exaggeration going on. Other more recent evidence of age exaggeration among American centenarians has been discovered by Rosenwaike (1979), who found significant discrepancies between ages recorded on death certificates and ages recorded in the census. In 1984 in the United States, there were five people who died with age 121 or over recorded on their death certificates (National Center for Health Statistics, 1987a), but as far as I can determine, their ages have not been verified by birth certificates. The family Bible and an affidavit in the 1930s for social security were the convincing pieces of evidence that Florence Knapp, who died in 1988 at the age of 114, was the longest living American on record. Knapp was a retired schoolteacher who had never married and had lived in the same house from the time of her birth on October 10, 1873, until 110 years later, when she moved into a nursing home (San Diego Union, 1988).

So we know that humans *can* live to age 120 and maybe even beyond; yet, very few people come close to achieving that age. Most, in fact, can expect to live only about half that long (life expectancy at birth for the world as a whole is 63 years). It is this concept, the age to which people *actually* survive, their demonstrated ability to stay alive as opposed to their potential, that we refer to as longevity.

Longevity

Biological Factors   Longevity is usually measured by *life expectancy*, the statistically average length of life, and is greatly influenced by the genetic characteristics with which we are born. The strength of vital organs, predisposition to particular diseases, metabolism rate, and so on, are biological factors over which we presently have little control. Many of the most severe biological weaknesses, though, tend to display themselves rather soon after birth, and, as a result, mortality is considerably higher in the first year or so of life than it is in the remainder of childhood and early adulthood.

After the initial year of life there is a period of time, usually lasting at least until middle age, when risks of death are relatively low. Beyond middle age, **mortality** increases at an accelerating rate. This pattern of death by age is illustrated in Figure 6.1, where you can see that the pattern is similar whether the actual death rates are high or low. The genetic or biological aspects of longevity have led many theorists over time to believe that the age patterns of longevity shown in Figure 6.1 could be explained by a simple mathematical formula similar perhaps to the law of gravity and other laws of nature. However, none of these theories has proven to be either valid or useful.

Despite our individual biological strengths and weaknesses, the actual levels of mortality for each sex at each age in each society appear to be due primarily to social factors that influence when and why death occurs.

Figure 6.1   The Very Young and the Old Have the Highest Death Rates

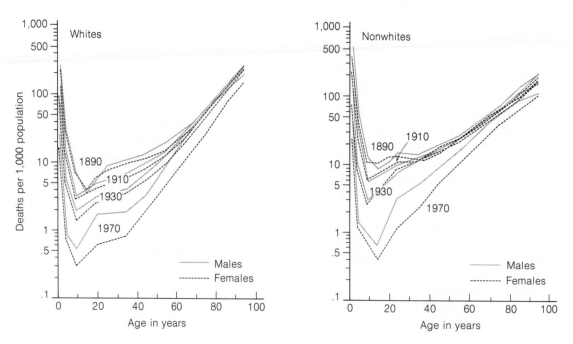

In 1890 the life expectancy at birth in the United States was less than 50 years, while in 1970 it was more than 70. Yet, even at such widely different levels of mortality, the risks of dying are highest at the very youngest and oldest ages. This is true regardless of such factors as sex and race. *Source:* A. Omran, 1977, "Epidemiological Transition in the U.S.," Population Bulletin 32(2), Figure 12. Reproduced courtesy of the Population Reference Bureau, Inc., Washington, D.C.

Social Factors   A good example of social influences affecting longevity is the case of the Abkhasian people in Russia. The Abkhasians live in the Caucasus mountain region in Russia and have recently been the subject of considerable study because they are reportedly the most long-lived people in the world. Although few of the people who say they are centenarians can verify their claim, it does appear that these people live to be older on average than most other people in the world. What is their secret? According to Sula Benet, an anthropologist who has studied them, their long life is a result of

> . . . the cultural, social and psychological factors that structure their existence. The most important are: the uniformity and predictability of both individual and group behavior, the unbroken continuum of life's activity, and integration of the aged into the extended family and community life as fully functioning members in work, decision making, and recreation. No less important are the culturally reinforced expectations of long life and good health; cultural mechanisms used in avoidance of stress and lack of intergenerational conflict (1974:103).

Thus, Benet believes that a lack of social stress combined with a positive motivation to live because of the respect accorded the elderly accounts in large part for the long lives of the Abkhasians.

Another village of long-living people has been discovered in Vilcabamba, Ecuador. Medical experts have attributed the longevity of these Ecuadorians to altitude (5,100 feet), diet (low in fat), and the clean air and water. There are, in addition, several features of social life that are strikingly similar to life among the Abkhasians. Life is simple, basically unchanging, and people remain physically and mentally active long past American ages of retirement. Martin reports that the people of Vilcabamba "seem free from fear and anxiety. Partners with nature and in tune with their surroundings, they know little of physical ailments or mental breakdowns" (1976:11). Lester Breslow, former Dean of the School of Public Health at the University of California, Los Angeles, believes that the keys to maximizing longevity are regular exercise, daily breakfast, normal weight, no smoking, only moderate drinking, 7 to 8 hours of sleep, and regular meal-taking (San Diego Union, 1981d). Most researchers who concern themselves with such matters would add an optimistic outlook on life to the list. James Birren, Director of the Andrus Gerontology Center at the University of Southern California, notes that "those who seem to do best with their lives are thinking ahead" (Locke, 1981). These suggestions, by the way, are not unique to the western world, nor are they particularly modern. A group of medical workers studying older people in southern China have concluded that the important factors for long life are fresh air, moderate drinking and eating, regular exercise, and an optimistic attitude (San Diego Union, 1980b). Similarly, note the words of a Dr. Weber, who was 83 in 1904 when he published an article in the *British Medical Journal* outlining his prescriptions for a long life:

> Be moderate in food and drink and in all physical pleasures; take exercise daily, regardless of the weather; go to bed early, rise early, sleep for no more than 6–7 hours; bathe daily; work and occupy yourself mentally on a regular basis—stimulate the enjoyment of life so that the mind may be tranquil and full of hope; control the passions; be

resolute about preserving health; and avoid alcohol, narcotics, and soothing drugs (quoted in Metchnikoff, 1908).

Other examples of the way in which social and psychological processes can apparently influence death have been given by David Phillips. In the first of a series of studies on suicide, Phillips (1974) found that mortality from suicide tends to increase right after a famous person commits a well-publicized suicide. Thus, some people seem to "follow the leader" when it comes to dying. Further, people do so in more invidious ways than just simple suicide. In follow-up studies, Phillips has found that the number of fatal automobile crashes (especially single-car, single-person crashes) goes up after publicized suicides (Phillips, 1977) and (incredibly enough) that private airplane accident fatalities also increase just after newspaper stories about a murder-suicide. It appears, then, "that murder-suicide stories trigger subsequent murder-suicides, some of which are disguised as airplane accidents" (Phillips, 1978:748). In a 1983 study, Phillips has demonstrated that mass-media violence can also trigger homicides. He discovered that in the United States between 1973 and 1978, homicides regularly increased right after championship prize fights. Furthermore, the more heavily publicized the fight, the greater the rise in homicides (Phillips, 1983).

It is easier, of course, to die than to resist death, adding interest to another angle of Phillips's research. He has found that there is a tendency for people who are near death to postpone dying until after a special event, especially a birthday. Phillips's findings are of sufficient interest to quote in detail:

> We have noted two sets of findings that are consistent with the notion that some people postpone death to witness a birthday because it is important to them. There is a death dip before the birth month and a death rise thereafter in four separate samples. We have noted also a consistent relation between the fame of a group and the size of its death dip and death rise: the more famous the group, the larger the death dip and death rise it produces. These results might be due to chance, but this possibility is sufficiently small that we would prefer some other explanation of these phenomena.
>
> There are indications that some people postpone dying in order to witness events other than their birthdays. There are fewer deaths than expected before the Jewish Day of Atonement in New York, a city with a large Jewish population. In addition, there is a dip in U.S. deaths, in general, before U.S. Presidential elections (1972:65).

These examples illustrate some of the more extreme ways in which social factors can influence death. Normally, however, social factors have less direct influence. In general, different patterns of social organization produce different levels of environmental protection against disease and death. For example, in Johannesburg, South Africa, in 1965 the death rate from tuberculosis among the black population was 48 per 100,000. In the same city at the same date, the death rate from tuberculosis for the white population was 4 per 100,000 (Boyden, 1972:418). Differences in general sanitation, medical diagnosis, and treatment undoubtedly accounted for the difference.

There is considerable variation in longevity around the world (see Figure 6.2), and social factors affect those differences to the extent that they influence intermediate variables—specific causes of death—analogous to the intermediate variables discussed in Chapter 4 with respect to fertility.

Figure 6.2   There Still Is Wide Variation in Longevity Around the World

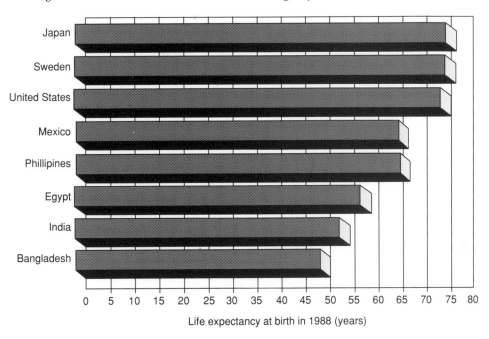

Less developed nations in Africa and Asia tend to be below the world average (dashed line) in terms of life expectancy. Latin American countries tend to be close to the world average, while the more developed countries in North America, Europe, and Asia are well above average. *Source:* Data courtesy of Population Reference Bureau, Inc., Washington, D.C.

CAUSES OF DEATH

In general, there are three major reasons why people die: (1) they degenerate; (2) they are killed by diseases that can be transmitted from one person to another (communicable diseases); and (3) they are killed by products of the social and economic environment.

Degeneration

Degeneration refers to the biological deterioration of a body. As a cause of death, the concept is really too general to be very useful, since deterioration tends to be a gradual process and, at least in American medicine, is generally treated as a disease under the category of chronic diseases. The major chronic diseases associated with degeneration, in order of importance as a cause of death, are **cardiovascular disease** or heart disease, cancer, stroke, arteriosclerosis, diabetes mellitus, cirrhosis of the liver, hypertension, and ulcers of the stomach and duodenum.

Table 6.1   Heart Disease Leads As a
Cause of Death in the United States (1984)

Cause of Death	Percent
1. Heart disease	38
2. Cancer	22
3. Cerebrovascular (especially stroke)	8
4. Accidents	5
5. Chronic obstructive pulmonary diseases	3
6. Influenza and pneumonia	3
7. Diabetes mellitus	2
8. Suicide	1
9. Cirrhosis of the liver	1
10. Atherosclerosis	1
11. Homicide	1
12. Other causes	15
	100

Source: National Center for Health Statistics, 1986, "Advance report of final mortality statistics, 1984," Monthly Vital Statistics Report 35(6):supplement, Table B.

The American Public Health Association defines **chronic diseases** as "all impairments or deviations from normal which have one or more of the following characteristics: are permanent, are caused by nonreversible **pathological** alterations, require special training of the patient for rehabilitation, or may be expected to require a long period of supervision, observation or care" (Blum and Keranen, 1966:xiii). Not all chronic diseases are degenerative; indeed, not all are necessarily fatal. Nonetheless, degeneration is treated as an illness even though it may be the result of natural irrevocable deterioration of bodily organs or functions.

In the United States in 1984, chronic diseases accounted for three fourths of all deaths. Heart disease alone accounted for 38 percent of all deaths, and cancer was responsible for 22 percent (see Table 6.1). I should note that as strange as it sounds, cancer (malignant neoplasm) technically is not fatal in most cases. Such neoplasms nourish themselves at the expense of the rest of the body, leaving the individual emaciated and in ill health. A study by Ambrus and others in Buffalo, New York in 1974 indicated that infections by antibiotic-resistant bacteria were the chief cause of death among cancer patients, followed by respiratory failure, blood clots or hemorrhaging, and cardiovascular insufficiency (Science, 1974).

Communicable Diseases

Communicable diseases (also known as infectious diseases) are those that can be transmitted from one person to another. Communicable diseases are, in fact, so dependent on human contact that the World Health Organization has suggested (somewhat whimsically perhaps) that if each person in the world were provided with a surgical-type "virus" mask to be worn for a month when in the company of other people, the great majority of communicable diseases would be eliminated. A major victory against communicable disease was scored in 1979 when smallpox was eliminated from the world. We had gone for 2 years without a reported case (and the World Health Organization had offered a $1,000 reward for any such report), and WHO officials thus declared the disease eradicated.

The major communicable diseases, in order of their current importance in the United States as causes of death, are: pneumonia, tuberculosis, influenza, syphilis, and infectious hepatitis. However, the list of potentially fatal communicable diseases that used to prevail in the United States and other developed nations prior to disease control is much longer, and many such diseases are still prominent causes of death in less developed nations. In alphabetical order, these diseases are: chicken pox, cholera, diphtheria, encephalitis, malaria, measles, meningitis, poliomyelitis, rubella (German measles), tetanus, typhoid, and whooping cough. In the United States, however, where sanitation and personal hygiene are good and people live at fairly low densities, death from communicable disease represents less than 5 percent of all deaths. Pneumonia alone accounts for more than two thirds of all deaths from communicable diseases. This is a bit misleading, however, since pneumonia often occurs as the fatal by-product of other diseases that leave a person bedridden and vulnerable. One such disease that has generated enormous public concern around the world is acquired immune deficiency syndrome (AIDS), which I discuss in the accompanying essay.

Products of the Social and Economic Environment

It is widely recognized that humans regularly introduce pollutants and chemicals into the environment that are known to speed up the process of biological deterioration. It is often disheartening for people to discover that many products designed to improve health or make life easier could produce cancer. An especially tragic example involves flame-retardant clothing, which helps to reduce burn injury and death, especially among children. Blum and Ames (1977) produced evidence that some of the flame-retardant chemicals (especially "Tris") could lead to cancer when ingested by a person, such as when children suck on their flame-retardant pajamas (and children do things like that). They might also be absorbed through the skin. When these and other chemicals are "disposed" of, they may find their way into the food chain, producing even more damage (Blum and Ames, 1977)—see Chapter 14 for more on this subject. It seems as though the progress of death control is increasingly sideways—we may be trading one problem for another, rather than actually improving our overall level of health.

There is a cause of death that is unrelated to disease of any kind—**accidental death.** Every time a person is killed in an automobile accident, slips and is killed in the bathtub, or is murdered by a mugger, that death is attributable to the social and economic environment. These deaths could occur even in the absence of degeneration or disease. The only types of accidents not directly attributable to the social and economic environment are those due to natural phenomena such as floods, tornadoes, avalanches, earthquakes, and others. However, in most of these instances deaths can be attributed to human risk taking even though the death certificate specifies drowning or suffocation, for example, as the cause of death. For instance, people die in an earthquake not from the quake itself, but from the building that falls

THE DEMOGRAPHY OF AIDS

At about the same time that we apparently rid the world of smallpox, another deadly viral disease came along to remind us of how tenuous is our control over mortality. I refer, of course, to AIDS (acquired immune deficiency syndrome). Unfortunately, this newer disease is worse than the one we eliminated. Classic smallpox (variola major) had a case fatality rate of about 30 percent (Gordon, 1965), which is certainly terrible, but AIDS appears to kill virtually *everyone* who develops its symptoms. AIDS is the most severe of several manifestations of infection with the human immunodeficiency virus (HIV), and, technically, AIDS is not a single disease but rather a complex of diseases and symptoms whose underlying causes are, as of this writing, still unknown. AIDS kills by attacking the immune system and rendering the victim susceptible to various kinds of infections and malignancies that then lead to death in a degenerative, disabling fashion.

AIDS was initially recognized as a specific cause of death in 1981 (Quinn, 1987), but at least one case appears to have shown up in the United States as early as 1969 (Associated Press, 1987). By April 1988 there had been 88,000 AIDS cases worldwide reported to the World Health Organization, a doubling since 1987 (Caballo, 1988). Nearly two thirds (62 percent) of these cases were in the United States, although it is believed that lack of diagnosis and lack of reporting lead to undercounting of AIDS cases elsewhere in the world, especially in Africa, where the disease is thought to have originated. Only about 12 percent of cases were reported in Africa, but it is suspected that infection rates in the population are alarmingly high in the central and eastern African countries of Zaire, Rwanda, Kenya, and Tanzania (Bertrand,

1988). An additional 12 percent of cases have come from Europe, with the remainder being divided nearly evenly between Asia and Oceania.

The reporting of AIDS cases is typically thought of as representing the tip of the iceberg, since some estimates suggest that for every identified case of AIDS there may be 50 additional persons with inapparent infections of HIV (Quinn, 1987). Between 20 and 50 percent of persons with HIV may eventually develop symptoms of AIDS, and 80 percent of those individuals will die within 2 years after their symptoms first occur. The potential invidiousness of the disease is obvious.

AIDS is spread when a person's bloodstream takes in the blood, semen, or possibly vaginal secretions of an infected person. There are three identified ways in which this is most likely to happen: (1) during sexual intercourse (especially anal or oral intercourse, during which an open sore or lesion might serve as the point of entry for the virus); (2) as a result of an injection of drugs using a contaminated needle; (3) during a blood transfusion with infected blood. The latter method of transmission, in particular, has diminished in importance in developing countries as tests have been devised to screen blood for AIDS prior to its use.

In theory, anyone *could* become infected, but reality is much different, especially in the United States. In the United States as of 1987, 93 percent of all AIDS victims were males, 70 percent of whom were homosexuals or bisexuals who were not users of intravenous (IV) drugs. An additional 8 percent of the males were homosexual or bisexual IV drug users, 15 percent were heterosexual IV drug users, 2 percent were heterosexual partners of peron top of them because it was unable to withstand the shaking. Nevertheless, buildings continue to be built and occupied very near, and in some cases right on top of, known fault lines. Likewise, floods generally kill those who unwisely build homes in flood plains or who venture away from secure areas. Tornadoes, too, tend to kill

---

sons with AIDS, 2 percent were victims of transfusions, and 3 percent were undetermined. Among the 7 percent of all victims who were women, the profile was very different. Virtually all women were either IV drug users or heterosexual partners of someone with AIDS. Most such women in the United States are prostitutes. Since most prostitutes are also mothers (Shedlin, 1988), it is not surprising that a small number of children are also infected with AIDS, largely as a result of having a mother who carried the AIDS virus during pregnancy.

The pattern of victimization that I have just described is found throughout the Americas and Europe, but in the Caribbean (especially Haiti) and in sub-Saharan Africa, the number of cases is about evenly divided between males and females, heterosexuals comprise the bulk of cases, and the incidence of AIDS in the population appears to be higher. This may be due to a combination of relatively high levels of heterosexual promiscuity, lower incidences of blood testing, and more uncontrolled use of needles among IV drug users (Population Information Program, 1986).

It is also true that AIDS disproportionately affects minority group members, especially in the United States. In 1987, 39 percent of all deaths occurred among blacks and Hispanics (who together account for less than 20 percent of the total U.S. population) (National Center for Health Statistics, 1988). This is primarily due to the fact that IV drug use is higher in these groups than in the Anglo population. In the latter group, homosexuality is a more important transmission source than is IV drug use.

AIDS is also found disproportionately among young people, which is not surprising, of course, since the young are more likely to be sexually promiscuous and to be IV drug users. Among young males in the United States, the importance of AIDS as a cause of death is exceeded only by that of accidents and other violent deaths, such as homicide and suicide. Throughout the world, the modal age category of people reported as having AIDS is 30–39, but the disease was probably acquired at an earlier age. There may be a lag of several years before the HIV infection turns into the clinical symptoms that we call AIDS. This fact has led to the concern that the rate of mortality from AIDS may accelerate during the next few years despite massive worldwide education programs. For many people who *now* know how to avoid AIDS, it is already too late. As of 1988, it was still true that the only "cure" for AIDS is prevention.

The outlook for the AIDS problem is, therefore, negative and positive at the same time. The down side is that we may expect a rise in the number of deaths from people already infected, and this increase could last through the early 1990s. On the positive side, it is probable that the number of new cases of infection is already declining as a consequence of worldwide publicity about "safe sex" and "safe drugs," along with improved scrutiny of the blood supply. Safe sex includes the avoidance of anal and oral sex, the avoidance of promiscuity, and the use of condoms during intercourse. Safe drug use mainly entails the use of sterile needles for an injection. Unfortunately, the likely high infection rate that already exists among some high-risk groups may lead to a diminution in the actual numbers of high-risk persons over time as they succumb to the disease. It also seems possible, however, that the massive resources that are being poured into research may yield a cure for AIDS.

those who do not take precautions and, for whatever reason, have not found a basement, ravine, or ditch to hide in. In the United States about 5 percent of all deaths are accidental, with motor vehicle accidents being the single most important cause.

Drunk Driving   Drunk driving has been called a national epidemic (Newsweek, 1982), one that kills more Americans every 2 years on the highways than died during the entire war in Vietnam. In the decade of the 1970s, Americans who were victims of this "invisible slaughter" (Wall Street Journal, 1982) numbered nearly a quarter of a million, a number equal to the total population of Rochester, New York or Akron, Ohio. So serious has the problem become that in 1981 President Reagan established a National Commission on Drunk Driving and in 1982 Congress passed a bill granting federal aid to states that tightened up their standards for defining drunk driving and that stepped up their enforcement of those laws. A particular focus has been placed on youths aged 16–24, who accounted for 35 percent of all alcohol-related accidents in 1981, while representing only 23 percent of the population of driving age. Concerted public effort in the 1980s helped to push down the percentage of fatal crashes attributable to 16- to 19-year-olds from 29 percent in 1982 to 21 percent in 1986.

Drunkenness is not a problem confined to the United States. Great Britain and Sweden also have tough laws on their books to try to crack down on alcohol-related fatalities, and in the Soviet Union an official of the state planning commission admitted in 1981 that three fourths of all violent crimes and two thirds of serious industrial, traffic, and household accidents in that country were attributable to alcohol abuse (Daily Californian, 1981a). Many of the factors often associated with alcohol abuse—anger, depression, loneliness, antisocial behavior—converge within some individuals to lead to suicide, another important cause of death associated with social factors rather than disease mechanisms.

Suicide   By world standards, the suicide rate is not unusually high in the United States—nearly every Scandinavian country, for example, has a rate at least twice as high. Interestingly enough, countries that are culturally similar to the United States, such as the United Kingdom, Canada, and New Zealand, have suicide rates similar to American rates (Klebba et al., 1974). In Figure 6.3 it is clear that the suicide rate in the United States rises though the teen years (a phenomenon that receives considerable publicity), peaks in the young adult ages, plateaus in the middle years, and then rises for males while it drops for females in the older ages. More specifically, the rate goes up among *white* males; it does not follow that pattern among nonwhite males. Although the reasons for this racial difference are not yet well defined, one explanation currently offered is that women and minority elders experience more adversity during their lives than do white males and thus may be better equipped to cope with the losses and frustrations that sometimes accompany old age (Miller, 1979).

The teenage suicide rate, although still lower than that for older men, has received a great deal of publicity for several reasons: (1) over time, the rate has been rising for teens while declining for the elderly; (2) the absolute number of teenage suicides is substantial, even if the rate is far below that of older men; and (3) the

Figure 6.3   Suicide Rates in the United States Are Highest for Older Men

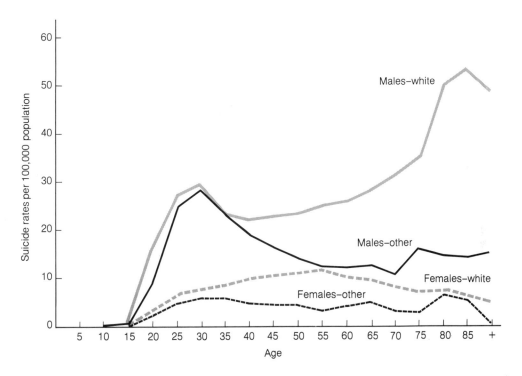

Sources: National Center for Health Statistics, 1984, Vital Statistics of the United States, 1979, Vol. II, Mortality, Part A (Hyattsville, MD: NCHS), Tables 1-8 and 1-25.

effects of ageism linger on in American society, causing people implicitly to place greater value on younger lives than on older, and thus to be more sorrowful and concerned about the death of youth than the death of the elderly.

Although Figure 6.3 shows official suicide rates, these data do not take into consideration the kinds of death, such as auto accidents (discussed earlier in the chapter), that may be disguised suicides. Nor do they show that at all ages women attempt more suicides than men, nor that young men attempt to take their lives more often than do older men, but are proportionately less successful (Resnick, 1974).

Now, before proceeding to an analysis of differences in mortality levels, we need to consider the methods by which mortality is usually measured.

MEASURING MORTALITY

In measuring mortality, we are attempting to estimate the **force of mortality,** the extent to which people are unable to live to their biological maximum. The ability to measure accurately varies according to the amount of information available, and as a consequence, the measures of mortality differ considerably in their level of sophistication, as was true for fertility measures (see Chapter 4). The least sophisticated and most often quoted measure of mortality is the crude death rate, completely analogous to the crude birth rate.

Crude Death Rate

The **crude death rate** (CDR) is the total number of deaths in a year divided by the average total population. In general form:

$$CDR = \frac{\text{Total deaths in a year}}{\text{Average total population in that year}} \times 1,000$$

It is called crude because it does not take into account the differences by age and sex in the likelihood of death. Nonetheless, it is frequently used because it requires only two pieces of information, total deaths and total population, which often can be estimated with reasonable accuracy even in the absence of costly censuses or vital registration systems.

Differences in the CDR between two countries could be due entirely to differences in the distribution of the population by age, even though the force of mortality was actually the same. Thus, if one population has a high proportion of old people, its crude death rate will be higher than that of a population with a high proportion of young adults, even though at each age the probabilities of death are identical. A good example of this is the difference in crude death rates between West Berlin and West Germany in 1967. In West Berlin the CDR was 18, while in West Germany it was 11, suggesting that in West Berlin mortality was 64 percent higher than in West Germany. Yet, in both places a female baby had nearly a 90 percent chance of survival to age 55. Thus, the force of mortality was identical, but the crude death rate was influenced by the fact that in West Berlin, 21 percent of the population was aged 65 or older, while in West Germany the percentage was only 12.

A different example is the comparison between the United States and Mexico in 1987. At that date Mexico's crude death rate of 7 per 1,000 was lower than the 9 per 1,000 recorded for the United States per 1,000 population. Yet in Mexico a baby at birth could expect to live 8 years less than a baby in the United States. The high birth rate in Mexico had produced an age structure with high proportions of young adults, thus lowering the crude death rate.

In order to account for the differences in dying by age (and sex), we must calculate age/sex–specific death rates.

Age/Sex–Specific Death Rates

To measure mortality at each age and for each sex we must have a vital registration system in which deaths by age and sex are reported, along with census data that provide estimates of the number of people in each age and sex category. The **age/sex–specific death rate** (ASDR) is measured as the number of deaths in a year of people of a particular age (usually ages x to $x + 5$) divided by the average number of people of that age in the population. In general:

$$\text{ASDR} = \frac{\text{Number of deaths in a year of people aged } x \text{ to } x + 5}{\text{Average number of people in that year aged } x \text{ to } x + 5}$$

In the United States in 1984, the ASDR for males aged 65–69 was 0.031 (if multiplied by 1,000, that would be 31 per 1,000), while for females it was 0.017, almost half that for males. In 1900, the ASDR for males aged 65–69 was 0.050, and for females, 0.055. Thus, we can see that in 84 years the death rates for males aged 65–69 dropped by only 38 percent, while for females the decline was 69 percent. To be sure, in 1900 the death rate for females was actually a bit higher than for males, whereas by 1984 it was well below that for males.

Often it is awkward or inconvenient to compare mortality on an age-by-age basis. We would like to have a single index that sums up the mortality experience of a population, while also taking into account the age and sex structure. A frequently used index is the expectation of life at birth. This measure is derived from a **life table**, which is a fairly complicated statistical device that I have saved for the Appendix, if you want to examine it. The important thing for you to know at this point is how to interpret a life expectancy at birth. It is the average age at death for a hypothetical group of people born in a particular year and being subjected to the risks of death experienced by people of all ages in that year. (If you think about it, you will realize that it is conceptually similar to the total fertility rate—a sophisticated measure of fertility discussed in Chapter 4.) The expectation of life at birth for U.S. females in 1984 of 78 years does not mean that the average age at death in that year for females was 78. What it does mean is that if all the females born in the United States in 1984 had the same risks of dying throughout their lives as those indicated by the age-specific death rates in 1984, then their average age at death would be 78. Of course, some of them would have died in infancy, while others might live to be 114, but the age-specific death rates in 1984 implied an average of 78. Note that life expectancy is based on a hypothetical population, just as is the total fertility rate. Analogously, the actual longevity of a population would be measured by the average age at death, just as actual fertility is measured by completed family size. Yet, since we do not usually want to wait decades to find out how long people are actually going to live, the hypothetical situation set up by life *expectancy* provides a useful, quick comparison between populations.

Having discussed the more prominent causes of death and the usual methods for measuring mortality levels, we are ready to analyze some important social factors associated with different causes of death and with correspondingly different levels of mortality—differences by social class, race or ethnicity, marital status, and rural or urban residence. In addition, we will examine two other important characteristics that influence mortality—age and sex.

SOCIAL CLASS DIFFERENTIALS IN MORTALITY

Differences in mortality by social class are among the most pervasive inequalities in modern society, yet there have been only a handful of studies on the subject. This is due primarily to the difficulty of obtaining data. Death certificates rarely contain information on occupation and virtually never on income or education, and when they do have occupation data, many indicate "retired" or "housewife," giving no further clues to social status. Thus, more circumlocutious means must be devised to obtain data on the likelihood of death among members of different social strata. The principal method used is record linkage, such as in the study by Kitagawa and Hauser (1973) for the United States. The only other country for which reasonably comparable data are available is England. In the record linkage approach, death certificates for individuals in a census year are linked with census information obtained for that individual prior to death. Age and cause of death are ascertained from the death certificate, while the census data provide information on occupation, education, income, marital status, and race.

Occupation

Data from both the United States and England indicate that as the prestige level of a group's occupation goes up, its death rate goes down. Among white American men aged 25–64 when they died in 1960, mortality rates for laborers were 19 percent above the average, while those for professional men were 20 percent below the average (Kitagawa and Hauser, 1973). Interestingly enough, agricultural workers had the lowest death rates, 24 percent below the average for all working males. Kitagawa and Hauser also grouped men into even broader occupational categories and found that mortality for white-collar workers was 8 percent below the average, while for blue-collar workers it was 7 percent above the average.

For England, Benjamin (1969) has put together similar information on occupational differences in mortality for 1951. He grouped occupations into five social class levels and found that in the highest class, mortality rates were 2 percent below average, while they were 18 percent above average in the lowest class. In the middle social class, death rates were 1 percent above average.

Since these data referred to men, Benjamin noted that they might reflect occupational hazards rather than something more generally inherent in the different lifestyles of various social classes. So he looked at the mortality levels of wives not exposed to their husbands' hazards of working. By using the wives as a control group, Benjamin was able to single out occupations that were clearly dangerous to the health of men. For example, in England in 1951, sandblasters and glassblowers had mortality rates that were substantially above average, whereas mortality rates for their wives were only slightly above average. In general, however, Benjamin found that mortality levels of wives followed the pattern of their husbands.

In examining causes of death by social class, Benjamin found that deaths from communicable diseases became increasingly common in lower social classes. For example, among working males aged 20–64, death rates from tuberculosis, bronchitis, and pneumonia were two to three times higher in the lowest social class than in the highest. On the other hand, death rates from chronic diseases such as coronaries, cirrhosis of the liver, diabetes, and stroke were uniformly higher in the higher social classes than in the lower. The most important aspects of occupation and social class that relate to mortality are undoubtedly income and education—income to buy protection against and cures for diseases, and education to know the means whereby disease risks can be minimized.

Income and Education

There is a striking relationship between income and mortality in the United States. Kitagawa and Hauser's data for 1960 show clearly that as income goes up, mortality goes down. Among white families, death rates for males aged 15–64 with incomes of $10,000 or more were almost half that for men in families with incomes of less than $2,000. A similar pattern existed for women.

In analyzing social class differences in mortality by specific causes of death, Kitagawa and Hauser looked only at education. However, they did note that the effects of income and education tended to be independent of each other. In other words, having both high income and high education was more advantageous than having only one or the other.

As with income, there is a marked decline in the risk of death as education increases. A white male in 1960 with an eighth-grade education had a 6 percent chance of dying between the ages of 25 and 45, whereas for a college graduate the probability was only half as high. For women, education makes an even bigger difference, especially at the extremes. A white female with a college education could expect, at age 25, to live 10 years longer than a woman who had 4 or fewer years of schooling.

For virtually every major cause of death, white males with at least 1 year of college had lower risks of death than those with less education. The differences appear to be least for the degenerative chronic diseases and greatest for accidental deaths. This is consistent with the way you might theorize that education would affect mortality, since it should enhance an individual's ability to avoid dangerous, high-risk situations.

Although few studies permit an expansion of this discussion, it should be apparent that every index of social class indicates that social status influences mortality. Other characteristics frequently associated with differences in social status are race and ethnicity.

Race and Ethnicity

In most societies in which more than one racial or ethnic group exists, one group tends to dominate the others. This generally leads to social and economic disadvantages for the subordinate groups, and such disadvantages frequently result in lower life expectancies for the racial or ethnic minority group members. This is certainly true in the United States.

The data for the United States in 1984 by the National Center for Health Statistics show that at every age up to 80, nonwhite mortality is higher than white mortality by more than 10 percent. Between ages 30 and 44, nonwhite death rates are more than double those for whites. Within the nonwhite category, however, there are important differences. Blacks in the United States have significantly higher death rates than whites, whereas the rates for Japanese-Americans are significantly lower. For example, at birth in 1979–81 in California (where such data are available), a white male could expect to live 6 years longer than a black male but 8 years less than a Japanese-American male. Differences were similar for females (California Center for Health Statistics, 1983). These disparities in mortality may be due at least partially to income levels, since in 1979, Japanese-Americans had a higher average family income than whites, whereas blacks had a lower than average income. However, income probably cannot account for all the mortality disadvantages experienced by nonwhites. Kitagawa and Hauser also found for the United States in 1960

Figure 6.4 Blacks Have Higher Death Rates Than Whites for Most Major Causes of Death (Females, 1984)

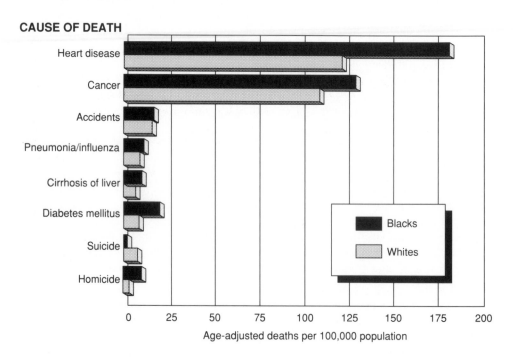

For almost all major causes of death, blacks have higher age-adjusted death rates than whites. These differences are probably accounted for in large part by the lower average socioeconomic status of nonwhites. *Source:* National Center for Health Statistics, 1986, "Advance report of final mortality statistics," Monthly Vital Statistics Report, 35(6):supplement: Table 12.

that within each broad social class grouping, mortality rates were still at least 20 percent higher for nonwhites than for whites. You can also see in Figure 6.4 that blacks have higher risks of death from almost every major cause of death than do whites.

The United States is one of the few countries for which recent data are available on ethnic differences in mortality, but earlier studies revealed that in India in 1931, members of a religious sect called Parsis had an expectation of life at birth that was 20 years longer than that of the total population of India. The difference apparently was due to the relatively high economic position of the Parsis (United Nations, 1953). Similarly, in the 1940s before Palestine was partitioned to make Israel, the death rate among Moslems was two or three times that of the Jewish population, probably due also to the higher economic status of the Jews (United Nations, 1953).

MARITAL STATUS DIFFERENTIALS IN MORTALITY

It has long been observed that married people tend to live longer than unmarried people. This is true not only in the United States but in other countries as well. A long-standing explanation for this phenomenon is that marriage is selective of healthy people; that is, people who are physically handicapped or in ill health may have both a lower chance of marrying and a higher risk of death. At least some of the difference in mortality by marital status is certainly due to this (Kisker and Goldman, 1987).

Another explanation is that marriage is good for your health. In 1973, Gove examined this issue, looking at cause-of-death data for the United States in 1959–61. His analysis indicates that differences in mortality of married and unmarried people "are particularly marked among those types of mortality where one's psychological state would appear to affect one's life chances" (1973:65). As examples, Gove notes that among men aged 25–64, suicide rates for single men are double those of married men. For women, the differences are in the same direction, but they are not as large. Unmarried males and females also have higher death rates from what Gove calls "the use of socially approved narcotics" such as alcohol and cigarettes. Cirrhosis of the liver is associated with heavy drinking, and single males have three times the death rate of married males from that disease; for divorced males, the rates are nine times higher. Again, the differences are less extreme for females. Lung cancer is associated with smoking, and single males have death rates 45 percent higher than married men; divorced men have three times the rate.

Finally, Gove notes that for mortality associated with diseases requiring "prolonged and methodical care" unmarried people are also at a disadvantage. In these cases, the most extreme rates are among divorced men, who have death rates nine times higher than married men. In general, Gove's analysis suggests that married people, especially men, have lower levels of mortality than unmarried people because their levels of social and psychological adjustment are higher.

You should not jump to any hasty decisions based on these data, however. If you are currently single, for example, don't get married just because you think it might prolong your life. Another study on the health (although not the death) of people by **marital status** suggests that single people are actually healthier than married people, even when you account for age (Wilder, 1976). The data from the National Health Survey of the United States for 1971–72 show that single persons have fewer restricted activity days per year, a lower incidence of acute conditions, and fewer visits to physicians and the hospital than married persons. However, separated, divorced, and widowed people were less healthy than the currently married. In recent years, of course, the fluidity of marital status has limited the usefulness of this comparison. Being single, in particular, may be more like being married if one is, in fact, cohabiting.

SEX DIFFERENTIALS IN MORTALITY

Women generally live longer than men do, and the gap is widening. In 1900 women could expect to live an average of 2 years longer than men in the United States, and by 1985, the difference had grown to 7 years. This phenomenon has attracted curiosity for a long time and it has been suggested facetiously that the early death of men is nature's way of repaying those women who have spent a lifetime with demanding, difficult husbands. However, the situation has been most thoroughly investigated by Retherford (1975) and Preston (1976).

Retherford points out that a large number of studies show that throughout the animal kingdom females survive longer than males, which could indicate a basic biological inferiority in the ability of males to survive relative to females. However, in human populations, although the survival advantage of women is widespread, it is not universal. This implies that there are social factors (Retherford calls them "external factors") that are also operating. One such factor is the status of women. It is in those countries where women are most dominated by men (especially the Islamic nations of the Middle East) where women are least likely to outlive men. In the United States, as in European and Scandinavian countries, the trend toward greater independence of women has also been accompanied by an increasing gap in life expectancy between the sexes, probably because women have been gaining in their knowledge of preventive health measures (such as proper nutrition and exercise) and because greater independence enhances the ability to seek proper medical care.

Another important social factor that has contributed to the sex differential in mortality, at least in the United States, is smoking. Since 1900, males have smoked cigarettes much more than have females, and this has helped to elevate male risks of death from cancer, degenerative lung diseases (such as chronic bronchitis and emphysema), and cardiovascular diseases (Preston, 1970).

By examining causes of death by age for each sex, Retherford was able to estimate the importance of each cause of death. He found that at very young ages (1–5) the declines in infectious and parasitic diseases in the United States from 1910 to 1965 actually narrowed the sex differences in mortality at young ages, although females still have the edge. Only at ages over 50 has the differential been widening substantially over time, and most of this difference is accounted for by cancer and cardiovascular diseases. This strongly suggests that in the United States (and probably in other Western nations as well) the widening sex differential in mortality is related to the effects of men's smoking patterns.

Over the next few decades, however, we will probably be seeing a lessening of that differential, or at least no further widening. The reason, of course, is that cigarette smoking by women increased after World War II and, as a result, women moving into the older ages now are more likely to be smokers than was true of earlier cohorts. In fact, in 1985 young women aged 20–24 were just as likely as young men to be smokers (the smoking version of gender equality), but fortunately the percentage of people who smoke has been steadily declining since the 1960s (National Center for Health Statistics, 1988). The result has been a fairly predictable rise in death rates from lung cancer among women. Between 1970 and 1985 age-adjusted death rates from lung cancer for men rose by 17 percent, but for women they rose by 124 percent (National Center for Health Statistics, 1988). In 1950 a woman was only one-fifth as likely to die from lung cancer as a man in the United States, but by 1985 that difference had dwindled to the point that a woman was two-fifths as likely as a man to die from lung cancer.

Smoking, of course, cannot explain the total difference between the sexes, and there is a growing body of research suggesting that the female hormone, estrogen, may in itself offer some form of protection against disease and death (Epstein, 1965; Newsweek, 1983a).

AGE DIFFERENTIALS IN MORTALITY

Infant Mortality

There are few things in the world more frightening and awesome than the responsibility for a newborn child—fragile and completely dependent on others for survival. In many societies, that fragility and dependency are translated into high **infant mortality** rates (the number of deaths during the first year of life per 1,000 live births). In some of the less developed nations, especially in equatorial Africa, infant death rates are as high as 175 deaths per 1,000 live births. That figure is for Sierra Leone, plagued by drought and famine in the 1970s and 1980s, but it is representative of that region of the world. By contrast, one of the lowest infant mortality rates in the world is in Sweden, where only 7 of every 1,000 babies die during their first year of life. Infant death rates for several different countries of the world are shown in Table 6.2.

In countries still characterized by high mortality, such as equatorial African societies, death in the first year of life may account for as much as one fourth of all deaths in a year. Deaths of children under 10 years old represent nearly two thirds of all deaths. However, as death rates decline and people start living longer, dying shifts to the older ages. In Sweden, for example, deaths of children under age 1 account for only 2 percent of all deaths, and the deaths of children up to age 10 account for less than 3 percent of the total.

Why do babies have higher death rates in some countries than in others? The answer is perhaps best summed up by mentioning the two characteristics common to

Table 6.2   The Top 20 and Bottom 10 Countries
in the World in Terms of Infant Mortality Rates (1988)

Country	Infant Mortality Rate
Infant Mortality Rates Are Lowest in the Following 20 Countries:	
1. Japan	5.2
2. Iceland	5.4
3. Finland	5.8
4. Sweden	5.9
5. Switzerland	6.8
6. Taiwan	6.9
7. Hong Kong	7.7
8. Netherlands	7.7
9. Canada	7.9
10. Luxembourg	7.9
11. France	8.0
12. Denmark	8.4
13. Norway	8.5
14. West Germany	8.6
15. Ireland	8.7
16. East Germany	9.2
17. Singapore	9.4
18. United Kingdom	9.5
19. Belgium	9.7
20. Australia	9.8
Infant Mortality Rates Are Highest in the Following 10 Countries:	
1. Afghanistan	183
2. Sierra Leone	175
3. Mali	175
4. Gambia	169
5. East Timor	166
6. Malawi	157
7. Guinea	153
8. Somalia	147
9. Mozambique	147
10. Niger	141

Source: Data courtesy of the Population Reference Bureau, Inc., Washington, D.C.

Note: Developed societies, especially Scandinavian nations, have the lowest rates of infant mortality, while less developed nations, especially in Africa and Asia, have the highest rates.

people in places where infant death rates are low—high levels of education and income. Education here can refer simply to knowledge of a few basic rules that would avoid unnecessary infant death. For example, one study in a rural Indian village revealed that tetanus was the major cause of infant death. Further investigation ascribed this to the fact that umbilical cords were often cut with instruments such as unsanitary farm implements, and the cord was dressed with ash from the cow dung fire typical of that part of the country (Bouvier and van de Tak, 1976).

Income is important in order to provide babies with a nutritious, sanitary diet that prevents diarrhea—an important cause of death among infants. Nursing mothers can best provide this service if their diet is adequate in amount and quality. Income is also frequently associated with the ability of a nation to provide, or an individual to buy, adequate medical protection from disease. In places where infant death rates are high, communicable diseases are a major cause of death, and most of those deaths could be prevented with medical assistance. For example, between 1861 and 1960, the infant death rate in England and Wales dropped from 160 to 20, with more than two thirds of that decline due to the control of communicable diseases.

Resistance to disease is, of course, closely related to the overall health of the child, which in turn is associated with the health of the mother (Bouvier and van de Tak, 1976). Mothers who are healthy while pregnant, and who maintain that good health after giving birth, are more likely to have healthy babies. Since levels of health are generally higher in the more advanced nations, infant mortality is generally lowest there. The relationship between income and health is not perfect, however. Consider that among fairly large countries (that is, excluding tiny oil-rich sheikdoms), Switzerland in 1985 had the highest level of per-person income and the fifth lowest level of infant mortality. Yet, the United States, while second in income, was only twenty-first in infant mortality. Much of this difference is perhaps accounted for by the fact that American women do not care for themselves as well as Swiss women do. Let me explain in more detail.

In advanced nations like the United States and Switzerland, prematurity accounts for a vast majority of deaths among infants, and in many cases prematurity results from lack of proper care of the mother during pregnancy. Pregnant women who do not maintain an adequate diet, who smoke or take drugs, or in general do not care for themselves have an elevated chance of giving birth prematurely, thus putting their baby at a distinct disadvantage in terms of survival after birth (Behrman, 1987).

In the United States, babies conceived illegitimately have a much higher risk of death than legitimately conceived babies, even if the mother marries before the baby is born (see Weeks, 1976). One of the things associated with this higher risk is, again, prenatal care. If a mother neglects her pregnancy, her child is more likely to die after birth. By and large these are deaths that could not have been prevented medically, but they could have been prevented if social pressure had been greater for the mother to care for herself more adequately during pregnancy.

The Soviet Union has had difficulty keeping its infant mortality rate low, and in recent years the rate there seems actually to have risen, a trend that "is unique in the history of developed countries" (Feshbach, 1982). Apparently to hide this health slippage from the rest of the world, the USSR stopped publishing detailed mortality data in 1974, but other data collected by Murray Feshbach at Georgetown University have made it clear that infants are at increasingly high risks of death, with a rate perhaps as high as 33 per 1,000. One of the explanations offered by Feshbach for this phenomenon is the widespread popularity of bottle-feeding in Russia, complicated by a shortage of fortified baby formula. Despite the fact that Abbott Laboratories of Chicago (makers of Similac, a popular infant formula) has built a new plant for the Russians outside of Moscow, there appears not to be an adequate supply. A 1983 editorial in the *Wall Street Journal* detailing Feshbach's findings drew an irate denial from the Soviet Ministry of Health, but they provided little data to rebut Feshbach's argument. In 1986, the Soviets resumed the publication of data on infant mortality following a ten-year hiatus. The figures suggest that at best, the situation was no better in 1985 than it had been in 1965 (Anderson and Silver, 1986).

The substitution of bottle-feeding for breast-feeding can be critical to an infant's health, and the introduction of supplements during lactation can also create health problems. Introducing supplements too early can cause diarrhea (the major health risk to infants), whereas waiting too long can cause malnutrition. "Ample data exist to indicate that the time of introduction of supplements has a profound effect on morbidity and mortality among infants and young children in poorer segments of the population in developing nations" (Prema and Ravindranath, 1982:295).

Although infant mortality measures infant deaths from birth through the first year of life, the most dangerous time for infants is just prior to and just after birth. There are special measures of infant death that take these risks into account. For example, **late fetal mortality** refers to fetal deaths that occur after at least 28 weeks of gestation. **Neonatal** mortality refers to deaths of infants within 28 days after birth. **Postneonatal** mortality then covers deaths from 28 days to 1 year after birth. In addition, there is an index called **perinatal** mortality, which includes late fetal deaths plus deaths within the first 7 days after birth.

In the United States, the late fetal death rate (late fetal deaths per 1,000 live births and late fetal deaths) declined from 14.9 in 1950 to 4.9 in 1985—a drop of 67 percent. The neonatal death rate (neonatal deaths per 1,000 live births) declined during that period from 20.5 to 7.0—a drop of 66 percent. The postneonatal death rate (postneonatal deaths per 1,000 live births) went from 8.7 in 1950 to 3.7 in 1985—a decline of 57 percent. The perinatal death rate (late fetal deaths plus infant deaths within 7 days after birth per 1,000 live births and late fetal deaths) went from 32.5 in 1950 to 10.7 in 1985—a drop of 67 percent (National Center for Health Statistics, 1988). Overall, you can see that progress had been made in helping infants to survive from the period of late gestation through the first year of life. Such progress is a reflection of the continual, albeit now rather slow, improvement in the overall level of living in the United States. Throughout the world, the infant mortality rate is a fairly sensitive indicator of societal development because as the standard of living goes up, so does the average level of health in a population, and the health of babies typically improves earlier and faster than at other ages (Hartley, 1972).

One interesting (and still controversial) explanation for the relative sensitivity of infant mortality to development is that in a poor society some infant deaths may be the result of a response by parents to too few resources (Scrimshaw, 1978; Simmons et al., 1982). If parents lack the foresight or the ability to control their fertility, the option always exists of controlling mortality by reducing the amount of food given to an infant, or by selective inattention to the health and medical needs of an unwanted child. Data from the European Fertility History Project have led to the conjecture that infant and child abuse in the nineteenth century may have been a result of the undesirability of large families (Cherfas, 1980), and an example of this is provided by an examination of family life in Paris. In that city in the nineteenth century, there was an increase in the percentage of women working outside the home (especially among middle-class artisans and shopkeepers). Before bottle-feeding, a woman with a baby who wished to continue working had to hire a wet nurse. Most wet nurses were peasant women who lived in the countryside, and a mother would have to give up the child for several months if she wished to keep working. Furthermore, infant mortality was as high as 250 deaths per 1,000 infants among those placed with wet nurses (Sussman, 1977). Yet, in the early 1800s nearly one fourth of all babies born in Paris were placed with wet nurses. Infants were a bother and the risk was worth taking.

In the modern world, Simmons and his associates (1982) have found evidence of disguised infanticide in India. "Female infants are much more likely to die in families where the wife has expressed a preference for no additional children or especially for no additional female children. Male children are also affected by family size desires, but the effect is much smaller" (1982:384). Apparently parents may deliberately let a child die in some instances, especially if it is a girl in a society in which girls are considered less desirable than boys. Indeed, this may be happening in China as a consequence of the one-child policy (which I will discuss in greater detail in Chapter 15). If a family is allowed only one child, many Chinese couples would prefer a boy, and female infanticide seems to occur in a startling fraction of cases when the parents prefer a son. The undesirability of a child may also help to explain the otherwise anomalous finding that "even in rich countries like the United Kingdom—where medical care is widespread and free—the fourth or fifth child in a family has a 25 percent greater chance of dying in infancy than the first-born" (Wigglesworth, 1983:7).

Birth can be a traumatic and dangerous time not only for the infant, but for the mother as well. Until the last few decades, pregnancy and childbearing were the major reasons for death among young female adults. Let us turn to an examination of mortality during that age period.

Mortality in Young Adulthood

Currently in the United States, young adults have very low risks of death. There is less than one chance in a hundred that a 25-year-old will die before reaching age 30—about one-ninth the risk experienced in 1900. For females at these ages, the decline in deaths associated with childbearing has been especially important. For example, in 1964, **maternal mortality** rates had declined to a level 9 percent of the 1900 level, and by the 1980s maternal mortality had been virtually eliminated as a cause of death, although it remains a tragically important cause of death in developing countries (Fortney, 1987).

Despite the important role played by declining maternal mortality, however, it was not the whole story. It was the decline in communicable diseases that actually led the drop in mortality over time at the young adulthood ages. Rarely do young adults, male or female, die from such causes today (see Table 6.3). Instead, those few who do die are much more likely to be victims of accidents, automobile or otherwise. Among women, accidents account for one third of all deaths between ages 25 and 30, and for males they account for two thirds of all deaths in this age range. This is a pattern that actually exists from early childhood on through the middle years of life, but by old age the pattern has changed considerably.

Mortality at Older Ages

It has been said that in the past parents buried their children; now, children bury their parents. In 1900, the vast majority of deaths occurred to people younger than 65—only one fourth of deaths in 1900 were to older people. By the 1980s, two thirds of all deaths were to people aged 65 or older. This postponement of death

Table 6.3   What Can Kill You?

| Selected Causes of Death | Death Rates per 100,000 People (United States, 1979) | | | | | |
| | Males | | | Females | | |
	20–24	50–54	70–74	20–24	50–54	70–74
All Causes	205	950	5,045	64	505	2,630
Tuberculosis	0	2	7	0	1	2
Cancer	9	248	1,291	6	215	664
Diabetes	1	12	77	1	11	77
Heart disease	4	368	2,151	3	110	1,082
Cerebrovascular	1	35	377	1	29	276
Influenza and pneumonia	1	12	99	1	5	42
Bronchitis, emphysema, and asthma	0	16	260	0	10	67
Cirrhosis of liver	1	48	58	0	24	25
Accidents	110	62	96	25	20	48
Motor vehicle	77	28	32	19	10	16
Other	33	34	64	6	10	32
Suicide	27	24	34	7	11	7
Homicide	31	16	7	8	3	4

Source: National Center for Health Statistics, 1984, Vital Statistics of the United States, 1979, Vol. II, Mortality, Part A (Hyattsville, MD: NCHS), Table 1-8.

Note: Young people, especially males, are much more likely to die accidentally than from any other cause. At the older ages, both males and females are more likely to die of heart disease and cancer than of anything else.

until the older ages means that the number of deaths among friends and relatives in your own age group is small in younger years and then accumulates more rapidly in the later decades of life.

By the time people move into their fifties, their chances of dying start to increase at an accelerating rate. At ages above 60, by far the largest number of people of both sexes die of cardiovascular diseases. Specifically, between two thirds and three fourths of all people of that age die from heart attack and stroke. It is probable that many, if not most, of the deaths from cardiovascular causes represent biological degeneration, although social factors, especially stress, are frequently implicated in connection with hypertensive heart disease, which is associated with chronic high blood pressure.

Running a distant second as a cause of death among the elderly is cancer—malignant neoplasms. They account for 13 percent of all deaths of females aged 60 or older and 16 percent of male deaths. Among the elderly, the cancers that produce the highest proportion of deaths are those of the digestive organs, especially the stomach, intestines, and pancreas. These account for one third of all deaths from cancer. The second most frequently encountered cancers are those of the breast and genitourinary system, which account for an additional one fourth of all cancer deaths. I might note that lung cancer, despite the amount of publicity it has received, accounts for only about 10 percent of all cancer deaths among the elderly and is a greater killer in the late fifties and early sixties than at older ages.

URBAN AND RURAL DIFFERENTIALS IN MORTALITY

Until a few decades ago, cities were deadly places to live. Mortality levels were invariably higher there than in surrounding areas, since the crowding of people into small spaces, along with poor sanitation and contacts with travelers who might be carrying disease, helped to maintain fairly high levels of communicable diseases in cities. For example, life expectancy in 1841 was 40 years for native English males and 42 years for females, but in London it was 5 years less than that. In Liverpool, the port city for the burgeoning coal regions of Manchester, life expectancy was only 25 years for males and 27 years for females. In probability terms, a female child born in the city of Liverpool in 1841 had less than a 25 percent chance of living to her 55th birthday, while a rural female had nearly a 50 percent chance of surviving to age 55. Sanitation in Liverpool at that time was atrociously bad. Pumphrey notes that "pits and deep open channels, from which solid material (human wastes) had to be cleared periodically, often ran the whole length of streets. From June to October cesspools were never emptied, for it was found that any disturbance was inevitably followed by an outbreak of disease" (1940:141).

In general, we can conclude that the early differences in urban and rural mortality were due less to favorable conditions in the countryside than to decidedly unfavorable conditions in the cities. Over time, however, medical advances and environmental improvements have benefited the urban population more than the rural, leading to the current situation of better mortality conditions in urban areas.

Urban death rates tend to be low today because public health measures have brought infectious diseases under control, and medical technology keeps infants and other high-risk persons alive. However, city life is often associated with its own particular patterns of death. San Francisco has a reputation as a hard-drinking town, and mortality data tend to bear out that reputation. The death rate from cirrhosis of the liver in San Francisco in 1973 was two and a half times the rate for the whole United States. Murder was also a more common cause of death in San Francisco than in the nation as a whole (National Center for Health Statistics, 1975). Several studies in the United States have also revealed that death rates from heart disease tend to be higher in urban than in rural areas, as is cancer from environmental pollution (Kitagawa and Hauser, 1973).

TRENDS AND LEVELS IN MORTALITY

Most of us take our long life expectancy for granted. Yet scarcely a century ago, death rates were higher in every part of the world than they are anywhere today.

Europe and the United States

Only since the beginning of the twentieth century have there actually been sharp declines in mortality in Europe and the United States. In Figure 6.5 are plotted the life expectancies in the United States from 1850 to 1978 (pre-1900 data actually refer only to the state of Massachusetts—no other information is available for the rest of the country). You can see that between 1850 and 1900 life expectancy for both males and females was increasing at a rate of 1.6 years per decade. On the other hand, between 1900 and 1950 life expectancy was increasing by 3.9 years per decade for males and 4.6 years per decade for females. Then, since 1950 there has been a slowdown in the improvement of life expectancy, with only 1.3 years added per decade for males and 2.0 for females. In the last two hundred years, then, the United States, like other developed nations, has undergone an **epidemiologic transition,** a long-term shift in health and disease patterns that has brought death rates from very high levels affecting virtually all ages to low levels with deaths heavily concentrated among the elderly (Omran, 1977). This is, of course, mortality's contribution to the overall demographic transition.

Although world mortality levels have declined most noticeably in the last century, there had been gradual improvement since the beginning of the Christian era. In the Roman Empire, the average expectation of life at birth was about 22 years. At that level of mortality, a female baby had only about a 15 percent chance of living to age 55. By the Middle Ages in England, life expectancy at birth was up to about 33 years, and by the middle of the nineteenth century, a few generations after the disappearance of bubonic plague in Europe, the expectation of life at birth in England had increased to about 43 years. A female baby then had about a 46 percent chance of living to age 55 (United Nations, 1953).

Figure 6.5   Life Expectancy in the United States, 1850–1978

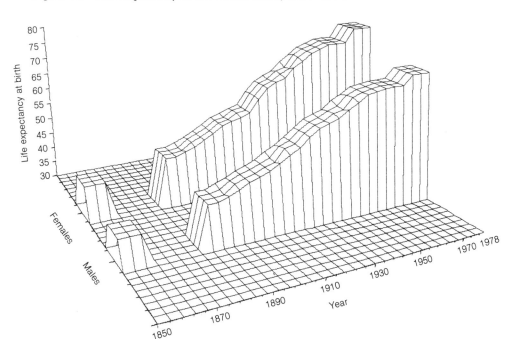

Source: U.S. Bureau of the Census, 1975, *Historical Statistics of the United States, Colonial Times to 1970, Bicentennial Edition, Part I* (Washington, D.C.: Government Printing Office), pp. 55–56; National Center for Health Statistics, 1982, *Vital Statistics of the United States, 1978, Vol. II, Mortality, Part A* (Hyattsville, MD: NCHS), Table 1-18.

Note: The early twentieth century was the period of most rapid improvement in life expectancy in the United States.

Between A.D. 1 and 1861 there was, then, an increase of 31 percentage points in the probability of survival to age 55. It took only another 79 years, from 1861 to 1940, for the probability of survival of English females to increase another 31 points to 77 percent, raising the life expectancy at birth in 1940 to 64 years. From the late nineteenth century to the present, deaths from infectious diseases such as tuberculosis, scarlet fever, typhus, whooping cough, measles, smallpox, cholera, and diarrhea have been drastically reduced, especially for young children.

Although death rates began to decline in the middle of the nineteenth century, at first improvements were fairly slow to develop for various reasons. Famines were frequent in Europe as late as the middle of the nineteenth century—the Irish potato famine of the late 1840s and Swedish harvest failures of the early 1860s are prominent examples. These crop failures were widespread, and it was common for local regions to suffer greatly from the effects of a poor harvest because poor transportation made relief very difficult. Epidemics and pandemics of infectious diseases, including the 1918 outbreak of the "swine flu," helped to keep death rates high even into this century (United Nations, 1953).

Until recently improvements in longevity were due primarily to environmental improvements, not to improved medical care. McKeown and Record (1962), who have done the pioneering research in this area, argue that the factors most responsible for nineteenth-century mortality declines were improved diet and hygienic changes, with medical improvements largely restricted to smallpox vaccinations. In addition, Boserup (1981) has noted that:

> Soap production seems to have increased considerably in England, and the availability of cheap cotton goods brought more frequent change of clothing within the economic feasibility of ordinary people. Better communication within and between European countries promoted dissemination of knowledge, including knowledge of disease and the ways to avoid it, and may help to explain the decline of mortality in areas which had neither an industrial nor an agricultural revolution at the time (1981:124–125).

The biggest declines in death rates occurred in Europe and the United States during the first half of the twentieth century as a result of the increased role of medical therapy (treatment of people already ill) combined with continued dietary and public health changes.

The experience of the American population has been generally comparable to that of Europeans, although there is some evidence that during the eighteenth and nineteenth centuries, mortality was slightly lower in the United States than in Europe. Nonetheless, by 1900 the expectations of life at birth were virtually identical in England and the United States, and they have remained that way since. Currently in the United States, there is more than a 90 percent chance that a female baby will survive to age 55. In fact, at current levels of mortality, with a life expectancy of about 77 years for women (for men it is lower than that), more than half of all women born will still be alive at age 80, and more than one fourth will still be alive at age 85. Trivial perhaps, but interesting, is the fact that mortality is currently low enough that more than 10 percent of all babies born in the United States could have a living great-great-grandmother (Keyfitz, 1977).

The death rate has persisted in its decline in developed nations, although at a slow rate, and a continuation of these downward trends will probably require that we persist in our life-style alterations. "It can be said unequivocally that a significant reduction in sedentary living and overnutrition, alcoholism, hypertension, and excessive cigarette smoking would save more lives in the age range 40 to 64 than the best current medical practices" (Kristein et al., 1977:461).

Less Developed Countries

As mortality has declined throughout the world, the control of communicable diseases has been the major reason. This is true for the less developed nations of the world today, just as it was for Europe and the United States before them. However, there is a big difference between the developed and developing countries in what precipitated the drop in death rates. Whereas socioeconomic development was a precursor to improving health in the developed societies, the less developed nations have been the lucky recipients of the transfer of public health knowledge and medical technology from the developed world. Much of this has taken place since World War II, although there is considerable unevenness in the pattern of mortality decline throughout the underdeveloped areas of the world. In general, it seems that those countries most heavily influenced by European culture have experienced the earliest and most pronounced declines in mortality. Among less developed nations, mortality tends to be lowest in Latin America, followed by Asia, with most African nations trailing behind in terms of their success at battling disease.

Prior to the Spanish invasion in the sixteenth century, the area now called Latin America was dotted with primitive civilizations in which medicine was practiced as a magic, religious, and healing art. In an interesting reconstruction of history, Ortiz de Montellano (1975) made chemical tests of herbs used by the Aztecs in Mexico and claimed by them to have particular healing powers. He found that a majority of those remedies he was able to replicate were, in fact, effective. Most of the remedies were for problems very similar to those for which Americans spend millions of dollars a year on over-the-counter drugs—coughs, sores, nausea, and diarrhea. Unfortunately, though, their remedies were not sufficient to combat the diseases that the Spaniards brought with them, and there is good evidence that contact with the Spaniards decimated the Mexican population. War and migration took a very small toll compared with the deadly effects of smallpox, bacterial infections, acute gastrointestinal disorders, measles, and typhus (Halberstein, 1973). Mortality remained very high throughout Latin America until the 1920s, when it started to decline at an accelerating rate.

Up to 1920, the life expectancy at birth was lower throughout Latin America than it had been in Europe in the Middle Ages. Since the 1920s, however, death rates have been declining so rapidly that by now, Mexico, as an example of the region as a whole, has reduced mortality to the level that the United States had achieved in 1945. In other words, it took half a century in Latin America for mortality to fall to a point that had taken at least five centuries in European countries. The slower decline represents the fact that in Europe and the United States mortality declines were closely associated with economic development, whereas in underdeveloped areas, including Latin America, this has been less true. Countries do not have to develop economically to improve their health levels if public health facilities can be emulated and medical care imported from European countries. As Arriaga noted: "Because public health programs in backward countries depend largely on other countries, we can expect that the later in historical time a massive public health program is applied in an underdeveloped country previously lacking public health programs, the higher the rate of mortality decline will be" (1970:33).

Included among those techniques that can be used to lower mortality even in the absence of economic development are eradication of disease-carrying insects and rodents, chlorination of drinking water, good sewage systems, vaccinations, dietary supplements, use of new drugs, and better personal hygiene (Arriaga, 1970). These factors have produced an especially rapid drop in death rates in Latin America as well as in many parts of Asia.

Among the high-fertility Asian countries most affected by declining mortality are Sri Lanka, the Philippines, Malaysia, and Thailand, where life expectancy at birth for females now exceeds 65 years. However, Asian countries to the west, including India and Pakistan, have life expectancies of about 10 years less, for an average of approximately 55 years. A major factor accounting for these differences in mortality levels is infant mortality. In India, a child has more than a 10 percent chance of dying in the first year of life, compared with a 4 percent chance in Malaysia.

In Africa, the area of the world least affected by industrialized societies, high death rates continue to prevail, although they are generally declining. Throughout most of Africa, life expectancies are generally below 50 years—a level not much higher than that common in preindustrial Europe dating back at least to the Middle Ages. It is a general rule that the higher the death rate, the lower the level of economic development and the smaller the amount of available information. Thus, we do not know as many details about the mortality of Africa as we would prefer, but we do know that high death rates there are generally a consequence of infectious diseases that kill not only infants but also significant proportions of people at all ages.

The decade of the 1950s was the period in which mortality declined most rapidly in the less developed nations. More recently, however, that improvement has slowed:

> This should not be surprising, because the pace of mortality decline during the 1950s was rather unique. It would be hard to maintain such a rapid rate of mortality change over a long period of time. The 1950s were the years of the application of low cost and massive health programs which produced a large decline in mortality, as the simpler causes of death were reduced. For continuation of rapid mortality decline, more expensive programs, including implementation of additional public health programs, would have been required (Arriaga, 1982:9).

The slower rate at which mortality is now declining, along with the continued prevalence of infectious disease in Africa, is a reminder to us all that these diseases still exist to threaten our lives if we relax our vigilance. Indeed, though bubonic plague may have disappeared from Europe centuries ago, it exists still in isolated corners of the United States. In 1982 two deaths were reported from the plague in rural New Mexico and one in rural Texas (San Diego Union, 1982c). Likewise, typhus, a fatal disease when untreated, also returned to the United States in 1976 after a 50-year absence, and 21 cases were confirmed between 1976 and 1981 (Daily Californian, 1981b). Typhus is harbored by body lice, and thus personal hygiene is a crucial factor in its control. Death control cannot be achieved and then taken for granted, for as Zinsser has so aptly put it:

> However secure and well-regulated civilized life may become, bacteria, protozoa, viruses, infected fleas, lice, ticks, mosquitoes, and bedbugs will always lurk in the shadows ready to pounce when neglect, poverty, famine, or war lets down the defenses. And even in normal times they prey on the weak, the very young, and the very old, living along with us, in mysterious obscurity waiting their opportunities (1935:13–14).

SUMMARY AND CONCLUSION

The control of mortality has vastly improved the human condition but has produced worldwide population growth in its wake. There are, however, wide variations between and within nations with respect to both the probabilities of dying and the causes of death. Differences in mortality by social class are among the most pervasive inequalities in modern society. For example, as prestige goes up, death rates go down. Likewise, as education and income levels go up, death rates go down. The social and economic disadvantages felt by minority groups often lead to lower life expectancies. This is certainly true in the United States, where nonwhite mortality is higher than white mortality by more than 10 percent. Marital status is also an important variable, with married people tending to live longer than unmarried people. Females have had a survival advantage over males at every age, and this mortality gap has widened over time.

In general, infancy—birth to 1 year—is the riskiest age until you are well into the retirement years. The vast majority of infant deaths in the United States are due to low birth weight. There is a very low risk of death in the United States during young adulthood, with accidental death the most likely cause. The risk of death accelerates at older ages and, among people over age 60, by far the most die from cardiovascular diseases. Historically, people of every age have had higher mortality in urban areas. However, since World War II urban mortality is as low or lower than rural mortality.

One point that I have made repeatedly is that mortality from communicable diseases is the major source of high mortality throughout the world. In those countries in which mortality is now low, the declines were brought about by improvements in the control of communicable diseases. Conversely, in those parts of the world where death rates remain fairly high, communicable diseases are a major reason. In general, improvements in health are more dependent on public health (preventive) measures than on medical (curative) measures.

We have now discussed two of the three demographic processes: fertility and mortality. In the next chapter we will complete our examination of the basics of population analysis with a discussion of migration.

MAIN POINTS

1. Lifespan refers to the oldest age to which members of a species can survive.

2. Longevity is the ability to resist death from year to year.

3. Although biological factors affect each individual's chance of survival, social factors are important overall determinants of longevity.

4. Most deaths can be broadly classified as a result of degeneration, communicable disease, or a product of the social and economic environment.

5. Degeneration is usually associated with chronic diseases, which account for about three fourths of all deaths in the United States. Heart disease is the most important of the chronic diseases as a cause of death.

6. The worldwide drop in mortality is due mostly to a reduction in deaths from communicable diseases.

7. Accidents are the most significant causes of death among teenagers and young adults.

8. Mortality is measured with the crude death rate, the age-specific death rate, and the expectation of life.

9. Rich people live longer than poor people on average (and they have more money, too).

10. Married people tend to live longer than unmarried people, and females generally live longer than males.

11. The single most vulnerable age in a person's life (at least until well beyond retirement age) is the first year. Reductions in infant mortality often account for a major part of the early mortality decline in a previously high-mortality society.

12. Living in a city used to verge on being a form of latent suicide, but now cities tend to have lower death rates than rural areas.

13. The role played by public health preventive measures in bringing down death rates is exemplified by the saying at the turn of this century that the amount of soap used could be taken as an index of the degree of civilization of a people.

14. Significant widespread improvements in the probability of survival date back only to the nineteenth century and have been especially impressive since the end of World War II. The drop in mortality, of course, precipitated the massive growth in the size of the human population.

SUGGESTED READINGS

1. Abdel Omran, 1977, "Epidemiologic transition in the United States," Population Bulletin 32(2).

   This report summarizes the reasons for and patterns of changing mortality in the world, tracing the changing causes of death at different ages over time.

2. David Phillips, 1983, "The impact of mass media violence on U.S. homicides," American Sociological Review 48(4):560–68.

   This is but one in a series of studies by Phillips analyzing the impact that the social world has on the risk of death.

3. Samuel Preston and P. Bhat, 1984, "New evidence on fertility and mortality trends in India," Population and Development Review 10(3):481–503.

   Anytime mortality changes (or does not change) in a nation as populous as India, it makes news. This article assesses recent trends in mortality and relates them to shifts in fertility to provide estimates of the rate of growth in India's population.

4. John Caldwell, 1986, "Routes to low mortality in poor countries," Population and Development Review 12(2):171–220.

Caldwell focuses specific attention on poor countries where mortality remains high by world standards and evaluates the prospects for future improvements in life expectancy.

5. Carl Mosk and S. Ryan Johansson, 1986, "Income and mortality: evidence from modern Japan," Population and Development Review 12(3):415–40.

Japan is an interesting case study for mortality decline. Although it is a non-Western, non-European nation that obviously was not influenced by the same cultural phenomena as was Europe, it has experienced many similarities in mortality decline. Note that the income referred to in the title refers to national income, that is, economic development rather than individual or household income.

CHAPTER 7
Migration

"The sole cause of man's unhappiness," quipped Pascal in the seventeenth century, "is that he does not know to stay quietly in his room." If this is so, unhappiness is enjoying unprecedented popularity as people are choosing to leave their rooms, so to speak, in record numbers. Sometimes they are fleeing from unhappiness; sometimes they are producing it. Since migration brings together people who have probably grown up with quite different views of the world, ways of approaching life, attitudes, and behavior patterns, it contributes to many of the tensions that confront the world, leading Kingsley Davis to comment that "so dubious are the advantages of immigration that one wonders why the governments of industrial nations favor it" (1974:105). Increasingly, they do not, and the popular literature reflects this ambivalence. Comments such as "Once, migration caused statues to be erected and poems to be written. . . . There is no monument, however, to the new immigrants" (Breslin, 1982; quoted by Sheppard, 1982:72); or "Emigration is an unnatural act — between consenting adults . . . an act of desperation, endured by immigrants and hosts alike without gratitude or sympathy, a placebo, not a cure" (Cornelison, 1980; quoted by Strouse, 1980:99) reflect the negative aura surrounding the influx of strangers into our midst.

Even if a country slams its doors to immigrants, however, will it work? More than 80 million people are being added to the world's population each year. What are they to do? As it becomes ever harder for a person to find a niche in the world economy, a would-be worker is often compelled to move. As an old Mexican saying goes, "Don't ask God to give it to you, ask Him to put you where it is." "Where it is" for many is the United States. "They arrive on foot, by rail, air and sea, coming from nearly every country. Some are smuggled in trucks, jammed together under terrible conditions" (Chapman, 1976). Though **illegal migrants** come from all over to the United States, about 85 percent come from Mexico. Today's pilgrims are from places such as Jalisco, Oaxaca, and Michoacán. They look to the border for relief from poverty (perhaps to increase their income by 800 percent—Louv, 1979), and some never return home.

Whether migration is legal or illegal, it can profoundly alter a community or an entire country within a short time. Although it is one of the three population processes (along with fertility and mortality), it is different in many respects beyond the obvious. To begin with, migration is very hard to measure, and consequently we know less about it than we do about mortality and fertility. That means, of course, that we understand even less about the complexities of why people migrate than we do about why they have babies (although that is a tough problem also) and why they die. Furthermore, despite the fact that there is much we do not know about who migrates and why, migration has been a subject of far more government control than has either fertility or mortality.

The United States is a nation of immigrants (both legal and illegal), and people have not stopped moving just because they made it in. We are a nation of people who are often "moving on" within the country in search of an almost mystical elsewhere that somehow promises more than we already have (Seidenbaum, 1976). As people move in and around, they contribute to population growth and change both in the short run and in the long run; and migration—when and where it occurs—is a population process of considerable importance.

I will begin this chapter with some comments on the definition and measurement of migration. Then I will move on to a discussion of some of the explanations that have been offered for why people move, followed by a review of some of the major consequences of migration (since the potentially dramatic results of migration are leading factors in the many attempts by governments to control the movement of people). That takes us to an examination of the actual patterns of migration: How many people move about within the United States, and where do they move? Who moves into and out of the United States, and what is happening elsewhere in the world?

DEFINING MIGRATION

Migration is defined as any permanent change in residence. It involves the "detachment from the organization of activities at one place and the movement of the total round of activities to another" (Goldscheider, 1971:64). Although the definition of migration seems fairly straightforward, the actual measurement of migration is confounded by its potential complexity. For openers, migration may or may not occur. Further, it may or may not recur, and if it does recur, it may be a return to the original point or another move to a new destination. In addition, to tangle the situation further, migration may involve more than a single individual—a family or even an entire village may migrate together. A ghost town, it has been suggested, does not necessarily signal the end of a community, only its relocation. People may move short or long distances, and they may or may not cross political boundaries (such as between states or between countries). In other words, the sheer act of migration is an amazingly difficult phenomenon to measure. Indeed, even the definition of migration is subject to some negotiation about what is meant by "permanent" and "residence." Those kinds of ambiguities obviously do not exist with births and deaths (except in very esoteric circumstances).

Migrants are usually categorized for research purposes according to whether they crossed political boundaries, and if so, what kind of boundary (county line, state line, international border), and also according to the points of origin and destination. The major distinction, however, is simply between **internal** and **international migration.**

Internal migration involves a permanent change of residence within national boundaries. The U.S. Census Bureau makes a further distinction by classifying as migrants only those people who moved between counties (obviously including people who moved between states) (Shryock et al., 1973). If you changed residence but stayed within the same county, then the Census Bureau would call you a **mover** (and maybe even a shaker), but not a **migrant.** In other words, all migrants are movers, but not all movers are migrants, at least by Census Bureau classifications. With reference to your area of origin (the place you left behind), you are an **out-migrant,** whereas you become an **in-migrant** with respect to your destination.

If you move from one country to another, you become an international migrant—an **emigrant** in terms of the area of origin and an **immigrant** in terms of the area of destination. The distinction between internal and international is important because the latter is usually more difficult to accomplish than the former, meaning that the motivation to move may have to be much stronger. In addition, the cultural impact of international migration is typically greater than that involved in internal migration. Crossing an international border is far more likely to involve a change of language, customs, and politics—in general, a change of life-style and world view— than is a move within a country.

MEASURING MIGRATION

Most of the information we have about migration into and within the United States is collected by asking people where they lived at a certain previous time. For example, the 1980 census on April 1, 1980 asked where people had lived on April 1, 1975 (similar questions have been asked on previous censuses). Thus, from those data we can tell whether a person is in the same house, county, or country as in 1975; however, we have no idea how many times, or to what places, that person may have migrated between those two dates. Also, the Current Population Survey each March asks a sample of Americans where they were living on March 1 the year before—again, we have the same problem of not knowing what happened in the interim. Much of the information that I discuss in this chapter, however, comes from these sources because they are the most detailed data available on migration.

The United States Immigration and Naturalization Service (INS) keeps track of legal immigrants but has essentially no record of people who emigrate. This stands in contrast to a few European nations which, as I mentioned in Chapter 1, maintain population registers and thus have a pretty accurate fix on the extent of both internal and international migration. Most countries, however, have little available information, and we either do not know what is happening or we have to rely on sample surveys or other indirect evidence (such as the number of foreign-born people counted in a census) to infer patterns of migration.

When data are available, migration is measured with rates that are similar to those we construct for fertility and mortality. The **crude net migration rate** is the net number of migrants in a year per 1,000 people in a population. We call it "net" because it is the difference between those who move in and those who move out. If those numbers are the same, then the net rate of migration is zero, even though in reality there may have been a lot of migration activity. The crude net migration rate (CNMR) thus is calculated as follows:

$$\text{CNMR} = \frac{\text{Total in-migrants} - \text{Total out-migrants}}{\text{Total midyear population}} \times 1,000$$

Since we rarely have complete sets of data on the number of in- and out-migrants, we often "back into" the migration rate by solving the demographic equation (see Chapter 2) for migration. This is known as the **intercensal component method** of measuring migration. The demographic equation, as you will recall, says that population growth between two dates is a result of the addition of births, the subtraction of deaths, and the net effect of migration (the number of in-migrants minus the number of out-migrants). If we know the amount of population growth between two dates, and we know also the number of births and deaths, then by subtraction we can estimate the amount of net migration. Let me give you an example. Based on the 1970 census of the United States, we can estimate that on July 1, 1970 there were 203,810,000 residents in the country. Between that date and July 1, 1980 there were 33,241,000 births and 19,296,500 deaths in the country. Thus, on July 1, 1980 we should have expected to find 217,754,500 residents, if no migration had occurred. However, the 1980 census suggests that there were, in fact, 226,505,000 people. That difference of 8,750,500 people we estimate to be the result of migration (note that a small fraction of the difference could also be due to differences in coverage error between the two censuses, as discussed in Chapter 1).

We can also calculate intercensal net migration rates for each age and sex group by combining census data with life-table probabilities of survival—a procedure called the **reverse survival method of migration estimation.** For example, in 1970 in the United States there were 14,551,000 males aged 20–29. Life-table values (see the Appendix) suggest that 98.04 percent of those men (or 14,266,000) should still have been alive at ages 30–39 in 1980. Yet, the 1980 census counted 15,536,000 men in that age group, 985,000 more than expected. We assume, then, that those "extra" people were migrants.

There are, by the way, no universally agreed-upon measures of migration that summarize the overall levels in the same way that the total fertility rate summarizes fertility and life expectancy captures a population's experience with mortality. However, one way of measuring the contribution that migration makes to population growth is to calculate the ratio of migration to natural increase. Thus, the **migration ratio** is:

$$\frac{\text{Net migration}}{\text{Births} - \text{Deaths}} \times 1,000$$

For example, again using the data for the United States from 1970 to 1980, we can calculate the migration ratio as (8,750,500 net migrants) divided by (33,241,000 births minus 19,296,500 deaths) times 1,000 equals 627 migrants added to the American population during the decade of the 1970s for each 1,000 people added through natural increase. Looked at another way, migrants accounted for 38 percent of the total population growth in the United States during that period of time.

Now, having worn you out trying to measure the nearly unmeasurable, let us move on to yet another difficult (but frequently more interesting) task—explaining why people migrate.

CAUSES AND CONSEQUENCES OF MIGRATION

General Explanations of Why People Move

Explaining migration requires an explanation of why some people do *not* move just as much as why some (indeed, most) do. Unfortunately, though, most analyses of why people move pay very little attention to why people do not move. The principal mode for developing explanations or theories has been to observe patterns of migration and then try to explain, after the fact, why people did move in given numbers and in a particular direction. Over time the most frequently heard explanation for migration has been the so-called **push-pull theory**, which says that some people move because they are pushed out of their former location, whereas others move because they have been pulled or attracted to someplace else. This idea was first put forward by Ravenstein (1889), who analyzed migration in England using data from the 1881 census of England and Wales. He concluded that pull factors were more important than push factors: "Bad or oppressive laws, heavy taxation, an unattractive climate, uncongenial social surrounding, and even compulsion (slave trade, transportation), all have produced and are still producing currents of migration, but none of these currents can compare in volume with that which arises from the desire inherent in most men to 'better' themselves in material respects." Thus, Ravenstein is saying that it is the desire to get ahead more than the desire to escape an unpleasant situation that is most responsible for the migration of people, at least in late nineteenth-century England. This theme should sound familiar to you. Is it not the same point made by Davis (1963) in discussing personal motivation for having small families (see Chapter 5)? Remember, Davis argued that it is the pursuit of pleasure or the fear of social slippage, not the desire to escape from poverty, that motivates people to limit their fertility.

In everyday language, we could label the factors that might push a person to migrate as stress or strain. However, it is probably rare for people to respond to stress by voluntarily migrating unless they feel that there is some reasonably attractive alternative, which we could call a pull factor. The social science model conjures up an image of the decision maker computing a calculated cost–benefit analysis of the situation. The potential migrant weighs the push and pull factors and moves if the benefits of doing so exceed the costs (Kosinski and Prothero, 1975; Stone, 1975). For example, if you lost your job, it could benefit you to move if there are no other jobs available where you live now, unemployment compensation and welfare benefits have expired, and there is a possibility of a job at another location. Or, to be more sanguine about your employability, the process may start, for example, when you are offered an excellent executive spot in a large firm in another city. Will the added income and prestige exceed the costs of uprooting the family and leaving the familiar house, community, and friends behind? In truth, whether or not you migrate will likely depend on a more complicated set of circumstances than this simple example might suggest. The decision to move usually occurs over a fairly long period of time, proceeding from a *desire* to move, to the *expectation* of moving, to the actual *fact* of migrating (Rossi, 1955). In Rossi's longitudinal sample of families in the 1950s, half of those interviewed expressed a desire to move, but only about 20 percent of them actually did so. Sell and DeJong (1983) have produced a set of longitudinal data for the 1970s that reinforce Rossi's findings—migration rates reflect a whole spectrum of attitudes, ranging from people who are "entrenched nonmovers" (who have no desire to move and no expectation of moving and who do not migrate) to "consistent decision-maker movers" (who desire to, expect to, and do migrate).

Between the desire to move and the actual decision to do so there also may be **intervening obstacles** (Lee, 1966). The distance of the expected destination, the cost of getting there, poor health, and other such factors may inhibit migration. These obstacles are hard to predict on any wide scale, however, and so we tend to ignore them and concentrate our attention on explaining the desire to move. Economic variables dominate most explanations of why people migrate. Analysis of data from the University of Michigan's Panel Study of Income Dynamics underscores the importance of job-related factors in influencing migration decisions. People who are unemployed and those who are dissatisfied with their present jobs are more likely than others to say they are planning a move, and to actually follow through with those plans (DaVanzo, 1976).

Migration associated with career advancement as happens so often in the military and in academics, illustrates a recent migration hypothesis appearing in the sociological literature—that migration decisions "arise from a system of strategies adopted by the individual in the course of passing through the life cycle" (Stone, 1975:97). If it is assumed that individuals spend much of their lifetimes pursuing various goals, then migration may be seen as a possible means—an **implementing strategy**—whereby a goal (such as more education, a better job, a nicer house, a more pleasant environment, and so on) might be attained. Although this is not a startling new hypothesis (it is little more than a modern restatement of Ravenstein's nineteenth-century conclusions), it is nonetheless a very reasonable one. Indeed, Lee (1966) has observed that two of the more enduring generalizations that can be made about migration are:

1. Migration is selective (that is, not everyone migrates, only a selected portion of the population).

2. The heightened propensity to migrate at certain stages of the life cycle is important in the selection of migrants.

One particular stage of life disproportionately associated with migration is that of reaching maturity. This is the age at which the demand or desire for obtaining more education tends to peak, along with the process of finding a job or a career, and getting married.

Migration by Age   Recent data for the United States illustrate this pattern very well. As you can see in Figure 7.1, young adults were much more mobile than people of other ages, and although these data are for the United States for 1980–85, the same pattern has existed in the United States in the past and holds true in other countries as well (Long and Boertlein, 1976).

The young adult ages, 20–34, are clearly those at which migration predominates. More than two thirds of all Americans who were 20–34 years old in 1985 had migrated across a county line since 1980. After the mid-thirties the propensity to migrate slackens off considerably. The fairly high rates for young children of course reflect the fact that families (especially those with preschool children), not just individuals, are often involved in the migration process. At the very oldest ages, the percentages of people moving reflect the fact that at least some Americans change location when they retire.

Using data from the Current Population Surveys, Long (1973) has estimated that, on the basis of data from 1966–71, the specific age at which an American is

Figure 7.1   Young Adults Are Most Likely to Be Migrants (United States, 1980–1985)

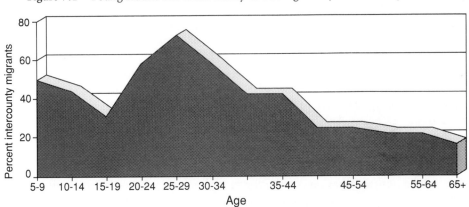

During the 1980–85 period (as during previous periods of American history), young adults were more likely to migrate than were people of any other age. For example, more than two thirds of persons aged 25–29 moved at least once during the 5-year period. *Source:* U.S. Bureau of the Census, "Geographical Mobility: 1985," Current Population Reports, Series P-20, No. 420, Table F.

most likely to migrate across county lines is 22, which not coincidentally corresponds with college graduation for many. A person is least likely to migrate at ages 60–61, a few years before retirement.

Migration by Marital Status   Migration differentials by marriage also help illustrate the relationship of migration to life-cycle stages, since there is a societal expectation that people will set up a new household on getting married (although migration to that new household may now very well precede the formal marriage). Since 1972 the Census Bureau has not published data on the mobility of Americans by recency of marriage, but data prior to that year show clearly that marriage and migration are closely related. For example, in the United States 90 percent of women aged 18–24 and marrying for the first time between March 1970 and March 1971 made a move during that year; 35 percent of them moved at least as far as between counties. This was much higher than the mobility of all women of that same age. Among women aged 25–34, 34 percent of the brides moved at least as far as between counties, compared with only 10 percent of all women of that age (U.S. Bureau of the Census, 1972).

Once married, the incidence of migration also varies according to the number and ages of children. Among young couples, the smaller the family and the younger the children, the greater the probability of migration. For example, among couples with the householder aged 25–34 in 1985, 32 percent of those with no children had migrated from one county to another between 1980 and 1985, dropping to 28 percent for couples with one child, and down to 27 percent for those with three or more children. So, the larger the family, the greater the barrier to migration. Furthermore, the likelihood of migration was greater if the oldest child was under 6 years old; once a child is old enough to start school, the temptation to move seems to go down (U.S. Bureau of the Census, 1987e). Migration, in its turn, may temporarily disrupt family-building activity. Data from Thailand, for example, reveal that the period just before migration, as people plan for their move, is a time of lower than expected fertility. It may be followed, however, by a "catch-up" time after migration is completed (Goldstein and Goldstein, 1981).

At older ages, the relationship between family cycle and migration changes. Among couples in which the householder was aged 45–54 in 1985, those with children under age 18 were just as likely to migrate as those with no children (U.S. Bureau of the Census, 1987e). Furthermore, the largest families were the most likely to move. This probably reflects at least three different phenomena: (1) as families grow larger, the need or desire for a larger house increases; (2) as families grow larger, the need to move to a better-paying job may increase; and (3) those persons with the highest incomes tend to be the most frequent movers (as we shall see). In general, we can observe that in the United States especially, the levels of migration go up as occupational levels rise, as income levels go up, and as educational attainment increases. Since the attainment of a particular educational level often sets up a whole chain of events leading to a certain occupation and income, it is a particularly crucial aspect of the life cycle, especially for the broad middle class of American society.

⌄ **Migration by Educational Attainment**   You can see in Figure 7.2 that there is a clear pattern for migration rates to go up as educational attainment goes up—a person (whether male or female) in the United States with a college degree had nearly three times the chance of migrating across county lines between 1980 and 1985 as a person with less than a high school education.

Since the differences between migration rates for males and females are not very great, the conclusion might be drawn that females are forced to tag along when their husbands (of presumably similar educational backgrounds) migrate. As more married women enter the labor force, we might well ask whether that life-cycle decision will affect a family's likelihood of migration in the same way and to the same degree that a man's occupation does. The answer seems to be maybe. Studies by DaVanzo (1976) and Duncan and Perrucci (1976) indicate that among wives who work, neither their occupational prestige nor their relative contribution to total family income affects the probability that a family will move. Nonetheless, Duncan and Perrucci found that the likelihood of family migration is closely related to the prestige of the husband's occupation—as prestige increases, so does geographic mobility. Furthermore, Lichter (1982), having analyzed data from the National Longitudinal Survey of Mature Women, concluded that a wife's job outside the home may indeed lower the chance of a family moving. Apparently, then, we must await more definitive studies before deciding for sure what impact there is on migration if both spouses are in the labor force.

A Conceptual Model

Most of the explanations for migration that I have discussed thus far are related to characteristics of individuals (such as age, sex, and education). But Gardner (1981) reminds us that the sociocultural environment in which a person lives is also

Figure 7.2 The Better Educated You Are, the More Likely You Are to Move (United States, 1985)

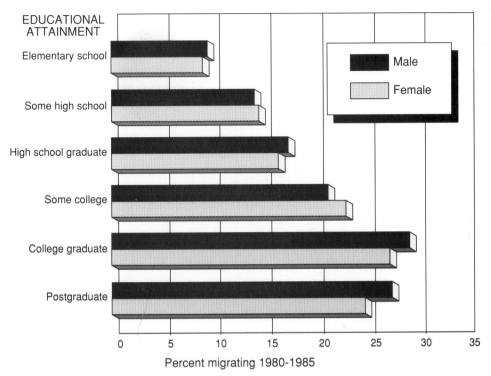

Between 1980 and 1985 college graduates were several times more likely to migrate across county lines than were people with no high school diploma. Data are for people aged 18 or older. *Source:* U.S. Bureau of the Census, 1987, "Geographical Mobility: 1985," Current Population Reports, Series P-20, No. 420, Table 17.

an important influence on the decision to move. One of the more coherent efforts to pull together all of the relevant variables—individual and societal—that affect migration is the conceptual model devised by Gordon De Jong and James Fawcett (1981), shown in Figure 7.3.

Beginning at the left of Figure 7.3, you can see that individual and household demographic characteristics are viewed as combining with societal and cultural norms about migration to shape the values that people hold with respect to migration. Such values or goals represent clusters of motivations to move, including the desires for wealth, status, comfort (better living or working conditions), stimulation (including entertainment and recreation), autonomy (personal freedom), affiliation (joining family or friends), and morality (especially religious beliefs). At the same time, personal traits (such as being a risk-taking person) combine with the opportunity structure for migration to affect one's value system with respect to migration. All of these personal and social environmental factors combine to affect a person's expectation of actually achieving the goals they have in mind that might be facilitated by migration. The amount of information a person has about the comparative

Figure 7.3   A Conceptual Model of Migration Decision Making

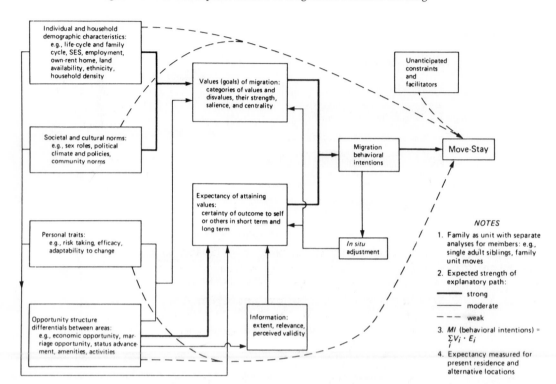

Source: G. De Jong and J. Fawcett, 1981, "Motivations for migration: an assessment and a value-expectancy research model," in G. De Jong and R. Gardner (eds.), Migration Decision Making (New York: Pergamon Press), Figure 2.2.

advantages of moving further contributes to the expectation of attaining migration values or goals. Goals and expectations jointly influence the intentions that a person has toward migration.

Given the intention to move, a person may discover that, by making adjustments in his or her current situation, personal goals can be achieved without having to move. "Such adjustments might include a change in occupation, alterations to the physical structure of the house, a change in daily and friendship patterns, or lifestyle changes" (De Jong and Fawcett, 1981:56). Finally, the intention to move (or to stay) leads ultimately to the act of moving (or staying) itself, although unanticipated events may affect that decision.

Continued research will have to determine whether all of the arrows in this model are heading in exactly the right direction, and whether the strength of influence among variables is similar to those proposed in Figure 7.3. However, despite its tentativeness, the model nicely brings together the major elements that are important in trying to explain why some people migrate and others do not. For example, it helps us to get a handle on the difference between internal and international migrants.

Differences Between Internal and International Migrants

Internal migration typically is "free" in the sense that people are choosing to migrate or not, often basing that decision on economic factors, as I have discussed. This is not to say that, within a country, people are never forced to move. Witness the migration of 250,000 Egyptians who were forced to relocate so that the Aswan Dam could be built, or the massive transmigration that Indonesia periodically attempts—moving people from the crowded island of Java to other, less populous islands. But such internal migration, though forced, is usually planned. People's needs are anticipated in advance and, presumably, the migration is expected to improve the lives of the people involved.

Migration across international boundaries is sometimes free, but it usually means that a person has met fairly stringent entrance requirements, is entering illegally, or is being granted refugee status, fleeing from a political, social, or military conflict. Each of these instances is apt to be more stressful than internal migration, and on top of that is heaped the burden of accommodating to a new culture and often a new language, being dominated perhaps by a different religion, being provided different types and levels of government services, and adjusting to different sets of social expectations and obligations.

Referring back to Figure 7.3, we can make the general statement that internal migration is more strongly influenced by individual characteristics of people, whereas international migrants are more apt to be influenced by the social and political climate and by the opportunity structure (especially the lack of barriers to migration). The kinds of migration goals that internal migrants have are also likely to differ somewhat from those of international migrants. In the former case, the desire for wealth, status, comfort, and stimulation may dominate, whereas among international migrants, the desire for autonomy, affiliation, and morality may be predominant.

Recognizing now that there are numerous and complex reasons for making the decision to move, we also need to bear in mind that when people migrate the impact is felt deeply at both the individual and the societal levels.

Individual Consequences of Migration

The process of migration has both individual and group consequences. For the individual, migration may result in stress, in the disorganization of daily life, or even in various forms of mental illness. The problems associated with, for example, a rural migrant's transition to a new setting in the United States have been well summarized by Rieger and Beegle:

> Normal relationships in the old community have been severed. The migrant often sustains a period of unemployment, engendering financial insecurity, if not dependency.

He may find people to be different from those with whom he was familiar, and he may be exposed to conditions and situations largely unprecedented in his past experiences. He is typically at some educational disadvantage in competing in the job market. Altogether, these conditions can produce anxiety, and even anomia, until such time as a satisfactory level of stability and security may be achieved (1974:43).

One of the ways in which migrants cope with a new environment is to seek out others who share their cultural and geographic backgrounds. This is often aided or even forced by the existence of enclaves or ghettos of recent and former migrants from the same or similar donor areas. In fact, the development of an enclave may facilitate migration, since a potential migrant need not be too fearful of the unknown. The host area has guides to the new environment in former migrants who have made the adaptation and stand ready to aid in the social adjustment and integration of new migrants. In some instances, such as the Mexican-American areas of Detroit, one area may serve both international and internal rural-to-urban migrants. A neighborhood to the southwest of downtown Detroit is the Mexican-American area (formerly a Lithuanian area), identifiable from the census data by the high proportion of Spanish-speaking people and identifiable in person by Mexican restaurants, a tortilla factory, a curio shop, and a Catholic church that is predominantly Spanish-speaking. This area has provided a settling-out point for Mexican-American migrant farm workers since 1920, and at the same time it has been a point of attraction for Mexican nationals migrating into the United States. Although it is referred to locally as a *barrio*, it is not a tightly knit area from which no escape is possible. Indeed, only a fraction of the Spanish-speaking population of Detroit now lives there, but most have lived there (or had parents or spouses live there) at some time (Weeks and Spielberg, 1979).

Although finding people of similar background may ease the burden of coping for a new migrant, there is some evidence to suggest that the long-run social consequences of "flocking together" (especially among relatives) will be a retardation of the migrant's adjustment to and assimilation into the new setting. A **longitudinal study** in Michigan by Rieger and Beegle (1974) indicated that new migrants may become integrated more quickly, at least into small communities, if there are no relatives present. In another longitudinal study in Arkansas, Hendrix (1976) found that while migration weakened kinship ties in the place of origin, kinship ties in the place of destination did not contribute to the integration of rural-to-urban migrants—a finding similar to that of Rieger and Beegle. Hendrix did find, however, that integration into a new area was promoted by strong acquaintance (not kinship) ties.

Social Consequences of Migration

Although the consequences of migration for the individual are of considerable interest (especially to the one uprooted), a more pervasive aspect of the social consequences of migration is the impact on the demographic composition and social structure of both the donor and host areas. The demographic composition is influenced by the selective nature of migration, particularly the selectivity by age. The

donor area typically loses people from its young adult population, those people then being added to the **host area.** Further, since it is at those ages that the bulk of reproduction occurs, the host area has its level of natural increase augmented at the expense of the donor area. This natural-increase effect of migration is further enhanced by the relatively low probability of death of young adults compared with the probability in the older portion of a population.

The selective nature of migration, when combined with its high volume, such as in the United States, helps to alter the patterns of social relationships and social organization. The extended kinship relations are weakened, although not destroyed, and local economic, political, and educational institutions have to adjust to shifts in the number of people serviced by each.

We can glimpse some of those changes by reviewing a study by Morrison (1974), in which he compared the migration into San Jose, California with the migration out of St. Louis, Missouri. San Jose is a city whose economy is expanding rapidly and whose population is rapidly increasing, largely as a result of migration. There are high levels of both in- and out-migration, causing a high rate of turnover. Morrison has suggested that the high rate of turnover may well be beneficial to future economic growth in the region, because a highly mobile population can quickly accommodate change. Shifts in local demand for different types of jobs can be met easily because of the turnover of people in the labor market.

The city of St. Louis, in contrast to San Jose, has been losing population since 1970, especially in the central city. This decline has been due primarily to a massive outward migration—largely a flight to the suburbs by whites and nonwhites alike. A result of this out-migration has been the now-familiar story of a relative accumulation of disadvantaged people in the city. Those who cannot leave are disproportionately racial and ethnic minority group members, poor people, the elderly, the unemployed, and welfare candidates. Part of the difference between San Jose and St. Louis is the extent of the city limits—St. Louis is a much older city with more circumscribed political boundaries than San Jose. But the general picture is widely repeated not only in the United States but in other areas of the world as well. In-migration both is stimulated by economic growth and contributes to that growth, as the influx of young adults brings a demand for a vast array of goods and services—jobs, food and shelter, and schools for children. On the other hand, out-migration is frequently associated with an economy that cannot handle its population size. Since the socially ambitious and educationally and occupationally talented people are among the most likely to leave such an area, their departure contributes to the potential for further economic stagnation or decline.

The dual processes of in-migration of one racial or ethnic group either preceded or succeeded by the out-migration of another racial or ethnic group illustrate one of the major social consequences of migration—its impact on **social stratification.** In-migrants tend to be improving their **socioeconomic status** by migrating in, just as out-migrants are improving their position by moving out.

In summary, migration has the greatest short-run impact on society of any of the three demographic processes. It is a selective process that always requires changes and adjustments on the part of the individual migrant. More important, when migration occurs with any appreciable volume, it may have a significant impact on the social, cultural, and economic structure of both donor and host regions. Because

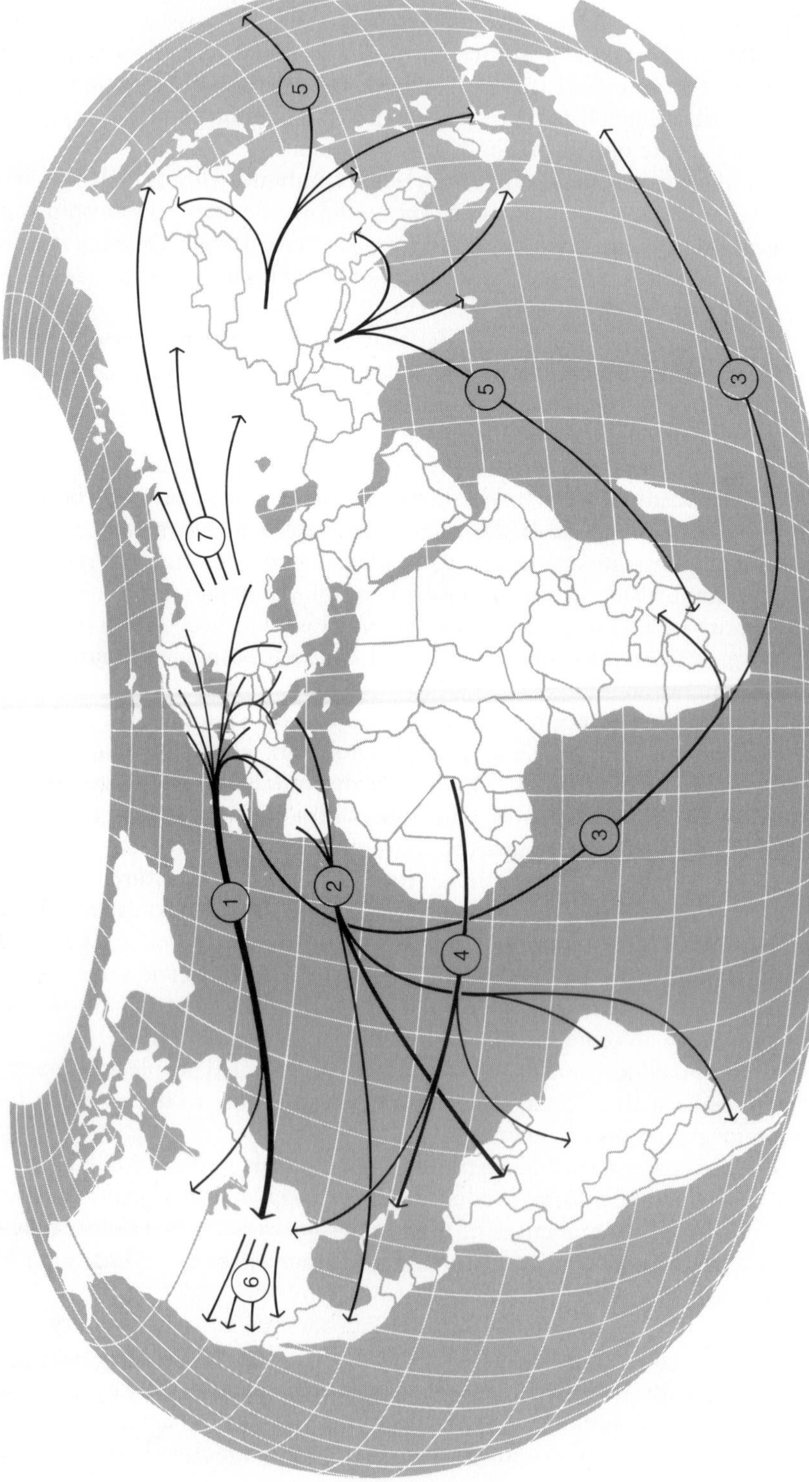

Figure 7.4 Main Currents of Intercontinental Migration (1500–1950)

of their potential impact, patterns of migration are harbingers of social change in a society.

PATTERNS OF MIGRATION ‒

Among the many things about migration that we do not know for certain is how many people move each year in the world. But we do know that migration occurs within every nation and between virtually all nations, even in tightly controlled societies such as the USSR and China. Humans seem almost by nature to eschew the completely sedentary life, and no nation exemplifies this characteristic better than the United States.

Migration Within the United States

The United States is a nation on the move, and it always has been. The Census Bureau has estimated that 90 million Americans (42 percent of the population) aged 5 and older in 1985 were living in a different house than in 1980. Many of the 91 million Americans had undoubtedly moved more than once during that 5-year period, so that represents a probable minimum of migration. Fewer than 4 million of those people were living abroad in 1980, so most of the migration was clearly internal. Almost half the migrants were living in the same metropolitan area in 1985 as they had been in 1980, but more than 18 million Americans had migrated to a different state (U.S. Bureau of the Census, 1987e).

Americans, though certainly very mobile, are not totally unique in that respect. In an international comparison of migration data, Long and Boertlein (1976) found that Australians actually have slightly higher rates of migration, and Canadians are only slightly behind Americans. On the other hand, residents in those three countries are much more likely to migrate than are the British or Japanese. Long and Boertlein

---

Major currents of intercontinental migration have been (1) from all parts of Europe to North America; (2) from Latin countries of Europe to Middle and South America; (3) from Great Britain to Africa and Australia; (4) from Africa to America; (5) from China and India abroad (partly intercontinental, partly intracontinental). Important currents of internal migration have been (6) the westward movement in the United States and (7) the eastward movement in Russia. Prior to the end of World War II, the main currents of migration were out of the more densely settled regions in Europe and Asia and into North and South America and Oceania. Major shifts since 1950 include a net flow of people back into Europe and a net flow out of many Latin American countries. *Source:* W. S. and E. S. Woytinsky, 1953, World Population Production (New York: The Twentieth Century Fund), p. 68. © 1953 by The Twentieth Century Fund, New York. Reprinted with permission.

argue that the United States, Australia, and Canada have high rates of geographic mobility because all three are nations of immigrants. Migration is thus not a new or innovative idea, but rather something learned "simply through knowledge of their ancestors" (Long and Boertlein, 1976:22). As a result, we are more likely to turn to migration as a life strategy than are people in countries where migration is less common.

Another interesting question discussed by Long and Boertlein is whether the large number of Americans who annually move is resulting in a deterioration of the quality of life. Is it true that we are "breeding a new race of nomads" (Toffler, 1970:75); that we have become "a nation of strangers" (Packard, 1972); that as a result of migration we are becoming alienated, lonely people (Keyes, 1973; Gordon, 1975)? The answer, say Long and Boertlein (1976), is no. They note that rates of **residential mobility** and migration have remained quite steady since the mid-1940s, and they suggest that the increased ease of transportation and communication may simply have raised our consciousness of the volume of migration (and, I might add, perhaps contributed to other problems, such as loneliness, as well).

Intimately bound up with the reasons for moving and the number of people who migrate is the question of where people go. Because migration is so often associated with life-cycle stages and represents attempts to improve the quality of life, migrants naturally tend to go where they perceive opportunities to be greatest. Economic motives dictate that migrants go where business is good and leave behind those places where it is not so good (Lee, 1966).

The history of international migration in the world suggests that opportunity has often been defined in terms of open territory, where land promised an economic reward (see Figure 7.4). More recently, opportunity has also meant city jobs and so there has been a prevalence of migration from **rural** (low income) to **urban** (higher income) areas (as I will discuss further in Chapter 12). Within the United States, there were several decades when migration was in the direction of the industrializing centers in the northeastern and north central states and to the rich farmland and industry in the western states. The strongest of these movements was the one westward (Shryock, 1964). At first this meant that the mountain valley areas west of the Atlantic seacoast were migration destinations; then the plains states were settled; and, especially since the end of World War II, the Pacific Coast states have been popular destinations.

Until about 1950 migrants had also been heading out of the southern states and into the northeastern and north central states. This generally represented rural-to-urban migration out of the economically depressed South into the industrialized cities of the North. In the 1950s this pattern of net out-migration from the South reversed itself (U.S. Bureau of the Census, 1975a), and the northeastern and north central states found themselves increasingly to be migration origins rather than destinations, as you can see in Figure 7.5.

Since the late 1960s, there have been two more significant reversals in the pattern of where Americans migrate. First, the strong westward movement has yielded to a strong southern movement (see Figure 7.6); while the West has become increasingly crowded, the South has become increasingly receptive to new business and new migrants. This is all part of the whole movement of Americans to the "Sun Belt," from southern California to Florida.

Figure 7.5   In the 1950s the Population Flow in the United States Was West and South

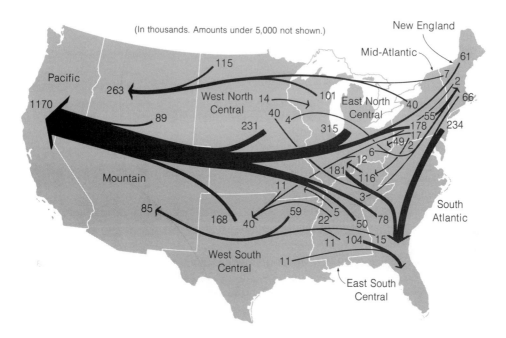

Between 1950 and 1960 there was an upsurge in migration into the South from the northern and midwestern states. Nonetheless, the strongest flow was still westward. By the 1970s, however, the South had taken the lead. *Sources:* Hope T. Eldridge and Yun Kim, 1968, The Estimation of Intercensal Migration from Birth-Residence Statistics: A Study of Data for the United States, 1950 and 1960 (Philadelphia: University of Pennsylvania, Population Studies Center), Analytical and Technical Reports, No. 7, February, Figure 7, p. 62; U.S. Bureau of the Census, 1961, U.S. Census of Population: 1960, Subject Reports, Lifetime and Recent Migration, Table 2.

Sun Belt Migration   The **Sun Belt** has a variety of definitions. Jeanne Biggar (1979; 1980) has included in her definition all those states along the United States border "from Virginia south and west through California, plus Oklahoma, Arkansas, and Missouri . . ." (1980:178). However, the flow of migrants actually has been concentrated in just four of the Sun Belt states: California, Arizona, Texas, and Florida. You might almost visualize the Mississippi River as the continental divide for migrants; migrants east of the Mississippi generally go to Florida, whereas those west of the Mississippi wind up in California, Arizona, or Texas. In absolute numbers, the states that gained the most people between the 1970 and 1980 censuses were California (3.7 million additional people), Texas (3.0 million), Florida (3.0 million), Arizona (nearly 1 million), and Georgia (875,000), while the states of New York and Rhode Island both lost population during that intercensal period.

If we look at smaller geographic units—counties—essentially the same pattern emerges. Harris County, Texas (which includes Houston) led the pack in the 1970–

Figure 7.6   In the 1970s and 1980s, the U.S. Population Was Heading South

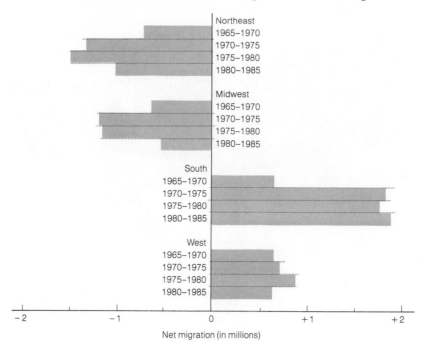

Net migration (in millions)

Between 1965 and 1970 the northeastern and midwestern states were losing migrants in numbers rather evenly distributed between the South and the West. But between 1970 and 1985 the volume of net migration out of the northern states picked up, as Americans headed in record numbers to the South. *Sources:* U.S. Bureau of the Census, 1987, "Geographical Mobility: 1985," Current Population Reports, Series P-20, No. 420, Table G.

80 period, adding 668,000 people, followed closely by Maricopa County, Arizona (Phoenix), Orange County, California (Anaheim), San Diego County, California, and Los Angeles, California. In fact, of the 20 counties that added the most people in the 1970s, 6 are in California, 5 are in Florida, 3 are in Texas, 2 are in Arizona, and 2 are in Nevada.

The move to the Sun Belt has partly been a result of the fact that many industries have moved south (including, I might add, the very bricks from older buildings, which are increasingly in demand in new areas) (San Diego Union, 1982b). Of course, it is easy to get into a chicken-and-egg situation. Migration of labor to the south encouraged industrial migration, which further encourages migration. "But it is not just the jobs but also the general climate, the cost of living, and the lifestyle which have brought people to the Sun Belt. Climate takes on increasing importance as people have more time and money to enjoy leisure activities. The Sun Belt offers both more 'sun' and more 'fun.' Outdoor living, informal entertaining, and golf the year-round—all afford the new lifestyles which Americans have adopted" (Biggar, 1979:26). Changing lifestyles, in conjunction with changing economic opportunities, help to account for another significant pattern of internal migration in the United States—the rural renaissance.

⌐The Rural Renaissance   In a major reversal of historical patterns, the population of nonmetropolitan areas of the United States grew by 15 percent between 1970 and 1980, compared with a 10 percent increase for metropolitan areas. In the 1950s only one tenth of the nonmetropolitan counties in the United States were growing as a result of net in-migration, whereas between 1970 and 1975 two thirds gained by migration (Morrison and Wheeler, 1976). Furthermore, these increases were not just the result of suburbanization and urban sprawl (although that was part of the explanation), since there was growth in remote areas as well. This renaissance of rural America has come at the expense of large metropolitan areas, especially (but not limited to) cities in the northeastern and north central states. Included among places that lost population between the 1970 and 1980 censuses are New York City, Philadelphia, Cleveland, Washington, D.C., Chicago, St. Louis, and Pittsburgh.

Why has this reversal taken place? Americans have long valued rural, pastoral life (Fischer, 1976), even if it means giving up an otherwise rapid advance in income (Heaton et al., 1979; Williams and Sofranko, 1979), although typically they have also preferred to be within easy range of a large metropolitan area (Fuguitt and Zuiches, 1975). Automobiles and superhighways have, of course, enhanced that possibility. Americans who leave the cities are not headed for small towns, by and large. Rather, they are typically moving to the open countryside and living in unincorporated areas (Long and DeAre, 1982). But that open land is not usually intended for use as a farm. Indeed, the number of farmers continued to decline in the 1970s. Most of the rural boom is strictly residential in nature (Kloppenburg, 1983). Several social and economic changes have aided the resurrection of rural life, including earlier retirement and more generous pensions that enable older people to move closer to places such as recreational facilities. Rural areas have also become more attractive as transportation and communication have improved and as municipal services have spread (Long and DeAre, 1982). But, perhaps even more importantly, there are "growth industries" springing up in rural areas that provide jobs that never before existed in the highly valued rural sector (Morrison and Wheeler, 1976; Williams, 1981; Long, 1983). The three basic specific industries they mention are: (1) industry, based on the growing number of retirees with more money than ever before moving to rural areas and needing services; (2) the recreation industry; and (3) energy—especially coal mining. In all likelihood, many jobs have followed people into the rural areas, rather than the other way around. Williams and Sofranko (1981) found, for example, that in a survey of 501 households who had moved from metropolitan to nonmetropolitan areas, improving the quality of life was the single reason most often given for the move. It may be that as the growth of income slowed down in the 1970s, a substantial fraction of Americans chose migration to the countryside as a way to upgrade their lives.

The repopulation of rural areas had already begun to slow down by the mid-1980s, reflecting the natural life cycle of most trends and fashions. As people become disenchanted with the new area, return migration occurs, since most migrants are still influenced by the prospect of a better life. Nowhere is this better illustrated than in the case of migration into the United States.

⇢ Migration Into the United States

Prior to World War I, there were few restrictions on migration into the United States, so the number of immigrants was determined more by the desire of people to move than anything else. Particularly important as a stimulus to migration, of course, was the drop in the death rate in Europe during the nineteenth century, which launched a long period of population growth, with its attendant pressure on Europe's economic resources. Economic opportunities in America looked awfully attractive to young Europeans who were competing with increasing numbers of young people for jobs. Voluntary migration from Europe to the temperate zones of the world—especially to the United States—represents one of the significant movements of people across international boundaries in history. The social, cultural, economic, and demographic impacts of this migration have been truly enormous (Davis, 1974).

Immigration to the United States reached its peak in the first decade of this century, when nearly 9 million entered the country, accounting for more than one in ten of all Americans at that time (see Table 7.1). "They came thinking the streets were paved with gold, but found that the streets weren't paved at all and that they were expected to do the paving" (Leroux, 1984:E1). As I will discuss in Chapter 15, the enormity of that migration led to restrictive immigration laws and, only 30 years later, during the Great Depression of the 1930s, the migration rate hit its lowest point. However, waves of refugees into the country following World War II, the Cuban Revolution, and the war in Vietnam, coupled with the liberalization of immigration laws in the 1960s, have led to a steady rise in the number of immigrants and in the immigration rates from the 1940s to the 1980s.

As the number of immigrants has fluctuated, so have the places from which they have come. Through the 1950s, Europeans had dominated migration statistics into the United States. In fact, Germany had sent more legal migrants (nearly 7 million) to the United States by the 1980s than any other single country (U.S. Immigration and Naturalization Service, 1977). Between 1820 and 1960, 82 percent of all legal immigrants had come from Europe, and as recently as the decade 1951–60, 60 percent were still from Europe. But since the 1970s, the number of European immigrants has declined while the number of Latin American and Asian immigrants has increased markedly. Thus, in 1986, 10 percent of legal immigrants were from Europe, whereas 40 percent were from Latin America (led by Mexico) and 45 percent were from Asia (led by the Philippines).

⇢**Migration from Mexico**   Although only one person is recorded as having migrated from Mexico into the United States in 1820, the number of Mexican immigrants has increased so tremendously since then that the legal and illegal immigrants from Mexico probably account for one in four of all foreigners now moving into the United States. Between 1820 and 1986 more than 2.6 million Mexicans migrated legally into the United States, with more than half of those people arriving since 1960. That increase coincided, of course, with the beginnings of the current rapid rate of population increase in Mexico. As Mexico's population has grown, so has the difficulty of finding adequate employment for the burgeoning number of young

Table 7.1   Immigration to the United States Peaked Early in This Century

Period	Thousands of Immigrants	Annual Migration Rate per 1,000 Population[a]
1820–30	152	1.2
1831–40	599	3.9
1841–50	1,713	8.4
1851–60	2,598	9.3
1861–70	2,315	6.4
1871–80	2,812	6.2
1881–90	5,247	9.2
1891–1900	3,688	5.3
1901–10	8,795	10.4
1911–20	5,736	5.7
1921–30	4,107	3.5
1931–40	528	0.4
1941–50	1,035	0.7
1951–60	2,515	1.5
1961–70	3,322	1.7
1971–80	4,493	2.1
1981–86	2,962	2.1
1820–1986	52,617	3.5

Source: U.S. Bureau of the Census, 1982, U.S. Statistical Abstract, 1982–83 (Washington, D.C.: Government Printing Office), Table 128; and unpublished data from the Immigration and Naturalization Service.

[a] Calculated as the number of immigrants in the 10-year period divided by the sum of the population in the 10-year period.

Note: More than 49 million people migrated legally to the United States between 1820 and 1979, with the number peaking during the decade 1901–10.

adults. That "push," accompanied by the "pull" of higher wages in the United States, has stimulated a tremendous migration stream.

Relative to all migrants into the United States, those from Mexico are typically younger, more apt to be males, and more likely to have a blue-collar occupation. Illegal Mexican immigrants certainly outnumber legal Mexican immigrants, since illegal entry is far quicker than going through legal channels, which may take up to 8 years (Rout, 1982). To be sure, Robert Warren and Jeffrey Passel have estimated that approximately 2 million undocumented aliens were counted in the 1980 census and that about 1 million of them were from Mexico (Warren and Passel, 1987). They believe that at least half of all undocumented persons were included in the census count, which would suggest that in 1980 there may have been 2 million undocumented persons from Mexico residing in the United States. This number, of course, would exceed the number of legal immigrants from Mexico entering the United States since 1960. Nonetheless, the two groups probably do not differ much—they all tend to be young, relatively unskilled, and eager to find a job (Blejer et al., 1978).

How massive is this migration of undocumented workers from Mexico? And are they really taking jobs away from American citizens? These are the two major issues that surround the migration of Mexicans into the United States. In the late 1970s and early 1980s the Immigration and Naturalization Service was apprehending an average of 700,000 deportable Mexican nationals per year. Using the "tip of the iceberg" theory, many people had argued that as many as 4 million Mexicans might well be added to the country each year. That theory, of course, was marred by the fact that many undocumented persons are picked up and deported several times each year and also by the fact that the number of out-migrants is ignored and thus the net effect of migration was being overestimated (Heer, 1979). Still, fears of the border being overrun by foreigners prompted Congress in 1986 to pass the Immigration Reform and Control Act (IRCA), whose main provisions were to punish employers who knowingly hire undocumented workers and to provide legalization for those undocumented people who could prove that they had been living in the United States continuously since January 1, 1982 (or seasonally, for certain kinds of agricultural workers). Thus, the intent was to provide amnesty for people who had become permanent residents of the United States without the benefit of papers but to close the door to future illegal migration by eliminating the availability of the biggest lure—the jobs. However, as of 1988, the bleak economic condition of Mexico seemed to suggest that some Mexicans were likely to continue coming to the United States whether or not they had proper documents.

The usual public image of the impact that illegal immigration has on the American labor force is conditioned by the belief that there is a fixed number of jobs and a fixed amount of income available to all workers to be shared among those who find the jobs. As migrants enter, the image continues, they take jobs from natives and income goes to immigrants instead of natives. Reality is apparently not so simple. It appears that most immigrants are actually employed in positions that natives do not want. Indeed, that is why those jobs are available—there is a demand for low-wage, relatively unskilled labor that the native labor force is not meeting (Wolin, 1982). Furthermore, many observers believe that if illegal immigrants were not available, then jobs either would be mechanized (as in the case of agriculture) or transferred to low-wage, third-world nations (as in the case of the garment industry) (Siegel, 1982). Jorge Bustamante, president of Mexico's El Colegio de la Frontera Norte (COLEF) believes that the size of Mexican immigration is a direct result of the demand by American businesses and households for inexpensive Mexican labor. At the same time, he notes, the transfer of American technology to Mexican business has mechanized many industries in that country, thus contributing to unemployment in Mexico (which turns a Mexican laborer's attention to the border) (Bustamante, 1983). Since studies done in both Mexico and the United States indicate that a high proportion of Mexican immigrants to the United States return to Mexico (Bustamante, 1983; Mines and Massey, 1982), the result may be seen as an implicit guest-worker program, rather than a large-scale wave of permanent migration. If this is true, then

Mexican migration to the United States is qualitatively different from Asian migration.

Migration from Asia   Asian immigration to the United States began in the middle of the nineteenth century, but a series of increasingly restrictive immigration laws (which I will discuss in Chapter 15) kept the number relatively low until the late 1960s, when the laws were substantially liberalized. In the entire decade 1841–50, there were fewer than 100 Asian immigrants, but in the following decade the demand for labor on the West Coast produced a 10-year total of 41,000 Asian immigrants, virtually all of whom were from China (all data in this section are from the U.S. Immigration and Naturalization Service, 1983). Between 1871 and 1880 the level of immigration from China climbed to 123,000, and that volume led to an unfortunate series of restrictive laws limiting the ability of Chinese to enter the country. As migration from China abated, migration from Japan increased. For example, in the decade 1901–10, there were only 21,000 Chinese immigrants, but there were 130,000 immigrants from Japan.

The National Origins Quota system, which went into effect in the 1920s (see Chapter 15) dramatically reduced migration from all parts of Asia. Thus, of the 528,000 immigrants to the United States between 1931 and 1940, only 16,000 were from Asia. However, following the 1965 revisions of the immigration laws in the United States, the picture changed. With migration from countries such as the Philippines and Korea, in addition to China and Japan, there were 428,000 immigrants from Asia between 1961 and 1970.

Immigration from the Philippines began in the 1920s, when free migration was permitted between the two countries. By 1930 there were 45,000 Pilipinos in the United States, almost all of them males. The vast majority of these men came without families and either returned home or stayed and married non-Pilipino women. Although migration was fairly heavy in the 1920s, it was stopped almost entirely during the Depression and World War II by discriminatory, anti-Pilipino legislation that stemmed from displeasure at the extent to which Pilipino men dated and married white women (Kitano, 1980). After World War II, however, that sentiment changed somewhat as a result of Americans' wartime experiences as allies and defenders of the Philippines, and there was an influx of Pilipino veterans after the war. But the biggest boon to Pilipino immigration was the change in the law in the 1960s that gave highest immigration preference to family members. Americans of Pilipino origin began to sponsor the immigration of their relatives (including especially parents and siblings). Thus, by 1980 virtually all of the 20,000 immigrants from the Philippines were relatives of U.S. citizens (U.S. Immigration and Naturalization Service, 1983).

Few Koreans immigrated to the United States prior to the change in immigration laws in the 1960s. Since then, however, there has been considerable movement of people from Korea, with established immigrants then helping their relatives to migrate. Like Pilipino immigrants, nearly all of the 20,000 Korean immigrants in 1980 were relatives of American citizens.

Although migration from Asia clearly increased during the 1960s, there were, amazingly, 1.6 million Asian immigrants between 1971 and 1980. The latter figure, of course, is swollen by the large number of Indochinese refugees who were resettled in the United States as a result of the war in Vietnam. Since the end of American involvement in the military conflicts of Southeast Asia in 1975, more than 850,000 refugees have fled Indochina for the United States (Office of Refugee Resettlement, 1987). Most (63 percent) of this population is Vietnamese (including ethnic Chi-

THE CONSEQUENCES OF IMMIGRATION FOR HONG KONG

In 1949 the Communist revolution in mainland China produced a flood of refugees into the tiny British colony of Hong Kong. The veritable tidal wave of humanity inundated Hong Kong in the early 1950s and increased the population from 1.5 million in 1950 to more than 3 million in 1960—a doubling in only a decade. Since a majority of the immigrants were young adults of parenting age, their migration led to further increases of Hong Kong's population as they settled down and had children. Thus, by 1985, the population had grown to more than 5 million.

The very rapid influx of migrants quickly led to a saturation of existing housing, and the immigrants resorted to putting up huts on vacant land (Agassi and Jarvie, 1959). In many places there were more than 50,000 huts, with an average of about six inhabitants per hut packed together in small areas. These makeshift communities were complete with shops and schools, and there was even some farming done on the unlivable slopes (Endacott, 1973). Sanitation was extremely poor, as you can imagine, and there was a constant threat of severe disease epidemics—situations that are still common in cities of less developed nations.

There was also an ever-present threat of fire, and on the eve of Christmas day in 1953 a disastrous fire in one of these immigrant camps caused 53,000 people to lose their homes. In reaction to that calamity, the government of Hong Kong established a Resettlement Council, which began building six-story concrete block apartment buildings. The standard "apartment" was really more like a college dormitory— a 10 × 12 foot room with minimum kitchen facilities. Each apartment was intended to

house a family of five or six people, and each floor had a community washing and latrine area. By 1972 there were about 1.5 million people living in these and similar apartment buildings.

In much of the discussion of the consequences of migration for society, I have stressed the potentially negative impact that may result. And, indeed, the incredible size of the migrant group and the extremely poor situation in which they found themselves might well lead you to suppose that the overall impact on the social and economic situation in Hong Kong was negative. But, until recently, that had not been so. The immigrants tended to be young, urban, and better educated than the average Hong Kong native—those people who felt they had the most to lose from the Communist regime. They also provided a cheap labor force, because there were so many of them competing for jobs. Those factors, combined with the trading advantages afforded by a good harbor and a good geographic location in Southeast Asia, have led Hong Kong to become one of the most commercialized and industrialized cities in Asia. The high fertility of the early immigrants has given ground to much lower levels of fertility—comparable to those of most southern European nations—and the low levels of life expectancy in the epidemic-prone squatter camps have given way to levels of life expectancy slightly higher than those in the United States.

The point is that immigration often has potentially beneficial consequences for the recipient area, especially if, as in the case of Hong Kong, the immigrants bring more rather than fewer skills, talents, and motivations to work than existed in the native population.

nese), with the numbers of Laotians, Cambodians, and Hmong being nearly equal. California has attracted at least one third of the refugees, and eight other states (Texas, Washington, Minnesota, Pennsylvania, Illinois, Oregon, Virginia, and New York) account for another third. The ethnic diversity of these new immigrants is

Unfortunately, this rosy picture was too good to be true for very long. By the 1970s the face of immigration had changed. No longer were migrants the cream of China's crop escaping communism; they now were almost all rural laborers drawn to the better economic life that Hong Kong promised. In 1974, the government of Hong Kong reversed its open-door policy and required new immigrants to show their exit cards from mainland China. But still the migrants came—legal and illegal alike. In 1978 Hong Kong refused to admit 2,000 Vietnamese refugees, and in 1980 tight immigration restrictions were announced, with the added feature that all illegal immigrants were to be repatriated. The government was so serious about this that all women having babies in Hong Kong hospitals were checked and those who were found to be illegal residents were sent back to China—without their babies (Parks, 1982a).

Hong Kong basically has reached its demographic saturation point and the government has decided that, no matter how beneficial earlier immigration might have been, further migration could be disastrous in terms of jobs, housing, and education. At the same time, Hong Kong has experienced its own version of the Baby Boom, with all of the problems attendant to such a phenomenon. The young people who migrated in the 1950s and 1960s had children, who moved through their teens and young adult years in the 1970s and early 1980s, creating a bulge in those ages that helped to raise the crime rate (see more on this topic in Chapter 8) along with a rise in the unemployment rate (Parks, 1982b). All of this happened at the same inopportune time that Hong Kong was feeling the effects of a world recession.

Some demographic relief may be found in out-migration. No sooner had Milton and Rose Friedman called Hong Kong the "modern exemplar of free markets and limited government" (quoted by Clark, 1983:33), than people began to look toward 1997 when Britain's lease on Hong Kong runs out and the People's Republic of China is expected to take control. This lays the city open to a future uncertain enough that at least one British investment executive has suggested that "the heyday of Hong Kong is over" (Gigot, 1982:1). Although the government of Hong Kong does not keep official track of emigrants, foreign consulates of Canada, Australia, and the United States have reported a surge of visa applicants among Hong Kong professionals since the early 1980s—people presumably trying to keep their options open by moving out if necessary. Those who cannot qualify occupationally to gain entrance to other countries have sometimes taken another tack by advertising for a spouse in the country of desired destination (Spaeth, 1983; Jones, 1988). Marriage to a foreigner would, of course, ensure an escape route out of Hong Kong.

The final lesson in Hong Kong's migration history is that too much of a good thing can be bad for the society. As the demographic characteristics of migrants changed from above-average skills to below average, their value to the colony diminished and they became less welcome. At the same time, as the area's political and economic future grows murky, the most skilled people are looking for the chance to migrate to other areas of opportunity.

matched by their socioeconomic and educational differences. Many of those who arrived in the "first wave" of immigration (1975–78) were highly skilled, educated, urban residents who had strong ties to the American government and Western culture. Those who arrive in the "second wave" are more rural in origin and have fewer occupational and educational skills. In addition, whereas many in the first group of refugees spent little time in Asian refugee camps, the large majority of post-1978 refugees have spent many months and years in profound hardship, both in their escape from Vietnam, Laos, and Cambodia, and in their tenure at the various camps in Thailand, Hong Kong, Malaysia, Indonesia, and the Philippines. For the Indochinese refugee population, the scars of the flight from Asia are bound to heal only slowly. Yet, the Indochinese refugees in the United States represent only a fraction of the estimated 12 million refugees throughout the world (U.S. Committee for Refugees, 1987). Indeed, the refugee movement has been characterized as "endemic to the contemporary world" (Keely, 1981:53).

Migration Out of the United States

The United States Immigration and Naturalization Service keeps track only of expatriates—those who renounce American citizenship—and these number no more than a few thousand people annually. However, there is a larger number of people who migrate out of the country each year, even though no records are kept for such individuals. We do know that in 1979 there were 312,000 people living abroad and receiving American social security benefits. Canada had the greatest number of such people (44,000), followed closely by Mexico (43,000) and Italy (42,000), and then by the Philippines (34,000), Germany (17,000), and Greece (17,000). An analysis of data for these older out-migrants has revealed that about 90 percent of them were not born in the United States, and most (95 percent) appear to have migrated back to their places of birth. Thus, it seems that many of the people who migrate to the United States at younger ages will work to build up a social security account and then retire, returning to their country of origin as older migrants (Kraly, 1982). Using data from the Current Population Surveys, the U.S. Government estimates that there are approximately 160,000 emigrants from the United States each year, of whom about 133,000 (83 percent) are foreign-born persons (probably returning to their country of origin) (Woodrow, 1988).

Migration Elsewhere in the World

The massive waves of international migration that characterized the nineteenth and early twentieth centuries have already been described in Chapter 2. They represented primarily the voluntary movement of people out of Europe into the "new" worlds of North and South America and Oceania. Restrictive immigration laws throughout the world (not just in the United States) and the worldwide economic depression between World Wars I and II severely limited international migration in the 1920s and 1930s. However, World War II unleashed a new cycle of European and Asian migration—this time a forced push of people out of war-torn countries as boundaries were realigned and ethnic groups were transferred between countries (United Nations, 1979). Shortly thereafter, the 1947 partition of the Indian subcontinent into India and Pakistan led to the transfer of more than 15 million people—Moslems into Pakistan and Hindus into India. Meanwhile, in the Middle East, the partitioning of Palestine to create a new state of Israel produced 700,000 Palestinian out-migrants and an influx of a large proportion of the Middle Eastern Jewish population into that area. Substantial migration into Israel from Europe, the Soviet Union, and other areas continued well into the 1960s. In the 1980s, the flow of migrants into Israel began to dry up, replaced by a small but steady stream of out-migrants. These changes in Israel were part of a new look taken on recently in international migration.

Recent General Patterns   Despite the relative paucity of good data on international migration, it is obvious to all but the most obdurate residents of industrialized nations that there has been a tremendous migration of people from less developed to more developed countries since the 1960s. Rapid population growth in less developed nations has put incredible pressure on resources in those nations, while declining rates of population growth in the more developed nations has, in many instances, heightened the demand for lower-cost workers from the Third World. In 1960 there were an estimated 3.3 million legal immigrants from less developed countries residing in developed countries, and by 1974 the number had jumped to 9.5 million (United Nations, 1979). Those are the most recent estimates compiled for the world, but it is certain that the number has continued to climb somewhat and, of course, the volume of illegal migration has almost certainly grown along with legal migration. While the general pattern is a flow from less developed to more developed nations, we can identify two major types of migration that are particularly involved—labor migration and refugee movements.

Labor Migration   Improved communication and transportation technology have greatly facilitated a time-honored way of solving short-term labor shortages—the importation of workers from elsewhere. The bracero guest-worker program opened the doors to the United States for many Mexicans in the 1950s, and guest-worker programs have also flourished in Europe, the Middle East, and Africa. Slow population growth combined with relatively good economic conditions in northern and western Europe in the 1960s through the mid-1970s to create a demand for substantial numbers of foreign workers. The labor pool was drawn primarily from southern Europe, northern Africa, and Turkey. By 1978, Western Germany and France both had nearly 4 million foreign residents, while Switzerland and Belgium had nearly 1 million each, and Sweden and the Netherlands each had close to one-half million (United Nations, 1982).

By the late 1970s, however, the demand for workers in Europe had slackened, as economies cooled in the face of higher oil prices. Most European nations responded by placing more restrictions on foreign immigration, but many of the migrants who had already been granted permanent residence decided to stay in Europe, creating new ethnic minorities in their adopted European homelands. Western Germany, for example, has a population of about 1.5 million Turks, changing the social landscape of Germany (Newman, 1983), while Great Britain's population now includes an estimated 2.5 million West Indians. Voices have been raised in both countries to send foreign workers home, and in 1984 the West German government did go so far as to offer $4,000 to any Turkish family that decided to leave. Such a decision was clearly a tormented one for many Turks. According to a Turkish psychiatrist in Germany, "These workers have ambitions of socially elevating themselves and their families, and to secure a higher social status position. This is more likely to occur if the workers eventually return home to Turkey where they are not considered as outsiders" (Babaoglu, 1982:116). In Britain, the **xenophobia** had reached a point even in 1975 that an American anthropologist commented that "there is a recognition that British racism has become less personal and more institutional in nature" (Midgett, 1975:78).

The Arab oil-producing nations, by contrast, were benefitting economically from the rise in oil prices and thus became centers of rapid immigration in the late 1970s and early 1980s. Libya and Saudi Arabia, in particular, became attractive destinations for Egyptian and Jordanian migrants, along with substantial numbers of Indians and Pakistanis. Kuwait also relies extensively on foreign workers for its labor force and, as in most nations receiving migrants, illegal immigration is substantial. In 1982 the Kuwaiti government decided that illegal immigrants posed a security threat and cracked down. The result was an immediate shortage of workers in the construction industry and a consequent boost in wages for the remaining, legally admitted foreign workers (Helal, 1982).

Guest-worker programs have also been historically common in sub-Saharan Africa, but the movement toward decolonization and the creation of independent states has altered some of those practices as governments attempt to control migration. In general, migration in Africa has involved males, who may be gone from their families for as long as 2 years while working in a resource-rich neighboring country. Despite the history of such labor migration, the government of Nigeria dramatically and heartlessly booted out 2 million foreign workers in January 1983. "Nigeria's President Shagari accused illegal immigrant workers of ruining his country's economy by taking needed jobs and draining the nation's wealth. He gave the foreign workers two weeks to clear out. The order sent immigrants rushing for the border in panic" (Newsweek, 1983b). Guest workers, whether legal or illegal, had been welcome in Nigeria during the oil-boom years from the mid-1970s to the early 1980s, and nearly all were from neighboring African countries, especially Ghana. But in late 1982, when oil prices fell, the welcome mat was yanked away and in short order a large-scale labor migration was transformed into a refugee exodus.

Refugee Migration   The 2 million refugees from Nigeria joined an estimated 10 million other refugees throughout the globe, a disproportionate share of whom were already in Africa (U.S. Committee for Refugees, 1987). The revolution in Ethiopia and civil war in Uganda had contributed significantly to the estimated 2.5 million African refugees before the Nigerian expulsion (Beyer, 1981). Asia, however, has the largest group of refugees, including about 2.5 million Afghans living in Pakistan and another 1.9 million being sheltered in Iran as a result first of a 1978 government coup in Afghanistan, then of the 1979 Soviet invasion. Farther east, Vietnam and Kampuchea (formerly Cambodia) have also produced a large number of refugees.

Besides the 850,000 Indochinese who had been resettled in the United States by 1987 and the tens of thousands who fled to France, many refugees were absorbed by neighboring Asian societies. China, for example, has accepted more than 265,000 Vietnamese refugees, almost all of ethnic Chinese background. This probably represents the largest migration ever into China and perhaps the largest ever into any communist society (Chen, 1984). Although most of these refugees were not farmers (they included shopkeepers, traders, miners, and so on), they have been resettled mainly into agricultural communes, because China's already populous urban areas could not absorb them. The transition was marred, as well, by the fact that the Chinese government allowed the refugees, whose average family size is about 6.5 children, to be exempted from the one-child policy (Chen, 1984).

In Central America, guerilla warfare has caused thousands of people to flee from El Salvador, Nicaragua, and Guatemala into Mexico and the United States. Mexico has faced the irony of coping with tens of thousands of refugees entering the country's southern border at the same time that thousands of Mexicans are illegally crossing the northern border into the United States. In fact, in the summer of 1983, Mexico decided to place restrictions on Central American refugees, arguing that they had taken jobs away from Mexicans and had added to the country's social pressures (San Diego Union, 1981b).

SUMMARY AND CONCLUSION

Migration is any permanent change of residence. It is the most complex of the three population processes because we have to account for the wide variety in the number of times people may move, the vast array of places migrants may go, and the incredible diversity of reasons there may be for who goes where, when. Although migration theory has had a rather low profile in past decades, an increasingly popular explanation for migration is that it occurs as an implementing strategy especially during the young adult years in the life cycle. Thus, if you were the archetypal migrant in the United States, you would be in your early twenties, recently married, well educated, and looking for a better job in a nonmetropolitan county in one of the Sun Belt states.

Migration has dynamic consequences for the migrants themselves, for the areas from which they came, and for the areas to which they go. Some of these consequences, especially for the areas of origin and destination, are fairly predictable if we know the characteristics of the migrants. For example, if in-migrants are well-educated young adults, they will be looking for well-paying jobs, they may add to the economic prosperity of an area, and they will probably be establishing families, which will further add to the area's population and increase the demand for services.

Throughout the world, population growth has induced an increase in the volume of migration, both legal and illegal. The United States passed legislation designed to limit the entry of illegal immigrants in 1986, whereas India had approached the issue more straightforwardly in 1983 by constructing a barbed-wire fence along its border with Bangladesh, designed to keep illegal migrants out of

India. "Temporary" labor migration has also increased throughout the world as jobs have become available in developed societies for workers from third-world countries. Understandably, workers are often reluctant to leave the higher-income countries, even when the economies in those places slow down and pressure builds for foreigners to go home. Such people are only a few steps away from the unhappily large fraction of the world's migrants who are refugees, seeking asylum in other countries after being forced out of their own. Of the approximately 12 million refugees scattered throughout the globe in the 1980s, disproportionate shares are found in Asia and Africa.

Although it is not always apparent, the quality of our everyday life is greatly affected by the process of migration, for even if we ourselves never move, we will spend a good part of our lifetime adjusting to people who have migrated into our lives and to the loss of people who have moved away. Each new person coming into our life greatly expands the potential size of our social network, especially since many people who move away do so physically but not symbolically; that is, we remain in communication.

In the next chapter I will examine the way in which migration, fertility, and mortality operate to shape the age and sex structure of a population—a structure that affects the lives of each of us by defining how many people of different ages and sex we must deal with.

MAIN POINTS

1. Migration is the process of changing residence and of moving your whole round of social activities from one place to another.

2. International migrants move between countries, whereas internal migrants do their moving within national boundaries.

3. Explanations of why people move typically begin with the push-pull theory, first formulated in the late nineteenth century.

4. Migration is selective and is associated especially with different stages in the life cycle, giving rise to the idea that migration is an implementing strategy—a means to a desired end.

5. Young adults are geographically more mobile than people of other ages.

6. Marriage is typically associated with a move, but children tend to slow parents down (in more ways than just migration).

7. The more highly educated you are, the more likely you are to migrate.

8. Americans are among the most mobile people in the world.

9. People generally move to places where they think business is good and they leave behind those places where it is bad.

10. In the United States so many people are moving to the Sun Belt that they may have to let it out a notch.

11. Migration can change the lives of individuals just as it can alter the social organization of both the host and donor areas.

12. Since the 1960s, large numbers of Mexicans have migrated legally and illegally to the United States, searching for relief from high unemployment rates in Mexico.

13. Labor migration from third-world countries to more developed nations substantially increased in volume during the 1970s.

14. In the late 1980s, there were an estimated 12 million refugees scattered throughout the globe, especially in Africa and Asia.

SUGGESTED READINGS

1. Everett Lee, 1966, "A theory of migration," Demography 3(1):47–57.

   This widely quoted article summarizes and updates the famous work of Ravenstein, who published a still influential treatise on migration in 1888.

2. Gordon DeJong and Robert Gardner (eds.), 1981, Migration Decision Making (New York: Pergamon Press).

   Amazingly little attention has been devoted to theories of migration in recent decades, but this volume brings together an excellent collection of the work that has been done.

3. Larry Long and D. DeAre, 1982, "Repopulating the countryside: a 1980 census trend," Science 217(1):1111–16.

   The U.S. Bureau of the Census is the major source of migration data for Americans, and this is one of a continuing series of important articles published by Census Bureau demographers as they chart the trends in the United States.

4. Robert Warren and Jeffrey Passel, 1987, "A count of the uncountable: estimates of undocumented aliens counted in the 1980 United States census," Demography 24(3):375–94.

   This article, which is as good a piece of demographic detective work as you are likely to find, has had considerable influence on the way demographers and policymakers view the issue of illegal migration to the United States.

5. Leon Bouvier and Robert Gardner, 1986, "Immigration to the United States: the unfinished story," Population Bulletin 41(4).

   This report provides an excellent overview of both legal and undocumented migration to the United States within the perspective of other demographic trends in the United States and the countries from which migrants come.

PART THREE
Population Structure and Characteristics

Thus far I have concentrated on the demographic perspective and on the three population processes: fertility, mortality, and migration. I have emphasized how social forces shape the trends and levels of each process, and, to a lesser extent, I have analyzed the social impact of changes in each of these processes. With this background, it is time now to turn to a more detailed analysis of other factors that are intimately intertwined with population processes. These factors are commonly called **population characteristics** and they include the distribution of a population by age, sex, race, marital status, education, occupation, and income.

I have divided these characteristics into two groups to discuss them in detail. Chapter 8 deals with age and sex, and Chapter 9 discusses the remaining characteristics. The rationale for this separation into two chapters is that the distribution of people in a society by age and sex is quite predictably associated with each of the three demographic processes. Also, since the age and sex structure can affect the distribution of other population characteristics, it makes sense to examine it first. On the other hand, the distribution of a population according to other characteristics is more likely to be influenced by purely social, rather than demographic, processes. Indeed, the number of people of a particular race, marital status, education level, occupation, or income will be a consequence of (1) the social and economic organization of society; (2) the levels of mortality, fertility, and migration; and (3) the age and sex structure.

Throughout the next two chapters the analysis will be two-pronged. We will be looking at the way in which population processes influence characteristics and the way in which those characteristics in turn affect population processes. By understanding these interrelationships—these feedback systems—you will enhance your own demographic perspective.

PART THREE
Population Structure and Characteristics

CHAPTER 8
Age and Sex Structure

You can't see a population grow in the same way that you can watch a crowd fill up a football stadium. If you leave a place for a few years and then come back, the change may be apparent to you—something akin to time-lapse photography. For the most part, however, we observe demographic changes by seeing their effect on the age and sex structure of an area—on the number of people of each age and sex. For example, recent changes in fertility influence the number of children in elementary school, whereas recent migration or prior fertility levels may affect the number of new apartments and houses being built (or vacated) to accommodate young families. In general, it is the interaction of fertility, mortality, and migration that produces the age/sex structure, which can be viewed as a key to the life of a social group—a record of past history and a hint of the future.

Population processes not only produce the age/sex structure but are, in turn, affected by it—another example of the complexity of the world when seen through your demographic "eye." I would not be exaggerating too much to say that changes in the age/sex structure affect virtually all social institutions and represent a major force in social change. In this chapter I will escort you through that complexity by first defining age and sex structures and examining how we measure and use them. Then I will look at the impact of each of the population processes on the age/sex structure, and finally I will examine the potential contributions that changing age/sex structures make to social change.

WHAT IS AN AGE/SEX STRUCTURE?

Strictly speaking, a structure is something that is built or constructed. In social science it refers more broadly to a pattern of interrelationships between parts of a society. An **age and sex structure** actually combines both definitions, since it represents the number of people of a given age and sex in society and is built from the input of births at age zero and deaths and migration at every age.

Age and sex influence the working of society in important ways because society assigns social roles and frequently organizes people into groups on the basis of their age and sex. Young people are treated differently from old people, and different kinds of behavior are expected of each. Women are treated differently from men and, like it or not, different kinds of behavior are expected from each. Regardless of your ideological position as to the rightness or wrongness of these distinctions, they do exist in every known human society. Further, at very young and very old ages, people are more dependent on others for survival, and so the proportions of people at these ages will influence how society works.

Measuring the Age Structure

A population is considered old or young depending on the proportion of people at different ages. In general, a population with more than about 35 percent of its people under age 15 is "young," and a population with more than about 10 percent of its people aged 65 or older can be considered "old." Further, as the proportion of young people increases relative to the total, we speak of the population as growing younger. Conversely, an aging population is one in which the proportion of older people is increasing relative to the total. There are three major ways in which we can graphically or statistically quantify the age structure. These include constructing a **population pyramid,** calculating the **average age of a population,** and calculating the **dependency ratio.**

Population Pyramids   A population pyramid (or **age/sex pyramid**) is a graphic representation of the distribution of a population by age and sex. It is called a pyramid because the "classic" picture is of a high-fertility, high-mortality society (which characterized most of the world until only several decades ago) with a broad base built of numerous births, rapidly tapering to the top (the older ages) because of high death rates in combination with the high birth rate. Two countries famous for their ancient stone pyramids, Egypt and Mexico, also have age and sex distributions that reflect the classic look of the population pyramids, as you can see in Figure 8.1. Developed countries such as the United States and West Germany have age/sex distributions that are more rectangular or barrel-shaped (see Figure 8.1), but we still call the graph a population pyramid. Later in the chapter I will return to a more detailed look at interpreting population pyramids.

While a picture may be worth a thousand words, there are times when we like to summarize an age/sex structure in only a few short words or, even better, in a few numbers. The average age and dependency ratio are two measures to help us do just that.

Average Age and Dependency Ratio   The average age in a population is generally measured by the median, which measures the age above which is found half of the population and below which is the other half. In Figure 8.1, the population pyramids of Egypt, Mexico, the United States, and West Germany reflect median ages of 17.6, 19.6, 30.0, and 36.7, respectively. Thus, the obvious differences in the shapes of the age distributions for less developed and more developed countries are reflected in the clear differences in median ages.

A frequently used index to measure the social and economic impact of different age structures is the dependency ratio—the ratio of the dependent-age population (the young and the old) to the working-age population. The higher this ratio is, the more people each worker is having to support; conversely, the lower it is, the fewer people there are dependent on each worker. Let me give you an example.

Suppose that a population of 100 people had 46 members under age 15, 3 people 65 or older, and the rest approximately of economically active ages (15–64). This is similar to the situation in Mexico, one of the higher-fertility nations in the world. You can see that there are 49 people of dependent age (0–14 and 65+) compared with 51 people of working age. Thus, the dependency ratio is 49/51 or 0.96, which means that there are 0.96 dependents per working-age person—a fairly heavy load, especially since in most societies you will not find everyone of working age actually working.

We can compare this dependency ratio of 0.96 with that for a population of 100 people in which 23 are under 15, 11 are 65 or over, and the rest (66) are of working age. As you may have guessed, this is typical of the United States. In this situation the

Figure 8.1 Age Pyramids Graphically Display a Country's Age/Sex Structure

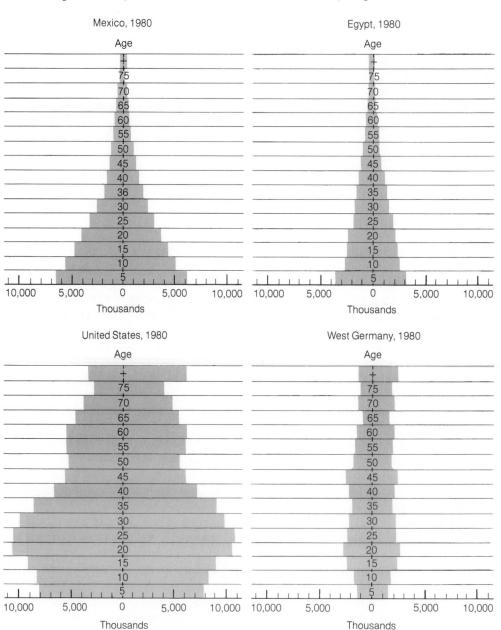

Source: United Nations, 1984, Demographic Yearbook, 1983 (New York: United Nations).

dependency ratio is 34/66 or 0.52, which means that one person of working age would be supporting about half the number of dependents as is supported in Mexico.

The dependency ratio does not capture all the intricacies of the age structure, but it is a useful indicator of the burden (or lack thereof) that some age structures place on a population. For individuals with large families, the impact of a youthful age structure, for example, will be immediately apparent. But even for the childless or those with only a few children, the effect may be higher taxes to pay for schools, health facilities, and subsidized housing. For those in business (whether government or private), an age structure that includes numerous dependents may mean that workers are able to save less, having to spend it on families, while government taxes must go toward buying food, housing, and education rather than to financing industry or economic infrastructure, such as roads, railways, and power and communications systems.

Measuring the Sex Structure

It is a common assumption that there are the same numbers of males and females at each age—actually, this is rarely the case. Migration, mortality, and fertility operate differently to create inequalities in the ratio of males to females (known as the **sex ratio**). For example, in some instances females are more likely to migrate (and thus to be added to or subtracted from an age/sex structure), and in other situations males are more likely to be the migrants and thus also produce inequalities in the age/sex structure.

Mortality creates sex inequalities because at every age males have higher death rates than females, as I discussed in Chapter 6. As mortality has declined, women have benefited disproportionately, and Western nations have thus become increasingly characterized by having substantially more older females than males. For example, in 1980 in the United States there were only 67 males aged 65 or older for every 100 females of that age; by age 85 there were only 44 males for every 100 females.

Fertility has the most predictable impact on the ratio of males to females (the sex ratio), since in virtually every known human society, more boys are born than girls. This is perhaps a biological adaptation to compensate partially for the higher male death rates. In the United States there are normally 105 boys born for every 100 girls, with the ratio of boys to girls being slightly higher for whites than blacks. Over time there has been a gradual increase in the sex ratio at birth for blacks in the United States, which is probably associated with improvements in health.

Let me also note that couples may soon have the ability to choose the sex of their offspring. It is already possible to manipulate the sex ratio at birth of nonmammalian vertebrates, and several techniques are being researched for applications to humans. The three most promising approaches appear to be (1) separating the X- and Y-bearing sperm and subsequently impregnating a woman through artificial insemination; (2) timing coitus through the ovulatory cycle so that it occurs either early or late, to enhance the probability of conceiving a male, or in the middle of the cycle, to increase the likelihood of conceiving a female; and (3) selective abortion after identifying the gender of the fetus (N. Bennett, 1983). A more drastic approach that is, of course, already available is infanticide. Westoff and Rindfuss (1974) believe that if these methods ever enjoyed widespread acceptance, there would be a short-run rise in the sex ratio at birth, since a preference for sons as first children (and for more total sons than daughters) is fairly common throughout the world (see Williamson, 1976; 1983). However, Westoff and Rindfuss also conclude that after an initial transition period, the sex ratio at birth would probably revert to the natural level of about 105 males per 100 females, since the disadvantage of too many or too few of either sex would be controlled by a shift to the other sex. The relatively strong preference for boys that we know exists in many developing societies, if coupled with sex selection, could actually work toward greater gender equality:

> If as a result of sex selection women become fewer, their relative position will change. They will become more desirable in marriage, and the dowry that has to be paid along with a daughter to obtain a suitable husband will drop, perhaps to zero, perhaps being replaced by a bride price. This drastic change in the marriage market will have effects on equality within the family—a woman who is badly treated will leave her husband, knowing that she can easily find a new one (Keyfitz, 1983:xii).

In Chapter 10 I will explore in greater detail this relationship between the sex ratio and women's status in society.

Ultimately, the effect of sex selection would likely be a return to the state of affairs exemplified by the current situation in the United States, where the excess of males over females prevails throughout the younger ages until higher male mortality takes its toll. In the United States in 1980, for example, there were more males than females at every age younger than 18, while females outnumbered males at every age from 18 on. Now that you have a feel for the essential ingredients of an age/sex structure, let us examine how those age/sex structures come about as a consequence of the three population processes.

IMPACT OF POPULATION PROCESSES ON THE AGE/SEX STRUCTURE

Each of the three population processes—migration, mortality, and fertility—makes its own imprint on the age/sex structure, and I list them in that order for a reason. Migration has the dramatic, short-term impact on the distribution of people by age and sex, but over the long run its influence is negligible. Mortality can have both short-run and long-run effects on the age/sex structure, but in neither case is the impact very dramatic. Finally, fertility has relatively little short-term effect, but in the long run it is by far the most important of the three population processes in influencing the shape of the age pyramid.

The Impact of Migration

A population experiencing net in- or out-migration (and virtually all populations—except the world as a whole—do experience one or the other) will almost certainly have its age/sex structure altered as a consequence. Since immigration has been especially important in the United States, it provides a good beginning for our analysis.

Impact of Immigration to the United States   We can assess the potential impact of international migrants into the United States by looking at the age/sex distribution of immigrants for a recent year. Figure 8.2 is an age pyramid of legal immigrants into the United States in 1984, where ages 20–29 stand out clearly as those most heavily influenced by migration. At each age under 40 men outnumber women, but the opposite pattern prevails at ages 40 and older. It seems that the impact of a group of nearly 544,000 legal immigrants (see Chapter 7) ought to be impressive and certainly socially consequential. However, the United States (as you well know by now) is a nation of nearly 250 million people, and so a few hundred thousand one way or the other really doesn't make much difference in the short run, despite the fact that they represent as many people as lived in the city of ancient Rome. If you consider that all Americans except the native American Indians are descendants of migrants, though, it becomes apparent that the effect of immigration on the United States has been substantial over the long run.

From an economic point of view, immigration can be a benefit to society, especially if adults without children are primarily involved. In those cases, some other group (the **donor area**) footed the bill for raising and educating the migrants,

Figure 8.2   Young Adults Are the Single Largest Category of Legal Immigrants to the United States (1984)

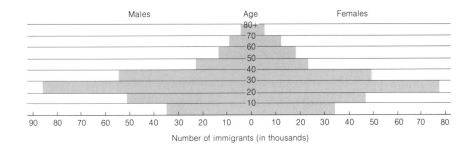

The age/sex pyramid reveals a preponderance of young adults. At the younger ages males outnumber females, but the reverse is true at ages 40 and above. *Source:* U.S. Immigration and Naturalization Service, 1986, 1984 Statistical Yearbook (Washington, D.C.: Government Printing Office), Table Imm 4.1.

while the **host area** gains the advantage of their economic productivity. Indeed, it is the loss of the economic productivity of young adults that tends to create so many problems for the area from which they left. These kinds of influences tend to be greatest in regions smaller than an entire country. In such instances the impact will probably be a result of internal migration, such as into or out of a state or local region like a city or even smaller areas within a city.

Impact of Internal Migration Within a City   The impact of migration on the age structure within a city is particularly noticeable when that area contains a social institution, such as a military base, college, or retirement community, which attracts a particular age group or sex. Examples of these situations are shown in Figure 8.3. Each of these age and sex distributions is drawn from areas of San Diego as measured by the 1980 census. The first example is the population in the Montezuma area near San Diego State University, where you can see the heavy bulges in the late teens and early twenties. There are rather severe dents in the age structures for both sexes in the thirties and among children, which indicates that there are relatively few married couples with young children. This is not an area conducive to young families, probably because the homes near the university have risen sharply in value since the demand for property has increased as the university's enrollment has grown to the largest in the state of California. The typical young adult couple with children thus cannot afford to move into the area, and homeowners tend to be older residents, as can be seen by the bulges at ages 45–60. This age pattern is by no means unique, however. Most American college towns are characterized by this kind of bipolar distribution—young students living side by side with (although typically not in contact with) older residents (often retirees) (Walsh, 1984).

Young families are located in adjacent parts of the city, which are slightly more **suburban** and of lower density than the area near the university. You can see in Figure 8.3 that in the Navajo area, for example, there are relatively few college-age persons and very few retired people. The area is composed primarily of middle-aged adults and their children.

The third example is the age and sex distribution for the city of Coronado, California, a suburb of San Diego. It is the city that serves the North Island Naval Air Station, and the influence of the military is seen in the heavy preponderance of males in the late teens through the twenties. Among females, the slight bulge in the early twenties probably reflects the in-migration of Navy wives and the trend toward recruiting women into the military.

The fourth example is the most bizarre, yet it is typical of the downtown central business districts of many cities. Downtown San Diego is heavily male in the ages up to retirement. Virtually everyone residing in this area lives in a hotel or apartment, many of which have been deliberately converted to residences serving the elderly. The excess of young males is again a reflection of the presence of the Navy, of sailors living in nearby, but off-base, housing. At the middle ages, the excess of males probably reflects a population of derelicts and other transients who move into the area for lack of anywhere else to go. At the retirement ages, the greater proportion of females is a consequence of the greater longevity of women, who have been attracted to the downtown area by the construction of new, high-security, high-rise, low-rent apartments.

Figure 8.3 Age Pyramids in Different Areas of San Diego (1980)

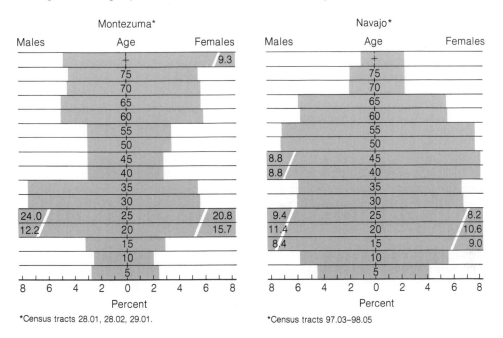

Montezuma*
*Census tracts 28.01, 28.02, 29.01.

Navajo*
*Census tracts 97.03–98.05

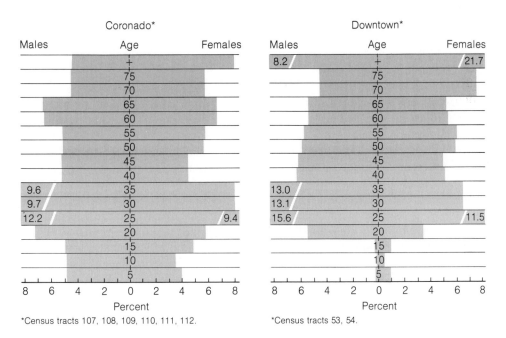

Coronado*
*Census tracts 107, 108, 109, 110, 111, 112.

Downtown*
*Census tracts 53, 54.

The age/sex structures of a city vary considerably, depending on the nature of social and economic activity in the neighborhood. See text for full discussion. *Source:* Recalculated from U.S. Bureau of the Census, 1980 Census of Population and Housing, Census Tracts, San Diego (Washington, D.C.: Government Printing Office), Table P-1.

These graphs show how the age and sex distributions in an area reflect the history of that area and reveal important social differences. In each case, the major determinant of the age/sex structure was migration, either in or out, and this illustrates the dramatic effect that migration may have on an area. Migration in two instances acted to produce bulges in the young adult ages, and in another instance to produce a bulge at the older ages. In one case, excessive male migration affected the structure of the population, while an excess of females was apparent in two of the examples. Migration, then, can affect either sex and can affect different ages to varying degrees. Of course, migration was not the only influence. Note that the abundance or lack of children in one area or another reflects high or low levels of fertility as well.

It is generally true that the more precisely you define a geographic area, the more likely it is that the age/sex structure will have been affected by migration, and the more likely it is that the area's "personality" will be affected by (and, of course, reciprocally influence) the age/sex structure. The age/sex structure for the state of California is very similar to that for the United States. As you narrow in on San Diego, local variations show up from the influence of the Navy (primarily) and the universities (there are three universities within the city limits). As you close in on specific sections of the city, as in Figure 8.3, the variations grow even wider. The character of each neighborhood begins to emerge, shaped by and helping to shape the age and sex distribution, which in turn affects and is affected by migration. Of course, the effects of the other two demographic processes, mortality and fertility, always go along with the effects of migration.

The Impact of Mortality

Long-Term Impact of Mortality Changes   Mortality is similar to migration in that it affects all ages and both sexes. But unlike migration, the age and sex pattern of dying is quite consistent from one society to the next, as I discussed in Chapter 6. In virtually all societies, the very youngest and the very oldest ages are most susceptible to death, and in modern societies (where maternal mortality is fairly low), males are more likely than females to die at any given age—a trend that accelerates with age.

Not only is there a fairly consistent pattern of mortality by age and sex, but when mortality levels change, all ages tend to be affected, even though some are affected more than others. Thus, improved health conditions in a society lower death rates at all ages, although the rates will be reduced proportionately more at the youngest and oldest ages. Similarly, if a famine or epidemic of disease strikes, death rates will rise at all ages, although again the youngest and oldest will be most affected.

The upshot of these facts is that severe alterations in the level of mortality in a society have far less dramatic consequences for the age and sex structure than does migration or, as we shall see, fertility. Over the long run, changes in mortality by themselves do not appreciably affect the age and sex structure of a society. However, to the extent that they do have an influence, albeit small, the effect of lower mortality is to make the population slightly younger—a seemingly paradoxical result, since it seems as though lower mortality should age the population by allowing people to live longer. But, instead, the disproportionately larger decline in infant mortality as overall levels of mortality decline tends to have the opposite effect. This impact of a mortality decline on the age/sex structure can be very noticeable in the short run if it is not accomplished by a decline in fertility.

Short-Term Impact of Mortality Changes   In the short run a decrease in mortality levels can substantially increase the number of young people, and one of the best studies of this effect is by Arriaga (1970) in his analysis of Latin American countries. Arriaga examined data from 11 countries for which information was available on the mortality decline from 1930 to the 1960s. He discovered that "of the 27 million people alive in all the eleven countries in the 1960s who would not have been alive if there had not been a mortality decline since the 1930s, 16 million—59 percent—were under 15" (1970:103). In relative terms, a lowering of mortality in Latin America noticeably raised the proportion of people at the young ages, slightly elevated the proportion at old ages, and lowered the proportion at the middle ages (14–64). However, in absolute terms, the number of people at all ages increased. Declining mortality had an impact similar to that of a rise in fertility, while also making a contribution to higher fertility.

The appearance of higher fertility is, of course, produced by the greater proportion of children surviving through each age of childhood. It is as though women were bearing more children, thereby broadening the base of the age structure. The actual contribution to higher fertility is generated by the higher probabilities of women (and their spouses) surviving through the reproductive ages, since under conditions of high mortality, a certain percentage of women will die before giving birth to as many children as they might have. When death rates go down, a higher percentage of women live to give birth to more children, assuming that social changes are not producing motivations for limiting fertility. The effect on fertility of changing mortality has been studied by Ridley et al. (1967), among others, and they were able to demonstrate that improved chances for survival increase the number of children ever born per woman and also increase the net reproduction rate.

Note that the only time that a change in mortality generates a change in the age/sex distribution is when the mortality shifts are different at different ages. If there is a change in the probability of survival from one age to the next that is exactly equal for all ages and for both sexes, then the age/sex structure will remain unchanged.

The Impact of Fertility

Both migration and mortality can affect all ages and differentially affect each sex. The impact of fertility is not quite the same. Fertility obviously adds people only at age zero to begin with, but that effect stays with the population age after age. Thus, if the birth rate were to drop suddenly in one year (as it did, for example, in Japan in 1966—see Chapter 5), then as those people get older, there will still always be fewer of them than there are people just older and (at least in the Japanese case) just younger. If fertility goes up, then there will be more people in each younger age group. Both of these situations—rising and declining fertility—have had strong influences on the age/sex structure of the United States, as I will discuss in a moment.

In general, the impact of fertility levels is so important that with exactly the same level of mortality, just altering the level of fertility can produce age/sex structures that run the gamut from those that might characterize primitive to highly developed populations. For example, let us suppose that we are looking at two countries with life expectancies of 70 years (such as Kuwait and Czechoslovakia). But one country (Kuwait) has very high fertility—a TFR of 6.2 (at least until very recently)—while the other has very low fertility—a TFR of 2.1. The respective age distributions of these two nations are already very different. In Kuwait 40 percent of the population was under age 15 in 1987, compared with only 24 percent of the Czech population. However, if each of these countries maintained these same levels of fertility and mortality for several decades, particularly in the absence of any migration, the differences would be even greater. In the long run, Kuwait would have nearly 46 percent of its population under age 15 and only 3 percent aged 65 and older (despite the low mortality). By contrast, only 21 percent of the Czech population would be under 15 in the long run, and fully 15 percent would be aged 65 and older. The average age of a Kuwaiti would be a mere 22, whereas the average Czech would be 38, and the wealth of the small nation-state of Kuwait would be put to the test with a dependency ratio of 0.96, while the economy of Czechoslovakia would be cruising with a dependency ratio of 0.56.

Having now discussed the way in which the age/sex structure is built on the foundation of migration, mortality, and fertility rates, it is worth spending a short while reminding you of the opposite side of that coin: How does the age structure influence rates of population growth?

IMPACT OF AGE STRUCTURE ON POPULATION PROCESSES

The actual rate of population growth is of course determined by the combination of fertility, mortality, and migration, and the rate of each of these is influenced by the age structure—a fact alluded to in earlier chapters, but worth repeating. A bulge in the age structure at the young adult (reproductive) ages will tend to raise the crude birth rate by producing a large number of children relative to the total population. As we shall see later in this chapter, even in an otherwise low-fertility society such as the United States, a large population of young women produces a substantial number of births. At the other extreme, a population with a relatively small proportion of young people, but with a high proportion of older people, will have a substantial number of deaths each year, even if life expectancy is high, just because there are so many people moving into those higher-risk years. This will generate a crude death rate higher than might otherwise be expected.

A young age structure produced by high fertility may also encourage a relatively large number of out-migrants. Each year such a population would produce a greater number of young adults, who are at greatest risk of migrating. Such migration, if it occurs, may well contribute to the sorts of massive changes almost invariably created by population growth. The question of social changes wrought by population processes leads us to examine the more general, and generally more interesting question: How do age/sex structures influence what a society is like?

THE DYNAMICS OF AGE/SEX STRUCTURES

It may seem mundane, if not downright boring, on the surface, but the age/sex structure of a population is actually one of the most potent forces of social change known to us. It is through this mechanism that all demographic changes are translated into a force with which we must cope. A high birth rate does not simply mean more people. It means that 6 years from now there will be more kids entering school than before; that 18 years from now there will be more new job hopefuls and college freshmen than before. An influx of young adult refugees this year means a larger than average number of older people 30 or 40 years from now (and it may mean an immediate sudden rise in the number of births, with all the attendant consequences). We study these phenomena by doing **population modeling.** This involves setting up hypothetical demographic situations—by constructing stable and stationary populations and projecting populations into the future, and doing so with specific models in mind. Then we look at those hypothetical demographic scenarios and ask what are the likely social, economic, and political ramifications of each. Let me go through the process to show you what I mean.

Stable and Stationary Populations

The long-run influences of mortality and fertility are best expressed by formal demographic models called stable and stationary populations. A **stable population** is one in which neither the age-specific birth rates nor the age-specific death rates have changed for a long time. Thus, a stable population is stable in the sense that the percentages of people at each age and sex do not change over time. However, a stable population could be growing at a constant rate (that is, the birth rate is higher than the death rate), it could be declining at a constant rate (the birth rate is lower than the death rate), or it could be unchanging (the birth rate equals the death rate). If the latter case prevails, we call it a **stationary population.** Thus, a stationary population is a special case of a stable population—all stationary populations are stable, but not all stable populations are stationary. The life table (discussed in Chapter 6) is one type of stationary population model.

For analytical purposes, a stable population is usually assumed to be closed to migration. Since 1760, when Leonhard Euler first devised the idea of a stable population, demographers have used the concept to explore the exact influence of differing levels of mortality and fertility on the age/sex structure. Such analyses are possible using a stable population model because it smooths out the dents and bumps in the age structure created by migration and by shifts in the death rate or the birth rate. Thus, if demographers were forced to study only real populations, we would be unable to ferret out all the kinds of relationships I discussed in previous sections. Demographers look at real populations and then apply stable population models to the real setting to understand the underlying demographic processes that influence the structure of a population by age and sex.

In Figure 8.4 I have employed stable population models to show how different fertility levels can affect the shape of the age/sex structure if everything else is held constant. Figure 8.4 assumes (as do most stable population models) that no migration is occurring. Then it assumes that mortality is constant, with a life expectancy of 71 years. The high fertility level is equivalent to a total fertility rate of 7.1 (similar to Tanzania). All other things being equal, a high-fertility, low-mortality society will have a very youthful age distribution. Indeed, the average age in the population is 20.7 years, with 48 percent of the population being under age 15. The median fertility level is equivalent to a total fertility rate of 4.3 children per woman (similar to Indonesia). This level of fertility still produces a youthful age structure, with an average age of 26.1 years and with 38 percent of the population under age 15. At the low fertility level, we are talking about a total fertility rate of 2.1, which is exact replacement. This population, which is close to the stable population model for the United States, has an average age of 37.9 years, and only 21 percent of the population is under age 15 (similar to France).

Figure 8.4   Different Levels of Fertility Have Dramatically Different Effects on the Age/ Sex Distribution

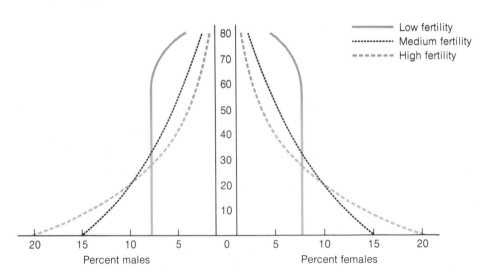

In this graph you can see the large impact that different levels of fertility have on the age/ sex structure of a population when mortality and migration are held constant. In all three cases the assumption is that there is no migration and that mortality is low. When fertility is also low, the age pyramid looks like a barrel, whereas the pyramidal shape is associated with higher levels of fertility.

Stable populations are also invaluable aids in estimating demographic measures. Let us suppose, for example, that we knew what the mortality and fertility rates were for a population, but no census had been conducted so we were unsure about the age and sex structure of the population. As I mentioned in Chapter 1, it is not uncommon for less developed nations to have such incomplete information. We do not have to give up or sit on our thumbs waiting for the United Nations Fund for Population Activities to finance a census. We can use a **model stable population**— the age and sex structure implied by an unchanging set of mortality and fertility rates (Coale and Demeny, 1983). A country that experiences little migration and has had relatively little change in mortality and fertility will have an age and sex structure similar to that of a stable population. Thus, if we know (or can reasonably estimate) two important facts, such as age-specific death rates and the rate of population increase, we can determine what the age and sex structure would almost certainly have to look like. For example, in 1988 it was estimated that the eastern African nation of Zimbabwe had a life expectancy of 57 years and an annual rate of population growth of 3.5 percent (Population Reference Bureau, 1988). Like many African nations, Zimbabwe has experienced relatively little in the way of fertility decline over the past several decades and, although mortality has been improving somewhat, levels are still well above the world average. Without detailed information yet from the 1982 census of Zimbabwe, but with knowledge of the mortality level and the growth rate, we can infer that the median age of the Zimbabwe population in 1988 was 16.3, with about 47 percent of the population under 15 and only about 3 percent aged 65 or older.

Stable population models are extremely useful in understanding the dynamics of population processes, and thus they are themselves aids in the development of demographic theory. However, we are usually interested in what we anticipate will happen in the real world, so we use our theories to project the population into the future to assess what we can most likely expect.

Population Projections

A **population projection** is the calculation of the number of persons we can expect to be alive at a future date given the number now alive and given reasonable assumptions about age-specific mortality and fertility rates (Keyfitz, 1968). In many respects, population projections are the single most useful set of tools available to us for demographic analysis. By enabling us to see what the future size and composition of the population might be under varying assumptions about the trends in mortality and fertility, we can intelligently evaluate what the likely course of events will be many years from now. Also, by projecting the population forward through time from some point in history, we are able to determine the sources of change in the population over time. A word of caution, however, is in order. Population projections always are based on a conditional future—this is what will happen *if* a certain set of conditions are met. Demographic theory is not yet sophisticated enough to be able to predict future shifts in demographic processes, especially fertility. Thus, we must distinguish projections from forecasts. As Nathan Keyfitz has observed, "Forecasts of weather and earthquakes, where the next few hours are the subject of interest, and of unemployment, where the next year or two is what counts, are difficult enough. Population forecasts, where one peers a generation or two ahead, are even more difficult" (1982:746).

There are four principal ways in which a demographer might project the population. The easiest way hearkens back to the formula that we used in Chapter 2 to derive an estimate of the doubling time of the population. In that problem, our concern was estimating the likely time that it would take a population to double in size when we knew the rate of population growth. By algebraically rearranging that equation, we can produce a formula that expresses the **logarithmic growth** of a population, assuming a constant rate of growth. This formula is as follows:

$$\text{Population at Time 2} = \text{Population at Time 1} \times e(rn).$$

Thus, if we know that the population of Mexico in 1988 (Time 1) was 84 million, and if we know that the rate of population growth (r) in Mexico in 1988 was 2.4 percent per year, we can project the population forward 12 years (n) to the year 2000 to estimate that if left unattended, the population in Mexico would grow to 112 million in 2000 (Time 2).

The logarithmic growth method of projecting population size is, in fact, nothing more than a relatively simple extrapolation of current trends into the future. A more complex method of extrapolation uses a statistical model known as *regression analysis* to examine variables that seem to be correlated with population growth. If we can measure these other variables, their change may hold clues to the likely path of future population growth, and we can use the statistical correlation of variables to estimate population size in the future (utilizing a model known as a linear regression equation). For example, in small geographic areas such as counties of the United States, population growth in an area is often tied to the creation or dissolution of jobs. Thus, if we survey employers and find out how many people they think they may be hiring or firing over the next year, we may then be able statistically to correlate that information to the likely change in the number of people in the area a year from now.

Notice that these methods of population projection that rely on an extrapolation of growth do not take into account births, deaths, or migration. If we have such information available, we can project a population using the **components of growth** method. This is actually an adaptation of the *demographic equation* discussed back in Chapter 2. The population of Mexico in the year 2000 will be equal to the population in 1988 plus all of the births that occur between 1988 and 2000, less all of the deaths during that interval, plus all of the in-migrants, less all of the out-migrants. However, since we rarely have a quick and easy way of calculating the future number of births, deaths, and migrants, the components of growth method is more often used to estimate the population between censuses, when we know already (from the vital statistics data and from other administrative records) how many births, deaths, and migrants there were.

None of the methods discussed so far allows us to estimate future births, deaths, and migrants, and none of them allows us to take account of the age/sex structure of society, which, as we have seen, is an important ingredient in the impact that population growth has on a society. What we need is a more sophisticated approach to population projection, and we find it in the *cohort component method*. To make a population projection using the cohort component method, we begin with an age and sex distribution (in absolute frequencies, not percentages) for a specific **base year.** Usually a base year is a year for which we have the most complete and accurate data—typically a census year. Besides age and sex distributions, you need to have base-year age-specific mortality rates (that is, a base-year life table); base-year age-specific fertility rates; and, if possible, age-specific rates of in- and out-migration. Data are usually arranged in 5-year intervals, such as ages 0–4, 5–9, 10–14, and so on, which facilitates projecting a population forward in time in 5-year intervals. For example, if we are making projections from a base year of 1980 to a **target year** of 2000, we would make intermediate projections for 1985, 1990, and 1995.

With the base-year data in hand and a target year in mind, we must next make some assumptions about the future course of each component of population growth between the base year and the target year. Will mortality continue to drop? If so, which age will be most affected and how big will the changes be? Will fertility decline, remain stable, or possibly rise at some ages while dropping in others? If there is an expected change, how big will it be? Can we expect rates of in- and out-migration to change? Note that if our population is an entire country, our concern will be with international migration only, whereas if we are projecting the population of an area such as a state, county, or city, we will have to consider both internal and international migration. However, since adequate data on migration are often not available, it is frequently ignored in population projections.

The actual process of projecting a population involves several steps and is carried out for each interval (usually 5 years, remember) between the base and target years. First, the age-specific mortality data are applied to each 5-year age group in the base-year population to estimate the number of survivors in that age range 5 years into the future. Thus, since there were 10,282,000 females aged 20–24 in the United States in 1980 and the probability of a female surviving from age 20–24 to age 25–29 (derived from the life table—see Chapter 6) is 0.92, then in 1985 there should be 9,973,000 women aged 25–29. This process of "surviving" a population forward through time is carried out for all age groups in the base-year population. The probabilities of migration (if such data are available) are applied in the same way as are mortality data.

In projecting a population forward at 5-year intervals, the task of fertility estimation is to (1) calculate the numbers of children likely to be born during the 5-year intervals, and (2) calculate how many of those born will also die during those intervals. The number to be born is estimated by multiplying the appropriate age-specific fertility rate by the number of women in each of the childbearing ages. Then we add up that total number of children and apply to that number their probability of survival from birth to the end of the 5-year interval. Experience suggests that fertility behavior frequently changes more rapidly (both up and down) than demographers may expect, so population projectionists now hedge their bets by producing high, medium, and low projections. A high estimate incorporates an assumption of the lowest likely decline (or greatest rise) in fertility and leads naturally to the largest likely population size. A low estimate incorporates the greatest decline (or lowest rise) and results in the smallest likely projected population size. A medium projection usually reflects the demographer's estimates of the most likely course of events. In sum, the differences between high, medium, and low estimates lie primarily in the underlying assumption about the course of fertility. In the short run, virtually all the differences, then, will be explained by differences in the number of young people. For example, in the projection of the population of Mexico made by the U.S. Bureau of the Census (1979e), the high projection for 1990 is 102,349,000, whereas the low projection is 88,103,000. Virtually all the difference (which is equivalent to the population of California) is found in the ages 0–14. Whether Mexico comes closest to the high or low estimate depends largely on the success of the current campaign in that country to lower the birth rate.

Population projections give us clues about the future by letting us view alternative age and sex distributions. From this demographic information we draw inferences about the impact on society by calling on our knowledge of how prior changes in the age structure have altered the fabric of social life. These kinds of interrelationships are well described by the perspectives of age stratification and cohort flow.

Age Stratification and Cohort Flow

The perspective of **age stratification** and **cohort flow** was first put forward as a cohesive package by Matilda White Riley, Marilyn Johnson, and Anne Foner; it has been expanded and detailed since then especially by Riley (1976a; 1979) and Foner (1975). The notion of age status is not new; Kingsley Davis noted in 1949 that "all societies recognize age as a basis of status, but some of them emphasize it more than others" (1949:104). Likewise, the importance of cohorts in analyzing social change is not unique to Riley, Johnson, and Foner; Norman Ryder suggested in 1964 that "social change occurs to the extent that successive cohorts do something other than merely repeat the patterns of behavior of their predecessors" (1964:461). What this perspective does is to integrate these concepts of age status and cohorts in a way that helps to explain social change, and thus helps us to understand how and why the status of older people has been shifting over time.

The age-stratification theory begins with the proposition that age is a basis of social differentiation in a manner analogous to stratification by **social class** (Foner, 1975). The term *stratification* implies a set of inequalities, and in this case it refers to the fact that societies distribute resources unequally by age. These resources include not only economic goods but also such crucial intangibles as social approval, acceptance, and respect. This theory is not a mere description of status, however; it introduces a dynamic element by recognizing that aging is a process of social mobility. Foner (1975) notes that "as the individual ages, he too moves within a social hierarchy. He goes from one set of age-related social roles to another and at each level receives greater or lesser rewards than before" (1975:156). Contrasted to other forms of social mobility, however, which may rely on merit, luck, or accident of birth, social mobility in the age hierarchy is "inevitable, universal and unidirectional in that the individual can never grow younger" (1975:156).

Age strata, though identifiable, are not viewed as fixed and unchanging. The assumption is that the number of age strata, and the prestige and power associated with each, are influenced by the needs of society and by characteristics of people at each age (their numbers and sociodemographic characteristics). European society of a few hundred years ago seems to have been characterized by three age strata—infancy, adulthood, and old age (Aries, 1962); and power (highest status) seems to have been concentrated in the hands of older people (Simmons, 1960). Modern western societies appear to have at least seven strata—infancy, childhood, adolescence, young adulthood, middle age, young old, and old old, with power typically concentrated in the hands of the middle-aged.

As we age from birth to death we are allocated to **social statuses** and **roles** considered appropriate to our age. Thus, children and adolescents are currently allocated to appropriate educational statuses; adults to appropriate positions of power and prestige; and the elderly to positions of retirement. We all learn the roles that society deems appropriate to our age, and we reward each other for fulfilling those roles and tend to cast disapproval upon those who do not fulfill the societal expectation. But neither the allocation process nor the overall **socialization** process is static (as I will discuss later in the chapter). They are in constant flux as changing cohorts alter social conditions and as social conditions, in turn, alter the characteristics of cohorts. This leads to the concept of cohort flow.

A cohort, in this case, refers to a group of people born during the same time period. As Riley (1976b) points out:

> Each cohort starts out with a given size which, save for additions from immigration, is the maximum size it can ever attain. Over the life course of the cohort, some portion of its members survive, while others move away or die until the entire cohort is destroyed. Each cohort starts out also with a given composition; it consists of members born with certain characteristics and dispositions. Over the life course of the individual, some of these characteristics are relatively stable (a person's sex, color, genetic makeup, country of birth, or—at entry into adulthood in our society—the level of educational attainment are unlikely to change). . . . When successive cohorts are compared, they resemble each other in certain respects, but differ markedly in other respects: in initial size and composition, in age-specific patterns of survival (or longevity), and in the period of history covered by their respective life span (1976b:194–195).

At any given moment, a cross section of all cohorts defines the current age strata in a society (see Figure 8.5). As cohorts flow through time, their respective sizes and characteristics may alter the allocation of status and thus the socialization into various age-related roles. Additionally, some characteristics of cohorts may change in response to changing social and economic conditions (such as wars, famines, and economic prosperity), and those changing conditions will influence the formation of new cohorts. This continual feedback between the dynamics of successive cohorts and the dynamics of other changes in society produces a constant shifting in the status and meaning attached to each age stratum.

The older population of the United States, for example, is currently being transformed by the changing characteristics of the new cohorts moving into old age. Cohorts of different sizes and backgrounds, and with different facets of social history having affected them, shape old age somewhat differently. For example, there were 8.7 million Americans aged 65–69 in 1980 (representing the birth cohorts of 1911 through 1915). Between 1911 and 1915, there were about 14 million Americans born, and, based on the known death rates for people born during those years,

Figure 8.5   Cohort Flow and Age Strata Are Closely Intertwined

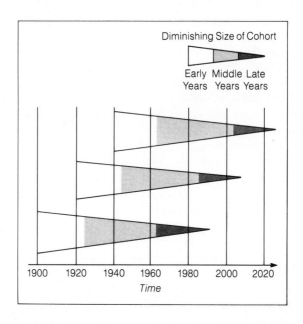

Source: Adapted from M. Riley, M. Johnson, and A. Foner, *Aging and Society: A Sociology of Age Stratification,* vol. III (New York: Russell Sage Foundation, © 1972), p. 10. Used by permission.

Note: Cohorts flow through time, gradually diminishing in size and impinging on society as they move through time. At any given date the number and characteristics of people in each life stage will influence the system of age strata.

we should have expected to find only about 8 million of them still alive in 1980. Where did the others come from? Europe, mainly, but also Asia, Latin America, and, to a much lesser extent, Africa. In 1980, there were more than half a million foreign-born people in the United States population aged 65–69; many were recent arrivals, but most had come as younger people and had grown old in the United States. The members of this birth cohort were youngsters during World War I and, though they were too young to go off to war, this generation was hit hard by the Depression that descended in the early 1930s, just as they were trying to find jobs. They were the young people who had to postpone childbearing and settle for fewer children than they desired because it was so costly to raise a family during the 1930s. Some of these people found themselves fighting World War II, and all of them were entangled in it in one way or another. Life was not completely bleak for this cohort, however. After the war this group provided leaders who forged the incredible rise in national wealth and personal income in the United States, and they became eligible for social security benefits at a time when those benefits hit record high levels. These people represent, in fact, the best-educated and highest-income group of older people so far in the United States, a topic to which I will return in Chapter 11.

One of the more widely discussed analyses of the impact of changing cohort size on a population is the "Easterlin hypothesis," which I discussed in Chapter 3. Yet, you need not accept all of Easterlin's assumptions about the effect of the relative size of cohorts to know that the Baby Boom generation has, through sheer cohort size, vastly influenced the social world of the United States. One example is the relationship between the age structure and the crime rate (see the Essay in this chapter). Another example is the unprecedented growth in the number of households in the United States between 1970 and 1980.

Between 1970 and 1980 the population of the United States living in households increased by 10 percent, but there was a 26 percent increase in the *number* of households (Sweet, 1984). This meant, of course, that the average household size was shrinking. The extraordinary increase in households was a bonus for the real estate, construction, and mortgage banking industries, as it was for people who furnish and service households, including manufacturers of housewares, furniture, appliances, carpeting, carpet cleaners, and household helpers. More than two thirds (69 percent) of the increase in the number of households was due to changing age structure. "The large baby boom cohorts have replaced the very small depression cohorts. In 1980 there were 39 percent more 20–34 year olds than in 1970" (Sweet, 1984:139). Additionally, continually declining mortality at the older ages contributed to the maintenance of a relatively large number of single-person households among the elderly.

The rest of the explanation for the increase in households is delayed marriage among younger people. Central to the Easterlin hypothesis is the idea that young people in a large cohort who have grown up in affluence will find it more difficult to simultaneously reach a high level of living on their own and also build a family. Competition for jobs, produced by the existence of so many other people of the same age, led the Baby Boomers to postpone marriage in order to get more education and to become more established in a career before being burdened with a family. Obviously, two single people produce twice as many households as would a married couple. Even though the proportion of people living together without being married more than tripled between 1970 and 1982 (U.S. Bureau of the Census, 1983b), those individuals still represented less than 2 percent of all single people.

Another example of the influence of the age structure on social phenomena is the change in the American suicide rate. This is a variation on the Easterlin theme that changing cohort size alters the fortunes of each cohort. Besides leading to delayed marriage, delayed parenthood, and slower social and economic mobility, changing cohort size may have contributed to a rise in the suicide rate, just as it did the crime rate. The Easterlin approach suggests that:

> When relative cohort size (the ratio of younger to older males) increases, it is expected to lead to an increase in suicide rates for young males (as their labor market position relative to their income aspirations deteriorates) and a decrease in suicide rates for older males (as their labor market position relative to their income aspiration improves) (Ahlburg and Schapiro, 1984:99).

The economic effect that is so crucial to the Easterlin perspective may be augmented by a sociopsychological effect:

> The large baby boom cohort, because of imperfect socialization arising from the rising child/adult ratio, was "saddled with expectations and beliefs which were less realistic, less suited to particular individual lives, less flexible in the face of adversity" (Carlson, 1980). Such imperfect socialization may be expected to result in an increase in the suicide rate (Ahlburg and Schapiro, 1984:100).

Ahlburg and Schapiro show that the data from the United States do, in fact, support the idea that between 1948 and 1976 the suicide rate went up among younger people as (1) the size of the younger cohorts increased relative to the older, and (2) the ratio of children to adults increased. Thus, the age structure itself may help to account for at least part of the dramatic rise in teenage suicides during the late 1960s and 1970s, and forecasts a rise in suicide rates for middle-aged and older males as the Baby Boom cohort flows through time.

Changes in household structure and in suicide rates occasioned by the changing age distribution of the United States represent two of numerous ways in which we can "read" an age structure and, in essence, try to tell a population's fortune. Let us do this in more detail for the United States.

Reading the American Age Structure

Changes Induced by Fertility Fluctuations   We can trace the recent history of fertility (and recount the economic situation of the time) in the age pyramid for the United States (Figure 8.6). Actually, above age 55 or 60 the effect of accelerating death rates obscures changes that might have occurred, but for slightly younger people, you can see the effect the Depression had on the birth rate. For example, people who were between 45 and 50 years old in 1980 were born between 1931 and 1936, which was the bottom of the Depression. In those years the birth rate was very low (below replacement level, as I discussed in Chapter 5), and you can see further that fertility had been declining since 1921–25. Had you looked only at the age distribution for males, you might well have jumped to the conclusion that the dent at those ages was due to World War II casualties, but a glance at the female side would cause you to reject that idea, since females were not engaged in actual combat.

In the late 1930s, the birth rate picked up a little and, of course, the Baby Boom occurred in the 1940s and 1950s as the economy recovered after World War II. You can spot the Baby Boom generation as roughly those people who were 20–34 years old in 1980. After 1960 the birth rate declined, with each year generally seeing fewer people added than the year before. Thus, in 1980 there were fewer people between ages 0 and 5 than there were in any 5-year age group up to age 35. That "birth dearth" or "baby bust" will be a feature of the age structure until the middle of the twenty-first century and will be a long-lived reminder of the inflation, tight job market, energy shortage, and female liberation from the late 1960s through the 1980s.

Figure 8.6   Age Pyramid for the United States (1980)

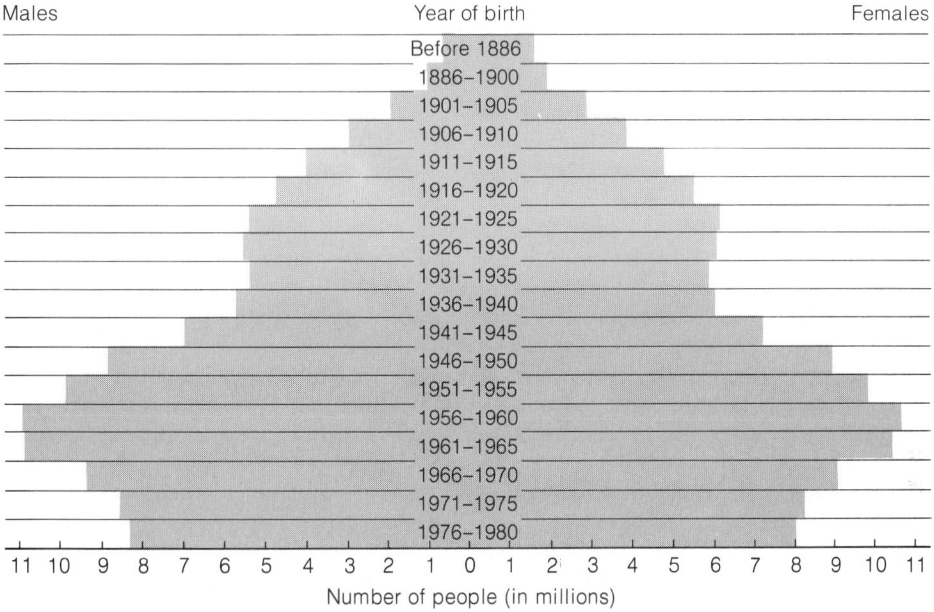

Males	Year of birth	Females
	Before 1886	
	1886–1900	
	1901–1905	
	1906–1910	
	1911–1915	
	1916–1920	
	1921–1925	
	1926–1930	
	1931–1935	
	1936–1940	
	1941–1945	
	1946–1950	
	1951–1955	
	1956–1960	
	1961–1965	
	1966–1970	
	1971–1975	
	1976–1980	

11 10 9 8 7 6 5 4 3 2 1 0 1 2 3 4 5 6 7 8 9 10 11

Number of people (in millions)

The age pyramid for the United States in 1980 clearly shows the impact of low birth rates during the Depression (births in 1931–40; ages 45–54 in 1980), the higher birth rate of the Baby Boom generation (births in 1946–60; ages 20–34 in 1980), and the decline in fertility since the 1960s. *Source:* U.S. Bureau of the Census, 1983, "Population Profile of the United States; 1982," Current Population Reports, Series P-23, No. 130, Table 3.

In the United States in 1980, 23 percent of the population was under age 15, so it was not exactly young, while more than 11 percent was 65 and older, putting it on the verge of old (remember my discussion earlier in the chapter). This might seem strange if you have grown up hearing that the United States has become a youth-oriented society. But in Figure 8.6 notice that the bulge of youth (the Baby Boom children) was centered around the late twenties and early thirties, with fewer people at the younger ages as a result of the decline in fertility from the early 1960s on. It was actually that decline in fertility that has aged the American population, rather than anything that has been happening to the aged themselves.

The distortions you see in the age structure have some interesting implications for the future, and in the following section I will talk about them in connection with two different sets of projections about the future course of birth rates. One projection assumes that birth rates were manipulated to achieve **zero population growth** (ZPG) in the 1980s, while the other assumes that fertility will remain unchanged from 1980 levels, thus eventually (rather than abruptly) leading to ZPG.

CRIME AND THE AGE STRUCTURE

There were 48 percent more arrests in the United States in 1980 than in 1970, according to the FBI (data from the U.S. Department of Justice, 1971; 1981). Had society fallen apart? Had the nation lapsed into a police state? Neither one. What happened was that the Baby Boom generation was moving through the late teen and early adult years, when crime rates are highest. They swelled those ages and crime went up at least partly because there were more people "at risk" of committing a crime. At these younger ages, a person's fancy seems to turn not just to love, but disproportionately to crime as well. In most societies crime is the province of the young, and it stands to reason that a youthful age structure will produce higher overall crime rates (that is, crude crime rates) than will an older age structure (Cohen and Land, 1987).

Calculating crime rates by age is a bit tricky for large geographic areas such as the United States, because not all regions of the country report crimes, nor do those reporting necessarily use the same criteria. Furthermore, you know the age of an alleged criminal only after you have caught him or her, so areas that are more efficient at catching criminals will have different data from those that are less efficient. Nonetheless, these limitations have not deterred me from comparing arrests in 1980 with those in 1970.

In the accompanying graph you can see the distribution of arrests by age in the United States in 1970 and 1980. It is obvious that crime (as evidenced by arrests) clusters between ages 15 and 24. The peak age was 16 in 1970 and 18 in 1980. Dividing the number of arrests by the midyear population at each age yields a set of age-specific crime rates, and the accompanying table shows these rates for 1970 and 1980. Comparing the graph with the table you will see that the arrest *rates* tended to go up in that intercensal period. Wouldn't that alone account for the rise in the number of arrests? Not quite. If we assumed that age-specific arrest rates had been the same in 1980 as in 1970, then applying those rates to the age distribution in 1980 tells us how many more arrests we would have expected in 1980 than in 1970, simply due to the increase in the number of people in the high crime years. The answer is that the changing age structure alone accounts for 1,353,786 more arrests in 1980 than in 1970, or 43 percent of the total increase. This is very similar to the findings of the 1967 National Crime Commission, which concluded that 40 to 50 percent of the increase in the U.S. crime rate between 1960 and 1965 was due to the changing age structure—the early impact of the Baby Boom.

The other 57 percent of the increase in arrests between 1970 and 1980 was due to other things besides the age structure. One possible explanation is that police were more likely to arrest people in 1980 than in 1970 because more money had been pumped into law enforcement in response to the crime siege brought on by the Baby Boomers. Another explanation is that the rise in the number of children per adult rose during the Baby Boom, potentially lowering the amount of social control exercised over each child, thus leading to more deviant behavior that resulted in arrest. Related to this is the fact that changing gender roles extends to criminal activity and the ratio of female to male arrests has steadily risen since 1960. In that year, for example, there were 12 females arrested for every 100 arrests of males. By 1980, the figure had risen to 19.

A less obvious, but potentially very important, aspect of the age structure's influence on crime is the fact that the age structure of the population of potential victims may also affect the opportunities for crime and thus the crime rate itself. In the United States in the 1970s, the high proportion of the population that was young, at work during the day, and affluent enough to own easily stolen and fenced goods rose dramatically, and thus the opportunity for crime rose during the 1970s. Cohen and Felson (1979) argue that this substantial increase in the opportunity to commit crime is, in fact, the most important explanation of the rise in the crime rate. If so, the age structure effect is less direct, but no less influential.

Another feature of the Baby Boom's potential impact on crime is seen in the arrest rates themselves. In 1980, no one aged 35 or older was a member of the Baby Boom cohort. In 1980, *arrest rates were lower at every age from 35 on up* than in 1970, whereas *at every age between 15 and 35 (the Baby Boomers) arrests were*

higher in 1980 than in 1970. Higher than average arrest rates may characterize the Baby Boom generation through its lifetime, but it is still true that the older you are, the less likely you are to commit a crime. Thus, with the aging of the Baby Boomers and the emergence of the Baby Bust generation into the prime crime years, we should expect crime to decline.

In 1982 the first signs of such a downturn appeared in the annual FBI statistics (U.S. Department of Justice, 1983). Violent crime declined by 3 percent that year, compared with 1981. Was it any coincidence that there were 3 percent fewer youths aged 15–19 in 1982 than in 1981? Was it just a coincidence that between

(continued on p. 244)

Arrests by Age, 1970 and 1980

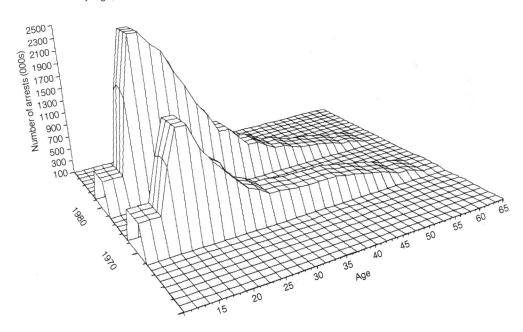

The number of arrests per age rose significantly at the younger ages between 1970 and 1980. *Sources:* U.S. Department of Justice, 1971, Crime in the United States, 1980 (Washington, D.C.: Federal Bureau of Investigation), Table 28; U.S. Department of Justice, 1981, Crime in the United States, 1970 (Washington, D.C.: Federal Bureau of Investigation), Table 32.

CRIME AND THE AGE STRUCTURE (Continued)

1980 and 1984 the total number of crimes in the United States dropped by 11 percent (U.S. Department of Justice, 1986), at the same time that the population aged 15–19 declined by 11 percent? Probably not, but law enforcement personnel are quite naturally wary of what they perceive to be an overemphasis on demographic explanations of the shifting crime rate. In 1984, Department of Justice officials announced that crime had dropped by 7 percent in 1983—the largest dip since 1960 (San Diego Union, 1984). Yet, the director of the Bureau of Justice Statistics was reluctant to accept the demographic inevitability. To do so would require that we ignore the important changes in law enforcement practices that have occurred over time. For example, between 1960 and 1970 the percentage of people arrested who actually went to jail went down significantly. This undoubtedly helped to increase the incidence of repeated arrests of the same people (recidivism), which could have helped to account for the rising crime and arrest rates, irrespective of changes in the age distribution. On the other hand, in the late 1970s and early 1980s, policy changes have reversed that downward trend. Increasing percentages of people arrested are winding up in jail. As a result the prison population is exploding in size, and this may help to account for the drop in the crime rate (Schlesinger and Sedgwick, 1984).

Probably the most interesting aspect of the debate over whether demography or law enforcement is responsible for the changing crime rate is that the relative im-

Arrest Rates by Age—
United States, 1970 and 1980

Age	Arrest Rates (per 1,000)	
	1970	1980
13–14	47.7	55.5
15–19	89.9	122.4
20–24	73.2	104.6
25–29	48.6	70.4
30–34	42.6	50.8
35–39	40.6	41.3
40–44	37.3	35.5
45–49	32.2	28.7
50–54	26.5	22.0
55–59	20.0	15.6
60–64	13.9	10.2
65+	5.2	3.7
All Ages Combined	32.6	42.6

Source: Calculated from data in U.S. Department of Justice, 1981, Crime in the United States, 1980 (Washington, D.C.: Federal Bureau of Investigation), Table 32.

portance of the two explanations has shifted in less than a decade. In the mid-1970s people were only beginning to accept the idea that crime bore any relation to the changing age structure. By the mid-1980s that influence was so widely accepted that law enforcement personnel were clamoring to remind us that demography does not explain everything. As usual, of course, the truth probably lies somewhere between those two extremes.

ZPG—Now or Later   The public worry over population growth in the United States quieted considerably in the 1970s after the commotion created in the 1960s. Interestingly enough, at the time of greatest public concern, about 1966–70, the U.S. birth rate had already begun to drop, and the concern was in many ways a belated reaction to the Baby Boom (as well as a corollary to other social concerns especially prevalent in the 1960s). However, the decline of interest in population issues in the United States in the 1970s was premature, since the population is almost certain to continue its increase into the next century.

At current levels of fertility and with relatively unchanging levels of migration and mortality, the U.S. population will stop growing around the year 2030. At that time the population will be larger by at least 55 million than it was in 1980—equivalent to adding another state with the population of California, New York, and Florida combined. There are those who have argued that the country cannot, and what's more should not, tolerate an additional 55 million people and that ZPG should be achieved immediately (see, for example, W. Davis, 1973). What are the consequences of these two different growth strategies? The contrast in the age/sex structure represents the single most important source of difference, and regardless of the path of future growth, age/sex structure changes will play a crucial role in the future development of the United States.

To bring these issues into sharper focus, I have made two projections for the U.S. population from 1980 to 2060. The first one (ZPG now) assumes that from 1980 on, the American population will not grow in size. The second (ZPG later) is based on the assumption that ZPG will come later as a result of a continuation of 1980 fertility levels.

For the sake of simplicity, I have assumed in both sets of projections that mortality will remain at the levels prevailing in 1980, and that the number of immigrants per year by age and sex will remain at the 1979 level. If mortality were to continue to decline from the 1980 levels, then my projections would be too low, since greater proportions of people would survive to each successive age. On the other hand, if significant restrictions were placed on legal immigration into the United States, the number of immigrants could drop from the 1979 levels. Over the long run, these two influences could roughly cancel each other in their effect on population size, although of course they would have differential effects on the age/sex structure. As you look at these alternative projections, keep in mind the old Chinese proverb: "Prediction is very difficult—especially with regard to the future."

1980 Let me put the projections into perspective by briefly reviewing the situation of 1980. The declining birth rate that followed the Baby Boom has forced adjustments in several segments of American society. During the early years of the Baby Boom there were too few classrooms and teachers, so new schools were built and new programs were developed to train teachers. But the drop in birth rates resulted in a bumper crop of unemployed teachers and, furthermore, companies that had made big profits on babies were forced to rethink their markets. The Baby Boom children were growing up and not having many babies. (This is the real story of how baby shampoo became a beauty shampoo for adults, as I discuss further in Chapter 16.) As the Baby Boom children hit the labor market, their annually increasing numbers put a severe strain on the ability of the economy to provide jobs, so it should be no surprise that during the 1970s unemployment rates were persistently high and that in the 1980s women were in the labor force in record proportions, helping to produce an adequate family income.

On the other hand, in the middle ages (40–54) we find cohorts of people who were among the most advantaged in American history. They were born during the Depression (and thus, you recall, there are not many of them) and they were too young for World War II, although some were involved in the Korean War. They were advantaged primarily in an economic sense, since they entered the labor market during a time of relative economic expansion. Because there were fewer of them than of older cohorts, they were absorbed into the labor force more quickly and had less competition for career advancement. Overall, the rise in their standard of living from childhood to mid-adulthood was probably greater than for any other generation of Americans.

At the oldest ages, near and above the age of retirement, the number of people was larger than at any time in history. The problems created by the Baby Boom generation, though, tended to steal the spotlight from the older generation, which lacked the political unity (although certainly not the numeric strength) to have a major voice in American policy making. Nonetheless, their increasing numbers have given rise to new construction of retirement communities, an expansion of employment opportunities servicing the elderly, and fears that the social security system will be bankrupted, topics to which I will return in Chapter 14.

Would the age/sex structure be more or less problematic in 2000 if ZPG had been achieved in 1980? Let us see.

2000   Zero population growth in the absence of migration means that the number of births in any given year just equals the number of people dying. Of course, with migration taken into account in the United States (where immigration exceeds emigration), there would have to be fewer births than deaths to maintain ZPG. This is reflected in Figure 8.7, where you can see that in 2000 the age structure would be heavily weighted toward the middle adult population, at the expense of the young, in order to achieve zero population growth. Indeed, in this model there are virtually twice as many people aged 35–44 as there are aged 0–9—nearly a complete turnabout from the early Baby Boom years.

To have achieved ZPG in the 1980s and maintained it until 2000 would have required a substantial reduction in fertility beyond the already low levels. Consequences of that rapidly falling fertility include the obvious fact that, after the bottom fell out of the higher education market and the number of new families formed dropped dramatically in the 1980s and 1990s, there would be only a slight rebounding by 2000. Since the number of large or growing families would be severely cut back, the housing construction industry would also be affected. However, there might be an increased demand for specialized housing and services for the elderly, whose numbers will, in all events, increase by 2005. The smaller numbers of people in the young-adult age cohorts, added to the prospect of even smaller cohorts younger than they, should provide the young adults with a relative advantage in entering the labor market. Rapid **upward mobility** would probably be rather difficult for those people, however, since the Baby Boom generation would still be glutting the market. In addition, the smaller family size might well add substantial proportions of women to the labor market, increasing competition for jobs and promotions. The problem of creating jobs and career opportunities might be compounded by the difficulty of expanding the economy in the face of no population growth. Americans (especially in the middle class) have generally taken progress for granted and tend to feel deprived when their standard of living is not materially improving, but it is possible that with ZPG, the quality of life would have to be measured in other than material terms.

It is probable, of course, that the future of American society will be a quest for nonmaterial progress whether we have ZPG now or later. The increasing worldwide demand for resources is placing ever-increasing constraints on the ability of Americans actually to improve their standard of living. Indeed there are some people (for example, Hernandez, 1974) who argue that material progress in the United States is really a sideways movement, not a real increase in the quality of life. The replacement of homemade cookies with snack foods and the popularity of fast-food restaurants and electronic games, for instance, represent changes in life-style but not necessarily improvements. A rise in the standard of living is perhaps better measured in the more standard terms of improved health, more comfortable housing, more and better education, and greater artistic achievement and appreciation. The future will in all probability see at least a measure of attention being focused increasingly on these aspects of the quality of existence rather than on simply diversifying consumer goods and services.

It should be obvious to you that in 2000 the only difference between the ZPG-now and ZPG-later positions would be the number of people at ages under 20. You can see from Figure 8.7 that with 1980 levels of fertility in the ZPG-later projection, there will be a slight rise in the number of births between 1980 and 1990, resulting in a slight rise in the number of people aged 10–20 in 2000. This is a result of the bulge of young women in 1980 moving through their reproductive ages; even at a rate of slightly less than two children per woman, there were so many young women in 1980 that their fertility increased the number of annual births. This would be offset in 1990–2000 by the relatively smaller number of young women (born in the 1960s and 1970s) moving through their reproductive years. This situation depicts the **momentum of population growth**; that is, high fertility in one generation has a certain momentum that carries it through time and results in high fertility in the next generation. Overall, however, the number of births in the ZPG-later projection is fairly stable and the social, political, and economic dislocations would probably be minimal. The price for the stability, of course, is a population that would still be growing. Between 1980 and 2000 the population of the United States would increase from 227 million to 262 million.

2020   By the year 2020, the number of old people will be rising each year and contributing to the possibility of rising fertility. In the ZPG-now projection the age structure broadens out slightly at the bottom as a new Baby Boom begins to replace the old boom generation, which by 2020 has almost reached, or is rapidly approaching, retirement age.

The economic and social makeup of society would be considerably different than it is now, being dominated by older middle-aged people but in the midst of a transition to a renewed emphasis on families and youth. The couples who had only one child to achieve ZPG could be thinking about a greater number of grandchildren. The economy then would have to be moving in two directions at once—accommodating both the increasing demands of children and the increasing needs of the elderly. It is conceivable that this would be a fairly rigid society in terms of social

Figure 8.7   ZPG-Now Age Pyramids Are More Distorted for the Future Than Those for ZPG-Later

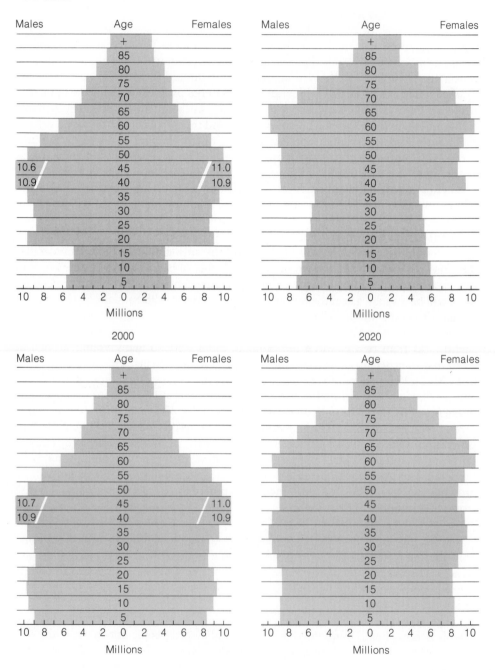

Projections over time of the U.S. population for 1980–2060 (assuming constant migration and mortality rates) show that the ZPG-later path would provide a smooth transition to nongrowth, whereas the ZPG-now path could create a new cycle of problems similar to the Baby Boom.

Figure 8.7   (continued)

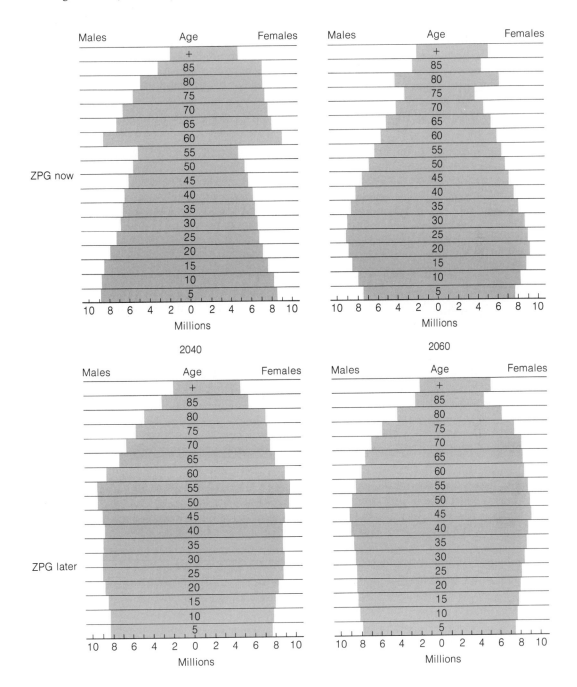

behavior, dominated by the older middle-aged adults. Indeed, from 1980 to 2020 the pattern is one of a lessening likelihood of innovative behavior on the part of the young as a consequence of the rise in the ratio of adults to children and the probable resulting increase in social control. On the other hand, the Baby Boom generation has been noted for its high degree of flexibility and innovativeness (see Jones, 1981), and it is reasonable to suppose that such behavior will be carried into older age (Weeks, 1984).

By the year 2020 the population in the ZPG-later projection would have grown to about 279 million people, a 23 percent increase over the 1980 population but only 6 percent larger than the 2000 population. It is at about this point that the population would finally stop growing (achieve ZPG) and would begin very slowly to decline in size. As you can see in Figure 8.7, the age structure suggests a population dominated numerically by people in their older middle ages. But unlike the ZPG-now population, the ZPG-later population in 2020 would have a fairly even distribution by age. The average age of the population would become steadily older, but the process is a gradual one, unencumbered by the fluctuations in the youthful population, which would be required at this date in the ZPG-now projection.

2040 and 2060   In the year 2040 ZPG now would produce an age structure from ages 0 through 55 that looks very much like an underdeveloped country (see Figure 8.7). Each year for five decades the number of babies born would have been greater to offset the increasing number of deaths generated by the burgeoning population of the elderly. This trend would actually continue for 5 more years. The number of young children (aged 0–4) now exceeds the number alive in 1980, adding to the dependency burden made awesome by the size of the retirement-age population. Everyone in the Baby Boom generation would be either dead or retired in 2040, and the retirees could represent an enormous social and political force in American society. Their power in society would be augmented by the fact that the retirement age would have to be virtually eliminated or else jobs could be begging in society.

Although dominated by the elderly, the American society of 2040 would have to start looking forward to the future (say, about 2060), when younger adults would again be a major influence in the economy, politics, and social fabric of the country, as they were in 1980.

In 2060 the United States would be dealing with a new Baby Boom generation of young adults, but a new Baby Bust phenomenon at the very youngest ages, and the ferris-wheel cycle of fertility would start all over again. That cycle would continue for as long as U.S. policy was oriented toward maintaining ZPG. By now, you may well have supposed that the massive shifting every decade or two in the numbers of people at each age might well have led to an abandonment of the ZPG policy in the interest of economic, political, and social stability. For example, the economic impact of the fluctuating age structure over time is evident in the dependency ratio. In Figure 8.7 you can see that with ZPG now, in the 40 years between 2000 and 2040 the dependency ratio would more than double, but in another 20 years (to 2060) the ratio would have dropped to nearly the 1980 level. The consequence would be a series of booms and busts in schools, retirement homes, job creation for youth, the demand for durable goods, and so forth.

As the ZPG-later projection progresses through time, the age/sex structure continues to smooth out to a population with a decreasing emphasis on children and youth and an increasing predominance of middle-aged and elderly persons. The vast majority of the population is of working age, and this could be more economically advantageous than the situation of ZPG now. The dependency ratios for the ZPG-later projections are lower than those of the ZPG-now projections every year from 2020 on, particularly in 2040 when the difference between the two projections is especially great.

We can conclude that over time the abrupt changes in fertility levels required just to bring the United States to ZPG now produce lifelong distortions in the age structure, which can create constant problems of adjustment for society. This is the dilemma that American society has had to face with the Baby Boom generation. At first there were the problems of schooling and jobs; the future will see problems of economic consumption (finding housing, getting promotions, and so on); and eventually there will be problems of retirement and providing social security and other retirement benefits.

SUMMARY AND CONCLUSION

The age/sex structure of a society is a subtle, frequently overlooked aspect of the social structure of a society. The number of people at each age and of each sex is an important factor in how a society is organized and how it operates. The age/sex structure is determined completely by the interaction of the three demographic processes. Migration can have a sizable impact, since migrants tend to predominate at particular age groups and, in addition, migration is frequently selective for one sex or the other. Mortality has the smallest short-run impact on the age/sex distribution, but when mortality declines suddenly (as in the less developed nations), the impact is to make the population more youthful. At the same time, a decline in mortality influences the sex structure at the older ages by producing increasingly greater numbers of females than males.

Changes in fertility generally produce the biggest changes in a society's age structure; a decline in fertility ages the population, just as a rise makes it more youthful. A rise in fertility also tends to produce a greater number of males than females, since there are more boys born than girls. For example, males in the world outnumber females, because continued high levels of reproduction have generated a youthful world age structure in which the excess of male babies at birth results in the overall majority of males.

We study the effects of population processes on the age/sex structure by calculating stable and stationary population models, which are types of population projections—one of the most useful methodological tools created in the field of population studies. Looking backward through time, we can see how different birth cohorts have flowed through time, being influenced differentially at each age by social events, and in turn have shaped events by their passage through the age structure.

Using population projections to look ahead, we can chart the potential course of change implied by different age/sex structures. The analysis of two alternative future patterns of population change in the United States (ZPG now and ZPG later) illustrates the impact that changing fertility could have on the age/sex structure and, by implication, on the overall structure of society. It is reasonable to suppose that distortions in the age structure could lead to changes in economic organization, political dominance, and social stability. In the next chapter, some of these interrelationships will be explored as we examine population characteristics.

MAIN POINTS

1. An age/sex structure represents the number of people of a given age and sex in society and is built from the input of births at age zero and from deaths and migration at every age.

2. A young population is one with a high proportion of young people, whereas an old population is one with a high proportion of elderly people.

3. The age structure is typically graphed as a population pyramid and measured by the median age or the dependency ratio.

4. More male babies than females are generally born, but the age structure is further influenced by the fact that at almost every age more males than females die.

5. Migration can have a very dramatic short-run impact on the age/sex structure of society, especially in local areas.

6. Migration most drastically affects the number of young adults.

7. Mortality has very little long-run impact on the age structure, but in the short run a decline in mortality typically makes the population younger.

8. Fertility is the most important determinant of the shape of the age/sex structure.

9. High fertility produces a young age structure, whereas low fertility produces an older age structure.

10. The age/sex structure is a powerful stimulant to social change.

11. The influences of fertility and mortality on the age/sex structure are usually understood by applying stable population models to real populations.

12. Population projections are developed from applying the age/sex distribution for a base year to sets of age-specific mortality, fertility, and migration rates for the interval between the base year and the target year.

13. The concepts of age stratification and cohort flow place age structures in their proper sociohistorical context.

14. In the United States, even with current low levels of fertility, a policy of zero population growth right now would produce rather severe dislocations in social organization as a result of changes in the age structure that would take place if the population suddenly stopped growing.

SUGGESTED READINGS

1. Jeanne Ridley, Mindel Sheps, J. Lingner, and Jane Menken, 1967, "The effects of changing mortality on natality," Milbank Memorial Fund Quarterly 55(1):77–97.

   The title of this article pretty well sums up the topic under discussion, but it fails to tell you that this was one of the first important statements of the link between mortality and fertility.

2. Ansley Coale and Paul Demeny, 1983, Regional Model Life Tables and Stable Populations (New York: Academic Press).

   This book pulls together more than two decades of ground-breaking work on stable population models and their usefulness in demography. Much of the discussion in the chapter you have just read owes a great deal to this work.

3. Carl Haub, 1987, "Understanding population projections," Population Bulletin 42(4).

   This is a well-written summary of the major types of population projections and their interpretations.

4. Matilda White Riley (ed.), 1979, Aging from Birth to Death (Boulder, CO: Westview Press).

   Riley is one of the world's foremost authorities on aging and is an innovator of the concept of age stratification. In this volume she has compiled papers by a variety of experts that expose you to the complex relationships between demographic processes and the age structure.

5. Landon Jones, 1981, Great Expectations: America and the Baby Boom Generation (New York: Ballantine).

   Although Jones is not a professional demographer, this is a well-researched book about the social impact of the great demographic anomaly of modern America—the Baby Boom. It was on the best-seller list for many weeks, and portions of the book have been reprinted in a variety of places, making it an influential interpreter of the demography of the Baby Boom generation.

CHAPTER 9
Population Characteristics and Life Chances

254

Have you ever given serious thought to the reasons why you may be seeking, or have achieved, a college education? How will your life be different because you are educated? What does it matter if you are black in the United States, Arab in Israel, Indian in Malaysia? Each of these different aspects of who you are will affect your life chances—your probability of having a high-prestige job, lots of money, a stable marriage, and a small family. These differences in life chances, of course, are not necessarily a reflection of your worth as an individual, but they are reflections of the social and economic makeup of society—indicators of the **demographic characteristics** that help to define what a society and its members are like.

In this chapter I will examine several of the most important characteristics—education, occupation, labor force participation, income, marital status, **race** and **ethnicity**, and religion. My purpose is not merely to describe how the population is divided up according to such characteristics (although I will certainly do that), but also to examine how your life chances are influenced by being on one path or another. Furthermore, I will show you how demographic characteristics affect population processes (looking especially at fertility) and how these differences in population processes in turn may influence your life chances by shifting you from one path to another.

Figure 9.1 illustrates what I mean by being on a particular track or path. We are born with certain **ascribed characteristics,** such as gender (which we discussed in the previous chapter) and race and ethnicity, over which we have essentially no control (except in extreme cases). These characteristics affect life chances because, as I have mentioned previously, virtually every society uses such identifiable human attributes to the advantage of some people and the disadvantage of others. Religion is not

Figure 9.1   Population Characteristics Affect Population Processes and Are Also Affected by Them

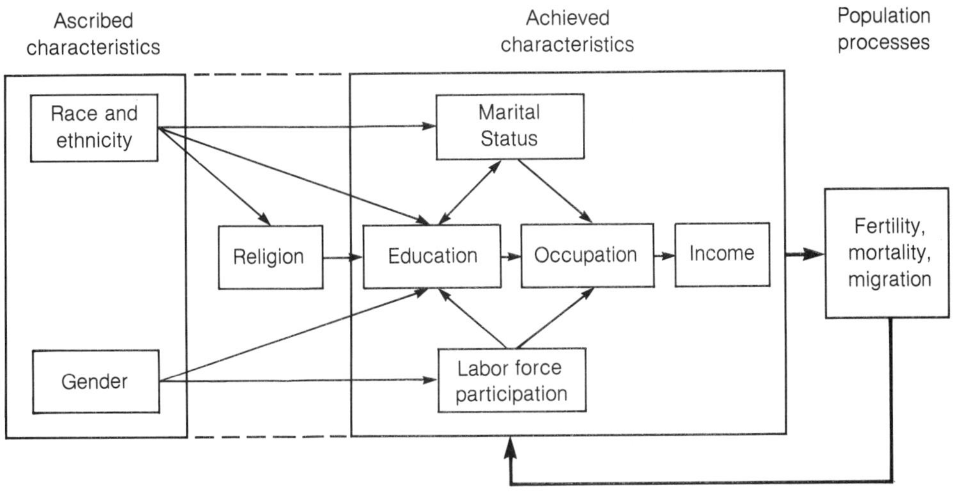

See text for discussion.

exactly an ascribed characteristic, but worldwide it is typically a function of race or ethnicity and, as with other ascribed characteristics, it is frequently a focal point for prejudice and discrimination, which influence life chances.

Life chances are more directly related to **achieved characteristics,** those sociodemographic characteristics such as education, occupation, labor force participation, income, and marital status, over which we do exercise some degree of control. In general, these are the characteristics that define what your life is apt to be. For example, the better educated you are, the higher is your occupational status apt to be, and thus the higher your level of income will likely be. Indeed, income is a crass, but widely accepted, index of how your life is turning out. Ascribed characteristics have their impact on your life chances primarily by affecting your access to achieved characteristics, which are the major ingredients of social status—education, occupation, and income. Population characteristics affect your own demographic behavior, especially fertility, although they also influence mortality and migration, as I have already discussed in Chapters 6 and 7, respectively. Demographic behavior then affects life chances through its ability to facilitate or retard your access to opportunities for higher education, a higher-status occupation, or a better-paying job.

With those words of introduction, let us press on to examine population characteristics, allowing you to see where you fit into the overall scheme of things. We will first look at the achieved characteristics, since our ability to shape them gives them particular interest. Then we will see how your life chances may be constrained by the ascribed characteristics.

EDUCATION

Becoming educated is probably the most dramatic and significant change that you can introduce into your life. It is the locomotive that drives much of the economic development throughout the world, and it is a vehicle for personal success used by generation after generation of people in the highly developed nations of the world. However, the relative recency with which advanced education has taken root in American society can be seen in Figure 9.2. In 1940, only one out of four Americans aged 25 or older had graduated from high school, and only one of ten had been to college. A historically short four decades later, two of every three people had high school diplomas and one of three had attended college. Even higher proportions of people are educated at the younger adult ages, where recent gains are primarily registered. In 1970, 46 percent of Americans aged 25–34 had attended college (16 percent had completed 4 or more years), but by 1980 an incredible 67 percent of all people of that age had been to college and 24 percent had completed at least 4 years.

The recent rapid rise in educational attainment has been shared by virtually all sociodemographic groups, so, despite the headway made by minority group members and women, white males continue to be the members of American society most likely to have attended college. If you fall into the category of white male, there was a 58 percent chance in 1980 that you had been to college. White women aged 25–34

Figure 9.2   Educational Attainment Has Increased Significantly over Time in the United States (1940 to 1980)

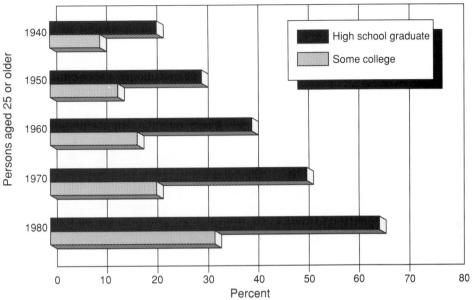

Source: U.S. Bureau of the Census, 1983, 1980 Census of Population, Vol. One, General Social and Economic Characteristics, U.S. Summary (Washington, D.C.: Government Printing Office), Table 83.

had a 43 percent chance of having attended college. By contrast, among blacks in that age group there was near equality by gender in the likelihood of having been to college in 1980—28 percent of black males and 27 percent of black females being in that position.

There are competing theories of why minority group members in the United States are less likely to attain as high an educational level as whites (see Jencks, 1972). Explanations range from the differing cultural emphases on the value of education to the impact of discrimination against minority group members. But, regardless of the reasons, there is little question about the fact. Indeed, if you are of Spanish origin, you are even less likely to have attended college than if you are black. However, that overall difference is accounted for by the lower level of educational attainment of Hispanic (Spanish-origin) women compared with black women. In the Hispanic population aged 25–34 in 1980, 29 percent of males but only 21 percent of females had ever attended college.

In general, women have been increasing their level of educational attainment relative to men. Although both sexes reached equality several decades ago with respect to graduating from high school, only since the 1970s has the college gap narrowed. In 1970, as in 1982, women were just as likely to graduate from high school as men (see Table 9.1). But in 1970, only 25 percent of women aged 25–34

Table 9.1 Women Have Been Improving Their
Educational Status Relative to Men in the United States

Educational Status	Males	Females
Percent aged 25–34 who were high school graduates in:		
1970	74	73
1982	87	86
Percent of high school graduates aged 25–34 who were also college graduates in:		
1970	35	25
1982	48	42

Source: U.S. Bureau of the Census, 1983, "Population Profile of
the United States: 1982," Current Population Reports, Series P-23,
No. 30, Table 18.

had gone on to complete college, compared with 35 percent of men. By 1982, 42 percent of women aged 25–34 had completed college and, although the figure was still lower than the 48 percent for men, the gender gap was narrower than in 1970. The educational gap between the sexes could disappear in the future, but the U.S. Bureau of the Census (1984b) believes that the cohort of men born between 1947 and 1951 may represent the historical peak of educational attainment among American men. This early Baby Boom group holds the record for college attendance, and it seems unlikely that future cohorts will achieve such high levels, partly because they will be composed increasingly of minority males, who have lower probabilities of graduating from high school and going on to college.

One of our primary demographic interests in education, of course, is that in the course of altering your world view, education tends to affect your reproductive behavior. Data from the World Fertility Survey show that nearly anywhere you go in the world, the more educated a woman is, the fewer children she will have had (see Jain, 1981). Not that education is inherently antinatalist; rather, it opens up new vistas—new opportunities and alternative approaches to life, other than simply building a family—and in so doing, it delays the onset of childbearing, which is a crucial factor in setting the tone for subsequent fertility (Marini, 1984; Rindfuss et al., 1980). Among recent cohorts of women in the United States there is, in fact, a striking relationship between higher education and childlessness (Bloom and Trussell, 1984). This is a point made in Chapter 5, but it is so important that it bears repeating. Even in the United States, where fertility levels are among the lowest in the world, there is a significant difference in childbearing behavior between the two extremes of educational attainment. Among women aged 25–34, when interviewed in 1986 by the U.S. Bureau of the Census, the average number of births to women who had not completed high school was 2.1, compared with 0.6 for women with 5 or more years of college. Even looking ahead to future births, the better-educated group expected to have 0.5 fewer children per woman than the less-educated group (U.S. Bureau of the Census, 1987b).

One of the ways in which education works its magic in society is by influencing the kind of occupation in which a person will wind up. Let us examine that connection more closely.

OCCUPATION

Occupational Categories

If you were a white adult male in 1980, you were more likely to have a managerial or professional occupation than were members of any other sociodemographic group (see Table 9.2). White women were more likely than others to be in what the Census Bureau calls "administrative support occupations, including clerical"; black males were more likely to be assembly line workers and similar laborers; and black females were more apt than others to be in service occupations.

Occupation is an especially important characteristic because it is without question one of the most defining aspects of a person's social identity in industrialized

Table 9.2   Whites Were More Likely Than Nonwhites to Be in White-Collar Occupations in the United States in 1980

| U.S. Census Bureau Occupation Category | Percent of the Labor Force in Each Occupation | | | |
| | Whites | | Nonwhites | |
	Males	Females	Males	Females
White-collar workers, total	45	70	27	52
Managerial and professional specialty occupations	25	22	12	17
Technicians and related support occupations	3	3	2	3
Sales occupations	10	12	4	6
Administrative support occupations, including clerical	7	33	9	26
Blue-collar workers, total	43	13	53	18
Precision production, craft, and repair occupations	21	2	16	2
Operators, fabricators, and laborers	22	11	37	16
Service occupations	8	16	17	29
Farming, forestry, and fishing occupations	4	1	3	1
Total (percent)	100	100	100	100

Source: U.S. Bureau of the Census, 1983, 1980 Census of Population, Vol. One, General Social and Economic Characteristics, U.S. Summary (Washington, D.C.: Government Printing Office), Table 89.

society. It is a clue to education, income, and residence—in general, a clue to life-style and an indicator of social status, pointing to a person's position in the social hierarchy. From a social point of view, occupation is so important that it is often the first (and occasionally the only) question that a stranger may ask about you. It provides information about what kind of behavior can be expected from you as well as how others will be expected to behave toward you. Although such a comment may offend you if you believe that "people are people," it is nonetheless true that there is no society in which all people are actually treated equally.

Since there are literally thousands of different occupations in every country, we need a way of fitting occupations into a few slots. The U.S. Census Bureau has devised such a classification scheme to divide occupations into several mutually exclusive categories; in Table 9.2 I have listed the occupational distribution of employed males and females in the United States in 1980. The first occupational category (typically the most prestigious) is labeled "managerial and professional specialties." Included are business executives, top-level bureaucrats, and profession-als such as physicians, nurses, lawyers, college professors and other teachers, engineers, and the like. In the United States in 1980, 25 percent of white males, 22 percent of white females, 17 percent of nonwhite females, and 12 percent of non-white males fell into this category (see Table 9.2).

The second category is "technicians and related support occupations." Dental hygienists represent the classic example of this group, which shows little difference from one gender and racial group to the other. Next comes "sales occupations," a self-explanatory category in which whites are more likely than blacks to find them-selves. This is followed by "administrative support occupations, including clerical," a category that recognizes that mechanization and computerization has changed the nature of the long-used term "clerk." Secretaries, word processors, file clerks, bank tellers, and similar workers fall into this group, and it is clear from Table 9.2 that women are far more likely to be in these kinds of occupations than are men.

The foregoing occupations fall into the broad category of white-collar work. Such workers totaled 45 percent of the white male labor force in 1980 but only 27 percent of the nonwhite male labor force. Most of the remaining occupations are blue-collar jobs, including "precision production, craft, and repair occupations" and "operators, fabricators, and laborers." These categories include plumbers, carpenters, assembly line workers, bus and truck drivers, and so forth. Note that men are far more likely than women to be found in these occupations. Finally, there are two remaining categories that are hard to classify as either white- or blue-collar—"service occupations," such as waitresses and waiters, laundry workers, pool cleaners, and so on, and "farm, forestry, and fishing occupations." Farming is very nearly a thing of the past as an American occupation, despite the fact that the United States has the most productive agricultural system in the world (as I will review in Chapter 14).

In 1980, working women represented 42 percent of the total United States labor force, but the distribution of women by occupational level reveals important differ-ences from the male pattern—a fact to which I have already alluded. As you can observe in Table 9.2, a higher percentage of nonwhite women than men were professional or technical workers, whereas for whites the percentages were almost identical for both sexes. That is misleading, however, since major subcategories within those groupings for women were elementary school teachers and nurses—occupations that are dominated by women but are often considered to be of lower prestige (and income) than "male" professions. Clerical work is the category in which one out of every three white women and one of four nonwhite women find themselves. There are also high percentages of women in service. In general, you can see that men are much more spread out occupationally than are women, and, as you might guess, that pattern is not peculiar to the United States; it is nearly universal.

One of the major characteristics distinguishing one occupational level from another is the amount of formal training (education) required. The close connection between occupation and education is illustrated by the fact that in 1980 nearly half of all white-collar workers aged 25–34 in the United States were college graduates, and two thirds to three fourths of all professional people had college degrees (see Table 9.3). On the other hand, fewer than one in ten blue-collar workers had completed college. As you can see in Table 9.3, women are less likely to be as well educated as men at each occupational level. Recall also from Table 9.2 that women are not as likely to even be in those higher occupational levels that require an advanced education. These patterns are changing, of course, as increasing proportions of women have been joining the labor force.

Table 9.3   Higher Occupational Status Goes
Hand in Hand with Higher Educational Attainment
(Full-Time, Year-Round Workers Aged 25–34—United States, 1980)

	Percent with College Degree	
Occupation	Males	Females
Executive, administrative, and managerial	55	38
Professional specialty	78	67
Technicians (engineering related)	20	26
Technicians (health related)	42	23
Sales	38	21
Administrative support	26	11
Precision production, craft, and repair	8	9
Operators, fabricators, and laborers	5	3
Service	14	7
Farming, forestry, and fishing	16	13

Source: U.S. Bureau of the Census, 1984, "Earnings by occupation and education," 1980 Census of Population, Vol. 2, Subject Reports (Washington, D.C.: Government Printing Office), Table 2.

Labor Force Participation

Women are working more, men are working less; this is the pattern that has emerged in the American labor force. Figure 9.3 shows clearly that at every age there were higher proportions of women participating in the labor force in 1980 than in 1940, while the opposite was true for men. As recently as 1960, white males accounted for six of every ten people in the labor force, but by 1980 just less than half of the labor force was composed of white males.

By far the biggest gain in employment over the past several years has been the movement of young women into the labor market. The Baby Boom women literally burst their way into the work force, and in 1985 more than 70 percent of women aged 20–34 had a job. This increase has been especially noticeable among young married women—a group that has traditionally been left out of the labor market. Working, as you might expect, cuts down on fertility under normal circumstances. For example, in 1986, among women aged 18–34, those in the labor force had given birth to an average of one less child than those not in the labor market. Women who do work outside the home tend to be optimistic about their future plans for having children, but even if we combine children already born with those that women

Figure 9.3   Women Are Working More; Men Are Working Less (United States, 1940 and 1980)

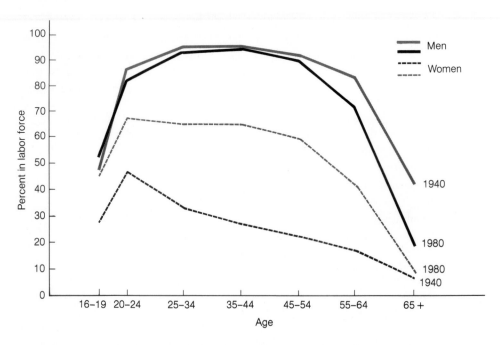

Source: U.S. Bureau of the Census, 1983, 1980 Census of Population, Vol. One, General Social and Economic Characteristics, U.S. Summary (Washington, D.C.: Government Printing Office), Table 87.

expect in the future, working women still have an average of half a child less (U.S. Bureau of the Census, 1987b).

The relationship between labor force participation of women and their fertility has always been clouded by a chicken-and-egg argument over which causes which—does low fertility produce greater opportunities for work, or does working cause a woman to reduce her family-building activity? The evidence suggests that, in truth, both factors are involved (Cramer, 1980; Groat et al., 1982). Traditionally, women who worked after marriage were disproportionately those who were subfecund. Thus, it was low fertility among such women that may have encouraged them to remain in or go back into the labor force. More recently, however, it is clear that a high proportion of women work before marriage, remain working after marriage, and adjust their fertility downward to accommodate their working. Still, necessity plays its role. In 1986, the female labor force participation rate was highest (85 percent) among divorced women with children aged 6–17, while it was lowest (48 percent) for married women with no children under age 18.

We must be cautious, however, about generalizing our findings from the United States to other countries. The data are, at best, mixed when it comes to cross-national studies of the influence of female labor force participation on fertility in less developed societies. It is apparent, for example, that only if a woman works outside the home (in the "impersonal market sector") will she be amenable to low-fertility pressures (Dixon, 1976). Furthermore, even in America, the greater the availability of child care, the less is the impact of working on fertility (Stolzenberg and Waite, 1984). Taiwan is a particularly interesting case in this regard, because there have been increasing opportunities for women to work outside the home, and fertility has declined over the past two decades, but the two events appear not to be statistically related. Data from Taiwan suggest little difference in fertility between women who work in the impersonal market sector and those who do not work at all (Stokes and Hsieh, 1983). One crucial factor that may limit the extent to which labor force participation affects fertility in Taiwan is that women are largely restricted to relatively unattractive and low-paying positions (Speare et al., 1973). It may be that it takes more than just work to induce women to lower their fertility preferences and limit fertility; it may require an adequate monetary reward for their labor. This certainly seems to be true in the United States.

A clear concomitant (if not cause) of the rise in female labor force participation in the United States has been a marked increase in women's wages. In fact, in the United States between 1947 and 1977, "female wage rates appear to be the dominant factor in explaining variations in fertility and female labor force participation . . . with increases in female earning leading to both depressed fertility and increased labor force participation of women" (Devaney, 1983:147). Another study using data from the National Longitudinal Survey of Young Women has shown that the higher the wages on her job, the less likely is a woman to quit because of a pregnancy (Felmlee, 1984).

Changing attitudes of employers toward women and of women as employees probably help account for the fact that by the 1980s the unemployment rate for women in the United States was lower than that for men, reversing a long-run pattern for females to be more vulnerable in the job market (U.S. Bureau of the Census, 1984k). This was true for blacks as well as for whites, although in general the unemployment rate for blacks has remained at a level about twice that of whites in the United States. Unemployment rates are strongly related to age—the older the age, the lower the rate, although that is partly accounted for by the definition of unemployment, which includes people looking for work, even if they have never worked before. At the younger ages there are considerable numbers of such people, whereas at the older ages people are more likely to give up on employment and seek a retirement pension as soon as it is available, if they experience difficulty finding a job. Age also interacts with race to produce the highly publicized unemployment rates for black teenagers (40 percent in 1985), while the lowest levels of unemployment are among whites aged 35 and older (4 percent in 1985).

Whether you are employed has an obvious bearing on your income, and since we know from much of our previous discussion that income is an all-around important factor in demographic behavior, let us look at it in greater detail.

INCOME

It has been estimated that shortly before his death in 1976, John Paul Getty, the oil magnate, had a *daily* income of $300,000. "Assuming a normal working day, this means that he earned $75,000 by the time the doughnuts arrived for his morning coffee break" (Dalphin, 1981:1). Even by 1988 only a tiny fraction of Americans made $75,000 in an entire year. Few (if any), of course, have matched Getty's income (much less his overall wealth), but there are business executives, star athletes, entertainers, and others in the United States whose annual incomes exceed $1 million—equivalent to the total lifetime earnings of the average American worker.

The very rich tend to be that way because of birth. Wealth and its attendant high income are essentially ascribed characteristics for those born into families that own huge homes, large amounts of real estate, and tremendous interests in stocks and bonds or other business interests. Indeed, for such people a good education may be a result of high income as much as it is a resource by which to improve their social standing. Huntington Hartford, heir to the A & P fortune, is said to have commented that although he was just a "C" student at St. Paul's (a posh prep school), he was automatically accepted at Harvard (Dalphin, 1981). But, for the rest of us, income is at least partially a consequence of the way in which we have parlayed a good education into a good job.

Although occupation may be the primary clue that people have about our social standing, our well-being is thought by most people to be a product of our level of income (Coleman and Rainwater, 1978). Based on their studies in Boston and Kansas City, Coleman and Rainwater conclude that "money, far more than anything else, is what Americans associate with the idea of social class" (1978:29). They suggest further that the principal indicators of having money include the kind of house in which you live, the car or cars you drive, the way your home is furnished, the clothes you wear, and the recreations and vacations you can afford.

It is no mystery that there is an uneven distribution of income in American society. In 1986 in the United States, the richest 5 percent of families earned 17 percent of the total income of the nation, while the poorest 40 percent earned 15 percent (U.S. Bureau of the Census, 1987c). This was a slight deterioration of the distribution that had prevailed only 5 years earlier, in 1977, when the top 5 percent also commanded 16 percent, but the bottom 40 percent shared 19 percent of the nation's income (U.S. Bureau of the Census, 1979m). Yet we must not confuse income distribution with absolute level of income. Since World War II (at least) the United States has been experiencing **structural economic mobility**; that is, the entire nation has been growing wealthier, even though the relative distribution of income has not changed a great deal. Between 1950 and 1986 the median family income in constant dollars (that is, holding purchasing power constant) nearly doubled in the United States. The median income in 1950 was equivalent to $14,874 at 1986 prices, while in 1986 the median income was up to $29,458—a 98 percent jump in only 36 years. This means that in terms of income, the average American family was twice as well off in 1986 as in 1950. However, as you can see in Figure 9.4, the average family was worse off in 1986 than in 1973.

One consequence of the long-term rise in income has been a change in the income gap between blacks and whites in the United States. In 1950, the average black family had $7,177 less income per year than the average white family (calculated in 1986 dollars). In 1960 the gap was $9,642, a wider dollar spread, although in percentage terms black income had grown by 40 percent, while white income had increased by 38 percent.

In 1970, the dollar gap between white and black families had grown to $10,502 (despite the fact that black incomes had been increasing by 54 percent per decade and white income by 34 percent), while in 1986 the income differential was $13,205. Thus, blacks have been in the peculiar position of having their incomes rise faster in percentage terms than whites, although in dollar terms they were falling further behind. This is one of the paradoxes that results from structural mobility— that situation in which an entire society is experiencing an upward mobility. That is the only time in which one group can improve itself socially or economically without forcing an absolute sacrifice from another group. When structural mobility ceased, then the gains of blacks also ceased, because at that point any rise in income would have resulted in a deliberate policy of conscious redistribution of income among ethnic groups.

I should add a word of caution about the comparison of family incomes of whites and blacks in the United States. Blacks have fewer earners per family than do whites (1.42 for blacks compared with 1.63 for whites in 1986), and thus have less family income on that account alone. Furthermore, 42 percent of black families are headed by a female, compared with 13 percent of white families (U.S. Bureau of the Census, 1987c). Since females tend to earn less than males, that too lowers black family income relative to whites. We can control for these factors by looking separately at the incomes of only those people who are year-round, full-time earners.

If we were to assume that every family in the United States had a male and a female year-round, full-time worker, each earning the median income for his or her sex and race, then we would find that in 1955 (the first year for which such data are available) white families would have had an average family income of $29,628 (in 1986 dollars), compared with $17,025 for black families. Thus, under these controlled circumstances, black families would have had $12,603 less money to spend

Figure 9.4 The Widening Gap in Income Between Blacks and Whites in the United
States

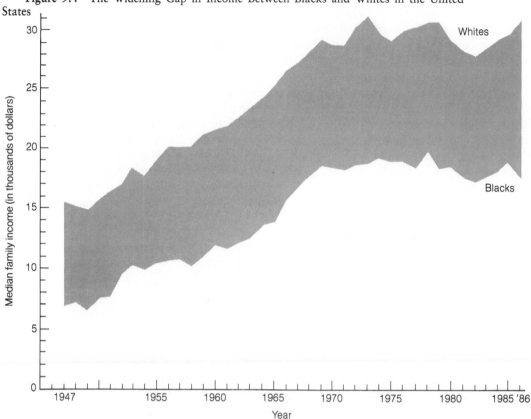

    Between 1947 (the first available year for these data) and 1986 the absolute dollar gap
between American blacks and whites widened. In 1947 the difference in median family
income was $7,573; by 1986 it had grown to $13,205, despite the fact that in relative terms
the growth of black income (122 percent) had been greater than the growth of white income
(99 percent). Data are in constant 1986 dollars. *Source:*   Adapted from U.S. Bureau of the
Census, 1987, "Money Income of Households, Families, and Persons in the United States:
1986," Current Population Reports, Series P-60, No. 156, Table 11.

each year—less than two thirds of the income of white families. By 1986, however,
the situation had definitely improved for everybody. White two-earner families
would have been making an average of $43,718, compared with $33,730 for black
families. That amounts to a difference of $9,988, with black family income at a level
that was 77 percent that of whites. Between 1955 and 1986, the average income of
these hypothetical white couples would have increased 48 percent, while the increase
for the hypothetical black couples during this time amounted to 98 percent! Furthermore, if all other things had been equal, the actual dollar income gap between blacks
and whites would have been cut by at least one fifth.

Things are rarely equal, however, and so we find that the comparison between actual families is not as rosy as in our controlled case. The disadvantage of blacks relative to whites in terms of family income is greatly exacerbated by the high rate of marital disruption among blacks, which I will discuss later in the chapter.

For any particular individual, of course, income is a product of many different factors, but especially of education and occupational level. Education facilitates earning a high income, and while that may be only one of many reasons for a person to pursue educational goals, its significance is undeniable. Education mainly does its income trick by allowing a person to translate educational attainment into occupational success, but even within occupational levels, it is true that the higher your educational level, the more money you will make, as I have already mentioned. In some occupations, acquiring more education (by taking extension classes, getting advanced degrees, and so on) is one of the most important criteria for moving up on an organization's income ladder.

Income's overall relation to education can be seen in Table 9.4. It is as perfect a positive relation as you could find; with each increment in educational attainment, earnings are higher. This is as true for females as it is for males, as true for blacks as it is for whites. These data, drawn from the Census Bureau's Survey on Income and Program Participation (SIPP), also reveal that the highest monthly earnings are

Table 9.4   The Better-Educated Earn Higher Incomes (United States, 1984; Persons 18 and Older)

Educational Attainment	Monthly Income (Spring 1984)
Doctorate	$3,265
Professional	3,871
Master's	2,288
Bachelor's	1,841
Associate	1,346
Vocational	1,219
Some college, no degree	1,169
High school graduate only	1,045
Not a high school graduate	693
All persons 18 and older	1,155

Source: U.S. Bureau of the Census, 1987, "What's It Worth? Educational Background and Economic Status: Spring 1984; Data from the Survey of Income and Program Participation," Current Population Reports, Series P-70, No. 11, Table 2.

Note: Each step in educational attainment will, on average, advance your income. In 1984, obtaining your bachelor's degree was worth an average of $796 per month (nearly $10,000 per year) more than if you had stopped your education after high school.

pulled in by people with professional graduate degrees in medicine, dentistry, and law. That probably does not surprise you. Indeed, a study conducted at the University of Michigan revealed that, among a wide range of variables, the amount of education is the most readily observable predictor of job status and incomes (ISR Newsletter, 1979).

If you have several children, however, the odds increase that your income will be below average, and if, on top of that, you are a divorced mother, the chance skyrockets that you will be living below the poverty level. In 1986, more than one in every three (35 percent) households headed by a woman (with no husband present) were below the poverty level. Yet among women in this situation with no children only 10 percent were below poverty, while 48 percent of those with two children, and 90 percent of those with five or more, were below the poverty level (U.S. Bureau of the Census, 1987c).

To imagine the struggle it is to manage successfully on so little money, it is necessary only to review the definition of the poverty level. The **poverty index** was devised initially in 1964 by Mollie Orshansky of the U.S. Social Security Administration. It was a measure of need based on the finding of a 1955 Department of Agriculture study showing that approximately one third of a poor family's income is spent on food, and on a 1961 Department of Agriculture estimate of the cost of an "economy food plan"—a plan defined as a minimally nutritious diet for emergency or temporary use (Orshansky, 1969). By calculating the cost of an economy food plan and multiplying it by 3, the poverty level was born, and since 1964 it has been raised at the same rate as the consumer price index.

Between 1960 and 1973 the percentage of American families below the poverty level was cut in half—from 22 to 11 percent. But since that time, as real incomes generally have slipped below their previous levels, the fraction of families in poverty has also increased—up to 14 percent in 1986.

Although income represents one aspect of status in society, it is only part of the broader concept of wealth, which is often measured as your net worth—the difference between the value of what you own and the value of what you owe. According to data from the SIPP in the United States, households headed by whites in 1984 had an average net worth of $39,135, compared with only $3,397 for blacks and $4,913 for Hispanics. Thus, although the average monthly income of black families that year was 62 percent of the income of whites, the level of wealth was only 9 percent of that of whites. Marriage is also an important ingredient in accumulating wealth (as long as you stay married) and thus we find that the highest level of net worth occurs among white couples ($54,184 in 1984), whereas the lowest occurs among Hispanic female-headed households (a paltry $478) (U.S. Bureau of the Census, 1987g).

MARITAL STATUS

Marriage

The financial ability of the head of the household to provide for a family has been variously implicated in the likelihood of marriage in the first place and of divorce once a marriage is accomplished. Marriage can occur sooner and more easily if the head of the household (often, but not always, the male) has a job with a good income. If employment is unsteady or the money turns out to be too little to make ends meet, divorce or separation (such as desertion—sometimes called the poor man's divorce) may result. If we look at the history of marital formation and dissolution in the United States, we find general support for these ideas.

In 1890, more than one third of all women aged 14 and older (34 percent) and close to one half of all men (44 percent) were single. Between 1890 and 1960, being single became progressively less common as women, and especially men, married at earlier ages. Only since the 1960s has there been a resurgence of delayed marriage. By 1986, the average age at marriage for females had risen to 23.1, the highest level since 1890, while for males it had increased to 25.7, a higher level than at any time since 1900. In fact, in 1986, 28 percent of all American women aged 25–29 were still single, a 168 percent increase over 1970, and 41 percent of all men of that age had not yet married, a 117 percent increase over 1970 (U.S. Bureau of the Census, 1987f). Changes in the popularity of early marriage have been roughly similar for both blacks and whites (Farley, 1970), although blacks have been more likely than whites to be single.

The increasingly younger ages at marriage throughout most of the twentieth century were probably a result of improved levels of living that meant earlier economic independence for men—an important precondition for marriage in most Western nations (Davis, 1972a). In addition, the greater knowledge and availability of contraceptive techniques helped to disentangle marriage from almost certain parenthood, and that also made it easier for couples to marry at an earlier age, since they knew they would not have to be saddled early with burdensome offspring.

Since the 1960s, however, the slowdown of economic growth, accompanied by the stiff competition for jobs brought about by the Baby Boom children growing up, has made it more advantageous for couples to postpone marriage to take maximum advantage of educational and career opportunities. Within marriage, couples find it advantageous to keep families small; and women find it desirable to have few or no children if they want to pursue a career of their own—a possibility only recently open to married women (see Chapter 10).

In general, in the United States the social penalties for early marriage have gradually eased as the economic well-being of the population has increased, divorce laws (and pressures against divorce) have eased, and fertility control has increased. On the other hand, fertility control has also altered the rewards of early marriage, since regular sexual activity that does not lead to pregnancy can involve a less formal obligation on the part of young couples. Furthermore, there is an economic penalty for early marriage, especially among upwardly mobile individuals. Back in 1948 the U.S. tax laws were rewritten to allow husbands and wives to file joint returns. This was thought of as a "marriage bonus," because it reduced the tax of a couple with only one worker by dividing the worker's pay by 2 (Shaw, 1984). At that time, however, only 22 percent of all married women worked. By 1982, however, 51 percent of all married women were in the labor force, and the joint return had become a burden rather than a bonus, serving as a source of discouragement for people to get married, especially if their incomes were high. In 1984, for example, a married man and woman, each of whom had $40,000 in taxable income, would have paid, as a couple, $23,568 in federal income taxes. Had they remained single, their combined tax bill would have been $19,498. Thus, remaining single would have saved the couple $4,070 in federal income taxes. This almost certainly led some couples to postpone marriage. Indeed, if they had waited until after the Tax Reform Act of 1987 went into effect, they would have found that under the revised tax code, remaining single would have saved them only $1,382 in federal income taxes. Still, the marriage penalty remains.

Although changes in marriage patterns over time have been similar by race, there are still actual differences in the likelihood of being married. If you are white you are more likely to be married and living with your spouse than if you are black, and you are less likely to be divorced or widowed. If we look at males aged 25–29, for example, we find that in 1986 in the United States, 52 percent of whites were married and living with their spouses, compared with 35 percent of blacks. The difference is even greater for females (62 percent compared with 35 percent) (U.S. Bureau of the Census, 1987f). Widowhood is not much of a problem at that age, but separation and divorce are, and in 1986, 9 percent of white males were divorced or separated, compared with 11 percent of blacks. Again the difference was even greater for females. Eleven percent of white females were separated or divorced, compared with 15 percent of black females. Similar comparisons can be made for other age groups, but I focused on ages 25–29 because at those ages children are especially likely to be present in a marriage and thus influenced by its disruption (or lack thereof).

Divorce and Widowhood

Divorce has become more common in the United States, reflecting many things, including the loosening hold of men over women and the longer lives we are leading, both of which may produce greater conflict within marriage. It has been estimated that husbands and wives now live together an average of 9 years longer than they did at the beginning of the century (assuming they stay married until one of them dies) (Glick and Parke, 1965). In 1857 in the United States, there was only a 27 percent chance that a husband aged 25 and a wife aged 22 would both still be alive when the wife reached 65, but for couples marrying 100 years later in the 1950s, the chances had exactly doubled.

Many marriages that in earlier days would have been dissolved by death are now dissolved by divorce. This seems apparent from the fact that the annual combined rate of marital dissolution from both the death of one spouse and divorce remained remarkably constant for more than a century. In Figure 9.5 you can see that the overall rate of marital dissolution was essentially unchanged between 1860 and 1970. As widowhood declined, divorce rose proportionately. Only with the rapid increase in divorce during the 1970s did that pattern begin to diverge. By 1980, the number of existing marriages dissolved by death dropped to an all-time low (not unexpectedly, of course, since death rates are at an all-time low), and for the first time in history, divorces accounted for more than half of all dissolved marriages. The increased frequency of divorce has shortened the average length of marriages in the United States from 36.4 years in 1960–66 to 25.2 years in 1972–76

Figure 9.5   The Annual Rate of Marital Dissolution Changed Little in the United States until 1965

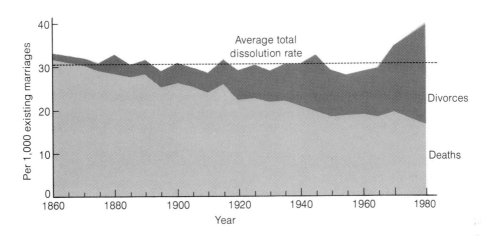

Although the divorce rate has been rising for a long time, it had been just offsetting the drop in marital dissolutions from death until about 1965. Thus, each year from the 1860s to mid-1960s, the number of total dissolutions per 1,000 existing marriages has remained remarkably stable. Since then the total dissolution rate has climbed. The dotted line represents the average total dissolution rate for the period 1860–1970. *Source:* Adapted from K. Davis, 1972, "The American family in relation to demographic change," in C. Westoff and R. Parke, Jr. (eds.), U.S. Commission on Population Growth and the American Future, Vol. 1, Demographic and Social Aspects of Population Growth (Washington, D.C.: Government Printing Office), Table 8, updated to 1980 by the author.

(Goldman, 1984). So dramatic was the rise in divorce in the 1970s that in the mid-1960s the elimination of divorce would have added an additional 6.7 years to the average marriage, whereas by the mid-1970s its elimination would have added 17.2 years (Goldman, 1984).

Divorce is not the only way in which a marriage may be disrupted without requiring that one spouse die. Blacks and Hispanics, for example, are more likely than whites to split up without a formal divorce. They show up in statistics among the people who are married but whose spouse is absent. In 1986, such people accounted for 3 percent of whites of marriageable age (15+) compared with 8 percent of blacks and 7 percent of Hispanics. One result is that marital disruption among blacks is almost twice as high as you would guess from looking only at divorce statistics. A second result is that, although divorce rates are lower among Hispanics than whites, the overall level of marital disruption is higher among Hispanics, because they are almost three times more likely to leave their spouse without getting a divorce (U.S. Bureau of the Census, 1987f).

As marital disruption has increased in frequency, the proportion of children in society whose lives are directly touched by it has also gone up. Bumpass (1984) has used data from the Current Population Reports to estimate that in 1977–79, 43 percent of all children were likely to have experienced the breakup of their parents' marriage by age 16, compared with only 22 percent in 1963–65. There were still substantial differences in the likelihood of being part of a disrupted family according to mother's education and the timing of her first birth. Only 36 percent of children born to college-educated mothers were likely in 1977–79 to see their parents' marriage dissolve by age 16, compared with 68 percent of children whose mothers had not completed high school. Similarly, divorce would be experienced by only 36 percent of children whose mothers had first given birth at age 25 or older, compared with 78 percent of children of teenage mothers. In general, these percentages tend to be lower for whites, but higher for blacks.

Because of remarriage, the majority of children of divorced parents wind up in a "new" family, but since the average length of time between marriages is greater than 5 years (Bumpass, 1984), at any given time there are substantial numbers of children living with only one parent. In 1986 in the United States, 16 percent of white children under 18, who were themselves not married, were living with their mothers only. Among black children under 18, however, more than half (54 percent) were living only with their mothers (U.S. Bureau of the Census, 1987f).

As death has receded to the older ages, the incidence of widowhood has steadily been pushed to the older years as well. You can see in Table 9.5 that divorce is a more important cause of not being married than is widowhood up to age 50, beyond which widowhood increases geometrically, undoubtedly compounded by the tendency of divorced women to change their status to widow on the death of a former husband. As is true with so many social facts in the United States, black women are disadvantaged relative to whites in terms of marital status. At every age, blacks are more likely to be either divorced or widowed—another indicator of the importance of race and ethnicity in the fabric of society.

Table 9.5 Widowhood Increases Dramatically with Age (United States, 1986)

	Percentage of Women Who Are Currently:				
Age	Single (Never Married)	Married, with Husband Present	Married, with Husband Absent	Divorced	Widowed
18–19	88	10	1	1	0
20–24	58	35	4	3	0
25–29	28	57	5	8	0
30–34	14	69	5	12	1
35–39	8	71	5	14	1
40–44	6	71	5	16	3
45–54	5	72	4	13	6
55–64	4	68	3	9	17
65–74	4	49	2	6	39
75+	6	23	1	3	67

Source: U.S. Bureau of the Census, 1987, "Marital Status and Living Arrangements: March, 1986," Current Population Reports, Series P-20, No. 418, Table 1.

RACE AND ETHNICITY

To be a member of a subordinate racial, ethnic, or religious group in any society is to be at jeopardy of impaired life chances. Blacks, Hispanics, Asians, and American Indians in the United States are well aware of this, as are the Tamils in Sri Lanka, Moslems in Israel or in India, Indians in Malaysia, and virtually any foreigner in Japan or China.

Blacks

In the United States, blacks represent by far the largest minority group, with a population of more than 26 million (12 percent of the total population), according to the 1980 census. Being black in the United States is associated with higher probabilities of death (until advanced ages), lower levels of education, lower levels of occupational status, lower incomes, and higher levels of marital disruption than for the white population.

Earlier in this chapter I noted that in recent decades income levels have risen proportionately at a more rapid rate for blacks than for whites in the United States. This fact, combined with a wide array of legal changes that protected the rights of minority group members, induced Wilson (1978) to talk of the "declining significance of race" in the United States: "Race relations in America have undergone fundamental changes in recent years, so much so that now the life chances of individual blacks have more to do with their economic class position than with their day-to-day encounters with whites" (Wilson, 1978:1). Hout (1984) has used data from the Occupational Changes in a Generation Surveys of 1962 and 1973 to support Wilson's claims. In particular, the public sector has provided substantial new opportunities for black males to move into the middle class. Nonetheless, Bianchi (1981) has cautioned us to be wary of overestimating the gains that have been made by blacks. If you are black, there is still a good chance that you will be earning less money than if you were white, even if everything else is the same. For example, in 1985 income for black families in which the head of the household had only a high school education was more than $10,000 less than for a comparable white family. Among families in which the head was a college graduate, the white income was about $12,000 more than for blacks (U.S. Bureau of the Census, 1987a). Why the difference? One reason may well be discrimination, which looms as a significant (although difficult to measure) factor, accounting for the fact that members of a minority group may not earn as much money as whites even when equipped with comparable educational levels and working at comparable occupational levels.

A good attempt to measure the effect of discrimination (albeit indirectly and inferentially) has been made by Hauser and Featherman (1974). They noted that in 1962, white males aged 35–44 earned $3,755 more per year on average than black males of the same age. By 1972 the income differential had dropped to $3,195. They then controlled for factors such as family background (father's education, father's occupation, and farm background); the number of siblings (too large a family might have cut down opportunity); education of the respondent; and occupational status, to see whether differences in those social structural factors could explain all the differences in income. They couldn't. In 1962 and 1972, nearly 40 percent of the income differential was left unexplained, and the researchers speculated that discrimination might be the missing factor.

The lower levels of educational attainment, occupational status, income, and marital stability for blacks than for whites in the United States have sometimes been attributed to the fact that blacks come from larger families on average than whites and thus are launched with fewer resources per person. Although the study by Hauser and Featherman (1974) just discussed did not lend much credence to that idea, it is nonetheless true that blacks tend to have more children, even though the difference is no longer very large. Over time the trend in fertility among blacks has tended to follow that for the rest of the population, but at a higher level (Reid, 1982). Black fertility declined during the Depression, but did not drop as low as for whites; it rose during the Baby Boom, and to a higher level than for whites, and it has declined since, as blacks have participated in the Baby Bust.

In 1986, white women aged 18–34 had an average of 1,060 births per 1,000 women, whereas black women of the same ages had borne an average of 1,476 children per 1,000 women—39 percent higher than for whites (U.S. Bureau of the Census, 1987b). In 1986 black women had nearly half a child more (on average, of course; it's pretty hard to have half a child) than did whites at every age (U.S. Bureau of the Census, 1987b). However, when asked, black women expected to have fewer additional children than whites. If women of each race actually wind up having the number of additional children they expect, then the total number of children already born plus those expected is nearly identical for blacks and whites. In other words, fertility preferences among younger women may have nearly converged for these two groups in the population. In particular, the fertility behavior of college-educated black and white females is virtually indistinguishable. However, it is important to note that expectations and actual behavior do not always coincide, and the fact that blacks begin childbearing at an earlier average age than whites suggests that lifetime fertility could continue to be higher for blacks than for whites (St. John, 1982).

Hispanics

People of Spanish origin (Hispanics) comprise the second largest minority group in the United States, with nearly 15 million counted in the 1980 census. "Hispanic" is a broad term, encompassing people of widely differing cultural backgrounds, including Mexican (9 million), Puerto Rican (2 million), Cuban (800,000), and a variety of others. According to a 1978 directive of the U.S. Office of Management and Budget, the term "Hispanic" describes a person of Mexican, Puerto Rican, Cuban, Central or South American, or other Spanish culture or origin, regardless of race (Washburn, 1984). The Hispanic population in the United States is the seventh largest population of Spanish origin in the world—behind Mexico, Spain, Argentina, Colombia, Peru, and Venezuela. In general, Hispanics have life expectancies lower than those of whites but higher than those of blacks, and they also fall in between whites and blacks with respect to income, as can be seen in Table 9.6. On the other hand, to show you how untidy the social world can be, average educational

Table 9.6 Asians and Blacks Represent the Two
Extremes in Sociodemographic Characteristics Among
Broadly Defined Racial/Ethnic Groups in the United States (1980)

Category	White	Black	Hispanic	Asian and Pacific Islander	American Indian
Total population (thousands)	188,372	26,495	14,609	3,500	1,479
Median family income	$20,840	$12,618	$14,711	$22,075	$13,678
% Persons below poverty level	9.4	30.2	23.8	13.9	27.5
% Persons 25+ who are college graduates	17	8	8	33	9
% Persons 16+ who are unemployed	3.6	6.9	5.8	3.2	13.0
% Females 16+ in the labor force	50	53	49	57	48
Children ever born to women ever married:					
15+	2.29	2.88	2.89	2.33	3.07
20–24	0.84	1.36	1.22	0.82	1.33
30–34	1.90	2.40	2.51	1.72	2.59
40–44	2.93	3.71	3.66	2.68	4.03
Life expectancy[a] at:					
Birth	74.9	69.9	75.5	82.5	64.0[b]
Age 10	65.9	61.6	66.6	73.0	60.4
Age 65	17.0	16.4	17.7	21.2	13.9

Sources: U.S. Bureau of the Census, 1984, 1980 Census of Population, Vol. One, General Social and Economic Characteristics, U.S. Summary (Washington, D.C.: Government Printing Office), Table 160; U.S. Bureau of the Census, 1984, 1980 Census of Population, Vol. One, Detailed Population Characteristics, U.S. Summary (Washington, D.C.: Government Printing Office), Table 270; California Center for Health Statistics, 1983, "California life expectancy: abridged life tables for California and Los Angeles, 1978–81," Data Matters, No. 83-01031, Tables 13–22.

[a] Data are for California.

[b] Estimates were made by the author by the application of model life tables to data for reservation Indians published in R. Kenen and C. Hammerslough, 1987, "Reservation and nonreservation American Indian mortality in 1970 and 1978," Social Biology 34(1–2), Table 1; data are for 1978.

levels are lower than for blacks or whites, while rates of marital dissolution are also lower than for either blacks or whites.

Since people of Mexican origin represent more than half of the Hispanic population in the United States, their levels of fertility have a substantial influence on the overall fertility pattern of Hispanics. You might expect to find that Mexican-Americans, having their origin fairly recently in a high-fertility society, would have birth rates noticeably higher than those for the population as a whole. In general, you would not be disappointed, since the data do indeed reveal that pattern, although birth rates have been declining for the Hispanic population, as they have for all groups in the United States. In 1986, Hispanic women aged 18–34 had given birth to slightly fewer children on average than blacks, but when you add their future expected births, Hispanics expect to complete their childbearing with nearly 200 children more per 1,000 women than is true for the non-Hispanic white population. Nonetheless, the evidence suggests that Hispanic fertility "has been falling in concert with that of all U.S. women since the mid-1950s. This suggests that the gap should eventually be closed" (Davis et al., 1983:17). I should add, however, that continued migration from Mexico could prevent the gap from closing, since women born in Mexico tend to have higher levels of fertility than U.S.-born Hispanics (Bean and Swicegood, 1985; U.S. Bureau of the Census, 1987b).

Asians and Pacific Islanders

The nearly 4 million people who comprise the Asian and Pacific Islander population in the United States represent an even more culturally heterogeneous group than the Hispanics. According to the 1980 census, Asians of Chinese origin were most numerous (806,000), followed by Pilipino (774,000), Japanese (700,000), Asian Indian (362,000), Korean (355,000), and Vietnamese (262,000). The number of Vietnamese and other Indochinese refugees (including those from Laos and Kampuchea (formerly Cambodia) has increased enormously since the 1980 census, both from continued immigration and from exceedingly high birth rates, and it is likely that by 1985 their number had surpassed 800,000 (Rumbaut and Weeks, 1985).

From the standpoint of sociodemographic characteristics, Asians and Pacific Islanders represent the most advantaged of the broadly defined racial/ethnic groups in the United States, as can be seen in Table 9.6. Data from the 1980 census reveal a median family income of $22,075, which exceeds the $20,840 for the white population. Furthermore, one out of every three Asian-Americans aged 25 and older is a college graduate, nearly double the percentage for any other group. Unemployment rates are lower, and female participation rates are higher than for any other group. Yet, the heterogeneity of this population is reflected in the fact that the percentage of people below the poverty level is higher than for whites. Indochinese refugees and some of the Pacific Islander groups, in particular, are less likely than the Chinese, Japanese, and Koreans to be sharing in the higher levels of education and income.

The more favorable demographic characteristics of the Asian and Pacific Islander population are accompanied by the fact that they are farther along the demographic transition in terms of low mortality and low fertility. The data in Table 9.6 show that recent fertility (that is, the number of children ever born to younger women) among Asian-Americans is lower than for any other group, and that life expectancy at birth, in childhood, and in old age is greater for Asians than for any other group.

American Indians

The least populous, and one of the most disadvantaged, of the major racial/ethnic groups in the United States is the American Indian population, which numbered 1.5 million in 1980. Looking at the data in Table 9.6 it is clear that, on average, the educational and income levels of American Indians are approximately the same as for blacks and Hispanics, while the rate of unemployment is the highest. At the same time, age-standardized death rates are approximately 30 percent higher than for the total U.S. population (Klimas, 1982), and fertility rates for ever-married women are 34 percent higher than for whites (see Table 9.6). The data in Table 9.6 hide the fact that there appear to be substantial differences in the life chances of urban versus rural American Indians—the latter being perhaps the most disadvantaged of all groups in the United States.

Arabs in Israel

The United States does not have a corner on the racial and ethnic minority market, nor are demographic differences by race and ethnicity peculiar to the United States. Perhaps the only feature of American society that is different internationally is the extent to which minority groups have been analyzed from a demographic perspective. Friedlander and Goldscheider (1984) have examined ethnic pluralism in Israel and have found that the Moslem Arab population in that country has been growing at twice the rate of the Jewish population and in 1982 represented 13 percent of the total—up from 8 percent in 1961. Like minority group members in the United States, the Moslem Arab minority in Israel is less educated, holds lower-status jobs on average, and has a lower life expectancy and higher fertility levels. Fertility has declined among Arabs in Israel since 1960, but the drop has been modest, and since Jewish fertility has also declined, the gap in fertility levels remains fairly wide. In 1982 the total fertility rate for the Jewish population was 2.8 children per woman, compared with 5.5 for the Moslem Arab population. However, high fertility in Israel is not simply a function of being Arab, since the Christian Arab minority (representing 14 percent of the total Arab population) has the lowest total fertility rate (2.3) of any group in Israel (Friedlander and Goldscheider, 1984). The contrast between Moslems and Christians takes us next into the realm of religion.

RELIGION

Virtually everyone is born into some kind of religious context, which is why I have likened religion to an ascribed characteristic. Yet, people can willingly change their religious preference during their lifetime, and so it is akin to an achieved status. Despite the appearance of choice, however, most people do not alter religious affiliation and so it is a nearly permanent feature of their social world. Like race and ethnicity, religion sets people apart from one another and is a frequent source of intergroup conflict throughout the world (Choucri, 1984). Since it is an often-discussed sociodemographic characteristic, religion has regularly come under the demographer's microscope, with particular attention being paid to its potential influence on fertility. What is the relationship between religion and fertility? The answer is complex and controversial.

America's history of **religious pluralism,** in which a wide variety of religious preferences have existed side by side, perhaps sensitized American demographers to the role of religion in influencing people's lives. A good deal of attention has been focused on the comparison between Protestants and Catholics. During the past century at least, Catholics have tended to want and to have more children than have Protestants in the United States, and internationally it has been true that predominantly Protestant areas (such as the United States and northern Europe) experienced low fertility sooner than did predominantly Catholic areas (such as southern and eastern Europe). More recently, however, data from the 1982 National Fertility Study in the United States have suggested that the long-time differences between Protestant and Catholic fertility levels have nearly disappeared (Goldscheider and Mosher, 1988).

Is religion less important now than it used to be? Are there other factors besides religion that explain the seeming differences sometimes noted between religious groups? Obviously, the relationship between religion and fertility is not a simple one, and, in fact, there are three major themes that run through the literature: (1) religion plays its most important role in the middle stage of the demographic transition; (2) religiosity may be more important than actual religious belief; and (3) religion and ethnicity are inextricably bound up with each other. Let us examine each of these ideas.

In a study of religious differentials in Lebanese fertility, Chamie (1981) concluded that a major effect of religion may be to retard the adoption of more modern, lower-fertility attitudes during the transitional phase of the demographic revolution. Adherents to religious beliefs that have been traditionally associated with high fertility will be slower to give ground than will people whose religious beliefs are more flexible with respect to fertility. In the United States, Jews have generally had lower fertility levels than the rest of the population. Trends in Jewish fertility have followed the American pattern (a decline in the Depression, a rise with the Baby Boom, a drop with the Baby Bust), but at a consistently lower level. "Widespread secularization processes, upward social mobility, a value system emphasizing individual achievement, and awareness of minority status have all been indicated as factors that are both typical of American Jews and conducive to low fertility" (DellaPergola, 1980:261). Indeed, it is not just American Jews whose fertility is low. DellaPergola (1980) points out that Jewish communities in central and western Europe have also been characterized by low fertility since as early as the second half of the nineteenth century, largely because contraception is readily accepted into the Jewish normative system. Leasure (1982) also found that in the United States fertility declined earliest in those areas dominated by more secularized religious groups. People who are more traditional in their religious beliefs tend to be less educated, have less income, and are thus more prone to higher fertility. Throughout the world, Moslems tend to have higher fertility than almost any other religious group, but a study in India showed that, after education and income are taken into account, Moslems and Hindus are almost equally likely to be practicing family planning (Population Crisis Committee, 1977). To show you how dangerous generalizations about religion can be, however, I offer data from Ghana, where a 1971 survey showed that Moslem women had lower fertility than any other group (Tawiah, 1984).

In looking at religious differentials in fertility it may be at least as important to examine the religiosity of people as to know their specific religious beliefs. It is likely, in fact, that fertility differences by religion will always exist in any society to some extent just because some groups inspire greater religious fervor than others and, in almost all instances, religious zealotry is associated with a desire for larger than average families because there is usually a desire to maintain or return to more traditional value systems in which large families are the norm. In many respects, this is the flip side of saying that secularism causes a decline in fertility. To eschew secularism generally means to maintain high fertility. A study in Guatemala revealed that while Roman Catholics are not less likely than others to know about or even use family planning, people of *any* denomination who consider themselves "very religious" are less likely to be family planners (Bertrand and Bogue, 1977). The same appears to be true in the United States and Canada. Although Catholic and Protestant fertility levels may be generally converging, women of both religious affiliations who are most religious (as measured by frequency of communion) have significantly higher fertility than those who are less religious (Mosher and Hendershot, 1984a; Balakrishnan and Chen, 1988). Furthermore, in a 1980 survey of high school sophomores and seniors, Blake (1984) found that "practicing Catholics, as compared with non-Catholics, expect larger families, rate having children as more important, are more traditional in defining the maternal role, and know less about birth control" (1984:338).

For the United States I have already discussed the high fertility of the Hutterites (see Chapter 4). Another, larger religious group whose average high level of religiosity seems to contribute to higher than average fertility is the Mormon Church. Mormons dominate the social, political, and demographic fabric of the state of Utah, explaining the fact that Utah's birth rate is the highest of any state—twice the national average—and Provo, Utah (the site of Brigham Young University, the principal Mormon institution of higher education) has the highest birth rate of any city in the United States. I should note in this regard that it is important to separate secular from sectarian education, because education in a religious setting (for example, Catholic or Mormon schools) can have the effect of reinforcing religious beliefs and helping to maintain higher levels of fertility (Janssen and Hauser, 1981; Johnson, 1982; Rosenhouse-Persson and Sabagh, 1983).

Finally, we must return to the theme that religion and ethnicity are often hard to disentangle as factors affecting demographic behavior (Bouvier and Rao, 1975). There is probably no more graphic a way to demonstrate this point than to look at the data presented in Table 9.7. By combining data from the 1973 and 1976 National Surveys of Family Growth in the United States, Mosher and Hendershot (1984b) were able to derive enough cases to look at fertility levels by racial and religious categories combined. Black Protestants actually exhibited the highest fertility levels (both in terms of children ever born and total births expected), whereas the fertility of black Catholics was lower than that of Hispanic Catholics. Jews had low fertility, but not as low as blacks and whites with no stated religious preference. To the extent that there is a cultural determinant of fertility, it goes beyond just race. Religion seems to interact with race (and, of course, a host of other factors) to produce the reproductive behavior we see reflected in the birth rates.

IS A COLLEGE EDUCATION WORTH THE TROUBLE?

You may already be familiar with the argument that Americans are "overeducated"—educated beyond the needs of society. It is increasingly rare for Americans to not complete high school, and each decade has brought a higher proportion of high school graduates who have completed college. But, is it also true that jobs have become ever more demanding of higher education, or are we educating too many people for the available number of professional and highly skilled positions in society? If the latter is true, won't that erode the potential earnings of a college graduate by forcing many such people into jobs that really do not require so much education?

The potential existence of problems such as these was brought to public attention in the mid-1970s by several researchers, especially Richard Freeman in his book *The Overeducated American* (1976). The theme was picked up by the news media and has been trumpeted almost annually since. Freeman's basic approach was to compare the earnings of people aged 25–34 who had only completed high school with those who had completed college. He concluded that the difference in income for college graduates had dropped so rapidly in the prior few years that college was no longer a very sound monetary investment. Analyses of other data from the Current Population Surveys have shown that, indeed, the proportion of college-trained people increased substantially between 1970 and 1980 in occupations for which there was almost certainly no increased requirement in skill level (Clogg and Shockey, 1984).

As you can probably see, there are at least two important issues in the controversy over whether Americans are becoming overeducated. The first relates to underemployment—are people being overtrained for the available jobs? The second relates to income—if underemployment exists, is it reducing the relative earning potential of a college degree?

The underemployment issue has been carefully analyzed by Clifford Clogg and James Shockey (1984), who developed a measure of occupational "mismatch." By looking at the average educational levels of people holding specific occupations in 1969, they were able to calculate deviations from that average from 1969 to 1980 and ask: How many people had more than the average level of education in 1980 compared with 1969? Applying this method to annual data compiled by the Current Population Survey, they documented a steady rise in the proportion of people whose educational levels were clearly above average for their occupational levels—an increase from 9.2 percent in 1969 to 17.4 percent in 1980. Within occupational groupings, the greatest increase in apparent underemployment was among managers—a rise from 10.6 percent in 1969 to 27.2 percent in 1980. Given the tremendous growth in enrollment in business schools throughout the United States in the 1970s, this should not be surprising. The size of the Baby Boom forced a high level of competition among its members, and this is another ramification of that fact. Managerial positions have more fluid educational requirements than do most of the professions and many young people, trying to gain a competitive edge, sought higher levels of education than had previously been customary.

Has the extra training paid off economically? Yes and no, depending on how you look at it. On the one hand, the greater proportion of people going to college has altered the life-styles of many young Americans. It has been accompanied by delayed marriage, delayed and a diminished amount of childbearing, and, consequently, higher per-person income among young adult householders. Young people today have more personal disposable income than almost any previous generation. But, at the same time, those sacrifices have simply meant that income of college graduates has just maintained its lead over income among people without a college education. Smith and Welch (1981), for example, calculated the ratio of the peak incomes of college graduates to peak incomes of high school graduates over a 10-year period, with the following results:

	1967	1970	1977
Weekly wages	1.57	1.55	1.55
Annual earnings	1.60	1.56	1.60

"The most reasonable description of these income patterns is that there exists no trend in the income ratios during the peak earning years of mature college workers relative to high school workers" (Smith and Welch, 1981:81). You may wind up being underemployed relative to your educational level, but these data suggest that your income as a college graduate will continue to be 60 percent higher at its peak than that of a person who only completed high school.

The classic case of an underemployed college graduate is the cab driver with a Ph.D. I know one (doesn't everybody?), and the 1980 census lists 3,797 taxi drivers who have 5 or more years of college (some of whom undoubtedly have earned a doctorate), and their income levels are not noticeably different from those of taxi drivers who did not even finish high school (who far outnumber the college graduates). Similar comments can be made for other blue-collar and lower-level service worker jobs for

which a college education is clearly not a prerequisite. In the arts, it might even be said that being too well-educated is an economic liability. Among actors and directors, the 1980 census (U.S. Bureau of the Census, 1984c) reveals that the highest average incomes are earned by high school dropouts. Among authors, college dropouts make more money than do college graduates (although the latter substantially outnumber the former among authors).

A different story can be told, however, for those occupations in which an education might logically be put to use. Let us look at the average pay of young (aged 25–34) legislators in the United States. In 1980, male legislators who were high school graduates earned $18,480 per year, compared with $23,927 for those legislators with 5 or more years of college—a 23 percent differential. Female legislators earn less than males, but those with 5 or more years of college earn 21 percent more than high school graduates—a difference that is nearly identical to that for males. Marketing managers, to look at a different example, earn more than legislators, regardless of educational level, yet in 1980 those marketing managers with 5 or more years of college earned 24 percent more than high school graduates. Among women, the income gap by education was even larger—35 percent.

In general, the data for nearly all professional, managerial, and skilled sales positions seem to point in the same direction: A college education pays off in a higher income. This is in addition, of course, to all of the myriad other ways in which an education enriches one's life. Such "psychic income" may boost your morale if you find yourself underemployed, but remember that even shoe salespeople with college degrees earn 27 percent more money each year than do people in shoe sales with only high school educations.

Table 9.7   Fertility Rates Differ by Race and Religion (United States, 1973–76: Combined 1973 and 1976 National Surveys of Family Growth)

Race, Origin, and Religious Affiliation	Weighted Number of Couples in Thousands	Children Ever Born	Total Births Expected
Total	27,085	2.12	2.70
Black Protestant	1,847	2.72	3.27
Hispanic Catholic	1,277	2.55	3.26
White Catholic	7,336	2.26	2.94
Black Catholic	174	2.26	3.00
White Protestant	15,317	2.05	2.58
Jewish	577	1.86	2.25
Other religions	420	1.69	2.51
Black, no religion	61	1.57	2.21
White, no religion	884	1.29	1.96

Source: W. Mosher and G. Hendershot, 1984, "Religions affiliation and the fertility of married couples," Journal of Marriage and the Family 46(3):671–77, Table 1.

SUMMARY AND CONCLUSION

Population characteristics are important clues to the social and economic life of a society. They are important to the study of population because they are often closely associated with population processes, both influencing and being influenced by fertility (which I discussed in this chapter) as well as mortality and migration. Differences in characteristics such as education, occupation, income, marital status, race and ethnicity, and religion reflect variations in the life chances of individuals.

The distribution of population characteristics in the United States indicates that higher educational status is associated with greater occupational prestige and higher income. Blacks and Hispanics are less likely than others to be highly educated, and this may contribute to their relative social and economic disadvantage in American society. On the other hand, Asian-Americans tend to have higher levels of education than other groups, which may help account for their higher levels of income (and higher life expectancies, as well).

Women have been increasing their levels of income, labor force participation, and occupational status relative to men, and there can be little question that this is related to declining levels of fertility in the United States. Substantial gaps remain in income by sex, but the greater ability of women to support themselves has helped many to avoid or extricate themselves from unhappy marriages. As a consequence, the divorce rate literally soared in the 1970s.

Our interest in population characteristics is especially connected to the way in which they may affect fertility. It is clear that education, occupation, and income are all negatively related to fertility. Minority group members, to the extent that they have less education, lower levels of occupational prestige, and lower income, also tend to have higher fertility. Religion, too, seems to play a factor in fertility. In general, it appears that the more religious is a group, the higher will be its level of fertility, almost regardless of the religious content (with the exception of groups like the Shakers, who forbade intercourse—and failed to survive long). Such cultural influences on fertility are issues of more than parochial concern (no pun intended), because they may influence the relationship between population growth and the status of women—the topic to which we turn in the next chapter.

MAIN POINTS

1. Demographic characteristics such as education, occupation, income, marital status, race and ethnicity, and religion help to define what a society is like.

2. In the United States, average educational attainment has increased substantially over time.

3. White males are still more likely than any other group in American society to have a high-status occupation.

4. Women represent more than 40 percent of all workers, but they are still concentrated disproportionately in clerical and service occupations.

5. Since 1940 the rates of labor force participation have risen for women while declining for men.

6. Americans of almost all statuses are wealthier in real absolute terms now than they were in the 1940s, but there have been only minor changes in the relative status of most groups.

7. The better educated you are, the more money you can expect to earn in your lifetime.

8. Even at comparable occupational levels, with similar educational backgrounds, blacks on average earn less money in the United States than whites.

9. If you are under 25 years old, the chance that you are also married is much higher than if you had been reading this book in 1890.

10. Marriages among blacks are much more prone to dissolution than those among whites, and children are much more likely to be involved.

11. Blacks, Hispanics, and American Indians tend to be disadvantaged compared with whites in American society, whereas Asian-Americans tend to be better off in socioeconomic terms.

12. Religiosity may slow down the adoption of modern, low-fertility attitudes, regardless of the substance of religious beliefs.

SUGGESTED READINGS

1. Richard Easterlin, 1987, Birth and Fortune: The Impact of Numbers on Personal Welfare, 2nd Ed. (Chicago: University of Chicago Press).

   In a book written for a general audience, Easterlin applies his relative income hypothesis (which was discussed in Chapter 3 of this book) to life chances in the United States.

2. Robert E. Kennedy, Jr., 1986, Life Choices: Applying Sociology (New York: Holt, Rinehart and Winston).

   Kennedy brings demographic analysis to bear on mainstream sociology to explore many of the ideas that are central to this chapter. Indeed, this could be thought of as a book-length version of the chapter you have just read.

3. Ronald Rindfuss, Larry Bumpass, and C. St. John, 1980, "Education and fertility: implications from the roles women occupy," American Sociological Review 45(3):431–47.

   This is a more technical article than the previous two readings, but it is well worth the effort if you want to appreciate the way demographers discover and test hypotheses about the relationship between demographic characteristics, such as education, and demographic processes, such as fertility.

4. Reynolds Farley, 1986, Blacks and Whites: Narrowing the Gap (Cambridge: Harvard University Press).

   This volume updates Farley's earlier work (The Growth of the Black Population), which was one of the most important modern treatises on the demography of blacks in the United States.

5. Robert Gardner, Bryant Robey, and Peter Smith, 1985, "Asian Americans: growth, change and diversity," Population Bulletin 40(4).

   Asian-Americans represent the most rapidly increasing group in the United States (as you now know); in this volume, you can "read all about it."

PART FOUR
Population and Contemporary Social Issues

Can women continue to free themselves from domination by men and the burden of too many children? Will the increasing number of older people throughout the world change the way we think about social security systems? What will happen to cities as they continue to absorb more and more people? Are underdeveloped countries trapped in a Malthusian dilemma of too many people and not enough resources? Is it possible to keep feeding billions of people each year? These are a few of the questions that confront the world and require a demographic perspective for a good understanding on our part. They are related to the major issues I will discuss in this section—the status of women, aging, the urban environment, economic development, and food production and distribution.

Each of these issues affects the lives of virtually all of us in one way or another. For example, small families and liberated women usually go together (Chapter 10). Is the status of women, then, the key to lower fertility throughout the world? As fertility and mortality decline, the elderly increase as a fraction of the population (Chapter 11). What kinds of social changes will be produced by a rapidly growing older population? Cities are the most rapidly growing areas on earth, and many questions have been raised about the impact of population growth on the urban environment (Chapter 12), not to mention the impact of urbanization on people. For example, is crowding harmful to human existence? Will urbanization help bring down birth rates?

People move to cities because they hope to better their lives. The desire of less developed nations to improve their levels of living (Chapter 13) has generated massive foreign debt for some countries, often (if not always) compounded by high rates of population growth, which produce ever-growing numbers of people competing for the world's desired and increasingly scarce resources. The most important of those resources is, of course, food (Chapter 14), and the ability of the world to feed everybody every year is obviously related to how rapidly the number of mouths increases.

CHAPTER 10
Population Growth, Women, and the Family

I swear I love my husband
and I love my kids
I wanted to be like my mother
but if I hadn't done it as soon as I did
   there might have been time to be me
      for myself
         for myself
(Barry Manilow and Enoch Anderson)

No time to be herself because the demands of children and her husband kept her too busy—a familiar story in human history and a poignant reminder of the intimate relationship between population growth and the roles that women play in society. For thousands of years—until the nineteenth century at the earliest—high mortality created a need for large families which, when combined with the relative dependency of women during pregnancy and the postnatal period, has been turned to the disadvantage of women. In recent years, however, significant changes have been occurring in the status and roles of women and also in the size and organization of the family unit, especially in industrialized societies.

Although there is no clear-cut cause-and-effect relationship linking population changes and changes in the roles of women and the organization of the family, a demographic perspective will enhance your understanding of the issues and provide you with a better view of current social change. To that end I will first examine those demographic factors that tend to facilitate the domination of women by men. Then I will look at the demographic factors that have, in my opinion, helped to erode that domination and thus helped to raise the status of women and alter their social roles. Next, I will turn the tables on that relationship and suggest to you the ways in which the changes in the status and roles of women can be important factors in maintaining low levels of fertility—an extension, really, of my discussion in Chapter 5. In the second half of the chapter, I will examine the interplay between demographic changes and shifts in the family structure, looking especially at changes in the family and alterations in the roles of women.

The demographic component is often ignored, and it is important; however, keep in mind as you read this chapter that I am not trying to create the impression that demographic change is necessarily the "prime mover" behind other social changes taking place, but rather that demographic changes are probably necessary, though not sufficient, causes of the changes occurring both in the family and in the lives of women. The women's movement as a social phenomenon in its own right is without doubt a major source of inspiration for change, and a whole range of social forces have influenced the reshaping of the family in industrialized societies. Granting that, my purpose in this chapter is fairly limited in scope. I will not examine all facets of the women's movement or all sides of family change. What I will do is provide for you an example of how a demographic perspective can add an important dimension to understanding a major contemporary social issue.

DEMOGRAPHIC CONDITIONS FACILITATING MALE DOMINATION

By now you are familiar with the fact that pronatalist pressures are especially strong in societies characterized by high mortality and high fertility. In those areas, several children must be born just to ensure that enough will survive to replace the adult membership. Thus, one component of the social status of women is that with a regime of high mortality, women are busy with pregnancy, nursing, and child care, and their status is closely tied to their performance in those activities.

Furthermore, high mortality means that childbearing must begin at an early age, because the risk of death even as an adult may be high enough that those younger, prime reproductive years cannot afford to be "wasted" on activities other than family building. In a premodern society with a life expectancy of about 30 years, fully one third of women aged 20 die before reaching age 45, making it imperative that childbearing begin as soon as possible. Of course, one irony of high-mortality societies is that the average age at menarche tends to be later than in modern low-mortality countries, due to dietary deficiencies and health problems. As a result, childbearing usually cannot start until the late teens, but once begun there tend to be strong pressures to continue bearing children.

Women who marry young and begin having children may be "twice-cursed"—having more years to be burdened with children and also being in a more vulnerable position to be dominated by a husband. Men need not marry as young as women since they are not the childbearers, and they also remain fecund longer. The older and more socially experienced a husband is relative to his wife, the easier it may be for him to dominate her; it is no coincidence that in the Moslem Middle East, where women are probably less free than anywhere in the world, men are about 8 years older than their wives on average. By contrast, in the United States husbands are only slightly more than 2 years older than their wives on average (National Center for Health Statistics, 1984a).

DEMOGRAPHIC FACTORS FACILITATING HIGHER STATUS FOR WOMEN

The Influence of Mortality, Fertility, and Urbanization

Three demographic processes—a decline in mortality, a drop in fertility, and increasing urbanization—have importantly influenced the ability of women to expand their social roles. A major factor influencing the rise in the status of women has been the more general liberation of humans from early death. In the first part of the nineteenth century, the expectation of life at birth for U.S. females was roughly 40 years, which meant that each girl baby had only about a 30 percent chance of reaching retirement age (age 65); and among every 100 women aged 20, only 45 could expect to be alive at age 65. On the other hand, by 1985 an American female at birth had an 84 percent chance of survival to retirement (as I discussed in Chapter 6); and of 100 women alive at age 20, 86 will still be around at age 65. Thus, since women and children have much higher probabilities of survival than they used to, lower mortality can reduce the pressure (or at least the need) to initiate childbearing at a young age and to have several children. The decline in mortality does not mean that pressures to have children have evaporated. That is far from the case, as I discuss later, but there is a greater chance that the pressures will be less; indeed, remaining single is more acceptable for a woman now than at any time in American history.

Most of a married American woman's lifetime is now spent doing something besides bearing and raising children, since she is having fewer children than in previous generations and she is also living longer. An average American woman bearing two children in her twenties would, at most, spend about 30 years bearing and rearing them. That many years is far fewer, of course, than she will actually have of relative (indeed increasing) independence from child-rearing obligations, since if her two children are spaced 2 years apart and the first child is born when she is 20, then by age 28 her youngest child will be in school all day, and she will still have 52 more years of expected life. Is it any wonder, then, that women have searched for alternatives to family building?

The declines in mortality and fertility that I have been discussing are both associated with economic development (see Chapter 13) which, in turn, is related to urbanization (see Chapter 12). Mortality declined in cities before it went down in rural areas (see Chapter 6), and the urban environment is almost always associated with lower levels of fertility than rural areas (see Chapter 12). In contrast to rural places, cities provide occupational pursuits for both women and men that encourage a delay in marriage (thus potentially lowering fertility) and lead to a smaller desired number of children within marriage. Other aspects of the urban environment, particularly the greater difficulty in finding spacious housing, may also help lower the family size in urban areas.

Urbanization initially involved migration from rural to urban areas. This meant that women, as they migrated, were removed from the promarital and pronatalist pressures that may have existed in their parents' homes. Thus, migration may have led to a greater ability to respond independently to the social environment of urban areas, which tends to devalue children. It is also true, from a mother's perspective, that in modern urban, industrial societies, the volume of migration may of itself shorten a mother's active daily involvement with her adult children and grandchildren. As I discussed in Chapter 7, young adults are especially prone to migration and every adult who moves may well be leaving a mother behind. Of course, that does not mean that she will be less happy (Campbell et al., 1974), but it does mean that she will have more time on her hands to look for alternatives and to question the social norms that prescribe a lower status and fewer out-of-the-home opportunities for women than for men.

It is probable that the process of urbanization in the Western world initially led to an increase in the dependency of women before influencing liberation (Nielsen, 1978). Urbanization is associated with a transfer of the workplace from the home to an outside location—a severing of the household economy and the establishment of what Kingsley Davis (1984b) has called the "breadwinner system," in which a member of the family (usually the male) leaves home each day to earn income to be shared with other family members. In premodern societies, women generally made a substantial contribution to the family economy through agricultural work and the marketing of produce (Boserup, 1970), but the city changed all that. Men were expected to be breadwinners (a task that women had previously shared), while women were charged with domestic responsibility (tasks that men had previously shared). From our vantage point in history, the breadwinner system seems "traditional," but from a longer historical view, it is really an anomaly:

> The breadwinner system develops slowly in the early phase [of development], characterizing the burgeoning but small middle class rather than the peasantry or the proletariat. Then, after reaching a climax in which virtually no married women are employed, the arrangement declines as more and more wives enter white-collar employment in offices, schools, hospitals, stores, and government agencies. In the United States the heyday of the breadwinner system was from about 1860 to 1920 (Davis, 1984b:404).

As the life expectancy of the urban woman increases and as her childbearing activity declines, the lack of alternative activities is bound to create pressures for change.

In Figure 10.1 I have diagrammed the major paths by which mortality, fertility, and urbanization influence the status of women and the breadth of gender roles considered appropriate for women. Again, I emphasize that these demographic conditions are necessary, but not sufficient, to initiate the current rise in the status of women in industrialized societies. What is also required is some change in circumstance to act as a catalyst for the underlying demographic factors. The women's movement has provided that catalytic force.

The United States As an Illustration

Although mortality and fertility have been declining since the nineteenth century in the United States and urbanization has been occurring throughout that time, it was during World War II that the particular combination of demographic and economic circumstances arose to provide the leading edge of a shift toward equality of the sexes.

The demand for armaments and other goods of war in the early 1940s came at the same time that men were moving out of civilian jobs into the military, and there was an increasing demand for civilian labor of almost every type. Earlier in American history, the demand for labor would have been met by foreign workers migrating into the country, but the Reed-Johnson Immigration Act passed in the 1920s (see Chapter 15) had set up national quotas that severely limited immigration. The only quotas large enough to have made a difference were those for immigrants from countries also involved in the war and thus not a potential source of labor.

With neither males nor immigrants to meet the labor demand, women were called into the labor force. Indeed, not just women per se, but more significantly, married women, and even more specifically, married women with children. Single women had been consistently employable and employed since at least the beginning of the century, as each year 45 to 50 percent of them had been economically active. But in the early 1940s there were not enough young single women to meet labor needs, partly because the improved economy was also making it easier for young

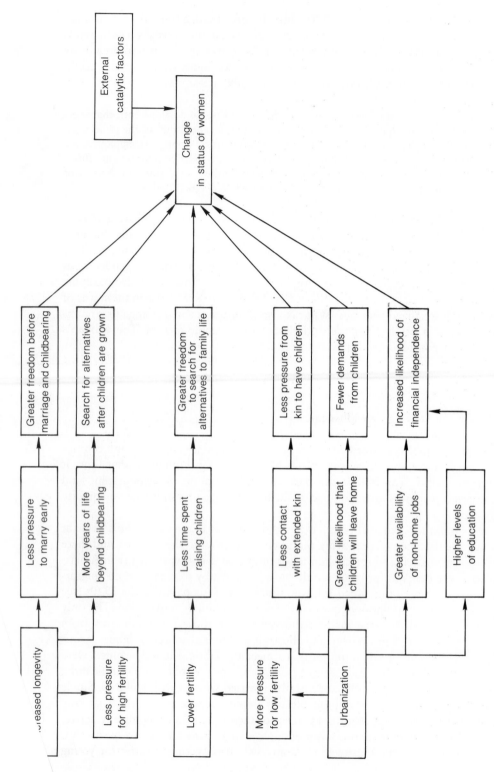

Components of the Changing Status of Women

Increased longevity, lower fertility, and urbanization are demographic processes that have contributed to the rise in the status of women in developed nations.

couples to get married and start a family. It was older women, past their childbearing years, who were particularly responsive to making up the deficit in the labor force (Oppenheimer, 1967). These were the women who broke the new ground in female employment in America, as you can see by the increases in the labor force activity rates for women between 1940 and 1950 (data from Oppenheimer, 1967:Table 2):

Age	Percent Change, 1940–50
14–24	+ 5.5
25–34	− 4.5
35–44	+32.0
45–54	+46.2
55–64	+39.3
65+	+ 2.8
Ages 14+	+12.4

Clearly the biggest change in the labor force rates was for women aged 45–54, and because more than 92 percent of those women were married, this obviously represented a break with the past. Who were these women? They were the mothers of the Depression, mothers who had sacrificed the larger families that they wanted (see Chapter 5) in order to scrape by during one of America's worst economic crises. They were women who had smaller families than their mothers and thus were more easily able to participate in the labor force. However, the ideal family size remained more than three children, and the improved economy permitted the low fertility of the 1930s to give way to higher levels in the 1940s and 1950s. Women with the small families from the Depression actually opened the door to employment for married women, but younger women were not ready to respond to those opportunities in the 1940s and 1950s. Indeed, looking at the preceding table, you can see that between 1940 and 1950 the labor force activity rates of women aged 25–34 actually declined by 4.5 percent. Those women were busy marrying and having children rather than becoming wage earners. Between 1940 and 1950 the percentage of women aged 20–24 who were married increased from 53 percent to 68 percent. In 1940 the total fertility rate in the United States was 2.3 children, and 10 years later it had gone up to 3.2—an increase of nearly one child per woman—and that was only the middle of the rise. By 1960 the total fertility rate had soared to 3.7 children per woman. The postwar Baby Boom, though, was an aberration in American history, a large bump on a long road toward low fertility, and in the late 1960s the number of babies women were having resumed its decline.

ECONOMIC INDEPENDENCE—A KEY TO STATUS

In most social systems, people who can take care of themselves and have enough money to be self-reliant have higher status and greater freedom than those who are economically dependent on others. Further, a pecking order tends to exist among those who are economically independent, with higher incomes being associated with higher status than are low incomes. Being independent, though, is definitely the starting point, and an increasing number of women are arriving at that point.

Between 1950 and 1985 there was a substantial increase in the number and proportion of American women who were in the labor force and earning independent incomes. In 1950, for example, there were 29 female, year-round, full-time workers for every 100 males in that category; by 1985, there were 64 females working full-time, year-round per 100 male workers (U.S. Department of Commerce, 1986). This increase in labor force activity was accomplished especially by younger women. Figure 10.2 shows the change in the pattern of labor force participation by successive cohorts of American women. Each cohort of women born before the Depression began adulthood with approximately one third of its members in the workplace. But the younger the cohort, the more rapidly did labor force involvement increase, especially beyond ages 25–34, after children are in school. The Depression and World War II cohort started out at higher levels of labor force

Figure 10.2   Labor Force Participation over Working Life of U.S. Women Born in Selected Time Intervals: 1886–1965

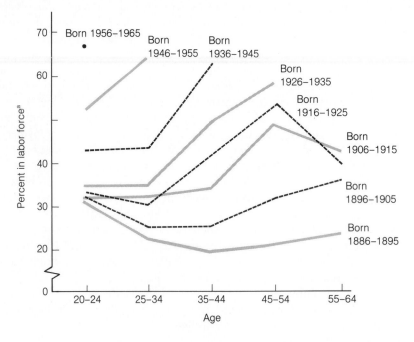

Source: L. Waite, 1981, "U.S. women at work," Population Bulletin 36(2), Figure 2.

[a] Number in labor force as percent of total noninstitutional population in group specified.

Note: For women born between 1886 and 1915, the first age plotted is 14–24 years. Each group (birth cohort) reaches each age interval according to the midpoint of their birth years. Thus, the cohort born in 1886–95 reached ages 25–34 in 1920 and ages 55–65 in 1950. The cohort born in 1916–25 reached ages 25–34 in 1950 and ages 45–54 in 1970.

participation than had previous groups, but its rapid increase coincided with the unprecedented increase in working experienced by the Baby Boom cohorts. Of course, having a job does not itself guarantee a person a satisfactory income. In 1986 the average female wage earner, working year-round, full-time, earned only 65 percent of the income garnered by males. This was an improvement from 1977 when pay for women was 58 percent of that for men, but it still meant that in 1986, 35 percent of families headed by women with no husband present were at or below the poverty level, compared with 11 percent of those headed by men with no wife present.

Why is there a differential in income by sex? The answer is that there is discrimination against women, in terms of what kinds of jobs they are hired for and what pay they receive (Halaby, 1979). As discussed in Chapter 9, women tend to wind up in a rather narrow set of occupational categories. There are very few self-employed female physicians or dentists in the United States and very few female construction workers, but most nurses, elementary school teachers, and bank tellers are women. Even within occupations, women generally earn less than men (U.S. Bureau of the Census, 1984d). In 1985, among full-time, year-round workers, women employed as accountants earned an average (median) of $20,369 per year, whereas men earned $30,098. Female engineers earned an average of $31,361, compared with $36,615 for males. Even among schoolteachers, where women tend to predominate numerically, women were earning $20,810 while men were earning $25,578. These differences suggest that even in the same occupations, women tend to have less power than men (England, 1979). It is of some interest to note that in the Soviet Union, where political ideology and the law both support equal pay for equal work, women still earn only about 65 percent as much as men (Swafford, 1978).

We must not, however, let the sex differential in pay cloud the fact that wage rates for women have increased substantially since the 1960s (Fuchs, 1983). Using time-series data from 1947 to 1977, Devaney (1983) has concluded that rising wage rates for women are the most important reason for the increase in labor force participation during the decades of the 1960s and 1970s, and that these two factors combine to help explain the decline in fertility during the same period.

WOMEN'S STATUS AND FERTILITY

From a demographic perspective, an important aspect of the rise in the status of women is its potential dampening effect on childbearing. As I examine that relationship, there are two questions for you to keep in mind: (1) Why should a change in gender role status affect fertility? (2) What evidence is there that this is really happening?

Why Might a Rise in Women's Status Affect Fertility?

The answer to this question is an extension of the theories of low fertility discussed in Chapter 5—a combination of the social and economic approaches to low fertility. The basis of the explanation is that if the costs of another child are seen as exceeding the benefits, then a woman with two children will decide not to have a third; if she has six, she will decide not to have a seventh; and so on. The emphasis is on rational decision making—a calculus of costs and benefits that are partly economic in nature (for example, income earned or lost) and partly social (status gained or lost, for instance) (see Blake, 1968; Hawthorne, 1970; Scanzoni, 1975). The balance between these costs and benefits measures the utility of the contemplated birth.

More specifically, the costs of having a child can be measured in terms of opportunities foregone—the education not completed, the career not fully realized, the income not earned, the leisure unavailable, and so on. There are two aspects to these costs, and each is related to women's status in a different way. Costs of such things as consumer goods (building a house, buying a boat, and so on) may be motivations for a *couple* to limit childbearing, regardless of the personal freedom of the wife. The desire of couples to obtain material goods and to achieve (and demonstrate through conspicuous consumption) a high standard of living has been an important component of the long-run trend in declining fertility in first-world nations. Those desires have played a role in influencing a rise in status by freeing the time and energy of women as *individuals* for nonfamilial activities, as I discussed earlier in the chapter. But as alternatives to family life have increased for women (that is, remaining single or childless or pursuing a career), a growing set of costs of childbearing and rearing has evolved.

When an advanced education, a prestigious career, and a good income were not generally available to women, then the lack of such things was not perceived as a cost of having children. But when those advantages are available, reducing or foregoing them for the sake of raising a family may be perceived as a sacrifice. Again, the reflexive nature of the fertility–women's status connection is apparent. As fertility has gone down, more time has become available for women to pursue alternate lifestyles; and as the alternatives grow in number and attractiveness, the costs of having children have gone up.

The benefits of having children are less tangible but no less important than the costs. They include psychological satisfaction and proof of adulthood, not to mention being more integrated into the family and community. The latter reasons reflect a broad category of reward that society offers for parenthood—social approval. In every society there exists considerable pressure to marry and have children, as I mentioned in Chapter 5, since not until a state of immortality is attained will a society be able to ignore reproduction. Obviously, a low-mortality society has less need for concern than a high-mortality society, but if any society is to continue to exist, a sufficient number of children must be born, raised, and socialized. To ensure that this happens, every society has institutionalized pronatalist pressures—pressures to marry and procreate—which tend to be pervasive, subtle, and usually taken for granted, so much so that the decision to bear children is often misconstrued as "voluntary." Nothing could be further from reality. As Blake (1972) has noted, childbearing is the prescribed behavior for American women—definitely the preferred norm or rule of conduct. "What leads us to abide by these rules? First of all, we are socialized from the beginning both to learn the rules and to believe they are right. Second, the everyday process of interaction with others puts us in constant contact with the norm-enforcement process, since other people have a stake in how we behave. They can reward us with approval, or punish us with rejection" (Blake, 1972:3).

In addition, most people are most comfortable in families with children, since by definition everyone was raised in a situation involving at least one child. Thus, having children may allow you to relive vicariously (and perhaps revamp) your own childhood, helping to recreate the past and take the sting out of any failures you may experience as an adult. In a more instrumental way, children tend to provide a means for establishing a network of social relationships in a community, through school, organized sports, and activity groups. The rewards of childbearing thus are greatest in terms of the personal and social satisfaction derived from them, since in American society there is certainly little, if any, economic advantage derived from having children.

From very early ages you have been exposed to the costs and benefits of child-bearing and child rearing, and one of the best indexes of the results of your internal calculation of the pros and cons of family life is your own **gender role** identification. This is generally conceptualized as a continuum from what might be called tradi-tional at one end to modern at the other (Scanzoni, 1975). If you are female, the traditional gender role identification is associated with the attitude that the benefits of marriage and the family far outweigh the costs. If you are traditional in outlook, you probably do not aspire to an advanced education, a career, or financial indepen-dence, but will find your personal fulfillment in the "traditional" ways of getting married (probably at a fairly young age) and having as many children as you and your husband feel you can afford.

If you are at the other end of the spectrum, you are a woman who perceives the costs of children to outweigh the benefits. You will probably delay marriage (if you marry at all) until you have completed your education and maximized your occupa-tional chances by keeping your options open. Your career and economic indepen-dence might well assure you of status equal to or greater than your husband (if, indeed, you marry), and you would be unlikely to want to confound that by having children.

Most American women probably fall in the middle range of that continuum. There are perceived costs of children in terms of opportunities foregone, but the benefits of children are also perceived as too great to ignore. This can produce many forms of compromise to keep fertility low without eliminating it altogether. Some of these options include postponing marriage and pursuing education and a career, but interrupting those pursuits to have a small family. Or you might marry early, have a small family, and then pursue an alternate life-style—an option made available by low mortality. Or, as is increasingly true, you might pursue a career and simulta-neously raise one or two children. Regardless of the particular path you choose, if you are a woman with a gender role identification that places dual emphases on minimizing the costs of children while maximizing the benefits, you are a person liberated from a total immersion in domestic life yet tied to the family as a source of social approval and personal gratification. Since in the United States the differences between an average of one child and an average of three is the difference between a declining population and one that will double in 47 years, the variation that might exist even among small families is important. In essence, the rise in the status of women is crucial to the future of family size and thus of population growth. As the costs of children exceed the benefits, indexed by greater "modernization" of gender role identification, family size declines. These costs rise as the alternatives to child-bearing increase in quantity and quality, and as women increase their ability to be independent.

Labor Force Participation and Fertility

It is by now a familiar theme that female labor force participation has a major bearing on fertility decisions. What may be less obvious is that the converse is no longer so true as it used to be; namely, having a child is no longer the impediment to working that it once was. In 1950 scarcely one in ten married women with children under 6 years of age was in the workplace. By 1984 more than half (52 percent) were working (U.S. Department of Commerce, 1986). This was facilitated by changes in the prevailing attitudes about the appropriateness of a woman with children being employed (Spitze and Spaeth, 1979). The liberalization of that attitude was influenced partly by a distinctly demographic factor—the decline in serious infant illness and death. Children are now much less likely to become ill for protracted lengths of time, thus requiring more intensive (and extensive) parental attention (Hoffman, 1975). Also, the rise in labor force participation of women with young children influences small-family norms. As I discussed in Chapter 5, the two-child family is now preferred in industrialized societies, and so a woman who decides to build a family is less apt to feel pressured to have more than one or two children. Even after childbearing begins, then, it no longer necessarily means a succession of children, and the woman is free to drop out of the labor force only briefly or perhaps not at all.

Despite the increase in the percentage of working mothers, it is still somewhat true that the social roles of parent and worker tend to be incompatible (Stolzenberg and Waite, 1977). In a study of women with babies less than a year old, Hock and her associates (1984) found that 66 percent planned to return to work by the baby's first birthday, but the majority said that they would prefer to be able to take care of their child. Women for whom the conflict between roles of mother and worker appears to be minimized are those who are especially involved in their work. The more enmeshed in her job a woman is, the less she seems to worry about leaving her infant (Pristag, 1984).

Using data from the National Longitudinal Study of the Labor Market Experiences of Young Women, Waite and Stolzenberg found that "plans to participate in the labor force at age 35 decrease a woman's expected family size by an average of 0.767 children below the number of children she would plan to bear if she did not expect to participate in the labor force at age 35" (1976:247). Their analysis further suggests that "childbearing and labor force participation plans tend to be formed before marriage, and that the relationship between [labor force participation plans] and [fertility expectations] is roughly the same for married young women as it is for single young women" (Waite and Stolzenberg, 1976:250). They have proceeded to develop the hypothesis that "the inverse effect of work plans on fertility expectations increases as women age from 19 to 29 because their knowledge of the demands of motherhood and their information about the labor market improve during that time.

. . . As a result, we reasoned that the extent to which women limit their expected fertility to accommodate their employment plans increases as they grow older" (Stolzenberg and Waite, 1977:780).

The relationship between labor force activity and fertility is complicated by the fact that not all jobs are the same; some are naturally more prestigious and require a higher commitment than others. Thus, Groat and associates (1976) found in a 1971 survey in Toledo, Ohio, that among white Protestants, even after controlling for age, education, and marital duration, professional women had borne an average of 1.9 children, compared with 2.4 for clerical and sales workers and 2.9 for women who were manual laborers. Income is closely related to job status and, again, the more a woman is paid, the fewer children she is likely to have. Thus, it may be that only the most personally gratifying jobs (which are especially those associated with higher education) will lead to lower fertility (Hoffman, 1975).

We can conclude that "both tangibly and intangibly education, job position, and earnings supply benefits [that is, to do without them would be a cost] that undercut the motivation to have children" (Scanzoni, 1975:158). It also appears from Scanzoni's analysis that those women who are employed are more likely to have a modern gender role orientation than those not employed; and among the employed, job prestige and earnings are also related positively to gender role modernity. It seems apparent, therefore, that freedom from the traditional women's role leads to lower fertility because children may impair a woman's education, job, and earning power (these are known as the *opportunity costs* of having children).

In the United States a good case can be built for the idea that equal status for women and men should help to maintain low fertility, even if it was not actually responsible for the decline in fertility. Now you might be asking whether we can expect a rise in the status of women to lower fertility levels in less developed, high-fertility countries when, in fact, it may have been a decline in fertility itself that helped to bring about the improved status of women in the United States. Is it possible for women to escape the domination of men prior to the kind of social and economic development that has occurred in the industrialized nations? The answer to both questions is a qualified yes. It seems to me that low levels of fertility are not required for the change in attitudes by and toward women, although lowered levels of mortality probably are. On the other hand, if you change the way people perceive the world (assuredly a monumental task), then you will probably have indirectly influenced the level of childbearing.

How can you influence people's perception of the world? A key element is education, and closely related to that is the freedom of women to remain single and childless long enough to get an education and assess their own alternatives. One of the greatest deterrents to female independence and thus to low fertility is undoubtedly teenage marriage, no matter which society you consider.

Teenage Motherhood

You learn the roles appropriate to your sex at an early age. Girls learn how to be women and boys to be men, girls to be mothers and boys to be fathers. The family is an inherently pronatalist institution since nearly all children, even if unplanned, are wanted at the time of their birth. That means that each child's parents tend to value parenthood, at least to some extent, and each child is likely socialized into the role models of parenthood. In other words, from a very early age the benefits of having children and the social approval accorded parenthood will be fairly obvious to most children. Not so obvious until later in life are the alternatives to childbearing and child rearing. Only as young people begin to disengage themselves from the family in which they grew up (their "family of orientation") are they likely to realistically assess the life-style options available to them as adults. The earlier you decide on a choice of alternatives (especially if you are a woman), the more likely it is that your choice will be marriage. Conversely, even if you eventually marry (as about 95 percent of Americans do—U.S. Bureau of the Census, 1975b), if you delay marriage past the teen years you are far more likely to acquire a liberated perception of your own gender role and are more likely to evaluate the costs and benefits of children in favor of a small family.

When a teenage girl gets married or has a baby, she may have significantly foreclosed many opportunities that could otherwise be available to her. The chance of her continuing her education, pursuing a professional career, or becoming financially independent are severely restricted; her chances of having a larger than average family, on the other hand, are considerably elevated. For instance, data from the 1970 U.S. census show that, among women first married in 1955–64, only 36 percent of women who had been 14–17 years old at marriage had completed high school by 1970. In other words, even 6–15 years after marriage the women who had been young teenagers as brides were still predominantly without a high school education. On the other hand, among women who delayed marriage only to age 18, 71 percent were at least high school graduates. However, only 2 percent of those women were also college graduates, whereas if you look at women who had delayed marriage to age 23 or 24, you find that 80 percent were high school graduates and 20 percent were college graduates as well. Comparable data from the 1980 census were not yet available at this writing.

There should be little question in your mind as to what the young brides were doing as their sisters continued on with an education. They were having babies. In 1986, for example, among women aged 25–29, those who had married at younger than age 18 had already given birth to 2,211 children per 1,000 women, compared with 1,854 children born to women married at ages 20–21. Among women aged 30–34 in 1986, those who had been teenage brides had nearly one child more on average than women married at ages 22 or older (U.S. Bureau of the Census, 1987b). I should point out that not only do teenage brides have more children than women who delay marriage, but their marriage is more likely to end in divorce, and their children (especially if conceived premaritally) have a greater likelihood of dying during infancy (see, for example, Kleinman and Kessel, 1987). Since the majority of births to teenagers are out of wedlock (a topic I return to later in this chapter) it is noteworthy that data from both the 1980 and 1982 Current Population Surveys confirm earlier findings that it is a difficult beginning for families in which the woman has experienced an out-of-wedlock pregnancy or birth. The lives of people in this situation tend to be marked by low education, low occupational status, high unemployment, and high dependence on welfare (O'Connell and Rogers, 1984).

Delaying childbearing past the teen years is an important component of freeing women from total immersion in child-rearing activities, and the trend since the early 1960s in the United States has been in that direction (National Center for Health Statistics, 1984b). In 1960, 44 percent of American women aged 15–19 were childless, while in 1965 the percentage had risen to 48, and in 1977 up to 50. By 1982, more than half (57 percent) of *married* women aged 15–19 had not yet borne a child (U.S. Bureau of the Census, 1984g). Similar trends have been apparent for women aged 20–24—young women have been delaying marriage and, more important, postponing childbearing. If this trend continues, we can reasonably anticipate an expansion of opportunities for women and a maintenance of low fertility in the United States; if it spreads to less developed nations (where young marriage and a quick succession of children are often the norm), then fertility will start declining rapidly. Any set of fertility and gender role changes like the ones I have been discussing are associated with a whole host of other changes in society. In American society there has been particular concern about the fate of the family in the face of this kind of social upheaval.

WOMEN'S STATUS AND THE FAMILY

In recent years we have heard rumors that the family is dying, or at least going out of style. Although these characterizations distort the situation, a major metamorphosis has been taking place in the structure of families in industrialized nations. In the following sections I will outline the nature of these changes and discuss them in the context of the preceding discussion about the changing status of women.

Five major changes are unfolding within the family structure of industrialized nations: (1) a delay in marriage, accompanied by (2) a rise in **cohabitation;** (3) a rise in illegitimacy; (4) a rise in the divorce rate; and (5) a continued high remarriage rate (Glick, 1979a; Westoff, 1978a).

Delay in Marriage

At its lowest ebb in 1956, the age at first marriage for females in the United States was 20.1 years, and for males it was 22.5. However, by 1986 the average age at marriage had risen to 23.1 for females (an increase of 3.0 years) and 25.7 for males (a rise of 3.2 years) (U.S. Bureau of the Census, 1987f). The impact of this rise in marriage age can be seen more dramatically if we look at the percentage of people who are remaining single. In 1960, 29 percent of American women aged 20–24 were single (never married), by 1970 that percentage had risen to 36, and by 1982 it had jumped to 58. In 1986, 34 percent of women aged 25 remained single—more than two and a half times the level of 1960. Similar trends have been apparent in other industrialized nations, especially in Sweden and Denmark, two countries that tend to set the fashion, so to speak, in these matters (Westoff, 1978b).

The ability of women to be economically independent helps to account for the delay in marriage, because that independence opens up alternatives to being married and having children and aids in a woman's ability to choose more freely the life-style she prefers. Of course, men make up half the marriage equation, and to men as well as women the economic burden and responsibility of marriage may seem less attractive in an era of higher material expectations and greater competition for jobs.

Rise in Cohabitation

As you may have guessed, a rising age at marriage has not meant that people are avoiding sexual unions altogether. Au contraire. The rise in cohabitation (living together, or "unmarried couple households," as the Census Bureau calls it) has indeed been one of the most prominent recent changes that have led to a belief that the family is dying. It is pretty easy to see why the demise seems imminent to some, since the number of unmarried couples in the United States more than tripled from half a million in 1970 to more than 2 million in 1986. The most dramatic increase, not surprisingly, has been among younger adults. The Baby Boom cohort increased the number of unmarried couples under age 45 twelvefold between 1970 and 1986. In 1970 there were only 89,000 unmarried couples under age 45, and they accounted for only 17 percent of all unmarried couples; by 1986, there were 1,768,000 unmarried couples in which both people were under 45, and they represented 80 percent of all unmarried couples. During that time there was little change in the incidence of living together among people aged 45 and older (U.S. Bureau of the Census, 1983b).

The increase in cohabitation is not due simply to the increase in the number of young adults. Note that in 1970 there were 72 million Americans aged 18–44 and the number increased to 103 million in 1986—a 43 percent increase. However, there was a 1,887 percent increase in the number of unmarried couples aged 18–44. Remember, though, that unmarried couples represent only a small fraction of all couples; in fact, in 1986 the 1,768,000 unmarried couples under age 45 represented only about 3 percent of all couples under 45. Yet it is likely that these figures on current cohabitation "considerably understate the percentage of young persons who will cohabit at some time during their lives. Eighteen percent of a 1974–75 sample of men in their twenties said they had lived with a woman without marriage for six months or more, even though only 5 percent were currently cohabiting" (Thornton and Freedman, 1983:12).

Since women now have the potential for greater independence, they may also be less willing to commit themselves to a relationship until they have tried it out for a while. For both sexes, cohabitation can be a way of avoiding the emotional and financial responsibility that might be involved in a marriage. The avoidance of family responsibility is, of course, facilitated by the now widespread use of effective contraceptives and abortion, and in the United States and most of western Europe levels of fertility tend to be lower among cohabiting couples than among the married (Klimas Blanc, 1984). In Sweden and Denmark, however, where as many as 20 percent of all couples may be cohabiting (Westoff, 1978b), childbearing within such unions is much more common.

Rise in Illegitimacy

As cohabitation has increased, so has the extent of illegitimacy. Between 1970 and 1986 in the United States, the birth rate for single women increased by 24 percent. Yet at the same time, the birth rate for all women declined by 25 percent (National Center for Health Statistics, 1987c). This, of course, has doubled the proportion of all births that are illegitimate, from 11 percent in 1970 to 22 percent in 1986. Since 1975 more than half of all black infants in the United States (61 percent in 1985) have been born out of wedlock (National Center for Health Statistics, 1987c). Interestingly enough, however, the rise in illegitimate births between 1970 and 1986 was composed of an increase among whites under age 25 but a decline among blacks at all reproductive ages.

To be sure, it is not cohabitation that has produced higher illegitimacy, but both are related to the society-wide relaxation of sexual norms, accompanied by earlier and more widespread premarital intercourse. As Zelnick and Kantner have said, "Although the majority of female teenagers have not had intercourse, the magnitude of that majority appears to be diminishing, so that more than one-half of those aged 19 in 1976 have had intercourse" (1980:80). That figure of a bit more than one half has probably remained stable since the latter part of the seventies (Zelnick and Shah, 1983; Bachrach and Horn, 1988).

Among younger women, conceiving a child outside of marriage is still sometimes a matter of ignorance about the menstrual cycle and the wide range of contraceptives available. In fact, the rise in one-parent households has been particularly great among young people with less than a high school education (Glick, 1979a). This is coupled with a general avoidance of responsibility for contraception on the part of young males. However, among women in their twenties or older, illegitimacy presumably reflects a desire to bear a child without a commensurate desire to be married. This view may be particularly characteristic of women who are relatively militant in their feminism (Nielsen, 1978).

Rise in Divorce Rate

Throughout the twentieth century the rise in the divorce rate has been a pervasive force in changing the family. Interestingly, the rise in the divorce rate is, at least statistically, closely related to an increase in longevity. Throughout this century, although the probability has increased that a husband and wife will survive to old age, the probability has decreased that they will still be married to each other when they do reach old age. Preston and McDonald (1979) have estimated that while 16 percent of all marriages made in 1915 ended in divorce, 36 percent of the 1964 marriages will end that way. If current trends continue, nearly one in two marriages from 1973 will wind up in divorce court (Thornton and Freedman, 1983). Indeed, since 1960, the rise in the population of divorced persons has been particularly astonishing. For example, in 1960, there were 9.2 divorces per 1,000 married women aged 15 and older—a rate that, despite fluctuations, had not changed much since the 1920s. However, by 1985 the rate had skyrocketed to 21.7 per 1,000 (National Center for Health Statistics, 1987d). In other words, by the 1980s more than 2 out of every 100 married women you might have known were likely to be on the threshold of divorce that year.

The factors that lead to cohabitation instead of marriage may also be important in the rising divorce rate. The greater ability of a woman to be independent has increased her ability to leave an unsatisfactory mate without suffering as disastrous a set of economic and social consequences as used to be the case. On the other hand, it has probably also loosened a man's feelings of responsibility to a marriage (especially if children are not involved) if he perceives it to be unsatisfactory.

Remarriage

For most of this century divorce has been followed quite closely by remarriage, leading to a popular belief that Americans were drifting toward **serial monogamy** (or perhaps *serial polygamy*). The prediction was premature, however, because the remarriage rate began to level off in the United States in the mid-1970s, just as it had done earlier in Sweden (Westoff, 1978a). By 1984 in the United States, the remarriage rate of 87 remarriages per 1,000 divorced women and 133 per 1,000 divorced men was below its 1971 peak of 133 for women and 231 for men (National Center for Health Statistics, 1987e). In general the rate of remarriage had been increasing for years, along with the divorce rate, because alternatives to marriage either were not socially acceptable or were too difficult financially. However, the growing acceptance of cohabitation and of fairly open nonmarital sexual relations, along with the acceptance (both legal and social) of single-parent families, the ability of a female-headed household to survive economically, and the settling in of the Baby Boomers, may all have contributed to lowering the remarriage rate.

In the United States, the changes taking place in the family structure are occurring mainly within the Baby Boom cohort, but similar changes have taken place earlier in Europe (especially Sweden and Denmark), where no Baby Boom occurred. Westoff has suggested that the institutions of marriage and the family show signs of change because

> The economic transformation of society has been accomplished by a decline in traditional and religious authority, the diffusion of an ethos of rationality and individualism, the universal education of both sexes, the increasing equality of women, the increasing survival of children and the emergence of a consumer-oriented culture that is increasingly aimed at maximizing personal gratification (1978b:53).

While the changes may seem readily explainable, we need to ask whether they are temporary or in fact represent more permanent changes in the familial landscape.

THE FUTURE OF THE FAMILY IN INDUSTRIALIZED NATIONS

Demographers are typically reluctant to predict the future, showing the same caution appropriate to all social sciences. Nonetheless, many trends in demographic change are persistent enough that we can venture out on a limb and suggest the probable future course of changes in the family. It seems likely that there will not be a reversal in the broad range of alternate living arrangements available. This follows from the fact that we are unlikely to see a reversal either in the status of women or in the low level of fertility.

The suggestion that fertility will remain low requires some explanation, since (1) I noted in Chapter 5 that the birth rate in the United States rose slightly in the late 1970s and early 1980s, and (2) the cohorts becoming adults in the 1990s in the United States will be smaller than the Baby Boom generation. If you followed Easterlin's argument closely in Chapters 3 and 5 you would conclude that as the smaller cohorts move into adulthood, men will have an easier time getting a job, and that will encourage women to marry and have children. That scenario is possible but unlikely, because the gains that women have made in the labor force and elsewhere in society will probably not be given up easily, even if economic uncertainty is alleviated. Indeed, we can expect continued pressure for sexual equality. Furthermore, the economic problems that have helped to prod women into the labor force show no signs of letting up in the foreseeable future. Worldwide population growth, which is a virtual certainty, will continue to put increased demand on resources, thus forcing prices to higher levels everywhere in the world. And, in the United States, as the younger cohorts reach adulthood they will continue to have competition from immigrants.

Let me add that I think the major changes in the family have already taken place and that future shifts will be small but in the same directions I outlined in the preceding sections. It seems unlikely to me that we will revert to the young ages at marriage characteristic of the 1950s. The trend toward higher levels of participation in higher education, especially for women, will probably help to maintain the higher age at marriage and also help to propel women into jobs that may compete with family-building activity.

The high cost of housing may also contribute to a delay in marriage and may encourage women to remain in the labor force. These pressures, when combined with the growing acceptance of cohabitation, may lead to a rise in that living arrangement, although perhaps not so dramatic a rise as in the 1970s. Pressure to keep fertility low for economic reasons, coupled with the clear ability to control fertility and combined with continued financial independence of women, add up to the likely continuance of the fairly high levels of single-parent households.

If economic pressures remain strong into the future, we may also find a rise in the number of multiple-generation households. Adult children even now appear to be staying home longer (or coming home again after a brief try on their own). It is also possible that young married adults may find it advantageous to live with one set of parents—an arrangement more likely if one or both sets of parents has only one or two children. Further, older members of society may find it advantageous to share their households with married grandchildren, with other relatives, or even with nonrelatives as a means of pooling resources in an expensive world.

In summary, it is likely that the major shift in the family occurred in the 1970s, and that future changes are likely to be less dramatic but in generally the same direction as those occurring in the 1970s. Bear in mind, however, that the vast majority (more than 90 percent) of Americans still marry, and that most residents of the United States (70 percent in 1986) are members of a household that includes a husband and a wife. Furthermore, most children under 18 (76 percent in 1986) live with both a mother and a father, although there is a huge differential by race—81 percent for whites but only 43 percent for blacks (U.S. Bureau of the Census, 1987f). Marriage and family living are not universal in the United States or in any other industrialized nation, but they continue to be the predominant living arrangement in all industrialized societies, as they also are in most less developed nations. In the latter places, however, the changes that are occurring are qualitatively different.

THE SITUATION IN LESS DEVELOPED COUNTRIES

One of the consequences of being a less developed nation in the modern world is, as I have suggested earlier in this chapter, that the movement from a premodern, agricultural society to a more technologically advanced stage typically witnesses the degradation (or even the *further* degradation) of women's status. In predominantly Moslem nations, the gap between men and women is especially wide, strengthened over the centuries by the Koran, which states that "man has authority over women because Allah made the one superior to the other" (quoted by Pool, 1972). Throughout the Third World, development is bringing about an increase in the breadwinner system (remember the earlier comments by Davis, 1984b) and is increasing the economic and political dependence of women. Charlton (1984) contends that in India, as a case study, modernization has been accompanied by a declining status of women. This is a story confirmed by the Report of the National Committee on the Status of Women in India (1975), which concluded that "to our dismay, we found that such disabilities [centers of resistance to change in the status of women] have sometimes been aggravated by the process of development itself" (1975:2).

The low status of women is perpetuated by the prevailing norms of youthful marriage, which often keep women very literally "barefoot and pregnant." In general, those countries with the highest levels of fertility also have the lowest average age at marriage for women (see Table 10.1). For example, in Europe and the United States, where low fertility prevails, the average age at marriage for women is consistently above 20; whereas in northern Africa, the Middle East, and South Asia, where high fertility prevails, the average age at marriage is consistently below 20. In Indonesia, nearly half of the women have had their first child by the time they are 17 (Wells, 1984). By contrast, in 1979 there were only 858 reported teenage pregnancies in the entirety of Japan, and of those, 70 percent ended in abortion (San Diego Union, 1980c). Youthful marriage and early childbearing force women to the sidelines of development and, with half of the population immobilized, development efforts are bound to falter (see Weinrich, 1979; Mehta, 1982; and Tillion, 1983).

In India, where the average age at marriage is less than 17 and where fertility is among the highest in the world, the percentage of women who are gainfully employed outside of agriculture is very low. Likewise, the alternatives to marriage and having a family are very few for those women—both a symptom of their domination by men and a source of their continued high levels of childbearing. Withholding from women a status equal to men is deeply ingrained in Indian culture, where in the mid-1960s there were only half as many girls as boys aged 11–14 enrolled in school (Mandelbaum, 1974). In a 70-nation survey conducted in 1976, George Gallup

Table 10.1 Women in High-Fertility
Countries Often Marry in Their Teens

Countries	Year	Percent of Brides and Bridegrooms Under Age 20 at Marriage	
		Brides	Bridegrooms
Low-fertility countries (CBR less than 20)			
Japan	1984	3	1
East Germany	1984	16	3
United Kingdom	1984	13	4
United States	1981	21	8
High-fertility countries (CBR greater than 30)			
Mexico	1982	41	17
Egypt	1980	46	9
Kuwait	1983	40	5
Philippines	1982	30	10

Source: United Nations, 1987, Demographic Yearbook, 1985 (New York: United Nations), Table 13.

Note: Brides in high-fertility countries are more likely to be teenagers than are brides in low-fertility countries. The same is true for bridegrooms, except in the Middle Eastern countries, where the difference in age between brides and grooms tends to be the widest. A bride's youthful marriage may militate against broader options for women.

found that only 56 percent of Indian women believed that women in their country had equal opportunities in education—one of the lowest percentages in any country studied (San Diego Union, 1977e). An improvement in the status of women in India would almost certainly lead to a decline in fertility. Indeed, India is a huge and diverse society and it is already apparent that fertility is lower in those states of India where, for a variety of historical and cultural reasons, women enjoy greater personal freedom (Dyson and Moore, 1983).

In India's Moslem neighbor, Bangladesh, only 3.3 percent of urban women are employed in nonagricultural activities. That small percentage of women who do work tend actually to have higher fertility than those not working—implying that economic necessity is most likely the main reason for their participation in the labor force.

Women's participation in economic activities in urban Bangladesh may depend, in the end, on changes in social values. Islam seems no longer to be a barrier to women's work outside the home, at least in cases of economic duress. But most men in Bangladesh still consider household and domestic activities as most suitable for women, whom they still see as subservient. Most families still educate their sons rather than their daughters on the assumption that boys are more of an economic asset than girls. Unless these values shift, we do not expect any major change in female participation in the labor force (Chaudhury, 1979:163).

HAS THE SEX RATIO AFFECTED THE GENDER REVOLUTION?

Throughout this chapter I have pointed out that the rise in the status of women in the United States has been aided by a series of long-term demographic events, but that a catalytic force such as the women's movement was necessary to unleash the power built into demographic forces. Ironically, many analysts (for example, Davis and van den Oever, 1982) have argued that the women's movement itself was triggered by one of the major demographic phenomena of the Baby Boom—the **marriage squeeze.** The marriage squeeze is "an evocative though imprecise term used to describe the effects of an imbalance between the number of males and females in the prime marriage ages" (Schoen, 1983:61). It is a by-product of the combination of different-sized cohorts and the fact that women do not usually marry men their own age.

You may recall from Chapter 8 that, while more boy babies are born than girl babies, higher male mortality evens the sex ratio by the late teens and early twenties. Thus, a young woman expecting to marry someone her own age would have virtually a 100 percent chance of finding someone. However, in the United States and in most other societies throughout the world, women usually marry someone older than themselves. Now, if there are fewer older males, due to the fact that the number of births had been lower prior to the woman's year of birth, her probability drops of finding someone of the usual marriageable age. Since men her own age may not be expecting to marry for another 2 to 3 years, she too may be forced to postpone marriage.

American women, on average, marry a man who is 2 to 3 years older, and over time the vast majority of American women have preferred marriage (at least at some point in life) to remaining single. Assuming that people will continue to want to marry, the imbalance in the number of males or females can lead to a delay in marriage for the sex that has the excess numbers. This is exactly what has happened to women of the Baby Boom. In the accompanying table you can see that in 1950 there were 98 men aged 22–26 for every 100 women 2 years younger (aged 20–24). Thus, there was near equality in the number of males and females of typical marriageable ages. If we assume that women preferred men 3 years older than themselves, the ratio was even closer to equity: There were 99 men aged 23–27 in 1950 per 100 women aged 20–24. But that ratio dropped precipitously through the years when the pre–Baby Boom and Baby Boom cohorts were reaching marriage age, because in nearly every year from 1937 through 1957 there were more people born than in the previous year. Women looking at the age group 2 to 3 years older kept seeing fewer men than there were women of their own age. The result, of course, was that many women were forced to postpone marriage, a phenomenon I have already discussed in this chapter.

By 1980 relative equity had been achieved again in the sex ratio at the usual marriage ages, but by that time some remarkable changes had already taken place in American gender roles. "The Women's Liberation Movement may be interpreted, on the one hand, as a collective means by which women helped themselves to reorient each other to the new lower compensation for the traditional female role and, on the other, as the means by which the increasing number of women outside of the traditional wife-mother role sought to combat the discrimination meted out to women in the job world" (Heer and Grossbard-Schechtman, 1981:49). Either interpretation can be viewed as women's responses to the demographic forces at work in the marriage market (Grossbard-Schechtman, 1985). In the late 1980s and early 1990s American males will be experiencing a marriage squeeze as the declining number of births through the 1960s and

The Sex Ratio of the Baby Boom Produced a Dearth of Potential Husbands

Cohort	Year				
	1950	1960	1970	1980	1990
Men aged 22–26 / Women aged 20–24	98	84	87	98	108
Men aged 23–27 / Women aged 20–24	99	86	85	96	111

Sources: U.S. Bureau of the Census, 1983, 1980 Census of Population, General Population Characteristics (Washington, D.C.: Government Printing Office), Table 2; and U.S. Bureau of the Census, 1982, "Projections of the Population of the United States: 1982 to 2050 (Advance Report)," Current Population Reports, Series P-25, No. 922, Table 2.

early 1970s produces a dearth of women of the usual marriage age (see the accompanying table). This should lead to a better bargaining position for women in the marriage market, and the new gender awareness brought about by the women's movement could aid women to achieve greater domestic equality in terms of shared housework and child care.

Guttentag and Secord (1983) have used the concept of sex ratio to develop a slightly different theory of gender relations. In general, their hypothesis is that a shortage of women relative to men encourages domesticity, marital stability, and a maintenance of male dominance over women. Conversely, a low sex ratio (more women than men) encourages women to find alternatives to traditional role models, since there are too few men of marriageable age. Guttentag and Secord use nineteenth-century America as an example. On the frontier the sex ratio was high and female roles were typically very traditional, with an emphasis on family building and family life. At the same time, the New England states had a much lower sex ratio and it was in that part of the country, perhaps not coincidentally, that the suffrage movement began.

American blacks have for several decades had a sex ratio lower than that of whites because of higher black male mortality from birth on. The sex ratio has been further lowered because of the higher proportion of black than white males in American prisons. Guttentag and Secord argue that this low sex ratio has led to greater independence among black women and to lower marital stability as well, because a relative surplus of women allows men to be choosier and thus more assertive.

As always in the social sciences, however, cause and effect is maddeningly hard to pin down. In those nations of the world where females are most oppressed, especially in the Middle East and Africa, sex ratios tend to be among the *highest* in the world, precisely because the low status of women leads to higher mortality among women than among men. So far, the high sex ratio has not helped to elevate the status of women in such cultures. Help may be coming, however. Schoen (1983) has noted that a number of third-world countries increasingly are experiencing marriage squeezes as a result of the declines in infant mortality since the end of World War II that have produced a demographic effect very similar to the American Baby Boom. The relative scarcity of husbands for third-world women may help lead to the delays in marriage that I have identified as being so crucial for women in avoiding the oppression of early motherhood and the maintenance of male domination.

Virtually every country in the world with a Marxist-style government has an official policy that the statuses of men and women are equal. But the key to low fertility is how a policy is implemented, not whether it exists. For example, in the Soviet Union and the People's Republic of China, the key to low and rapidly declining fertility is that women really do have nearly equal access to all occupations. In Mexico, where the birth rate is showing signs of a decline, women officially have equal status with men, but changes have been slow to occur in practice (especially in the labor market) to bring life to that policy and thus have a more dramatic impact on fertility. Less than one fifth of the women in Mexico are in the labor force, and more than half those women are single (Lustig and Rendon, 1979). Thus, Mexico is following the pattern that prevailed in the United States earlier in this century in which women work until married but are not likely to work after family building has begun.

It is wise, perhaps, to end on a note of caution. Pushing women into the labor force may not have a noticeable effect on either their status in society or their fertility. Women working in low-level, unstable jobs in less developed countries are usually there out of economic necessity, and work is frequently done within a context that minimizes the conflict between job and family—hours may be staggered or irregular, and family members may assist in child care (Mason and Palan, 1981; Gurak and Kritz, 1982). On the other hand, when women are pulled into the workplace by expanding job opportunities and higher wages, more radical shifts in demographic behavior can be expected (S. Ho, 1984).

SUMMARY AND CONCLUSION

The status of women has been influenced by several demographic factors, especially declining mortality, declining fertility, and urbanization. Women have become less dependent on men as they have begun to live longer and spend more of their lives without children in an urban environment, where there are alternatives to childbearing and family life. In turn, the rise in the status of women appears to play a key role in keeping fertility at low levels, and it has the potential for being an important factor in reducing fertility in less developed nations. This seems to operate by increasing the costs of children (both direct and opportunity costs) while at the same time heightening the awareness of benefits of having children. An especially crucial factor in broadening a woman's social roles may be postponing marriage and childbearing past the teenage years, thus providing a greater chance for alternatives to develop.

Population growth and the status of women are important factors underlying the changes that have been taking place in the family. The financial independence of women and economic pressures have combined with a range of other social changes such as greater openness about sex and less social control over the family to produce delays in marriage, a rise in cohabitation, a rise in illegitimacy, a rise in the divorce rate, and a general decrease in the size of the family. It is probable that the 1970s witnessed the most rapid change in the family and that the future will probably see a continuation of the current shifts in the family without dramatic alterations.

The future will, however, witness a dramatic alteration in at least one segment of society—its older population. In the next chapter we will examine the relationship between population growth and aging.

MAIN POINTS

1. Under conditions of high mortality, the societal demand for childbearing may contribute to the domination of women by men.

2. The older a husband in relation to his wife, the more dominant he may be and the more children she may have.

3. Declining mortality has helped to contribute to a freeing of women from childbearing responsibility and has provided more years of prereproductive and postreproductive time.

4. Urbanization has helped to improve the status of women by providing opportunities for nonfamilial activities.

5. In the United States during World War II, a combination of demand for labor and too few traditional labor force entrants created an opening for married women to move into jobs previously denied them.

6. In broad terms, it was the grandmothers of the Baby Boom children who helped open the door to the increased labor force participation of American women, but it has been Baby Boom women themselves who have taken the greatest advantage of those opportunities.

7. Although low fertility may contribute to the rise in the status of women, it is clear that the greater independence of women will lead to lower levels of fertility.

8. The costs of having children can be measured both in real dollar terms and in terms of the opportunities foregone. The latter costs are especially important for women.

9. The benefits of having children in modern society are measured almost entirely in units of "psychic income"—the satisfaction derived from them and the "strokes" received from family and friends for conforming to the social pressures for having children.

10. The archetypal low-fertility woman in the United States is highly educated and employed in a high-status occupation.

11. The archetypal high-fertility woman, even in American society, is one who married as a teenager and began bearing children before knowing what the alternatives might be.

12. Changes in the status of women and the decline in fertility in industrialized societies have been associated with a delay in marriage, a rise in cohabitation, a rise in illegitimacy and a rise in the divorce rate.

13. It is likely that changes in the structure of the family will be less dramatic in the future than they were in the 1970s.

SUGGESTED READINGS

1. Ester Boserup, 1970, Women's Role in Economic Development (New York: St. Martin's Press).

   In this seminal work, Boserup focuses on the role of women in modern developing societies, but there are also lessons here for understanding the role of women in the economic and demographic history of any human society.

2. Ruth Dixon, 1976, "The roles of rural women: female seclusion, economic production, and reproductive choice," in Ronald Ridker (ed.), Population and Development: The Search for Selective Intervention (Baltimore: The Johns Hopkins University Press).

   This is a careful analysis of some of the same themes that Boserup discusses, but with a more distinctly demographic flavor.

3. Linda Waite, 1981, "U.S. women at work," Population Bulletin 36(2).

   There is no better summary of the history of the movement of American women into the labor force—a phenomenon that is having a major demographic impact on society (as well as having deep demographic roots itself).

4. Martin O'Connell and C. Rogers, 1984, "Out-of-wedlock births, premarital pregnancies and their effect on family formation and dissolution," Family Planning Perspectives 16(4):157–62.

   Two experts from the U.S. Bureau of the Census evaluate the evidence linking out-of-wedlock fertility to some of its consequences for society and for the individuals involved.

5. Robert Schoen, 1983, "Measuring the tightness of the marriage squeeze," Demography 20(1):61–78.

   The marriage squeeze is one of the more fascinating ways in which demography influences social relations, and this article provides you with important details about the American situation.

CHAPTER 11
Population Growth and Aging

Most old people are pretty much alike—they have no interest in sex, they are miserable most of the time, they cannot work as effectively as younger people, and they have incomes below the poverty level. Now, if you believe all that, I have some swampland in Florida you might want to buy! The truth is that older people in the United States—or anywhere else, for that matter—are not all pretty much alike. On the contrary, exposure to several decades of history and countless different patterns of social interaction tends to make older people even less alike than people at younger ages. Thus, we find a wide range of interest in sex among older people, a wide range of life satisfaction (from miserable to extremely happy), a wide range of worker effectiveness, and a wide range of income. This means that you stereotype older people at your own risk; indeed, at an increasing risk, because the older population of the world is growing at a rapid rate, especially in the industrialized nations.

The decline in mortality throughout the world has even broader implications than more babies surviving to adulthood; it means more adults surviving to old age as well. Consequently, the same societies that have been pressed to provide education, jobs, and food for their burgeoning young populations are also faced with caring for a growing number of elderly as those youngsters progress in ever greater numbers through the life cycle. In this chapter I will examine both the causes and the consequences of this growing number of older people. I will begin by defining what an older population is, and then I will examine the size and geographic distribution of the older population in the world, discussing why and at what rate the older population is growing. Next, I will focus on the situation in the United States, examining not only the growth in numbers and proportions of older people but also their demographic characteristics. In the process of seeing what older people are like, I will pave the way for a discussion of how the aging process will likely influence the future course of society, particularly in the United States.

WHAT IS OLD?

Age as we usually think of it is a social construct—something we talk about, define, and redefine on the basis of social categories, not purely biological ones. A good way to visualize this concept is to contemplate Satchel Paige's famous question: "How old would you be, if you didn't know how old you was?" or even the well-worn cliché: "You're only as old as you feel." These quotes illustrate the point that age takes on its meanings from our interaction with other people in the social world. If we are defined by others as being old, we may be treated like an old person regardless of our own feelings about whether or not we are, in fact, old.

There is no inherent chronological threshold to old age; however, in the United States and much of the world, old age has come to be defined as beginning at age 65. The number 65 assumes its almost mystical quality in the United States because it is the age at which important government-funded benefits such as social security and Medicare are fully available. In 1935, when the present social security benefits were designed, the eligibility age was set at 65, "more because of custom than deliberate design. That age had become the normal retirement age under the few American pension plans then in existence and under the social insurance system in Germany" (Viscusi, 1979:96). The Older Americans Act passed by the U.S. Congress in 1965 did provide benefits in some programs for people aged 60 and over, but age 65 is a milestone firmly entrenched in the Western world, and so I too will adopt that definition in this chapter. However, remember that the number is arbitrary, and people obviously will not fit neatly into any senior citizen mold on reaching their 65th birthday. In fact, most do not think of themselves as being old until well beyond that age.

Our demographic interest in the older population comes from the fact that as the number and proportion of older people increase, changes are wrought in the organization of society. Legal, political, educational, familial, and economic institutions all undergo change as the emphasis in society shifts even subtly in the direction of older people. The reason for this is that aging introduces both biological and social changes in the lives of individuals.

Biological Aspects of Aging

Biological aging represents a set of concurrent processes known as **senescence**— a decline in physical viability accompanied by a rise in vulnerability to disease (Atchley, 1977). Some important generalizations about physical aging are: (1) the physiological changes that take place tend to be steady but gradual through adulthood into old age; (2) the more complex the bodily function, the more rapid is its rate of decline; (3) individuals age at different rates, and different tissues and systems within one person also may age at different rates; (4) aging brings with it a lowered ability to respond to stress; and (5) aging brings a diminished ability to resist disease (Weg, 1975).

There are several theories in vogue as to why people become susceptible to disease and death as age increases. These include the **wear and tear theory,** the **error theory,** and the **programmed time clock theory.** Wear and tear is one of the most popularly appealing theories of aging and likens humans to machines that eventually wear out due to the stresses and strains of constant use (Shock, 1974). The theory gains support from studies showing that blue-collar workers (who are presumably exposed to greater wear and tear) typically die younger than white-collar workers (see, for example, Benjamin, 1969). But the theory fails to tell us which biological mechanisms might actually account for the wearing out. The error theory jumps in to argue that "as cells continue to function, random error may occur somewhere in the process of the synthesis of new proteins" (Rockstein and Sussman, 1979:42). Protein synthesis involves a long and complex series of events, beginning with the DNA in the nucleus and ending with the production of new proteins. At several steps in this delicate process, it seems possible that molecular errors can occur that lead to irreversible damage (and thus aging) of a cell.

The programmed time clock theory of aging is based on the idea that each of us has a built-in biological time clock that ticks for a predetermined length of time and then is still. It essentially proposes that you will die "when your number is up," because each cell in your body will regenerate only a certain number of times and no more (Hayflick, 1979). Which of these theories makes most sense? Good question. If you had a solid answer, you could bottle it and retire. Short of that, let me remind you that "there is no generally accepted theory about the cause or causes of aging" (Moment, 1978:6). Current evidence points to two basic conclusions: (1) aging is much more complex than we have previously assumed, and each of the theories may fill in part of the puzzle; and (2) we have not yet discovered the basic, underlying mechanism of aging that (if it exists) would explain everything.

As we discuss human aging it is important not to confuse senescence, the biological process of aging, with **senility.** Senility (or *senile dementia,* as it is known formally) has often been used as a derogatory term applied to forgetfulness or seemingly erratic behavior on the part of older people. We now know, however, that senility is not a normal part of aging. Instead it represents the consequences of several different organic brain disorders, especially **Alzheimer's disease.** In recent years a great deal of federally funded research has been aimed at the identification of exact disease mechanisms so that a treatment or cure can be found.

The physical changes that actually take place as we age are often exaggerated in our minds when we are younger. The gradualness with which changes occur usually provides ample time to learn to cope with them, and actual changes may well occur later or be different from what we suspected when we were younger. For example, one of the most blatant stereotypes of aging has to do with sexual functioning in old age. As a matter of fact, sexual activity tends to remain fairly strong well into old age, at least until death removes a person's partner (Pfeiffer and Davis, 1974). The frequency and enjoyment of sexual relations in old age seem to be more closely related to individual preference than to age itself. Thus, people who enjoyed sex and were sexually active when younger will likely remain that way when older. Though your physical capacity to engage in intercourse may diminish with age, your level of sexual activity will likely be influenced more by social factors than by biology.

Social Aspects of Aging

The social world of the elderly is different from that of younger people because virtually every society has some built-in system of age stratification—the assignment of social roles and social status on the basis of age. As people age, their sets of social obligations and expectations change, and certain kinds of behavior are deemed appropriate for some ages but not for others. I discussed this phenomenon in general terms in Chapter 8, but here I will highlight the importance of age stratification for the older population.

Perhaps the most crucial aspect of age stratification in Western nations is the relegation of the elderly to a lower status than younger people. Indicators of status such as access to economic resources, policy-making influence, and breadth of social relations all suggest the decline in status accompanying old age in Western society. How does this arise? Why are Western, industrialized nations different in this respect from traditional, agrarian societies? The most widely discussed explanation for this phenomenon is offered by Donald Cowgill (1979). His theory presents the causal model illustrated in Figure 11.1 in which four basic factors involved in

Figure 11.1   How Is the Status of the Elderly Influenced by Modernization?

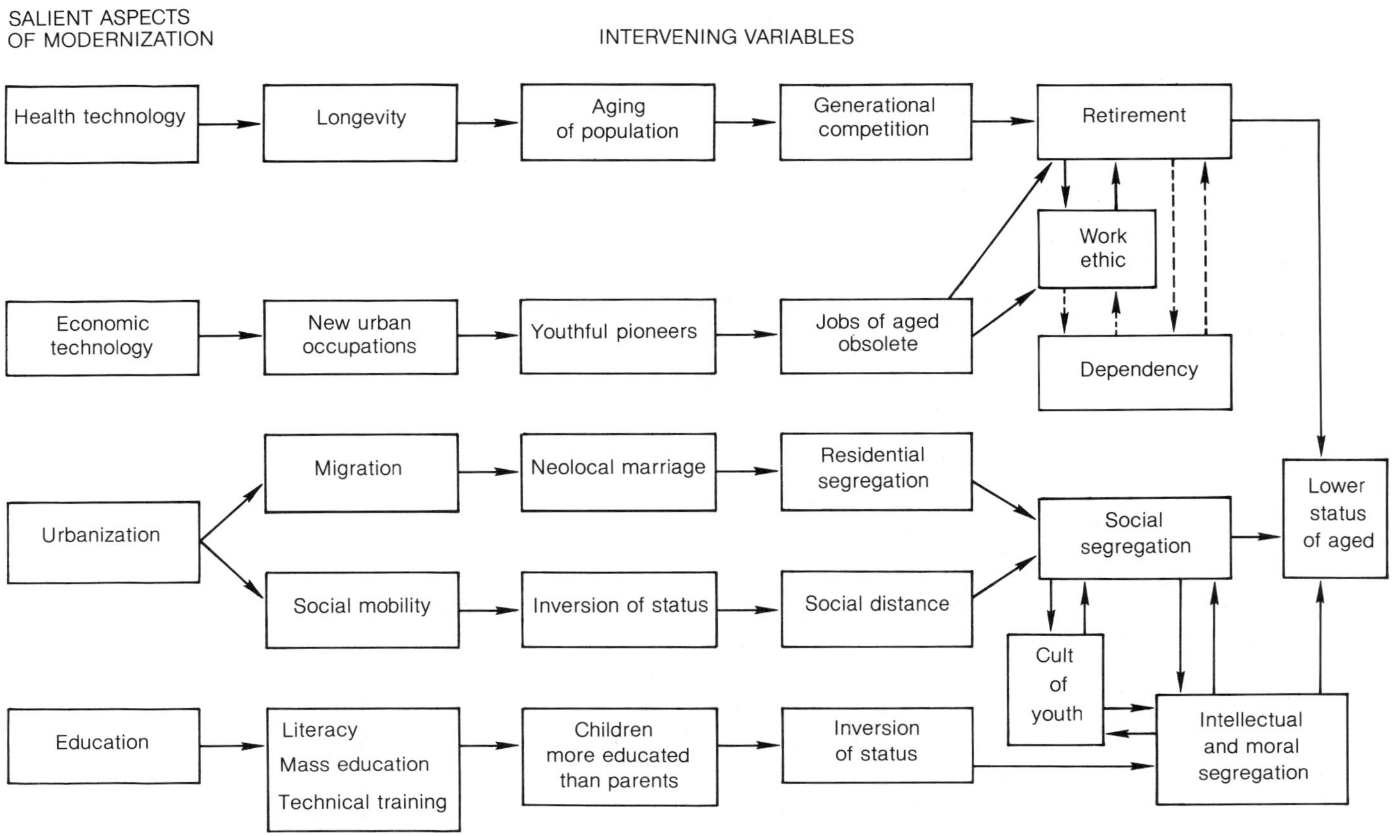

Donald Cowgill's framework is an attempt to explain the lower status of the elderly in modernized societies as the end result of the combined influence of changes in health technology, economic technology, urbanization, and education. *Source:* Donald Cowgill, 1979, "Aging and modernization: a revision of the theory," in J. Gubrium (ed.), Late Life: Communities and Environmental Policy (Springfield, Illinois: Charles C Thomas, Publisher), figure 5. Reprinted with permission.

modernization—health technology, economic technology, urbanization, and education—combine to lower the status of the elderly.

The health technology accompanying modernization increases longevity, as you well know. That greater longevity in turn creates intergenerational competition for jobs, because people are no longer so likely to die and create room for the young to enter and advance within the labor market. This competition has led to the phenomenon we call retirement. Work itself is a valued activity in society, since work produces income; because income is a major source of status, retirement leads inexorably to decreased status.

The economic technology that accompanies modernization is closely associated with the creation of new, especially urban, occupations. Because the young are more likely to migrate to cities than are the old (as you no doubt remember from Chapter 7), and since urban occupations tend to pay more than those in rural areas (as I will discuss in the next chapter), there results "an inversion of status, with children achieving higher status than their parents instead of merely moving up to the status of their parents as in most pre-modern societies" (Cowgill, 1979:59).

The third factor that Cowgill mentions as leading to a decline in the status of the elderly is urbanization. In addition to its relationship to mobility and the inversion of status, which were mentioned previously, urbanization produces a segregation of residence of the young and the old. In turn, that produces a greater social distance between generations, relegating aging parents to a more peripheral role in the lives of children. The greater physical distance between generations thus accelerates the already inverted social distance and further depresses the status of the elderly.

The process of modernization is closely bound with an increase in formal education. In preliterate societies education is based especially on the recitation of life's experiences by the older people. The school of hard knocks prevails, and experience is the best teacher—a feature of life that enhances the status of the elderly. Modernization, though, tends to bring with it institutionalized, formal, mass education, and the content is more technical than experiential. The main targets of such educational programs are always the young, and this leads to the young being better educated than their parents. This further exacerbates the status of the older person because it leads to a greater intellectual and moral (or value) distance between the generations. Education brings with it (indeed is part of) changes in the value system of society, and the constant upward spiral of education has led to shifting values and intellectual levels from one generation to the next.

As historical forces shape and influence the status of the elderly in a society, those same forces are shaping the character of the older people themselves. This is the basis of the concept of cohort flow, which I discussed in Chapter 8. Thus, in an era of rapid social change, such as we have experienced throughout the last century, we should expect that each new generation of people moving into the old ages will be substantially different from the previous one. This has tremendous implications for the future of society, as I will discuss toward the end of the chapter, because it implies that social change and innovation are not solely the province of the young. We are beginning to appreciate that the social changes experienced by younger people will also transform the older population as those cohorts flow into old age.

HOW MANY OLDER PEOPLE ARE THERE?

In 1988 there were 300 million people in the world aged 65 and older. Indeed, if they all lived together under one flag, they would have represented the third largest nation in the world. As a fraction of the total world population, the elderly account for 6 percent. Bear in mind, however, that this percentage varies considerably from one part of the world to another. For example, in 1988 only 24 percent of the total population of the world lived in more developed nations, yet 48 percent of the world's population aged 65 or older lived there.

These gross regional differences in the number of older people are influenced, of course, by disparities in mortality. In the more developed nations, the average expectation of life at birth is 73 years, compared with 59 years in the less developed nations. Total population size also plays a role. For example, the population of mainland China is so large that although only 5 percent of the total population is 65 or older (compared with an average of 12 percent in the more developed nations), China still has the world's largest population of elderly—65 million in 1988. The USSR and the United States tie for second place with nearly identical numbers of older persons, approximately 29 million. India, although second in total population, comes in fourth on the list of older people with 28 million. Overall, 45 percent of all people aged 65 and over in the world live in the world's four most populous nations.

The proportion of a country's population 65 and over is, as I discussed in Chapter 8, influenced more by the birth rate than anything else. A low birth rate elevates the relative proportion of older people, whereas a high birth rate lowers the proportion. Nonetheless, mortality (and to a lesser extent migration) also has some influence on the proportion of elderly. Thus, the highest proportion of older people will be found in a society with a low birth rate, a low death rate, and net out-migration (since migrants tend to be young adults). A good example is Sweden, which meets these three criteria and has the world's highest national percentage of people over 64 (17 percent). Conversely, the lowest percentage of older persons will be found in a society with a high birth rate, a high death rate, and net in-migration. Mali, located in the drought-ridden, northern African region along the Niger River, fits at least the first two criteria and has one of the lowest proportions of older people in the world—less than 3 percent of its 8 million people are 65 or over. Indeed, as a region, Africa has the lowest proportion of older people among its population, with an average of only 3 percent.

GROWTH OF THE OLDER POPULATION IN THE UNITED STATES

In 1900 the United States had only slightly more than 3 million people aged 65 and over and only 122,000 people aged 85 and over (U.S. Bureau of the Census, 1978b). By 1987, the estimated number of people aged 65 and over had grown to 29 million—a ninefold increase over 85 years—whereas the population aged 85 and over had grown to nearly 3 million—a twenty-five-fold increase (Torrey et al.,

1987). By the end of this century there will be nearly 35 million older Americans, and more than 5 million of them will be over 84 years old. From 1950 to 1980, when the total world population was "exploding" at a rate of 2 percent per year, the older population in the United States was increasing by 2.3 percent per year. In fact, the population aged 85 and older in the United States was growing at a rate of 4.2 percent per year between 1950 and 1980. These numbers represent the reasons for the rapid rise in concern over the condition of life among the elderly and the rapid rise also in government spending for benefits to the elderly in the United States.

In examining the probable future growth of the older population in the United States, we can make very reasonable projections for at least 65 years down the road, since these people are already born and it is unlikely that major changes in mortality will occur during that period. The low birth rate during the Depression means that as people born then reach their sixties at the end of this century, there will be a temporary slackening in the increase in the older population. Between 1990 and 2000, it is projected that the population aged 65 and over will increase by only 3 million (from 32 to 35 million), compared with the 5 million increase each decade during the 1970s and 1980s. Of course, as the Baby Boom generation reaches the older years in the period 2010 to 2030, the population of elders will undergo a boom, increasing from 39 million in 2010 to 64 million in 2030. After that, the low fertility of the late 1960s and 1970s will produce a stabilization in the size of the older American population (data from U.S. Bureau of the Census, 1984h).

DEMOGRAPHIC CHARACTERISTICS OF THE ELDERLY

In the next several pages I will explore the demographic characteristics of the older population. The focus will be on the United States, because we have more data for American older people than for most; however, I will draw on information from other societies where it is available. I will look at the age and sex distribution within the population aged 65 and older and examine levels of education, occupation and labor force activity, and income. I will also look at marital status, living arrangements, and race and ethnicity.

Age and Sex

Remember that the older population rarely represents a homogeneous group. Defining the older population as being 65 and older means that we have a wide range of ages under consideration. For example, it is not uncommon in the United States for people to reach age 65 and still have at least one parent alive (Keyfitz, 1971). As the younger generation grows older it will be even more common, because the average age at which a woman completes her childbearing has been declining (as I mentioned in Chapter 5), resulting in fewer years of difference in age between parent and child and a greater likelihood of joint survival to old age. Thus, the "generation gap" that probably seemed so obvious when parent and child were young may still exist in interpersonal relations yet may be obscured by the fact that now both parties are "senior citizens."

From society's standpoint, the distribution by age and sex of the older population affects the type and level of services that must be provided to maintain the quality of life. Since health typically deteriorates more rapidly after about age 75 than before, the size of the "young-old" population compared with the "old-old" population has considerable importance. Furthermore, since women tend to outlive men, the number of widows at older ages significantly affects the social structure—marital status, living arrangements, income, and patterns of social interaction—of the older population.

Age Distribution of the Older U.S. Population   In 1980, 34 percent of the U.S. population aged 65 and older was in the 65–69 category, 57 percent was 70–84, and 9 percent was in the oldest category—85+ (U.S. Bureau of the Census, 1983a). These figures show a considerable aging of the older population compared with 1950, when 41 percent were in the 65–69 age group and 5 percent were 85 and older. As you can see in Table 11.1, the trend over time in the United States from 1950 through 2000 will be for a gradual aging of the older population. The trend will abate as we move into the twenty-first century, as the post-Depression babies begin to reach the retirement years.

Even though the absolute number of older people will be increasing in the near future at a slower pace than, for example, between 1950 and 1980, the fact that the older population will itself be growing proportionately older will continue to put pressure on the need for resources for the elderly. The need will grow for health care, long-term care facilities, transportation, subsidized housing, day-care services, prepared meals, personal care, and housekeeping assistance.

Table 11.1   The Age Distribution of the Older Population Is Changing (United States, 1950–2020)

	Percent 65–69	Percent 70–84	Percent 85+	Ratio $\dfrac{65-69}{85+}$
1950	41	55	5	9
1960	38	57	6	7
1970	35	58	7	5
1980	34	57	9	4
1990	32	58	11	3
2000	26	59	15	2
2010	30	53	17	2
2020	32	53	14	2

Source: U.S. Bureau of the Census, 1984, "Demographic and Socioeconomic Aspects of Aging in the United States," Current Population Reports, Series P-23, No. 138.

Note: Over time, the older population of the United States will itself be growing older (that is, higher percentages aged 85+), at least until the Baby Boom generation reaches old age.

In 1977, an average of $1,745 was spent per person aged 65 and older for health care in the United States. Although the money came from a variety of sources—private insurance, federal and state governments, and the individuals themselves—most of it (indeed, 67 percent) came from public funds (Gibson and Fisher, 1979). In all, $41 billion was spent in 1977 to provide health care to the elderly in the United States. This was a dramatic rise from the $8 billion spent in 1966, and the amount will continue to increase, as Gibson and Fisher have observed:

> Within the group aged 65 and older, the proportion of persons aged 75 or older is growing. Since older persons tend to suffer chronic conditions—about half of all persons aged 65 and over are limited in activity because of one or more chronic conditions—and since illness and injury have greater impact on the elderly, they are hospitalized more frequently and for longer periods (1979:15).

As an example, in 1986 there were 337 short-stay hospital discharges per 1,000 people aged 75 and older in the United States, compared with 236 per 1,000 at ages 65–69 and only 142 at ages 45–64. In that year, the average hospital cost per patient per day was nearly $500. Since the average stay is about 2 days longer for a person aged 65 or older than for a person under age 65, the rise in health expenditures as age increases is obvious. Nursing homes are another expensive source of care for the elderly for which usage goes up dramatically with age. In 1985, 22 percent of people aged 85 and older were residing in a nursing home, whereas only 1 percent of persons aged 65–74 in the United States were in such places (National Center for Health Statistics, 1988). Since the major portion of the cost of such hospitalization for the elderly is borne by the public, it is clear that the aging of the older population, as well as the overall increase in the number of older persons, will result in a continued increase in demand for public funds.

Sex Distribution of the Older Population   It is well known that women tend to outlive men (see Chapter 6). In the United States there are about 149 women aged 65 and over for every 100 men of those ages; by age 85 and over there are 238 women for every 100 men. This is typical in industrialized societies, indeed in westernized societies generally. In Sweden in 1981 there were 131 women aged 65 and older for each 100 men, in Japan the ratio was 131 : 100, and in Mexico it was 113 : 100. In most societies women have an edge in survivability from the moment of conception, and in most developed countries the differences widen with age. However, the pattern is not universal for all societies.

In India in 1981 there were only 93 women aged 65 and older for every 100 men of that age. India is, in fact, one of 28 nations in which the older male population outnumbers the older female population, as you can see in Table 11.2. Of those 28 countries, 25 are in either Africa or western Asia, Asia, and the Middle East. They are almost all countries in which local "traditional" religions or Islam predominate—a matter of importance, since the status of women tends to be lower in such societies. In at least four cases Islam is the official state religion, and included in the list are the second and third most populous Moslem nations in the world, India and Bangladesh. As I noted in Chapter 10, in Africa (especially the northern portion) and the western portion of Asia (including the Middle East) the status of

Table 11.2   Nations in Which Older Men Outnumber Older Women

Country	Most Recent Data Available	Males Aged 65+ per 100 Females Aged 65+
Africa		
Benin	1975	130
Central African Republic	1975	113
Chad[a]	1978	102
Comoros[a]	1973	125
Ethiopia	1982	123
Liberia	1977	143
Libya	1973	112
Madagascar	1978	115
Rwanda	1978	102
Senegal	1976	113
Sierra Leone	1974	109
Tunisia	1979	119
Tanzania	1978	114
Upper Volta	1975	119
Latin America		
Cuba	1981	105
Dominican Republic	1980	102
Asia		
Afghanistan	1979	136
Bangladesh	1981	107
Brunei	1981	110
India	1981	108
Iran	1976	111
Jordan	1979	138
Qatar	1981	122
Sri Lanka	1981	111
United Arab Emirates	1977	133
Andorra	1981	109
Oceania		
Cook Islands	1981	106
Solomon Islands	1978	163

Source: United Nations, 1984, Demographic Yearbook, 1982 (New York: United Nations), Table 7.

[a] Aged 60+

Note: Most countries in which men outnumber women at the older ages are societies in which the status of women is significantly lower than men. This would explain these data even if they only represent the undercounting of older women.

women is particularly low by world standards. Thus, it is probable that women in these countries are disadvantaged with respect to nutrition and health care (including protection against the risks of maternal mortality in high-fertility countries), and this disadvantage means that lower proportions of women survive to old age.

Marital Status and Living Arrangements

The unbalanced sex ratio at the older ages in most societies signals a change in marital status, which in turn means a change in living arrangements for many people as they grow older. In the United States in 1986, 71 percent of all women aged 35–39 were married and living with their spouse; by ages 65–74, the percentage had dropped to 49; and by ages 75 and older, only 23 percent were married and living with a spouse (U.S. Bureau of the Census, 1987f). Indeed, at ages 75 and older, more than two thirds of all American women are widows. The United States tends to mirror the rest of the world in these terms, as you can see in Table 11.3. Males, of course, are less likely to experience a change in marital status as they grow older, because they are more likely to be outlived by their wives.

Does a change in marital status affect living arrangements? The answer is yes, because it means especially that more women wind up living alone. On the other hand, the fairly common notion that old people are packed off to the "home" is, as you might imagine, a myth. Only about 5 percent of older people in the United States live in group quarters designed for the elderly (U.S. Bureau of the Census, 1984h). Thus, for women in the United States, old age more likely means living alone than being institutionalized or living in a group environment with other seniors. In 1982, 36 percent of all women aged 65–74 were living alone, and at ages 75 and older 52 percent were living alone (U.S. Bureau of the Census, 1983b). For men, living alone is less common. At ages 65–74, 12 percent of men were living alone, whereas at ages 75 and above, 21 percent were living alone. In American and European societies, older people are much more separate from their children than in Asian societies such as Japan. In Japan it is common not only for a parent whose spouse is gone to live with her (or his) children, but more than three fourths of older couples live together with a child (Palmore, 1975). Such a living arrangement is common to less than 20 percent of older couples in the United States. Will the Japanese become westernized

Table 11.3 Changes in Marital Status with Age

| Year | Percent Married with Spouse | | | |
| | Females | | Males | |
	35–39	75+	35–39	75+
United States, 1982	73	23	78	71
Sweden, 1981	73	21	66	57
Japan, 1980	91	16	89	67
Mexico[a], 1978	84	32	88	67
Indonesia, 1980	88	17	95	73

Source: United Nations, 1984, Demographic Yearbook, 1982 (New York: United Nations), Table 40.

[a] Includes consensual unions.

Note: Greater longevity of women than of men means that older women are much less likely than men to remain married and with a spouse into the older years.

and alter the pattern of elders living with their children? Maybe, but it is likely to be a slow process, since the respect and dignity afforded older people in Japan are not likely to be eroded in a single generation. Although the proportion of older parents living with children in Japan is decreasing, especially in urban areas and among the highly educated (as we might expect from Cowgill's theory), at its current rate "over two-thirds of the aged will still be living with their children in the year 2000" (Palmore, 1975:40).

Education

Throughout the world today, older people have lower levels of education than do younger adults. In the United States in 1982, for example, people aged 25–34 were almost twice as likely to be high school graduates as were people aged 65 and older, and these young adults were almost three times as likely to be college graduates (U.S. Bureau of the Census, 1983c). The reason, as I mentioned earlier, is that the older individuals grew up in an era when it was not so common to go to college or even to finish high school. In fact, in just the 12-year span between 1970 and 1982, the proportion of people aged 65 and older in the United States who were high school graduates rose from 28 percent to 44 percent (U.S. Bureau of the Census, 1983c). This rise was due solely to the higher educational levels of the people moving into the older years, not to the recent, but still sparse, attempts to bring older people back into the educational system.

On average, older people are not less well educated because they are less competent, less able to achieve higher levels of education, or even less ambitious. Rather, it is because the world has been experiencing an upward spiral of literacy and education for the last few hundred years, with the result that each generation tends to be better educated than the previous one. For example, in Italy in 1881, less than 20 percent of the women aged 71 and older were literate, compared with almost 40 percent literacy among women aged 21–30. Comparisons were similar for men, and they were also similar for other European nations in the nineteenth century (Cipolla, 1969).

Using the traditional method of educating the young as a guide, we can project the educational level of people aged 65–74 and older in the year 2015 by examining the level of educational achievement of people aged 30–39 in 1980 (which would imply that more than three fourths will be high school graduates and one fifth will be college graduates). However, if that model of education were modified so that people of all ages could have greater access to the educational process, then in the future we would see smaller differences between the older and younger populations in terms of education.

Labor Force Activity and Income

In industrialized societies, old age is stereotypically a time of retirement from labor force activity. Indeed, when the Social Security Act was passed in the United States in the middle of the Great Depression in the 1930s, it was designed quite literally to encourage people to leave the labor force. At the time the idea was to remove older workers from the work force to replace them with younger workers and thus lower the rate of unemployment among younger people. The arbitrarily chosen age of 65 became etched in stone as the age of retirement (Segerberg, 1974). Most companies and government entities alike turned age 65 into a mandatory age of retirement. More than half of all workers since the early 1960s have avoided mandatory retirement (which is now 70, rather than 65) by retiring early. In 1956 for women, and in 1961 for men, Congress allowed reduced social security pensions to be available at age 62, and this has been a popular option.

Once retired, it tends to be in a person's best economic interest to remain out of the labor force. Between ages 62 and 70, a person cannot earn more than a few thousand dollars a year in working wages and still collect his or her full social security benefits. (Note that income from pensions and investments are not counted—thus the rich do not suffer as much from this rule.) Not until age 70 can a person work full-time and also receive full social security benefits. As a means of taking older people out of the labor force, the policy, when combined with mandatory retirement, has worked well; in 1890, 75 percent of all men remained in the labor force past age 64, whereas in 1982 only 18 percent were still employed at that age (Viscusi, 1979; U.S. Bureau of the Census, 1983c).

The decline of older people in labor force activity actually has been quite precipitous in recent years. For example, in 1960 more than 33 percent of all men aged 65 and older were in the labor force (at least part-time), compared with 18 percent in 1982. The employment rate of older women has also declined, although not so much. In 1960, 11 percent of older women were active in the economy, compared with 8 percent in 1982 (U.S. Bureau of the Census, 1983c). The pattern is similar for both white and black men, although black women are almost half again as likely to be employed at older ages than are white women. A male, married and living with his spouse, is more likely to be employed than is any other category of older person (U.S. Department of Labor, 1983).

Needless to say, when people drop out of the labor force their income is likely to decline. This is certainly true for older people. The minimum social security benefit is below the poverty level, although in 1974 the establishment of Supplemental Security Income (SSI) for older persons meant that most old people in the United States are now guaranteed an income no lower than the poverty level. Indeed, between 1959 and 1986, the percentage of people aged 65 and older with poverty-level incomes in the United States dropped from 35 percent to 12 percent (U.S. Bureau of the Census, 1987c).

How much money do older Americans have to live on? In 1986, the median income of families in which the head of the household was 65 years or older was $19,932 per year, about two-thirds the $29,458 average for all families. That difference is due in large part to the fact that older people are not in the labor force. Note that in 1986 people aged 65 and older whose only income was from a job had an average family income of $39,439 per year—very close to the average for people of all ages ($37,509) (U.S. Bureau of the Census, 1987c). By contrast, older families living on social security alone averaged only $5,170 per year in income. Fortunately, in 1982 only 10 percent of American households where the householder was 65 and older relied solely on social security income for a living. Almost all families are able to combine social security with other sources of income such as a pension, dividends or interest income, property income, earnings from a job (including self-employment), or public assistance (principally SSI). In-kind benefits such as food stamps and Medicare are available to shore up impoverished elders (Preston, 1984), and for the better-off, security in old age may be bolstered by homeownership, since 70 percent of all older people in the United States own their own houses (Segerberg, 1974).

Not all older people, of course, live in families. Many, especially those in the eighth and ninth decades of life, live alone as unrelated individuals—almost half the older population in the United States in 1982. The average income for these individuals was only $6,424, compared with $9,977 for unrelated individuals of all ages in the United States (U.S. Bureau of the Census, 1984f). Of these older, unrelated people, 26 percent survived only on social security income, while the remainder had at least one additional source of income. For the most part, the conclusion is inescapable that relying solely on social security will almost guarantee that your income in old age will hover near the poverty level.

How can a person most likely arrive at an advantageous position in old age? The answer is to be in an advantageous position when you are young and to plan well for your future. Educational attainment, for example, is closely related to income in old age. In 1985 in the United States, males aged 65 and older who had completed 5 or more years of college were earning an average (median) income of $23,976 per year. Indeed, 18 percent of these people were still in the labor force on a full-time, year-round basis. In contrast, people who had gone no further than their high school graduation were living on an average of $12,686 per year, and only 9 percent were full-time, year-round labor force participants. Each year of college education brings with it an average (in 1985 dollars) of as much as $2,258 more per year in income beyond age 65 (U.S. Bureau of the Census, 1987a).

For at least one segment of the American population, however, a decent living in old age has been made more difficult because opportunities to do well in younger years were not always available. These are the minority elderly.

Minority Elderly

Persons who are both old and members of an ethnic minority group are said to be in double jeopardy. As minority group members, they spent their lives dealing with prejudice and discrimination; as older persons, they also face the prejudice and discrimination that may befall a person just because of being old. In fact, minority group members are less likely to reach old age at all than are majority group members. Once they do reach old age, minority elders are less likely than their counterparts in the majority to be doing well economically.

The economic plight of older minority group members can be appreciated by noting the percentage below the poverty level. In 1986, when 11 percent of whites aged 65 and over lived below the poverty line, 31 percent of black elders lived at that level, as did 23 percent of the older Hispanics (U.S. Bureau of the Census, 1987c).

In terms of income, the patterns for older people are similar to those for younger people, but the levels are lower. From the Current Population Survey in the United States, we have data for the two most populous ethnic minority groups—blacks and

Hispanics. In 1985 the average (mean) family income for Hispanic families with a householder aged 65 and over was $19,871, compared with $15,651 for older black men. As a comparison, white families with a householder aged 65 or older had a mean income of $25,934.

THE AMERICAN BABY BOOM AND SOCIAL SECURITY

Back in 1935, when President Roosevelt's Committee on Economic Security was putting the finishing touches on the social security legislation, two committee members met to discuss the projections that had been made for social security expenditures for 1935 through 1980. Treasury Secretary Henry Morgenthau, Jr., and Harry Hopkins, head of the Federal Emergency Relief Administration, were aware of possible problems ahead, as is evidenced by their comments at the meeting (quoted in Graebner, 1980:256):

> Hopkins: *Well, there are going to be twice as many old people thirty years from now, Henry, than there are now.*
>
> Morgenthau: *Well, I've gotten a very good analysis of this thing . . . and I want to show them* [other members of the committee] *the bad curves.*
>
> Hopkins: *That old age thing is a bad curve.*

That bad curve referred to the ratio of workers to retirees, which, though quite favorable in the early years of social security, could be foreseen to worsen over the years as the small birth cohorts of the early 1930s tried to support the numerically larger older cohorts. Despite the fact that reference is often made to the term "trust fund," most of you are probably aware that social security systems in most countries, including the United States, were never designed to have the government actually deposit money in an account with your name on it and have the money accrue principal and interest until you retire and start withdrawing your pension. Rather, almost every system is "pay as you go"—current benefits are paid from current revenue. Morgenthau's data suggested that by 1980, social security expenditures would have risen to one billion dollars (in 1935 currency) (Graebner, 1980). This curve looked bad then, but in truth it turned out to be even sharper than expected: life expectancy has increased; the Baby Boom has injected a large cohort that will ultimately have to be dealt with in retirement (but that in the meantime has helped to delay the funding crisis because of its members' payroll contributions); and Congress has regularly expanded social security coverage and raised benefits.

The demographic impact on the social security system was felt keenly through the 1980s as the older population grew more rapidly than the number of younger workers. By 1990, for example, there will be 9 percent *more* people aged 60–69 (people moving into retirement) in the United States than in 1980, yet there will be 6 percent *fewer* people aged 20–29 (people moving into the labor force). These changes, of course, had been projected for some time, and in the mid-1970s (and again in the 1980s) Congress made adjustments to increase payroll taxes and cut back on the annual allowable increase in social security payments. These measures (along with a little borrowing from the disability and Medicare trust funds) allowed the system to survive the 1980s. In 1987 the social security old-age trust fund took in $211 billion while disbursing $188 billion.

The positive cash flow of the late

Lower incomes have a variety of life-style consequences for the minority elderly, including the kinds of housing that are available to them. The highly visible retirement homes for older people have a much smaller proportion of minority elders living in them than you would expect from their relative proportions in the popula-

1980s is expected to blend into a decade that has been dubbed "The False Era of Good Feelings" (Fialka, 1981). The new money being pumped into the social security system from the higher payroll taxes will be accompanied in the 1990s by a hiatus in the increase of new retirees as the Depression-era cohorts reach old age. For example, between 1990 and 2000, the number of people aged 60–69 in the United States will actually decline by 6 percent. This will ease the pressure of expenditures while revenues rise. However, Robert Myers, who served as the Social Security Administration's chief actuary from 1947 to 1970, sees a danger in the social security system's projected funding surpluses in the 1990s. "That may not be good politically, because Congress will be tempted to spent it" (quoted in Fialka, 1981). By spending it, he means that Congress might increase benefits or roll back some of the changes made to struggle through the 1980s. Myers's concern came from having been there before. He left the Social Security Administration in 1970 over a dispute about the wisdom of expanding benefits. Congress felt generous because the Baby Boom cohort was supplying an influx of new workers to pay taxes, and inflation was showering social security with unexpected revenue. In 1972, Congress boosted retirement benefits by 20 percent and built in an automatic adjustment to keep benefits increasing each year along with inflation.

If Congress were to use the growing surplus of the 1990s to increase benefits (or to lower taxes, as Congressman Jack Kemp suggested in 1988, or to pay off the national debt, as the social security trust-

ees themselves suggested in 1988—Auerbach, 1988), such a course of action could be disastrous because just after the turn of the coming century—around 2010—the Baby Boom generation will really crunch the pension system. Between the years 2000 and 2010, there will be nearly a 50 percent increase in the population aged 60–69—an unprecedented rise in the number of people who might be retiring—and this increase will continue until 2030. If declines in mortality at older ages were to accelerate, the increase could be even greater. Recent reductions in smoking, for example, could add substantially to the number of people surviving to old age and collecting their social security pensions. In any event, by 2030 the ratio of taxpaying workers to pension-receiving retirees will be only 3:1, compared with 5:1 in 1960. This ratio means, in essence, that the workers will be paying heavily for their elders' retirement—a twist on the effects of the age structure on the dependency ratio in a population. The building up of a surplus in the Social Security Trust Fund is widely viewed as a hedge against the potential for intergenerational conflict as the Baby Boom cohort retires and places heavy demands on the relatively smaller Baby Bust cohort. Another hedge, less predictable, of course, is for the economy to be growing fairly rapidly in the next century as the Baby Boom generation reaches retirement age. As I discussed in Chapter 9, the kind of structural mobility (when the economic situation of everyone is improving) that has typically accompanied rapid economic growth in the United States would permit the transfer of money from the younger to the older generation to be a little less painful.

tion. The disproportionately low number could be due partly to a lack of desire on the part of minorities to live in such places (although there is little evidence to support such an idea), or it could be due to discrimination (and there is some evidence to suggest this). The most important factor, however, is probably neither the acceptability of such facilities nor the issue of discrimination, but rather the economic realities of how much a retirement home costs (Weeks, 1979). The cost of housing also affects the ability of minority group members to be homeowners in their old age. In the United States in 1983, 78 percent of all whites aged 65 and older owned their own homes, compared with 64 percent for blacks and 58 percent for Hispanics (estimates derived from U.S. Bureau of the Census, 1985b).

Because the number of minority elderly is increasing, levels of income, kinds of housing, helping networks, and availability and appropriateness of public benefits will all be increasingly important issues in the future. Indeed, since the entire older population in the United States is growing larger both numerically and proportionately (while the older population of the world is also certainly increasing in numbers if not yet proportionately), the future will likely be more influenced by older people than was any previous time in history.

AGING AND THE FUTURE OF SOCIETY

The United States

What will the future be like for the elderly? How will the growing numbers of older people influence the future of society? Both sides of this coin are of considerable interest, since both old age and the future beckon to all of us. Because these questions are so closely interrelated, I will treat them together.

In the United States, the future will include many more people aged 75 and above and many more minority elderly. Adjustments will have to be made to accommodate these increases; adjustments may be in the family system or in public support systems or, more likely, in both. It is possible that the growth of the older population, coupled with the low fertility of the 1970s and 1980s, will cause the focus of attention within families to shift somewhat away from the young and onto the old. This may lead simultaneously to an increase in the intensity of social interaction between young and old generations and more emphasis on making policy oriented toward the elderly.

One landmark policy decision has already been made by Congress with the passage of legislation in 1978 ending mandatory retirement at age 65 for all but a few professional categories. Thus it is no longer possible for a company to force a person to retire solely on the basis of age (until age 70, that is). We could witness a return to the longer work lives characteristic of the pre-Depression years, which would accentuate even more the ability of older people to remain financially independent well into old age. This may be especially true for older women, since they make up a disproportionately large part of the older population (Campbell, 1979). As long as the birth rate remains low and the number of new entrants into the labor force does not greatly exceed the number of jobs available, the intergenerational conflict over access to the labor force should be minimal. However, if new entrants to the labor force (including many younger women) find their job opportunities blocked by the retention of older people in the work force, the possibility of conflict would rise.

A major benefit of this longer potential work life is, of course, that the social security system could find some relief. As the Baby Boom generation moves into old age and becomes eligible for old-age benefits, the ratio of those eligible for benefits to workers will be very large. Thus, as I described in Chapter 8, the financial (tax) burden on the younger generation (people now in childhood or just being born) will be enormous, as I discuss in the essay accompanying this chapter. As a result, there may be considerable pressure on the elderly to be more self-sufficient—not only to work longer but also to become involved in mutual self-help organizations that could relieve some of the burden on the public agencies. It is ironic indeed that the social security system, which was designed in large part to encourage older people to leave the work force, may in the future be bailed out because people can stay in the labor force longer.

The options available to older people are already increasing. These include the ability to work longer, the growth in lifelong learning opportunities—college courses designed for people of all ages, and travel discounts for seniors that may open up opportunities previously closed. These trends are likely to continue almost unabated well into the next century as a result of the previously mentioned cohort flow. For example, the greater participation of women in the labor force and the resulting increase in female financial independence will likely mean a greater sense of personal freedom for these women as they grow older.

Further, the high level of political advocacy of youth in the 1960s will almost certainly be translated into greater political advocacy among the elderly when those people reach old age. Already people aged 65–74 are the most likely to vote in national elections, followed closely by people aged 55–64 (U.S. Bureau of the Census, 1987d). As the current generation of younger people grows older, we should find the older population becoming more tolerant of a wide range of life-styles and more understanding of the problems and issues facing older people. All in all, it appears that the status of the older population in the United States and in other developed societies is on the rise. The cohorts of people now moving into the older ages may have abandoned their own parents in the countryside and may have helped contribute to a slide in status for earlier generations of elderly, but they themselves generally have a different life-style. They tend to be in closer touch with their children, perhaps partly because, as I discussed in Chapter 3, the flow of wealth in developed societies is from parents to children, even into the older ages. Indeed, the older population is increasing its share of national wealth through its holdings in stocks, bonds, real estate, and other assets. For example, *Forbes* magazine regularly identifies the 400 wealthiest Americans. Among the Forbes Four Hundred in 1983, four of the ten richest people were 65 or older, and seven of the top ten were 60 or older. Overall, 43 percent of the wealthiest 400 people were 65 years of age or older (Forbes, 1983). This is consistent with the fact that in 1984 the American households with the highest average net worth ($410,252) were those in which the head of household was aged 70–74 and still earning $4,000 or more a month (U.S. Bureau of the Census, 1987g). Overall, average net worth (or household wealth) peaks at age 55–64 in the United States, and even at age 70–74 it is still higher than at any age younger than 55. To the extent that wealth, status, and power go together, they all seem to be rising for the elderly. In less developed nations, however, events seem to be leading the elderly in the opposite direction.

Less Developed Nations

It is consistent with Cowgill's modernization theory that as less developed societies go through the process of modernization the status of their older population should drop, much as it did in the now developed regions of the world. So it is that in country after country the complaint is being heard that the elderly, increasing numerically with each new cohort, are being left behind by the younger generation and forgotten by the rest of society. As we move into the twenty-first century, nearly two out of every three older people in the world will be in the less developed nations (Oriol, 1982), and their plight will be a significant factor in world affairs. At the 1982 United Nations World Assembly on Aging, held in Vienna, Austria, representatives from third-world nations talked about their perceptions of the status of the elderly in their countries. From Pakistan came the opinion that "the social and family fabric will inevitably break up because of new stresses"; from the Philippines came survey results showing that the elderly "expressed feelings of loneliness, helplessness and worthlessness coupled with feelings of rejection and neglect by their families. Strained relationships between the elderly and family members was also an identified problem"; and from Kenya came the opinion that "due to modern changes, the traditional family commitment of caring for the aged is slowly dying" (Oriol, 1982:34–35). In another African nation, Zimbabwe, the elderly are described as being at the edge of destitution (Hampson, 1983). In rural Zaire, "the traditional and still widely held view that having many children allows one to rely upon them as a source of labor and financial support is in fact largely a myth" (Masamba, 1984:26), because most of the younger villagers have migrated to urban areas.

As modernization occurs, the process of urbanization, combined with education and a redefinition of the labor force, pushes the elderly aside (Cohn, 1982). At the same time the older people themselves begin to redefine their own expectations, anticipating less from their children in the way of old-age support (Coombs and Sun, 1981). This is the crucial moment of change in the obligations and expectations that the old and the young have toward each other that may be the tipping point in the generational flow of wealth, in the perceived value of children, and ultimately in the birth rate. Over the long run, of course, we would expect the status of the elderly to rise again in the less developed nations, as their achievement of higher standards of living and lower birth rates elevates the demographic and social profiles of the older population, as has happened in the more developed nations of the world.

SUMMARY AND CONCLUSION

As fertility and mortality remain at low levels in the developed nations, the populations are becoming older. Changes occur in many aspects of social organization as a population ages, because the aging process brings with it numerous changes in individuals themselves, both biological and social. The biological changes are related to the gradual decline in physical functioning and the concomitant rise in susceptibility to disease. Social changes are related especially to the system of age stratification, which in modern industrialized societies has relegated the elderly to a lower status than was formerly true or than is true is less developed, agrarian societies. The downgrading of status seems to be a combined result of greater longevity, which has led to retirement (which has lower status than work); economic technology, which renders the skills of the elderly obsolete; urbanization, which segregates the generations and reinforces the inversion of status between generations engendered by the upward spiral of technology; and improvements in education, which mean that children tend to be better educated than their parents. Related to these historical changes is the fact that each cohort is unique in its social and historical experiences as it moves through the life cycle. This introduces a dynamic element into the process of aging, signaling future changes in the demographic characteristics and life-styles of the elderly.

The older population in the United States is characterized by an unbalanced sex ratio, because male mortality is higher than female mortality. This means that as women age they are increasingly susceptible to widowhood and the prospect of living alone. Old age also brings with it a fairly dramatic drop in income as people are encouraged or forced to leave the labor force. Minority elders are in double jeopardy since they, as younger people, were less likely to have had access to the higher educational and occupational levels that are associated with high incomes among the elderly.

The future prospects for the elderly differ according to the level of development of a society. If Cowgill's theory of modernization and the status of the elderly is correct, then we should expect continued modernization of the developing nations to lead to a future decline in the status of old people in those nations. On the other hand, in developed nations, the future rise in the number and proportion of older people, combined with the changes that will occur as the younger cohorts age, will undoubtedly reelevate the status of the elderly. Already government policies designed to improve the lives of older people in the United States have been fairly swift in coming and reasonably effective in their impact, especially in urban areas. Indeed, although cities harbor some of society's most difficult problems, they have also given birth to some of its great triumphs. The next chapter examines the demographic components of the modern wishing well of society—the urban environment.

MAIN POINTS

1. A major consequence of the worldwide decline in mortality is an increase in the number of people surviving to old age.

2. Although social age and chronological age rarely seem to coincide, it has become customary to define an old person as one who is 65 or older.

3. Biological aging refers to a decline in physical abilities accompanied by an increased risk of illness.

4. Socially, aging carries with it a changing set of obligations and role expectations.

5. Increased longevity, higher levels of education, urbanization, and economic technology may all have conspired to alter the status of older persons in industrialized nations.

6. There are currently 300 million people in the world aged 65 and older. In the United States the older population numbers 29 million.

7. The population of older persons in the United States is growing at a rapid rate, especially in the ages 85 and older.

8. In most societies females outnumber males at the older ages. The exceptions are nations in which the social status of women tends to be clearly inferior to that of men.

9. The older ages are typically characterized by an increase in widowhood and an increase in the proportion of people who live alone.

10. The upward spiral of literacy and education over the last few hundred years has meant that each generation of older people tends to be less well-educated than younger people.

11. In industrialized nations old age is characterized by retirement from full-time employment and by a subsequent drop in income.

12. Minority elders are said to be in double jeopardy, discriminated against both for their minority status and for their age.

13. In the future, societies will be much more influenced by the presence of older people than was ever true in the past.

SUGGESTED READINGS

1. Donald Cowgill, 1986, Aging Around the World (Belmont, CA: Wadsworth Publishing Co.).

   Cowgill popularized the modernization theory of aging, which has a heavy demographic emphasis, and in this work he puts the theory into global perspective.

2. John R. Weeks, 1984, Aging: An Introduction to Concepts and Social Issues (Belmont, CA: Wadsworth Publishing Co.).

   This book actually began as an expansion of the chapter you have just read; it is an attempt to put the aging process into its proper social and demographic perspective.

3. Barbara Torrey, K. Kinsella, and C. Taeuber, 1987, "An aging world," U.S. Bureau of the Census International Population Reports, Series P-95, No. 78.

Three demographers from the U.S. Bureau of the Census have compiled and briefly described demographic data on aging for a number of countries around the world. This is an excellent source of comparative data.

4. Beth Soldo, 1980, "America's elderly in the 1980s," Population Bulletin 35(4).
This volume focuses on the social impact of the demography of aging in the United States.

5. Samuel Preston, 1984, "Children and the elderly: divergent paths for America's dependents," Demography 21(4):435–57.
In this very thought provoking article, Preston shows how the demography of aging in America is on a potential collision course with the demography of youth—at least with respect to public policy.

CHAPTER 12
Population Growth and Urbanization

The majority of Americans live in—indeed were born in—cities, and most people of the Western world share that urban experience. Some of us take the city for granted, some curse it, some find its attractions irresistible, but no one denies that urban life is the center of Western industrial civilization. Cities, of course, are nothing new, and their influence on society is not a uniquely modern feature of life; however, the widespread emergence of urban life—the explosive growth of the urban population—is very much a recent feature of human existence. Consider that at the beginning of the nineteenth century less than 3 percent of the world's population lived in cities, whereas 45 percent of the world's population is urban today. In the United States, about 75 percent of the population is now urban. By the end of this century, it is projected that one out of every two human beings will live in an urban area.

The rapid **urbanization,** or redistribution of people from countryside to city, is one of the most significant demographic movements in world history—at least as important to the world as the population "explosion" itself. Rafael Salas, who before his death in 1987 was executive director of the United Nations Fund for Population Activities, commented in 1983 that, in his view, the continuing process of urbanization will be the dominant feature of the global population picture in the future (Population Action Council, 1983a). What are the demographic components of urbanization, and what are the demographic consequences for society of an ever-increasing concentration of people in urban areas? These are the questions I will focus on in this chapter. Clearly the city is implicated in a wide range of problems, issues, and triumphs in all societies, but my intention here is not to review life in the city (which could, and has, filled volumes). Rather, I want to provide you with a demographic perspective on urbanization. To accomplish that, I will begin with an analysis of the demographic components of urbanization, looking especially at the way in which migration, mortality, and fertility interact with the process of urbanization, and emphasizing the role of urban life in lowering fertility. Finally, I will turn to the question of whether urbanization may do as much harm as good; is crowding harmful to human existence? Before launching into the chapter, however, let me briefly define "urban."

WHAT IS URBAN?

An **urban** place can be defined as a spatial concentration of people whose lives are organized around nonagricultural activities; the essential characteristic here is that urban means nonagricultural. A farming village of 5,000 people should not be called urban, whereas a tourist spa or an artist colony of 2,500 people may well be correctly designated an urban place. You can appreciate, then, that "urban" is a fairly complex concept. It is a function of (1) sheer population size, (2) space (land area), (3) the ratio of population to space (density or concentration), and (4) economic and social organization.

The definitions of urban used in most demographic research unfortunately rarely encompass all the above ingredients. Due to limitations of available data and sometimes due simply to expediency, researchers (and government bureaucrats as well) typically define urban places on the basis of population size alone. Thus, all places with a population of 2,000, 5,000, 10,000, or more (the lower limit varies) might be considered urban for research purposes. Of course you should recognize that an arbitrary cutoff disguises a lot of variation in human behavior. Although the difference between rural and urban areas may at first appear to be a dichotomy, it is really a continuum in which we might find an aboriginal hunter-gatherer near one end and an apartment dweller in Manhattan near the other. In between there will be varying shades of difference. Indeed, the next time you drive from the city to the country (or the other way around), you might ask yourself where you would arbitrarily make a dividing line between the two.

Another essential ingredient of being urban is economic and social life organized around nonagricultural activities. Thus, there is an explicit recognition that urban people order their lives differently than rural people do; they perceive the world differently and behave differently. These differences in behavior are usually subsumed under the label "urbanism," which describes the city dweller's way of life, a topic I will return to later. Now, however, let me discuss the demographic aspects of the process whereby a society is transformed from rural to urban—the process of urbanization.

DEMOGRAPHIC COMPONENTS OF URBANIZATION

Urbanization refers to the change in the proportion of a population living in urban places; it is a relative measure ranging from 0 percent, if a population is entirely agricultural, to 100 percent, if a population is entirely urban (see Figure 12.1 for examples). Urbanization can occur as a result of internal rural-to-urban migration, natural increase, international urban migration, reclassification of places from rural to urban, or combinations of these processes.

Internal Rural-to-Urban Migration

The migration of people within a country from rural to urban places represents the classic definition of urbanization because it is intuitively the most obvious way by which a population can be shifted from countryside to curbside. There is no question that in the developed countries, rural-to-urban migration was a major force in the process of urbanization. Over time the agricultural population of these countries has tended to decline in absolute numbers, as well as in relative terms, even in the face of overall population growth. In less developed countries, though, rural-to-urban migration is occurring in large absolute terms but without a consequent depopulation of rural areas. The reason, of course, is the difference in the rates of natural increase in less developed countries compared with rates in the developed nations.

Figure 12.1　Industrialized Nations Are Highly Urbanized

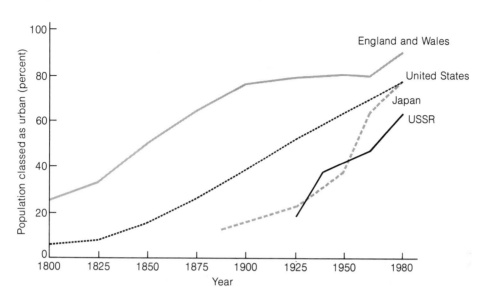

The process of urbanization is closely associated with industrialization. England and Wales began to industrialize before the United States did, and so their urban fraction increased sooner. On the other hand, Japan began to industrialize and urbanize in the late nineteenth century, whereas those two processes were delayed in Russia until after the revolution. *Source:*　Kingsley Davis, 1965, "The urbanization of the human population," Scientific American, 213(3):47. Copyright © 1965 by Scientific American, Inc. All rights reserved; and World Bank, 1984, World Development Report, 1984 (New York: Oxford University Press), Table 22.

Natural Increase

Even without a physical redistribution of people from rural to urban areas, the proportion of any population living in urban places will increase if the rate of natural increase is greater there than in rural areas. This situation rarely arises, but it is worth knowing about because exactly the opposite is responsible for the lack of rapid urbanization in many developing nations in spite of high rates of rural-to-urban migration. When the rate of natural increase is very high in rural areas, migration to cities may only keep the population relatively balanced between urban and rural places, rather than increasing the proportion of people living in urban places.

International Urban Migration

Although it is not widely recognized as important, international migration also operates to increase the level of urbanization, because most international migrants move to cities in the host area regardless of where they lived in the donor area. From the standpoint of the host area, then, the impact of international migration is naturally to add to the urban population without adding significantly to the rural population, thereby shifting a greater proportion of the total to urban places. Certainly, most immigrants to the United States wind up as urban residents. For example, in the United States in 1980, 92 percent of the foreign-born population lived in cities, compared to 72 percent of the native-born population. A similar situation has prevailed in Latin America, especially in Argentina, Uruguay, Chile, and Venezuela (Browning, 1958).

Reclassification

It is also possible for "in-place" urbanization to occur. This happens when the absolute size of a place grows so large, whether by migration, natural increase, or both, that it reaches or exceeds the minimum size criterion used to distinguish urban from rural places. In the United States, any incorporated town that exceeds 2,500 is considered urban because, back in the 1920s when the current definition was devised, any place that large seemed urban to the people living in the surrounding countryside. Thus, in 1980, the tiny village of Troy, North Carolina became an urban area, to be included in the same category as New York City. Note that reclassification is more of an administrative phenomenon than anything else and is based on a unidimensional (size only) definition of urban places, rather than also incorporating any concept of economic and social activity. Of course, it is quite probable that as a place grows in absolute size it will at the same time diversify economically and socially, probably away from agricultural activities into more urban enterprises. This tends to be part of the social change that occurs everywhere in response to an increase in population size; an agricultural population can become quickly redundant and the lure of urban activities (such as industry, commerce, and services) may be strong under those conditions.

Another administrative trick that can lead to rapid city growth is annexation. City boundaries are almost constantly changing, and the effect is often to bring into the city limits people who might otherwise be classified as rural. Urban growth rates can thus be misleading. For example, "The city of Houston grew 29 percent during the 1970s—one of the most rapidly growing large cities in the country. But the city also annexed a quarter of a million people. Without the annexation, the city would have grown only modestly" (Miller, 1984:31).

Metropolitanization

In countries such as the United States, cities have grown so large and their influence has extended so far that a distinction is often made between metropolitan and nonmetropolitan counties, rather than the more vague but still useful distinction between urban and rural. In 1949 the U.S. Census Bureau developed the concept of standard metropolitan area (SMA). An SMA consists of a county with a core city of at least 50,000 people and with a population density of at least 1,000 people per square mile. The concept proved useful and was subsequently revised to be called the **standard metropolitan statistical area (SMSA)**. In 1983 the U.S. Office of Management and Budget ordered a new revision, and the United States is now divided into MSAs (**metropolitan statistical areas**), CMSAs (**consolidated metropolitan statistical areas**), and PMSAs (**primary metropolitan statistical areas**). An MSA is a county with an urbanized area with at least 50,000 people. "However, there is virtually always a wide border zone of mixed rural-urban territory around the urbanized area, mostly open country but also containing considerable scattered suburban development" (Forstall and Gonzalez, 1984:24). In fact, in 1970 over 30 percent of the nation's rural population lived in metropolitan areas and over 40 percent of the nonmetropolitan population was classified as urban (Alonso and Starr, 1982).

In 1984 there were 257 MSAs that stood alone without being part of a wider metropolitan region (Carlson, 1984). However, there also was a large number of metropolitan areas that were contiguous to one another and thus formed consolidated metropolitan areas—groupings of the largest metropolitan areas. In 1984 there were 23 such places, the largest of which was the New York–Long Island–Southwestern Connecticut–Northern New Jersey CMSA with 17 million people. The MSAs within each of the CMSAs are given a special notation—they are the Primary MSAs. Thus, New York City is one of the PMSAs within the nation's largest CMSA. In 1984 there were 78 PMSAs included within the 23 CMSAs. Despite the shifting of definitions, the metropolitan population of the United States has essentially stopped growing since 1970 (Holdrich, 1984), although there has been a lot of reshuffling of people within the metropolitan areas, as I will discuss later in the chapter.

IMPACT OF POPULATION PROCESSES ON URBANIZATION

Beginnings

The earliest cities were not very large, because most of them were not demographically self-sustaining. The ancient city of Babylon might have had 50,000 people, Athens possibly 80,000, and Rome as many as 500,000; but, as Davis has put it, such cities were "urban spots in a sea of rurality" (1968). They were symbols of civilization, visible centers that were written about, discussed by travelers, and densely enough settled to be later dug up by archaeologists. Our view of ancient history is colored by the fact that our knowledge of societal detail is limited primarily to the cities, although we can be sure that those populations represented only a tiny fraction of the total.

Early cities had to be constantly replenished by migrants from the hinterlands, since they had higher death rates and lower birth rates than did the countryside, usually resulting in an annual excess of deaths over births. The self-sustaining character of modern urban areas began with the transformation of economies based on agriculture (produced in the country) to those based on manufactured goods (produced in the city). Control of the economy made it far easier for cities to dominate the rural areas politically and thus ensure their own continued existence in economic terms. A crucial transition in this process came between about 1500 and 1800 with the discovery of new lands, the rise of mercantilistic states (that is, based on goods rather than landholdings), and the inception of the Industrial Revolution. These events were inextricably intertwined, and they added up to a diversity of trade that gave a powerful stimulus to the European economy. This was a period of building a base for subsequent industrialization, but it was still a preindustrial and largely pre-urban era. During this time, for example, cities in England were growing at only a slightly higher rate of growth than the total population, and thus the proportion of urban population was rising only very slowly. Between 1500 and 1800 London grew from about 80,000 people to slightly more than 1 million—an average rate of growth considerably less than 1 percent per year; also during this span of 300 years, the London population increased from 2 percent of the total population of England to 10 percent—significant, but not necessarily remarkable. In 1801 only 18 percent of the population in England lived in cities of 30,000 people or more, and nearly two thirds of those urban residents were concentrated in London. Thus, on the eve of the Industrial Revolution, Europe (like the rest of the world) was predominantly agrarian.

Neither England nor any other country was at that time urbanizing with any speed, because industry had not yet grown sufficiently to demand a sizable urban population and because cities could not yet sustain their populations through natural increase. Not until the nineteenth century did urbanization take off, with a timing closely tied to industrialization and the decline in mortality that triggered population growth.

The ancient cities of Rome and Tenochtitlán (the capital of the Aztec Empire in Mexico) obviously did not derive their size from the attraction of industry but rather because their system of social organization could produce the surplus food necessary to sustain a large urban (administrative, artistic, service-producing) population. Likewise, London's growth to a city of 1 million people in 1801 was due more to the preliminaries of industrialization (commerce and finance, for example) than to industrialization itself.

As economic development occurred, cities grew because they were economically efficient places. For example, commercial centers bring together in one place the buyers and sellers of goods and services. Likewise, industrial centers bring together raw materials, laborers, and the financial capital necessary for the profitable production of goods. They are efficient politically because they centralize power and thus make more efficient the administrative activities of the power base that supports them. In sum, cities perform most functions of society more efficiently than is possible when people are spatially spread out. Mumford says it well: "There is indeed no single urban activity that has not been performed successfully in isolated units in the open country. But there is one function that the city alone can perform, namely the synthesis and synergy of the many separate parts by continually bringing them together in a common meeting place where direct fact-to-face intercourse is possible. The office of the city, then, is to increase the variety, the velocity, the extent, and the continuity of human intercourse" (1968:447).

Cities are efficient partly because they reduce costs by congregating together both producers and consumers of a variety of goods and services. By reducing costs, urban places increase the benefits accruing to industry—meaning, naturally, higher profits. Those profits translate into higher levels of living, and it is no surprise that as cities have industrialized their death rates have declined.

People living in and near cities now enjoy health benefits never previously available and, as a result, the populations of cities are growing at an unprecedented high rate. Indeed, Davis has noted that "during the 1950–70 period, the world had to accommodate nearly four times as many urban inhabitants each decade as it had accommodated during the previous half century . . . and the city population today is approaching the magnitude of the world's population in 1800" (1972b:57). In the two decades between 1950 and 1970, nearly 700 million people were added to the world's urban population, and about 460 million of those were added to cities with 100,000 or more people. Davis has also shown that in 171 less developed nations, the average annual growth rate in cities of 100,000 or more was substantially higher between 1950 and 1970 than in the United States, England, France, or Russia at comparable stages of urbanization.

In 1950 only two of the ten largest urban agglomerations in the world were located in less developed nations—Shanghai, China, and Calcutta, India. But, as you can see in Figure 12.2, projections by the United Nations suggest that by the year 2025 nine of the top ten largest agglomerations will be in third-world nations—and the magnitude of their projected population sizes is almost incomprehensible. Mexico City, which in 1985 was the world's second largest urban area with 18 million

Figure 12.2   The World's Largest Urban Agglomerations Will Have Changed Dramatically Between 1950 and 2025

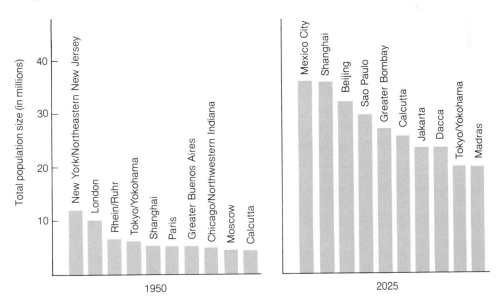

Source: United Nations, 1982, Estimates and Projections of Urban, Rural and City Populations, 1950–2025. The 1980 Assessment (New York: United Nations), Table 8.

people (Tokyo/Yokohama was largest in 1985 with 22 million), is projected to double in size by the year 2025 to an amazing 37 million people (United Nations, 1982c).

Rates of natural increase are higher in the cities of developing countries than they ever were in the developed nations, and so are rates of increase in the countryside. Thus, since substantial rural-to-urban migration is still occurring, the transformation of less developed societies into predominantly urban populations is proceeding at a rapid pace. Because the interrelationships between urbanization and the process of migration, mortality, and fertility have changed somewhat over time, let me review the relationships for you.

Migration to Cities

Had it not been for migration, cities of the nineteenth century could not have grown in population size. In fact, in the absence of migration, the excess of deaths over births would actually have produced deurbanization. Of course, migration did occur, since economic development created a demand for an urban population that was met by the eventual emptying out of the countryside. Industrial cities drew the largest crowds, but commercial cities, even in nonindustrial countries, also generated a demand for jobs and created opportunities for people to move from agrarian to urban areas. The cities of most colonized countries bear witness to this fact. For example, migration accounted for 75 to 100 percent of the total growth of nineteenth-century cities in Latin America (Weller et al., 1971). The growth of cities in southern Asia and western Africa was also stimulated by the commercial contacts of an expanding European economy. Naturally, in the highly industrialized, highly urbanized countries the agricultural population is so small that cities (also nations) now depend on the natural increase of urban areas rather than migration for population growth.

In third-world countries, where cities are growing so rapidly, the question is often raised about the causes of the high rate of rural-to-urban migration. Is urban economic development attracting people away from the countryside, or is population pressure so intense in the rural areas that people are being pushed toward the cities? The answer seems to be that both processes are working simultaneously to stimulate urban growth in developing countries. Kelley and Williamson (1984) examined data for 40 less developed countries going back to 1960 and, using a complex statistical model, suggested that third-world urbanization is more a function of opportunities in the city than it is of pressure from the countryside. But Firebaugh (1979) had earlier used data from 27 Asian and Latin American countries to conclude that, in fact, adverse rural conditions do make an important contribution to the cityward flow of migrants. In reviewing these and other studies, Bradshaw (1987) has concluded that the cities of developing countries are often the areas where disproportionate societal resources are spent. This leaves the rural sector lagging economically in comparison with cities, where opportunities are typically seen to be more numerous. No matter how bad life appears to be in the city, it is frequently worse in the countryside, and so a reasonably good conclusion is that both rural push and urban pull continue to explain migration to cities in developing nations.

Although important in its own right, migration is also related to fertility, since migrants tend to be young adults of reproductive ages. Furthermore, migrants from rural areas typically wind up having levels of fertility lower than those in the rural areas from which they left but still higher than levels in the urban areas to which they have moved (Ritchey and Stokes, 1972; Zarate and de Zarate, 1975; Goldstein and Goldstein, 1981). To some extent, of course, the fertility impact of the migrants will depend on whether males or females (or neither) predominate in the migration stream.

Sex Ratios in Cities

Females tend to be more mobile in North and South America and Europe, whereas in Africa and Asia more men than women migrate from rural to urban places. The differences in the sex ratios of migrants are determined largely by the employment opportunities for women. Among the developing regions of the world, Latin America is the only area where women outnumber men in the migrant stream, and it is also the area in which employment opportunities are better for women in urban than in rural areas (see Boserup, 1970). The pattern of agricultural labor in Europe, North America, and South America has been for males to do most of the outside-the-home work, relegating women to domestic work for the most part; whereas in Africa and Asia (including Arab countries and India), the role of women in regular agricultural work (especially commercial enterprises associated with agricultural produce bazaars, and so on) has been more prominent. Thus, it is at least a reasonable thesis that as an economy develops and urban opportunities arise, females will be more responsive than males to these opportunities if they are less actively involved in the agrarian labor force. For example, in countries of Europe, North America, and South America, where women have not been very active in agriculture, the cities have a feminine sex ratio. You can see in Table 12.1, where I have shown data for a few such countries, that urban areas, in contrast to rural areas, have consistently fewer males than females. On the other hand, in Asian and African countries, urban sex ratios are higher (that is, more masculine) than rural sex ratios. In recent years, however, East Asian women have been heading for the cities in increasingly greater proportions, stimulated by the new availability of jobs in electronics, textiles, and other industries in which there has been a demand for cheap labor (Khoo, 1984; Smith et al., 1983). It appears that female migration in Asia is associated with improving female literacy and postponement of marriage—much as you might expect.

Urbanization and Mortality

Kingsley Davis (1973) has estimated that in the city of Stockholm, Sweden, in 1861–70, the average life expectancy at birth was only 28 years; for the country as a whole at that time, the life expectancy was 45 years. I discussed in Chapter 6 that the ability to resist death has been passed to the rest of the world by the industrialized

Table 12.1 Urban and Rural Sex Ratios

Country	Year	Urban Sex Ratio[a]	Rural Sex Ratio[a]	Urban/Rural
United States	1980	0.93	1.00	.93
Sweden	1980	0.96	1.12	.86
Netherlands	1985	0.96	1.03	.93
Mexico	1979	1.00	1.06	.94
Guatemala	1981	0.92	1.03	.89
Zimbabwe	1982	1.14	0.91	1.25
India	1986	1.13	1.05	1.08
Indonesia	1980	1.00	0.98	1.02

Source: Data are calculated from United Nations, 1988, Demographic Yearbook, 1986 (New York: United Nations), Table 7.

[a] Males per females.

nations, and the diffusion of death control has usually started in the cities and spread from there to the countryside. This pattern of diffusion was similar in the now developed countries, but there was an important difference. When mortality declines as a response to economic development, there are also structural changes that tend to reduce fertility; but when death control is introduced independently of economic development, mortality and fertility declines lose their common source, and mortality decreases while fertility remains stable. This results in fertility levels being higher today in the less developed countries (urban and rural places alike) than they were at a comparable stage of mortality decline in the currently advanced countries.

Urbanization and Fertility

It is almost an axiom in population studies that urban fertility levels are lower than rural levels; it is also true, of course, that fertility is higher in less developed than in developed nations. Putting these two generalizations together, you can conclude that urban fertility in less developed nations will be lower than rural fertility but still higher than the urban fertility of cities in the industrialized nations. High fertility persists in the cities of less developed nations partly because the urban environment is less hostile to reproduction than it used to be. Less developed nations often have systems of public welfare, subsidized housing, free education, and accessible maternal and child health clinics. Nonetheless, the lower fertility that almost always prevails in urban places deserves closer scrutiny.

We can usually anticipate that people residing in urban areas will have fairly distinctive ways of behaving compared with rural dwellers. So important and obvious are these differences demographically that urban and rural differentials in fertility are among the most well documented in the literature of demographic research.

John Graunt, the seventeenth-century English demographer whose name I first mentioned in Chapter 1, concluded that London marriages were less fruitful than those in the country because of "the intemperance in feeding, and especially the Adulteries and Fornications, supposed more frequent in London than elsewhere . . . and . . . the minds of men in London are more thoughtful and full of business than in the Country" (quoted by Eversley, 1959:38).

In 1940 in the United States there were substantial differences in the number of children women had according to where they lived. Rural farm women, for example, at every age over 19 had at least twice as many children as urban women (see Figure 12.3).

In rural areas large families may be useful (for the labor power), but even if they are not, a family can "take care of" too many members by encouraging migration to the city. Once in the city, people have to cope more immediately with the problems that large families might create and, besides, the city offers many more alternatives to family life than do rural areas. In recent decades the once wide divergence in urban and rural fertility levels has narrowed as rural fertility has decreased relative to urban levels, reflecting the growing dependence of rural places on urban production and an urban life-style.

The difference between city and country fertility levels may not be what it used to be in the United States, but it does still exist. In 1986 fertility was still highest in rural areas. In the cities, women in the suburbs had fewer children on average than those in the central cities, as you can see in Figure 12.4, although the differences are very small.

Figure 12.3 Rural Women Had More Children Than Urban Women in the United States in 1940

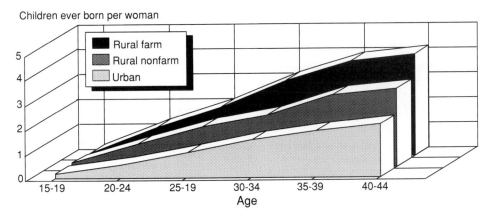

Children ever born per woman

In 1940, U.S. rural farm women at all ages over 19 had about twice as many children on the average as did urban women. *Source:* Adapted from C. Kiser, W. Grabill, and A. Campbell, 1968, Trends and Variations in Fertility in the United States (Cambridge: Harvard University Press), Table 5:2.

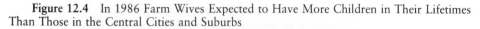

Figure 12.4 In 1986 Farm Wives Expected to Have More Children in Their Lifetimes Than Those in the Central Cities and Suburbs

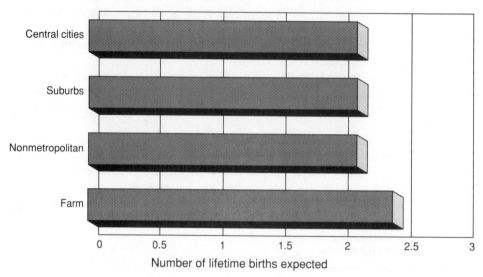

Number of lifetime births expected

In 1982, U.S. married farm women were bearing more children on average than women in cities. However, the differences are not nearly so large as they were even a decade ago. *Source:* U.S. Bureau of the Census, 1984, "Fertility of American Women: June 1982," Current Population Reports, Series P-20, No. 387, Table 11.

An Illustration from Mexico

The impact of population processes on urbanization is illustrated by what has happened to people in one small village in Mexico—Tzintzuntzan. For nearly 400 years the population of Tzintzuntzan stayed right about 1,000 people (Foster, 1967). In the mid-1940s, at about the time that Foster began studying the village, the population size was starting to climb slowly, since death rates had started to decline in the late 1930s. In 1940 the population was 1,077 and the death rate was about 30 per 1,000 while the birth rate of 47 per 1,000 was leading to a rate of natural increase of 17 per 1,000. For some time there had been small-scale, local out-migration from the village to keep its population in balance with the limited local resources, but by 1950 the death rate was down to 17 per 1,000 and the birth rate had risen. Better medical care had reduced the incidence of miscarriage and stillbirth, and in 1950 the village had 1,336 people (Foster, 1967). By 1970 the population had leveled off at about 2,200 (twice the 1940 size); however, were it not for out-migration draining away virtually all the natural increase of Tzintzuntzan, the population would double again in about 20 years (Kemper and Foster, 1975).

What, you ask, does growth in a small Mexican village have to do with urbanization? The answer, of course, is that the migrants headed for the cities. Seventy percent of those people who leave Tzintzuntzan go to urban places, with Mexico City (230 miles away) being the most popular destination (Kemper and Foster, 1975). In Chapter 3, in discussing the theory of demographic change and response, I indicated that one of the easiest demographic responses that people can make to population pressure is migration, and in Mexico, as in most countries of the world, the city has been the receiving ground. Furthermore, the demographic characteristics of those who go to the city are what you would expect; they tend to be younger, slightly better educated, of higher occupational status, and more innovative than nonmigrants (Kemper, 1974).

For Tzintzuntzeños, migration to Mexico City has raised the standard of living of migrant families, altered the world view of both adults and their children toward greater independence and achievement, and, indirectly, "urbanized" the village they left behind. This last effect is due to the fact that having friends and relatives in Mexico City is one factor that leads the villagers to be aware of their participation in a wider world. These factors all make it easier for each generation to make the move to Mexico City, since they know what to expect when they arrive and they know people who can help them.

The whole process of mortality decline and the cityward movement of Tzintzuntzeños began in the late 1930s, when a government project gave the village electricity, running water, and a hard-surfaced highway connecting it to the outside world (Kemper and Foster, 1975). More recently, government expansion of the local school system may actually be encouraging migration through its effect of raising aspirations (Turner, 1976).

However, what is lacking so far in the process of urbanization of the Tzintzuntzeños is a documented decline in fertility. Although little is known about the fertility of those who migrate, birth rates remain high in the village. One of the major factors in lowering the fertility of migrants is for women to find employment; however, in Mexico, labor force participation rates for women are very low (Mexico, 1982), so that effect is minimal. In general, of course, the demographic impact of a woman migrating is twofold, since she brings not only herself to the city but her potential children as well. If she is economically active, then her level of fertility is depressed relative to nonworking women, and that helps to dampen the impact of her migration. If young women cannot find jobs, however, they may be more likely to get married and turn to childbearing. This appears to be what happened, for example, in Chile during the 1950s, when birth rates rose substantially in the large metropolitan areas while rising barely at all in rural areas. Between 1952 and 1960 the total fertility rate rose from 3.42 to 4.46 in Santiago, the capital city of Chile, whereas it rose only from 4.76 to 5.05 in the nonurban places. An important reason for the rise in the birth rate seemed to be that the slow growth of the economy, relative to population increase between 1952 and 1960, reduced the opportunities for women to work (Weeks, 1970). As the proportion of women actively employed decreases, a large number are left to devote themselves to families, and fertility will rise.

I have examined the demographic inputs to the urbanization process by looking at the way in which mortality, migration, and fertility interact to produce city growth and transform a society from rural to urban. But what are the consequences of urbanization for the human condition?

IMPACT OF URBANIZATION ON THE HUMAN CONDITION

The benefits of cities, of course, are what make them attractive, and they at least partially explain the massive transformation of the United States, for example, from a predominantly rural to a primarily urban nation within a few generations. The negative impact of urbanization on the human condition represents the set of unintended consequences that may prevent the city from being as attractive as it might otherwise be.

The efficiencies of the city have generally been translated into higher incomes for city dwellers than for farmers. In fact, it even tends to be true that the larger the city, the higher the wages (Hoch, 1976). Wage differentials undoubtedly have been and continue to be prime motivations for individuals to move to cities and stay there. That is not to say that people necessarily prefer to live in cities; the reverse may actually be true. Throughout American history the sins and foibles of urban life have been decried, and the city is often compared unfavorably with a pastoral existence (see Fischer, 1976:chap. 2). Of course, people recognize the advantages of the city, and Americans prefer to be near a city though not right in it. In a study done for the U.S. Commission on Population Growth and the American Future, Zuiches and Fuguitt point out that public opinion polls since 1948 have shown that a vast majority of Americans indicate a preference for living in rural areas or small cities and towns. When, however, in 1971 Zuiches and Fuguitt added for the first time a survey question about the desire to be near a large city, those rural preferences became more specific. Their data show that of all the people who say they prefer living in rural areas or in small cities, 61 percent also want to be within 30 miles of a central city. In general, Americans like it both ways. They aspire to the freedom of space in the country but also prefer the economic and social advantages of the city. The compromise, of course, is the suburb, and it turns out that the average American is already living in this preferred location (Howell and Frese, 1983).

Suburbanization in the United States

In 1899, Adna Weber noted that American cities were beginning to **suburban-ize**—to grow in the outlying rings of the city. It was not until the 1920s, however, that suburbanization really took off. Hawley (1972) has noted that between 1900 and 1920 people were still concentrating in the centers of cities, but after 1920 the suburbs began regularly to grow in population at a faster pace than the central cities. Two factors related to suburbanization are the desire of Americans to live in the less crowded environment of the outlying areas and their ability to do so—a result of increasing wealth and the availability of buses and automobiles (Tobin, 1976). Such transportation has added an element of geographic flexibility not possible when suburbanites depended on fixed-rail trolleys to transport them between home in the suburbs and work in the central city.

From the 1920s through the 1960s the process of suburbanization continued almost unabated in the United States (as indeed in most cities of the world). To illustrate the impact of the automobile, note that in 1980, 85 percent of all workers drove to work in an automobile (car, truck, or van). On average, American workers drive 9 miles to work and it takes an average of 22 minutes to get there (U.S. Bureau of the Census, 1984i). Over time, however, the fabled commute from suburb to central city has given way to a commute from one suburb to another as businesses have followed the people out of the central city. In 1975, for example, 12 percent of all workers were traveling each day from the suburb into the central city, 25 percent were going from suburb to suburb, 5 percent headed from the central city to the suburb, and the remainder followed some other kind of pattern.

Since 1970 two new wrinkles have been added to the process of suburbanization—growth beyond the suburbs (**exurbanization**) and the return of some elite suburbanites to older city areas (**gentrification**). As I touched on in Chapter 7, the emptying out of nonmetropolitan areas in the United States ceased in the 1970s, and those areas began witnessing new vigor, growing almost as fast in percentage terms (although not in absolute numbers) as the suburbs. At least part of this growth may represent a further suburbanization of the suburban elite. Some evidence for this speculation is that the movement to nonmetropolitan areas is typically made by people with higher incomes than those who were moving into the metropolitan areas (U.S. Bureau of the Census, 1979k). It has been suggested that exurbanization is at least partly an attempt by native suburbanites to find locations that resemble their former suburbs at an earlier, less crowded time because, in fact, the suburbs have *become* the city (Newitt, 1984). Shopping centers, corporate headquarters, many new high-technology industries, and traffic gridlock have all relocated to the suburbs, leaving some central cities to be little more than residential areas for low-income people. At the same time, older suburban areas are facing problems that used to be associated with the inner city. "The aging of suburbia is causing radical changes in the character and politics of countless bedroom communities. It is leading to school closings, property-tax revolts, and demands for new or expanded housing, transportation and recreation services for the elderly" (Lublin, 1984:1). This is not a uniquely American experience, I should note. Similar changes are occurring in England as well (Otten, 1981).

The Baby Boom generation in the United States grew up in the suburbs to a greater extent than any previous cohort, but as they reached an age to buy homes, Baby Boomers found themselves caught in the midst of spiraling housing costs. One innovative response to higher housing prices in the 1970s was the purchase and rehabilitation of abandoned homes in older sections of central cities—especially in the older cities in the eastern half of the nation. Younger people, typically without children, were buying homes that were sometimes mere shells and were thus sold very cheaply, and then renovating them and moving in. Since these innovative renovators tended to be white and upwardly mobile, they were likened to the gentry moving back into the city, and thus the term gentrification was applied. Yet, despite the radical transformation of a few neighborhoods in places like New York City, Chicago, Baltimore, and Washington, D.C. (see, for example, Blum, 1982) gentrification apparently never involved enough people to counter the continuing movement of people out of the central cities and into the suburbs (Newitt, 1983; Chall, 1984).

Residential Segregation

Although suburbia has become a legendary part of American society, suburbanization has been disproportionately engaged in by whites. For examples, in 1970 in 15 large areas studied by Farley (1976), 58 percent of the whites lived in the suburbs compared with 17 percent of the nonwhites. As suburbs have grown, the color composition of central cities has also changed dramatically. Since the 1930s the proportion of whites living in central cities has declined steadily and the proportion of blacks has risen steeply (Schnore et al., 1976); the black population has undergone a very rapid urbanization at the same time that whites have been suburbanizing.

During the period 1910–30, there was a substantial movement of blacks out of the South destined for the cities of the North and West. The urban population of blacks grew by more than 3 percent per year during that 20-year period, whereas the rural population declined not only relatively but in absolute terms as well. The reasons for migration out of rural areas were primarily economic, with the decline in the world demand for southern agricultural products providing the *push* out of the South. But there were concurrent *pull* factors as well in the form of demands in northern and western cities for labor, which could be met cheaply by blacks moving from the South (Farley, 1970). During the Depression there was a slowdown in the urbanization of blacks, but by the beginning of World War II half the nation's blacks lived in cities, reaching that level of urbanization 30 years later than whites had. After World War II the urbanization and rural depopulation of blacks resumed at an even higher level than after World War I, and by 1960 the black population was 58 percent urban in the South and 95 percent urban in the North and West. Recent urbanization has been associated not only with the economic recovery after the war but also with the severely restricted international migration (see Chapter 15), which meant that Europeans no longer were entering the labor force to take newly created jobs, thus providing a market for black labor.

The concentration of blacks in older central locations within cities is aggravated by the higher rates of natural increase that characterize blacks compared with whites (Schnore et al., 1976)—see Chapter 9. Since U.S. death rates tend to be only slightly higher for blacks than for whites (see Chapter 6), the entire explanation for the higher rate for natural increase is the significantly elevated fertility levels among inner-city blacks. In 1986, for example, fertility among ever-married black women aged 18–34 living in central cities was 1,761 children ever born per 1,000 women, compared with 1,300 for whites (U.S. Bureau of the Census, 1987b). The consequence of the urbanization of blacks, their urban rates of natural increase, and the relatively higher rates of suburbanization of whites is increasing segregation of black and white populations within cities.

The segregation of people into different neighborhoods on the basis of different social characteristics (such as ethnicity, occupation, or income) is a fairly common feature of human society (Farley, 1976; Zlaff, 1973). However, in the United States residential segregation by race is much more intense than segregation by any other measurable category. For example, Farley (1976) has demonstrated that in both predominantly white and predominantly black areas there is a fair amount of residential segregation by education, occupation, and income—whether you look at central cities or suburbs. A representative illustration is Detroit, where in 1970 you would have had to move more than one third of all college graduates (whether black or white) to other parts of the city to achieve an even residential distribution of college graduates. Yet, you would have had to move 91 percent of all black college graduates to achieve racial residential integration of college graduates (Farley, 1976).

Of course, the demographic components of suburbanization do not explain residential segregation; they merely point to its existence. The explanations are essentially social in nature, and one of the prevailing ones is based on the idea that "status rankings are operationalized in society through the imposition of social distance" (Berry et al., 1976:249). In race relations, the social status of American blacks has been historically lower than that of whites. That status ranking used to be maintained symbolically by such devices as uniforms, separate facilities, and so forth, which were obvious enough to allow social distance even though blacks and whites lived in close proximity to each other. However, as blacks left the South and moved into industrial urban settings, many of those negative status symbols were also left behind. As a result, spatial segregation serves as a means of maintaining social distance "where 'etiquette'—the recognition of social distance symbols— breaks down" (Berry et al., 1976:249). Thus, as blacks have improved in education, income, and occupational status, whites have maintained social distance by means of residential segregation facilitated by suburbanization.

Will the situation change in the future? Probably not. The black population of the United States is currently experiencing a rising rate of suburbanization, but whites are continuing to suburbanize at equally high rates (Goodman and Streit- weiser, 1982). The result is a general loss of population in central cities (Long, 1983), with a shift among all groups to the suburbs where patterns of residential segregation tend to persist (Schnore et al., 1976). Farley has commented that "it is difficult to imagine abrupt changes in these patterns in the immediate future" (1976:36). That sentiment has been echoed by Berry and his associates, who com- mented that "substantial residential integration by race is unlikely to emerge either in central city or in suburb in years to come" (1976:262), and by Frey, who has concluded that "recent lifecourse migration patterns do not imply an eventual met- ropolitan-wide integration of races" (1984:803). Of course, it is worth adding that residential segregation is not entirely a case of whites imposing their power on others. Lieberson and Carter (1982) have noted that at least some fraction of segre- gation results from the preference of blacks to live in neighborhoods with a high proportion of blacks. This is consistent with findings by Portes and co-investigators (1982) that Cuban and Mexican-Americans tend to be economically more successful when they live in ethnic enclaves, and it is consistent also with the greater success that Indochinese refugees in the United States have had when concentrated in a few geographic regions rather than being widely dispersed (Rumbaut, 1985).

Other Aspects of the Urban Environment

Not all people are wary of the city. City lovers may be in the minority, but they are also a select group of American society (this can be generalized to other populations as well). The people who most prefer to live in cities tend to be younger, better educated, and have higher-status jobs than those who prefer to move away from the metropolitan areas. The selectivity of migrants is indicative of the city's rewards—education, high-status jobs, and the opportunity for social mobility, especially for the young.

These qualities increase the desirability of migrating to the city in many parts of the world. In Africa, for example, the key to social mobility has been education, and according to numerous surveys, that is a very important motivation there to migrate from rural to urban settings (Hance, 1970). The love that Americans and Europeans seem to have for rural areas is not common in Africa. According to Hance, many Africans "who receive even a primary education feel that farm work (or sometimes any physical labor) is no longer an appropriate occupation. Indeed, some youth see the life of the peasant as the most miserable that exists, one that subjects the individual to physical forces beyond his control, while town life appears to offer rapid social advance and liberation" (1970:181).

Although cities offer economic and social opportunities that are unavailable anywhere else, city dwellers often weigh those advantages against one of the most widely perceived disadvantages of increasing urbanization—crowding.

The Impact of Urban Crowding

For centuries the crowding of people into cities was doubtless harmful to existence. Packing people together into unsanitary houses in dirty cities raised death rates. Furthermore, as is so often the case, as cities grew to unprecedented sizes in nineteenth-century Europe, death struck unevenly within the population. Mortality went down faster for the better off, leaving the slums as the places where lower-income people were crowded into areas "with their sickening odor of disease, vice and crime" (Weber, 1899:414).

When early students of the effects of urbanization such as Weber and Bertillon discussed crowding and overcrowding, they had in mind a relatively simple concept of **density**—the number of people per room, or per block, or per square mile. Thus, Weber quotes the 1891 census of England, "regarding as overcrowded all the 'ordinary tenements that had more than two occupants to a room, bedrooms and sitting rooms included'" (1899:416). The prescription for the ill effects (literally) of overcrowding was fairly straightforward as far as Weber was concerned. "The requirement of a definite amount of air space to each occupant of a room will prevent some of the worst evils of overcrowding; plenty of water, good paving, drainage, etc. will render the sanitary conditions good."

Crime and vice are also often believed to be linked to urban life and, as a matter of fact, crime rates are higher in cities than in the countryside, at least in the United States (Mayhew and Levinger, 1976). But what is it about crowding that might lead to differences in social behavior between urban and rural people? To examine that question, you have to ask more specifically what crowding is.

The simplest definition of **crowding** is essentially demographic and refers to density—the ratio of people to physical space. As more and more people occupy a given area, the density increases and it becomes therefore relatively more crowded. Under these conditions, what changes in behavior can you expect? In a 1905 essay, Georg Simmel suggested that the result of crowding was an "intensification of nervous stimulation" (1905:48), which produced stress and, in turn, was adapted to by people reacting with their heads rather than their hearts. "This means that urban dwellers tend to become intellectual, rational, calculating, and emotionally distant from one another" (Fischer, 1976:30). Here were the early murmurs of the "urbanism" concept—that the crowding of people into cities changes behavior—a concept frequently expressed with negative overtones.

Perhaps the most famous expression of the negative consequences of the city is Louis Wirth's paper "Urbanism as a Way of Life" (1938), in which he argued that urbanism will result in isolation and the disorganization of social life. Density, Wirth argued, encourages impersonality and leads to people exploiting one another. For two decades there was little questioning of Wirth's thesis and, as Hawley has put it, "in one short paper, Wirth determined the interpretation of density for an entire generation of social scientists" (1972:524). The idea that increased population density had harmful side effects lay idle for a while, but it was revived with considerable enthusiasm in the 1960s following a report by Calhoun on the behavior of rats under crowded conditions.

Crowding Among Rats   Although he initiated his studies of crowding among rats in 1947, it was not until 1958 that Calhoun began his most famous experiments (published in 1962). In a barn in Rockville, Maryland, he designed a series of experiments in which rat populations could build up freely under conditions that would permit detailed observations without humans influencing the behavior of the rats in relation to one another.

Calhoun built four pens, each with all the accoutrements for normal rat life and divided by electrified partitions. Initially eight infant rats were placed in each pen, and when they reached maturity Calhoun installed ramps between each pen. At that point the experiment took its own course in terms of the effects of population growth in a limited area. Normally, rats have a fairly simple form of social organization, characterized by groups of 10 to 12 hierarchically ranked rats defending their common territory. There is usually one male dominating the group, and status is indicated by the amount of territory open to an individual.

As Calhoun's rat population grew from the original 32 to 60, one dominant male took over each of the two end pens and established harems of 8 to 10 females. The remaining rats were congregated in the middle two pens, where problems developed over congestion at the feeding hoppers. As the population grew from 60 to 80, behavior patterns developed into what Calhoun called a "behavioral sink"— gross distortions of behavior resulting from animal crowding. Behavior remained fairly normal in the two end pens, where each dominant male defended his territory by sleeping at the end of the ramp, but in the middle two pens there were severe changes in sex, nesting, and territorial behavior. Some of the males became sexually passive; others became sexually hyperactive, chasing females unmercifully; and still another group of males was observed mounting other males as well as females. Females became disorganized in their nesting habits, building very poor nests, getting litters mixed up, and losing track of their young. Infant mortality rose significantly. Finally, males appeared to alter their concept of territoriality. With no space to defend, the males in the middle two pens substituted time for territory, and three times a day the males fought at the eating bin.

Calhoun's study can be summarized by noting that among his rats, crowding (an

WHITE FLIGHT FROM THE CITIES: A CASE STUDY IN RESIDENTIAL SUCCESSION

The premise that school busing leads to white flight—the movement of whites into the suburbs from central cities where school desegregation is occurring—was a hotly controversial issue in the 1970s and early 1980s, and the evidence seems sufficiently inconclusive that people have been able to believe whatever suited their particular political inclinations. For example, University of Chicago sociologist James Coleman (1979) argued that white flight does occur when school desegregation plans are implemented, and he further noted that the process is accelerated if the district has a high proportion of blacks and if there are white suburban school districts nearby to provide convenient flight destinations. His conclusion was that the long-term demographic consequence of school desegregation is to further exacerbate residential segregation.

Opponents of the white-flight theory used a variety of statistical techniques to show that while a relationship exists between school busing and white suburbanization, no causal linkage could be established statistically, even though it may be inferred. That is, although whites were indeed moving out, it could not be proved that busing was the reason. One of every five households moves each year in the United States, and this level of mobility provides the principal mechanism by which neighborhoods change over time. There can also be no dispute that the white population in the United States has been suburbanizing at a fairly rapid pace since World War II, but what is perhaps less obvious is whether the so-called white flight is real or simply part of a more widespread process of residential succession.

White flight assumes that whites have been pushed rather than pulled to the suburbs and implies further that they were being replaced by nonwhites. Unfortunately, the data about why people continue to suburbanize are sparse for the 1980s. The most complete studies refer to the late 1960s and 1970s, but they still provide very important insights. In an extensive analysis of residential mobility patterns in 39 SMSAs in the United States between 1965 and 1970, Frey (1979) found that the development of suburban areas (pull factors) tended to be a more important determinant of the flight to the suburbs than were push factors such as school desegregation, racial disturbances, and center-city decline. Frey hypothesizes that the major influence of such factors as center-city deterioration and school desegregation is not so much to push whites out of the city but rather to discourage the white portion of that large pool of movers (that one in five mentioned earlier) from going into the center city as households change residence from one metropolitan area to another. Thus, perhaps the attractiveness of the suburbs is at least as important as the growing unattractiveness of the central city in explaining white suburbanization.

I have noted in this chapter that blacks were suburbanizing during the 1970s, but not as rapidly as whites. A study of 35 major metropolitan areas in the United States by Goodman and Streitweiser (1982) suggests that between 1970 and 1980 white flight was as much a case of blacks deciding *not to move* as it was a case of whites deciding *to move*. To fill the picture in more completely, it is interesting to investigate just how much neighborhoods really increase in the number of rats within a fixed amount of space) led to the disruption of important social functions and to social disorganization. Related to these changes in social behavior were signs of physiological stress, such as changes in the hormonal system that made it difficult for females to bring pregnancies to term and care for the

change as a result of residential mobility; that is, when one household moves, does the household that succeeds it have different social and economic characteristics? The most complete analysis of this question is provided by two U.S. Bureau of the Census demographers, Larry Long and Daphne Spain (1979), using overlapping data from the Current Population Surveys. They found that during the study period (1969–71) in the United States, 94 percent of all household moves did not involve a change in race, 3 percent involved white-to-black succession, and 1 percent involved black-to-white succession (the remainder involved other racial combinations).

There were, however, significant differences in residential succession patterns between central cities and suburbs. In the central cities, Long and Spain found that 6 percent of all household changes involved blacks replacing whites, compared with 2 percent in the metropolitan suburbs and less than 1 percent in nonmetropolitan areas. The rates of racial succession were also found to be highest in the northeastern region of the country and lowest in the West.

When viewed only from the perspective of the black family rather than from that of the total population, a slightly different picture emerges. When a black household moves, there is a 30 percent chance that it will be replacing a white family. In the Northeast and West there is more than a 40 percent chance that a black household move involves racial succession. The figure is lowest (17 percent) in the South.

When black households replace white households, the black and the white households tend to share more social and economic characteristics than is true for any other combination of movers. In general, it is black husband-wife families with children who lead the way in replacing whites; further, they tend to have higher incomes and higher levels of education than do other black movers. On the other hand, the whites who are being replaced tend to be older (around age 45) and appear to be couples whose children have already left home.

Because blacks who replace whites are quite similar in socioeconomic characteristics to the whites they replace, it appears that racial succession per se does not create a substantial change in the socioeconomic character of a neighborhood. This means that if a neighborhood declines over time, it is principally due to changes in population characteristics between in-movers and out-movers of the same race. Thus, a deteriorating neighborhood is more a result of lower-status whites replacing relatively higher-status whites, or lower-status blacks replacing relatively higher-status blacks, than it is due to blacks replacing whites.

The decline of neighborhoods in central cities is then due less to racial succession than to a constant flow of lower-status migrants into the central city tending to replace the higher-status households that are heading for the suburbs. This almost centrifugal force of the central city affects all groups in society, even though it may be most obvious for the numerically larger white population.

young. More recent studies have shown that not only rats, but monkeys, hares, shrews, fish, elephants, and house mice also tend to respond to higher density by reducing their fertility (Galle et al., 1972). Now the important question must be raised: Does the behavior of rats and other animals signal an analogous response to crowding on the part of humans?

Humans at the Macro Level   Although the severe distortions of behavior that Calhoun witnessed among rats have never been replicated among humans, recent studies have suggested that at the macro (group) level there have been some fairly predictable consequences of increasing population density (mainly as a result of increases in population size). For example, Mayhew and Levinger note that violent interaction can be expected to increase as population size increases; "the opportunity structure for murder, robbery, and aggravated assault increases at an increasing rate with aggregate size" (1976:98). There are more people with whom to have conflict, and there is an increasingly small proportion of people over whom we exercise direct social control (which would lessen the likelihood of conflict leading to violence). Increasing size leads to greater superficiality and to more transitory human interaction, that is, greater anonymity. Mayhew and Levinger point out that "since humans are by nature finite organisms with a finite amount of time to devote to the total stream of incoming signals, it is necessarily the case that the average amount of time they can devote to the increasing volume of contacts . . . is a decreasing function of aggregate size. This will occur by chance alone" (1976:100).

Since no person has the time to develop deeply personal relationships (primary relations) with more than a few people, the more people there are entering a person's life, the smaller the proportion that one can deal with in depth. This often leads to personal stress as people try to sort out the vast array of human contacts. The more people there are, the greater is the variety both of expectations that others have of you and of obligations that you have toward others. The problems of not enough time to go around and of contradictory expectations lead to "role strain"—a perceived difficulty in fulfilling role obligations. Most of these problems of size seem to arise naturally in large metropolitan areas and, indeed, the problems are most intense there. But even rural communities experience an increase in the density of social interaction as they grow in size.

Since growth is associated with more intense interaction, nongrowth should ease the situation. In a study of the impact of nongrowth on American metropolitan areas, Rust revealed that such communities often have strong church, family, and ethnic ties. "The incidence of stress diseases was low. They were relatively safe from crime. Housing was cheap, plentiful, and to a large extent owner-occupied" (1975:218).

Social research commonly produces mixed results, of course, and the study of crowding is no exception. Thus, Choldin (1978) reviewed the literature on density and its effects and concluded that "when social structural differences among neighborhoods are considered [held constant], population density appears to make a trivial difference in predicting pathology rates" (1978:109). On the other hand, a study of rural villages in India has suggested that high density does appear to dampen fertility levels (Firebaugh, 1982)—a finding consistent with studies among other animals. Size and density do not, however, tell the whole tale when it comes to crowding; it is more a process than a state of being and is experiential in nature, rather than just a matter of high human density (Baum and Davis, 1976). In other words, if crowding is harmful, it is because you and I react differently when we feel crowded than we do otherwise. The way we react to an increased concentration of people will depend on our perception of that situation as being crowded and on our previous experience in dealing with such a situation. This aspect of crowding is an individual, or micro-level, phenomenon.

Humans at the Micro Level   From Weber to Calhoun, studies of crowding emphasized a measure of density defined in terms of two variables: physical space and population. The works of Somer (1969) and Hall (1966) added personal space to the concept of physical space, which is the idea that you have something akin to a bubble surrounding you that, when penetrated, produces distress. That bubble of **personal space** is thought of as being a socially derived phenomenon that differs from one culture to another. Thus, two Turks will be almost face to face for a friendly chat, whereas Americans might be 3 feet apart.

With the addition of the personal space concept, we can note a fairly long list of studies (see Fischer, 1976 for a discussion) that show how people react to violation of their expectation of closeness. People are not necessarily distressed on a crowded subway or elevator as long as they know what to expect, but it is distressing to have a stranger stand right next to you when the two of you are the only passengers on an elevator, and equally disconcerting to have someone sit right next to you at an otherwise deserted library, restaurant, or picnic area. In these instances our personal space has been violated; people have behaved in an unaccustomed way and it makes us uncomfortable. As long as there is an escape, however, our discomfort is easily assuaged. This leads to the addition of yet another element in the definition of crowding—namely, time.

Crowding refers to the number of people per space per unit of time. We frequently use the term *congestion* to refer to very high densities that occur for relatively short periods of time—traffic at rush hour, lunch counters at noon, department stores before the holidays. It was precisely that kind of congestion that was associated with Calhoun's "behavioral sink"—congestion from which there was no escape. The importance of escape is that it provides an immediate way of relieving anxiety or stress that might be produced by increasing levels of crowding. In other words, it provides for an immediate return to a situation of less crowding. As people move to cities, though, or as family size grows with the birth of children, the absolute level of crowding may increase on a daily basis with less possibility of escape.

Cultural factors undoubtedly influence how crowded a person must be before the effects of crowding are felt. Also important is the distinction between high density (which is primarily what we have been discussing so far) and overcrowding (which is usually defined as an excessive number of people per room) (Jacobs, 1961). Most researchers do, in fact, "assume that the greater the number of persons per household, the greater the number of role obligations and experienced demands and hence the greater experience of crowding" (Gove et al., 1979:61). To test the effects of such personal crowding (defined simply as the number of persons per room), Gove and his associates (1979) conducted a sample survey in Chicago, obtaining data from 2,035 respondents. They found that the higher the level of crowding, the greater is the negative impact on social relationships within the home and mental health generally. These relationships held even when such factors as race, sex, age, education, income, and marital status were taken into account (Gove and Hughes, 1983).

Despite the apparent validity of the analysis by Gove and his associates, their finding of a deleterious impact of crowding on human behavior is more the exception to the rule than the rule itself. Most researchers have been rather unsuccessful in establishing that kind of relationship.

Why is there not more evidence of physiological and sociopsychological harm? Probably because of our ability as humans to cope—to adapt to new structures of human interaction (Choi et al., 1976). It is during that process of adaptation that anxieties and stress occur; if crowding is harmful to human existence, it is perhaps the *process* of crowding, not high density per se, that produces the deleterious effects. Thus, the process of crowding can be viewed in the same way that any other change—social, demographic, or otherwise—can be viewed. Adjustment is required when someone close to you dies, just as the birth of a child creates problems of family reorganization, and just as migration requires learning a new round of social activities. The crowding of people into cities is not a unique phenomenon, and it is unlikely that it is any more harmful to human existence than other changes in a person's life.

SUMMARY AND CONCLUSION

Urbanization is the process whereby a society shifts from being largely bound to the country to being bound to the city. It is a process that is almost always the close companion of economic development, which, of itself, suggests the close theoretical connection of urbanization with demographic processes. Although rural-to-urban migration is a major aspect of urbanization, mortality and fertility are importantly associated as well, as both causes and consequences. Population pressures created by declining mortality in rural areas, combined with the economic opportunities offered by cities, have been historically linked to urbanization. On the other hand, mortality now tends typically to be lower in cities than in rural areas, which permits higher rates of urban natural increase than in the past.

The development of the industrialized countries is replete with examples of how urban life helps to generate or ignite the first two of Ansley Coale's three preconditions for a fertility decline—the acceptance of calculated choice as an element in personal family size decisions and the perception of advantages to small families (see Chapter 5). Fertility levels are still lower in American cities than in rural areas; but in cities of the less developed nations, urban fertility, which is lower than rural fertility, is often much higher than in the cities of the developed world. As a result, cities in third-world nations are growing very rapidly without a proportionate shift in the percentage of people living in urban places. As a consequence, city growth and economic development are not as closely tied to each other as are urbanization and development.

Nonetheless, the high level of urbanization in the industrialized nations and the increasing levels in less developed nations signal the importance of this phenomenon. In general, it seems that the most readily identifiable beneficial consequences are those associated with higher standards of living in cities than in rural places. The detrimental consequences (crime, impersonality, and so on) appear to be due more to sheer population size than to some sort of harm resulting from crowding. Although cities are by definition places of high density, it appears that severe metabolic or social distress is not a human response to high density, or else humans have never been exposed to analogously high levels of crowding as were the famous rats studied by Calhoun. We humans seem to adapt to high density by defining and defending our own personal space.

My purpose in this chapter has been to analyze the demographic components of urbanization—one of the world's abiding social issues. In the next chapter I will continue in this vein by applying the demographic perspective to the debate over economic development.

MAIN POINTS

1. The world is rapidly approaching a situation in which one of every two people lives in an urban area.

2. Urbanization refers to the increase in the proportion of people living in urban places.

3. Urbanization can occur as a result of internal rural-to-urban migration, higher rates of natural increase in urban than in rural areas, international urban migration, and reclassification of places from rural to urban.

4. One of the most striking features of urbanization is its recency in world history. Highly urban nations like England and the United States were almost entirely agricultural at the beginning of the nineteenth century.

5. Until the twentieth century, death rates in cities were so high and fertility was low enough that cities could not have grown had it not been for the migration of people from the countryside.

6. In virtually every society, fertility levels are lower in cities than in rural areas.

7. Despite lower fertility in cities, cities in less developed nations almost always have higher fertility levels than cities in developed nations.

8. People are generally attracted to cities, and they remain there because wages are higher there than in agricultural sectors.

9. Population growth in cities has given rise to fears about potential harmful effects of crowding. These fears were heightened by a study of rats in which crowding did lead to some bizarre behavior patterns.

10. Evidence relating to humans suggests that the process of crowding in cities may be stressful but that humans adapt fairly well to living in crowded circumstances.

SUGGESTED READINGS

1. James L. Spates and John J. Macionis, 1982, The Sociology of Cities (New York: St. Martin's Press).

This is but one among many good textbooks on cities and the process of urbanization. This particular volume provides an international perspective and includes case studies from all over the globe.

2. Y. Bradshaw, 1987, "Urbanization and underdevelopment: a global study of modernization, urban bias, and economic dependency," American Sociological Review 52(2):224–39.

This is an excellent example of the type of research required to understand the complex relationship between urbanization, population growth, and economic development.

3. Claude Fischer, 1984, The Urban Experience (San Diego, CA: Harcourt Brace Jovanovich).

This is an updated version of one of the most insightful and well written books ever published on the subject of urban life.

4. Douglas Massey and Nancy Denton, 1987, "Trends in the residential segregation of blacks, Hispanics, and Asians: 1970–1980," American Sociological Review 52(6):802–25.

The title of this article pretty well sums up its contents.

5. Walter Gove and M. Hughes, 1983, Overcrowding in the Household: An Analysis of Determinants and Effects (New York: Academic Press).

The authors review the literature and contribute their own research findings to this intriguing aspect of the social consequences of urban population concentration.

CHAPTER 13
Population Growth and Economic Development

Is the control of population growth a necessary precursor to economic development? Most developed countries argue that underdeveloped countries will be unable to move out of the vicious cycle of poverty unless population growth is brought under control. Some less developed nations, especially those with socialist governments, insist on pushing the population issue aside, objecting that economic exploitation and political domination by the developed countries are the real reasons for their relative poverty. This very debate was featured at the World Population Conference in Bucharest in 1974, which was attended by government officials from all over the world, and it surfaced for reexamination at the more recent 1984 International Population Conference in Mexico City. The 1974 conference resulted in a "world plan of action" (see Table 13.1) that developed nations hoped would give high priority to family planning programs to combat what they saw as the potentially serious barrier to economic development posed by population growth. However, an interesting coalition of Catholic and socialist countries fought off that proposal, and ultimately the role of population growth as an impediment to improving the human condition was considerably downplayed.

In 1984, when delegates met in Mexico City to assess progress since 1974 and to make recommendations for the future, the United States added its own wrinkle to the proceedings by reversing the earlier American view that slowing down the rate of population growth was the key element in promoting economic development. Instead, the U.S. delegation, influenced by the views of Julian Simon (whom I will discuss later in this chapter), asserted that population growth was not necessarily bad and that a free economic environment was the magic ingredient in both development and fertility control. Just as world opinion had seemed headed toward a consensus that economic development was impeded by population growth, the 1984 International Population Conference had to reckon with the U.S. position that maybe the two were not so inextricably linked after all. This is one of the most crucial policy issues that world leaders face, and the position you take in this argument will heavily influence the kind of population and development policies that you, as a decision maker, would advocate. In this chapter I will examine several facets of the debate, with an eye toward seeing how each side of the issue may lead to different policy alternatives. The chapter begins with a discussion of economic development, a concept that I have mentioned but not really analyzed yet. Then I will examine three sides of the debate: (1) population growth is a stimulus to economic development; (2) population growth is not an important factor related to economic growth; and (3) population growth is a hindrance to development. I will discuss the policy implications of each of these positions and conclude with a brief look at Mexico as a case study in some of the concepts and policies introduced in the chapter.

WHAT IS ECONOMIC DEVELOPMENT?

The most common definition of **economic development** is that it represents a growth in average income, usually defined as per capita (per person) income (World Bank, 1974). A closely related idea is that economic development is occurring when

Table 13.1   Highlights of the World Population Plan of Action

In 1974 representatives from nations all over the world met at the United Nations–sponsored World Population Conference. Out of that conference came a World Population Plan of Action that became a set of benchmarks for discussion at the 1984 International Population Conference (again sponsored by the United Nations).

Some of the resolutions agreed to that are especially relevant to the issue of population growth and economic development include:

1. Governments should develop national policies and programs relating to the growth and distribution of their populations, if they have not already done so, and the rate of population change should be taken into account in development programs.

2. Countries should aim at a balance between low rather than high death rates and birth rates.

3. Highest priority should be given to the reduction of high death rates. Expectation of life should exceed 62 years in 1985 and 74 years in 2000. Where infant mortality continues high, it should be brought down to at least 120 per 1,000 live births by the year 2000.

4. Because all couples and individuals have the basic human right to decide freely and responsibly the number and spacing of their children, countries should encourage appropriate education concerning responsible parenthood and make available to persons who so desire advice and means of achieving it.

5. Family planning and related services should aim at prevention of unwanted pregnancies as well as elimination of involuntary sterility or subfecundity to enable couples to achieve their desired number of children.

6. Countries that consider their birth rates detrimental to their national purposes are invited to set quantitative goals and implement policies to achieve them by 1985.

7. Governments should ensure full participation of women in the educational, economic, social, and political life of their countries on an equal basis with men.

8. Countries that wish to increase their rate of population growth should do so through low mortality rather than high fertility, and possibly immigration.

9. To achieve the projected declines in population growth and the projected increases in life expectancy, birth rates in the developing countries should decline from the present level of 38 to 30 per 1,000 by 1985, which will require substantial national efforts and international assistance.

10. In addition to family planning, measures should be employed that affect such socioeconomic factors as reduction in infant and childhood mortality; increased education, particularly for females; improvement in the status of women; land reform; and support in old age.

11. National efforts should be intensified through expanded research programs to develop knowledge concerning the social, economic, and political interrelationships with population trends; effective means of reducing infant and childhood mortality; new and improved methods of fertility regulation to meet the varied requirements of individuals and communities, including methods requiring no medical supervision; the interrelations of health, nutrition, and reproductive biology; and methods for improving the administration, delivery, and utilization of social services, including family planning services.

12. The Plan of Action should be closely coordinated with the International Development Strategy for the Second United Nations Development Decade, reviewed in depth at 5-year intervals, and modified as appropriate.

Source: Reprinted by permission of the Population Crisis Committee.

the output per worker is increasing; since more output should lead to higher incomes, you can appreciate that they are really two sides of the same coin. Of course, if you are holding down two jobs this year just to keep afloat in the face of rising prices, you know that producing more will not necessarily improve your economic situation. Rather, it may only keep it from getting worse. Thus, a more meaningful definition of economic development refers to a rise in *real* income—an increase in the amount of goods and services that you can actually buy.

Indeed, an important aspect of development is that it is concerned with improving the welfare of human beings. It includes more than just increased productivity; it includes the resulting rise in the ability of people to consume (either buy or have available to them) the things they need to improve their level of living. Included in the list of improvements might be higher income, stable employment, more education, and better health and nutrition; consumption of more food and better housing; and increased public services such as water, power, transportation, entertainment, and police and fire protection (see Kocher, 1973).

ECONOMIC GROWTH AND ECONOMIC DEVELOPMENT

Economic growth refers to an increase in the total amount of wealth in a nation (or whatever your unit of analysis might be) without regard to the total number of people, whereas economic development relates that amount of wealth to the number of people. For example, in 1988 in the United States, the total national income was $4.3 trillion (Population Reference Bureau, 1988). For the 246 million Americans in 1988 that averaged out to $17,500 per person per year in income. In Switzerland in 1988, national income was "only" $118 billion, but since there are far fewer Swiss (a little less than 7 million), average (per capita) income was higher in Switzerland ($17,840) than in the United States.

In contrast to those two wealthy nations is a country like India, whose total estimated income in 1988 of $220 billion was higher than Switzerland's, but the far larger number of people in India (more than 800 million) reduced the per person income to $270 per year. Thus, the "average" American (if there is such a person) has 65 times the income of the "average" Indian. National income in India, even in constant dollars (controlling for inflation), was 44 percent higher in 1985 than it was in 1975, but the population also was growing very quickly and, as a result, per capita income increased only 18 percent in that 10-year span (United Nations, 1988).

So far I have discussed economic development in terms of average income, but those averages frequently hide inequalities and disparities in the distribution of income. It may happen that the per capita increase in productivity profits only a few people rather than the entire population, and, in fact, some economists argue that a concentration of income is the only way that enough money can be saved for further investment and further economic growth. Kuznets (1965), for example, has suggested that income inequality characterizes the early phases of economic development when capital formation is so crucial; only later is it possible to spread the income around. A loose analogy might be made to a family that wants to "develop economically" by purchasing a home. Assuming that a substantial amount of cash must be saved for the down payment and closing costs, the members of the family may well have to do without things they would like to consume, because all the extra money is being accumulated for the house purchase. Only when the house has been bought can the sacrifice cease and the family income be spread around more among its members. The analogy is not perfect, but it illustrates a point well known to early industrial entrepreneurs—a delay of gratification is required if income is going to be reinvested for further growth.

Economic growth often involves the introduction of machines that work more efficiently and cheaply than humans, which can lead to the paradoxical situation in which per capita income in a nation may rise (that is, economic growth occurs) but the actual standard of living of almost the entire population may fall (that is, a general lack of economic development). Bauer (1972) has discussed this difference between growth and development and has noted that the opposite paradox could also occur—per capita income could go down, but the level of living could rise as a result of income redistribution. Of course, in this latter example, real economic development occurs only if the improved standards of living can be maintained.

In sum, economic development in its broadest sense means a sustained increase in the socioeconomic welfare of a population. There is a major problem, though, in the measurement of economic development, since for the most part the data we have refer only to levels of income, not to the distribution of income. Thus, we have to use those data to make inferences about the nature of the changes occurring within a society. As a matter of fact, if we could accurately measure economic development as I have defined it, the entire debate about its relationship to population growth might be resolved.

THE DEBATE—STATISTICAL BASES

There is an almost indisputable statistical association between economic development and population growth; that is, when one changes, the other also tends to change. As you no doubt already know, though, two things may be related to each other without one causing the other. Furthermore, the patterns of cause and effect can conceivably change over time. Does population growth promote economic development? Are population growth and economic development only coincidentally associated with each other? Or is population growth a hindrance to economic development? That is the debate.

The problem is that the data presently available lend themselves to a variety of interpretations. In Table 13.2 I have compared 1986 **per capita gross national product** (a common measure of income) with rates of population growth in 133 countries. You can see that in general, countries in which average income levels are low tend to be clustered around the high end of population growth rates. Of the 90 countries with rates of growth at or above the world average (1.7 percent), 81 of them had per capita incomes less than $4,000 per year. In 1965 Kuznets defined an

Table 13.2   Low Rates of Population Growth Do Not
Necessarily Mean High Incomes (Data for 133 Countries, 1988)

Per Capita Gross National Product	Annual Rate of Natural Increase				
	to 0.7	0.8–1.7	1.8–2.7	2.8+	Totals
$0–399	0	1	12	21	34
400–3,999	6	11	24	24	65
4,000–7,999	1	7	2	2	12
8,000+	17	0	3	2	22
Totals	24	19	41	49	133

Source: Data courtesy of Population Reference Bureau, Inc., Washington, D.C.

Note: In 1988 there was a tendency for low-income countries to also have rapidly growing populations. But rapid population growth did not prevent high average income in oil-rich nations, nor did slow growth necessarily bring high incomes with it. Per capita GNP data refer to 1986.

underdeveloped nation as one with a per capita income less than $100 in 1952–54 prices (1965). Allowing for an approximate quadrupling of prices between then and 1986 suggests a cut-off of about $400 for a country to be considered **underdeveloped** (as opposed to the more general term *less developed*). By that definition, you can see in Table 13.2 that 34 of the 35 underdeveloped countries had populations growing at or above the average world rate. The only exception was China, in which a concerted governmental effort has lowered the birth rate, despite the very low level of per person income ($300 per year in 1986).

Conversely, high-income countries tend to have low rates of population growth; of the 22 countries with average incomes of $8,000 or more, 17 were growing at rates below the world average. Nonetheless, the relationship does not always hold. Five oil-rich nations have high incomes and high growth rates, while eighteen nations (mainly from southern and eastern Europe and the Caribbean) have low rates of growth but also low levels of income. Clearly, a low rate of population growth is no assurance of a high income, and vice versa. Further, such data, taken from just one point in time, cannot be used to establish a cause-and-effect relationship, and to date no one has been able to produce a convincing set of data to establish the validity of one position or another. Thus, the data you see in Table 13.2 can be interpreted in several different ways, depending on your ideological predilections.

THE DEBATE—IDEOLOGICAL BASES

The debate, then, over population growth and economic development is three-cornered. In the first corner, arguing that population growth stimulates development, you will typically find **nationalists**—people seeking freedom for their country from economic and political exploitation by more powerful nations. A frequent corollary of nationalism is the idea that more people will bring more productivity and greater power.

In the second corner you will find Marxists (and others, as well) arguing that social and economic injustice result simultaneously from the lack (or slowness) of economic development and the (erroneous) belief that there is a population problem. The Marxist position maintains that no cause-and-effect relationship exists between population growth and economic development—that poverty, hunger, and other social welfare problems associated with lack of economic development are a result of unjust social and economic institutions, not population growth.

Finally, in the third corner you find those who have historically antagonized the Marxists, namely the neo-Malthusians. They are, of course, latter-day advocates of the thesis that population growth, unless checked, will wipe out economic gain. The difference between Malthus and the neo-Malthusians is that Malthus was opposed to birth control, as you will recall from Chapter 3, whereas neo-Malthusians are strong advocates of birth control as a preventive check to population growth. Let me examine these three positions in more detail.

Is Population Growth a Stimulus to Economic Development?

Probably the best-known exponent of the idea that population growth is the trigger of economic development is a British agricultural economist, Colin Clark. Clark (1967) insists that, in the long run, a growing population is more likely than either a nongrowing or a declining population to lead to economic development. He points to the history of Europe, in which the Industrial Revolution and the increase in agricultural production were accompanied almost universally by population growth. Clark's argument is based on the thesis that population growth is the motivating force that brings about the clearing of uncultivated land, the draining of swamps, and the development of new crops, fertilizers, and irrigation techniques, all of which are linked to "revolutions" in agriculture (Clark, 1967). The kernel of Clark's argument, which is advanced also by Boserup (1965; 1981), has often been repeated around the world (especially by the Catholic Church) and is well stated in the following quotation:

> [Population growth] is the only force powerful enough to make such communities change their methods, and in the long run transforms them into much more advanced and productive societies. The world has immense physical resources for agriculture and mineral production still unused. In industrial communities, the beneficial economic effects of large and expanding markets are abundantly clear. The principal problems created by population growth are not those of poverty, but of exceptionally rapid increase of wealth in certain favoured regions of growing population, their attraction of further population by migration, and the unmanageable spread of their cities (Clark, 1967:preface).

This same line of reasoning is part of a strategy of development forwarded by Hirschman, who has argued as follows: (1) An increase in population size will lower a population's standard of living unless people reorganize their lives to increase production. (2) It is "a fundamental psychological postulate" that people will resist a lowering in their standard of living. (3) " . . . the activity undertaken by the community in resisting a decline in its standard of living causes an increase in its ability to control its environment and to organize itself for development. As a result, the community will now be able to exploit the opportunities for economic growth that existed previously but were left unutilized" (1958:177).

The thesis that population growth is beneficial to economic development does have some foundation in fact. In Europe and the United States there is a reasonable amount of evidence to suggest that development may well have been stimulated by population increase. Indeed, some historians regard preindustrial declines in death rates in Europe, associated partly with the disappearance of the plague (perhaps also with the introduction of the potato) as the spark that set off the Industrial Revolution. The reasoning goes that the lowered death rates created a rise in the rate of population growth, which then created a demand for more resources (Clark, 1967, has given a review). An analogous example of population growth influencing development is the case of the American railroad, which opened up the frontier and hastened resource development in the United States. Fishlow (1965) has demonstrated that the railroad (which helped to accelerate the economic development of the western states) was actually following people westward rather than the other way around.

Although history may show that population growth was good for development in the now highly industrialized nations, statistics also reveal very important differences between the European-American experience and that of modern, less developed nations. The less developed countries today are not, in general, retracing the steps of the currently developed nations. For example, less developed nations are building from a base of much lower levels of living than those that prevailed in either Europe or the United States in the early phases of economic development (Kuznets, 1965; Boserup, 1981). Furthermore, although the rate of economic growth in many underdeveloped countries has recently been higher than at comparable periods in the history of the developed nations, population growth is also significantly higher. They have much higher rates of population growth than European or American countries *ever* had, with the possible exception of the colonial period of American history. In fact, the rates of population growth in the underdeveloped world seem to be virtually unparalleled in human history.

It appears that population growth may have helped to stimulate economic growth in the developed countries "by forcing men out of their natural torpor and inducing innovation and technical change, or by speeding up the replacement of the labour force with better educated labor" (Ohlin, 1976:9). The less developed nations of today, however, do not seem to require any kind of internal stimulation to be innovative. They can see in the world around them the fruits of economic development, and quite naturally they want to share in as many of those goodies as possible—a situation often referred to as "the revolution of rising expectations." People in less developed nations today know what economic development is, and by studying the history of the highly industrialized nations they can see at least how it used to be achievable. If it was ever true that more people meant a greater chance of producing the genius that will solve the world's problems, it is a difficult argument to sustain today. As Nathan Keyfitz has pointed out, "the England that produced Shakespeare and shortly after that Newton held in all 5 million people, and probably not more than one million of these could read or write. . . . The thought that with more people there will be more talent for politics, for administration, for enterprise, for technological advance, is best dismissed. . . . For the most part, innovation comes from those who are comfortably located and have plenty of resources at their disposal" (quoted in United Nations Fund for Population Activities, 1987:16). In any event, it seems unlikely that a spark such as population growth is necessary any longer, although there really is little solid evidence one way or another.

Controversy is always fed by contradictory evidence, and in 1981 Julian Simon, an economist at the University of Maryland, popularized his thesis that a growing human population is the "ultimate resource" in the search for economic improvement. Eschewing the Malthusian idea that resources are finite, Simon suggests that resources are limited only by our ability to invent them and that, in essence, such inventiveness increases in proportion to the number of brains trying to solve problems. Coal replaced wood as a source of energy only to be replaced by oil, which may ultimately be replaced by solar energy—if we can figure out how to do it properly. From Simon's vantage point, innovation goes hand in hand with population growth, although he is quick to point out that *moderate,* rather than fast (or very slow) population growth is most conducive to an improvement in human welfare.

Simon, however, makes a crucial assumption: To be beneficial, population growth must occur in an environment in which people are free to be expressive and creative. For him, that means a free market or capitalist system. Marxists, of course, balk at such a suggestion.

Is Population Growth Unrelated to Economic Development?

The usual Marxist view is that population problems will disappear when other problems are solved, and that economic development can occur readily in a socialist society. Marx (and Engels) believed that each country at each historical period has its own law of population, and that economic development is related to the political-economic structure of society, not at all to population growth. Indeed, Marx seemed to be arguing that whether or not population grew as a nation advanced economically was due to the nature of social organization. In an exploitive **capitalist** society, the government would encourage population increase to keep wages low, whereas in a socialist state there would be no such encouragement. Socialists argue that every member of society is born with the means to provide his or her own subsistence; thus, economic development should proportionately benefit every person. The only reason why it might not is if society is organized to exploit the workers by letting capitalists take large profits, thereby depriving laborers of the full share of their earnings.

Leaders of less developed nations have argued that the world economic system operates the same way. The developed nations of the West "are charged with buying raw materials cheap from developing countries and selling manufactured goods dear, thus putting developing countries permanently in the role of debtors and dependents" (Walsh, 1974:1144). They have suggested further that if the economic power of the developed nations could be reduced and theirs enhanced, the boost to development in their nations would dissipate problems such as hunger and poverty that are currently believed to be a result of too many people. At such time the population problem will disappear because, they argue, it is not really a problem after all. The socialist view, then, is that when all other social problems (primarily economic in origin) are taken care of, people will deal easily with any population problem if, indeed, one occurs. This was obviously the attitude of Friedrich Engels, who wrote in a letter in 1881, "If at some stage communist society finds itself obligated to regulate the production of human beings . . . , it will be precisely this and this society alone, which can carry this out without difficulty" (quoted in Hansen, 1970:47).

Supporters of this position have some evidence to which they can appeal. In Russia in the 1920s after the Communist revolution, Lenin repealed anti-abortion laws and abolished the restrictions on divorce in order to free women; the result was a fairly rapid decline in the birth rate (although it turned out to be too rapid for the government's taste and in the 1930s abortions were again made illegal). On the other hand, the Cuban response to a Marxist government was exactly the opposite. Shortly after the Cuban revolution in 1959, the crude birth rate soared from 27 births per 1,000 population in 1958 to 37 per 1,000 in 1962. A Cuban demographer, Juan Perez de la Riva, has explained that after the revolution, rural unemployment disappeared, new opportunities arose in towns, and an exuberant optimism led to a lowering of the age at marriage and an abandonment of family planning (Stycos, 1971)—an ironically "Malthusian" response to a Marxist reorganization of society. Since then the birth rate has reestablished its prerevolutionary decline, facilitated by the easing of restrictions on abortion and the increasing availability of contraceptives (Hollerbach, 1980). The underlying causes of the more recent decline in fertility are similarly non-Marxist in nature: (1) increasing modernization, especially of the rural population, and (2) an economy that deteriorated after the initial flush of revolutionary success (Diaz-Briquets and Perez, 1981).

In sum, the evidence from Marxist countries such as Russia, Cuba, and, indeed, China (see Chapter 15 for more on China) suggests that a revolution may alter the demographic picture of a nation, but the relationship to economic development is somewhat cloudy. That overcast is also reflected in recent empirical work that seems to support a non-Marxist, but still "neutral," view of the relationship between population growth and per capita income. Using data for developing societies for the period 1965–84, Bloom and Freeman (1986) have concluded that despite rapid population growth, the labor markets in most developing countries were able to absorb the large population increase at the same time that per worker incomes were rising and productivity was increasing. In other words, just as Davis had pointed out in the theory of demographic change and response, a society's initial response to rapid population growth is to work harder to support its new members. But can that be sustained? Preston (1986) has argued that it could be in those areas that have sufficient natural resources and, more importantly, are making increasingly efficient use of the major societal resource—human capital. This means not simply more people (as Simon seems to infer) but a better-educated and better-managed labor force, combined with improved methods of communication and transportation (the economic infrastructure). Small, oil-rich nations have been able quickly to increase their per person wealth through the sale of a highly valued resource, and they have done so without much concern over their high rates of population growth. At the same time, there are other areas of the world in which problems are so deeply rooted and resources are so scarce that every additional human being will likely aggravate the economic condition of the society. In Bangladesh, it appears that real agricultural wages in the 1970s were actually below the level of the 1830s, and much of this decline occurred after population growth accelerated in the 1950s (Preston, 1986). For such a country, it is fairly easy to make the case that population growth is probably detrimental to economic development.

Is Population Growth Detrimental to Economic Development?

In the industrialized world it is popular to support the neo-Malthusian position that economic development is hindered by rapid population growth. In its basic form, it is a simple proposition. Regardless of the reason for an economy starting to grow, that growth will not be translated into development unless the population is growing slower than the economy. An analogy can be made to business. A storekeeper will make a profit only if his expenses (his overhead) add up to less than his gross sales. For an economy, the addition of people involves expenses (a **demographic overhead**) in terms of feeding, clothing, sheltering, and providing education and other goods and services, and if the demographic overhead equals or exceeds the national product, then no improvement (that is, no profit) will have occurred in the overall standard of living.

Let me illustrate the point further with a few numbers and a graph—see Figure 13.1. Between 1970 and 1980 the total national income of Mexico increased by a rather phenomenal 90 percent even after adjusting for inflation (United Nations, 1983). Yet during this time the population was increasing in size by more than one third, and as a result the rise in per person income was about 28 percent. Thus, population growth consumed 69 percent of the total improvement in national income. During that same period in the United States, national income rose by 27 percent, but only 11 percent of that rise was eroded by population increase. So, U.S. per capita income rose by 24 percent, nearly as much as in Mexico, but the economy had to grow only one-third as fast to accomplish the feat. Be aware, of course, that income per person is only an average, and obviously not everybody shared in that rise in wealth, either in the United States or in Mexico. This was particularly true in Mexico, where the economic rise could not be sustained. Indeed, it was based heavily on borrowing against future oil sales, but the price of oil fell and the Mexican economy stumbled badly in 1982. Of course, the population continued to increase, so per capita income in Mexico in 1986 was lower than it had been in 1980.

Figure 13.1 Population Growth Caused the Mexican Economy to Work Harder Than the American Economy for the Same Per Person Increase Between 1970 and 1980

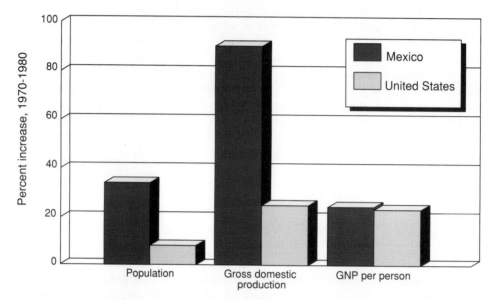

Sources: United Nations, 1983, Demographic Yearbook, 1981 (New York: United Nations), Table 7; United Nations, 1983, Yearbook of National Accounts Statistics, 1981 (New York: United Nations), Table 1.

The situation seems simple enough. If populations were growing more slowly, then economic development could take place more easily, and so the neo-Malthusian concludes that population growth is detrimental to economic development. Demeny has gone so far as to suggest that material progress in less developed nations "is so hindered by current demographic patterns and prospective demographic developments that in the foreseeable future a further widening of the . . . income gap [between developed and less developed nations] is highly probable" (1981:308). This position is so prevalent in Western society that I will discuss it in more detail, looking at the relationship from both sides.

Economic Development As a Source of Population Change   So far I have been looking at only one side of the relationship between population growth and economic development, that is, the consequences of economic change when population changes. If we are to fully understand the position that population growth is a hindrance to economic development, we need to look at the other side of the coin as well. You will recall from Chapter 2 that most available data suggest it was economic development that spurred the declines in mortality and eventually helped motivate the decline in fertility in the industrialized countries. In other words, economic development was a stimulus first to a rise in the rate of population growth and then to a slowing in its growth rate. It is this relationship that underlies the theory of the demographic transition and that is pointed to by Marxists in rebuttal of the neo-Malthusian argument.

These relationships were clearly outlined in 1958 by Ansley Coale and Edgar Hoover in a study that is unprecedented in its impact on theory and research on population growth and economic development. They note that economic development led to a mortality decline in the developed countries, and that it was also the economic development of those countries that has led to mortality declines in the rest of the world. This is true whether or not you accept my earlier suggestion that population growth may have initially stimulated the economic growth that led to the Industrial Revolution. The important point here is that the demographic transition theory suggests that the same economic development that lowered death rates will have within it the motivation for couples to lower birth rates. Yet, since the death rates in the less developed nations dropped as a result of someone else's economic development, why should we expect a rise in motivation to limit fertility without similar intervention? More important, why should we care whether fertility declines? What difference will it make to the future well-being of a population to continue with high birth and low death rates? Neo-Malthusians, of course, answer that it may make a big difference.

Impact of Population Growth Rates on Economic Development   Population growth can make a difference in how many resources are consumed in the world—how much we have to pay for things like food and gasoline, and how much elbow room we have in the world. Population growth anywhere in the world may well threaten the quality of our own existence, as well as inhibit the improvement of life in those countries struggling to develop economically under the burden of daily-increasing numbers of people. Actually, at least three different aspects of population change affect the course of economic development—rates of growth, population size, and the age structure.

The starting point of economic development is the investment of **capital.** Capital represents a stock of goods used for the production of other goods rather than for immediate enjoyment. While capital may be money spent on heavy machinery or on an assembly line, it can better be thought of as anything we invest today to yield income tomorrow (Spengler, 1974). This means not only equipment and construction, but also investments in education, health, and, in general, the accumulation and application of knowledge. For an economy to grow, the level of capital investment must grow. Clearly, the higher the rate of population growth, the higher the rate of investment must be; this is what Leibenstein (1957) called the "population hurdle." If a population is growing so fast that it overreaches the rate of investment, then it will be stuck in a vicious Malthusian cycle of poverty; the economic growth will have been enough to feed more mouths but not enough to escape from poverty.

The problem is complicated by the fact that in today's rapidly growing populations poverty is already rampant, thus impeding the ability of a nation to save enough money for the investment required to push its economy into rapid growth. Furthermore, most of the less developed nations in the world today have histories of being colonized and dependent on other countries for their economic and political fortunes. Often this has meant that "not only were economic problems neglected but the native leadership was trained in political conflict rather than economic states-manship" (Kuznets, 1965:182). Heavy reliance is therefore placed on foreign capi-tal—money earned and saved by slower growing, richer nations. In those countries, of course, the initial capital investment required for development was much less in relative terms than it is today. There are several reasons for this, including the facts that the developed nations started out with considerably lower rates of population growth and they did not have to jump into a well-advanced world economic system that requires high levels of technology to compete.

The less developed nations face a different set of world circumstances in trying to improve economically than did the developed nations. Many of these circum-stances are probably (although not necessarily) hurdles. One example is energy—where will it come from? Vast amounts of energy, of course, are required for agriculture, manufacturing, transportation, and daily living. Water, wood, and coal were early resources cheaply converted to energy, but the world has become increas-ingly dependent on oil and, as you know, the price of oil has increased dramatically since the early 1970s. Countries that are hardest hit are, of course, the less developed nations that have few energy resources themselves. Only if oil-producing nations invest their profits in those countries that are hardest hit can the less developed nations hope to keep their economies growing. Marxists would argue that such an issue has no relevance to population growth, since a Communist world would distribute resources justly among those who need them. Neo-Malthusians, on the other hand, would point out that regardless of the economic order prevailing in a nation or in the world, a rapidly growing population will make it harder for an economy to find its way than would a slowly growing population.

Impact of Population Size on Economic Development   As a population grows larger, the ability to garner resources for development may grow progressively smaller. This is true for individual nations just as it is true for the entire world. Although we can conjure up images of standing room only at the point at which all economic activity most certainly would have to stop, in reality the limit is far less than that. But how much less? This is a question that is still puzzling but has been the object of a good deal of scrutiny, as researchers have tried to define an **optimum population size** for the earth or for a particular country. In trying to determine an optimum size, we ask how large a population can be before the level of living begins to decline.

It is widely recognized that there are economies of scale associated with size; that is, too few people may retard economic development as surely as too many people might. The world is much better off economically with 5 billion people than it was with 1 billion. General Motors can produce a car far more cheaply than you or I could build one, precisely because they sell so many cars that they can afford the expensive assembly plants that reduce production costs per car. Granting that larger is sometimes more economical, a population may grow too large to be efficient or so large that, at a given level of living, it will exhaust resources. When it reaches that point, it is said to have exceeded its **carrying capacity**—that size of population that could theoretically be maintained indefinitely at a given level of living.

The carrying capacity will vary according to which level of living you might choose for the world's population. The lower that level, the greater the number of people that can be indefinitely sustained. On the other hand, if the desired level of living is too high, you may well exceed the carrying capacity and start draining resources at a rate that will lead to their exhaustion. Once you have done that, you lower the long-run carrying capacity. For example, if you and everyone else in the world were content to live at the level of the typical South Asian peasant, then the number of humans that the world could carry would be considerably larger than if everyone were trying to live like the board of directors of General Motors. Indeed, it is highly doubtful that the world has enough resources for 5 billion people to ever approach the level of living of a successful business executive.

The most elaborate and well-known empirical investigation of an optimum population size for the world is the Club of Rome study, *Limits to Growth* (Meadows et al., 1972; Meadows, 1974). Their study addressed the question of what size of population will enable the earth to maximize the socioeconomic well-being of its citizens.

After building a computer model simulating various paths of population growth and capital investment in resource development, this team of social scientists came to the conclusion that the world's population is so large and is consuming resources at such a prodigious rate that by the year 2100 resources will be exhausted, the world economy will collapse, and the world's population size will plummet. After introducing their most optimistic assumption into the model, the Meadows' team describes the potential result in the following way:

> Resources are fully exploited, and 75 percent of those used are recycled. Pollution generation is reduced to one-fourth of its 1970 value. Land yields are doubled, and effective methods of birth control are made available to the world population. The result is a temporary achievement of a constant population with a world average income per capita that reaches nearly the present U.S. level. Finally, though, industrial growth is halted, and the death rate rises as resources are depleted, pollution accumulates, and food production declines (1972:147).

This was the gloomiest forecast of the impact of population size on economic development since the publication of Ehrlich's *Population Bomb* (1968), in which worldwide famine and war were seen as almost inevitable results of continued increases in the world's population. It was another variation on the Malthusian theme that the growth of population tends to outstrip resources, and, taken at face value, it could be viewed as so discouraging that there would be no point in worrying any longer; the population that we have at hand is already too large and has too much momentum for continued growth to permit further sustained improvements in the human condition. Of course, as the authors of *Limits to Growth* freely acknowledge, their models do not replicate the complexities of the real world, nor are they attempting to predict the future. Nonetheless, the study demonstrates the possibility that for the world as a whole, the optimum population is probably no larger than the present level.

The implications of this position are rather striking. Meadows and associates discuss the need for "dynamic equilibrium" in which population and capital remain constant, while other "desirable and satisfying activities of man—education, art, music, religion, basic scientific research, athletics, and social institutions . . ." also flourish (1972:180). In 1977, President Carter directed that a study be conducted "of the probable changes in the world's population, natural resources, and environment through the end of the century" (Council on Environmental Quality, 1980). The result was the "Global 2000" report, released in 1980, and containing equally dreary conclusions:

> If present trends continue, the world in 2000 will be more crowded, more polluted, less stable ecologically, and more vulnerable to disruption than the world we live in now. . . . Barring revolutionary advances in technology, life for most people on earth will be more precarious in 2000 than it is now. . . . At present and projected growth rates, the world's population would reach 10 billion by 2030 and would approach 30 billion by the end of the twenty-first century. These levels correspond closely to estimates by the U.S. National Academy of Sciences of the maximum carrying capacity of the entire earth (Council on Environmental Quality, 1980:1–3).

There is little comfort here for countries not yet fully developed, since for them, the implication is that they should cease growing demographically and hope for a redistribution of income from the wealthier nations.

Before you take those gloomy forebodings too seriously, let me offer a comment on the idea of a population decline in the wake of economic collapse. Van de Walle (1975) has noted that the *Limits to Growth* model assumes historical reversibility—that mortality rates could rise in the future just as they declined in the past. Van de Walle feels that is an unwarranted assumption, since our knowledge of nutrition would not be lost, nor would we lose our ability to reorganize life around different standards of living that could maintain health despite a reduced supply of food. Let me remind you as well of Simon's argument that specific resources, such as oil, may be finite, but in broad, generic terms, energy as a resource may be infinite—we just need to be clever enough to unlock the mysteries of the universe.

The Malthusian specter of sheer numbers of people exhausting available resources is rather overwhelming, and as a result it disguises other, more subtle negative consequences that population growth has for economic development—consequences that are far more certain to be problems than are worldwide famine, war, or economic collapse. The consequences to which I refer are those associated with the age structure of rapidly growing populations.

Impact of Age Structure on Economic Development   A rapidly growing population has a young age structure. As you will remember from Chapter 8, this means that a relatively high proportion of the population is found in the young ages. Two important economic consequences of this youthfulness are that the age structure affects the level of dependency, and it puts severe strains on the economy to generate savings for the investment needed for industry and for the jobs sought by an ever-increasing number of new entrants into the labor force.

Dependency   A major theme of the Coale and Hoover (1958) study of economic development (which I mentioned earlier in the chapter) is that a high rate of population growth leads to a situation in which the ratio of workers (people of working age) to dependents (people either too young or too old to work) is much lower than if a population is growing slowly. This means that in a rapidly growing society each worker will have to produce more goods (that is, work harder) just to maintain the same level of living for each person as in a more slowly growing society. This may seem like an obvious point. The father of six children will have to earn more money than the father of three just to keep his family living at the same level as the smaller family. But it goes deeper than that. A nation depends at least partially on savings from within its population to generate investment capital with which to expand the economy, regardless of the kind of political system that exists. With a very young age structure, money gets siphoned off into taking care of more people (buying more food, and so on) rather than into savings per se (Kelley, 1973). As Kelley has pointed out, a very old age structure may also be conducive to low levels of saving, since in the retirement ages people may be taking money out rather than putting it in.

Entry into the Labor Force   In a growing population the number of prospective entrants into the labor force is also growing every year, as each group of young people matures to an economically active age. If economic development is to occur, the number of new jobs must at least keep pace with the number of people looking for them. The expansion of jobs is, of course, related to economic growth, which in turn relies on investment, which may be harder to generate with a young age structure.

There is an added wrinkle when rates of population growth are high. The combination of larger families, typically the responsibility of the mother, and the stiffer competition for jobs is likely to discourage employment of women. As Ester Boserup (1970) has shown, the jobs that women have in most human societies are those that men do not want, and with high rates of population growth the level of unemployment tends to be high, leaving fewer jobs that a man will refuse. We may suspect this to be another path to the vicious cycle of national poverty. When fertility is high and death rates low, a woman's family will be large and the probability of employment low. Without the prospect of obtaining a job, a woman may have few incentives for a life-style that precludes marriage and childbearing, and she may be held rather tightly in the web of the family.

POLICY IMPLICATIONS OF THE DEBATE

I have tried thus far to summarize the main aspects of each of the three major positions in the world debate over population growth and economic development. Ultimately, of course, each of these positions must be reconciled with the fact that population growth cannot continue for very long, regardless of its short-run impact on economic development. In the long run, the rate of population growth must go to zero, because the planet simply cannot tolerate growth indefinitely. Furthermore, virtually no one would dispute that as the growth rate of the world's population subsides, it is vastly preferable that it do so because the birth rate has gone down, not because the death rate has gone up. Thus, ultimately fertility must go down if the human condition is to be maximized. None of the three positions discussed is inconsistent with a long-run decline in fertility, but each has different approaches to dealing with birth rates in the short run.

If you believe that population growth is good for societal development, then you are probably a pronatalist and argue that birth control will have to wait until your country increases its population. If you are a Marxist, you will most likely suggest that the only reasonable use of birth control is to free women from the domination of men. If you are a neo-Malthusian, you will no doubt argue that family planning is a necessary precursor to economic development, and that a few dollars spent on family planning may be worth a hundred dollars in industrial investment. In other words, you will believe that it is less costly and more economically advantageous to spend money preventing births than to spend it trying to raise and find jobs for more people (Enke, 1960; Demeny, 1971).

MEXICO AS A CASE STUDY

In their classic study of population growth and economic development, Coale and Hoover (1958) looked briefly at the situation in Mexico, although their major effort was devoted to an examination of India. Unlike India, the first country in the world to institutionalize family planning programs as a national government policy, Mexico was until the mid-1970s pronatalist in its official policy. Since Mexico had one of the highest rates of natural increase in the world until very recently, it is of considerable interest to ask if population growth has been a stimulus or a hindrance to development. And what has been the government's position with respect to population programs?

The Analysis by Coale and Hoover

When Coale and Hoover began their analysis in 1958, the Mexican population was already growing very rapidly as a result of declining mortality and sustained high fertility. Indeed, Mexico's population growth dates back to at least 1930, when mortality began to decline. By 1955 the life expectancy at birth (for both sexes) was about 53 years. This was equivalent to a crude death rate of 14 per 1,000 population, and the rate of natural increase was 30 per 1,000, or 3 percent per year—well above the world average. Coale and Hoover made projections of future population size in Mexico, assuming that mortality would decline steadily so that by 1985 the life expectancy at birth would be 70 years. They made three different projections, based on three alternate assumptions about future trends in fertility: (1) it would remain unchanged; (2) it would decline by 50 percent between 1955 and 1980; and (3) it would decline by 50 percent between 1965 and 1980. They then examined the differential impact on future economic growth and development.

In 1955 Mexico had a population of about 31 million, and the projected population by 1970 was 50 million; only if fertility had dropped dramatically from 1955 through 1970 would the population have been less than that. Coale and Hoover argued that the higher the rate of population growth and the larger the population, the more difficult economic development would be. With sustained high growth, (1) Mexico would have potential difficulty in maintaining its agricultural self-sufficiency; (2) exports would have to be curtailed; (3) the import of consumer goods would rise at the expense of capital goods; and (4) foreign investment would also decline as the high rates of population growth made the future of economic growth more uncertain. In general, more people means more consumption, less investment, and ultimately a lower level of per capita income. The lower the fertility rate, the faster per person output will rise, simply because more money can be used for development of the economy rather than for maintenance of the population. Coale and Hoover saw no reason to expect a decline in fertility in Mexico, at least not as a consequence of government action. However, they did see some possibility, since the Mexican population was more than one-third urban, and urban fertility is lower than rural fertility. In general, their analysis suggested that population growth would be a substantial deterrent to economic development in Mexico. Has it been?

What Has Happened?

In the 1970 Mexican census the population was listed as about 51 million, 1 million more even than the maximum estimate by Coale and Hoover based on the 1955 population. Mortality declined slightly faster than they had anticipated; their estimate suggested that the life expectancy at birth for Mexican males in 1970 would be 61 years, and the actual figure was 64 years. They anticipated the continued high fertility, and their model had suggested an average annual rate of population growth of 3.4 percent per year by 1970, compared with the observed rate of 3.3 percent. Out-migration to the United States probably kept the growth rate lower than it might otherwise have been. By 1988 the population of Mexico was estimated to be 84 million, with a growth rate of about 2.4 percent per year (Population Reference Bureau, 1988).

While it is true that fertility levels in cities in Mexico are lower than those in the rural areas, fertility is still high in urban places. According to the National Fertility and Health Survey in 1987, the total fertility rate for urban areas of Mexico was estimated to be 3.7, compared with 5.6 in rural areas (Urbina, 1988). In 1986 the total fertility rate for the entire nation was estimated to be 3.8, a substantial decline from 6.7 in 1960, and even an amazing decline from 6.0 in 1975. However, this was still far above the fertility rate of the United States, as you can see in Figure 13.2, and it was accompanied by continued high rates of overall population growth. What has been its relationship to economic development?

Earlier in the chapter I indicated that the rate of economic growth in Mexico was quite high during the 1970s but has suffered considerably since 1982. Nonetheless, the average Mexican in 1988 was nearly 20 percent better off economically than in 1978, even after controlling for inflation, so by that criterion economic development was taking place even in the face of rapid population growth. On the other hand, per person income was lower in 1988 than in 1982, so a real question must be raised about the future development of the Mexican economy.

Figure 13.2   Fertility Is Much Higher in Mexico Than in the United States

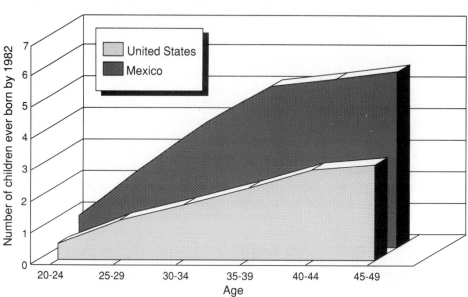

Mexico is growing much more rapidly than the United States because women there are having so many more children. In 1982, Mexican women at each age had already borne substantially more children than had Americans. For example, by her mid-thirties the average Mexican woman had three more children than the average American woman. *Sources:* Adapted from Consejo Nacional de Poblacion, Mexico, Resultados Principales de la Encuesta Nacional Demografica de 1982, Table III.11; and U.S. Bureau of the Census, 1983, "Population Profile of the United States: 1982," Current Population Reports, Series P-23, No. 130, Table 13.

Let's look more deeply into the situation by examining four important ways in which economic growth might be altered and economic development slowed by population growth, according to the Coale and Hoover model: (1) Has there been difficulty in maintaining agricultural self-sufficiency? (2) Have exports been curtailed? (3) Has the level of imports risen? (4) Has foreign capital investment diminished?

Agricultural Self-Sufficiency   In the decade of the 1960s, agricultural production climbed upward in Mexico as a result of the **Green Revolution** (see Chapter 14), but by the early 1970s the rate of expansion had slowed considerably. Between 1960 and 1970 the agricultural sector was increasing its productivity by 4.5 percent per year, but it increased at a slower rate, 3.4 percent, between 1970 and 1982 (World Bank, 1984a), and even more slowly (2.0 percent) between 1982 and 1985 (Food and Agriculture Organization, 1986a).

Throughout the 1960s and into the 1970s, agriculture had been the slowest growing sector in the entire Mexican economy, and Mexico had not been able to maintain food self-sufficiency. When Jose Lopez Portillo took office as President of Mexico in 1976 he made self-sufficiency in basic foodstuffs a primary goal of his administration (Gibbs, 1982). When he relinquished his position to Miguel de la Madrid in 1982 Mexico had not quite reached that point, but in 1982 the amount of grain imported was 24 percent less than it had been in 1974 (World Bank, 1984a). This was occasioned by the fact that annual food production in 1981, for example, was 55 percent higher than in 1970, while the population had increased by 37 percent. To help increase production Mexico has been increasing the amount of land under cultivation and, more importantly, has increasingly mechanized agriculture. Between 1974 and 1984 the number of tractors in Mexico increased by 57 percent and the number of harvester-threshers went up by 36 percent (Food and Agriculture Organization, 1986a), and the amount of fertilizer used by Mexican farmers increased by 271 percent between 1970 and 1981 (World Bank, 1984a).

Have Exports Been Curtailed and Have Imports Risen?   The 1970s were golden years for Mexico as the country floated in newly discovered reserves of oil. With oil to sell, Mexico decided to mortgage its future by borrowing heavily against future oil sales in order to finance further economic development. Thus, the level of imports rose substantially in the 1970s—more quickly than exports—leading to a trade deficit every year from 1970 through 1981. The fiscal crisis of 1982 turned things around in a rather perverse way from the Mexican perspective. Every year since 1982 Mexico has had more exports than imports, so there is the appearance of a favorable trade surplus (United Nations, 1987). Unfortunately for the average Mexican, the majority of those exports represented the payment of debts that had been built up during the 1970s. Of course, this situation is not necessarily attributable to population growth per se. It could be called the consequences of previous bad planning, but the pressure of a growing population was certainly an aggravating factor in the Mexican government's decision to spend more money than it had during the 1970s.

Has Foreign Capital Investment Diminished?   Coale and Hoover argued that as the balance-of-payments situation became less and less favorable (that is, as the total value of goods and services imported increasingly exceeded the value of exports), foreign investors would take their capital elsewhere, and this did happen in Mexico in the early 1970s. The foreign investment and balance-of-trade problems were so bad in 1976 that the Mexican government decided to devalue the peso—allowing it to drop from its previous value of 8¢ (American) to about 5¢. By 1988 the value of the peso had dropped to a tiny fraction of a U.S. penny. The initial impact was for many wealthy Mexicans to transfer their money to other countries, thus drawing away more of Mexico's capital (San Diego Union, 1977b). By 1981, Mexico's oil reserves had attracted renewed foreign investment (69 percent of it from the United States—Robinson, 1982), but only a year later, after the drop in world oil prices, Mexico was deeply in debt and in need of foreign investment, more for short-term economic survival than for long-term development. By 1985, Mexico was second only to Brazil in the net flow of capital out of the country.

Distribution of Income   There has been little change in the distribution of income in Mexico since 1950 (Nagel, 1978) and, according to the latest data from a survey in 1977 (World Bank, 1987), the income is less evenly distributed in that country than in the United States. For example, in the United States in 1978, the wealthiest 20 percent of families had 50 percent of the total American income; in Mexico, the top 20 percent controlled 58 percent of the total income. At the other end of the continuum, the lowest 20 percent in Mexico had only 3 percent of the nation's income, compared with 5 percent in the United States. A comparison of

AGE STRUCTURE AND ECONOMIC DEVELOPMENT IN INDONESIA

In this chapter I have argued that the age structure of a growing population may be an impediment to economic development since it carries with it a high demographic overhead, which drains resources away from development. However, there is another side to the coin, as Keyfitz (1965) has suggested in analyzing the situation in Indonesia, one of the most populous and, until recently, poorest nations in the world, where population is growing at the world average rate, while per capita income is only about $500 per year.

After World War II and the Indonesian revolution of the 1950s, the death rate went down (while the birth rate possibly rose), leading to a very young population; by 1961 42 percent of all Indonesians were under age 15. This meant that the number of people entering the labor force would more than double between 1961 and 1971. Could the economy handle such an onslaught of people? Wouldn't the prognosis be an economic crisis? Keyfitz thought the answers to these questions could easily be yes and no, respectively. He reasoned that since the level of literacy had risen sharply in Indonesia during the 1950s, the rural youth who were better educated would move toward the city "where opportunity seems to beckon" (Keyfitz, 1965:664). If these young people could be put to work productively, they would represent a tremendous source of human capital from

which the economy could draw as Indonesia tries to establish a nation out of a group of formerly colonized islands. It is, of course, the young who are economically and politically malleable and mobile, and in Indonesia the "shock" of a sudden, dramatic rise in the number of entrants into the labor force could be beneficial in jolting the economy into a spurt of greater productivity.

The 1961 census showed 7.7 million people aged 15–19 (that is, essentially the age of joining the labor force). The 1971 population of that age was 11.4 million (United Nations, 1975)—a 48 percent increase; and in 1980 there were more than 15 million Indonesians aged 15–19. Has this shock wave of troops into the labor force been beneficial or calamitous? The answer seems to lie somewhere in between. Despite the enormous increase in population in a nation that already is the world's fifth most populous, the literacy rate has continued to climb for both males and females, and labor force participation rates have also increased over time, especially for females (U.S. Bureau of the Census, 1979b; World Bank, 1987). Furthermore, between 1980 and 1985, rice production rose by 31 percent, staying well ahead of the population increase of 11 percent. Overall, from 1980 to 1985, food production increased by 19 percent in Indonesia (compared, for example, with a rise of 9 these data with an earlier (1968) survey of income distribution in Mexico suggests that in the period from 1968 to 1978 the Mexican economy became less equitably distributed.

Dependency Ratios   In 1960 the dependency ratio (the ratio of people aged 0–14 and 65+ to people aged 15–64) was 0.90 in Mexico, and by 1979 it had increased to 0.94. Thus, the dependency burden increased in Mexico even while per person income was rising by 55 percent, demonstrating that a rising dependency

percent in Mexico); and the production of all commodities increased by 21 percent during that time (compared with 5 percent in Mexico) (World Bank, 1987). In fact, between 1970 and 1982 the annual rate of growth in manufacturing in Indonesia was one of the highest in the world (much as had been true for Mexico in the period 1960–70—World Bank, 1984a).

Per capita income also rose in Indonesia during the 1970s, increasing by 66 percent between 1970 and 1980. But not everything that was going up was necessarily beneficial. For example, the number of unemployed Indonesians increased by 1,200 percent between 1970 and 1982—from 31,000 to 368,000. Furthermore, inflation in Indonesia in the 1970s was one of the highest in the world. Between 1965 and 1980 prices were increasing by 34 percent per year compared, for example, with a 6 percent per year increase in the United States during that same time (World Bank, 1987).

The case of Indonesia illustrates that, at least in the short run, increases in the younger ages of a population may be associated with a stimulated economy, but whether that effect can be maintained in the face of yearly increases in the foreseeable future is something you will want to watch for. Indeed, the case of Mexico, which I discuss in some detail in this chapter, is perhaps a model with respect to portending the future for Indonesia. Mexico, like Indonesia, experienced rapid economic growth at the same time that its population was making an initial spurt in size. But the momentum of population growth is much greater than that of economic growth, and Indonesia, like Mexico, has discovered that sustained economic development is very difficult in the face of rapid population growth. The economy may bend with world price fluctuations, but population momentum yields only to far greater pressures.

Until the mid-1960s, when the Sukarno government was replaced, Indonesia's population policy was officially pronatalist. However, the Suharto government inaugurated a family planning program on the main island of Java in 1969, and it has been spreading to the other islands since then (Sinquefield and Sungkono, 1979). By 1982 an estimated 53 percent of Indonesian women were contraceptive users (the pill is the favorite), and the total fertility rate had declined from 5.6 in 1970 to 3.3 in 1988. Even so, current projections indicate that by the year 2020 there will be as many Indonesians as there are Americans, and only time will tell whether the Indonesian economy can continue to develop as it absorbs an additional 37 million people between 1988 and the end of this century.

ratio did not foreclose the possibility of economic development. But Coale and Hoover had also foreseen that possibility, suggesting that "Mexico may be able to achieve rising economic welfare for 30 years or even for a half-century without major declines in fertility" (Coale and Hoover, 1958:335). However, they argued that the relative deterioration of the economy (which is at least aggravated by high fertility) would eventually catch up with Mexico. In a study in 1973, Isbister concluded that a decline in fertility in Mexico would almost certainly stimulate savings and thus the economy, but continued high fertility would tend to undermine both. Coale himself reevaluated the situation in Mexico in the late 1970s and again in the 1980s and drew essentially the same conclusions (1978; 1986). By 1988 the dependency ratio had declined to .85, entirely a result of the fairly dramatic drop in fertility that has been occurring in Mexico since the 1970s. Mexico has thus experienced a multiphasic response to population growth. The first response was for the economy to expand to meet the needs of the multiplying numbers of people. This was accompanied by migration from rural to urban areas (especially to Mexico City, as I discussed in Chapter 12), and migration out of the country (especially to the United States, as I discussed in Chapter 7). The more recent response has been for the birth rate to drop, a phenomenon that has been aided by public policy.

Population Policy Implications

It is by no means certain that population growth is holding back economic development in Mexico, but the suspicion is certainly there (Urquidi, 1975; 1987). The Mexican government has the same suspicion, and in 1973 it took an initial step toward population control. In 1970 President Luis Echeverria had campaigned on a pronatalist platform, but in 1973 that policy was reversed and the government launched a program of voluntary family planning. The Mexican constitution was modified in January 1974 to guarantee every couple the right to plan their family freely (Rowan, 1976), and birth control information and services have been made available in hundreds of health clinics throughout Mexico. The result has been a surprisingly swift reaction on the part of the Mexican population. Faced with inflation, recession, and high levels of unemployment, Mexicans have turned rather dramatically to contraception to ease their burdens by limiting family size. In 1977 there were nearly a million new acceptors of contraception (primarily the pill), compared with only 44,000 in 1972, the year before the government changed its policy (U.S. Bureau of the Census, 1979c). As a result, between 1974 and 1981 the age-specific birth rates dropped by 31 percent among women aged 30–34, by 32 percent among women aged 25–29, and by 28 percent among women aged 20–24. While it is still true that only an estimated 48 percent of the women are using contraceptives, the changes in fertility are clearly under way. Be mindful, however, that the battle is far from over for Mexico. The birth rate is still high even though it is declining, and between 1988 and the year 2000 the population of Mexico could increase from 84 million to 105 million, based solely on the momentum to growth from the people already born. Even with a rapid decline in fertility, Mexico's population will not likely stop growing until well into the twenty-first century, at which time its population could easily be larger than that of the United States. Needless to say, the economy of Mexico will be fully exercised by that time.

SUMMARY AND CONCLUSION

The relationship between economic development and population growth is currently a star attraction of world debate. Statistics clearly indicate that the two are associated with each other, but which is cause, which is effect, and could they actually be only coincidentally related (no cause and effect whatever)? That set of questions is at the center of the debate, which has three principal sides: (1) nationalists see population growth as a stimulus to economic development, (2) neo-Malthusians see it the other way around, and (3) Marxists say that population problems will disappear if economies are developed according to a socialist model. There is evidence to support each position, but in industrialized nations much research has recently gone into the idea that population growth must slow down before economic development (measured as an increase in average income per person) can occur. Economic development may be influenced not only by rates of population growth, but also by its size and the resulting age structure.

Examining Mexico as a case study in population growth and economic development, I noted that the economic welfare of the average Mexican has been rising (although the distribution of income is such that those at the top have undoubtedly benefited much more than those at the bottom) even in the face of very rapid population growth. However, in the 1970s the economy was experiencing an unfavorable balance of trade and difficulty attracting investors. For a brief period in the late 1970s and early 1980s, the economy was booming in Mexico while the birth rate was dropping noticeably. A decline in world demand for oil lowered the boom on the economy, so to speak, but fertility continues to drop while Mexico struggles to retain the economic gains made in the previous decade.

In examining the recent development of Mexico's economy in the face of incredibly rapid population growth, I noted that a major issue has been the ability to be self-sufficient for food. As you know, the issue of food production and consumption is of vital concern to the entire world, not just Mexico, and it is to this subject that I turn next.

MAIN POINTS

1. Economic development represents a growth in average income—a rise in the material well-being of people in a society.

2. Economic growth often occurs in conjunction with population growth, but economic development may be hampered by a high rate of population growth.

3. Data for the world indicate that high levels of average income are almost always associated with low rates of population growth, whereas high rates of population growth typically are accompanied by low levels of average income.

4. The worldwide debate over the relationship between population growth and economic development has three main ideological sides, which can roughly be characterized as nationalism, Marxism, and neo-Malthusianism.

5. Nationalists often argue that population growth is a stimulus to economic development—"the more the merrier" and "they're cheaper by the dozen."

6. The Marxist view is that population growth is actually unrelated to economic development, and that development along Marxist lines would negate the seemingly problematic nature of population growth.

7. Neo-Malthusians argue that population growth is detrimental to economic development.

8. It may be that high rates of population growth are detrimental to economic development, whereas low rates of growth are either not harmful or may in some cases actually be a stimulus to development.

9. Ultimately, continued population growth would lead to a population too large for the world's resources.

10. High rates of population growth lead to a young age structure, which may create demographic overhead costs that are too high for a developing economy.

11. Mexico is a country in which early population growth was accompanied by economic development; but more recently the sustained increase in size has created an economic strain, leading the government to advocate family planning.

SUGGESTED READINGS

1. World Bank, 1984, World Development Report 1984 (New York: Oxford University Press).

   The World Bank annually publishes a World Development Report, which includes a useful compendium of demographic information. In 1984, however, they produced a report devoted exclusively to population problems, timing its publication to coincide with the International Conference on Population held in Mexico City.

2. Ester Boserup, 1981, Population and Technological Change: A Study of Long-Term Trends (Chicago: University of Chicago Press).

   Boserup's work has been extremely influential in the field of population growth and economic development, and this volume will show you why.

3. Ansley Coale and Edgar Hoover, 1958, Population Growth and Economic Development in Low-Income Countries (Princeton, NJ: Princeton University Press).

   This book is such a classic in the area of the demography of economic development that it is the basis of comparison for evaluating virtually all theories and research findings.

4. Donald Meadows and associates, 1972, The Limits to Growth (New York: New American Library).

   You should read this more as history than as current research, but keep in mind that it was a controversial and widely debated attempt to quantify how close we were to population-induced ecological and economic disaster. This was the first of its kind in modern computer models of the future.

5. Thomas J. Goliber, 1985, "Sub-Saharan Africa: population pressures on development," Population Bulletin 40(1).

   Sub-Saharan Africa is the region where population is growing most quickly and economic development is occurring most slowly. This review of the situation provides you with a good background on the population/development dilemma.

CHAPTER 14
Population Growth and Food

"When food is abundant, it is wasted or treated as a commodity. But when food is scarce, it is regarded as the staff of life and its distribution becomes a highly emotional issue" (Abelson, 1975b:501). Is it really possible to feed everybody when the population is growing so rapidly? Will there be enough food in the year 2000 for the estimated 6 billion people who will be sharing the planet? I will devote the first half of this chapter to looking for answers to these questions, but the relationship between population growth and food is more complex than simply finding out how much grain there is or can be. The production of food for an ever-increasing number of people has among its costs pollution, which may restrict the ability of people to grow food and at the same time may lower the overall quality of life. It is this dilemma that I will consider in the second part of the chapter.

How, you ask, has the world come to find itself in this predicament, where it is not only hard to produce enough food, but where doing so may also be harmful to our health? How can it be that as you read this page, half a billion people are chronically undernourished (Lowenthal, 1982), and just in the time it takes you to read the rest of this page one person will have died of hunger while 32 babies were being born somewhere in the world? Part of the explanation is obviously related to population growth, part to economic development (or the lack of it) in agriculture, and part to the peculiarities of social organization (that is, the way food is distributed and the environment is handled). In this chapter I will analyze the pattern of food production in the world with a brief historical review from the Agricultural Revolution to the Green Revolution, looking closely at the relationship between food production and population growth. With this perspective in hand, I will turn to that often-asked and ever-troubling question: Will there ever be enough food to feed all of us adequately? Finally, I will examine the harmful side effects of attempting to increase agricultural yield, effects that may very well determine the upper limit of how many humans can be fed.

THE AGRICULTURAL REVOLUTION

It was roughly 10,000 years ago that humans first began to domesticate plants and animals, thereby making it possible to grow food and settle down in permanent villages. The domestication of plants, of course, hinged on the use of tools to work the ground near the settlement site, and the invention of those tools and their application to farming can be traced to many different areas of the world. Some of the earliest known sites are in the Dead Sea region of the Middle East (Cipolla, 1965), where the **Agricultural Revolution** apparently took place around 8000 B.C. From the eastern end of the Mediterranean, the agricultural innovations spread slowly west through Europe (being picked up in the British Isles around 3000 B.C.) and east through Asia.

Plants and animals were also domesticated in the Western Hemisphere several thousand years ago (Harlan, 1976), resulting in an increase in the amount of food that could be produced per person. As you can guess, increased food production was associated with population growth (possibly as a cause, possibly as a consequence).

Overall, the Agricultural Revolution "created an economy which, by . . . giving men a more reliable supply of food, permitted them to multiply to a hitherto unknown degree" (Sanchez-Albornoz, 1974:24). The classic Malthusian view, of course, is that the cultivation of land was the cause of population increase by lowering mortality and possibly raising fertility. Another view is that independent increases in population size, perhaps through a long-run excess of births over deaths, led to a need for more innovative ways of obtaining food, and so of necessity the revolution in agriculture gradually occurred (see Chapter 13). Once the increase in agricultural yield started, for whatever reason, it became possible for more people to be supported in a given locale; so even if independent increases in population size led to the Agricultural Revolution (in the way that necessity is the mother of invention), it may still be true that the economic changes fed back (literally) to encourage population growth.

Regardless of whether or not population growth triggered agricultural changes, the result of the Agricultural Revolution was undoubtedly to provide sustenance for more people than before. It is to that fact that you can attribute the slow but fairly steady growth of population in most areas of the world for several thousand years preceding the Industrial Revolution.

AGRICULTURE AND THE INDUSTRIAL REVOLUTION

The Industrial Revolution of the nineteenth century was preceded by, indeed made possible by, important changes in agriculture that significantly improved output (Clough, 1968). In Europe and North America those factors helping to increase agricultural productivity in a relatively short time included (1) mechanization of cultivating and harvesting processes, (2) increased use of fertilizers and irrigation, and (3) reorganization of land holdings (Poleman, 1975; Walsh, 1975).

The Industrial Revolution generated a host of mechanical devices, especially mechanical reapers, to greatly speed up harvesting. Drawn first by horses or oxen, reapers were pulled later by an even more efficient energy converter—the tractor. Overall, the mechanization of agriculture vastly increased the number of acres that one or a few people could farm, and also increased the amount of land that could be devoted to more than one crop per growing season, since land could be cultivated and harvested so much more easily.

Although mechanization was certainly a prime mover of increased productivity in agriculture, especially in North America where land was plentiful in relation to people, it is not an absolute requirement. The only requirement is an **intensification of agriculture,** that is, getting more out of the land than you used to, whether by mechanical means, people power, or whatever. In North America, where population density was low and labor was scarce, the increase in energy needed to intensify agriculture came from mechanical devices. In Japan, on the other hand, where even at the beginning of industrialization labor was at a surplus, the increase in energy came from people—people working harder and more efficiently on the land (Gordon, 1975).

One method of intensifying agriculture is to **multiple crop,** that is, to grow more than one crop per year on the same plot of ground. Multiple cropping, as well as making more intensive use of single-cropped land by using it every year (rather than letting it lie fallow), has been greatly aided by increased use of fertilizers and more extensive irrigation of areas previously too dry to cultivate.

Many agricultural innovations have also been made possible by reorganizing agricultural land. Collecting farms into large units and using meadows and pastures for cultivation rather than extensive grazing have increased production, particularly in the United States and Europe, since large farms introduce economies of scale that permit investment in expensive tractors, harvesters, fertilizers, irrigation systems, and the like. In the United States this is a process that has a long history and is still continuing; for example, between 1950 and 1978 the number of small farms (less than 180 acres) in the United States decreased from 4,120 to 1,349, a 67 percent decline (U.S. Department of Commerce, 1986). This does not mean that the number of acres under cultivation has declined very much, but rather that there is an increasing trend toward large commercial farms and away from small family farms. Let me add that the commercialization of farms is not so widely associated with large corporate holdings as is often believed. In 1982 only 31 percent of U.S. farmland was owned by corporations, most of which were family held.

While it may be intuitively obvious, it bears repeating that industrial expansion cannot occur unless agricultural production increases proportionately. Industrialization is typically associated with the migration of people out of rural and into urban areas, naturally resulting in a shift of workers out of agriculture and into industry. Therefore, those workers left behind must be able to produce more—enough for themselves and also for the nonagricultural sector of the population. Thus, you can see that the Industrial Revolution would have been impossible if agricultural production had not increased. Adam Smith, the classical economist, once remarked that "when by the improvement and cultivation of land . . . the labor of half the society becomes sufficient to provide food for the whole, the other half . . . can be employed . . . in satisfying the other wants and fancies of mankind" (quoted by Nicholls, 1970:296).

In the modern world those wants and fancies are usually related to economic development, which is vastly improved if a nation's agricultural sector can move into the modern era of high productivity per person, since without that high productivity a nation will be forced to import food. At best, importing food can tide a country over until agricultural development can take place, but as the population continues to grow at a rapid pace, the pressures mount to produce more food. This has been the case in many less developed countries in recent decades, where the attempt to increase food production quickly has generated the Green Revolution.

THE GREEN REVOLUTION

What Is It?

The **Green Revolution** began quietly in the 1940s in Mexico at the Rockefeller Foundation's International Maize and Wheat Improvement Center. The goal was to provide a means to increase grain production, and under the direction of Norman Borlaug, new **high-yield varieties** (HYV) of wheat were developed that are known as dwarf types, because they have shorter stems that produce more stalks than do most traditional varieties. In the mid-1960s these varieties of wheat were introduced into a number of countries, notably India and Pakistan, with spectacular early success—a result that had been anticipated after what the researchers saw in Mexico (Chandler, 1971). In 1954 the best wheat yields in Mexico had been about 3 metric tons per hectare, but the introduction of the HYV wheat (now used in about 90 percent of Mexico's wheat land—Karim, 1986) raised yields to 6 or even 8 tons if crops were carefully managed. A major difference was that the more traditional varieties were too tall and tended to lodge (fall over) prior to harvest, thus raising the loss per acre, whereas the dwarf varieties (being shorter) prevented lodging. This is critical, because lodging can be devastating; it destroys some ears of grain and damages others. Furthermore, resistance to lodging makes possible the heavy fertilization and irrigation necessary for high yields (Wortman, 1976).

The Green Revolution was not restricted to high-yield wheat, and in 1962 the Ford Foundation began to research rice breeding at the International Rice Research Institute in the Philippines. In a few short years a high-yield variety of dwarf rice had been developed that, like HYV wheat, dramatically raised per acre yields. Rice production was increased in India and Pakistan, as well as in the Philippines, Indonesia, South Vietnam, and several other less developed countries.

The rise in the number of acres devoted to HYV rice and wheat in the 1960s was significant enough to deserve a name, and so in 1968 the term "Green Revolution" was coined by the U.S. Agency for International Development (Brown, 1973). In 1965 only 200 acres of land in the world were planted in HYV wheat, but by 1971 the acreage had increased to 50 million. In India, wheat production rose from 11 million tons in 1965 to 27 million tons in 1968 (Brown, 1973); increased by 51 percent between 1970 and 1980 (Food and Agriculture Organization, 1981a); and rose another 28 percent between 1980 and 1985 (Food and Agriculture Organization, 1986a). There is, however, a catch in the Green Revolution—success requires more than simply planting a new type of seed. These plants require fertilizers, pesticides, and irrigation in rather large amounts, a problem compounded by the fact that fertilizer and pesticides are normally petroleum-based and the irrigation system requires fuel for pumping. These are expensive items, and the price of oil (and thus products derived from oil) has risen dramatically since the early 1970s. Thus, for a developing country to have its own Green Revolution, it has to have enough wealth to purchase the fertilizers, pesticides, and irrigation systems necessary to produce high yields, since without these accessories the yields from the HYV rice and wheat are about comparable to those from many traditional varieties. Because of these difficulties and others, it is reasonable to question how much of a "revolution" the Green Revolution really is.

How Much of a Revolution?

The Green Revolution, to be effective in all parts of the world, would require major changes in the way social life is organized in rural areas, not just a change in the plants grown or the fertilizers used. This is because the Green Revolution is based on Western (especially American and Canadian) methods of farming, in which the emphasis is on using expensive supplies and equipment and on the high-risk, high-profit principle of economies of scale—plant one crop in high volume and do it well (Wade, 1974).

If you are a traditional, subsistence farmer, that kind of agriculture will not necessarily appeal to you. You will be accustomed to growing a variety of crops, not only to round out your diet but also to lower your risk of failure, since even in poor seasons there is a good chance that something can be salvaged. Of course, in minimizing your risks you minimize your profit (that is, the ability to grow a big surplus) as well. Let me add that the major risk lies in the vagaries of nature—particularly bad weather (which I discuss later in the chapter), but also new kinds of pests and new kinds of diseases; an early frost can wipe out a crop and so can heavy rains. Furthermore, although HYV plants are bred to resist the most important diseases, and pesticides are effective against most pests, the life cycle of immunity is only about 5 years. After that time, new forms of pests and diseases have had a chance to establish themselves and can wipe out a crop. Obviously, if all your eggs are in one basket, so to speak, a crop failure can be economically disastrous. This kind of risk taking is commonplace in Western societies but requires a new way of thinking about the world for subsistence farmers in less developed nations.

Another important danger inherent in planting one crop or very few crops is nutritional deficiency. The HYVs are not much different in nutritional value from the earlier varieties of wheat and rice (Wade, 1974), and they may wind up replacing more nutritious crops such as beans, peas, and lentils. Poor nutrition can retard physical and mental growth, creating health and social problems for a society, which compound the difficulties of trying to increase agricultural productivity and economic development. Thus, the kinds of changes that Western farmers might make to increase the food supply could (indeed, already have in some cases) lower the quality of existence in some areas of the less developed world (Lappé and Collins, 1977).

The Green Revolution is, then, more than just a breakthrough in plant breeding. To be effective it requires large-scale planting (which may require altering land tenure arrangements) and other forms of social organization. Furthermore, it demands massive doses of energy-dependent products such as fertilizers, pesticides, and irrigation. A group of American agricultural scientists has estimated that producing an acre of high-yield corn requires an amount of energy equivalent to 80 gallons of gasoline (Brown, 1973). In less developed countries, a subsistence farmer's entire annual income might have to be spent to participate in the Green Revolution, and the price of participation has been rising. In 1970 it took one bushel of wheat to buy a gallon of gasoline, but by 1980 the price had risen to six bushels (Brown, 1981). Obviously, no farmer is likely to pay such a high price unless credit is extended on fairly easy terms, and such credit is not readily available in many areas of the world. Energy costs were not an issue during the developmental phases of the Green Revolution, and so it should not surprise you that the biggest points were scored prior to the rise in fuel prices.

During the late 1960s and up to 1972, the developing nations grew enough of their own food so that, although they did not become completely self-sufficient, their relative dependence on developed nations did not increase. At the same time, food production in the developed countries considerably outstripped population growth, providing for an increase in the amount people could eat at home while still leaving a surplus for developing nations (see Figure 14.1). Between 1960 and 1974 the world's population increased by 33 percent—from 3 to almost 4 billion; at the same time, the world's production of grain increased by 48 percent (Abelson, 1975a). Yet the figures for the world obscure the regional problems. For example, in 1965 India had to import 11 million metric tons of grain to feed its population. Then production rose as the Green Revolution worked its wonders, and in 1972 India was nearly self-sustaining. Unfortunately, the momentum has been hard to sustain, largely due to the vagaries of the weather, which influences how good the crops will be. As you are

Figure 14.1   Population and Food Production Growth

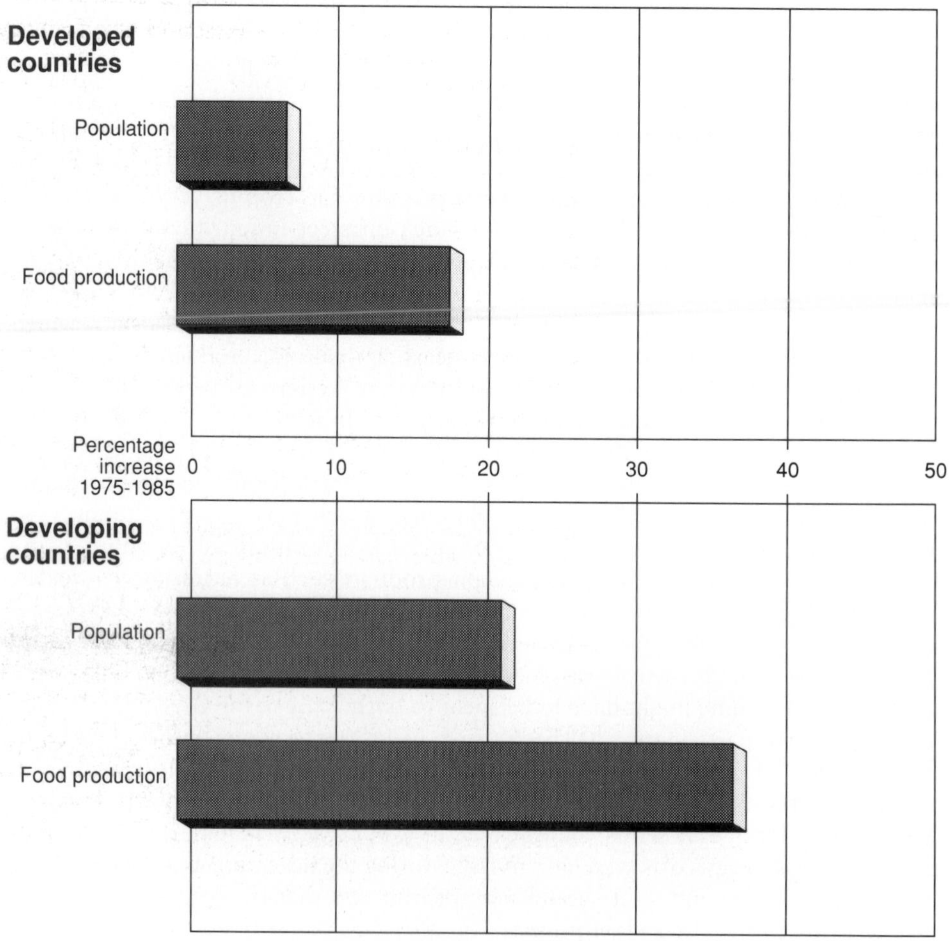

Data from the Food and Agriculture Organization of the United Nations show that food production stayed ahead of population growth from 1975 to 1985, even in the developing nations of the world. *Source:*   Adapted from data in Food and Agriculture Organization of the United Nations, 1986, Production Yearbook, 1985 (Rome: FAO), Tables 3 and 4.

no doubt aware, scarcity of food has been a particular problem in sub-Sarahan Africa. At least five rapidly growing sub-Saharan countries (Ethiopia, Mozambique, Namibia, Réunion, and South Africa) produced less food in 1985 than they had 5 years earlier, and most African nations have not been able to keep production levels increasing as rapidly as the population (Food and Agriculture Organization, 1986a).

In general, however, world food security has been high on the list of the United Nations' priorities since the 1970s, and globally the food supply has been expanding at a faster pace than the population, due largely to the spread of the Green Revolution. In fact, in 1985, developing nations were having to import food at only half the rate of 1980 (Food and Agriculture Organization, 1986b). China, in particular, has been striving for food self-sufficiency. The Chinese managed to reach that goal in 1984 through 1986, but they have discovered (as has India) that the constant pressure from population momentum makes self-sufficiency difficult to hang on to, especially in the face of constantly uncertain weather. The world's biggest food importer, however, is not a poor, developing nation at all but rather the Soviet Union, whose agricultural quandaries (including a series of below-average harvests and general mismanagement) have been compounded by the desire of the Soviets to increase consumer beef consumption, which requires more grain to feed the cattle.

Although imports of food into developing countries have been rising, the number of countries exporting grain is very limited, and you might well ask about the prospects for feeding people in those countries that are not agriculturally self-sufficient. The current very young age structure of the world implies a high growth momentum even if fertility should decline immediately all over the world, and so we know that the world will have to provide food for a few billion more people in the foreseeable future than there are already. Can food production meet this demand?

HOW CAN FOOD PRODUCTION BE INCREASED?

There are two aspects to increasing the amount of food grown. One problem is to grow enough food; the second is to grow food where the need is greatest (that is, in poor and rapidly growing nations). I deal here primarily with the first problem—the global issue. There are several different approaches to increasing the total food resources available, and they can be categorized into two broad groups: increasing the amount of land under cultivation and increasing the yield per acre. There is also a short-run solution—to distribute food more equitably.

Increasing Farmland

Only 11 percent of the world's land surface is readily suitable for crop production, and most of it is already under cultivation. This was the first response to growing more food for more people. In 1860 there were an estimated 572 million hectares of land in the world cleared for agricultural use. As the populations of

Europe and North America expanded in the late nineteenth century, the amount of farmland in these regions virtually doubled. More recently, the population pressure in developing countries has been accompanied by an expansion of farmland in those parts of the world. All of this adds up to a total of 1,414 million hectares of farmland in the world today—nearly a tripling since 1860 (Revelle, 1984). I should note that the portion of the globe not yet under cultivation remains that way because either it is too wet, too cold, too dry, or too shallow (not enough topsoil) or it has chemical problems (too acidic or alkaline) (Hendry, 1988). If that list of problems is not dismal enough, consider that the amount of good farmland is actually shrinking. In some parts of the world this is a result of soil erosion or desert encroachment, while in many other places it is a consequence of urban sprawl. The sites of most major cities are in abundant agricultural regions that can provide fresh food daily to the city populations; only recently have transportation and refrigeration lessened (but not eliminated) that need. As cities have grown in size, nearby agricultural land increasingly has been graded and paved for higher-profit residential or business uses. For example, in the United States about 40 million acres of land are in urban use, and about half of that was at one time cropland. In addition, there are about 32 million acres of land in the United States that are covered by highways and roads (Pimentel et al., 1976). The uses of good farmland in the United States for nonagricultural purposes has become enough of an issue so that in 1979 two federal agencies (the Department of Agriculture and the Council on Environmental Quality) commissioned a joint 18-month study to investigate the problem. The conclusion was that the United States is losing 3 million acres per year (an area roughly the size of Connecticut) of actual or potential cropland through conversion to nonfarm use.

> The allure of farm land to the developer is clear: it's generally flat and well-drained, thus good for building. It's probably outside town limits and therefore taxed at cheaper county rates. And the land is probably family-owned, an important factor with farming costs going up, children moving to the city and nonfarming family members pressuring for a quick sale (Carlson, 1981:25).

Such conversion is extremely difficult to reverse and, as the Assistant Secretary of Agriculture of the United States said in 1980, "When farmland goes, food goes. Asphalt is the land's last crop" (quoted by the Environmental Fund, 1981:1). The problem is not peculiar to the United States. Chinese officials reported in 1982 that 16.5 million acres of land (6 percent of the total in China) had been lost in the previous year to farming through conversion to urban and other uses (San Diego Union, 1982d).

Soil erosion is a major problem throughout the world, as more than 26 billion tons of topsoil are washed or blown away each year, often as a result of deforestation, which leaves the ground unprotected from rain and wind (Brown et al., 1988). Thus we are losing ground (quite literally) at the same time that few places in the world still await the plow. Some notable exceptions are portions of sub-Saharan Africa and areas in the interior of South America. Those regions are the most feasible for cultivation of the remaining unused land, but they could hardly be considered choice. To farm sub-Saharan Africa, the tsetse fly would have to be eradicated; and for the interior of South America to be farmed, the jungle would have to be tamed. Besides, in many jungle areas, clearing the land has revealed very thin topsoil unsuitable for farming (Ehrlich and Ehrlich, 1972; Brown 1981). In North America, much of the land that used to belong to the "soil bank" has already been brought back into production, and the land that remains is marginal in the sense that vast amounts of time and money would be required to prepare it for cultivation. Even then expected yields per acre would still be less than in the prime agricultural zones (Pimentel et al., 1976), and it has been estimated that marginal land would cost an average of $2,000 per acre to be brought under cultivation. In the United States there are about 127 million acres of land that could be farmed if push came to shove. But to develop that land would require that swamps be drained, deserts irrigated, and land graded—all at very high cost in both dollars and energy (Brewer, 1981). As Lester Brown, President of Worldwatch Institute, has commented, "If you are willing to pay the price, you can farm the slope of Mt. Everest" (Newsweek, 1974:62).

It has also been suggested that a viable source of "land" is the sea—mariculture, or the "blue revolution," as some have called it. Farming the sea includes both fishing and harvesting kelp and algae for human consumption, but the expense of growing kelp and other plants is again so great that it does not appear to be an economically viable alternative to cultivating land. Fish, of course, are an excellent source of protein, and fish by-products include a fairly cheap form of fertilizer, making them an attractive resource. Between 1950 and 1970 the annual yield of fish increased from 21 to 68 million tons (Brown, 1981), and the supply of fish seemed almost inexhaustible. But the catches dropped off significantly in the 1970s, due at least in part to overfishing, and between 1974 and 1984 the catch of fish increased at almost exactly the same rate as has the population, thus just maintaining the status quo (Food and Agriculture Organization, 1986c). Furthermore, as the fish catch ran into trouble, the level of conflict between fishing nations increased, especially over the issue of territorial limits. The United Nations attempted to deal with this in 1982 by adopting the Convention on the Law of the Sea. Whereas previously most fishing stocks in the ocean were viewed as the common property of all nations, the new Law of the Sea provides each nation with jurisdiction over fish catches within 250 miles of its coast. In practice, this encompasses about 90 percent of the world's fish catch, and it has generated considerable readjustment of the world's fishing industry (Food and Agriculture Organization, 1986c). The new territorial limits may enhance some new approaches to mariculture that are being tested by scientists at the Smithsonian Institution. Their work involves growing algae on underwater screens; the algae is to be the food for fish that are kept in large underwater cages. Studies in the Caribbean have shown promising results for these maritime fisheries (ISR Newsletter, 1988).

Ehrlich and Ehrlich commented that "biologists have carefully measured the riches of the sea, considered the means of harvesting them, and have found them wanting as a solution to the food problem" (1972:125). In the same vein, the Global 2000 report concluded that "on a per capita basis, fish may well contribute less to the world's nutrition in 2000 than today" (Council on Environmental Quality, 1980:23). Thus, the evidence all seems to point to the fact that with current levels of food from the sea, and if all available land were to be cultivated at current yields per acre, that still would not be enough to feed the world's population in the year 2000 (Pimentel et al., 1976). There are about 4 billion acres of natural (not including marginal) farmland in the world, and there are more than 5 billion people—roughly eight tenths of an acre of **arable** land per person. The average American diet, though, currently requires 1.25 acres of production per year (Pimentel et al., 1976). Thus, at present levels of production, there is only enough land to support 3.2 billion people on an average American diet, even if all that land were used. In other words, unless the developed nations drastically reduce their food consumption, the growing world's population virtually demands a substantial increase in the yield from the land.

Increasing per Acre Yield

There are several different ways that output from the land can be increased, and frequently methods must be combined if substantial success is to be realized. Those methods include plant breeding, increased irrigation, and increased use of pesticides and fertilizers. In addition, I will comment on some problems, relating especially to land reform and financing, that may limit the motivation or ability to implement these means of raising per acre yield.

Plant Breeding   I mentioned the fact that plant breeding was the cornerstone of the Green Revolution. The plants involved have been principally wheat and rice, but there is the potential, of course, for breeding HYV soybeans, peanuts, and other high-protein plants. Since HYV grains (wheat and rice) have already found wide acceptance throughout the world, though, you probably should not look to an overwhelming increase in HYV planting as a solution. About 35 percent of the world's cropland devoted to wheat and rice is currently utilizing HYV technology (Karim, 1986), but the adoption rate has slowed considerably because of the tremendous social and cultural changes that accompany the Green Revolution, as I have already mentioned.

One possible avenue of genetic research is to raise the nutrient levels of crops now being cultivated. Remember that HYV wheat and rice are about equal nutritionally to the wheat and rice they replace, so if foods can be developed that offer more nutrition per plant, then we will have improved the ability to reduce malnutrition even without increasing per acre yields. An example is the development of synthetic species such as **triticale,** which is derived from a cross of wheat and rye (Wittwer, 1975). Another candidate is the winged bean, sometimes known as "a supermarket on a stalk" because the plant combines the desirable nutritional characteristics of the green bean, garden pea, spinach, mushroom, soybean, bean sprout and potato—all on one plant that is almost entirely edible, save the stalk (National Research Council, 1982). It is already being grown in parts of Africa and South Asia.

At least as important as the nutritional aspect of plant breeding is the development of disease and pest resistance. The rapid change in pest populations requires constant surveillance and alteration of seed strains. Insects are very much our competitors for the world food supply, and it has been estimated that pests of all kinds may wipe out as much as a third of all crops in the world each year (Wittwer, 1977). The pesky devils are a problem both before and after the crops are harvested. In addition, other major obstacles to the increase in yield per acre even with (or especially with) HYV seeds include the availability of water, fertilizers, and pesticides (in order of usual importance).

Water The high-yield seeds generally require substantial amounts of water to be successful. Irrigation, of course, requires a water source (such as a reservoir created by a dam), an initial capital investment to dig canals and install pipes, and energy to drive the pumps. Each of these elements is in increasingly short supply. With respect to water sources, "from 1950 to 1970 there was a great expansion . . . in irrigated areas as large new irrigation projects were undertaken in China, India, and numerous other developing countries. The total irrigated area was expanding by nearly three percent per year, but the annual increase from now until the end of the century will be scarcely one percent since most of the choice dam sites have already been exploited" (Brown, 1975:1058). To give you some sense of the magnitude of the water issue, it takes about half a million gallons of water to grow an acre of rice, and in the United States agriculture accounts for 96 percent of the water consumed (Pimentel et al., 1976). The tremendous expense of providing irrigation (estimated to be more than $4,000 per acre in Africa—World Bank, 1984a) imposes serious limits to any sizable future increase in the amount of land being irrigated in developing nations.

Fertilizers and Pesticides In order to maximize yields, plants must also be fed (fertilized) and protected (sprayed with pesticides). Fertilizers are, to repeat, growing increasingly expensive, which means they are increasingly difficult to obtain in less wealthy nations. In fact, in 1970 about three fourths of all fertilizers were used in the United States and Europe and less than one fourth were used in less developed nations. By 1984, farmers in developing nations were more than twice as likely to be using fertilizers than in 1970, but two thirds of all fertilizer was still being used by farmers in developed nations (Food and Agriculture Organization, 1986c). Pesticides are in even shorter supply, which is a problem for high-yield production but perhaps a blessing in disguise for the world's ecosystem, as I will discuss later in the chapter. The availability of fertilizer is not a technological problem; we know how to make the stuff. It is rather an issue of being able to afford it and finding the social and economic institutions to produce and distribute it. At present, almost all chemical fertilizers are produced in the developed nations, since it is there that the incentives of high profits tend to exist for increased production.

Incentives for Increasing Yields I have discussed the fact that subsistence farmers, who proliferate in less developed nations, tend to operate by minimizing risks, which generally also means that they are not producing even near maximum capacity. What will motivate them to increase production? The answer may be land reform, since a fairly high probability of increased profit could be an important motivation for greater output, and one way to achieve this is to put the ownership of the land into the hands of the people who are doing the work (Gordon, 1975). This means permitting the risk takers to also be the profit makers rather than giving profits to absentee landowners. Land reform seems to have aided agricultural productivity in Mexico and Taiwan, although it is claimed that in many parts of South

Asia, production has been achieved without it (Crosson, 1975). Nonetheless, it is reported that in China, where large-scale collective farms are common, the private plots represent only 5 percent of the land but produce 20 percent of the food (Gordon, 1975).

Another potential method for increasing incentives is to subsidize the farmer's risk taking. This can be accomplished by government subsidies in the form of credits and price supports. Without institutional support (from governments or large cooperatives) it is unlikely that yields per acre can be systematically increased. The flip side of this coin is that agricultural production is enhanced when governments do not implicitly *discourage* it. In many less developed nations, especially in sub-Saharan Africa, the governments' need for cash has led to policies that encourage the growing of exportable, nonfood cash crops at the expense of basic foodstuffs. The result is that farmers have a greater risk of losing money if they grow the usual food crops. Increasingly, governments have become aware of these problems and efforts to alter policy have resulted in increased food production (World Bank, 1984b).

Reducing Waste   A subtle, but effective, way of getting more out of each acre of food production is to waste less. There are two ways of doing that—not eating more than you need to and not throwing food away. Americans could eat less beef and still be well nourished. It takes several pounds of grain to produce one pound of red meat, and there are other, more efficient ways to get protein (such as soybeans, peanuts, peas, and beans). The **amino acids** found in meat, but not in the vegetable proteins, may possibly be obtained from such things as **lysine**-enriched corn (Gordon, 1975). Cutting back on animal protein could then free up the production of grain for human rather than animal consumption. Of course, most Americans would not welcome that suggestion, since eating beef is as much a part of American culture as not eating meat is in India. Thus, in the United States there is resistance to the idea of meatless meals just as in India many people resist killing cows, monkeys, and even rats in the belief that all living things are sacred.

The issue of rats is central to a more invidious kind of waste—the destruction of food after it is produced. In India this happens at least partly because rats get the food before humans do. Ehrlich and Ehrlich (1972) report that it would take a train almost 3,000 miles long to haul the grain eaten by rats in a single year in India. In 1975, when India had a good harvest, the rats (which outnumber humans by 8 to 1) had a field day eating the stored grain (Time, 1976). In China, the government reportedly has tried to keep its rat population under control with a rat poison that seems to kill off the rat's natural enemies—cats and weasels—faster than it exterminates the rodents. The rat eats the poison, the cat eats the rat, and both die. Rats breed faster than cats or weasels, however, so the rat population is still growing, while cats are disappearing. Since 1983 a firm in California has been marketing a pill that acts as a male rat contraceptive if nibbled in small doses and will kill the rat if taken in a large quantity. Its use appears to be spreading (Hughey, 1983), but not at a rapid enough rate. By 1986 the rats were still consuming enough grain to feed 50 million humans in China each year, and the government, in a desperation measure, began publishing recipes to promote rats and mice as mealtime delicacies (San Diego Union, 1986).

It has been suggested that people in wealthy nations may literally throw away up to 25 percent of the food they buy (Newsweek, 1974). In the United States alone, food distributors may throw away as much as $6 billion worth of food each year— packages that were short-weighted or damaged, overstocked, or poorly marketed (San Diego Union, 1981e). Similarly, in Mexico it is reported that more than one fourth of the perishable agricultural products harvested in 1984 never made it to the dinner table because they rotted in the backs of delivery trucks or in warehouses (San Diego Union, 1985b).

Currently, enough food may be produced in the world to eliminate malnutrition if food were not wasted and were distributed evenly around the world, even though there is not enough to feed everyone an American diet (Reutlinger and Selowsky, 1976; Food and Agriculture Organization, 1982b). The truth is, of course, that food is not distributed equally around the world, a fact that raises at least two questions: (1) who has the food, and (2) whose responsibility is it to provide food for the world?

WHO HAS THE FOOD?

About half of all food eaten in the world is based on grain (wheat, corn, and rice, for example), so if you know who has or does not have grain, you have a pretty good handle on the food situation. In the 1970s and 1980s, the United States, Canada, Argentina, and Australia were the only exporters of grain, while most other areas of the world were net importers of grain (see Figure 14.2). For example, although Americans represent 4 percent of the world's total population, American farmers produce 15 percent of the world's wheat, 43 percent of the world's corn, and 59 percent of the world's soybeans. Additionally, Americans slaughter 19 percent of the world's meat (Food and Agriculture Organization, 1981a).

While rich and poor countries alike fall into the importer category, there are important demographic differences between them. The richer nations are growing only very slowly in population size; thus, their demand for food is increasing more because of a desire to improve their diet than because of more mouths to feed. Furthermore, the developing nations have a younger population with a great need for a nutritious, higher calorie diet in order to maximize the health and productivity of the labor force. Yet many developing countries are struggling just to maintain their current caloric intake per person, much less improve on it. Food, then, should represent a high-priority item on every developing country's agenda, although a World Bank study has estimated that the world's serious hunger exists in only nine countries (Zaire, Ethiopia, Brazil, India, Bangladesh, Indonesia, Pakistan, the Philippines, and Cambodia) (Timmer and Falcon, 1983). But, high priority or not, unless a country can build up and maintain an annual surplus (not just keep up with population growth), it will always be at the mercy of the most important foe or friend of agriculture—the weather.

Figure 14.2 The World Is Increasingly Dependent on North American Grain

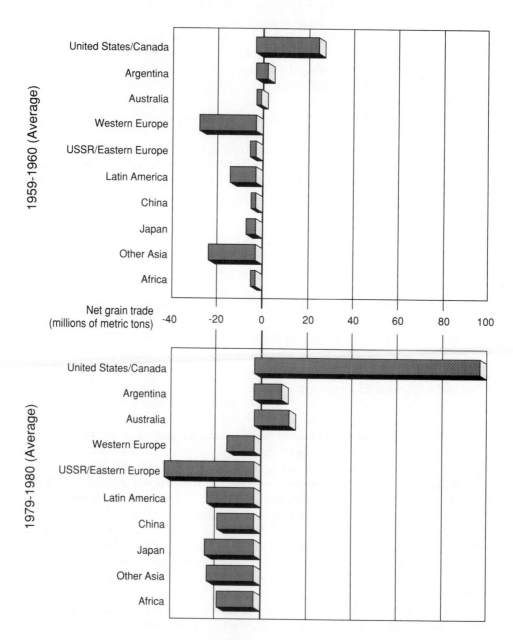

In the two decades between 1959–60 and 1979–80, the world became more dependent on North America for its grain. The United States, Canada, Argentina, and Australia are virtually the only major net exporters of grain. The rest of the world must import at least some grain to feed the population. *Sources:* Food and Agriculture Organization of the United Nations, 1966, Trade Yearbook, 1965, Vol. 19 (Rome: FAO), Table 29; Food and Agriculture Organization of the United Nations, 1982, Trade Yearbook, 1981, Vol. 35 (Rome: FAO), Table 36.

FAMINE AND THE WEATHER

Drought and famine have hit Africa with frightening regularity over the centuries and the most recent bout began in the late 1960s and early 1970s in the area just south of the Sahara Desert, in the countries of Chad and Niger. In northern Chad, an area "seared by eight years of drought, one group of parents implored a United Nations relief official not to send drugs when a diphtheria epidemic broke out. It was better, they explained, for their children to die straight off than to suffer further from hunger—or to grow up with their minds stunted and their spirit crippled by lingering malnutrition" (Newsweek, 1974).

In the mid-1980s the drought spread to many other African nations (among which Ethiopia cornered the greatest amount of attention) and relief aid was mobilized on a massive scale. We are usually prone to take weather for granted and neglect its impact on agricultural development, but recent research has increasingly called attention to weather as a factor affecting the relationship between population growth and the food supply. For example, a team of anthropologists working in Niger found that the demographic impact of the drought was not quite what they expected. Faulkingham and Thorbahn (1975) discovered that, in a village considered by them to be representative of the region, the population actually grew by 11 percent during the drought period. Despite the drought and near famine conditions, the death rate was not abnormally high for the region, and women were bearing an average of more than six children each. In the African sahel south of the Sahara, drought occurs with devastating predictability, and for the more than 2,000 years that people have lived there, they have learned to combat drought and high mortality by having large families (see Chapter 5 on the need to replenish society). In the years just before the drought of the 1970s, the death rate had been declining, especially as a result of the better care women had been giving their children—an influence of a maternity hospital in the vicinity of the village. The impact of the drought was to slow down the decline in the death rate, while it had no apparent effect on the birth rate (Faulkingham and Thorbahn, 1975).

Let me note that Africa is not unique in its demographic adaptation to the weather. In a review of evidence linking weather to population changes in the preindustrial world, Galloway has concluded that "an important driving force behind long term fluctuations in populations may very well be long term variations in climate and its effects on agricultural yields and vital rates" (1984:27). Historical data for China and Europe suggest that, much as you would expect, bad weather contributes to poor harvests, higher mortality, and slower population growth, whereas good weather has the opposite effect. In Africa bad weather has led to a situation in which the population is generating a demand for more food without the area necessarily being able currently to produce the food that people need. Whose responsibility is it, then, to feed them?

WHO SHOULD PROVIDE THE FOOD?

I raise this question not to answer it for you (because it is a moral, not a scientific, question) but rather to provide you with the major competing perspectives. For example, the Environmental Fund has argued that American generosity has encouraged an attitude on the part of many less developed nations that "the hungry nations have the right to produce as many children as they please" while "others have the responsibility to feed them" (1976:2). It then argues that the real crisis is population growth and adopts a neo-Malthusian perspective, calling on less developed nations to cut their birth rates as a response to the growing need to find food.

Others, such as Bread for the World (1976) and Berg (1973), have argued that the most important responsibility of developed nations is to provide food and other developmental assistance to other countries, because only if they are assured that

FOOD AND POPULATION POLICY

Food could be used as a weapon of foreign policy, and such a policy could, of course, have major demographic consequences. The withholding of food supplies could force a country to adopt a vigorous program to lower its birth rate. This amounts to blackmail based on the assumption that "necessity is the mother of invention" when it comes to lowering family size. The Environmental Fund felt so strongly about this issue that in April 1977 it took out a two-page advertisement in several major national publications to publicize its advocacy of a modified program of triage. It urged Congress to establish a moratorium "on all U.S. food aid and technical assistance to any country if its population growth rate is above the world average, *unless* it officially acknowledges that its national birth rate must be lowered and unless it adopts stringent measures to control population growth."

Could such a policy work? Ignoring the ethical issues involved in implementing (or not implementing) such a strategy, you must reckon with the fact that U.S. food reserves are dwindling, and thus the American position has hardened in terms of food aid to recipient countries (Srivastava et al., 1975). Through the 1960s the reserve stocks and idle lands in the United States meant a reserve of an amount equal to about 105 days of world grain consumption, while by early 1976 it was down to 35 days (Population Crisis Committee, 1976).

Thus, the United States does face a decision about who might get surplus food. Indeed, a CIA report in 1976 concluded that the world's growing dependence on U.S. surpluses "portends an increase in the U.S. power and influence" which might help the United States to "regain the primacy in world affairs it held in the immediate post–World War II era" (quoted in the San Diego Union, March 13, 1977).

Would a population policy be a viable part of that influence? Possibly, but the difficulty lies in the short-term nature of American politics compared with the long-term consequences of population growth. It is true, as the Environmental Fund argues, that in the long run the increasing demand for resources by an ever-growing population overshadows all other concerns. But in the short term of a 4-year presidency or 2-year congressional seat, the more immediate political uses of food are to gain desired trade advantages rather than to influence world population trends. For example, in 1975 and 1976 the United States sent rice to Indonesia in exchange for oil and to South Korea in exchange for a restriction on textile exports to America (Morgan, 1976); and in 1980 the United States attempted an embargo of grain exports to the Soviet Union as a protest against their invasion of Afghanistan.

What these and other food aid policies of the American government suggest is that the United States is already practicing an their children will live and have enough food will they ever be motivated to limit family size. That position has the built-in catch-22 that it implicitly encourages further population growth, at least for some transition period. For example, in a rural village in Punjab, India, agricultural modernization in the late 1960s led to a rise in the birth rate, causing even more rapid population increase (Schultz, 1971).

A third position, much more extreme than the other two, is called **triage**— nations with food selecting those hungry nations most likely to survive and concentrating available food aid on them (Environmental Fund, 1976). This position has led at least one writer (Morgan, 1976) to suggest that food may be the American

---

implicit policy of using food as a tool of foreign policy. To be sure, food aid from the United States has for years been aimed at countries that are strategically important for American foreign policy, rather than at those that are necessarily the hungriest (Lappé et al., 1982). All that is missing is an explicit government announcement that food aid will no longer be available to those countries that, because of rapid population growth or other reasons, cannot pay the increasingly high prices for American surpluses.

As with most issues, there is another side to this one. It has been suggested that one reason why American food aid to poor countries in the past has not helped to solve their problems is precisely because the United States has not given them enough food nor given it consistently enough to enable poor countries to count on it and use it as part of a development strategy (Srivastava et al., 1975). Food aid for poor countries often comes as charity in times of crisis and has been called the famine relief theory of food aid (Singer, 1977). For example, in 1979 the United States was willing to send food to Cambodia to aid the millions of starving people being victimized by opposing political groups. The offers were rebuffed, however, resulting implicitly in governmentally sanctioned famine and genocide—a horrid, sordid example of the way in which a lack

of food is typically a problem more of social organization than of human ability to produce food.

The widely accepted neo-Malthusian belief (and it is only a belief, because the evidence is not conclusive) is that shared by Norman Borlaug, who in a 1976 interview reportedly suggested that American food aid may have "adversely affected the will of developing nations to invest in food programs" (quoted in the San Diego Union, March 13, 1977).

Regardless of the consequences of U.S. food aid programs, it is increasingly obvious that at some point in the future "the politics of food will become the central issue of every government" (Idso et al., 1977:19); and an imperative demographic element in those politics will be a consideration of the demand side of the food problem—namely, how many people are there? The bigger and more rapidly growing a population is, the harder it will be for that population to be self-sustaining and, at the same time, the less likely that food reserves will be available in sufficient quantity to feed the hungry. The future seems to hold all the elements for a Malthusian moral dilemma.

Will we run out of food and find the death rate rising, or will the rising prices of food act worldwide as an incentive to drastically lower the birth rate?

strategic weapon of foreign policy in the not so distant future. In other words, the United States can pressure a country into a particular course of action by threatening to cut off its supply of corn or wheat or soybeans. On the other hand, the United States is already involved in trying to help countries raise their agricultural productivity wherever possible. A 1984 report by the United Nation's Food and Agriculture Organization suggested that most developing areas of the world have the *capacity* to feed several times their current population, but in general they lack the *capability*.

Regardless of short-run possibilities, you have to come back to the fact that in the long run the only solution is to halt population growth; at some point the finite limit to resources will close the gate on population growth. One factor already at work to limit future food production, which will also endanger human health and thus produce a deteriorating human condition, is the degradation of the environment—pollution—especially related to the attempt to be ever more productive agriculturally and produce more energy. It is ironic that some techniques that offer the greatest hope for increasing the supply of food and improving the level of living may be changing the very **ecosystem** that could have made more food possible.

FOOD AND POLLUTION

Almost every step of improving agricultural productivity has its environmental costs—from irrigation to the use of fertilizers and pesticides to the creation of energy sources and the production of machinery.

Degrading the Agricultural Environment

If not carefully managed, farming can lead to an actual destruction of the land. For example, improper irrigation is one of several causes of soil erosion, to which valuable farm land is lost every year (Gordon, 1975). In the United States alone it is estimated that during the past 200 years, at least one third of the topsoil on croplands has been lost, ruining as much as 100 million acres of cultivated land (Pimentel et al., 1976; Brown et al., 1988). Even if cropland is not ruined, its productivity is lowered by erosion, because there are few good chemical additives that can adequately replace the nutrition of natural topsoil. Unfortunately, the push for greater yield per acre may lead a farmer to achieve short-term rises in productivity without concern for the longer-term ability of the land to remain productive (Brewer, 1981).

Crop rotation and the application of livestock manure help to reduce soil erosion, but in some parts of the world the land is robbed even of cow dung by the need of growing populations for something to burn as fuel for cooking and staying warm. The eroded soil has to go somewhere, of course, and its usual destinations are river beds and lake bottoms, where it often causes secondary problems by choking reservoirs (Gordon, 1975). Desertification and deforestation are ecological disasters associated with the pressure of population growth on the environment. The southern portion of the Sahara desert has been growing in size as overgrazing (complicated by drought) has denuded wide swaths of land (Goliber, 1985). In the Philippines, the growing population is pushing rural villagers further up the hillsides in search of farmland, and deforestation is increasing (McCue, 1982).

Deforestation contributes to soil erosion by removing physical barriers that prevent wind and water from carrying the topsoil away. The loss of topsoil not only lowers an area's potential agricultural productivity, but it may also contribute to the spread of carcinogens that have been added to that soil as by-products of the use of fertilizers and pesticides.

Health Hazards in Food Production

There are three important aspects of increased food production (and consumption) that warrant attention for their potentially harmful side effects—the use of pesticides, fertilizers, and food additives. In each case, products have been used that are now known to be either poisonous or carcinogenic (cancer producing).

Much of the success in increasing food production during and after World War II has been achieved by applying chemical pesticides. No matter how much water and fertilizer you apply to a crop, it will be for naught if pests damage or destroy the crops either before or after harvest. DDT was the first widely used pesticide, but the buildup of its toxicity throughout the food chain, culminating in increased likelihood of death for humans, was most poignantly publicized by Rachel Carson's book, *The Silent Spring*, which first appeared in 1962. Since then DDT has been banned in the United States and is no longer widely used in the world. However, many chemical pesticides that have replaced DDT have also come under attack, and in 1974 aldrin and dieldrin—two chlorinated hydrocarbons widely used against soil pests in cornfields—were also put on the banished list by the U.S. Environmental Protection Agency. Repeated tests had shown that these two substances cause liver cancer in mice, and there was a reasonable inference that they could do the same to humans. Unfortunately, the product that replaced aldrin and dieldrin on the market, heptachlor, is also suspected of being a carcinogen (Carter, 1974a).

In 1979 the EPA reduced the allowable amount of the pesticide pronamide, which is used commonly on lettuce. Although it was suspected of causing cancer in laboratory mice, the pesticide was not banned by the EPA, because lettuce growers argued that they would lose $17 million of crops each year if they were forbidden to use it (San Diego Union, 1979a). The EPA did, however, ban two herbicides in 1979, both of which contained TCDD (dioxin), which is strongly suspected of causing miscarriages and birth defects.

These examples illustrate a major problem associated with food production, especially in North America and Europe where pesticides have been most widely used, because the chemicals not only are in the plants and the soil but are also washed into rivers and underground streams and eaten by other animals that humans may in turn eat, and at each stage the buildup becomes more highly concentrated. The chemical industry has really been around only since the early 1940s (Carson, 1962), and the substantial rise in chemical pesticides has obviously been even more recent than that. Since the effect on your health may be delayed for 20 to 30 years or even longer, we have only recently moved into an era when pesticide use may have a discernible effect on mortality (and, of course, there are many who point out that the cancer rate *is* rising—although the cause-and-effect relationship is not firmly established). In the meantime, seed breeders have continued to look for organic sources of pesticides, since the problem of controlling pests remains a major issue in food storage and production.

The rapid rise in the use of fertilizers, especially nitrogen fertilizer, has also raised the question of *its* potential effect on the environment. In 1950 the world used only 2 million tons of nitrogen fertilizer, but the Green Revolution changed all that, and in 1984 the world used 66 million tons; by the year 2000 it might be more than triple that (Food and Agriculture Organization, 1986c). There is some evidence that the fertilizer undergoes a transformation in the soil that turns it into a kind of gas that could deplete the earth's **ozone layer.** That, in turn, would lower our protection from the hazards of ultraviolet light, a subject I will return to later.

There are yet other potential dangers involved in the production of some foods, namely additives. Especially in developed nations, chemical substances are added to food to protect its nutritional value, to lengthen its shelf life (preservatives), and to change or enhance flavors and colors. Additives in some cases greatly aid the process of feeding people by keeping food from spoiling and helping to preserve its value. This has aided in the mass distribution of food and has made it possible for people to live considerable distances from food sources. The use of preservatives is one means of deterring the spoilage of food by microorganisms, and worldwide food shortages could be at least partially alleviated by their more widespread use. For example, the World Health Organization estimates that about 20 percent of the world's food supply is lost to microorganism spoilage. Nonetheless, preservatives have increasingly been attacked as potential cancer agents. Sodium nitrate, used for centuries in curing meat to prevent botulism, is now suspected of being a carcinogen, at least in some dietary combinations. In addition, it has been suggested that some kinds of preservatives may cause nutritional imbalances that can lead to behavioral disorders (Charaskin et al., 1974). In 1984 the U.S. Food and Drug Administration approved the use of low doses of irradiation as a new form of food preservation. Approved earlier by a United Nations panel, the method involves exposing food to low levels of irradiation, which kills insects that can cause infections, as well as killing food-spoiling bacteria, fungi, and other parasites (Koenig, 1984). As always, of course, the concern among potential consumers of irradiated food is how dangerous (if at all) is it? Preliminary data suggest that it is about as safe as food prepared in a microwave oven.

Before you swear off all food and drink because you think you will die from them sooner or more horribly than from starvation, consider the analysis by Efron (1984), lambasting what she calls the overemphasis on environmental and industrial causes of cancer. Her point is that 70 percent of all cancers remain essentially unknown (only smoking has been definitely nailed down as a cause) and that the evidence is very weak that fertilizers, pesticides, and food additives are important cancer-causing agents. Time will tell.

Other Environmental Hazards

In countries where pesticides, fertilizers, tractors, and other industrial goods are produced, pollution is a by-product that threatens not only human life but other animal and plant life as well. It is common for extraction industries (mining for coal and minerals and drilling for oil, for example) and manufacturing industries (chemical plants, steel mills, and so on) to produce wastes that can pollute the air and water. Many of these pollutants are mild irritants to humans, while many are known carcinogens that may shorten our life expectancy. A well-publicized case is that of the Reserve Mining Company, located north of Duluth, Minnesota, which extracts magnetite or iron oxide from taconite, a low-grade iron ore. From 1955 to 1974 the company daily dumped thousands of tons of taconite tailings into Lake Superior, the earth's largest body of fresh water, which, because of its purity, was used for drinking water without filtration by Duluth and other cities around the lake. However, in 1973 it was discovered that the drinking water in Duluth contained asbestos fibers, which were traceable to the taconite dumpings. Since nearly 50 percent of all asbestos workers die of cancer (compared with 18 percent for the general population in the United States), it seems apparent that asbestos is a carcinogen. Asbestos particles were found not only in the water but also in the air (Carter, 1974b; 1977), yet the plant continued to operate because there was not overwhelming evidence of the extent of health hazard.

In another well-known case, drinking water polluted by industrial waste and dumped into the Mississippi River was implicated in the 1970s as a health hazard in Louisiana. Researchers have found a statistically significant relationship between cancer mortality rates and drinking water obtained from the Mississippi River (Page et al., 1976).

These are only two cases among many, but they are part of the evidence that industrial by-products are detrimental to human health. Less well understood is the impact of such pollution on the potential food-producing capacity of the earth. There is evidence that polluted water can alter marine life, killing fish and other sources of marine food; there is also scattered evidence that air pollution may inhibit agricultural production. For example, in the United States "smog" or ozone and other oxidants are known to have caused plant damage in California as well as in the Northeast from Boston to Washington, D.C. Crops known to be susceptible to damage by air pollution include potatoes, sweet corn, tomatoes, green beans, pinto beans, lima beans, grapes, oranges, tobacco, spinach, peanuts, soybeans, and alfalfa (Marx, 1975). Industrial pollutants, especially coal residue, have generated "acid rain" in the northern Midwest and eastern parts of the United States, Canada, and Northern Europe, as well. These contaminants have negative effects on forests and plants and may also pollute the area's water (Hopkins et al., 1982; Brown et al., 1988).

There is increasing evidence that a wide range of human activities can disturb the ozone layer in the atmosphere, which shields us from the potentially harmful effects of ultraviolet light from the sun. Most notable on the list are nitrogen fertilizer and catalytic agents released by SSTs, nuclear explosions, and chlorofluorocarbons (such as are used in spray cans and in refrigerants) (Hammond and Maugh,

1974; Brown et al., 1988). Some scientists believe that increased radiation from the sun associated with ozone depletion could retard the growth of major food crops, although at present the scant available evidence relates to only tomatoes, lettuce, peas, and millet. Although there is presently no concrete evidence, there is the suggestion that stratospheric pollution could alter the climate, a factor that could greatly affect food-producing patterns.

SUMMARY AND CONCLUSION

The world's rapidly growing population naturally requires an equally rapid increase in food production. Since the world is about out of land that can be readily cultivated, increases in yield per acre seem to offer the only hope for the future. Indeed, that is what the Green Revolution has been all about—combining plant genetics with pesticides, fertilizer, irrigation, crop rotation, and multiple cropping to get more food out of each acre. At current levels of technology it is reasonable to suppose that the world's population could be fed for many years to come if food can be properly distributed, and if farmers in less developed nations are able to reach their potential for production. Whether that happens is more a political, social, and economic question than anything else.

I have also indicated that food production and consumption are paradoxically associated with potential health hazards. Many ingredients that go into increased yields, increased storage time, and increased palatability of foods may be inadvertently lowering the overall quality of life. The health costs must be added to the costs of irrigation, fertilizers, pesticides, development of new HYV seeds, and other costs that will have to be incurred if food production is going to be maintained at its current pace. It appears almost inconceivable that all the people in the world will ever be able to eat as Americans do. In fact, the diet of Americans may have to undergo significant shifts over the next few decades in response to competing demands for U.S. food production. Since with current technology it would not be possible to feed the whole world the equivalent of the average American diet, the world may already have exceeded its optimum size—may already have surpassed its carrying capacity. Whether that is true only time will tell, but one thing we can be sure of is that in many areas of the world there are people who are the victims of rapid population growth that has outstripped the local food supply; they simply don't have enough to eat.

Demographers, of course, cannot provide solutions to the problems of feeding the population, but they have wrestled mightily with the task of slowing down the rate of population growth, as I discuss in the next chapter.

MAIN POINTS

1. The Agricultural Revolution provided the first opportunity for an increase in the number of humans—involving as it did the domestication of plants and animals.

2. Population growth during the Industrial Revolution also was associated with increased agricultural output.

3. The Green Revolution is a recent phenomenon involving an increase in grain yields through the development of new strains of plants.

4. The high-yield varieties of wheat and rice that formed the basis of the Green Revolution produced early spectacular success, but more recently the gains have been slower because of the increased costs of pesticides and fertilizers.

5. Food production will obviously have to continue to increase in order to feed the inevitably larger world population.

6. Food production can be increased by increasing farmland or per acre yield. The latter can be accomplished by continued plant breeding and increased use of irrigation, fertilizers, and pesticides.

7. In India it is reported that rats eat stored grain and are, in turn, eaten by snakes. However, the food chain tends to stop there, since the snakes in India are rarely eaten by humans.

8. It is estimated that the world could not grow enough food for the entire population to eat an average American diet.

9. Not all nations can supply their populations with a diet even far lower in calories and nutrition than the U.S. diet; who has the responsibility to feed those people?

10. One side effect of the effort to grow more food is degradation of the environment.

11. Soil erosion and air and water pollution are all products of increased agricultural yields.

SUGGESTED READINGS

1. Food and Agriculture Organization of the United Nations, 1986, The State of Food and Agriculture, 1985: A Mid-Decade Review (Rome: FAO).

   The FAO is the single most important source of information about food productivity and trade in the world. This review gives you a global perspective on virtually all important aspects of the food situation, often relating it to demographic trends.

2. Lester Brown and associates, 1988, State of the World, 1988 (New York: W. W. Norton & Co.).

   Despite the rather grandiose title, the focus in this annual volume produced by Worldwatch Institute is on the food supply and the ecological problems facing a world that is trying to produce ever more food for ever more humans. Each year's volume has a slightly different focus, but there is an underlying theme of the demographic dimension of global problems.

3. Peter Hendry, 1988, "Food and population: beyond five billion," Population Bulletin 43(2).

This wraps up in a fairly concise fashion many of the policy implications of the world food and demographic situations alluded to in the prior two readings.

4. S. Wortman, 1976, "Food and agriculture," Scientific American 23(3):30–39.

If you still feel yourself on shaky ground with respect to understanding agriculture because you have not been exposed to it beyond the produce section of the supermarket, you will find this article very readable and enlightening.

5. Rachel Carson, 1962, The Silent Spring (Boston: Houghton Mifflin Co.).

This best-selling book helped to alert the world to the fact that we were inadvertently killing ourselves in the process of feeding more and more human beings.

PART FIVE
Using the Demographic Perspective

One of my major purposes in this book has been to provide you with a demographic perspective that will help you understand the past, cope with the present, and contemplate the future. Population growth has been, is, and will continue to be an integral part of your world, and the more you know about it (realizing the myriad ways in which it can influence social change), the better you can handle it. Most people, at least in the developed nations, feel that indeed we should do more than just cope; we should actively work toward reducing population growth. To do so demands that you develop a population policy by putting your demographic perspective into action to influence the future course of events.

Those of you who decide to have no children or only a few, as well as those who decide to have several, are putting a personal population policy of sorts into practice. However, in the next chapter I will be discussing the large picture—the population policies (both explicit and implicit) of governments that affect where and how populations grow. What can be done to influence or directly induce a change in the rate of growth or the distribution of a population? What has been done in the past? Those are two of the questions that I will be examining in Chapter 15, and I hope that uppermost in your mind as you read is the question: What would I do?

Formulating and implementing population policies, however, are not the only (nor necessarily even the most frequent) uses to which demographic perspectives are put. People engaged in private business, in public social planning, and in the broader realm of politics have increasingly been using demographics to understand who their clients, constituents, or prospective customers are, where they live, and how they might be reached. These applications of population perspectives and methods may do more to educate you about the issues of population growth and change than all the other awareness campaigns put together, because they help make the direct connection between your life and the seemingly anonymous demographic events swirling around you. In Chapter 16 (the last chapter) I show you how businesses and other organizations apply demography to help illuminate and solve their problems.

CHAPTER 15
Population Policy

What can you do about it if you think the population is growing too rapidly or too slowly? In this chapter your demographic perspective will be put to work trying to find answers by examining how others have tried to influence demographic events. This is an important use to which a demographic perspective can be put—employing your understanding of the causes and consequences of population growth to improve the human condition, including your own.

I will begin with a discussion of what a policy is, so that you will appreciate the fact that the complexity of policy making leads to an almost inevitable lack of agreement about what should be done. The disagreement has led to the development of several different types of policy orientation to pursue the basic goals of retarding growth, promoting growth, or maintaining growth. As the chapter proceeds, I will introduce you to some of these different policy orientations and also to specific proposals that have been or could be implemented to achieve the desired goals. First, though, what is a policy?

WHAT IS A POLICY?

A policy is a formalized set of procedures designed to guide behavior. Its purpose is either to maintain consistency in behavior or to alter behavior, in order to achieve a specified goal. Population policy represents a strategy for achieving a particular pattern of population change. The strategy may consist of only one specific component—a single-purpose goal—such as to lower the crude birth rate by 10 points during a 5-year period. Or it may be multifaceted, such as an attempt to "rationalize" or "modernize" reproductive behavior. Naturally, in both cases the objective requires a policy only if there is some indication that the goal may not be achieved unless a policy is implemented. Note that in the foregoing situations I am referring to a *direct* population policy, one aimed specifically at altering demographic behavior. There are also *indirect* population policies, which are not necessarily designed to influence population changes but wind up doing so anyway. I will return later in the chapter to a brief discussion of indirect policies and will focus here only on the direct ones.

I have outlined the basic elements of analyzing policy formulations in Figure 15.1. Your first step is to assess carefully the current demographic situation, a technique that I have tried to illustrate in virtually every chapter of this book. This is obviously a crucial task, since you have to know where you are now if you expect to chart a course for the future. Assuming that you can accurately measure (or even carefully estimate) the present situation, your next step is to analyze what the future would bring if society were left to its own devices.

Assessing the Future

We humans have been preoccupied with looking into the future for centuries, since knowledge of what is coming gives us the power to prepare for it or possibly to change it. Predicting or forecasting the future, though, is an almost impossible task

Figure 15.1   Formulating a Population Policy

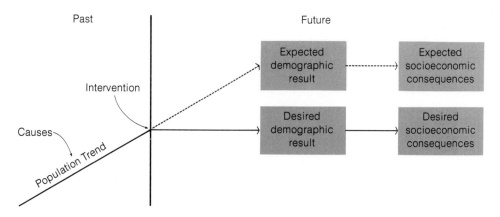

The formulation of a population policy requires an assessment of current trends (requiring an understanding of the causes of population change) and an evaluation of the expected consequences of current trends. If the expected consequences differ from the desired result, then you must intervene to alter the course of demographic events. *Source:* Kingsley Davis, 1975, "Demographic Reality and Policy in Nepal's Future," Workshop Conference on Population, Family Planning, and Development in Nepal, University of California, Berkeley, p. 2. Used by permission.

except in very general terms, because of the amazing complexity of the social and physical world. As a result, demographers rarely stretch their necks out to predict the future but rely instead on projections, which are statements about what would happen under a given, specified set of conditions. Indeed, throughout the book I have made frequent implicit references to projections (see especially Chapter 8). For example, when I say that in 1988 the world's population was growing so fast that it would double in 41 years, that is a projection. In other words, if neither birth rates nor death rates changed from their 1988 levels, there would be twice as many people in the world in the year 2029 as in 1988. I am not saying that there necessarily will be that many people; there might be fewer (if fertility continues to decline or if mortality rises) or there might be more (if mortality declines further without a compensatory drop in fertility); I am only indicating the consequences of current rates.

Projections also permit you to ask questions about other possible paths into the future if conditions change. For example, in Chapter 8 I projected the U.S. population into the twenty-first century using two different assumptions: (1) that current trends would remain unchanged, and (2) that the United States would have achieved ZPG in 1980. Thus, by looking at an array of alternatives, you can lay the groundwork for anticipating different courses of events.

It is at this stage, in deciding what the future might look like, that most attempts at policy making (whether in the area of population or anything else) break down. Because most of us have different insights and perceptions of the world (even though differences may be small), it is sometimes impossible to reach a consensus about anything much beyond how many 19-year-olds there will be in the United States next year. However, if you try to avoid the issue of assessing the future, you void the possibility of implementing a policy because you won't have established a case for it. This is what happened to the U.S. Commission on Population Growth and the American Future, a body legislated into existence in 1969, which presented its findings and policy recommendations in 1972. The commission sidestepped an assessment of the probable future and thereby lost much of its political clout:

> For our part, it is enough to make population, and all that it means, explicit on the national agenda, to signal its impact on our national life, to sort out the issues, and to propose how to start toward a better state of affairs. By its very nature, population is a continuing concern and should receive continuing attentions. *Later generations, and later commissions will be able to see the right path further into the future.* In any case, no generation needs to know the ultimate goal or the final means, only the direction in which they will be found" (Commission on Population Growth and the American Future, 1972:8). (Emphasis is mine.)

If a policy is to be implemented with the expectation of producing predictable results (and controllable side effects), you must get a bead on the most likely future. If you do, then not only is your policy well grounded, but you are in a position to decide later if your assessment was wrong, and then either abandon your policy as incorrect or alter it in accordance with your revised estimate of where your society is going.

Establishing a Goal

Once you have an idea of what the future may be, or at least a range of reasonable alternatives, you are in a position to compare that with what you aspire to in demographic and social terms. Establishing a goal is not an easy task, and it grows more difficult as the number of people involved in setting the goals grows. As a result, goals are usually general and idealistic in nature; those related to population issues might include improving the standard of living, eliminating hunger and racial tension, preserving international peace, and promoting personal freedom.

In Chapter 13 I discussed the World Plan of Action laid out by delegates to the 1974 World Population Conference in Bucharest and I mentioned the follow-up International Conference on Population held in Mexico City in 1984. At that more recent meeting, delegates from 147 nations reassessed world demographic trends and rededicated themselves to the basic goals established 10 years earlier. I have reproduced in Table 15.1 the declaration approved by delegates at the conclusion of the meetings in Mexico City.

The demographic future is assessed primarily with an eye toward determining whether projected demographic trends will enhance or detract from the ability to achieve other broad goals. In other words, population control is rarely an end in itself but rather an "implementing strategy" that helps to achieve other goals. This is analogous to my comment in Chapter 5, that, for individuals, having children is typically a means to other ends, rather than being intrinsically a desired goal. Thus,

Table 15.1   Mexico City Declaration on Population and Development

The following declaration was approved by acclamation at the conclusion of the International Conference on Population in Mexico City on August 14, 1984:

1. The International Conference on Population met in Mexico City from 6 to 14 August 1984, to appraise the implementation of the World Population Plan of Action, adopted by consensus at Bucharest, ten years ago. The Conference reaffirmed the full validity of the principles and objectives of the World Population Plan of Action and adopted a set of recommendations for the further implementation of the Plan in the years ahead.

2. The world has undergone far-reaching changes in the past decade. Significant progress in many fields important for human welfare has been made through national and international efforts. However, for a large number of countries it has been a period of instability, increased unemployment, mounting external indebtedness, stagnation and even decline in economic growth. The number of people living in absolute poverty has increased.

3. Economic difficulties and problems of resource mobilization have been particularly serious in the developing countries. Growing international disparities have further exacerbated already serious problems in social and economic terms. Firm and widespread hope was expressed that increasing international co-operation will lead to a growth in welfare and wealth, their just and equitable distribution and minimal waste in use of resources, thereby promoting development and peace for the benefit of the world's population.

4. Population growth, high mortality and morbidity, and migration problems continue to be causes of great concern requiring immediate action.

5. The Conference confirms that the principal aim of social, economic and human development, of which population goals and policies are integral parts, is to improve the standards of living and quality of life of the people. This Declaration constitutes a solemn undertaking by the nations and international organizations gathered in Mexico City to respect national sovereignty to combat all forms of racial discrimination including *apartheid,* and to promote social and economic development, human rights and individual freedom.

* * * *

6. Since Bucharest the global population growth rate has declined from 2.03 to 1.67 per cent per year. In the next decade the growth rate will decline more slowly. Moreover, the annual increase in numbers is expected to continue and may reach 90 million by the year 2000. Ninety per cent of that increase will occur in developing countries and at that time 6.1 billion people are expected to inhabit the Earth.

7. Demographic differences between developed and developing countries remains striking. The average life expectancy at birth, which has increased almost everywhere, is 73 years in developed countries, while in developing countries it is only 57 years and families in developing countries tend to be much larger than elsewhere. This gives cause for concern since social and population pressures may contribute to the continuation of the wide disparity in welfare and the quality of life between developing and developed countries.

8. In the past decade, population issues have been increasingly recognized as a fundamental element in development planning. To be realistic, development policies, plans and programmes must reflect the inextricable links between population, resources, environment and development. Priority should be given to action programmes integrating all essential population and development factors, taking fully into account the need for rational utilization of natural resources and protection of the physical environment and preventing its further deterioration.

(continued)

Table 15.1   (continued)

9. The experience with population policies in recent years is encouraging. Mortality and morbidity rates have been lowered, although not to the desired extent. Family planning programmes have been successful in reducing fertility at relatively low cost. Countries which consider that their population growth rate hinders their national development plans should adopt appropriate population policies and programmes. Timely action could avoid the accentuation of problems such as overpopulation, unemployment, food shortages, and environmental degradation.

10. Population and development policies reinforce each other when they are responsive to individual, family and community needs. Experience from the past decade demonstrates the necessity of the full participation by the entire community and grass-roots organizations in the design and implementation of policies and programmes. This will ensure that programmes are relevant to local needs and in keeping with personal and social values. It will also promote social awareness of demographic problems.

11. Improving the status of women and enhancing their role is an important goal in itself and will also influence family life and size in a positive way. Community support is essential to bring about the full integration and participation of women into all phases and functions of the development process. Institutional, economic and cultural barriers must be removed and broad and swift action taken to assist women in attaining full equality with men in the social, political and economic life of their communities. To achieve this goal, it is necessary for men and women to share jointly responsibilities in areas such as family life, child-caring and family planning. Governments should formulate and implement concrete policies which would enhance the status and role of women.

12. Unwanted high fertility adversely affects the health and welfare of individuals and families, especially among the poor, and seriously impedes social and economic progress in many countries. Women and children are the main victims of unregulated fertility. Too many, too close, too early and too late pregnancies are a major cause of maternal, infant and childhood mortality and morbidity.

13. Although considerable progress has been made since Bucharest, millions of people still lack access to safe and effective family planning methods. By the year 2000 some 1.6 billion women will be of childbearing age, 1.3 billion of them in developing countries. Major efforts must be made now to ensure that all couples and individuals can exercise their basic human rights to decide freely, responsibly and without coercion, the number and spacing of their children and to have the information, education and means to do so. In exercising this right, the best interests of their living and future children as well as the responsibility towards the community should be taken into account.

14. Although modern contraceptive technology has brought considerable progress into family planning programmes, increased funding is required in order to develop new methods and to improve the safety, efficacy and acceptability of existing methods. Expanded research should also be undertaken in human reproduction to solve problems of infertility and subfecundity.

15. As part of the overall goal to improve the health standards for all people, special attention should be given to maternal and child health services within a primary health care system. Through breast-feeding, adequate nutrition, clean water, immunization programmes, oral rehydration therapy and birth spacing, a virtual revolution in child survival could be achieved. The impact would be dramatic in humanitarian and fertility terms.

16. The coming decades will see rapid changes in population structures with marked regional variations. The absolute numbers of children and youth in developing countries will continue to rise so rapidly that special programmes will be necessary to respond to their needs and aspirations, including productive employment. Aging of populations is a phenomenon which many countries will experience. This issue requires attention particularly in developed countries in view of its social implications and the active contribution the aged can make to the social, cultural and economic life in their countries.

Table 15.1   (continued)

17. Rapid urbanization will continue to be a salient feature. By the end of the century, 3 billion people, 48 per cent of the world's population, might live in cities, frequently very large cities. Integrated urban and rural development strategies should therefore be an essential part of population policies. They should be based on a full evaluation of the costs and benefits to individuals, groups and regions involved, should respect basic human rights and use incentives rather than restrictive measures.

18. The volume and nature of international migratory movements continue to undergo rapid changes. Illegal or undocumented migration and refugee movements have gained particular importance; labour migration of considerable magnitude occurs in all regions. The outflow of skills remains a serious human resource problem in many developing countries. It is indispensable to safeguard the individual and social rights of the persons involved and to protect them from exploitation and treatment not in conformity with basic human rights; it is also necessary to guide these different migration streams. To achieve this, the co-operation of countries of origin and destination and the assistance of international organizations are required.

19. As the years since 1974 have shown, the political commitment of Heads of State and other leaders and the willingness of Governments to take the lead in formulating population programmes and allocating the necessary resources are crucial for the further implementation of the World Population Plan of Action. Governments should attach high priority to the attainment of self-reliance in the management of such programmes, strengthen their administrative and managerial capabilities, and ensure co-ordination of international assistance at the national level.

20. The years since Bucharest have also shown that international co-operation in the field of population is essential for the implementation of recommendations agreed upon by the international community and can be notably successful. The need for increased resources for population activities is emphasized. Adequate and substantial international support and assistance will greatly facilitate the efforts of Governments. It should be provided wholeheartedly and in a spirit of universal solidarity and enlightened self-interest. The United Nations family should continue to perform its vital responsibilities.

21. Non-governmental organizations have a continuing important role in the implementation of the World Population Plan of Action and deserve encouragement and support from Governments and international organizations. Members of Parliament, community leaders, scientists, the media and others in influential positions are called upon to assist in all aspects of population and development work.

* * * *

22. At Bucharest, the world was made aware of the gravity and magnitude of the population problems and their close interrelationship with economic and social development. The message of Mexico City is to forge ahead with effective implementation of the World Population Plan of Action aimed at improving standards of living and quality of life for all peoples of this planet in promotion of their common destiny in peace and security.

23. IN ISSUING THIS DECLARATION, ALL PARTICIPANTS AT THE INTERNATIONAL CONFERENCE ON POPULATION REITERATE THEIR COMMITMENT AND REDEDICATE THEMSELVES TO THE FURTHER IMPLEMENTATION OF THE PLAN.

Source: United Nations Fund for Population Activities, 1984, Document No. E/CONF.76/L.4.

WHATEVER HAPPENED TO THE RECOMMENDATIONS OF THE COMMISSION ON POPULATION GROWTH AND THE AMERICAN FUTURE?

In 1969, President Nixon proposed and Congress legislated into existence a commission to examine the growth of population in the United States, to assess the impact of that growth on the American future, and "to make recommendations on how the nation can best cope with that impact" (Commission, 1972:preface). Before producing its findings in 1972, the commission spent 3 years gathering information, listening to the public and to experts, and deliberating. Its essential conclusion was that "no substantial benefits would result from continued growth of the nation's population" (Commission, 1972:1), and its principal recommendation was that the United States pursue a policy of population stabilization (that is, of ZPG later—see Chapter 8). But how should that be accomplished?

The commission made a number of specific recommendations that would help to stabilize population while also maintaining freedom of individual choice. I have listed some of them here and have indicated what their fate was as of 1988.

1. *States ought to ratify the Equal Rights Amendment to the Constitution so that women would have the same legal rights as males, thereby potentially expanding their ability to be financially and socially independent.* The ERA was initially passed by Congress in 1972 and required approval by 38 states before it could become part of the U.S. Constitution. After 10 years without ratification, the ERA expired in 1982, only to be reintroduced into the House and then defeated there in 1983. President Reagan argued that a constitutional amendment was not needed to fight sexual bias, and a majority of congressional members apparently agreed.

2. *Abortion should be legalized and performed on request by duly licensed physicians under conditions of medical safety.* This change in American law did take place in January 1973 when a U.S. Supreme Court decision essentially legalized abortion on demand during the first 3 months of pregnancy. In 1977, however, Congress passed a law forbidding the use of federal funds for abortion, whereas in 1983 the Supreme Court invalidated a series of city and state laws that had been designed to make abortions more difficult to obtain. The battle between "pro-choice" and "pro-life" groups escalated in 1984 and 1985 with the bombing of several abortion clinics in the United States. In 1986, the U.S. Supreme Court struck down a Pennsylvania law that had restricted access to abortion and, in doing so, reaffirmed the Court's 1973 decision.

3. *Congress should immediately consider the serious situation of illegal immigration and pass legislation to impose civil and criminal sanctions on employers of illegal border-crossers or aliens in an immigration status in which employment is not authorized.* Legislation that would accomplish this was introduced into Congress in the early 1980s and, although an early version was defeated in Congress in 1984, a modified version was passed in 1986. Known as the Immigration Reform and Control Act of 1986, the bill provided for amnesty to long-term undocumented workers, along with employer sanctions for hiring undocumented workers.

4. *The nation ought to give the highest priority to research in reproductive biology and to the search for improved methods by which individuals can control their fertility.* Yet a Ford Foundation report released in 1976 suggested that support for research in this area has been dwindling, not growing (Greep et al., 1976). Indeed, it has been argued that while the research costs have soared, due partly to stiffer Food and Drug Administration testing requirements, a truly successful contraceptive would

have to be very cheap. Thus, the economic reward for developing such a device is rather small. By the 1980s there had been at least one major development in contraception—NORPLANT (see Chapter 4)—which was partially supported by public funding. Still, a study in 1985 indicated that funding for reproductive and contraceptive research and evaluation had been declining in constant dollars during the 1980s (Atkinson et al., 1985).

5. *Sex education ought to be available to everyone.* This is still a highly controversial issue, since many people feel that teaching teenagers about sex encourages early indulgence. In some areas, such as California, the state encourages, but does not require, the establishment of sex education programs, and the law specifically permits parents to withhold their children from such programs.

6. *States should permit minors to receive contraceptive and prophylactic information and services.* Though the myth dies hard that the availability of contraception leads, of its own accord, to early and promiscuous sexual behavior, in 1979 the Supreme Court ruled that minors do have the right to obtain medically prescribed contraceptives on their own consent. The court thus struck down all state statutes forbidding such practices. Earlier, in 1976, the U.S. Supreme Court ruled that "mature minors have a right to obtain an abortion on their own consent, and that immature minors must be provided with a swift and confidential alternative to parental involvement" (that is, some form of counseling) (Paul and Pilpel, 1979:302). In 1982 the Reagan administration tried to establish a policy ordering clinics to tell parents whenever a teenage girl was given a prescription for birth control. However, the U.S. federal courts struck down that requirement in 1983. In 1987 a little bit of information about fertility control hit the

media as television, radio, and magazines began to advertise condoms. Of course, the target was "safe sex" to avoid AIDS, but safe sex also avoids unwanted teenage pregnancies.

7. *In order to provide improved legislative oversight of population issues, the commission recommends that Congress assign to a joint committee responsibility for specific review of the area.* Although no joint committee was established, the House did establish a Select Committee on Population, which was chaired by Representative James Scheuer and began work in September 1977. The committee's deliberation consisted of a series of hearings covering such issues as whether development aid should be linked to population policies, whether injectable contraception should be banned, and whether illegal immigration should be slowed. This last issue duplicated work of the House Select Subcommittee on Immigration, Refugees, and International Law, and that may have been a reason for the House Select Committee on Population going out of existence in April 1979, barely a year and a half after its inception.

Despite the spotty record in implementing the recommendations of the Commission on Population and the American Future and despite the lack of an official American population policy, the birth rate remains low in the United States, at least for the time being. The lesson seems to be a familiar one: Even in the face of government inaction or opposition, the birth rate can be low if individuals see small families as being most advantageous for them. The low birth rate in the United States compensates for a fairly high rate of illegal immigration, which seems increasingly difficult to limit without police-state tactics, which, of course, most everyone would find unacceptable.

when you look at the future course of demographic events, you might ask whether projected population growth will undermine the ability of an economy to develop. Will projected shifts in the age/sex distribution affect the ability of an economy to provide jobs, thereby leading to lower incomes or a greater welfare burden? Will projected growth and urbanization in one ethnic group or another lead to greater intergroup tension and hostility? Will the projected growth of the population lead to a catastrophic economic-demographic collapse that will drastically restructure world politics?

Whatever your goal, if it is discrepant with the projected future, you can use demographic knowledge to propose specific policies to avert unhappy consequences. Your work does not end there, of course, because once your policies are implemented, you have to continually evaluate them to see whether they are accomplishing what you had hoped and to make sure they are not producing undesirable side effects.

Who Needs a Population Policy?

The process of policy formulation outlined in Figure 15.1 assumes a country oriented toward the future and anticipating change. If a population or its government leadership is "traditional" and expects tomorrow to be just like today, policies aimed at altering behavior are not likely to be adopted. If demographic policies exist at all in such a country (and they are not likely to), they may have as a goal the maintenance of the status quo and are probably coercively pronatalist; that is, they might forbid divorce or abortion, impede the liberation of women, and so forth. In general, they would probably discourage the kind of innovative behavior that might lead to demographic change. However, the dynamics of population growth are often such a powerful stimulus to social change that there is really no country, scarcely any community, that can really afford to be complacent or traditional. Almost every region in the world must anticipate a future that will be influenced to some degree by population change.

To avoid looking at the potential for change and at the likelihood of that change being different from what people might want is a treacherous omission in public policy. Fortunately, nearly every country in the world has come to that realization in recent years. That does not mean, of course, that all goals are the same or that all countries with similar goals agree on the need for, or means of, implementing population policy. It only means that most countries are aware that population change will be an important part of the future.

There are several different basic policy orientations that can be adopted to close the gap, or maintain the fit, between goals and projections. These orientations include (1) retarding growth, (2) promoting growth, and (3) maintaining growth. Each policy orientation offers a wide variety of specific means that can be implemented to achieve the desired kind of demographic future. The most controversial and widespread of those three policy orientations is retarding growth; I will discuss it first and in greater depth than the others.

RETARDING GROWTH

The major policies advocated for (and in) most areas of the world are those that will slow down population growth. In previous chapters I have indicated that since no nation's population can grow indefinitely, a policy to slow growth may produce more desirable results than letting demographic, social, and economic events take their respective courses. This seems to be particularly true if economic development is also a desired goal. Growth can be retarded by attempting to manipulate one or more of the three population processes of mortality, migration, and fertility.

Influencing Mortality

Although no nation advocates it, it is possible for population growth to be slowed by returning to former high levels of mortality. It has been argued, at least facetiously, that since the dramatic drop in mortality in less developed countries precipitated current world concern about population growth, if fertility levels do not come down, mortality levels should be "allowed" to rise. The "lifeboat ethic" and "triage" are two orientations that would retard growth by selectively raising death rates.

The lifeboat ethic is based on the premise that since a lifeboat holds only so many people and any more than that will cause the whole boat to sink, only to those with a reasonable chance to survive (those with low fertility) should be allowed into the lifeboat. Withholding food and medical supplies could drastically raise the death rates in less developed nations and thus provide a longer voyage for those wealthier nations already riding in the lifeboat. A closely related doctrine is that of *triage*, which is the French word for sorting or picking, and refers to an army hospital practice of sorting the wounded into three groups—those who are in sufficiently good shape that they can survive without immediate treatment, those who will survive if they are treated without delay, and those "basket cases" who will die regardless of what treatment might be applied (Demerath, 1976:13). As with the lifeboat ethic, it translates into selectivity in providing food and economic aid should the day come when supplies of each are far less than demand. It means sending aid only those countries that show promise of being able to bring their rates of population growth under control and abandoning those nations that are not likely to improve.

In my view, raising mortality is better grist for a science fiction novel than for population policy. However, there is another aspect of mortality control that *is* often an integral part of policies aimed at controlling growth—lowering mortality. Despite a lowering of mortality in most countries of the world, death rates are still often higher in rapidly growing, less developed nations than in the more highly advanced countries. Thus, most governments find it difficult to commit time and money to any policy aimed at reducing growth without also paying attention to lowering mortality—a policy that, of course, exacerbates the problems of growth. Although there is no necessary link between lowering fertility and lowering mortality, the two programs are often linked administratively because of the emphasis on female birth control aids, which are typically dispensed through health clinics as a fertility control policy in much of the world. I will comment more on that later.

It has been argued that fertility will not come down until parents are sure that their children will survive (Berg, 1973; Brewer, 1977). If women actually do bear more children than they want just to overcome high mortality, then it is reasonable to propose that lowering infant mortality will lower the need for children. This would hopefully be translated into a demand for birth control.

Such a proposal was put forth at one time by India's former health minister S. Chandrasekhar, who suggested that "because many babies are born, many die in infancy, and the large number of children born is apparently in response to the high number of infant deaths. Therefore, any attempt to evolve the small family norm in India must involve a serious policy to reduce the infant death rate" (1972:10). His argument suggests that if you lower infant mortality, the family size will go down because people will finally perceive that they no longer need have large families to ensure at least one surviving son to bury them (as is desirable under Hindu religious ideology). In fact, this causal link is implied by the usual theories offered to explain the demographic transition from high birth and death rates to low birth and death rates (see Chapter 3). Chandrasekhar notes that small families are associated with lower levels of infant mortality, and that if Indian couples were aware of that fact, they might be further motivated to have small families on the assumption that a higher proportion would survive to adulthood.

The difficulty with lowering infant mortality as a means of ultimately lowering fertility is that it assumes that people are having more children than they actually want simply to overcome the effect of high mortality. I discussed the dubiousness of that proposition in Chapter 5, and in India it is a particularly questionable assumption. For example, in the world's first global opinion poll, George Gallup (1976) surveyed the opinions of 10,000 people in 70 different countries. One of his findings was that despite population pressures in India, half its citizens would like to see the population increase even more! The consequence is that a further decline in infant mortality could have the unintended (but certainly predictable) effect of raising, not lowering, the rate of population growth. Indeed, this is what happened in one of India's largest states between 1951 and 1975 when infant and childhood mortality declined noticeably. Even with an official family planning program, the fertility levels showed little sign of change (Srinivasan et al., 1978). Data for Guatemala suggest that it may take at least two generations for the reduction in infant and child mortality to influence the level of fertility (Pebley et al., 1979). In fact, it may be that the relationship works the other way around—that the best way to lower infant mortality is to develop a comprehensive family planning program. Couples throughout the world have known for a long time that the health of infants is improved by greater spacing between births (Gadalla, 1978). The use of modern contraception can supplant or supplement traditional methods of child spacing and thus help to lower infant mortality.

For the most part, it seems that manipulating mortality is inhumane, politically infeasible, or a potentially unsuccessful means of attempting to deliberately slow down rates of population growth. Indeed, the focus on mortality is almost always to lower it as a means of improving the human condition for individuals, regardless of social side effects. Thus, you must look elsewhere for a viable policy alternative. Perhaps migration can be manipulated.

Influencing Migration

Migration is the most easily controlled of the three population processes, at least in theory. You cannot legislate against death (except against death as a punishment), and few have dared try to legislate directly against babies. But you *can* set up legal and even physical barriers to migration. In practice, of course, controlling migration is difficult if people are highly motivated to move. Nonetheless, local and national governments often try. In the following sections I first will look at efforts to control international migration, and then will examine policies directed at internal migration.

International Migration   Migration between countries is fraught with the potential for conflict among people of different cultural backgrounds and, as technology has made transportation and thus migration easier, policies to deal with international migration have come into sharper focus. Nowhere is this more true than in the United States, where international migration has been a way of life for more than two centuries and toward which a majority of the annual volume of world's international migrants still head.

Historical Background in the United States   Prior to World War I there were few restrictions on migration into the United States, so the number of migrants was determined more by the desire of people to come than anything else. Particularly important as a stimulus to migration, of course, was the drop in the death rate in Europe during the nineteenth century, which launched a long period of population growth. Free migration from Europe to the temperate zones of the world—especially North and South America and Oceania—represents one of the most significant movements of people across international boundaries in history. The social, cultural, economic, and demographic impacts of this migration were enormous (Davis, 1974).

Recognition of the problems created by free migration led to a new era of restrictions around the time of World War I, when numerous controls were established by the host countries—the destinations of international migrants. The United States and Canada led the restrictive movement (Boyd, 1976). The ideology behind the control of entering migrants was ethnic purity, and the sentiment of the time is perhaps best expressed as "not too tired, not too poor, and not too many."

The discovery of gold in California in the mid-nineteenth century prompted a demand for labor—for railroad building and farming—that was met in part by the migration of indentured Chinese laborers. However, in 1869, after the completion of the transcontinental railroad, American workers came west more readily and the Chinese showed up in the east on several occasions as strikebreakers. Resentment against the Chinese built to the point that in 1882 Congress was willing to break a recently signed treaty with China and suspend Chinese immigration for 10 years

(Stephenson, 1964). The law was challenged unsuccessfully in the courts and, over time, restrictions on the Chinese, even those residing in the United States, were tightened (indeed, the Chinese Exclusion Acts, as they were called, were not repealed until 1943). The exclusion of the Chinese led to an increase in the 1880s and 1890s of Japanese immigration, but by the turn of the century hostility was building against them, too, and against several other immigrant groups.

By the late nineteenth century the ethnic distribution of immigrants to the United States had shifted away from the predominance of northern and western Europeans toward an increase in migration from southern Europe, especially Italy. In 1890, 86 percent of all foreign-born persons in the United States were of European origin, but only 2 percent were from southern Europe—almost exclusively Italy. Only 30 years later, in 1920, it was still true that 86 percent of the foreign-born were Europeans, but 14 percent were southern Europeans—a sevenfold increase (U.S. Bureau of the Census, 1975d).

The immigrant processing center in New York City was moved to Ellis Island in 1892 to aid in screening people entering the United States from foreign countries (Stephenson, 1964), since the changing mix of ethnicity had led to public demands for greater control over who could enter the country. In 1891 Congress legislated that **aliens** were not to be allowed into the country if they suffered from "a loathsome or dangerous contagious disease" (Auerbach, 1961:5) or if they were criminals. Insanity was added to the unacceptable list in 1903, and tuberculosis joined it in 1907. In 1917 a highly controversial provision was passed that established a literacy requirement, thus excluding aliens over age 16 who were unable to read (Auerbach, 1961).

In 1921 Congress passed the first act in American history to put a numeric limit on immigrants. The Quota Law of 1921 "limited the number of aliens of any nationality to three percent of foreign-born persons of that nationality who lived in the U.S. in 1910" (Auerbach, 1961:9). For example, in 1910 there were 11,498 people in the United States who had been born in Bulgaria (U.S. Bureau of the Census, 1975a), so 3 percent of that number, or 345, would be permitted to enter each year from Bulgaria. Under the law about 350,000 people could enter the United States each year as quota immigrants, although close relatives of American citizens and people in certain professions (for example, artists, nurses, professors, and domestic servants) were not affected by the quotas (Auerbach, 1961). That law was passed because after World War I, Europe was unsettled and in the midst of economic chaos, and there was a widespread belief that "millions of war-torn Europeans were about to descend on the United States—a veritable flood which would completely subvert the traditional American way of life" (Divine, 1957:6).

The law of 1921 remained in effect only until 1924, when it was replaced by the Immigration Quota Act. The 1924 law was even more restrictive than that of 1921, because public debate over immigration had unfortunately led to a popularization of racist theories claiming that "Nordics [people from northwestern Europe] were genetically superior to others" (Divine, 1957:14). Initially, the 1924 law established quotas on the basis of 2 percent of the foreign-born in the 1890 census, when about 70 percent of the foreign-born were from northwestern Europe, as opposed to using the 1910 census (used in the 1921 law) when only about 50 percent were from northwestern Europe (Divine, 1957). To avoid the charge that the immigration law was deliberately discriminatory, though, a new quota system—the National Origins Quota—was adopted in 1929 (Auerbach, 1961). This was a complex scheme in which a special Quota Board took the percentage of each nationality group in the United States in 1790 (the first U.S. Census) and then traced "the additions to that number of subsequent immigration" (Divine, 1957:28). The task was not an easy one, since by and large the necessary data did not exist, so a lot of arbitrary assumptions and questionable estimates were made in the process (Divine, 1957). Once the national origins restriction had been established, the actual number of immigrants allowed from each country each year was calculated as a proportion of 150,000, which was established as the maximum number of all immigrants. Thus, if 60 percent of the population was of English origin, then 60 percent of the 150,000 immigrants, or 90,000, could be from England. The number turned out to be slightly more than 150,000, since every country was allowed a minimum of 100 visas. Furthermore, close relatives of American citizens continued to be exempt from the quotas. In Canada, a similar immigration act was passed in 1927 (Boyd, 1976). Congress, of course, retained the ability to override those quotas if the need arose, as it did during and after World War II when refugees from Europe were accommodated.

In 1952, in the middle of the anti-Communist McCarthy era, another attempt was made in the United States to control immigration by increasing the "compatibility" of migrants and the established North American society. The McCarran-Walter Act, or the Immigration and Naturalization Act of 1952, retained the system of national origin quotas and added to it a system of preferences based largely on occupation (Keely, 1971). The McCarran-Walter Act permitted up to 50 percent of the visas from each country to be taken by highly skilled persons whose services were urgently needed. Relatives of American citizens were ranked next, followed by people with no salable skills and no relatives who were citizens of the United States. Thus, even from those countries with an advantage according to the national origins quota system, the freedom of migration into the United States was severely restricted. The same was true in Canada, which passed similar legislation in the same year.

Canada, I should note, had at least two reasons for echoing the immigration policies of the United States. In the first place, it shares much of the sociocultural heritage of the United States, and second, it shares a border with the United States. This cultural similarity and close proximity would have left Canada inundated with migrants excluded from the United States had Canada not passed its own restrictive laws.

Contemporary American Immigration Policy   In the 1960s the ethnically discriminatory aspects of North America's immigration policy ended, but its restrictive aspects were maintained. The Immigration Act of 1965 (the Kennedy-Johnson Act) ended the nearly half-century of national origins as the principal determinant of who could enter this country from non–Western Hemisphere nations. Again, related changes occurred in Canada in 1962.

Although the criterion of national origins is gone, restrictions on the numbers of immigrants remain, including a limit on immigrants from Western Hemisphere as well as non–Western Hemisphere nations. The 1965 act set an annual limit of

120,000 persons from the Western Hemisphere; in addition, there is a maximum limit of 170,000 from non–Western Hemisphere nations, with no more than 20,000 allowed from any single country. Congress again retained the right to grant exemptions from those limits for any special groups, such as the Vietnamese refugees (of whom there were more than 800,000 in 1985) (Rumbaut and Weeks, 1985). A system of preference was retained but modified to give first crack at immigration to relatives of American citizens. Parents of U.S. citizens could migrate regardless of the quota. In addition, a certification by the Labor Department is now required for occupational preference applicants to establish that their skills are required in the United States. In 1976 the law was amended so that parents of U.S. citizens had highest priority only if their child was at least 21 years old. The intent of that change was to eliminate the fairly frequent ploy of a pregnant woman entering the country illegally, bearing her child in the United States (the child then being a U.S. citizen), and then applying for citizenship on the basis of being a parent of a U.S. citizen.

It is almost certain that the restriction of immigration in the Western Hemisphere contributed to the number of people who have become undocumented workers or illegal immigrants to the United States, especially from Mexico. The requirement of labor certification, as well as a numeric quota on Western Hemisphere nations (dominated by Mexico), came at a time when the population of Mexico was growing much more rapidly than the Mexican economy could handle, especially in terms of jobs (as I discussed in Chapter 13). Thus, there are distinct push factors in Mexico. Migration of unskilled labor to the United States from Mexico had been an alternative from the 1950s through the 1960s as part of the bracero program, which California growers had pushed as a means of obtaining cheap labor. In the 1960s, however, Mexican-Americans lobbied successfully for a halt to the bracero program, and that followed on the heels of the more restrictive labor requirements. Thus, it is no surprise that illegal migration from Mexico was fairly high in the 1970s and 1980s.

As undocumented migration from Mexico continued, the cry was often heard that the southern border of the United States was "out of control," and it was widely believed that undocumented workers were taking jobs from U.S. citizens and were draining the welfare system. Typically, reality was less dramatic. The number of undocumented workers in the United States is less than many people imagined (as I discussed in Chapter 7), and "studies of labor market impact have found that the effects of immigrants (both legal and undocumented) on the wages and earnings of other labor force groups are either nonexistent or small (and sometimes positive)" (Bean et al., 1987). Yet the widespread public perception of negative consequences of undocumented migration helped push Congress to pass the 1986 Immigration Reform and Control Act. From the standpoint of the undocumented immigrant, this was a "good news/bad news" piece of legislation. The good news was that the law offered "amnesty"—relief from the threat of deportation and the prospect of legal resident status for undocumented workers who had been living continuously in the United States before January 1, 1982. The bad news was that in order to curtail new workers from entering the country without documentation, it is now unlawful for an employer to knowingly hire such a person. The teeth of the law include fines for employers beginning at $250, with the prospect of much larger fines and even jail sentences for employers who are repeatedly found to be hiring undocumented workers. Notice that this law was aimed entirely at curtailing illegal immigration and had no impact on the pattern of legal migration.

It should be apparent that over time the immigration policy of the United States, and to a lesser extent Canada, has been that of gatekeeping—keeping out those people considered undesirable. Those people generally considered most desirable are professionals: physicians, scientists, engineers, teachers, lawyers, and others. Indeed, one interesting aspect of the abolition of the national origins criterion is that the proportion of all legal immigrants who are professionals has actually increased. In 1961–65, the last 4 years of the national origins system, 20 percent of the economically active immigrants were professionals, whereas in 1968–72 it rose to 30 percent (Keely, 1974). This was more than twice the percentage in the U.S. labor force at the time. A major reason for this seems to be a type of "brain drain" from countries whose people were previously excluded, or nearly so, from the United States. For example, in 1961–65 less than 9 percent of all immigrants were from Asia and Africa, but in 1968–72 nearly 30 percent were from those continents, primarily Asia. Disproportionate numbers of these migrants were professionals (Keely, 1974).

With the American gatekeeper being less restrictive than in the past, the composition of ethnic origins has changed drastically in recent years. The number of Europeans entering the United States each year declined by 45 percent between 1965 and 1986, whereas there was a 1,200 percent increase from Asia. Although Mexico topped the list of nations sending immigrants to the United States in 1986, four of the top ten countries were in Asia.

Most countries currently experiencing high rates of population growth are not experiencing substantial immigration. If they were, establishing barriers to migration would be a good first step to retarding growth. The countries that are experiencing sizable immigration tend to be the developed nations in North America and Europe. Some of the countries, particularly England and the United States, are concerned with the level of migration, but most concerns are with the social and economic consequences of migration—the varying cultural and economic backgrounds of the migrants, not population growth per se.

Other Countries   Out-migration is obviously not a viable solution to relieving worldwide population pressure. Although it was suggested as a possibility at the time Americans first landed on the moon (raising speculation about establishing colonies in space), the cost and problems of social organization and technological development are too immense to give it more than a passing thought.

For specific nations and groups of people, however, migration has been useful in the past to relieve pressure by sending people from densely settled areas to less populated regions. Indeed, this is the basic policy that Plato advocated centuries ago in his *Republic,* in which he suggested an optimum population of 5,040 for a Greek community, and then suggested that new colonies be set up to handle population growth.

In earlier chapters I discussed out-migration as a frequent response to population growth. Europeans migrated to the Western Hemisphere, Indians have migrated throughout Asia and Africa, Jamaicans have headed for Great Britain, and Mexicans continue to migrate to the United States. But in none of these instances or any others has out-migration been a response to deliberate policy. Why not? Because, as you saw in Chapter 7, migration is a highly selective process—selective often of better-educated, highly motivated people, and those are generally not the people that a society wants to lose. Governments of countries experiencing out-migration are worried about a drain of their brain power, and governments of cities experiencing out-migration are worried about a drain of their higher-income tax base. As the more highly skilled workers leave a city, industry may follow (and vice versa), robbing a city of its major sources of income. Thus, a city experiencing net out-migration will have to respond to the fact that "the migration system is distilling the more mobile, economically 'rational' people into the faster growing places while the less mobile . . . people are being concentrated in the slower growing ones" (Rust, 1975:216). In sum, past patterns of out-migration suggest that the most economically skilled and highest-income people are those who are likely to leave an area.

The question of who would be encouraged to leave under a policy of out-migration is, of course, a thorny ethical problem. History is replete with examples of forced out-migration, but generally the purpose was not to control population growth but rather to control political or religious dissent. One aspect of improving the human condition as conceptualized in the Western world is, in fact, to minimize people's fear that they will be wantonly uprooted from their homes and forced elsewhere. As a direct population policy, such a possibility seems remote.

Migration need not be forced, of course; it need only be encouraged in indirect ways. This could be accomplished by raising taxes, reducing or cutting off services to residents or businesses in particular areas, and so forth. But here again such repressive measures are likely to be responded to most readily by those with the most marketable skills who can most easily move elsewhere.

Internal Migration   Despite the political importance of international migration, at least an equally important issue is the internal redistribution of populations. The question is, how can a government (at any level) influence individual choices to achieve the most desirable pattern of population distribution through migration? In the late 1960s and early 1970s the United States was being sensitized to the issue of world population growth and at the same time the Baby Boom generation was making itself felt as a factor in American demographic change. Many communities responded by passing laws and zoning restrictions designed to limit the influx of people. One of the earliest of these limits to growth policies was established in Petaluma, California in 1972. An ordinance passed that year limited construction of large housing developments and apartment houses to 500 units a year. Although challenged in court, the ordinance was ultimately upheld by the U.S. Supreme Court. By the 1980s, however, the ordinance had become largely symbolic because the population pressure was never as great as planners had feared. Of course, it may be that the publicity over the area's concern about growth diverted potential buyers toward other communities (Guenther, 1983). That does mean that limits to growth did not continue to be a concern. Throughout the United States, the increase in the number of two-earner families since the 1970s has meant that almost every American community has been experiencing an uncomfortable rise in the volume of traffic. To the average person, more traffic means more people, and that calls for limits to growth, or at least better control over growth. Enter, then, the Growth Management Act of 1985 in Florida, which was designed to guarantee that population does not grow faster than the physical means to support it (Carlson, 1987). That is but one of literally hundreds of local plans that have been drawn throughout the United States to curtail or control population growth (Rose, 1987).

The state of Oregon had also tried to isolate itself from population growth in the 1970s. In 1971, when Tom McCall was governor of that state, he said, "Visit us often, but for heaven's sake, don't move here to live" (Vicker, 1982). McCall later claimed that the comment was made in jest, but state policies in the 1970s did, in fact, discourage new industry and new migrants. The result was a depressed economy, and by the 1980s Oregon's gates were again beginning to open. The dean of Oregon State University's engineering school capsulized the change in attitude: "One's perception of life changes when one's pocketbook is squeezed" (quoted by Vicker, 1982:50).

In some countries, such as Brazil, a long-term problem has been to encourage migration to the interior of the country to develop the resources of that region and relieve the demographic and economic pressures along the seacoast. Throughout the less developed regions of the world, the major problem faced by governments is excessive migration out of rural areas into the already crowded, large urban centers. Nearly three fourths of the governments of less developed countries have implemented population redistribution policies aimed at diverting rural migrants from large metropolitan areas and attempting to disperse them to other, less densely settled areas (Findley, 1977). Thus, less developed nations are attempting to promote patterns of internal migration similar to those being pushed in the United States, where a typical problem is that faced by areas wanting to slow down the influx of new people.

In Indonesia in the 1950s the government began experimenting with transmigration—resettlement from the main island of Java to other, less densely settled islands. The goal has been to provide jobs for landless peasants and improve the economy of those islands (Widjojo, 1970). Since 1969 the Indonesian government has stepped up its transmigration program, moving hundreds of thousands of people in the process (Krunholz, 1983). But, to be effective in reducing population density on the main island of Java, millions more would have to be relocated (van der Wijst, 1985). Thus, the program so far has been only modestly effective.

The overall impact of migration as a means of population control in Indonesia specifically, or anywhere generally, has been investigated in some detail by Keyfitz. He notes that "getting people to move requires overcoming the contemporary disinclination to pioneer settlement, as well as heavy expenditure in support of each settler for at least the first year or two. Because of the difficulty of recruitment and support, the number of such settlers needed to substitute effectively for birth control in the crowded areas is of interest" (1971:63). Keyfitz notes that crucial aspects of migration are the ages and sex of the migrants. In terms of maximizing the long-run impact of out-migration, women aged 15–19 are the optimum candidates for moving. For example, Keyfitz used the 1966 data for the country of Mauritius to estimate that the out-migration of 1,000 women aged 15–19 would have been equivalent to the out-migration of 1,983 babies.

Migration is, of course, only a temporary solution to population growth, since the empty spaces people are moving to will eventually fill up. Furthermore, tremendous numbers of people would have to move for such a policy to be effective. For example, in Indonesia, if the island of Java were to lower its growth rate to zero by sending migrants to other islands, fully 57 percent of each group of young people each year would have to migrate (Keyfitz, 1971). To date, the success of attempts to limit immigration has been highly variable at best, and in the final analysis the most effective means by which you can retard growth is to nip it in the bud (or indeed, before)—to limit fertility.

Limiting Fertility

Limiting fertility is the best way to slow down population growth in any population, but it is also the most complex. Two important aspects must be considered when trying to limit fertility: (1) the desire of individuals to limit family size, and (2) the ability to limit family size. To ignore the first aspect is to invite failure in any proposed policy; to ignore the second aspect is to miss an opportunity to slow down or stop population growth more quickly. Unfortunately, most national policies oriented toward limiting fertility have been aimed only at the second aspect—enhancing the ability of couples to control their fertility. Programs like that fall under the general heading of family planning.

Family Planning   One of the internationally most popular population policies to limit fertility is to provide each woman with the technological ability to have the number of children she wants. Family planning involves the provision of birth prevention information, services, and appliances. It also involves teaching women (sometimes men as well) about their bodies and teaching them how to prevent births, usually with contraceptives but sometimes also with abortion or sterilization.

An early assumption of family planning programs was that women were having large families because they were uninformed about birth prevention or lacked access to the means for preventing births. Even though that assumption has been increasingly questioned in the past few years, family planing programs have remained the most popular means of implementing a policy to slow down population growth.

A major reason for the widespread prevalence of family planning is, as I mentioned before, the fact that it is usually associated with health programs, which are almost universally acceptable. This is an important point, because many issues surrounding reproduction are very sensitive politically, if not socially. Indeed, Bachrach and Bergman (1973) have argued that because of its basic political conservatism, the family planning approach was most acceptable to the U.S. Commission on Population Growth and the American Future. In order to "stabilize population growth" in the United States, the commission recommended various measures by which "freedom of choice" can be achieved—mainly (although not exclusively) by enlarging the size and scope of family planning programs and services.

In 1965 there were only 21 countries in the world that admitted to actively supporting family planning programs. By 1983 the number had soared to 127. In about half of these countries, explicit recognition was given to the idea of fertility limitation (Isaacs and Cook, 1984). As you can see, the spread of family planning services and technology around the world has taken place fairly rapidly since about

1965, and according to Demerath it has been "attributable to the efforts of a few wealthy people and perhaps 300–400 professionals, principally Americans" (1976:29). The actual diffusion has been the work largely of the U.S. Department of State (mainly the Agency for International Development), the United Nations Fund for Population Activities, the World Bank, and the International Planned Parenthood Federation. Somewhat akin to the Green Revolution, the family planning movement has been an attempt to transmit Western (especially American) behavior and technology to less developed nations.

A typical example of a family planning approach to population policy is in Guatemala, which is trying "to achieve a substantial decline in the birth rate by expanding the government family planning programs to rural areas" (Nortman, 1975:29). The Ministry of Health provides family planning services as part of maternal and child health care and, in addition, each year the ministry is graduating about 40 rural health technicians trained in family planning. With a total fertility rate of 5.8 in 1988, Guatemala still has a long way to go, and after two decades of government support for family planning, only 25 percent of ever-married women are estimated to be using any form of contraception. Nonetheless, Contraceptive Prevalence Surveys in 1978 and 1983 in Guatemala have indicated "a strong relationship between exposure to family planning messages and contraceptive use" (Bertrand et al., 1982; Montieth et al., 1985).

Governmentally supported family planning programs generally evolve from the efforts of private citizens. In Egypt, for example, private, voluntary organizations opened family planning clinics in urban areas as early as the 1950s. These clinics distributed contraceptive foams and jellies to women as long as they met three preconditions: (1) they already had three children; (2) they had their husband's permission; and (3) they could show a health or economic reason that established the need for birth control (Gadalla, 1978). As quaint as that sounds, it helped set the stage for the far more massive government effort currently underway in Egypt, in which government health clinics dispense pills, IUDs, and other contraceptives, and outreach workers distribute contraceptives in rural areas.

Since family planning programs represent the major type of population policy to retard growth in the world, it is important to ask, do they work? Or are they mere palliatives—policies adopted to smooth relations with more powerful industrialized nations that, after all, provide much of the funding and guidance for the programs?

Do Family Planning Programs Work?   In a 1975 review of family planning services, Mauldin concluded that "the performance of family planning programs to date has been mixed, ranging from poor to moderately good to nearly spectacular" (1975:35). In 1981, after analyzing data for 81 countries, Cutright and Kelly concluded that family planning programs clearly do have an important effect on fertility. Lapham and Mauldin (1984) followed up with a more extensive analysis of nearly 100 countries and drew the same conclusion. Both studies used a measure of family planning program effort developed in 1972 by Lapham and Mauldin, relating effort to the observed decline in the birth rate, while controlling for such things as the level of social and economic development. Success in lowering the birth rate has been demonstrated especially in Hong Kong, Taiwan, Singapore, Mauritius, South Korea, and China. In each case social and economic development has been occurring, and the data suggest that organized programs have enhanced a fertility decline that would have occurred anyway (Sherris, 1985).

Other countries in which birth rates have declined moderately with (although not necessarily as a result of) family planning programs include Thailand, Colombia, Cuba, Malaysia, Brazil, Indonesia, Jamaica, Venezuela, Guatemala, Mexico, and Turkey. In each of those (and similar) countries, birth rates remain high even after a clear decline, and new policies that "go beyond family planning" (see the next section) may be required to sustain or accelerate the decline.

In many countries, such as Kenya, Ghana, Bangladesh, India, Indonesia, Iran, and the Dominican Republic, family planning programs have had little observable impact. In Africa especially, Caldwell (1975) has suggested that programs have been so poorly funded, badly organized, and thus so low-profile that success should not have been expected. Since the early 1980s there has been considerable international assistance provided to population control programs in sub-Saharan Africa (see World Bank, 1986).

In general, there are three categories of countries in which you will find family planning programs: those in which fertility was already low before the advent of organized programs (primarily in Europe and North America), those in which a family planning program promoted or enhanced a decline in fertility (mainly in East Asia and Latin America), and, finally, those in which family planning programs exist on a very small scale and/or have yet had little (or no) impact on the birth rate (largely in Africa, the Middle East, and South Asia). Let me provide you with an example from each category.

Fertility Decline Without Organized Family Planning—The United States
Fertility declined in the United States up to the 1940s without a widespread family planning program. Nonetheless, the family planning or planned parenthood movement in the United States in fact has a fairly long history, dating back to the nineteenth century, when many of the early efforts were aimed at removing legal restrictions on the distribution and sale of contraceptives and on abortions. In 1873, after production of the condom had begun and in the midst of a general decline in U.S. fertility, Congress passed the Comstock Law prohibiting the distribution of contraceptives through the mails. According to Westoff and Westoff, "Anthony Comstock, for whom the law was named, formed the New York Society for the Suppression of Vice . . . (and) was responsible for seven hundred arrests, the suicide of a woman abortionist, and the seizure of thousands of books and contraceptives" (1971:47). The Comstock Law was not repealed until 1970, although it had been toned down by court order in 1936 (Jaffe, 1971).

Jaffe has also noted that "it was not until 1958 that the ban on prescribing contraceptives in public hospitals was lifted in New York City and the way opened for publicly financed health institutions to provide family planning services. It was not until 1965, when the Supreme Court struck down the Connecticut statute barring the use of contraceptives, that a number of states repealed their restrictive laws" (1971:119).

Congress has provided federal funding for family planning programs in the United States since 1967, but the Family Planning Services and Population Research

Act of 1970 specifically forbade funds to any organization that provided abortion services, even though several states already had liberalized abortion laws at that time. In 1973 the Supreme Court struck down restrictive laws in the United States and one of the last obstacles to free choice in birth prevention was hurdled. In the United States, as in other parts of the world, a decline in fertility did not wait for the legal restrictions to be removed from contraception and abortion; nor did it await government programs to develop new contraceptive technologies such as the IUD and the pill (both were privately financed), or for the government to provide free or subsidized birth control measures. Fertility declined dramatically from the nineteenth century to World War II, went up briefly, and then again declined dramatically. Only on the second decline was a wide range of birth prevention means readily available to women; in essence, the means were part of the rise in the standard of living. The same goal of family limitation can now be accomplished more easily and more confidently than ever before.

Fertility Decline Enhanced by a Family Planning Program—Taiwan   One of the countries that was an early showpiece of the success of family planning programs was Taiwan, which was heralded in the 1960s as a nation that had responded to a highly organized family planning program with a dramatic fertility decline. However, a close inspection of the data reveals that the general fertility rate was already declining before World War II, during the period of Japanese occupation. The withdrawal of the Japanese after the war removed most of the skilled personnel, but factories and a labor force accustomed to industrial work remained, and, as a result, the Taiwanese were able to take advantage of these resources fairly quickly. As the economy expanded, mortality fell and birth rates declined in an almost perfect replication of the demographic transition model.

Since the early 1950s both the economy and the population of Taiwan have been growing quite rapidly. Between 1952 and 1967, for example, the income per person doubled, and although the population was growing, fertility was in the midst of a decline. There was a baby boom just after the war, but the birth rate has declined quite steadily again since about 1951, whereas the family planning program did not start until 1959 and only became fully organized in 1963 (Davis, 1967). Not until 1968 did the government actually adopt an official policy condoning and encouraging family planning (Nortman, 1974). During the period 1963–68 the total fertility rate fell from 5.3 to 4.3, largely as a result of a delay in marriage, and by 1988 it was down to 1.7 (below replacement level) as contraceptive use reached the saturation level (Chang et al., 1987).

Thus, family planning has without doubt helped to sustain, and possibly to accelerate, the decline in fertility in Taiwan. In a wide-reaching program, hundreds of thousands of women have been fitted with IUDs, been given other contraceptives (especially the pill and the condom), or been sterilized, but only after the Taiwanese were generally motivated to have smaller families.

Fertility Little Influenced by a Family Planning Program—India   In 1952 India began experimenting with family planning programs to keep the population "at a level consistent with requirements of the economy" (Samuel, 1966:54). Although initial progress was pretty slow—the Indian government was moving cautiously—by 1961 there were about 1,500 clinics in operation, providing condoms, diaphragms, jellies, foam tablets, and other services, largely free (Demerath, 1976).

In 1963 the birth rate still was not responding and the government, now with the advice of the Ford Foundation, reorganized its family planning effort, mainly in an outreach effort to spread the birth control message to more people. Still the birth rate did not go down, so in 1966 there was another reorganization, and in 1967 S. Chandrasekhar, a demographer, was named Minister of State for Health and Family Planning (Demerath, 1976). Chandrasekhar boosted the use of the mass media, offered transistor radios to men undergoing vasectomy, pushed through a legalization of abortion, and generally brought about more family planning action than had occurred in all the previous years of family planning. Male sterilization, being both permanent as well as the cheapest method of birth control, has been especially pushed by the Indian government, and between 1967 and 1973 (when Chandrasekhar left his position) 13 million persons had been sterilized in India.

Did the birth rate respond accordingly? I mentioned in Chapter 2 that the birth rate in India *may* have declined ever so slightly between 1961 and 1971, but the death rate sank even more, so by the mid-1970s the Indian population was growing faster than ever before. Why had the family planning efforts failed? Because family planners had not taken into account the broader social context within which reproduction occurs. It was naive to think that family planners could, of their own accord, generate the kind of social and cultural revolution required to make small family norms an everyday practice throughout India (Demerath, 1976).

By 1976 the Indian government was beginning to show signs of desperation at being unable to slow the rate of population growth, and it became the first government in the world to lean definitely toward compulsory measures. Dr. D. N. Pai, director of family planning in Bombay, has reportedly said, "Ninety percent of the people have no stake in life. How do you motivate them? They have nothing to lose. The only way out of the situation is compulsion" (Rosenhause, 1976).

Compulsion was considered by several states, led by Maharashtra (whose capital is Bombay), where debate centered on a bill that would have imposed a fine or jail sentence for couples not submitting to sterilization within 6 months after the birth of their third child. Although that piece of legislation was not passed, the Indian government in 1976 ordered its employees to limit the size of their families to three children, presumably with a threat of job loss if they did not comply (San Diego Union, 1976b). As a result of the policy of enforced sterilization, the number of people (largely male) who were sterilized in India jumped from 13 million in 1976 to 22 million in 1977. By contrast, I should note, there were fewer than 4 million users of the IUD or the pill (only 3 percent of the total population of married women; U.S. Bureau of the Census, 1978a). Although her campaign effectively raised the level of sterilization, Indira Gandhi's policies generated violent hostility (San Diego Union, 1976c), and in 1977 she was defeated in her bid for reelection. Her successor, 82-year-old Morarji Desai, professed support for family planning, but only half-facetiously suggested that self-control (that is, abstinence), rather than birth control, was the solution to India's high rate of population growth (Bhatia, 1978). Gandhi was reelected in 1979, but she kept a relatively low profile with respect to her support for family planning, right up to the time of her assassination in 1984. Interestingly enough, that was a period of time in which the birth rate did appear to be dropping, although survey results have shown that no change in desired family size took place between 1970 and 1980 (Khan and Prasad, 1985). It would no longer be fair to call the family planning program a failure in India, but it is apparent that the program has lacked consistent direction and has failed to offer couples the most flexible forms of birth control. Even in the early 1980s, the distribution of oral contraceptives was only a small portion of the family planning effort in India (Soni, 1983).

In 1984 Indira Gandhi's son, Rajiv, was elected prime minister of India. He had been actively involved in the family planning movement during his mother's administration and in 1985 he declared that the nation was on "war footing" to reduce its rate of population growth to a two-child family norm by 2000 (Population Action Council, 1985:1). A 5-year, $3.6 billion program was unveiled that included monetary rewards to women who limited their family size (see the discussion later in this chapter of similar motivational schemes) and a broadening of the scope and quality of the nation's family planning services. Whether such an ethnically diverse democratic society can achieve the kinds of results implied by a two-child family in the year 2000 is still an open question in India, but a government commitment to such a proposal is an important starting point. Specific steps that have been suggested to help bring about a two-child norm in India include a delay in the average age at marriage, an increase in literacy among India's young women, an increase in communication throughout the country (where thousands of villages are still physically isolated but can be reached by radio and television), and a system of monetary incentives (Tata, 1987).

The problem of bringing the birth rate down does not seem to lie simply with the Indian government's approach to population policy. Two culturally similar and geographically contiguous neighbors—Pakistan and Bangladesh—have officially adopted population control policies and have family planning programs in place, but in neither case has there been a significant measurable decline in fertility.

Why Don't They Always Work?   The conclusion to be drawn from the preceding three case studies is one that I have repeated earlier in the book: A decline in fertility is as dependent on motivation as it is on technology and government administrators. Consider also that in 1963, in discussing the rapid decline of fertility in Japan, the United Nations noted that "the important lesson to be learned from the Japanese experience is that the desire for fewer children spreads quickly if a strong motivation exists, but without this, family planning programmers are not likely to achieve their aims" (United Nations, 1963:33).

A stronger and widely reproduced statement of the same theme is that by Davis, who noted that "by sanctifying the doctrine that each woman should have the number of children she wants, and by assuming that if she has only that number this will automatically curb population growth to the necessary degree, the leaders of current policies escape the necessity of asking why women desire so many children and how this desire can be influenced" (1967:733).

Again, the assumption that underlies family planning programs and that lends them credence as a policy designed to limit fertility is that millions of women in the world (including the United States) have more children than they want because they are ignorant of, or lack access to, effective methods of birth control. Furthermore, family planning is designed to improve the *ability* of women to have the number of children they want (whether that number is zero or eight), but it does little to influence a couple's *desire* to have children. In places like India, Pakistan, Bangladesh, Nepal, and Kenya—where fertility remains high and family planning programs remain ineffectual—it is easy to argue that the problem is a weak family planning program. Indeed, all those countries *do* have weak programs (Sherris, 1985). But it has become increasingly accepted throughout the world that a good family planning program must work in the context of a changing social environment that encourages couples to have fewer children and/or discourages them from having large families. A family planning program will not lower fertility in the absence of the desire for smaller families; to be effective, a population policy must go beyond family planning.

BEYOND FAMILY PLANNING—ENGINEERING SOCIAL CHANGE

In Chapters 5, 9, and 10 I discussed the kinds of social factors that motivate people to want smaller families. How can the desire for children be altered? Since people have children because the perceived benefits exceed the costs, a policy must be aimed at raising costs and lowering benefits—a policy or set of policies that are tantamount to engineering social change. Costs can be raised directly by government action imposing fines or taxes or eliminating deductions or allowances for children, or indirectly by restricting the availability of housing or keeping prices on child-oriented consumer goods artificially high. Benefits of children can be lowered directly by making child labor illegal and indirectly by lifting the pronatalist pressures that currently exist in virtually every society and lifting the penalties for antinatalist behavior that also currently exist (Blake, 1969).

Lifting pronatalist pressures will especially involve a change in the sex roles taught to boys and girls, giving equal treatment to the sexes in the educational and occupational spheres. If a woman's adulthood and femininity are expressed in other ways besides childbearing, then the pressures lessen to bear children as a means of forcing social recognition. Likewise, if a man's role is viewed as less domineering, then the establishment of a family may be less essential to him as a means of forcing social recognition. Required, of course, are alternatives to children and families in general as bonds holding social relationships together, indeed as centers of everyday life. This does not require the abolition of the family, but it does involve playing down its importance, which may (perhaps I should say "will") require massive social change—a virtual revolution in the way social life is organized.

Any policy aimed at affecting motivation will, by definition, have to alter the way people perceive the social world and how they deal with their environment on an everyday basis. It will have to involve a restructuring of power relationships within the family, a reordering of priorities with respect to sex roles, a reorganization of the economic structure to enhance the participation of women, and a concerted effort to raise the level of education for all people in the society. History suggests that most of these changes have evolved somewhat naturally in the course of economic development, at least in Western nations. However, they are not inherently dependent on development and, as a result, could be part of a deliberate policy even before large-scale development occurs. In fact, it is probable that those are the very kinds of social changes that would help accelerate economic development, leading, as they would, to a substantial improvement in the human condition, at least by Western standards.

Lifting the penalties for antinatalist behavior also starts with the redefinition of sex roles—a more positive evaluation of single or childless persons. But there are more specific items that could be mentioned with reference to almost any country, such as: (1) to alter tax systems in which single people pay higher taxes than married people, (2) to stop giving tax exemptions for children or for child care, (3) to eliminate or reduce maternity benefits, and (4) to stop providing larger allowances (such as welfare and health benefits) to people with children than to those without.

One of the first plans to use monetary incentives in a positive way to affect the desire for children was that proposed for the Indian government by Stephen Enke.

A Direct Economic Incentive

In 1959 Stephen Enke calculated that in many countries, such as India, the resources invested in children (food, clothing, medical care, education, and so on) do not earn as high a return as resources invested in ordinary capital projects (a factory, an irrigation dam, and others). In those countries, Enke proposed that the government could afford to pay a money bonus to men and women for each birth permanently prevented (Enke, 1960). India was a prime candidate for such a scheme, since at that time in India there were already state governments and private companies offering employees a free vasectomy plus a small bonus.

Enke argued for a larger bonus, perhaps as high as $100 (more than a year's income in India), and recommended sterilization rather than contraception, since it requires a one-time-only cost, and for men rather than women, since vasectomy is the cheapest form of sterilization. His justification for the larger bonus was that "it may be several hundred times more advantageous to invest money in preventing births—in the ways suggested here—than in traditional development projects" (1960:346).

It was an innovative idea, but Enke ignored two important corollary problems and gave short shrift to a third. In the first place, and perhaps most important, he failed to indicate what society had planned for the women now cut adrift from a large family. Would they be allowed access to schools and jobs or would they simply slip a notch lower in social esteem? Second, and related to the first point, he failed to ascertain whether a larger cash bonus would be sufficient motivation for a large enough number of men to have vasectomies to make a difference in the growth rate. Finally, he grappled only incompletely with the problem of how the money for vasectomies and bonuses would be raised; he proposed only that the money could be obtained "from additional tax receipts." Enke's plan was a positive suggestion for a social program aimed specifically at limiting fertility, but its shortcomings were still the reasons for its lack of adoption. It failed to grapple with the desire of couples to have children, which, as I have often repeated, is the necessary precursor to any decline in fertility levels.

Enke also proposed an alternative plan that in his estimation would be less effective but had the advantage of not requiring immediate cash payments. This was a scheme to put money into a retirement trust fund for women for every year that passes without a child being born. This plan is currently being used by private employees on several tea plantations in India and has received the endorsement of the World Bank (1974). An evaluation of its demographic impact after several years of operation revealed that the program is not as dramatically successful as had been hoped, but appears nonetheless to be having a negative impact on fertility (Ridker, 1980; World Bank, 1984a). A similar experimental program has been initiated in Bangladesh, offering savings bonds to couples who volunteer for sterilization after having two or three children. "The scheme has several attractive features. It provides for old-age security, the lack of which is one reason the poor have many children. By providing a mortgageable bond, the scheme increases access to credit for the poor. Yet its immediate financial costs are small" (World Bank, 1984a:126). A review of all of India's incentive programs concluded that in general, they do help to increase the level of contraceptive use (Satia and Maru, 1986).

Few governments have been willing to commit energy and resources to the type of direct economic incentive programs that India and Bangladesh have tried experimentally. However, two countries—China and Singapore—have been notably successful in using an array of incentives and disincentives to influence directly the number of children that couples have.

China and Singapore

Since the Communist revolution in 1949, the population of the People's Republic of China has more than doubled. The Chinese government realizes that the population problem is enormous, and they are in the midst of implementing the largest, most ambitious, and most significant policy to slow population growth ever undertaken in the world. The 1978 constitution of the People's Republic of China declared that "the state advocates and encourages birth planning," and the reasons for this were spelled out in 1979 by Vice Premier Chen Muhua (Chen, 1979). She argued that there are three major explanations for the fact that in China population control is now "dictated and demanded by the socialist mode of production" (1979:94). These are: (1) too rapid an increase in population is detrimental to the acceleration of capital accumulation, (2) rapid population increase hinders the efforts to quickly raise the scientific and cultural level of the whole nation, and (3) rapid population growth is detrimental to the improvement of the standard of living. These arguments are, of course, basically those I outlined in Chapter 13 in discussing the relationship between population growth and economic development.

The goal of the Chinese government is, incredibly enough, to achieve ZPG by the year 2000, with the population stabilizing at 1.2 billion people. As you know from Chapter 8, to do so will require that the one-child family become the norm, since the current youthful age structure in China places a high proportion of people in the childbearing ages. How are they trying to achieve this goal? The first step is to convince women not to have a third child (third or higher-order births accounted for 30 percent of all births in 1979—Chen, 1979). The second step is to promote the one-child family. These goals are being accomplished partly by increased social pressure (propaganda, party worker activism) and partly by the increased manufacture and distribution of contraceptives. The heart of the policy, though, is a carefully drawn system of economic incentives (rewards) for one-child families and disincentives (punishments) for larger families.

In the cities, couples with only one child who pledge that they will have no more (and are using some form of fertility limitation) may apply for a one-child certificate. The certificate entitles the couple to a monthly allowance to help with the cost of child rearing until the child reaches age 14. Furthermore, one-child couples receive preference over others in obtaining housing and are allotted the same amount of space as a two-child family; their child is given preference in school admission and job application; and when they retire they will receive a larger than average pension.

In the countryside, the incentives are a bit different. One-child rural families receive additional monthly work points (which determine the rural payments in cash and kind) until the child reaches age 14. These one-child families also get the same grain ration as a two-child family. In addition, all rural families receive the same size of plot for private cultivation regardless of family size, thus indirectly rewarding the small family. Each province in China is encouraged to tailor specific policies to meet the particular needs of its residents, and some of the more popular policies include an increasingly heavy tax on each child after the second, and the expectation that for each child after the second, parents will pay full maternity costs as well as full medical and education costs.

There is no question that the policies are working in China, as you can see in Figure 15.2. The crude birth rate dropped by 43 percent between 1972 and 1982 (Sherris, 1985)—a decline exceeded only by Cuba and matched only by Singapore (see the following). Furthermore, the policies are working not only in urban areas where the motivations for small families might be greatest, but in rural areas as well. The total fertility rate in rural China reportedly fell from 6.7 in the mid-1960s to 2.9 in 1982 (Lavely, 1984; Z. Ho, 1984). Lavely (1984) studied a rural commune in Sichuan Province, which is admittedly a model demonstration project (see Lin and Zhou, 1981), but which nonetheless has experienced a remarkable decline in fertility, with the total fertility rate going from nearly 7 to almost 1 in less than two decades. "Fertility before the decline was high and uncontrolled, corresponding to a pattern of natural fertility. The onset of the decline can be dated almost precisely in 1966, apparently in response to government efforts to promote birth planning" (Lavely, 1984:365).

The birth rate in China went up slightly in 1981, perhaps in response to the relaxation of a law prohibiting early marriage, and the government responded in 1983 by trying to rebuild momentum for a fertility decline with a "New Mobilization" for comprehensive planned reproduction (Tien, 1984). Qian Xinzhong, Minister-in-Charge of the State Family Planning Commission of China, noted in 1983 that "individuals are not moved by statistics, but by emotions" (quoted in Population Action Council, 1983b). By the late 1980s the fertility rate in China was still stalled at a level above the replacement rate (in 1988 the total fertility rate was 2.4 children

Figure 15.2   The Birth Rate in China Has Responded to Government Programs

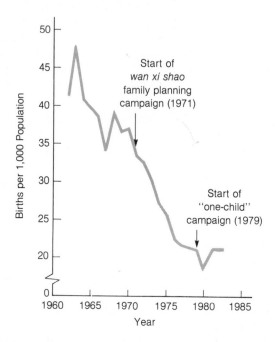

Source: J. Sherris, 1985, "The impact of family planning programs on fertility." Population Reports, J-29, Population Information Program, Johns Hopkins University, Figure 4. Used by permission.

per woman), and the government was moving to emphasize the *incentives* to have only one child, while playing down the *disincentives*. This was necessary at least in part because slowly rising incomes in China have allowed a larger number of couples to pay the price for a second child, thus undermining the official policy. At the same time, the government subtly, but importantly, changed the demographic target from no more than 1.2 billion people in the year 2000 to *about* 1.2 billion (Greenhalgh, 1986).

The one-child policy in China was never intended to be anything more than an interim measure that would finally put the brake on population growth in that country (Greenhalgh, 1986). From the beginning, the plan had been to ease back to a two-child family after hitting the 1.2 billion level of population size. Even a quick glance at Figure 15.2 calls into question whether the one-child policy was ever a real instrument for fertility decline or whether it mainly helped to publicize a fertility decline that was already well under way. Several researchers have concluded that socioeconomic development in China has been a more important factor than government policy in motivating couples to want fewer children (see Poston and Gu, 1987), although the government's attitude has certainly facilitated and enhanced those motivations. It is also intriguing to note the cultural similarities between mainland China and Taiwan (which, as you know, is actually claimed by China as part of its territory) and the coincidence of rapid fertility declines in the two countries.

While China has been emphasizing both strong incentives for small families and penalties for large families, the small (but growing) republic of Singapore has emphasized disincentives to large families since 1969. Singapore is a city-state that used to be part of Malaysia and now has a population of a little more than 2.5 million. Interestingly enough, nearly three fourths of its population are ethnic Chinese. On independence in 1965, the government of Singapore realized that its rapid rate of population growth would make it impossible to continue developing economically. At first, the approach was the traditional family planning programs, emphasizing the distribution of contraception through clinics and hospitals (Salaff and Wong, 1978). After 4 years of family planning, however, the government grew restless at the slow pace of the decline in the birth rate. The result, in 1969, was a liberalization of the abortion law and concomitant establishment of some economic disincentives to encourage adoption of the idea that "two is enough." These measures included steeply rising maternity costs for each additional child, low school enrollment priorities for third and higher-order children, withdrawal of paid 2-month maternity leave for civil service and union women after the second child, low public housing priority for large families, and no income tax allowance for more than three children.

Have these basically coercive measures worked? Yes. Between 1966 and 1988 the total fertility rate in Singapore dropped from 4.5 children per woman to 1.4. The data suggest that the disincentives have been particularly effective in lowering the fertility of older women (aged 30 and older), and they appear to have the indirect effect of delaying marriage among younger women.

The impact on fertility has been greater among the wealthier, educated women than among poorer women, as you might expect, but this classic case of differential fertility worried Singapore's prime minister Lee Kuan Yew. In 1983 he became concerned that not enough bright Singaporans were being born and he argued, "In some way or other, we must ensure that the next generation will not be too depleted of the talented. Get our educated women fully into the life cycle. Get them to replace themselves" (quoted by Leung, 1983:20). However, the only policy designed to implement pronatalism among the better-educated women has been the promise that if they have more than two children, the children will be given priority in admission to schools. Realistically, few women are likely to respond to such a modest incentive to bear more children, and so the country began promoting selective sterilization in 1984 to specifically discourage the less-educated from having many children. In the nation's first move toward a real incentive for family size limitation, women with no diploma and family income of less than 1,500 Singapore dollars per year (about 675 U.S. dollars) were offered 10,000 Singapore dollars (about $4,500 in American money) if they were sterilized after their first or second birth. This selective policy was revoked in 1986, ostensibly because the government of Singapore was fearful of eventual shortages of skilled and unskilled labor if too many uneducated women took advantage of the offer (Evans, 1987).

Indirect Policies That Influence Fertility

While China and Singapore have been struggling to alter social organization to bring down the birth rate, eastern European countries have found that some of their economic and housing policies have brought fertility to an even lower level than they would like. As recently as 1920, the crude birth rates in Bulgaria, Hungary, Poland, Romania, Yugoslavia, and Russia were still as high or higher than the rates in western and northern Europe 100 years earlier; but from the early 1950s to the present a downward trend in fertility has taken place—most of it attributable to abortion. For example, it is estimated that in the 1980s approximately 70 percent of all pregnancies in the USSR were being aborted. The percentages were 54 in Hungary, 36 in East Germany, and 19 in Poland (Kaufman, 1986). The importance of abortion was illustrated in Romania in 1966. In that year the Romanian government decided to halt the downward trend in the birth rate (which was being accomplished primarily by abortion) by establishing a policy that made abortions illegal except under extreme circumstances. The government also discouraged the use of other contraceptives by stopping their importation and by making them available only for medical reasons. The result was that the birth rate skyrocketed from 14 per 1,000 population in 1966 to 27 per 1,000 in 1967. Although it did begin to fall again after 1967 as women resorted to illegal abortions and found other means of birth control (primarily rhythm and withdrawal), by 1988 the total fertility rate of 2.3 was still higher than the 1.9 level of 1966. It is also obvious that the demography of Romania includes a baby boom effect similar to the American experience after World War II.

Throughout eastern Europe, levels of fertility seem disconcertingly low to national Marxist government officials. However, motivations for family limitations are strong. Since the end of World War II there has been a labor shortage in this part of Europe, created by the great loss of men during the war coupled with high rates of industrialization. In eastern Europe, prevailing Marxist ideologies emphasize the equality of the sexes and minimize the importance of family and kinship relationships, which has made it fairly easy for women to respond to the demand for labor, and having families tends to interfere with working. Furthermore, lack of housing has limited the desire of many couples to have children, as has the slowly increasing prosperity that forces a Hungarian family, for instance, to decide "*kicsi* or *kocsi?*"— a child or a car?

We are faced with the irony of a world situation in which some countries have high birth rates and their governments attempt to bring them down, whereas in other countries the birth rates are low and government officials would prefer them to be higher.

PROMOTING OR MAINTAINING GROWTH

Europe

Several developed nations, especially in eastern Europe, are pursuing policies either to maintain their low levels of growth (without letting them get any lower) or actually to slightly raise their growth rate. Besides Romania, which I have just discussed, Hungary has a policy of trying to raise fertility up to the replacement level by 2000. Their approach is to offer a variety of incentives to women to have children, including monthly allowances, generous maternity and sick leave benefits, a partial down payment on a house, and subsidies on baby products. At the same time the government has made abortions much harder to get, although it has compensated for this by making contraception more readily available (in contrast to the more restrictive policy in neighboring Romania) (World Bank, 1984a).

The Soviet Union has also sought a boost in its birth rate, and in 1981 the cash bonuses were increased, as were other benefits to women who have several children. The government has continued its program of granting medals of honor to "hero mothers" who have ten or more children, while encouraging single women to contemplate motherhood rather than seek abortions (Wall Street Journal, 1981c). France, which has experienced a low birth rate for longer than almost any other existing society, has also maintained its policy of providing monthly allowances to couples who have a second or higher-order child, despite the lack of evidence that such allowances have had any measurable impact on the birth rate. In 1985, a government committee in Norway recommended that fertility be encouraged in order to avoid a population decline. Suggestions included the usual incentives of extended maternity leave and subsidized child care (Wall Street Journal, 1985a).

Perhaps more significant are the less developed nations that are either actively pronatalist or satisfied with their present demographic situation. In the latter case, I should note that no decision making is also essentially a policy decision—a decision that there is little discrepancy between projected changes and desired changes.

Africa and the Middle East

In the 1970s there were several African countries, including Chad and Niger, in which there was an active desire to increase population size. This seems to have been motivated by " a desire to achieve economies of scale through increasing population densities and to have a larger domestic market" (National Academy of Sciences, 1973:59). By the 1980s population policy was still a weak agenda item in most of sub-Saharan Africa, despite the high rates of population growth throughout the continent. In 1980 there were five countries in Africa—Libya, Guinea, Gabon, the Central African Republic, and Equatorial Guinea—in which the government policy was that fertility was too low and should be raised (United Nations, 1982b). Perhaps as significant, however, is the fact that 24 additional African nations (including Chad and Niger) indicated satisfaction with their current fertility levels. Worldwide, then, 29 of the 67 countries (43 percent) reporting to the United Nations that their birth rates are either too low or just right are located on the African continent.

Among all sub-Saharan African nations, only Kenya has a lengthy history of family planning programs (it launched the first sub-Saharan national family planning program in 1967, but not until the 1980s did it begin to receive full government support). In 1985 President Daniel arap Moi announced a four-child policy for his country (PopLine, 1985). This may not seem too drastic to you, since even in 1988 a four-child norm would have placed Kenya no lower than the average for less developed nations in the world. Nonetheless, when you begin with a total fertility rate of eight children per woman and have a population that is doubling in size every 17 years, such a policy is a rather important break from current levels. As of 1988, however, the specific details of the plan to achieve a four-child family norm were still rather vague. Family planning clinics and contraceptives were to be made more available, and the president has threatened to fire government workers who continue to have children (Population, 1988), but these efforts alone are unlikely to have a precipitous impact on the birth rate.

A World Bank report in 1986 noted that "most African couples want and have large families. Total fertility rates exceed six children in most Sub-Saharan countries, and in many countries desired family size exceeds seven children. But the situation is changing rapidly. More and more governments are expressing concern, and the idea of family planning is gaining acceptance" (World Bank, 1986:4). Zimbabwe now has a National Family Planning Council, supported in part by the U.S. Agency for International Development, and the Marxist government in Tanzania has also begun to seek international assistance for its family planning efforts. Nonetheless, it appears that in many African countries the lack of strong political leadership in population control is a reflection of popular ambivalence toward the issue.

In the Middle Eastern nations (encompassing both northern Africa and West Asia), the countries that favor lower rates of growth are far outnumbered by those that either seek higher birth rates or are satisfied with the status quo. Only Egypt, Tunisia, Morocco, Algeria, Bahrain, and Jordan are actively pursuing policies designed to limit fertility. The remaining 11 countries are virtually all Islamic, oil-producing nations, and at present they are not interested in promoting family planning, although they do not actively discourage it.

Asia and Latin America

East and South Asia represent the area of the world in which deliberate policies to limit fertility have probably been most successful, as I have discussed earlier in this chapter. Thus, it may surprise you to learn that there are three countries, Democratic Kampuchea (formerly Cambodia), the Lao People's Democratic Republic, and Malaysia, in which governments are actively trying to encourage population growth. Both Laos and Democratic Kampuchea claim that more people are needed for reconstruction and development. In Kampuchea, of course, it is sadly ironic that there is a push for population growth only a few years after one of the most brutal genocidal campaigns in world history, in which 2 to 3 million Cambodians were killed by the Pol Pot regime. In Laos, the government is paying women to get married and then providing an allowance after the birth of each child (United Nations Fund for Population Activities, 1985).

The situation in Malaysia is quite a policy turnaround from the recent past. The country has experienced fairly rapid economic development during the past two decades, accompanied by a significant decline in fertility that was certainly accelerated by the presence of a reasonably strong family planning program. In 1984, however, Prime Minister Mahathir Mohammad declared that the country needed a more rapidly growing population in order to provide an adequate labor force (Malaysia has a large population of foreign workers) and to help stimulate the national economy through a growing home market. By 1988 the policy had not yet gone beyond rhetoric, and the nation's family planning program had not been affected.

Latin America has witnessed a reversal in the other direction since the 1970s. Brazil was once actively pronatalist, but in the early 1980s the government relaxed that stance and began to promote a program integrating health care of women and children with the provision of birth control. The government also approved legislation permitting the local production of IUDs. The birth rate has responded to these efforts; by 1988 the total fertility rate had dropped to 3.4 children per woman. In Chile, however, the situation remains pronatalist. The counterrevolutionary government in Chile has also been calling for a significant increase in population to protect the country from population growth in neighboring Latin American nations; however, events have been working in the opposite direction. Since overthrowing Allende's socialist government in 1973, the regime of Pinochet has imposed a level of austerity that has cut incomes and raised the levels of unemployment. This has in fact encouraged out-migration, postponement of marriage, and the widespread use of contraception within marriage—not a great way to increase the population.

In strife-torn Central America, virtually all governments are nominally in favor of slowing down the explosive rate of population growth, but implementation of appropriate policies is often slow or may even be opposed by detractors of the prevailing political regime. In 1981, the executive director of the Salvadoran Demographic Association (an organization working for family planning and women's rights in El Salvador) was murdered by four gunmen as she was leaving her home for work one morning. A friend noted that "she could have been killed by either side. What she was doing was unpopular with both the left and the right" (Population Action Council, 1981:2). What was she doing? She was championing the cause of population control. She had been quoted as arguing that El Salvador's "principal problem has been a disorderly growth of population; it has been a lack of attention to the demographic factor in development policies. Our situation has been brought about by a blindness that refused to adopt measures, however urgent, necessary or important they were. . . . In our country, it [the population time bomb] has already gone off. Do not permit the same thing to happen to you. . . ." (Population Action Council, 1981:2). An editorial in the *Wall Street Journal* in 1984, just prior to the International Conference on Population, argued that "the population debate can get so heated because what's really at issue are competing visions of our future. [One] view is dark and pessimistic. There are limits to growth. Another person is another hungry mouth to feed. The alternative view is more optimistic. People, even poor people, are assets. Given enough incentive—in other words, enough freedom—the poor even more than the well-off will work hard and eventually prosper. Which view is more ennobling," asked the *Journal*, "and more likely to find converts in the Third World?" (1984a:16). That is a good question, of course, but the better question is, which view is *correct*? That is for you to decide.

SUMMARY AND CONCLUSION

One of the major uses of demographic science is as a tool for shaping the future, for trying to improve the conditions, both social and material, of human existence. To do that requires a demographic perspective—an understanding of how the causes of population change are related to the consequences. Throughout the previous 14 chapters, I have explored the ins and outs of those causes and consequences: how and why mortality, fertility, and migration change; how they affect the age and sex structure of society; how population characteristics are influenced by and in turn affect demographic changes; how women's liberation can influence fertility levels; how demographic changes affect the process of growing old in developed societies; and how population growth affects the urban environment, economic development, and food resources. Implicit in all those discussions is the idea that an understanding of what has happened in the past and what is happening now will provide you with insights about the future, which is, of course, your first step toward advocating or promoting a population policy.

On the basis of what you now know about population change, you should be able to make some reckoning of what the future will be like if things do not change. If what you see upsets you and you want to advocate a policy to slow down the rate of population growth, I have tried to provide you with ideas about what can be done to curtail population increase. If what you see does not worry you, then perhaps you should reread the book. Either way, I encourage you to go on to the next chapter, in which I chart for you a different kind of demographic path—one that applies demographic theory and methods to issues of business, social, and political planning strategies.

MAIN POINTS

1. A population policy is a strategy for achieving a particular pattern of demographic change.

2. Population policies are rarely ends in themselves but are designed to bring about desired social changes.

3. Policy orientations to close the gap or maintain the fit between goals and projections include retarding growth, promoting growth, and maintaining growth.

4. Growth in population size could be retarded by raising mortality—as expressed in the lifeboat and triage ethics.

5. Retarding growth can also be accomplished by encouraging emigration or, at a minimum, discouraging immigration.

6. The U.S. immigration policy used to say that it was illegal to be an undocumented worker, but it was not illegal to employ one. As of 1986, it became unlawful to be in either category.

7. Most policies are oriented toward limiting fertility, especially by providing family planning services.

8. Most evidence suggests that family planning programs are primarily effective when they take place in the context of economic and social change.

9. The most extensive way to limit fertility is by promoting the kinds of social change that alter a couple's motivation to have a large family.

10. India has been relatively ineffective in implementing a population policy, whereas a combination of economic incentives for small families and disincentives for large families is having a significant impact in China.

11. Governments that want to promote or maintain growth can do so primarily by encouraging a further decline in the death rate and by making it difficult for women to obtain family planning services.

12. If you have been reading this book at the pace of one chapter per hour, 150,000 people will have been added to the world's population between the time you started reading and now. That is the equivalent of about 500 full flights on a Boeing 747, or more than 33 flight loads of people per chapter.

SUGGESTED READINGS

1. Jane Menken (ed.), 1986, World Population and U.S. Policy: The Choices Ahead (New York: W. W. Norton & Co.).
This is an excellent set of papers by a group of distinguished demographers convened in 1986 by the American Assembly at Columbia University.

2. Robert Lapham and W. Parker Mauldin, 1984, "Family planning program effort and birthrate decline in developing countries," International Family Planning Perspectives 10(4):109–18.
This updated version of the authors' innovative methodology quantifies the impact of family planning programs on fertility declines in developing countries.

3. Anrudh K. Jain, 1985, "The impact of development and population policies on fertility in India," Studies in Family Planning 16(4):181–98.
A prominent Indian demographer reviews the extent to which development and family planning programs have contributed, and may continue to contribute, to fertility declines in that country.

4. World Bank, 1986, Population Growth and Policies in Sub-Saharan Africa (Washington, D.C.: World Bank).
This is an overview of the extent to which population growth in Sub-Saharan Africa has encouraged, if not forced, many nations to develop and implement population policies.

5. Kingsley Davis, Mikhail S. Bernstram, and Rita Ricardo-Campbell (eds.), 1986, Below-Replacement Fertility in Industrial Societies, supplement to Population and Development Review 12.
The other side of the population policy coin is that some developed nations have fertility that is lower than what governments might prefer. This collection of essays reviews that situation and surveys the field of population policy in the process.

CHAPTER 16
Demographics

Our market research showed that the youthful image of the new decade had a firm basis in demographic reality. Millions of teenagers, born in the postwar baby boom, were about to surge into the national marketplace. Here was a market in search of a car. Any car that would appeal to these young customers had to have three main features: great styling, strong performance and a low price (Iacocca, 1984:64).

The result was Ford's Mustang, brought out in the 1960s; and the rest, as they say, is history. Another piece of history was being written by General Motors at about the same time. The economical, mid-sized Chevrolet Nova was introduced in Mexico, with high hopes of tapping into a lucrative market. The result: appallingly low sales figures (Frost and Deakin, 1983). The reason: In Spanish, *No va* means "it doesn't go"! The lesson: Some of the world's best decisions have a solid demographic base; some of the worst do not.

The insights into the social world offered by the demographer are extremely valuable not only to business executives but to social planners and political strategists as well—individuals who often are less concerned with trying to change demographic trends than with using information about those trends to improve their company's profit margin, improve the provision of publicly funded services, or plot campaign and legislative strategy. It is no great exaggeration to say that every piece of information you have gleaned from the previous 15 chapters could be of great value to people who seek solutions to many practical dilemmas, and it is my purpose in this chapter to show you how to mine this treasure trove. To this end I begin with a definition of **demographics** (the popular name for applied demography) and then move to a discussion of its uses. These include planning in business (marketing, investment, and management demographics) as well as planning for social purposes (such as education, public services, and health services) and political planning (such as legislative analysis and campaign strategy). To help inspire you to find a useful purpose in your own life for demographic information, I conclude the chapter with a discussion of applied demography as a career choice.

DEFINING DEMOGRAPHICS

Throughout this chapter I will use the terms "demographics" and "applied demography" interchangeably, even though the former term is clearly the most popular. Despite the term you use, it has been defined as the "branch of the discipline that is directed toward the production, dissemination, and analysis of demographic and closely related socioeconomic information for quite specific purposes of planning and reporting" (Rives and Serow, 1984:1). The major difference between demographics and the field of demography more generally is that the latter is concerned more with producing new knowledge and understanding of human behavior, whereas the former is concerned more with the use of existing knowledge and techniques to identify and solve problems. Thus, in this chapter you will not necessarily learn anything about demographic behavior that I have not already discussed in earlier chapters, but you *will* learn new ways to apply that information and bring solutions to problems that have a demographic component. What might those problems be?

THE USES OF DEMOGRAPHICS

There are at least three major uses to which demographics are regularly put by people in business: marketing strategies, investment decisions, and management of human resources. Marketing demographics answer questions such as: Who buys my product, and where are those people located? Investment demographics answer questions like: What are the potentially most profitable kinds of products in the future? What other countries might have a market for my products or services? Human-resource management demographics look at questions such as: Is my company hiring the proper racial and ethnic mix of employees? Will future labor force shortages prompt me to discourage older employees from retiring?

Social agencies have also recognized the value of demographics for planning. School districts ask: How many students will there be next year? Or: Do we need to redraw school attendance areas? Police departments need to ask what the changes in population growth might portend for criminal activity in their areas. Health officials plan services by identifying specific high-risk populations (people who have an unusually high need for particular services) and attempting to meet their needs: Where is the best location for a new skilled nursing facility? Or: Does the community hospital really need an additional 40 beds?

Demographics have also worked their way into the political process. Legislators ask questions about how population growth and distribution influence the allocation of tax dollars. Will the increase in the older population bankrupt the social security system? Would federal subsidies to inner-city areas help lower the unemployment rate? Are illegal aliens creating an undue burden on the educational and welfare systems? Politicians are not completely altruistic, of course, and have been known to use demographics for their own personal use when campaign time rolls around. What are the characteristics of a candidate's supporters and where are these voters located? Important and interesting though the uses of demographics for social and political planning may be, however, the most extensive use of demographics is clearly in business.

BUSINESS PLANNING

Making a profit in business requires, among other things, having an edge on your competitors. This may mean that your product or service is better or at least different in some meaningful way, or it may mean that you have been able to find potential customers that your competition has ignored. In either case, effective marketing is the answer to higher profits, and demographics aid in that process, as I will discuss first. Then I will turn your attention to a related aspect of business—deciding when and where to invest in order to realize long-term productivity—in which demographics are often an important consideration. Finally in this section, I will examine the way in which demographic information assists in the management of any business's most important set of resources—its workers.

Marketing Demographics

One of the most impressive (and profitable) ways in which demographics are employed in business is for marketing. A prime example of this is the use of demographics to help a company properly segment and target the market for a product.

Segmenting and Targeting Populations   **Segmentation** refers to the manufacturing and packaging of products or the provision of services that appeal to specific sociodemographically identifiable groups within the population. In the early 1980s, for example, the Ralston Purina Company had a subsidiary called Foodmaker which, in turn, had two divisions. One of them, Jack-in-the-Box, is a fast-food hamburger and taco chain aimed at that segment of the population interested in a quick meal at minimal expense. The second division, Continental Restaurant Systems (which Ralston Purina has since sold) is a series of theme restaurants with names like Stag and Hound, Tortilla Flats, and Quimby's Cricket Club. These places are tailored to that segment of the adult market interested in having an expensive lunch or dinner surrounded by interesting decor. By segmenting, or dividing, the market into two different levels and targeting different types of restaurants to meet those needs, Foodmaker hoped to capture a larger share of the whole "let's eat out" market than it might otherwise be able to. In this example, a market has been identified (people like to go out for meals) and the question is how best to match the appropriate restaurants to the needs of different people with different life-styles and tastes living in different areas.

Alternatively, a company may have developed what it hopes or believes is a good product or service. Now the question is: How many people are there who might be interested? What are they like? And, Where are they located? This is called **targeting** and it involves picking out particular sociodemographic characteristics of people who might purchase what you have to offer, and then appealing to the consumer tastes and behavior reflected in those particular characteristics. The phone should now be ringing on a demographer's desk somewhere. One of the demographer's first questions of a client would likely be: What are the characteristics of the people to whom a fast-food meal might appeal? We cannot answer this directly with our usual arsenal of demographic tools, however. The answer requires a bit of survey research. A sample of households in an area might be selected for a survey in which people would be asked to indicate their preferences for various kinds of restaurants (including fast-food). Basic demographic data would also be collected in this survey and the results might reveal, for example, that a fast-food chain appeals to low- to middle-income families with younger children. An up-scale, sit-down restaurant, on the other hand, might be found appealing to middle- to upper-income, two-earner families with older or no children. The picture might be rounded out with a **psychographic** analysis of the potential consumer, a profile of a person's lifestyle, values, attitudes, and personality traits (Russell, 1984).

The next task is to find where the "right" types of people abide so that the appropriate restaurant can be located nearby. Here is where census data come into their own. As you know from Chapter 1, the census can provide data on the distribution of households by income, household structure, ages of children, and a lot of other relevant categories, and it can do so for relatively small geographic areas. By mapping these data you can pretty well pinpoint the location of clientele most apt to patronize a fast-food place and those most likely to take advantage of a more expensive, theme restaurant. Armed with all this information, the chance of success is greatly enhanced. Remember, however, that behavior changes over time and thus regular updating of research is necessary in order to maintain market success.

It is rare, of course, for a single person (demographer or otherwise) to do all of this research. Much of it is handled by teams of people at one of the many demographic companies that have sprung up in the United States. A directory published by *American Demographics* in 1985 listed 66 American firms offering demographic products and services. Figure 16.1 illustrates the type of information available from one of the largest of these companies.

Targeting by Sociodemographic Characteristics   One of the most important tasks a business can undertake is to know its clientele in order to maximize its appeal. Goya Foods is the top producer of food aimed at Hispanics, with a line of 700 specialty foods.

> Despite its $150 million in sales last year, the family-owned concern still operates like an old-time wholesale grocer. Its 120 salesmen deal directly with their 9,300 grocery-store clients and pay special attention to the mom-and-pop shops that dot Hispanic neighborhoods. The company produces its own Spanish-language advertising with consumers by appealing to old-country values. "Goya really knows its market," says Kathryn Curran, a New York marketing consultant who has worked with Goya. "It speaks directly to the Spanish population" (Lowenstein, 1982:1).

Originally, the company overcame the problem of cultural diversity within the Hispanic population by focusing on the Caribbean immigrant group. More recently it has been forced to alter its marketing practices because of "the changing demographics of its market. Younger, more assimilated Hispanics are moving to the suburbs or away from the East Coast, and Goya is going after them" (Lowenstein, 1982:16). Campbell Soup is chasing the same people, hoping to grab a share of the rapidly growing Hispanic consumer market in the United States. In 1983 Campbell bought a Puerto Rican firm called Casera Foods (in Spanish, *casera* means "home-cooked") and introduced a line of Hispanic food in New York and Miami (Corchado, 1988). Partly in response to the competition, Goya has since begun aiming its products at young adult Anglos, among whom Mexican food has become popular. Similar demographics have been spotted by the auto industry. In 1985 Ford unveiled the Taurus model, "aimed squarely at one of the fastest-growing parts of the U.S. car market: young professionals with children" (Buss, 1985:18).

Government deregulation combined with new, computerized technology created new business opportunities for banks and thrift institutions in the 1980s.

> The challenge to banks [has been] to find the most profitable customers—typically upscale customers with large financial portfolios and favorable demographic characteristics—and offer them personalized and comprehensive financial management services, while less profitable, small-deposit customers are offered low-cost services through electronic funds transfer technology (Walsh, 1983a:40).

Enter the demographic detective, this time in the shape of Mathematika Policy Research, a Washington, D.C. company that has merged several data bases, including the Current Population Survey, the Pension Survey of the President's Commission on Pension Policy, the Federal Reserve Board's Survey of Consumer Finances, and several market surveys. This merged file, when combined with the company's computer software, allowed Flagship Banks of Florida to target the people who were its prime customers, with age and occupation turning out to be the key indicators (Walsh, 1983a).

Although age and occupation may represent the most important sociodemographic characteristics for banks, any of a whole set of variables (such as I discussed in Chapters 8 and 9) may solve other kinds of puzzles. Let me discuss five sociodemographic characteristics—gender, age, education, income, and race and ethnicity—to further illustrate the role that demographics may play in marketing decisions.

Gender   Women represent a demographic category increasingly targeted by businesses, and advertisements reflect the change in strategy. Consider, for example, that more than half of all married women are now working, compared with one in four only 40 years ago. "The dimensions of this shift and its abruptness have meant profound differences not only in the buying power of the average household but in the goods that go into the typical market basket" (Linden, 1983b:8). "Ads of the 1950s were replete with housewives whose greatest pleasure seemed to be seeing their faces reflected in well-scrubbed floors and polished furniture. In the 1970s, the housewives gave ground to images of impeccably dressed women executives dashing off to fancy French restaurants" (Bralove, 1982:33). In the 1980s, the imagery changed again, to a new type of woman who is "fully dimensional . . . she cares about her home but isn't obsessive about it. If she has a career, it isn't necessarily as a TV anchor woman" (Bralove, 1982:33).

As the status and roles of women change, there are complementary shifts in the male population that require adjustments in marketing strategy. Increasing proportions of men are remaining single, with attendant problems of housekeeping and cooking, and married men are also increasingly likely to involve themselves in domestic affairs. The change is evident in advertising and marketing. Taster's Choice, for example, replaced the image of a woman on its instant coffee label with that of a man, while Swanson repackaged its frozen dinners as Hungry Man meals, and Reggie Jackson showed up as "the face behind the Panasonic microwave oven" (Prescott, 1983).

One aspect of gender is sexual preference, and some businesses are targeting the growing ranks of the openly homosexual. In San Francisco (Where else, you say)

Figure 16.1 A Variety of Products and Services Are Now Available from Private Companies to Help Businesses Use Demographics for Marketing

---

Instant
Demographics

Census Profile Report

This report contains two full pages of all the important census, demographic and socio-economic characteristics for your trade area.

The Census Profile Report answers a wide range of your needs.

- Do the residents of this area fit my customer profile?

- How "upscale" are the residents, based on income, occupation, education and housing value?

- How old is the actual housing stock in the neighborhood?

- Are they renters or homeowners?

- Do they have children?

- Are they family people?

CACI 1815 North Fort Myer Drive, Arlington, VA 22209 • (800) 336-6600, ext. 7807 • (703) 841-7800, ext. 7807

"Atlas Savings and Loan primarily seeks out homosexuals for clients. The strategy appears to be paying off; during 1982 its deposits rose to $18.4 million, from $1.2 million, while the number of depositors rose to 8,505, from 874" (Wall Street Journal, 1983a:1).

Age   It is a well-known fact that age is an important determinant of consumer behavior. People at different ages have different needs and tastes for products, meaning that companies that were profitable during the peak of the Baby Boom by catering to the small fry have had to change their pitch. The Nestle Company, a major maker of baby formula, decided to market its products in less developed countries where, you will recall, there are lots of babies, but with results that were not always welcomed (as I discussed in Chapter 4). Johnson & Johnson has flourished by convincing adults that baby shampoo is as good for football players as it is for babies and by diversifying its product line in a demographically relevant way, including acquiring the ownership of Ortho Pharmaceuticals (the largest U.S. manufacturer of contraceptives—helping to keep the birth rate low—and a large manufacturer of drugs to treat chronic diseases associated with aging) and the ownership of Tylenol (one of the world's most popular pain relievers) (Smith, 1981).

Another successful adaptation to the aging population has been made by Procter & Gamble.

> The Cincinnati-based company practically invented the disposable-diaper industry with Pampers and, with the subsequent addition of premium-priced Luvs [diapers elasticized around the legs], has muscled well ahead of every competitor in the throwaway diaper trade. But since products dependent on sales to a baby market are beginning to make marketers uncomfortable, Procter & Gamble forged ahead in 1978 with a product called Attends (Span, 1981:D1).

Attends are diapers for incontinent adults, including many older people or those recovering from surgery or some forms of cancer therapy. Procter & Gamble estimates that there is a potential market of more than 1.5 million people who could use $6 billion worth of Attends each year. Gerber Products, on the other hand, tried marketing baby food to almost every other age group (Bronson, 1981; Span, 1981), but with little success. Not until the baby boomlet of the early 1980s did their sales rise, although their profits were augmented by acquisitions of other companies, including an insurance firm and a chain of day-care centers (American Demographics, 1984).

It is dangerous business, however, to be lulled into believing that every company dealing with baby products will *necessarily* live or die on the peaks and troughs of birth cycles. In 1984 there were 600,000 fewer births than in 1964, but there were 500,000 *more* first births in 1984 than in 1964. If you have hung around new parents and new grandparents, you know that people react differently to first births than to others. In particular, they open their pocketbooks wider for pay for cribs,

---

Note: This is a page from a brochure by CACI, INC., one of the largest of the demographic companies, advertising some of its products and services. *Source:*   Reprinted by permission from CACI, INC.–FEDERAL, Arlington, Virginia.

buggies, strollers, and even diaper service. These businesses, then, are as sensitive to birth order as they are to the absolute volume of births.

Companies that keep on top of demographic trends will find themselves constantly open to change. Arnold Hiatt, president of Stride Rite Corporation (a company built on the manufacture of children's shoes), was well aware of the declining birth rate in the 1970s and began diversifying in that decade to reduce the company's dependence on children's shoes. By 1982 the children's line accounted for less than 40 percent of sales and the company's earnings rose 24 percent, even though domestic shoe production fell 13 percent and 20,000 shoe workers lost their jobs (Roberts, 1983).

Of course, as both birth and death rates have had a long-term decline, the population has aged and we now find that "gray-haired models have assumed an increased importance in recent years as retailers began to gear marketing campaigns toward an older audience. This trend also reflects two deeper developments—the growing economic power of older Americans and the changing perceptions of their lifestyle" (Bell, 1982:12). Indeed, in 1985, 30 percent of all income in the United States went to households in which the head was 55 or older (U.S. Bureau of the Census, 1987a), and an advertising agency survey in 1980 suggested that 50 percent of all disposable income in the United States was in the hands of householders between the ages of 45 and 64 (Bell, 1982). As a result, Lauren Bacall has advertised High Point coffee, Frank Sinatra has advertised Chrysler cars, and three older women starred in the successful "Where's the beef?" commercial by Wendy's. Furthermore, Wilson Sporting Goods has developed a line of golf clubs designed to accommodate the physical limitations of the older golfer, and the bowling industry, stung by the fact that housewives have gone to work and have left the lanes vacant during the daytime, are promoting bowling among seniors by offering discounts and promotions (Allan, 1981).

Education and Income   Education is an important sociodemographic variable, as you already know, and is a particularly potent predictor of consumer tastes. In 1986 there were 24 million households in the United States in which the head had at least some college education. That represents a market larger than the total population of most countries of the world. "Today's generation of consumers, accordingly, is more sophisticated, more knowledgeable, and more receptive to the new—suggesting the need for continuous reassessment of marketing strategies, ranging from product design to the advertising message and the selection of media" (Linden, 1983a:8). Magazine editorial boards have been watching these trends, and several have either upgraded their image or started special editions "aimed at their high-demographic readers, as identified by the zip codes of prosperous communities" (Machalaba, 1982:34). In 1981 *Apartment Life* magazine changed its name to *Metropolitan Home* and shifted its format to appeal to more affluent and educated consumers. Within a year its readership was dramatically different and its sales of advertising pages had risen by 8 percent. On the other hand, when *House and Garden* went up-scale in 1982 Seagram's decided to withdraw its advertising because it reasoned that the wealthier new readers would probably prefer imported, rather than its domestic, gins (Machalaba, 1982). They probably also prefer wine. "There is little disagreement among surveys that the best wine customers in the

United States are the well educated and affluent" (Walsh, 1983b:34). The demographics of the wine industry thus seem favorable, since there has been a long-term rise in both education and income in the United States.

These long-term changes are noted carefully by marketers. The analysis by Jill Himonas, vice president of a large advertising firm in Los Angeles, is a case in point. In 1982 she took note of the age structure changes, especially the maturing of the Baby Boom cohort, and the move away from the youth orientation that had dominated the previous two decades. Then she commented on the likely continued trend toward small households, inhabited by better-educated people—an increasing proportion of whom will be women. Her conclusion was that these demographic trends forecast

> . . . an era of extraordinary change in consumer lifestyles, attitudes, and needs. Consider this: the so-called "typical" American family—working father, mom at home, with two children under 18—now represents less than 10 percent of American households! Clearly we cannot talk or sell to today's Americans the way we did to Ozzie and Harriet in the past. . . . For each group and each need to be satisfied in the 80s, the product or service must convey the benefit of top quality. A new, rich class of two-income families and a newly affluent blue-collar class has spawned a new elite among consumers—an audience with a taste for the top of the line (Himonas, 1982:13–14).

Shooting for just that elite group has helped golfer Jack Nicklaus increase his fortune. As his business manager, Charles Perry, has said, "The demographics of golf make it a very marketable field. If you're trying to sell a $500 sport coat, you're generally not going to sell it to a bowler" (Greene, 1983:58).

Race and Ethnicity   Ethnic groups provide another identifiable target for marketers, as I have already noted with respect to Hispanics. A study in 1979 pointed out that "the United States contains the best-educated, wealthiest and, except in Nigeria, the largest black population of any nation in the world" (Novak, 1979:B11). Even though they are disproportionately clustered at or below the poverty level, blacks represent a $100 billion market—by anyone's standards a large group of consumers to be targeted by marketers. The National Black Network syndicates radio programs aimed specifically at blacks, with advertising oriented toward black consumers. In 1984 researchers for Wendy's International (a fast-food chain) concluded that blacks have a higher prospensity to eat out than whites and so Wendy's hired an advertising agency that specializes in marketing to blacks to promote the message that black communities are important to them (Alsop, 1984).

There is little wonder that Hispanics have caught the attention of marketers when you consider that the number of Hispanics will have increased by more than 35 percent between 1980 and 1990. Virtually all top advertising agencies in the United States now have in-house Hispanic departments that produce culturally appropriate advertising aimed at one or more of the three major groups that comprise the Hispanic market—Mexican-Americans (centered in Los Angeles), Puerto Ricans (primarily in New York City), and Cuban-Americans (concentrated in Miami). Each group has its own demographic implications for marketing. Mexican-Americans, for example, have birth rates nearly twice those of Anglos. Thus, manufacturers of baby products find a denser market there than among Anglos. Puerto Ricans have high fertility, but also a high proportion of broken families and a very high incidence of poverty. Therefore, marketing is better reserved for basics such as food and clothing. Puerto Ricans are a prime target, for example, of Goya Foods, whose company goal is "putting beans on every table" (Lowenstein, 1982:16). Cuban-Americans, on the other hand, have low fertility and the greatest amount of discretionary income of any of the Hispanic groups, and are most likely to purchase expensive consumer durables such as color televisions and stereo equipment (Russell, 1983).

Asian-Americans represent a smaller, yet growing, ethnic market in the United States and though businesses cater to their particular needs, Asian products (like goods and services originally aimed at other ethnic groups) have on occasion been retargeted to gain wider appeal. In 1975, for example, tofu (a soybean product) made the leap from the Asian-American market to the mainstream market. Ever since, manufacturers have been busy doing demographic research to determine how far tofu can go. "Marketing tofu is a matter of matching tofu's virtue to each targeted market, whether it be to 'peasant-style' natural food users, trendy Oriental food buffs, upscale gourmet chic fanciers, calories-obsessed dieters, or the diet-restricted elderly" (Leviton, 1983:39).

Tofu is neither the first nor the last ethnic food added to the American diet as a result of migration. The story goes that at Plymouth Rock a Mayflower passenger was asked to attend to the ailing American Indian chief Massasoit. The passenger revived the chief with some English fruit jam and a bit of English soup. "Since then, immigrants have been arriving like guests at a covered-dish supper, contributing their specialties to the new communal table" (Sheraton, 1985:98). But to each new food, be it sauerkraut, pita bread, guacamole, or tofu, is put the question that precedes the food to your lips: Will it play in Peoria?

Will It Play in Peoria?   Segmenting and targeting products means ignoring the masses in favor of particular groups, yet sometimes it is the averages that marketers are after. Where are the sociodemographically average people in the country? Why do we care? Because many producers are more interested in mass appeal than in targeting and, further, such areas represent fertile ground in which potential mass-marketed goods can be tested for their appeal. For decades, Peoria, Illinois was the quintessential average community in the United States with respect to age, income, education, and other relevant factors. Thus, it was sort of a United States in minia-ture. "If a new brand of soap or antifreeze plays well in Peoria, the theory goes, there's a good chance it will be a sales winner across the country" (Carlson, 1983:29). Alas, in 1983 the advertising agency that maintains a vigil on such aver-ageness (I will refrain from saying mediocrity) dropped Peoria from its list of average U.S. cities because its demographics finally shifted away from center—high unem-ployment upset the balance. Fortunately, a major strike at Caterpillar Inc. was settled in 1985 and Peoria regained its place as a demographic model of America, along with places like Minneapolis–St. Paul and Portland, Oregon (Wall Street Journal, 1988; Carlson, 1985).

From marketing, it is only a short step to using demographic data to help make investment decisions.

Investment Demographics

To invest is to put your money to use for the purpose of securing a gain in income. Companies invest in themselves by ploughing their profits back into the company in order to develop new products or expand or change markets; individuals (and companies also) invest by buying stocks or bonds of those companies that are viewed as having a profitable future, or by purchasing real property whose value is judged to rise in the future. Clearly, a wide range of factors goes into the decision to invest in one product line, a particular company, or a specific piece of property, but one very important consideration is future demographic change. Companies that plan for demographic shifts have a better chance at success than those that do not. In fact, it has been said that "Wall Street uses demographics to pinpoint opportunity" (Nordberg, 1983:23). James Morton, vice president of Chase Special Equities in New York, has noted that the flip side is that "if you don't know demographics, and they're not in your favor, you're in trouble" (quoted by Nordberg, 1983:24). As Cheryl Russell, editor of *American Demographics,* has commented:

> No one claims that demographics are a perfect marketing tool, or the only marketing tool. But demographics are the best predictors of consumption, and of national moods, preoccupations, and well-being. They are a starting point in marketing, and they are a framework for corporate planning. Following trends is like a long-term financial investment. No one gets rich overnight mining demographic statistics. But over the years, an investment in demographics will mature, yielding high returns at no risk (1985:7).

Basically, making sound investment decisions (as opposed to lucky ones) involves peering into the future, forecasting likely scenarios, and then acting on the basis of what seems likely to happen. For example, in 1985 the outlook was weak for industries that dealt with teenagers, but as the baby boomlet children move into the late childhood and early teen years in the late 1980s and early 1990s, the demand should pick up for amusement parks, bicycles, and franchise foods. Looking at the changing age structure of the United States led the *Wall Street Journal* to suggest a variety of stock-picking decisions, including food companies, restaurants and fast-food chains, resorts and travel, home entertainment, and toys and games (Smith, 1986).

Small entrepreneurs can also use demographics to make decisions about setting up a new business. Louis Pol, one of the few academically trained demographers teaching in a school of business in the United States, has pointed out that demographics help small businesses make appropriate site selections, identify market areas, forecast demand and sales, and estimate market share (Pol, 1987).

You know already that population is a major push behind social change and so it is that crystal-ball gazing inevitably reveals the importance of demographics. Forecasting is one of the cornerstones of corporate planning, and many large companies employ futurists (usually in the marketing department) whose job it is "to foresee the future by examining the past" (Toffler, 1970:71). Demographics do not tell the entire tale, of course. Harold M. Levine, vice president of E. F. Hutton, has a rule of thumb that in making an investment decision, 20 percent is based on demographics, 30 percent on the economic situation, and 50 percent on the characteristics of the individual company (Nordberg, 1983). These proportions may shift a little, however, depending on whether the investment decision is domestic or international in nature.

Domestic Demographics   Because you are reading this book, you already have a good feel for the shape of things to come demographically. Most people do not. Thus, the demographic insights provided by John Naisbitt in his best-selling book, *Megatrends* (New York: Warner Books, 1982), may have seemed remarkable to the average reader. Naisbitt is an American trend-watcher, a futurologist with one eye on the present and the other on the future. By doing content analysis of news stories in papers of the major metropolitan areas, Naisbitt and his colleagues have charted the ten major (and therefore "mega") trends that seem to be unfolding in the United States, three of which, as it turns out, are distinctly demographic in nature— a 30 percent fraction that may reflect the relative importance of demographics in long-range investment planning.

Naisbitt argues that our economy is becoming part of a global structure in which the vast bulk of manufacturing, even of American products, is done outside of the United States, primarily in less developed nations, where the work force is increasing at an extremely rapid pace. The net result is that workers in less developed nations are producing the bulk of products sold in the United States, but we hear little about it because the goods are sold with familiar trade names such as Sears and J.C. Penney. The Mexican side of the U.S.–Mexico border is dotted with thousands of *maquiladoras*—factories set up by U.S. companies to take advantage of cheap labor in Mexico but whose products are shipped back to the United States (Magnuson, 1985).

The second demographically related megatrend (Naisbitt's number nine) is that the North–South shift in the United States is real and irreversible. This refers to the obvious movement of the American population out of the Northeast and toward the Sun Belt. This migration, which hit its peak in the 1970s, has signaled a life-style alteration for the United States and changed the thinking about where economic opportunity is abundant. The Northeast and Midwest have experienced a brain drain to states such as California, Florida, and Texas, and both population and economic growth rates are expected to be higher in these states than in most of the others. Such demographic changes can be crucial for companies, especially high-technology enterprises, as you may remember, because as companies grow they may need to hire employees who have specialized skills. "A company's inability to find such fundamental resources when they are needed can greatly influence its success" (Posner, 1982:95).

The third demographically related trend identified by Naisbitt is that we no longer live in an either-or, chocolate-or-vanilla world—people have demanded and are getting a multitude of choices. This, of course, relates to the changing sociodemographic characteristics of the American population, especially those related to the changing status of women. As a consequence of this social movement, both women and men have more choices in their personal lives, creating a more diversified society that may require new marketing strategies for those businesses that will survive and prosper. I have already discussed these issues in looking at marketing demographics, but it is perhaps worth reminding you that marketing and investing are closely interrelated. If there is a market for a product, then it may be worth investing in that product. That is as true domestically as it is internationally.

International Demographics   When you combine the fact that the American population represents only 5 percent of the world's total with the fact that 90 percent of the world's population growth in the foreseeable future will occur in the less developed nations, it is not surprising that many companies look around the world for investment possibilities. Take soft drinks, for example, sales of which are enhanced by hot weather and lots of teenagers. 1980 witnessed a cool summer in the United States and the number of American teenagers was smaller than the year before, yet Coca-Cola's sales were on the rise. Why? Because the United States accounts for less than half of world soft drink sales (Bauder, 1981) and there are millions of thirsty teenagers all over the globe. In 1981 Donald Keough, president and chief executive officer of Coca-Cola, remarked that "In Latin America, where we have a dominant position, the demographics for any consumer product that people can afford are highly favorable. In Brazil, the median age is under 18" (quoted in American Demographics, 1982a:1). Coke has also moved into China. The company signed an agreement to reenter the country in 1978 (shortly before the U.S. government reached its own agreement to renew relations with China). Initially, soft drinks were bottled only for tourists, but in 1984 Coke began to cooperatively develop China's soft-drink industry. PepsiCo, Inc., has been selling cola in the world's third most populous nation (USSR) since the early 1970s.

Soft drinks represent a good international product because they are basic (everyone has to drink *something*) and they are affordable. By contrast, the market for automobiles grows more slowly because of the high cost. The market for new cars is no larger in India than in Denmark, for example, despite the fact that India's population is 146 times as big. Cars are expensive and per person income in India is only one fiftieth that in Denmark (Population Crisis Committee, 1978).

Many companies shy away from less developed nations because of the risks inherent in potential economic and political instability. Others are willing to take a chance because of the huge demographic potential that can mean enormous profits (as a sign on the floor of the Pacific Coast Stock Exchange says: "No guts, no glory"). One such gambling company is H. J. Heinz, whose president has said, "Much of our planning stems from an awareness that we serve only 15 percent of the world's population. There's huge potential to expand our markets to the remaining 85 percent" (quoted by Hymowitz, 1983). Thus, in 1983 Heinz became the first post-revolution foreign investor in Zimbabwe, acquiring majority interest in a cooking-oils company (Mufson, 1985).

A relatively safe third-world investment was made in China in 1985 by Nabisco when they negotiated a joint venture with a Chinese firm to make Ritz crackers for China's billion appetites (Bennett, 1985). CBS television also has an agreement with the China Central Television network to provide programming to be seen on that nation's 16 million television sets, with revenues to be split between CBS and the Chinese network. Other American companies, including Chrysler Corporation,

Nike, Inc., Avon Products, Beatrice Foods, Heinz, and R. J. Reynolds Tobacco, are also selling their wares in China (Wall Street Journal, 1983b; 1984; 1985b; 1985d; 1987).

Demographics of Human-Resource Management

Whether or not a firm uses demographics in its marketing or investment decisions, nearly all firms must cope with the fact that their employees are drawn from differing sociodemographic strata. A recognition of these differences (sometimes called "internal demographics"—Walsh and Lloyd, 1984) may well enable managers to deal more humanely and successfully with their human resources. Furthermore, knowledge of the optimal sociodemographic characteristics for a firm (for example, males or females, certain preferred racial or ethnic groups, certain required level of educational attainment or background) can be crucial in helping a company decide where it should locate a new plant or facility.

Sensitivity to the needs of workers is viewed by most management professionals as a prerequisite for maximizing employee morale and productivity, and the underlying demographic makeup of a company will influence what sorts of needs exist. A company that employs a large number of women may find itself dealing with the potential effects of maternity leaves, with the desirability of opening a child-care center, and with protecting employees from sexual harassment and the higher crime risk that might be associated with working late and leaving for home after dark. A company that counts on immigrants or resident aliens for its labor force will find itself needing bilingual supervisors and a set of policies recognizing that different cultural backgrounds demand different kinds of inducements to productivity.

Effective managers also need to be aware of the possible impact of demographic trends ("external demographics") on their work force. One reason for relatively low levels of worker productivity in the 1970s, for example, was the fact that the labor force was inundated with new, relatively inexperienced workers—Baby Boomers and women of all ages (Weber, 1982). As the Baby Bust generation moves into the labor force in the 1980s and 1990s, these smaller-sized cohorts will create greater competition among companies for the best workers, keeping unemployment low (all other things staying the same) and pushing up entry-level wages and salaries. This shrinking supply of younger workers could produce shortages among nurses, engineers, computer programmers, and other professionals, leading perhaps to more part-time employment of people (such as young mothers and the elderly) who are not presently in the labor force in high proportions (Lublin, 1982). In particular, it has forced some companies to think about ways to stem the long-run trend toward early retirement (Walsh and Lloyd, 1984).

In the meantime, the Baby Boomers are clogging up the middle management levels, significantly slowing the rate of promotion and leading to executive frustrations. Between 1980 and 1990 the number of middle-manager candidates from the Baby Boom will increase by 42 percent, while the number of managerial jobs is expected to grow by only 19 percent (Gottschalk, 1981). Top management at large corporations is struggling to maintain high job satisfaction for younger executives in the face of the diminished promotion prospects. BMC Industries, an electronics firm in St. Paul, Minnesota, has tried to keep "Baby Boomer executives" happy by offering "a menu of flexible perks worth up to 10 percent of base pay—including spousal travel, day care, a personal-computer lease, a home security system, an athletic club membership, financial counseling, and legal services" (Wall Street Journal, 1985c:A1).

If such efforts fail, companies risk losing valuable employees. Indeed, Eric Flamholtz, professor of management at the University of California at Los Angeles, sees more and more business-school graduates "becoming entrepreneurs and moving to smaller firms as they get fed up with waiting for advancement in big corporations" (quoted by Gottschalk, 1981:16). A side effect of this phenomenon is that it has created a growth industry out of executive search firms whose job it is to find bright, talented young managerial types and lure them away from their present employers—a task made easier by the lower firm loyalty that may stem from limited opportunities for promotion.

Corporate relocation is another aspect of business that often is enhanced by a demographic perspective. Part of the decision-making process with respect to moving a company should involve asking if a proposed new site has the right mix of potential workers. High-technology firms in the United States have tended to cluster in places like the "Silicon Valley" (Santa Clara County, California, south of San Francisco) because of the ready availability of computer and other engineering specialists. By contrast, the 1980 census lists no one in South Dakota with a doctorate in computer science. Nonetheless, the higher cost of housing (and of other space, as well) since the 1970s has slowed down the pace of company moves and of within-company job transfers. Furthermore, job transfers are increasingly complicated by two-career households, which may lead to some resistance to relocation. In 1982, for example, when Georgia-Pacific moved its headquarters from Portland, Oregon to Atlanta, Georgia, nearly half of its employees chose to stay behind (Calonius and Larson, 1982). Such a move, of course, has its own demographic implications: taking people out of one state and adding them to another. Tracking these and other population trends represents another use for demographics—social planning.

SOCIAL PLANNING

Demographics are widely used in American society to chart population movements and plan for social change. When such planning breaks down, as it often does in cities of third-world nations where rapid population growth is occurring, the result can be a certain amount of chaos, social foment, and even political upheaval. We can identify three major areas in which a demographic perspective aids in the planning process—education, public services, and health services. Although there are, to be sure, other social planning uses of demographics, I will focus on these three for illustrative purposes.

Education

Perhaps most obvious in its need for demographic information is the educational system. Public elementary and secondary school districts cannot readily recruit students or market their services to new prospects; they rise and fall on demographic currents that determine enrollment. As the Baby Boom gave way to the Baby Bust between 1975 and 1985, school enrollment in the United States dropped 15 percent, whereas some empty seats were taken in the late 1980s by the children of the more recent baby boomlet. It is doubtful, however, that in this century we will ever return to the enrollment levels of the 1960s.

There is variation among and between individual school districts and they have a need for fairly precise information, since even within a district some geographic areas may be growing while others are diminishing in the number of school-aged children. Do you close some schools and open new ones elsewhere? If so, what do you do with the old schools, and how do you pay for the new ones? Should children be bused from area to another? If so, how is that to be organized and paid for? Can teachers be retrained to fill classes where demand is growing? These and a host of related questions push school-district demographers to pore over questionnaires about the number of younger, pre–school-aged siblings reported by currently enrolled students; to examine birth records to see where the families are that are having babies; and to talk to realtors to assess the potential for home turnover and to evaluate the likely number of children among families moving in and out. From these data they construct enrollment projections, which are a vital part of public education planning.

> The consequences of failing to project public school enrollments accurately are clear. Underestimates may result in crowded classrooms, shortages of education personnel, and outmoded facilities. The quality of education suffers as a result. On the other hand, overestimates may lead to excess capacity in capital resources and to underutilized educators (Espenshade and Hagemann, 1977:1).

Educators must also bear in mind the important influence that economic conditions have on job opportunities and, thus, on the likelihood that people will be moving in or out. A sidelight to that issue is the potential drop in educational quality in the United States, occasioned at least partly by demographic trends themselves. Some of the less qualified teachers in public schools are people who were hastily recruited in the 1960s and early 1970s to meet the rise in demand for teachers created by the Baby Boom. Now these teachers have tenure and are locked into the educational system. Potentially better teachers began to choose other careers as the women's liberation movement (aided by declining fertility) opened new and more financially rewarding doors. Further, many younger teachers were laid off in the early 1980s as declining enrollments cost them their jobs. Typically, the best and the brightest of these found jobs elsewhere and may be lost forever to the educational system (Chase, 1983). The picture for teachers will brighten in the 1990s, however, when demand surges as a result of retirements of older teachers just as a resurgence in school enrollments (from the baby boomlet cohort) is expected.

Neither are colleges and universities immune to the effects of demographics. The threat of declining enrollments from the Baby Bust cohort has combined with belt-tightening budgets to force the cutback of some academic programs and thus deflect many younger doctoral candidates away from academics into other, higher-paying jobs. In general, however, higher education has been spared the full brunt of declining enrollment in secondary schools, because each year higher proportions of high school seniors have gone on to college. These same shifting demographics that complicate life for educators also make life hard for people whose job it is to plan for public services.

Public Services

Public services include such things as police and fire protection, the provision of water and sewers, power (gas and electricity), road maintenance, libraries, parks, and recreational facilities, all of which are typically funded, or at least subsidized, by public taxes. Changing demographics will affect both the tax base for, and the local needs that must be met by, public services. Local planners need to track not only total population size, but also the age, sex, and employment characteristics of the population in order to know what is needed and where. Data for this undertaking come primarily from the U.S. Census Bureau, funneled through state and regional data centers that disseminate demographic information to local communities. This is all part of the Federal-State Cooperative Program for Population Estimates, jointly undertaken by the U.S. Bureau of the Census and by state organizations. In Virginia, for example, the Tayloe Murphy Institute at the University of Virginia is the agency officially responsible for producing population estimates for that state's 136 counties and independent cities (Martin, 1985). In New Jersey, the state data center is actually a network of 90 different agencies, headed by the Office of Demographic and Economic Analysis of the New Jersey Department of Labor (Hughes, 1985).

Local population estimates allow planners to decide how much water needs to be stored in local reservoirs, where new sewage pipes need to go, which surrounding areas might be candidates for annexation, and how many firefighters and police officers should be recruited and trained. In 1982, for example, the San Diego Police Department held a conference on police issues—a gathering of social science experts who were asked to do a bit of forecasting about possible community changes with which the police would have to cope in the future (Henson and Zadorozny, 1982). Demographic changes were highlighted, since San Diego is a rapidly growing metropolitan area with a tremendous cultural mix of both internal and international migrants. Changes in the types of crimes committed and the areas of the city in which crime might decline or increase were identified. High-density areas populated by young, childless individuals represent areas of high crime opportunity with which police must deal, while older areas with high proportions of older people constitute another set of criminal opportunities. Additionally, areas in which one ethnic group is displacing another were seen as representing potential hot spots of juvenile violence. Indeed, virtually every policy shift that was proposed for future policing activities had an underlying demographic basis because, as I touched on in Chapter

8, criminal arrest and victimization rates tend to vary by socioeconomic status, by age, and by ethnicity.

Demographic factors are also key elements in planning decisions made for one of the most important societal resources—health services.

Health Services

Are you planning to have a baby? You might consider going to Las Vegas, where in 1983 the Sunrise Hospital (one of that city's three major hospitals) cut its maternity ward fees nearly in half in order to increase business (Witt, 1983). That is a far cry from the 1950s and 1960s, when babies were being delivered in the halls of nearly every medical facility in the nation because hospitals simply could not keep up with the demands placed on maternity wards.

Not only hospitals but physicians are having to "reposition" themselves in a classic marketing sense in order to meet the needs of a society that is changing demographically. For example, Dr. George McCollum of Pittsburgh, Pennsylvania found in 1982 that it was becoming worth his while to make himself known to older patients at a local hospital and to elderly residents of nursing homes and boarding houses (Toman, 1982). Such a strategy certainly makes sense given the aging of the population and the fact that the elderly utilize health services far more frequently than younger people. Those aged 65 and older are more than twice as likely than those aged 18–44 to be admitted to a hospital, and they spend an average of 7 more days each year in the hospital (National Center for Health Statistics, 1987b). In fact, "an estimated 40 percent or more of physician office time and 33 percent of hospital time are devoted to older patients" (Butler, 1978:200). Despite this enormous proportion of all health care that is devoted to the elderly, medical schools and teaching hospitals were slow to pick up the demographic trends. A survey in 1977 revealed that in the United States there were fewer than 700 geriatric medical specialists— physicians trained specifically in the medical needs of the elderly (Nelson, 1981).

Not only do older people have greater medical needs, they are also more likely to go to a physician for any particular ailment than are younger people. The Baby Boom generation is America's best-educated cohort, and that has boosted the transformation to greater reliance on self-care. Particularly among young, urban professionals (the "yuppies") there has been a booming market in fitness and health care publications along with a spate of new self-diagnosis tests and devices. Members of this young cohort tend to view physicians as experts to go to when you are in dire need of help but not for routine health problems, which can be handled effectively at home (Edmondson, 1985). So, when Huguley Hospital in Fort Worth, Texas opened a new Health Fitness Center in 1984 they decided that it would take some work to attract the attention of the demographic group they were initially interested in targeting—those aged 30–55 with incomes of $35,000 or more. With the assistance of a local firm they were able to locate people with those characteristics and successfully use a direct-mail approach to find prospective clients (Walsh, 1985b).

Unfortunately, broad health issues and problems often transcend the ability of local communities to find a remedy. Infant death resulting from low birth weight (which I discussed in Chapter 6) is a national issue, even though it must be dealt with at the local level. Likewise, the preference of older persons to remain at home even if they suffer from severe chronic illness is a national issue with repercussions at the community level. In general, the provision of health services is so costly, and the training of health personnel so lengthy and expensive, that legislative action is often required to permit the system of health services to respond adequately to demographic changes. This takes us into the sphere of political planning.

POLITICAL PLANNING

The original purpose of the Census of Population in the United States was, in reality, political planning—to determine how membership in the House of Representatives should be distributed. Though that is still the single most compelling reason to conduct the census, the American federal government has increasingly tied the distribution of revenue to population counts. Thus, the number of people in an area and their sociodemographic makeup (especially in terms of ethnicity and income) are critical factors in the amount of federal money received by local communities—an aspect of legislative analysis in which demographics play a role.

Legislative Analysis

Demographics underlie many of the major social issues that confront national and state legislators, as you know from the previous chapters. As Peter Morrison has said, "Demographic change bears directly on the formulation of social policy because it determines in large part whose wealth or income is redistributed" (Morrison, 1980:85). The demographics of the Baby Boom, for example, probably helped fuel inflation during the 1970s. Government policies in that period were oriented toward creating new jobs for the swelling numbers of labor force entrants, directly contributing to inflation through government expenditure and indirectly having an effect because Congress' attention was turned away from combating inflation (Freund, 1982).

The influence of the Baby Boom was felt in another way in many states in the late 1960s and early 1970s through pressure to lower the legal drinking age from 21 to 18. The result, unfortunately, has been an increase in alcohol-related deaths in that age group, and in the mid-1980s there were signs that some states were going back to the higher limit.

One of the more controversial aspects of political planning that is tied closely to demographics is the issue of social security and other benefits for the elderly. In general, as the older population has grown in size in the United States and the number of children has declined, the political clout of those groups has followed suit. Programs for elders have risen to record levels of public funding, while public financing of children's programs has been rolled back (Preston, 1984). Looking to the future, we can see that between the years 2000 and 2010 there will be nearly a 50 percent increase in the population aged 60–69. The Baby Boom generation will be squeezing the social security system. It is clear that legislative action will be required to make long-run changes in the financing and benefit structure of social security if the system is to survive. Changes will be made, of course, even if their exact shape is difficult to forecast. What seems likely, however, is that people who are aged 30–40 in the 1980s will pay increasingly high social security taxes for the next two decades, only to find reduced benefits when they decide to retire.

If people continue to retire disproportionately to Sun Belt states, particularly along the Gulf Coast of the United States (Florida through Texas), the elderly will indirectly contribute to the government expenditure that has grown with the population—protection against hurricanes. The government cannot legislate the weather, but population growth in potentially hard-hit areas has forced the government to spend considerable resources developing elaborate warning systems and evacuation plans in order to minimize injury and death if a major hurricane does strike. Six thousand people died in a hurricane in Galveston in 1900; today that region has many times the population of 1900, while hurricane prediction is only slightly better (Calonius, 1983).

In the meantime, another concern of demographic origin has cropped up with regard to the social security system. Does it "rip off" minority group members? And, if so, should different criteria be used for calculating benefits for different racial and ethnic groups? Let me concentrate on the first question. If we assume that people enter the labor force at age 20, and if we focus our attention momentarily on males (for the sake of simplicity), we find that in 1982, 59 percent of blacks aged 20 could expect to still be alive at age 65, compared with 73 percent of white males. (For females the figures are 76 percent for blacks and 87 percent for whites.) Thus, the argument goes, blacks will pay into the social security system all their working lives, but the probability is lower that they will live long enough to collect a pension check. Is that fair? Probably not, but a book of this sort is not the place to deal with that, which is as much a political issue as it is a social one. It is, in fact, the kind of topic that might well be discussed by political candidates—a group of people that makes increasing use of demographic information as a part of campaign strategies.

Campaign Strategy

Demographics are used extensively by politicians seeking office. After researching the sociodemographic characteristics of voters in their constituency, they must either match their election platform to the political attitudes of such voters or realize that they will face an uphill battle to convince people to vote for them. Politicians, of course, are typically concerned about appealing only to potential voters in their own geographic district, so the term **geodemographics** has been created to refer to demographic data that are for carefully defined geographic regions. In 1983, Edward Schneider, vice president and research director of Market Opinion Research, wrote that "a burgeoning industry is forming to supply the demand for applying geodemographics to political campaigns. . . . Geodemographics methods are likely to be an integral part of every aspect of a campaign" (quoted in American Demographics, 1983).

In truth, the strategies for "packaging and selling" a candidate are not unlike those used for any other product or service. Census and survey data are used to map the demographic characteristics of voters in a candidate's area and an appropriate plan of action is prepared, quite possibly using the psychographic approach that I discussed earlier with reference to marketing. Remember, though, that to be elected, a candidate must appeal to voters, not necessarily to all people who reside in an area. Since not all residents may be eligible to vote (because they are too young, are not citizens, or are convicted felons) and since not all who are eligible will actually vote, these differences may be crucial. Effective campaign strategy must take into account demographic intelligence such as the fact that the older you are the more likely you are to actually vote. Voting also goes up with education (U.S. Bureau of the Census, 1983g). Young women (under age 45) have also become a particularly enthusiastic segment of the electorate in the 1980s (Carlson, 1984b).

Those candidates who pay attention to demographics may have a greater chance of winning the opportunity to put their demographic literacy to work in effective legislation. My own belief is, not unexpectedly, that you should be aware of the underlying influences of demographics in nearly every aspect of your life—from the probability of finding a suitable mate to the probable size of your retirement check. If you take this interest in population change seriously, you may even wish to consider a career in demographics.

SHOULD YOU PURSUE A CAREER IN DEMOGRAPHICS?

The demographics of higher education preclude an abundance of academic jobs in most social science fields (including demography) until at least the mid-1990s, as you know from the previous discussion. But, an increasing awareness on the part of businesses that demographics represents a useful (and thus profitable) resource means that an increasing number of job opportunities exist in the field of applied demography. The U.S. Department of Labor suggests that in the 1990s "increased demand for sociologists is likely to arise from demographic research and the need to evaluate and administer programs designed to cope with social and welfare programs. . . . Additional demographers may be sought to help businesses plan marketing and advertising programs and to help developing countries analyze censuses, prepare population projections, and formulate long-range public planning programs" (U.S. Department of Labor, 1986:109).

By the late 1980s a number of large companies in the United States already had demographers on their payrolls. At the Chesapeake and Potomac Telephone Companies, as at Pacific Gas and Electric, demographers project the formation of new households and the size and composition of households in order to estimate future demand for utilities. General Motors hired a demographer to ease its search for engineers, especially minorities and women, while Westinghouse Health Systems, a division of Westinghouse Electric Corporation, created an active consulting business

THE DEMOGRAPHICS OF JURIES—A CASE STUDY

The Sixth Amendment to the U.S. Constitution guarantees every American accused of a crime the right to be tried by a jury of peers. A "jury of peers" means that the jury must be chosen from a panel of people that represents a demographic cross section of the community, according to a 1975 U.S. Supreme Court ruling in the case of *Taylor* v. *Louisiana*. By that broad definition, of course, you can easily imagine that the makeup of a jury could become exceedingly complex (for example, finding the proportionate numbers of "butchers, bakers, and candlestick makers"). So, in 1979, in *Duren* v. *Missouri,* the Supreme Court established a three-pronged test to determine whether a jury panel is a fair cross section of the population. To successfully argue that it is *not,* a defendant must be able to show that (1) the group alleged to be excluded or underrepresented is "distinctive" or "cognizable"; (2) the underrepresentation is not reasonable given the number of such "distinctive" persons in the community; and (3) the underrepresentation is a result of some systematic bias in the jury selection process.

Obviously, if a defendant has no quarrel with the jury panel, it is unlikely that any existing demographic unrepresentativeness will be challenged. On the other hand, if you, as a defendant, are a member of a group that you think is either excluded from or underrepresented on the jury panel, you are more likely to challenge the jury panel, based on the assumption that people who share your sociodemographic characteristics will be more apt than others to sympathize with your plight. In such a case, the first step is to make sure that these sympathetic (you hope) people are adequately represented in the pool of potential jurors.

Over time, courts have consistently agreed that blacks and Hispanics in the United States represent distinctive groups, where distinctive (or "cognizable," as the court rulings usually say) is defined as "a group of citizens who share a common perspective gained precisely because of membership in the group, which perspective cannot be adequately represented by other members of the community" (*Rubio* v. *Superior Court* [California, 1979]). The demographer's job, then, becomes to examine whether or not blacks and/or Hispanics are underrepresented on specific jury panels and, if so, to assess whether the reason for the underrepresentation is found within the jury selection system (and thus is remediable).

Although there is some evidence that blacks historically had been deliberately kept out of juries in a few southern states (Benokratis, 1982), one of the first major legal tests of the issue occurred not in the South but in California, in the case of *People* v. *Rhymes*. Deborah Rhymes is a black woman who was convicted of a crime in Pomona (a community in southern California) in 1979. She immediately appealed the conviction, however, on the grounds that she had been denied a jury of her peers—only two blacks had been in the pool of jurors, and none had been seated on the jury hearing her case.

The court of appeals agreed to hear the case in 1982, and her lawyer called on Edgar Butler, a social demographer in the Department of Sociology at the University of California, Riverside. He testified that the 1970 census showed blacks to represent 10.8 percent of the population in the county of Los Angeles (the 1980 census data had not yet been tabulated at the time of the hearing), whereas a survey of prospective jurors that he had conducted showed that only 6.2 percent were black. Thus, there were only 57 percent as many blacks in the pool of jurors as one would have expected given the demographic makeup of the community.

Why the disparity? Other defense witnesses testified that the process of selecting jurors was biased because at that time in California jurors were drawn exclusively from lists of registered voters. Yet blacks (as well as Hispanics) are less likely than members of most other groups in the population to be registered voters. In 1982, for example, 66 percent of whites aged 18 and older interviewed nationally in the Current Population Survey reported that they were registered to vote, compared with 59 percent of blacks and only 35 percent of Hispanics (U.S. Bureau of the Census, 1983g). The logical conclusion was that minority group members were disproportionately missing from the voter registration rolls and therefore were disproportionately less likely to be called in for jury duty. The court concluded that Rhymes had, indeed, been denied a fair trial and ordered her freed on her own recognizance pending a retrial on the same charges, but with a new jury.

In the meantime, this and several similar cases throughout California prompted the state legislature to revamp the source lists from which jurors are selected. Beginning in 1984, each judicial district in California was required to merge data from lists of people obtained not only from the Registrar of Voters but also from the Department of Motor Vehicles (from which people obtain driver's licenses and identification cards). Although that change did improve the demographic cross section of jury panels in California (as has occurred in other states where similar changes have been introduced), it did not solve all of the potential problems.

In 1988 I was called to provide testimony about jury demographics in the case of *People* v. *Ware* in the Santa Monica branch courthouse of the Los Angeles Superior Court. Charles Ware, the defendant, had been charged with killing two people while burglarizing a home, and he was facing the death penalty. His lawyers were concerned that Ware, who is black, would be tried by a predominantly white (and

possibly less sympathetic) jury because they believed that juries in Santa Monica tended to be disproportionately white and were underrepresentative of blacks.

A survey of 2,553 people showing up for jury duty at the Santa Monica courthouse in late 1987 and early 1988 revealed that in fact, 81 percent identified themselves as white, whereas only 5.8 percent identified themselves as black. To begin to unravel the mystery, you need to know that in Los Angeles County, the Office of the Jury Commissioner draws jurors from an area within a 20-mile driving radius of a particular courthouse. Analysis of the 1980 census data showed that 18.7 percent of the population aged 18 and older within a 20-mile driving radius of the Santa Monica courthouse was black.

The difference between 18.7 percent black in the community and 5.8 percent in the jury survey does not automatically lead to the conclusion that a disparity exists. Not everyone who is 18 or older is necessarily eligible to serve on a jury. To qualify, you must be a citizen and you must be adequately proficient in English. In a large, cosmopolitan area such as Los Angeles, many people are noncitizens or, especially if they are recently naturalized citizens, may not be sufficiently proficient in English to be able to serve on a jury. Using information available from the 1980 Census Public Use Microdata Sample (PUMS)—a detailed 1 percent sample of individuals counted in the 1980 census—I was able to find out how many people in each racial and ethnic category were "jury eligible"— 18 years of age or older, a citizen, and a speaker of English. These data revealed that in Los Angeles County, 95 percent of whites aged 18 and older are likely to be eligible for jury duty, compared with 98 percent of blacks but only 52 percent of Asians and 47 percent of Hispanics. After adjusting the data for these estimates, it turned out that 21.9 percent of the jury-

THE DEMOGRAPHICS OF JURIES—A CASE STUDY (Continued)

eligible population within a 20-mile radius of the Santa Monica courthouse was black. This is substantially higher than the 5.8 percent black population actually showing up at the courthouse. So why the big disparity this time?

With further analysis I discovered that a majority of blacks who lived within a 20-mile radius of the Santa Monica courthouse *also* lived within a 20-mile radius of the downtown courthouse in Los Angeles. Additionally, the jury commissioner's office had a policy of generally allowing people to serve in the courthouse nearest their home, and, for most blacks in the region, downtown was closer than Santa Monica. As a result, there were actually more blacks showing up for jury duty downtown than would have been expected based on the percentage of jury-eligible blacks within the 20-mile driving radius. It was apparent, then, that there were too few blacks on jury duty in Santa Monica at least partly because there were too many blacks on jury duty downtown.

On hearing the evidence, the court decided that blacks (a "distinctive" group) were unfairly underrepresented in the Santa Monica courthouse and that the cause of the disparity was the way in which jurors were assigned to different courthouses. The court therefore ordered the jury commissioner to redirect black jurors from downtown Los Angeles to the Santa Monica courthouse for Mr. Ware's trial. He was subsequently convicted of murder, but spared the death penalty.

For the typical defendant coming to trial in the United States, it is doubtful that the demographic composition of the jury will make a difference in the way in which evidence is weighed, arguments are perceived, and judgment is rendered. But, for a few people, demographics could be the key to a fair trial, and it is likely that a consideration of jury demographics will remain a useful tool to help ensure justice for all.

---

to do such things as project demand for school buildings and medical institutions. You may recall that Westinghouse has also been involved in more traditional demographic research through its worldwide program of Contraceptive Prevalence Surveys. Dayton-Hudson Corporation in Minneapolis uses demographic insight regularly in its planning for Dayton and Hudson stores as well as for Mervyn's, B. Dalton Bookseller, and Target Stores (Finch, 1986).

In 1982 the Population Association of America created a Committee on Business Demography, and in 1983 that group published a brochure in which committee members (most of whom are privately employed demographers) shared their insights into the employment of applied demographers. "Demographers are found in a variety of businesses . . . Fortune 500 companies, trade associations, newspapers, public utilities, private data companies, banks, consumer goods manufacturers, and pharmaceutical companies" (Population Association of America, 1983:2). Although titles of demographers vary, the following are illustrative: corporate planner, demographer, economist, information analyst, market analyst, market researcher, research analyst, and survey analyst.

What background should you have, besides reading this book, if you want to pursue a career in demography? The Population Association of America suggests that "a strong background in *demographic techniques* is recommended, especially in the areas of estimates, projections, and trend analysis. In addition, several companies are concerned with international demography, so coursework that includes the analysis of international data is helpful. A thorough understanding of *census geography* enables private-sector demographers to use U.S. demographic data correctly and effectively. *Research methods,* with an emphasis on the analysis of secondary data sources, is advocated. Finally, the study of *migration* theory, especially as it relates to internal migration, is also recommended" (Population Association of America, 1983:3).

Unfortunately, the training of applied demographers has not kept up with the growth of demographics as a field of activity (Merrick, 1985). For example, as of 1984 there were 16 universities in the United States that offered graduate programs in applied demography, but a survey the year before had shown that only 39 percent of people doing demographic analysis in the private sector had ever taken any kind of course in demography (Russell, 1984). That leaves a lot of room for improvement, and it may well be that as greater numbers of people enhance their own demographic perspective, as you have now done, the entire field of demographics will grow in sophistication and scope.

SUMMARY AND CONCLUSION

Until the 1980s business did little business with demography, but the computerization of census data has changed all that. Demographics has found a comfortable and important niche in the business world, especially in marketing, where demographic information permits more accurate segmentation of markets and the targeting of specific groups of consumers. Investors also pay attention to the way demographic trends point to future market growth and thus to potential profits. Human-resource managers are learning the value of knowing the demographics of their employees and of the labor force in general.

Before business got its hands on demographics, the major application of demographic theory and methods had been in planning—social planning, especially in education, but also in public and health services. Political planners have picked up on demographics, too, using it both for analysis of potential legislation and for strategy in election campaigns.

The applied uses of demography may help keep demography in front of you for the rest of your life. You are likely to encounter demographics in magazines, newspapers, television, and in the course of your work, no matter what it might be. As that happens, I hope that you will not fail to use your demographic perspective (your demographic literacy, if you will) in its broadest scope to keep track of local, national, and international population trends, because demographic events will contribute to many of the major social changes you will witness over your lifetime, just as you will continue to contribute to those population trends with your own behavior.

MAIN POINTS

1. Demographics is the application of population theory and methods to the solution of practical problems.

2. A major use of demographics is in the marketing of products and services in the private sector.

3. Marketing demographics involve segmenting markets (tailoring products and services to a specific demographic group) and targeting (aiming the advertising of a product or service to a specific demographic group).

4. A wide range of sociodemographic characteristics are used in targeting, including gender, age, education, income, and race and ethnicity.

5. Investors use demographics to pinpoint areas of potential market growth, since population is a major factor behind social change (and thus opportunity).

6. Human-resource managers use demographics to help increase their awareness of the special qualities and needs that exist among their present and prospective employees.

7. Education is the area of social planning in which demographics have been used most extensively.

8. Public agencies use demographics to plan for the adequate provision of services for their communities.

9. Health planners pay close attention to demographics because sickness and health are affected by sociodemographic characteristics and because the demand for services shifts with demographic trends.

10. Politicians find demographics helpful in the analysis of legislation and in the strategy for their own election to office.

11. You, too, could become a demographer. See your local professor for more details.

SUGGESTED READINGS

1. Thomas Merrick and Stephen Tordella, 1988, "Demographics: people and markets," Population Bulletin 43(1).
    This is an excellent overview of the field of applied demography written by two demographers from an organization that provides such services to commercial customers.

2. David B. Hill and Mary M. Kent, 1988, "Election demographics," Population Trends and Public Policy, No. 14 (Washington, D.C.: Population Reference Bureau).
    This is a very informative guidebook to the way in which demographic information can be used in political campaigns.

3. Louis G. Pol, 1987, Business Demography: A Guide and Reference for Business Planners and Marketers (New York: Quorum Books).

This is meant to be an all-purpose introduction to demography for business students, but the last third of the book is a fine summary of the application of demographic concepts and techniques in the business environment.

4. Wendy Manning and William O'Hare, 1988, "The best metros for Asian-American businesses," American Demographics 10(8):34–37.

This is one among many articles on demographics published each month in American Demographics, the most important publishing outlet for research on applied demography.

5. Norfleet W. Rives, Jr., and William J. Serow, 1984, Introduction to Applied Demography: Data Sources and Estimation Techniques (Beverly Hills, CA: Sage Publications).

This was the first book published on the specific topic of applied demography. Although it is largely concerned with quantitative methods in applied demography, it is a useful reference and background resource.

EPILOGUE

More than 5 billion humans occupy the earth now—twice as many as there were 40 years ago, yet only half as many as there could be 40 years from now. In this historically tiny fraction of time, humans have indulged in a binge of reproduction and accumulation of wealth and knowledge totally without precedent in the million or so years of human existence. The result is that the world has "shrunk"; we are not isolated from others but are intimately bound up with events taking place all over the world. In a sense, you and I live in a world that is much smaller than the worlds of Plato, Michelangelo, or Thomas Jefferson. The daily addition to the world's population of nearly a quarter of a million people affects each one of us, even if we may not live in a country with a rapidly increasing population. Your ability to get a job, buy a home, have a nutritious meal, travel, and know about the world around you are now, and will be increasingly in the future, limited by population growth and the demands made by more people for a share of the resources of this earth.

I am not an alarmist who anticipates a catastrophic collapse of the world economic and political structure as a result of sustained population growth. That view is analogous to the straw that broke the camel's back. My own view is that population growth is slow and insidious, hard to see on a daily basis, but readily apparent if you apply a little mental time-lapse photography—if you stand back and compare the world, or perhaps even your own community, now with what it was like 10 years ago. Now project that image another 10 years into the future to imagine what life will be like when there almost certainly will be 1 billion more people competing for energy to drive cars, heat homes, and run factories; for lumber to build houses; for jobs; for food; or just for a place to put down your beach blanket.

Are you a helpless victim, or is there something you can do? The answer is that adjustments will have to be made by both governments and individuals as events foreclose many of the options we enjoy today. Yes, to a certain extent you are a victim of the tremendous momentum for future growth that exists in the world today, and there is virtually nothing you can do to prevent the American or world population from being larger 10 to 20 years from now than it is today. On the other hand, neither are you totally a victim. Remember that population growth is the result of billions of individual decisions, including your own, about childbearing in particular but also about health care and migration. Your decisions, and your influ-

482

ence on the decision making of others, will contribute to future patterns of population growth and change.

Now in response to the second part of my question—yes, there are things that can be done. In the first place, the demographic perspective you have acquired by reading and studying this book should enable you to do a better job coping with future change. You now understand that world population growth began as a result of the decline in the death rate but is sustained by a relatively slow change in reproductive behavior. You understand that migration plays a very important role in influencing population growth in local areas, and that migration and fertility changes are especially crucial in shaping the age/sex structure of society—which in turn influences the way in which that society will be organized. You understand that characteristics such as income, education, race, and ethnicity usually influence demographic behavior and that when you meet someone with specific demographic characteristics, you may well expect to find certain patterns of migration, childbearing, and health problems. You understand that population growth may stimulate economic development in some instances, but that in the long run it probably inhibits the ability of a society to improve the overall level of the human condition. You understand that with prevailing technologies it would not be possible for everyone in the world to eat as Americans do, and that continued efforts to feed the world's population may be partly offset by the resulting damage to the environment. You understand that people all over the world are crowding into cities, and that while crowding itself may not be harmful, the very process may be fraught with considerable human trauma. You understand that improving the status of women is important in lowering fertility levels in the future, but you also understand that the desire to limit births is not accepted worldwide as a reasonable policy for people to engage in or for governments to pursue. You understand that as the less developed nations beget more children, the industrialized nations are growing at the other end of the age structure, and the attention of those concerned about the human condition will become divided between the needs and demands of the old and the needs and demands of the young.

The poor person who sees little hope for improvement in life may see children as the only potential escape. Perhaps one of his or her children will be able to escape from poverty and pull along the other family members. The nationalist or racial or ethnic chauvinist may see a strength in numbers that overrides any other concern about population growth. A Marxist may choose to ignore population growth and concentrate instead on effecting a social revolution which, he or she would contend, would bring people and resources into proper alignment. Others may subscribe to a faith of unfounded optimism—"God will provide," even though it is not apparent now what form those heavenly provisions will take.

There are certainly obstacles to any worldwide implementation of population control, but that does not mean that birth rates cannot or will not decline substantially. It is people, not just governments, who must change, and even a small dose of demographic perspective can go a long way in influencing behavior. It is my hope that in reading this book you have established in your own mind a framework for the kind of demographic behavior that will best help to achieve the future you want, and that you can share that insight with others, thereby reducing the number of people who are helpless victims of population growth.

APPENDIX
The Life Table,
Net Reproduction Rate,
and Standardization

In the preceding 16 chapters I have referred to the expectation of life, the probabilities of survival, the level of generational replacement, and standardization of vital rates. Although you should be familiar with the concepts, the actual measurements are somewhat complex and so I have reserved them for this appendix rather than sidetracking you (and maybe derailing you) earlier on. The expectation of life and the probabilities of survival are derived from a set of statistical calculations called a life table, while the level of generational replacement is measured by the net reproduction rate—a statistic that requires data from a life table in its calculation. Standardization is a procedure that permits us to control for the effects of other variables when we compare crude birth or death rates.

THE LIFE TABLE

The **life table** is a somewhat complex statistical device for summarizing the mortality experience of a population. It is a basic demographic tool and has a wide range of applications beyond the study of mortality. Life-table techniques have been used to study divorce (see Schoen and Nelson, 1974), migration (see Long, 1973), school dropouts, labor force participation, fertility, family planning, and other problems (see Chiang, 1984). It is the backbone of the insurance industry, since actuaries use life tables to estimate the likelihood of occurrence of almost any event for which an insurance company might want to issue a policy.

The life table has been around since the middle of the seventeenth century, when an Englishman, John Graunt, developed it as a means to show the different patterns of mortality in London, as I mentioned in Chapter 1. He found, for example, that some parts of London had consistently higher levels of mortality than other areas. At the time it was an important discovery, because it helped to explode the myth that death was totally capricious. I might note that since the life table is based on death, it perhaps should be called a death table. It is, however, typical of our culture to resist morbid topics just as we resist death, and so we call it a life table.

The major goal of the life table, as it is applied to the study of mortality trends and levels, is to calculate the average remaining lifetime, or expectation of life as it is usually called. It is an index of the number of additional years beyond the current age that a typical individual can expect to live if mortality levels remain unchanged. It is an average, representing the potential experience of a hypothetical group of people. In that sense it is analogous to the total fertility rate, an index of fertility discussed in Chapter 4.

In discussing each part of the life table, reference will be made to Tables A.1 and A.2, life tables for U.S. females and males in 1985. Life-table calculations begin with a set of age/sex–specific death rates (see Chapter 6), and then the first step in calculating expectations of life is to find the probabilities of dying during any given age interval. Note that in the following examples I will be referring to an **abridged life table,** rather than a **complete life table**. The former groups ages into 5-year categories, while the latter uses single years of age. The calculations are slightly different for the two different kinds of life tables, but the interpretation of the results is identical.

Table A.1 Life Table for U.S. Females (1985)

(1) Age Interval	(2) Age-Specific Death Rates in Age Interval (per 1,000)	(3) Probability of Death (proportion of persons alive at beginning who die during interval)	Of 100,000 Hypothetical People Born Alive			Number of Years Lived		(8) Expectation of Life
			(4) Number Alive at Beginning of Interval	(5) Number Dying During Age Interval	(6) In the Age Interval	(7) In This and All Subsequent Age Intervals		Average Number of Years of Life Remaining at Beginning of Age Interval
x to $x + n$	$_nM_x$	$_nq_x$	l_x	$_nd_x$	$_nL_x$	T_x		e_x^0
0–1	9.32	0.0094	100,000	935	99,199	7,818,820		78.2
1–5	.44	0.0017	99,065	173	395,846	7,719,621		77.9
5–10	.21	0.0011	98,892	105	494,174	7,323,775		74.1
10–15	.21	0.0010	98,787	100	493,719	6,829,601		69.1
15–20	.46	0.0023	98,687	229	492,899	6,335,882		64.2
20–25	.53	0.0026	98,458	260	491,652	5,842,983		59.3
25–30	.60	0.0030	98,198	294	490,270	5,351,331		54.5
30–35	.78	0.0039	97,904	385	488,602	4,861,061		49.7
35–40	1.10	0.0055	97,519	540	486,340	4,372,459		44.8
40–45	1.74	0.0087	96,979	842	482,946	3,886,119		40.1
45–50	2.86	0.0142	96,137	1,364	477,523	3,403,173		35.4
50–55	4.64	0.0229	94,773	2,169	468,779	2,925,650		30.9
55–60	7.21	0.0355	92,604	3,287	455,287	2,456,871		26.5
60–65	11.20	0.0547	89,317	4,883	435,088	2,001,584		22.4
65–70	16.71	0.0806	84,434	6,801	406,058	1,566,496		18.6
70–75	25.99	0.1229	77,633	9,545	365,528	1,160,438		14.9
75–80	40.94	0.1875	68,088	12,768	310,027	794,910		11.7
80–85	69.58	0.2993	55,320	16,557	236,363	484,883		8.8
85 and over	143.43	1.0000	38,763	38,763	248,520	248,520		6.4

Source: National Center for Health Statistics, 1988, Vital Statistics of the United States, 1985, Volume II—Mortality, Part A, Table 1-8; Volume II—Section 6, "Life Tables," Table 6-1.

Table A.2 Life Table for U.S. Males (1985)

(1) Age Interval	(2) Age-Specific Death Rates in Age Interval (per 1,000)	(3) Probability of Death (proportion of persons alive at beginning who die during interval)	(4) Number Alive at Beginning of Interval	(5) Number Dying During Age Interval	(6) In the Age Interval	(7) In This and All Subsequent Age Intervals	(8) Average Number of Years of Life Remaining at Beginning of Age Interval
x to $x + n$	$_nM_x$	$_nq_x$	l_x	$_nd_x$	$_nL_x$	T_x	e_x^0
0–1	11.97	0.0120	100,000	1,196	98,966	7,119,925	71.2
1–5	.58	0.0023	98,805	226	394,692	7,020,759	71.1
5–10	.28	0.0014	98,578	140	492,508	6,626,067	67.2
10–15	.35	0.0017	98,438	169	491,882	6,133,559	62.3
15–20	1.15	0.0057	98,269	560	490,092	5,641,677	57.4
20–25	1.65	0.0082	97,709	802	486,583	5,151,585	52.7
25–30	1.67	0.0083	96,907	807	482,495	4,665,002	48.1
30–35	1.90	0.0095	96,100	908	478,257	4,182,507	43.5
35–40	2.35	0.0118	95,192	1,121	473,299	3,704,250	38.9
40–45	3.33	0.0166	94,071	1,560	466,725	3,230,951	34.3
45–50	5.14	0.0254	92,511	2,347	457,124	2,764,226	29.9
50–55	8.36	0.0409	90,164	3,688	442,187	2,307,102	25.6
55–60	13.42	0.0651	86,476	5,631	419,094	1,864,915	21.6
60–65	20.62	0.0985	80,845	7,965	385,341	1,445,821	17.9
65–70	30.62	0.1429	72,880	10,414	339,342	1,060,480	14.6
70–75	47.48	0.2135	62,466	13,338	279,746	721,138	11.5
75–80	71.43	0.3044	49,128	14,955	208,385	441,392	9.0
80–85	110.25	0.4315	34,173	14,744	133,156	233,007	6.8
85 and over	183.25	1.0000	19,429	19,429	99,851	99,851	5.1

Source: National Center for Health Statistics, 1988, Vital Statistics of the United States, 1985, Volume II—Mortality, Part A, Table 1-8; Volume II—Section 6, "Life Tables," Table 6-1.

Probability of Dying

The probability of dying $(_nq_x)$ between ages x and $x + n$ is obtained by converting age/sex–specific death rates to probabilities. You will recall that such death rates relate deaths in a single year to the total (usually midyear) population in the given age group. However, a probability of death relates the number of deaths during any given number of years (that is, between any given exact ages) to the number of people who started out being alive and at risk of dying. For most age groups, except the very youngest and oldest, for which special adjustments are made, death rates $(_nM_x)$ for a given sex for ages x to $x + n$ may be converted to probabilities of dying according to the following formula:

$$_nq_x = \frac{(n)(_nM_x)}{1 + \frac{1}{2}(n)(_nM_x)}$$

I should point out that this formula is only an estimate of the actual probability of death. Rarely do we have the data that would permit an exact calculation, but the difference between the estimation and the "true" number will seldom be significant. The principal difference between reality and estimation is the fraction that, in the above equation, is shown as $\frac{1}{2}$. This fraction implies that deaths are distributed evenly over an age interval and thus the average death occurs halfway through that interval. This is a good estimate for every age above 4, regardless of race or sex (Chiang, 1984). At the younger ages, however, death tends to occur earlier in the age interval. Chiang (1984) suggests that the appropriate fraction for ages 0–1 is $\frac{1}{10}$ and for ages 1–4 it is $\frac{4}{10}$. Another special case is the oldest age group (85+ in Tables A.1 and A.2) because it is open-ended, going to the highest age at which people might die. Thus it is obvious that the probability of death in this interval is 1.000—death is certain.

In Tables A.1 and A.2 the age-specific death rates for 1985 are given in column (2). In column (3) they have been converted to probabilities of death from exact age x (for example, 10) to exact age $x + n$ (for example, $10 + 5 = 15$).

Deaths in the Life Table

Once the probabilities of death have been calculated, the number of deaths that would occur to the hypothetical life-table population is calculated. The life table assumes an initial population of 100,000 live births, which are then subjected to the specific mortality schedule. These 100,000 babies represent what is called the radix (l_0). During the first year, the number of babies dying is equal to the radix (100,000) times the probability of death. Subtracting the babies who died $(_1d_0)$ gives the number of people still alive at the beginning of the next age interval (l_1). These calculations are shown in columns (4) and (5) of Tables A.1 and A.2. In general:

$$_nd_x = (_nq_x)(l_x)$$

and

$$l_{x+n} = l_x - {_n}d_x$$

Although we have not yet calculated the expectation of life, we already have some very useful information in column (4). This column indicates how many of the original 100,000 people are still alive at the beginning of any given age interval. Thus, since in Table A.1 92,604 women (out of the original 100,000) are still alive at age 55, we can say that the probability of surviving to age 55 is almost 93 percent for U.S. females in 1985. In other words, a female baby born in that year would have a 93 percent chance of living to age 55 if her mortality risks were exactly those experienced by the female population of the United States in 1985.

Number of Years Lived

The final two columns that lead to the calculation of expectation of life are related to the concept of number of years lived. During the 5-year period, for example, between the fifth and the tenth birthdays, each person lives 5 years. If there were 98,000 people sharing their tenth birthdays, then they all would have lived a total of $5 \times 98,000 = 490,000$ years between their fifth and tenth birthdays. Of course, if a person died after the fifth but before the tenth birthday, then we add in only those years that were lived prior to dying. This concept is analogous to the frequently used measure "person-years" as an index of the cost of something. For example, we might be told that a huge dam required 1,000 person-years to build. That does not mean that it took 1,000 years to build the dam, but rather that it could have been built if 1,000 people worked on it for a year, or if 2,000 people worked on it for half a year, and so on. With respect to mortality, we are interested in the fact that the lower the death rates, the more people will survive through an entire age interval and the greater the number of years lived will be. Since at all age intervals except the first and last we can assume that people die on average halfway through the interval, the number of years lived $({_n}L_x)$ can be estimated as follows:

$$_nL_x = n(l_x - \tfrac{1}{2}{_n}d_x)$$

Again I must comment that the fraction "½" is good for all age groups except 0–1 (for which we should use $\frac{1}{10}$) and 1–4 (for which we should use $\frac{4}{10}$). Furthermore, this formula will not work for the oldest, open age interval (85+), since there are no survivors at the end of that age interval and we have no data as to how many years each person will live before finally dying. All is not lost, however. We can estimate the number of years lived by dividing the number of survivors to that oldest cohort (l_{85}) by the death rate at the oldest age (M_{85}):

$$L_{85} = \frac{l_{85}}{M_{85}}$$

Let me warn you that these formulas will not exactly replicate the numbers shown in the life tables in Tables A.1 and A.2. This is because the National Center for Health Statistics actually uses single-year-of-age data to calculate $_nL_x$ and then abridges those data into 5-year intervals. However, the preceding formula will yield very close estimates of the official numbers.

The results of these calculations are shown in column (6). Then we add up the years lived, cumulating from the oldest to the youngest ages. These calculations are shown in column (7) and represent T_x, the total number of years lived in a given age interval and all subsequent intervals:

$$T_x = \sum_{i=x}^{\infty} {}_nL_x$$

Expectation of Life

Finally we arrive at the expectation of life, or average remaining lifetime. It is the total years remaining to be lived at exact age x and is found by dividing T_x by the number of people alive at that exact age (l_x). In column (8), we find that

$$e_x^0 = \frac{T_x}{l_x}$$

Thus, for U.S. females in 1985, the expectation of life at birth (e_0^0) was 7,818,820/ 100,000 = 78.2, while at age 55 a female could expect to live an additional 26.5 years. For males the comparable numbers are 7,119,725/100,000 = 71.2 as the expectation of life at birth in 1985; and the expectation of life at age 55 in 1985 was 21.6.

Although it has required some work, we now have a sophisticated single index that summarizes the level of mortality prevailing in a given population at a particular time.

Other Applications of the Life Table

The life table as a measure of mortality is actually a measure of duration—of the length of human life. We can apply the same techniques to the measurement of the duration of anything else—marriage, widowhood, employment, or contraceptive use, to use examples close at hand. However, by adding to the mathematical complexity of the table, we can gain additional insights into some of these phenomena by separating out specific events or by combining events. In the former instance we produce a *single-decrement* table and in the latter case we get a *multiple-decrement* table.

A single-decrement table can, for example, isolate the impact of a specific cause of death on overall mortality levels. Preston and his associates (1972) found that in

1964 the expectation of life for all females in the United States was 73.8 years. Deleting heart disease as a cause of death would have raised life expectancy by 17.1 years, to 90.9; whereas deleting cancer as a cause of death would have produced a gain of 2.6 years in life expectancy, to 76.3. A multiple-decrement table goes beyond the one-cause-at-a-time approach and allows you to look simultaneously at how deaths are distributed among several causes of death (see Keyfitz, 1977). Alternatively, we can examine different kinds of events that may go together. What are the probabilities at each age of leaving the labor force before death? Of dying before your spouse? Or of discontinuing a contraceptive method and becoming pregnant?

So far, I have mentioned only those situations in which people in the life table exit only once, through death or some other event. A next level of sophistication is to allow for a succession of possible contingencies—several migrations; entering and leaving the labor force, including periods of unemployment and retirement; school enrollment, with dropouts and reentries; moving through different marital statuses; and moving from one birth parity to another. Elaborate discussion of these techniques is, of course, beyond the scope of this book, but you should be aware that such methods do, in fact, exist to help untangle the mysteries of the social world.

NET REPRODUCTION RATE AND MEAN LENGTH OF GENERATION

The **net reproduction rate** (NRR) is a measure of generational replacement. Its lowest possible value is 0, meaning that there will be no next generation if things remain as they are. A value of 1 means that the next generation will be exactly replaced, no more and no less. Values greater than 1, of course, indicate that the next generation will be larger in size than the current one. More specifically, the NRR measures the average number of female children that will be born to the female babies born in a given year, assuming no change in the age-specific fertility and mortality rates (and ignoring the effect of migration).

To calculate the NRR for the United States for 1985, for example, we need the age-specific birth rates, the proportion of births that are females, and a life table for 1985 (we will use the data from Table A.1). From the life table we need to know the probability that a female will still be alive at a particular age. If she is alive, then she may be at risk of having a child.

The calculation of the net reproduction rate for the United States in 1985 is illustrated in Table A.3. Palmore and Gardner (1983) have succinctly described the process:

> We first enter the age-specific fertility rates including only female live births [column (3) of Table A.3]. Next, we enter the values for the number of person-years lived in each age interval, using the $_5L_x$ column from an abridged life table for females in the current period [in column (4) are data derived from Table A.1 for U.S. females in 1985]. Since the rates in column 3 are expressed per 1,000 women, we express the $_5L_x$ values per woman so that we do not multiply by 1,000 twice. We then take the product of the $_5L_x$ values and the age-specific rates [column (3) multiplied by column (4)]. The $_5L_x$ values

Table A.3 Net Reproduction Rate (United States, 1985)

(1) Age	(2) Midpoint of Interval	(3) Female Births per 1,000 Women per Year[a]	(4) Person-Years Lived in Age Interval $(_5L_x/l_0)$	(5) Female Births per 1,000 Women for 5-Year Period [Column (3) × Column (4)]	(6) Column (2) × Column (5)
10–14	12.5	0.57	4.93719	2.81	35.12
15–19	17.5	29.88	4.92899	147.28	2577.40
20–24	22.5	51.73	4.91652	254.33	5722.42
25–29	27.5	52.49	4.90270	257.34	7076.85
30–34	32.5	32.54	4.88602	158.99	5167.18
35–39	37.5	11.35	4.86340	55.20	2070.00
40–44	42.5	1.90	4.82946	9.18	390.15
45–49	47.5	0.10	4.77523	0.48	22.80
Sum		180.56[b]		NRR = 885.61	23,061.92[c]

Sources: National Center for Health Statistics, 1988, Vital Statistics Report of the United States, 1985, Volume II—Mortality, Part A, Table 1-8; Volume II—Section 6, "Life Tables," Table 6-1; National Center for Health Statistics, 1988, Health, United States, 1987, Table 2 (Hyattsville, MD: NCHS).

[a] Calculated by multiplying the proportion of all female births in each group by the age-specific fertility rate for that age group.

[b] Gross reproduction rate (GRR) = [sum of column (3)] × 5 = 902.80.

[c] Mean length of generation = [sum of column (6)] ÷ NRR = 23,061.92 ÷ 885.61 = 26.04.

refer to a 5-year period, and therefore we do not need to multiply by 5 to get the NRR . . . [which] is simply the sum of the products of columns 3 and 4 (1983:91,93).

You can see that for the United States in 1985 the net reproduction rate was less than 1, indicating that if fertility and mortality remain exactly the same, the cohort of babies born in 1985 will not quite replace itself as it moves through the reproductive ages.

Another measure of replacement that follows easily from the calculations performed for the net reproduction rate is the mean length of generation. This measure answers the question: On the average, how many years after birth does a woman replace herself with female children? The measure is designed to give an indication of the speed with which each woman replaces herself with potential mothers.

The length of a generation is a weighted sum of the female births per 1,000 women for each five-year period, all divided by the net reproduction rate—that is, it is the average age of women at the birth of their children. The weights used are the ages of the women (Palmore and Gardner, 1983:95).

Table A.3 illustrates the calculation for the United States for 1985. You multiply the midpoint of each age interval [column (2)] by the female births per 1,000 women for that age interval [column (5)] and then you divide the result by the net reproduction rate [the sum of column (5)], yielding a figure of 26.04 years.

> The length of a generation is important, because it affects the rate of growth of a population independently of the number of children born as measured by the net reproduction rate. This is so because the more rapidly a generation replaces itself, the more rapidly it will add new members to the population (at whatever rate *per generation* prevails). The net reproduction rate tells us how much a population is growing per generation. It does not tell us how long the generation is (Palmore and Gardner, 1983:98).

STANDARDIZATION

In discussing crude birth and death rates in Chapters 4 and 6, respectively, I noted that they were "crude" because they failed to take the age and sex structure into account. I then went on to suggest other measures, such as the life table and the total fertility rate, which allow us to correct for these shortcomings, as long as the necessary data are available. The issue does not die there, however, because we can conceive of several other factors besides age and sex that could affect overall death and birth rates.

We know from Chapter 6 that death rates can be influenced not only by age and sex, but also by urban/rural residence, education, occupation, income, and marital status. Fertility rates are affected by these same variables, as you learned in Chapter 5. One way to take these or any other characteristics into account is through *standardization*—a set of calculations that statistically control for the effects of an external factor. In demography, the variable most often taken into account with standardization is, in fact, age. So I will use it in the following example, which illustrates the use of the standardization procedure as applied to the crude death rate. Remember, however, that an analogous set of procedures could be applied to any variable that the researcher thinks may be muddying up a comparison of overall crude rates.

There are two common ways of computing standardized rates. "One consists of applying different age-specific rates to a standard population; this is called (for no very good reason) in English and American usage, 'direct standardization.' The other consists of applying a standard set of rates to different populations by age; this is called 'indirect standardization.' In both types, the object is to calculate the number of deaths to be expected in one population, on the basis of some information from another population. This number of 'expected deaths' is used in calculating the standardized death rate" (Barclay, 1958:161). Both the direct and indirect methods are described in Barclay (1958) and Shryock, et al. (1976). In the following example I use the direct standardization procedure to calculate the age-standardized (also

Table A.4   Age-Standardized Death Rates for Mexico
(Females, 1980) Using the 1980 U.S. Population as the Standard

(1) Age	(2) Death Rates for Females, Mexico, 1980 (per 1,000)	(3) Standard Population (U.S., 1980) (in thousands)	(4) "Expected" Deaths in Mexico (2) × (3) (in thousands)
0–4	10.0	7,986	80
5–9	0.7	8,160	6
10–14	0.6	8,925	5
15–19	0.9	10,413	9
20–24	1.3	10,656	14
25–29	1.5	9,816	15
30–34	1.9	8,884	17
35–39	2.8	7,104	20
40–44	3.5	5,961	21
45–49	4.7	5,702	27
50–54	6.9	6,089	42
55–59	9.0	6,134	55
60–64	13.8	5,417	75
65–69	20.5	4,880	100
70–74	33.1	3,948	131
75–79	52.7	2,946	155
80+	153.2	3,474	532
Crude Death Rate in Mexico 1980 (Females)	5.3		
Total Standard Population (000's)		116,495	
Total Number of Expected Deaths (000's)			1,303
Crude Death Rate in the Standard Population		7.9	
Age-Adjusted Death Rate Mexico, 1980			(1,303/116,495) = 11.2

Sources: United Nations, 1988, *Demographic Yearbook 1986* (New York: United Nations): Table 14; and United Nations, 1985, *Demographic Yearbook 1983* (New York: United Nations): Table 7.

called the *age-adjusted*) death rate for Mexican females in 1980, compared with U.S. females in the same year. I will use the 1980 female population of the United States as the standard population.

In 1980 the crude death rate for females in Mexico was 5.3 deaths per 1,000 population. In the United States in the same year, the crude death rate for females was 7.9 per 1,000. Although Mexico had been developing at a rapid rate in the 1970s, you would probably suspect that the overall risk of death was still greater in Mexico in 1980 than it was in the United States. Because of the higher fertility in Mexico, the age structure in that country is younger than in the United States, putting disproportionate numbers of people in the relatively low-risk ages, even though the actual risk of dying at each specific age was higher. Age-standardization permits us to see how much of the difference in the crude death rate between Mexico and the United States is due to the differences in those two nations' age structures.

In Table A.4, you can see that the process of standardization begins with a listing of age-specific death rates for Mexican females in 1980 (column 2). These data are drawn from the *United Nations Demographic Yearbook*. We then apply those rates to the standard population (column 3) to see how many deaths would result in the standard population, given the risk of death at each age. This produces column 4, which is the expected number of deaths at each age in the standard population, given Mexico's age-specific death rates. Our interest is in the sum of this column—the total number of expected deaths, which we divide by the total number of people in the standard population to yield our age-adjusted or age-standardized death rate. The result is an age-adjusted death rate of 11.2 deaths per 1,000 among Mexican females when applied to the U.S. age structure. Thus, we can conclude that since the Mexican crude death rate (unadjusted) was lower than that in the United States, whereas the age-adjusted rate is higher (indeed, 42 percent higher), the observed difference in the crude death rates between the two countries is attributable entirely to the age structure.

GLOSSARY

This glossary contains words or terms that appeared in boldface type in the text. I have tried to include terms that are central to an understanding of the study of population. The chapter notation in parentheses refers to the chapter in which the term is first discussed in detail.

abortion the expulsion of a fetus prematurely; a miscarriage—may be either induced or spontaneous (Chapter 4).

abridged life table a life table (see definition) in which ages are grouped into categories (usually five-year age groupings) (Appendix).

accidental death loss of life unrelated to disease of any kind but attributable to the physical, social, or economic environment (Chapter 6).

achieved characteristics those sociodemographic characteristics such as education, occupation, income, marital status, and labor force participation, over which we do have some degree of control (Chapter 9).

age/sex pyramid graph of the number of people in a population by age and sex (Chapter 8).

age/sex–specific death rate the number of people of a given age and sex who died in a given year divided by the total number of people of that age and sex (Chapter 6).

age-specific fertility rate the number of children born to women of a given age divided by the total number of women that age (Chapter 4).

age stratification the assignment of social roles and social status on the basis of age (Chapter 11).

age structure the distribution of people in a population by age (Chapter 8).

Agricultural Revolution change that took place roughly 10,000 years ago when humans first began to domesticate plants and animals, thereby making it easier to settle in permanent establishments (Chapters 2 and 14).

alien a person born in, or belonging to, another country who has not acquired citizenship by naturalization—distinguished from citizen (Chapter 7).

Alzheimer's disease a disease involving a change in the brain's neurons, producing behavioral shifts; a major cause of senility (Chapter 11).

ambivalence state of being caught between competing pressures and thus being uncertain about how to behave properly (Chapter 5).

amenorrhea temporary absence or suppression of the menstrual discharge (Chapter 4).

amino acids building blocks from which proteins are formed (Chapter 14).

anovulatory pertaining to a menstrual cycle in which no egg is released (Chapter 4).

antinatalist based on an ideological position that discourages childbearing (Chapter 3).

arable describes land that is suitable for farming (Chapter 14).

ascribed characteristics sociodemographic characteristics such as gender and race and ethnicity, with which we are born and over which we have essentially no control (Chapter 9).

average age of a population one measure of the age distribution of a population—may be calculated as either the mean or the median (Chapter 8).

Baby Boom   the dramatic rise in the birth rate in the United States following World War II and lasting until well into the 1950s (Chapter 5).

base year   the beginning year of a population projection (Chapter 8).

birth control   regulation of the number of children you have through the deliberate prevention of conception; note that birth control does not necessarily include abortion (Chapter 4).

bracero   a Mexican laborer admitted legally into the United States for a short time to perform seasonal, usually agricultural, labor (Chapter 7).

capital   a stock of goods used for the production of other goods rather than for immediate enjoyment; anything invested to yield income in the future (Chapter 13).

capitalism   an economic system in which the means of production, distribution, and exchange of wealth are maintained chiefly by private individuals or corporations, as contrasted to government ownership (Chapter 3).

capitalist   based on capitalism (Chapter 13).

cardiovascular disease   a disease of the heart or blood vessels (Chapter 6).

carrying capacity   the size of population that could theoretically be maintained indefinitely at a given level of living (Chapter 13).

celibacy   permanent nonmarriage. A celibate is a person who never enters a sexual union, whether legal or not (Chapter 4).

census of population   an official enumeration of an entire population, usually with details as to age, sex, occupation, and so on (Chapter 1).

child-woman ratio   a census-based measure of fertility, calculated as the ratio of children aged 0–4 to the number of women aged 15–49 (Chapter 4).

chronic disease   disease that continues for a long time or recurs frequently (as opposed to *acute*)—often associated with degeneration (Chapter 6).

cohabitation   living together without benefit of legal marriage (Chapter 10).

cohort   persons who share something in common, typically their year of birth (Chapter 4).

cohort flow   the movement through time of a group of people born in the same year (Chapter 11).

communicable disease   (also called *infectious disease*) a disease capable of being communicated or transmitted from person to person (Chapters 2 and 6).

complete life table   a life table (see definition) based on data by single years of age (Appendix).

components of growth   a method of estimating and/or projecting population size by adding births, subtracting deaths, and adding net migration occurring in an interval of time, then adding the result to the population at the beginning of the interval (Chapter 8).

condom   a thin sheath, usually of rubber, worn over the penis during sexual intercourse to prevent conception or venereal disease (Chapter 4).

consolidated metropolitan statistical areas (CMSAs)   groupings of the very largest Metropolitan Statistical Areas in the United States (Chapter 12).

content error   an error caused by inaccuracy in the data obtained in a census; possibly an error in reporting, editing, or tabulating (Chapter 1).

contraception   the prevention of conception or impregnation by any of various techniques or devices; birth control (Chapter 4).

coverage error   the extent to which people are not included in the census (Chapter 1).

crowding   the gathering of a large number of people closely together; the number of people per space per unit of time (Chapter 12).

crude birth rate   the number of births in a given year divided by the total population in that year (Chapters 2 and 4).

crude death rate   the number of deaths in a given year divided by the total population in that year (Chapters 2 and 6).

crude net migration rate   a measure of migration calculated as the number of in-migrants minus the number of out-migrants divided by the average (midyear) population (Chapter 7).

deductive logic   a method of establishing an explanation for a particular phenomenon prior to having adequate facts to support the explanation (Chapter 3).

de facto population   the people actually in a given territory on the census day (Chapter 1).

degeneration   the biological deterioration of a body (Chapter 6).

de jure population   the people who "belong" in a given area whether or not they are there on the census day (Chapter 1).

demographic change and response   the theory that the response made by individuals to population pressures is determined by the means available to them (Chapter 3).

demographic characteristics   indicators of the social and economic organization of society such as race and ethnicity, education, occupation, income, and marital status (Chapter 9).

demographic overhead   the general cost of adding people to a population caused by the necessity of providing goods and services (Chapter 13).

demographic perspective   a way of relating basic information to theories about how the world operates demographically (Chapter 3).

demographics   the application of demographic science to practical problems; any applied use of population statistics (Chapter 16).

demographic structure   the organized pattern of demographic behavior that characterizes a population at a particular time (Chapter 1).

demographic transition   the process whereby a country moves from high birth and high death rates to low birth and low death rates with an interstitial spurt in population growth (Chapter 3).

demography   the science of population (Chapter 1).

density   the ratio of people to physical space (Chapter 12).

dependency ratio   the ratio of people of dependent age (0–14 and 65 +) to people of economically active ages (15–64) (Chapter 8).

diaphragm   a thin, dome-shaped device, usually of rubber, inserted in the vagina and worn over the uterine cervix to prevent conception during sexual intercourse (Chapter 4).

doctrine   a principle laid down as true and beyond dispute (Chapter 3).

donor area   the area from which migrants come (Chapters 7 and 8).

douche   (as a contraceptive) washing of the vaginal area after intercourse to prevent conception (Chapter 4).

economic development   a rise in the average standard of living associated with economic growth; a rise in per capita income (Chapters 10 and 13).

economic growth   an increase in the total amount of wealth in a nation without regard to the total number of people (Chapter 13).

ecosystem   a system formed by the interaction of a community of organisms with their environment (Chapter 14).

emigrant   a person who leaves one country or region to settle in another (Chapter 7).

epidemiologic transition   long-term shifts in health and disease patterns as mortality moves from high to low levels (Chapter 6).

error theory   a theory of human aging based on the notion that random error occurs in the synthesis of protein, leading to irreversible damage (and thus aging) of a cell (Chapter 11).

ethnic group   a group of people of the same race or nationality who share a common and distinctive culture while living within a larger society (Chapter 5).

ethnicity   the ethnic quality of a particular group (Chapter 9).

ethnocentric   characterized by a belief in the inherent superiority of one's own group and culture accompanied by a feeling of contempt for other groups and cultures (Chapter 3).

expectation of life   the average duration of life beyond any age, of persons who have attained that age, calculated from a life table (Chapter 6).

exponentially   (increasing) in a compound fashion (Chapter 2).

exurbanization   nonrural population growth beyond the suburbs (Chapter 12).

fecundity   the physical ability to reproduce (Chapter 4).

fertility   reproductive *performance* rather than the mere capacity to do so; one of the three basic demographic processes (Chapter 4).

force of mortality   the extent to which people are unable to live to their biological maximum (Chapter 6).

gender role   a social role considered appropriate for a person of one sex or the other (Chapter 10).

general fertility rate   the total number of births in

a year divided by the number of women in the childbearing ages (Chapter 4).

gentrification restoration and habitation of older homes in central city areas by urban or suburban elites (Chapter 12).

geodemographics use of demographic data specific to a particular geographic region (Chapter 16).

gestation the process of carrying a fetus in the uterus during the period from conception to delivery (Chapter 4).

Green Revolution an improvement in agricultural production begun in the 1940s based on high-yield–variety strains of grain and increased use of fertilizers, pesticides, and irrigation (Chapter 14).

gross reproduction rate the total fertility rate multiplied by the proportion of all births that are girls. It is generally interpreted as the number of female children that a female just born may expect to have in her lifetime, assuming that birth rates stay the same and ignoring her chances of survival through her reproductive years (Chapter 4).

high growth potential the stage in the demographic transition in which a population has a relative lack of voluntary control over births and deaths (Chapter 3).

high-yield varieties (HYV) dwarf types of grains that have shorter stems and produce more stalks than most traditional varieties (Chapter 14).

host area the destination area of migrants; the area into which they migrate (Chapter 7).

illegal migrants migrants coming into a country without proper government approval (Chapter 7).

immigrant a person who moves into a country of which he or she is not a native for the purpose of taking up permanent residence (Chapter 7).

implementing strategy a possible means whereby a goal might be attained (Chapter 7).

incipient decline a stage in the demographic transition when a country has moved from having a very high rate of natural increase to having a very low (possibly negative) rate of increase (Chapter 3).

inductive logic a method of establishing a general explanation for a phenomenon based on the examination of specific facts (Chapter 3).

Industrial Revolution the totality of the changes in economic and social organization that began about 1760 in England—later in other countries—characterized chiefly by the replacement of hand tools with power-driven machines and by the concentration of industry in large establishments (Chapter 2).

infanticide the deliberate killing of an infant—often through neglect or abandonment (Chapter 2).

infant mortality death during the first year of life (Chapter 6).

infecundity the inability to produce offspring (Chapter 4).

in-migrant a person who moves into an area. This term usually refers to an internal migrant; an international migrant is an immigrant (Chapter 7).

intensification of agriculture the process of increasing crop yield by any means—mechanical, chemical, or otherwise (Chapter 14).

intercensal component method a method of measuring net migration between two censuses by comparing actual population growth with that which would have resulted solely from the demographic components of birth and death (Chapter 7).

intercensal years the years between the taking of censuses (Chapter 1).

intermediate variables means for regulating fertility; the variables through which any social factors influencing the level of fertility must operate (Chapter 4).

internal migration permanent change in residence within national boundaries (Chapter 7).

international migration permanent change of residence involving movement from one country to another (Chapter 7).

intervening obstacles factors that may inhibit migration even if a person is motivated to migrate (Chapter 7).

intrauterine device (IUD) any small, mechanical device for semipermanent insertion in the uterus as a contraceptive (Chapter 4).

late fetal mortality fetal deaths that occur after at least 28 weeks of gestation (Chapter 6).

life expectancy see expectation of life.

lifespan the longest period over which an organism or species may live (Chapter 6).

life table an actuarial table showing the number of persons who die at any given age, from which the expectation of life is calculated (Chapter 6 and Appendix).

logarithm the exponent indicating the power to which a fixed number, the base, must be raised to produce a given number (Chapter 2).

logarithmic growth the concept that human populations have the capacity to grow in a logarithmic fashion, increasing geometrically in size from one generation to the next (Chapter 2).

longevity the ability to resist death (Chapter 6).

longitudinal study a study in which the subjects are followed through time (Chapter 7).

lysine a crystalline, basic amino acid essential in the nutrition of humans and animals (Chapter 14).

Malthusian pertaining to the theories of Malthus, which state that population tends to increase at a geometric rate, while the means of subsistence increase at an arithmetic rate, resulting in an inadequate supply of the goods supporting life, unless a catastrophe occurs to reduce the population or the increase of population is checked by sexual restraint (Chapter 3).

marital status the state of being married, single, separated, divorced, widowed, or living in a consensual union (Chapter 9).

marriage squeeze an imbalance between the numbers of males and females in the prime marriage ages (Chapter 10).

Marxist an adherent of Karl Marx or his theories, which assert that throughout history the state has been a device for the exploitation of the masses by a dominant class (Chapter 3).

maternal mortality the death of a woman as a result of childbearing (Chapter 6).

menarche the first menstrual period; the establishment of menstruation (Chapter 4).

menopause the time when menstruation ceases permanently, usually occurring between the ages of 45 and 50 (Chapter 4).

mercantilism the theory or practice of commercial pursuits (Chapter 2).

metropolitan area see standard metropolitan statistical area.

metropolitan statistical area (MSA) a "stand-alone" metropolitan area composed of a county with an urbanized area of at least 50,000 people (Chapter 12).

migrant a person who makes a permanent change of residence substantial enough in distance to in-

volve a shift in that individual's round of social activities (Chapter 7).

migration the process of changing residence from one geographic location to another; one of the three basic demographic processes (Chapter 7).

migration ratio the ratio of the net number of migrants (in-migrants minus out-migrants) to the difference between the number of births and deaths—measuring the contribution that migration makes to overall population growth (Chapter 7).

model stable population a population whose age and sex structure is implied by a given set of mortality rates and a particular rate of population growth (Chapter 8).

modernization the process of societal development in terms of urbanization, industrialization, standard of living, education, and health that we often associate with a Western or European lifestyle and world view (Chapter 3).

momentum of population growth the potential for future increases in population size that is inherent in any present age/sex structure (Chapter 8).

moral restraint according to Malthus, the avoidance of sexual intercourse prior to marriage and the delay of marriage until a man could afford all the children his wife might bear; a desirable preventive check on population growth (Chapter 3).

mortality deaths in a population; one of the three basic demographic processes (Chapter 6).

mover a person who moves within the same county and thus, according to the U.S. Bureau of the Census definitions, has not moved far enough to become a migrant (Chapter 7).

multiple crop to grow more than one crop per year on the same plot of ground (Chapter 14).

nationalist a person seeking freedom for his or her country from economic and political exploitation by more powerful nations (Chapter 13).

natural fertility fertility levels that exist in the absence of deliberate birth control (Chapter 7).

natural increase the excess of births over deaths. The difference between the crude birth rate and the crude death rate is the rate of natural increase (Chapter 2).

neo-Malthusian a person who accepts the basic Malthusian premise that population growth tends to outstrip resources, but (unlike Malthus) believes that birth control measures are appropriate checks to population growth (Chapter 3).

neonatal pertaining to the first 28 days after birth (Chapter 6).

net reproduction rate a measure of generational replacement; specifically, the average number of female children that will be born to the female babies who were themselves born in a given year, assuming no change in the age-specific fertility and mortality rates and ignoring the effect of migration (Chapter 4 and Appendix).

norms socially defined rules for behavior (Chapter 5).

optimum population size the number of people that would provide the best balance of people and resources for a desired standard of living (Chapter 13).

out-migrant a person who leaves an area with the intention of changing residence. This term usually refers to internal migration, whereas *emigrant* refers to an international migrant (Chapter 7).

ozone layer the region in the earth's upper atmosphere that protects the earth from the ultraviolet rays of the sun (Chapter 14).

pathological in biology, the term refers to disease; it also has been used to refer to deviant forms of behavior (Chapter 6).

per capita gross national product a common measure of average income in a nation, calculated by dividing the total value of goods and services produced in a nation by the total population size (Chapter 13).

perinatal pertaining to the time from shortly before birth to 7 days after birth (Chapter 6).

period see period data or period rates.

period data population data that refer to a particular year and represent a cross section of the population at one specific time (Chapter 4).

period rates rates referring to a specific, limited period of time, usually 1 year (Chapter 4).

personal space a "bubble" surrounding each person that when penetrated produces stress; a socially derived phenomenon differing from one culture to another (Chapter 12).

physiocratic describing a reaction against mercantilism and an emphasis on the powers of nature as the source of public wealth (Chapter 3).

population characteristics traits or qualities that differentiate one individual from another, including age, sex, race, ethnicity, marital status, occupation, education, and income (Chapters 8 and 9).

population explosion a popular term referring to the rapid increase in the size of the world's population, especially the increase since World War II (Chapter 3).

population modeling using the techniques of projecting populations to evaluate the possible consequences of different combinations of population processes (Chapter 8).

population processes fertility, mortality, and migration; the dynamic elements of demographic analysis (Chapters 4, 6, and 7, respectively).

population projection the calculation of the number of persons we can expect to be alive at a future date, given the number now alive and given reasonable assumptions about age-specific mortality and fertility rates (Chapter 8).

population pyramid see age/sex pyramid.

population register a vital registration system in which data for each individual in the country are recorded on a list (Chapter 1).

positive checks a term used by Malthus to refer to factors (essentially mortality) that limit the size of human populations by "weakening" or "destroying the human frame" (Chapter 3).

postcensus local review the practice by the U.S. Bureau of the Census of allowing local officials to review preliminary census results to comment on their accuracy (Chapter 1).

postneonatal pertaining to the period from 28 days after birth to 1 year of age (Chapter 6).

postpartum following childbirth (Chapter 4).

poverty index a measure of need based on the premise that one third of a family's income is spent on food; the cost of an economy food plan multiplied by 3. Since 1964, it has increased at the same rate as the consumer price index (Chapter 9).

preventive checks in Malthus's writings, any limits to birth, among which Malthus himself preferred moral restraint (Chapter 3).

primary metropolitan statistical area (PMSA) MSA within a CMSA (Chapter 12).

programmed time clock theory a theory of aging based on the idea that each person has a built-in biological time clock; barring death from accidents or disease, cells still die because each is programmed to reproduce itself only a fixed number of times (Chapter 11).

pronatalist   favoring the encouragement of childbearing (Chapter 3).

prudential restraint   a Malthusian concept referring to delaying marriage without necessarily avoiding premarital intercourse (Chapter 3).

psychographics   description of a person's lifestyle, values, attitudes, and personality traits—used in conjunction with marketing demographics (Chapter 16).

push-pull theory   a theory of migration that says some people move because they are pushed out of their former location, whereas others move because they have been pulled, or attracted, to another location (Chapter 7).

race   a group of people characterized by a more or less distinctive combination of inheritable physical traits (Chapter 9).

racial genocide   the deliberate extermination of people who belong to a particular racial group (Chapter 9).

religious pluralism   the existence of two or more religious groups side by side in society, without any domination of one group over any others (Chapter 9).

residential mobility   the process of changing residence, whether it be over a short or long distance. This term is essentially synonymous with migration (Chapter 7).

reverse survival method of migration estimation   a method of estimating migration between two censuses by combining census data with life table probabilities of survival between the two censuses (Chapter 7).

rural   of, or pertaining to, the countryside. Rural populations are generally defined as those that are nonurban in character (Chapter 7).

sample surveys   a method of collecting data by obtaining information from a sample of the total population, rather than by a complete census (Chapter 1).

secularization   a spirit of autonomy from otherworldly powers; a sense of responsibility for one's own well-being (Chapter 3).

segmentation   the manufacturing and packaging of products or the provision of services that appeal to specific sociodemographically identifiable groups within the population (Chapter 16).

semen   the male reproductive fluid (Chapter 4).

senescence   a decline in physical viability accompanied by a rise in vulnerability to disease (Chapter 11).

senility   an outdated term implying a loss of mental abilities (Chapter 11).

serial monogamy   a series of marriages, each with only one partner at a time (Chapter 10).

sex ratio   the number of males per the number of females in a population (usually multiplied by 100 to get rid of the decimal point) (Chapter 8).

sex structure   the distribution of people in a population according to sex (Chapter 8).

social class   a group of people in a society who have more or less similar levels of income, education, and occupational prestige (Chapters 5 and 8).

social institutions   sets of procedures (norms, laws, etc.) that organize behavior in society in fairly predictable and ongoing ways (Chapters 3 and 5).

socialist   a person who advocates an economic system whereby the community as a whole (i.e., the government) owns the means of production and a social system that minimizes social stratification (Chapter 3).

socialization   the process of learning the behavior appropriate to particular social roles (Chapter 8).

social roles   the set of obligations and expectations that characterize a particular position within society (Chapter 8).

social status   relative position or standing in society (Chapter 8).

social stratification   a system of social inequality through which members of society are ranked in status from high to low (Chapter 7).

socioeconomic status   a person's status in society as determined by that individual's combination of social and economic characteristics (Chapter 7).

spermicide   a chemical agent with the ability to kill sperm (Chapter 4).

sponge   a disposable contraceptive containing a spermicide that acts as a chemical barrier after insertion in the vagina (Chapter 4).

stable population   a population in which the percentage of people at each age and sex does not change over time (Chapter 8).

standard metropolitan statistical area (SMSA)   an area defined by the U.S. Bureau of the Census as a county or group of contiguous counties that contain at least one city of 50,000 inhabitants or more and any contiguous counties that are socially and economically integrated with the central city or cities. In the New England states SMSAs consist of towns and cities instead of counties (Chapter 12).

standardization   a set of procedures for controlling for the effects of external factors influencing overall crude birth or death rates (Appendix).

stationary population   a type of stable population in which the birth rate equals the death rate (Chapter 8).

sterile   biologically incapable of reproduction. This term is synonymous with *infecund* (Chapter 4).

sterilization   the process of rendering a person sterile (either voluntarily or involuntarily) (Chapter 4).

structural economic mobility   the situation in which most, if not all, people in an entire society experience an improvement in living levels, even though some people may be improving faster than others (Chapter 9).

subfecundity   a reduced ability to reproduce (Chapter 4).

suburban   pertaining to populations in low-density areas close to and integrated with central cities (Chapter 12).

suburbanize   to become suburban—a city suburbanizes by growing in its outer rings (Chapter 12).

Sun belt   the area in the southern part of the United States that is a popular destination for migrants; in particular, California, Arizona, Texas, and Florida (Chapter 7).

symptothermal method   method of fertility control based on avoiding intercourse during the fertile period, as determined by observation of changes in a woman's cervical mucus along with the taking of basal body temperature (Chapter 4).

synthetic cohort   a measurement obtained by treating period data as though they represented a cohort (Chapter 4).

targeting   a marketing technique of picking out particular sociodemographic characteristics and appealing to differences in consumer tastes and behavior reflected in those particular characteristics (Chapter 16).

target year   the year to which we project a population forward in time (Chapter 8).

theoretical effectiveness   with respect to birth control methods, the probability of preventing a pregnancy if a method is used exactly as it should be (Chapter 4).

theory   a system of assumptions, accepted principles, and rules of procedure devised to analyze, predict, or otherwise explain a set of phenomena (Chapter 3).

theory of relative income   a theory developed by Easterlin and based on the idea that the birth rate responds not to absolute levels of economic well-being, but rather to levels that are related to those to which one is accustomed (Chapter 3).

total fertility rate   an estimate of the average number of children that would be born to each woman if the current age-specific birth rates remained constant (Chapter 4).

transitional growth   that period of time during the demographic transition when death rates have dropped but birth rates are still high. During this time, population size is increasing steadily—this is the essence of the "population explosion" (Chapter 3).

triage   as applied to population studies, the selection by those nations with food of those hungry nations most likely to survive and the concentration of available food aid on them (Chapter 14).

triticale   grain that is produced by crossing wheat with rye (Chapter 14).

underdeveloped   describes those nations with very low average levels of income. This is sometimes a euphemism for a poor country, but the term also implies that the country has the potential to raise its level of living (Chapter 13).

upward mobility   the process of improving one's socioeconomic status, of moving from one social class to a higher one (Chapters 5 and 8).

urban   describes a spatial concentration of people whose lives are organized around nonagricultural activities (Chapters 7 and 12).

urbanism   the changes that occur in life-style and social interaction as a result of living in urban places (Chapter 12).

urbanization   the process whereby the proportion of people in a population who live in urban places increases (Chapters 2 and 12).

use effectiveness   the actual pregnancy prevention performance associated with the use of a particular birth control measure (Chapter 4).

vasectomy   a technique of male sterilization in which each vas deferens is cut and tied, thus preventing sperm from being ejaculated during intercourse (Chapter 4).

vital statistics   data referring to the so-called vital events of life, especially birth and death, but usually also including marriage and divorce and sometimes abortion (Chapter 1).

wealth flow   a term coined by John Caldwell to refer to the intergenerational transfer of income (Chapter 3).

wear and tear theory   the theory of aging that argues that humans are like machines that eventually wear out due to the stresses and strains of constant use (Chapter 11).

withdrawal   a form of fertility control that requires the male to withdraw his penis from his partner's vagina prior to ejaculation; also called coitus interruptus (Chapter 4).

xenophobia   fear of strangers (Chapter 7).

zero population growth (ZPG)   a situation in which a population is not changing in size from year to year, as a result of the combination of births, deaths, and migration (Chapter 8).

BIBLIOGRAPHY

Abelson, P.

14   1975a "The world's disparate food supplies." Science 187: editorial.

14   1975b "Food and nutrition." Science 188 (4188):501.

4   Adelman, C.
1982 "Saving babies with a signature." Wall Street Journal, 28 July.

5   Adlakha, A., and D. Kirk
1974 "Vital rates in India 1961–71 estimated from 1971 census data." Population Studies 28(3):381–400.

7   Agassi, J., and I. C. Jarvie
1959 Hong Kong. London: Oxford Press.

8   Ahlburg, D., and M. Schapiro
1984 "Socioeconomic ramifications of changing cohort size: an analysis of U.S. postwar suicide rates by age and sex." Demography 21(1):97–105.

3   Ahmad, S.
1977 "Population myths and realities." Race and Class 19(1):19–29.

4   Akin, J., R. Bilsbarrow, D. Guilkey, B. Popkin, D. Benoit, P. Cantrelle, M. Garenne, and P. Levi
1981 "The determinants of breast-feeding in Sri Lanka." Demography 18(3):287–308.

4   Akpom, C., K. Akpom, and M. Davis
1976 "Prior sexual behavior of teenagers attending rap sessions for the first time." Family Planning Perspectives 8:203–6.

16   Allan, C.
1981 "Measuring mature markets." American Demographics 3(3):13–17.

1,12   Alonso, W., and P. Starr
1982 "The political economy of national statistics." Social Science Research Council Items 36(3):29–35.

16   Alsop, R.
1984 "Firms still struggle to devise best approach to black buyers." Wall Street Journal, 25 October.

7   American Council for Nationalities Service
1983 Refugee Reports. Washington, D.C.: ACNS.

American Demographics

16   1982a "The demographic future." The Monthly Report of International Demographics (brochure).

16   1983 "Here comes 1984." American Demographics 5(6):11.

16   1984 "Gerber and Levi Strauss diversify." American Demographics 6(12):17.

6   Anderson, B., and B. Silver
1986 "Infant mortality in the Soviet Union: regional differences and measurement issues." Population and Development Review 12(4):705.

15   Applebaum, R.
1976 "City size and urban life: an inquiry into some consequences of growth in American cities." Urban Affairs Quarterly 12:139–68.

8   Aries, P.
1962 Centuries of Childhood. New York: Vintage Books.

4   Arnett, G.
1981 "A national trend in birth control." San Diego Union, 6 April.

Arriaga, E.

6,8   1970 Mortality Decline and Its Demographic Effects in Latin America. Institute of International Studies, University of California, Berkeley.

6   1982 "Changing trends in mortality in developing countries." Paper presented at the

505

annual meeting of the Population Association of America, San Diego.

5 Aso, T.
1972 "Fertility control transition from abortion to contraception in Japan since 1948." Paper read at the annual meeting of the Population Association of America, Toronto.

6 Associated Press
1987 "AIDS suspected 18 years after teen died." San Diego Union, 26 October.

11 Atchley, R.
1977 The Social Forces in Later Life, 2nd edition. Belmont, CA: Wadsworth.

15 Atkinson, L., R. Lincoln, and J. Forrest
1985 "Worldwide trends in funding for contraception research and evaluation." Family Planning Perspectives 11(3):67–76.

15 Auerbach, F.
1961 Immigration Laws of the United States, 2nd edition. New York: Bobbs-Merrill.

11 Auerbach, I.
1988 "No social security bonanza for the federal debt." Wall Street Journal, 9 August.

7 Babaoglu, A.
1982 "Some social and psychiatric aspects of uprooting among Turkish immigrant workers in West Germany." In R. Nann (ed.), Uprooting and Surviving. Boston: D. Reidel.

10 Bachrach, C., and M. Horn
1988 "Sexual activity among U.S. women of reproductive age." American Journal of Public Health 78(3):320.

15 Bachrach, P., and E. Bergman
1973 Power and Choice: The Formulation of American Population Policy. Lexington, MA: Lexington Books.

4 Bader, M.
1976 "Breast-feeding: the role of multi-national corporations in Latin America." International Journal of Health Science 6(4):609–26.

9 Balakrishnan, T., and J. Chen
1988 "Religiosity, nuptiality, and reproduction in Canada." Paper presented at the annual meeting of the Population Association of America, New Orleans.

10 Baldwin, W., and Nord, C.
1984 "Delayed childbearing in the U.S.: facts and fictions." Population Bulletin 39(4).

Banco de Mexico
13 1966 Informe Anual, 1965. Mexico, D.F.
13 1974a Informe Anual, 1973. Mexico, D.F.

13 1974b La distribucion del Ingreso en Mexico: Encuesta sobre los ingresos y gastos de las familias: 1968. Mexico, D.F.
13 1976 Informe Anual, 1975. Mexico, D.F.
13 1978 Informe Anual, 1977. Mexico, D.F.

5 Banks, J. A.
1954 Prosperity and Parenthood: A Study of Family Planning among the Victorian Middle Classes. London: Routledge & Kegan Paul.

5 Banks, J., and O. Banks
1964 Feminism and Family Planning in Victorian England. Liverpool: Liverpool University Press.

1 Baskin, Y.
1980 "U.S. Census chief says alien suit could delay count at least a year." San Diego Union, 7 January.

16 Bauder, D.
1981 "Growth slows, but soft drink future sparkles." San Diego Union, 12 January.

13 Bauer, P. T.
1972 Dissent on Development. Cambridge: Harvard University Press.

12 Baum, A., and G. Davis
1976 "Spatial and social aspects of crowding perception." Environment and Behavior 8:527–44.

7 Bean, F., A. King, and J. Passel
1983 "The number of illegal migrants of Mexican origin in the United States: sex ratio-based estimates from 1980." Demography 20(1):99–109.

9 Bean, F., and G. Swicegood
1985 Mexican American Fertility Patterns. Austin: University of Texas Press.

15 Bean, F., E. Telles, and B. Lowell
1987 "Undocumented migration to the United States: perceptions and evidence." Population and Development Review 13(4):671–90.

9 Beaujot, R., K. Krotki, and P. Krishnan
1982 "Analysis of ethnic fertility differentials through the consideration of assimilation." International Journal of Comparative Sociology 23(1/2):62–70.

5 Becker, G.
1960 "An economic analysis of fertility." In National Bureau of Economic Research, Demographic and Economic Change in Developed Countries. Princeton, NJ: Princeton University Press.

6 Behrman, R.
1987 "Premature births among black women." New England Journal of Medicine 317:763.

Barclay, G. W.
1958 Techniques of Population Analysis. New York: John Wiley & Sons, Inc.

16 Bell, C.
1982 "Models in gray." Parade, 21 November.

5 Belmont, L., and F. Marolla
1973 "Birth order, family size, and intelligence." Science 182:1096–1101.

5 Benedict, B.
1972 "Social regulation of fertility." In G. A. Harrison and A. J. Boyce (eds.), The Structure of Human Population. Oxford: Clarendon Press.

6 Benet, S.
1974 Abkhasians: The Long-Living People of the Caucasus. New York: Holt, Rinehart & Winston.

10 Bengelsdorf, C., and A. Hageman
1978 "Emerging from underdevelopment: women and work in Cuba." Race and Class 19(4):361–78.

6,11 Benjamin, B.
1969 Demographic Analysis. New York: Praeger.

Bennett, A.
15 1983 "China cajoles families and offers incentives to reduce birth rate." Wall Street Journal, 6 July.
16 1985 "U.S. firms rush through China's open door." Wall Street Journal, 8 April.

8 Bennett, N.
1983 "Sex selection of children: an overview." In N. Bennett (ed.), Sex Selection of Children. New York: Academic Press.

16 Benokratis, N.
1982 "Racial exclusion in juries." Journal of Applied Behavioral Science 18(1):29–47.

Berelson, B.
15 1974 Population Policy in Developed Countries. New York: McGraw-Hill.
15 1979 "Romania's 1966 anti-abortion decree: the demographic experience of the first decade." Population Studies 33(2):209–22.

4,15 Berg, A.
1973 "Nutrition, development, and population growth." Population Bulletin 29(1).

5 Bernhardt, E.
1972 "Fertility and economic status—some recent findings on differentials in Sweden." Population Studies 26(2):175–84.

12 Berry, B., C. Goodwin, R. Lake, and K. Smith
1976 "Attitudes toward integration: the role of status." In B. Schwartz (ed.), The Changing Face of the Suburbs. Chicago: University of Chicago Press.

6 Bertrand, J.
1988 "AIDS and its implications for family planning programs in developing countries." Paper presented at the 16th Annual Psychosocial Workshop, New Orleans.

9 Bertrand, J., and D. Bogue
1977 "A research-based system for improving family planning adoption: the Guatemalan study." Intercom 5:8–9.

15 Bertrand, J., R. Santiso, R. Cisneros, F. Mascarin, and L. Morris
1982 "Family planning communication and contraceptive use in Guatemala, El Salvador, and Panama." Studies in Family Planning 13(6/7):190–99.

7 Beyer, G.
1981 "The political refugee: 35 years later." International Migration Review 15 (1/2):26–34.

15 Bhatia, P.
1978 "Abstinence—Desai solution for baby boom." San Francisco Chronicle, 11 June.

9 Bianchi, S.
1981 Household Composition and Racial Inequality. New Brunswick: Rutgers University Press.

Biggar, J.
7 1979 "The sunning of America: migration to the sunbelt." Population Bulletin 34 (1).
7 1980 "Reassessing elderly sunbelt migration." Research on Aging 2(2):177–90.

Blake, J.
5 1967 "Family size in the 1960s—a baffling fad?" Eugenics Quarterly 14:60–74.
10 1968 "Are babies consumer durables?" Population Studies 22:5–25.
15 1969 "Population policy for Americans: is the government being misled?" Science 164:522–29.
10 1972 "Coercive pronatalism and American population policy." In C. Westoff and R. Parke (eds.), Social and Demographic Aspects of Population Growth and the American Future. Washington, D.C.: Government Printing Office.
5 1974 "Can we believe recent data in the United States?" Demography 11(1):25–44.
2 1979 Lecture at San Diego University (July).
5 1981 "The only child in America: prejudice

versus performance." Population and Development Review 7(1):43–54. **5,6, 13**

9   1984   "Catholicism and fertility: on attitudes of young Americans." Population and Development Review 10(2):329–40.

9   Blauner, R.
        1972   Racial Oppression in America. New York: Harper & Row.

7   Blejer, M., H. Johnson, and A. Porzecanski
        1978   "An analysis of the economic determinants of legal and illegal migration to the United States." In J. Simon (ed.), Research in Population Economics, Vol. 1. Greenwich: JAI Press.

4   Bloom, D.
        1982   "What's happening to the age at first birth in the United States? A study of recent cohorts." Demography 19(3):351–70.

13   Bloom, D., and R. Freeman
        1986   "The effects of rapid population growth on labor supply and employment in developing countries." Population and Development Review 12(3):381–414.

9   Bloom, D., and J. Trussell
        1984   "What are the determinants of delayed childbearing and permanent childlessness in the United States?" Demography 21(4):591–612.

6   Blum, A., and B. Ames
        1977   "Flame-retardant additives as possible cancer hazards." Science 195:17–23.

12   Blum, D.
        1982   "Youthful professionals without any children transform city areas." Wall Street Journal, 1 February.

6   Blum, H. L., and G. M. Keranen
        1966   Control of Chronic Diseases in Man. New York: American Public Health Association.

2   Bogue, D.
        1967   "The end of the population explosion." The Public Interest 7.

Bongaarts, J.
4   1978   "A framework for analyzing the proximate determinants of fertility." Population and Development Review 4(1):105–32.

4   1982   "The fertility-inhibiting effects of the intermediate fertility variables." Studies in Family Planning 13(6/7):179–89.

Boserup, E.
13   1965   The Conditions of Agricultural Growth. Chicago: Aldine.

10, 1970   Woman's Role in Economic Development. New York: St. Martin's Press.
12,
13

5,6, 1981   Population and Technological Change: A Study of Long-Term Trends. Chicago: University of Chicago Press.
13

9   Bouvier, L., and S. L. H. Rao
        1975   Socioreligious Factors in Fertility Decline. Cambridge: Ballinger.

6   Bouvier, L., and J. van de Tak
        1976   "Infant mortality—progress and problems." Population Bulletin, 31 April.

15   Boyd, M.
        1976   "Immigration policies and trends: a comparison of Canada and the United States." Demography 13:83–104.

6   Boyden, S.
        1972   "Ecology in relation to urban population structure." Chap. 20 in G. A. Harrison and A. J. Boyce (eds.), The Structure of Human Population. Oxford: Clarendon Press.

3   Brackett, J.
        1967   "The evolution of Marxist theories of population: Marxism recognizes the population problem." Paper read at the annual meeting of the Population Association of America, Cincinnati, Ohio.

11   Bradshaw, Y.
        1987   "Urbanization and underdevelopment: a global study of modernization, urban bias, and economic dependency." American Sociological Review 52(2):224–39.

16   Bralove, M.
        1982   "Advertising world's portrayal of women is starting to shift." Wall Street Journal, 28 October.

4   Brandes, S. H.
        1975   Migration, Kinship, and Community. New York: Academic Press.

14   Bread for the World
        1976   "World hunger: too little food or too many people." Reply, in Environmental Fund, World Hunger: Too Little Food or Too Many People? Washington, D.C.: Environmental Fund.

3   Brentano, L.
        1910   "The Doctrine of Malthus and the increase of population during the last decade." Economic Journal, September.

7   Breslin, J.
        1982   Forsaking All Others. New York: Simon & Schuster.

Brewer, M.
15   1977   "Slowing population growth with food aid." In P. G. Brown and H. Shue (eds.), Food Policy. New York: Free Press.

14   1981   "The changing U.S. farmland scene." Population Bulletin 36(5).

7   Briggs, V.
    1976   "Illegal immigration and the American
           labor force." American Behavioral Scien-
           tist 19(3):351–63.

16 Bronson, G.
    1981   "Baby food it is, but Gerber wants teen-
           agers to think of it as dessert." Wall
           Street Journal, 17 July.

    Brown, L.
14 1973   "Population and affluence: growing
           pressures on world food resources."
           Population Bulletin 29(2).

14 1975   "The world food prospect." Science
           190:1053–59.

14 1981   "World food resources and population:
           the narrowing gap." Population Bulletin
           36(3).

1   Brown, L., W. Chandler, C. Flavin, J. Jacobson, C.
    Pollock, S. Postel, L. Starke, and E. Wolf
    1988   State of the World, 1988. New York:
           W. W. Norton & Co.

12 Browning, H.
    1958   "Recent trends in Latin American urban-
           ization." Annals of the American Acad-
           emy of Political and Social Science
           316:111–20.

4   Bullough, V.
    1981   "Age at menarche: a misunderstanding."
           Science 213:365–66.

9   Bumpass, L.
    1984   "Children and marital disruption: a rep-
           lication and update." Demography
           21(1):71–82.

5   Burch, T.
    1975   "Theories of fertility as guides to popula-
           tion policy." Social Forces 54(1):126–
           39.

5   Busfield, J., and M. Paddon
    1977   Thinking About Children. Cambridge:
           Cambridge University Press.

11 Business Week
    1979   "Inflation forces retirees into new ca-
           reers." 20 August, p. 119.

16 Buss, D.
    1985   "Ford to unveil 2 cars aimed at young
           professionals with children." Wall Street
           Journal, 28 January.

7   Bustamante, J.
    1983   "Immigration into the San Diego-Ti-
           juana Region." Lecture at San Diego
           State University, 16 November.

16 Butler, R.
    1978   "The doctor and the aged patient." In
           W. Reichel and M. Schechter (eds.), The
           Geriatric Patient. New York: HP.

3   Butz, W., and M. Ward
    1979   "Will U.S. fertility remain low? A new
           economic interpretation." Population
           and Development Review 5(4):663–88.

6   Caballo, M.
    1988   "Global epidemiology of AIDS." Paper
           presented at the 16th Annual Psychoso-
           cial Workshop, New Orleans.

5   Cain, M.
    1981   "Risk and fertility in India and Bangla-
           desh." Population and Development Re-
           view 7(3):435–74.

    Caldwell, J.
15 1975   "The containment of world population
           growth." Studies in Family Planning
           6(12):429–36.

3   1976   "Toward a restatement of demographic
           transition theory." Population and De-
           velopment Review 2(3–4):321–66.

3   1980   "Mass education as a determinant of the
           timing of fertility decline." Population
           and Development Review 6(2):225–
           56.

3,5 1982   Theory of Fertility Decline. New York:
           Academic Press.

12 Calhoun, J.
    1962   "Population density and social pathol-
           ogy." Scientific American 206:139–46.

9   California Center for Health Statistics
    1983   "California life expectancy: abridged life
           tables for California and Los Angeles,
           1978–81." Data Matters, No. 83-
           01031.

11 Calloway, N.
    1973   "Medical aspects of the aging American
           black." Proceedings of Black Aged in the
           Future (Durham: Duke University Press).
           Summarized in Black Aging, 1977,
           3(1,2):36–38.

16 Calonius, L.
    1983   "Hurricane experts say the state of their
           art can't avert a disaster." Wall Street
           Journal, 14 October.

16 Calonius, L., and E. Larson
    1982   "Georgia-Pacific's trek from west to
           south rattles many workers." Wall Street
           Journal, 30 September.

15 Camp, W.
    1961   Marriage and the Family in France since
           the Revolution. New York: Bookman
           Associates.

5   Campbell, A.
    1969   "Changing patterns of childbearing in
           the United States." In National Institutes
           of Health, The Family in Transition.
           Washington, D.C.: Government Printing
           Office.

10 Campbell, A., P. Converse, and W. Rodgers
    1974   "Measuring the quality of life in Amer-

510   Bibliography

11 ica." Institute for Social Research News-
    letter.
    Campbell, S.
    1979 "Delayed mandatory retirement and the
          working woman." The Gerontologist
          19(3):257–63.

8   Carlson, Elwood
    1980 "Divorce rate fluctuations as a cohort
          phenomenon." Population Studies
          33:523–36.

    Carlson, Eugene
14 1981 "Governments struggle to keep farms
          away from developers." Wall Street
          Journal, 23 June.

16 1983 "Peoria isn't average enough for one ad
          agency anymore." Wall Street Journal,
          27 September.

12 1984a "Changes in population game hurt some
          big-city players." Wall Street Journal, 14
          February.

16 1984b "Electorate reflects population changes
          as voters go to polls in record numbers."
          Wall Street Journal, 7 November.

16 1985 "Peoria gets an 'A' for average in passing
          test-market exam." Wall Street Jour-
          nal, 24 December.

15 1987 "Floridians ponder implications of
          state's new planning law." Wall Street
          Journal, 20 October.

14 Carson, R.
    1962 The Silent Spring. Boston: Houghton-
          Mifflin.

    Carter, L.
14 1974a "Controversy over new pesticide regula-
          tion." Science 186:904.

14 1974b "Pollution and public health: taconite
          cases pose a major test." Science
          186:31–36.

15 1976 "Dade county: the politics of managing
          urban growth." Science 192:982–85.

19 1977 "PR man helps select author of book on
          pollution case." Science 195:468.

1   Cassedy, J.
    1969 Demography in Early America, Begin-
          nings of the Statistical Mind, 1600–
          1800. Cambridge: Harvard University
          Press.

12 Chall, D.
    1984 "Neighborhood changes in New York
          City." American Demographics 6(10):
          18–23.

9   Chamie, J.
    1981 Religion and Fertility. Cambridge: Cam-
          bridge University Press.

14 Chandler, R.F.
    1971 "The scientific basis for the increased

          yield potential of rice and wheat." Chap.
          2 in Thomas Poleman and Donald Free-
          bain (eds.), Food, Population and Em-
          ployments: The Impact of the Green
          Revolution. New York: Praeger.

2   Chandler, T., and G. Fox
    1974 3000 Years of Urban Growth. New
          York: Academic Press.

15 Chandrasekhar, S.
    1972 Infant Mortality, Population Growth
          and Family Planning in India. Chapel
          Hill: University of North Carolina
          Press.

15 Chang, M-C., R. Freedman, and T-H. Sun
    1987 "Trends in fertility, family size prefer-
          ences, and family planning practice: Tai-
          wan, 1961–85." Studies in Family Plan-
          ning 18(6):320–37.

7,15 Chapman, L.
    1976 "Illegal aliens: time to call a halt!" Read-
          ers Digest 109(654):188–92.

14 Charaskin, E., W. M. Ringsdorf, and A. Brecker
    1974 Psychodietetics. New York: Bantam
          Books.

3   Charles, E.
    1936 The Twilight of Parenthood. London:
          Watt's and Co.

10 Charlton, S.
    1984 Women in Third World Development.
          Boulder, CO: Westview Press.

16 Chase, M.
    1983 "California's teachers, once among the
          best, slump in competency." Wall Street
          Journal, 1 April.

10 Chaudhury, R.
    1979 "Marriage, urban women and the labor
          force: the Bangladesh case." Signs
          5(1):154–63.

7   Chen, K.
    1984 "When a quarter million flee to China."
          Wall Street Journal, 19 March.

15 Chen, M.
    1979 "Birth planning in China." International
          Family Planning Perspectives 5(3):92–
          101.

6   Cherfas, J.
    1980 "The World Fertility Survey Conference:
          population bomb revisited." Science 80,
          November:11–14.

A   Chiang, C.
    1984 The Life Table and Its Applications.
          Melbourne, FL: Krieger.

8   Chilton, R., and A. Spielberger
    1971 "Is delinquency increasing? Age struc-
          ture and the crime rate." Social Forces
          49:487–93.

1 Ching, F.
   1982 "Abacuses are out, computers are in in Chinese census." Wall Street Journal, 7 July.

12 Choi, S., A. Mirhafari, and H. Weaver
    1976 "The concept of crowding: a critical review and proposal of an alternative approach." Environment and Behavior 8:345–63.

12 Choldin, H.
    1978 "Urban density and pathology." Annual Review of Sociology 4:91–113.

1,9 Choucri, N.
     1984 "Perspectives on population and conflict." In N. Choucri (ed.), Multidisciplinary Perspectives on Population and Conflict. Syracuse: Syracuse University Press.

3 Cicourel, A.
   1974 Theory and Method in a Study of Argentine Fertility. New York: Wiley.

   Cipolla, C.
2,14 1965 The Economic History of World Population. Middlesex: Penguin Books.

11 1969 Literacy and Development in the West. Baltimore: Penguin Books.

13 Clark, C.
    1967 Population Growth and Land Use. New York: St. Martin's Press.

7 Clark, L.
   1983 "Hong Kong exemplifies the power of an idea." Wall Street Journal, 11 October.

9 Clogg, C., and J. Shockey
   1984 "Mismatch between occupation and schooling: a prevalence measure, recent trends and demographic analysis." Demography 21(2):235–57.

14 Clough, S.
    1968 European Economic History. New York: Walker.

   Coale, A.
5 1973 "The demographic transition." Proceedings of the International Population Conference, Liege. Volume 1, pp. 53–72.

2 1974 "The history of the human population." Scientific American 231(3):40–51.

13 1978 "Population growth and economic development: the case of Mexico." Foreign Affairs 56(2):415–29.

13 1986 "Population trends and economic development." In J. Menken (ed.), World Population and U.S. Population Policy: The Choice Ahead. New York: W. W. Norton & Co.

8 Coale, A., and P. Demeny
   1983 Regional Model Life Tables and Stable Populations. New York: Academic Press.

5,13 Coale, A., and E. Hoover
      1958 Population Growth and Economic Development in Low-Income Countries. Princeton, NJ: Princeton University Press.

5 Coale, A., and M. Zelnick
   1963 Estimates of Fertility and Population in the United States. Princeton, NJ: Princeton University Press.

8 Cohen, L., and M. Felson
   1979 "Social change and crime rate trends." American Sociological Review 44(4):588–607.

8 Cohen, L., and K. Land
   1987 "Age structure and crime." American Sociological Review 52(2):170.

11 Cohn, R.
    1982 "Economic development and status change of the aged." American Journal of Sociology 87(5):1150–61.

12 Coleman, J.
    1979 "School desegregation in large cities: a critique of the Coleman 'White Flight Thesis'; response to Professors Pettigrew and Green." Harvard Educational Review 64(2):217–24.

9 Coleman, R., and L. Rainwater
   1978 Social Standing in America. New York: Basic Books.

5 Colvin, T.
   1982 "Students halt 19-year slide in test scores." San Diego Union, 22 September.

3,15 Commission on Population Growth and the American Future
      1972 Population and the American Future. Washington, D.C.: Government Printing Office.

15 Comprehensive Planning Organization of the San Diego Region
    1974 Population Growth Policy Study, Final Report.

1 Cook, R.
   1964 "Outdoor recreation threatened by excess procreation." Population Bulletin 20(4):89–94.

8,11 Coombs, L., and T. Sun
      1981 "Familial values in a developing society: a decade of change in Taiwan." Social Forces 59(4):1229–55.

16 Corchado, A.
    1988 "Campbell Soup is seeking to be numero uno where Goya reigns." Wall Street Journal, 28 March.

7 Cornelison, A.

1980   Strangers and Pilgrims. New York: Holt, Rinehart & Winston.

13, 14 Council on Environmental Quality
1980   The Global 2000 Report to the President, Volume 1. Washington, D.C.: Government Printing Office.

11 Cowgill, D.
1979   "Aging and modernization: a revision of the theory." In J. Hendricks and C. D. Hendricks (eds.), Dimensions of Aging. Cambridge: Winthrop.

9 Cramer, J.
1980   "Fertility and female employment: problems of causal direction." American Sociological Review 45(2):167–190.

14 Crosson, P.
1975   "Institutional obstacles to expansion of world food production." Science 188:519–24.

15 Cutright, P., and W. Kelly
1981   "The role of family planning programs in fertility declines in less developed countries, 1958–1977." International Family Planning Perspectives 7(4):145–51.

Daily Californian
6 1981a "30% to 40% of Soviets are too drunk or groggy to work Monday." 6 June.
6 1981b "Epidemic typhus reappears after an absence of 50 years." 17 August.

9 Dalphin, J.
1981   The Persistence of Social Inequality in America. Cambridge, MA: Schenkman.

5 Daly, H.
1971   "A Marxian-Malthusian view of poverty and development." Population Studies 25(1).

9 Darity, W., C. Turner, and H. Thiebaux
1971   Race Consciousness and Fears of Black Genocide As Barriers to Family Planning. Population Reference Bureau Selection No. 37.

7 DaVanzo, J.
1976   "Why families move: a model of the geographic mobility of married couples." Rand Report #R-1972-DOL. Santa Monica, CA: Rand Corporation.

9 Davis, C., C. Haub, and J. Willette
1983   "U.S. Hispanics: changing the face of America." Population Bulletin 38(3).

Davis, K.
3 1945   "The world demographic transition." The Annals of the American Academy of Political and Social Science 237(January):1–11.
5 1949   Human Society. New York: Macmillan.

5 1951   The Population of India and Pakistan. Princeton, NJ: Princeton University Press.
3 1955   "Matlhus and the theory of population." In P. Lazarsfeld and M. Rosenberg (eds.), The Language of Social Research. New York: Free Press.
3,5,7 1963   "The theory of change and response in modern demographic history." Population Index 29(4):345–66.
5,15 1967   "Population policy: will current programs succeed?" Science 158:730–39.
12 1968   Personal communication.
2,9 1972a   "The American family in relation to demographic change." Pp. 237–65 in C. Westoff and R. Parke, Jr. (eds.), U.S. Commission on Population Growth and the American Future, Vol. 1, Demographic and Social Aspects of Population Growth. Washington, D.C.: Government Printing Office.
12 1972b   World Urbanization 1950–1970, Vol. II: Analysis of Trends, Relationships, and Development. Berkeley: University of California Population Monograph Series, No. 9.
12 1973   "Cities and mortality." Proceedings of the International Population Conference, Liege.
2,7, 15 1974   "The migration of human populations." Scientific American 231.
15 1975   "Demographic reality and policy in Nepal's future." Workshop—Conference on Population, Family Planning, and Development in Nepal. University of California, Berkeley.
1 1984a   "Demographic imbalances and international conflict." Paper presented at the annual meeting of the American Sociological Association, San Antonio.
10 1984b   "Wives and work: the sex role revolution and its consequences." Population and Development Review 10(3):397–418.

4 Davis, K., and J. Blake
1956   "Social structure and fertility: an analytic framework." Economic Development and Cultural Change 4:211–35.

10 Davis, K., and P. van den Oever
1982   "Demographic foundations of new sex roles." Population and Development Review 8(3):495–511.

8 Davis, W.
1973   "Overpopulated America." In E. Pohlman (ed.), Population: A Clash of

Prophets. New York: New American Library.

2   Deevey, E.
    1960   "The human population." Scientific American 203(3):194–205.

7   DeJong, G., and J. Fawcett
    1981   "Motivations for migration: an assessment on a value-expectancy model." In G. DeJong and R. Gardner (eds.), Migration Decision Making. New York: Pergamon Press.

9   DellaPergola, S.
    1980   "Patterns of American Jewish fertility." Demography 17(3):261–73.

3   Demeny, P.
    1968   "Early fertility decline in Austria-Hungary: a lesson in demographic transition." Daedalus 97(2):502–22.

13 1971   "The economics of population control." In National Academy of Science, Rapid Population Growth. Baltimore: Johns Hopkins University Press.

2   1979   "On the end of the population explosion." Population and Development Review 5(1):141–69.

13 1981   "The North–South income gap: a demographic perspective." Population and Development Review 7(2):297–310.

15 Demerath, N.
    1976   Birth Control and Foreign Policy: The Alternatives to Family Planning. New York: Harper & Row.

2   Demos, J.
    1965   "Notes on life in Plymouth Colony." William and Mary Quarterly 22:264–86.

2   Desmond, A., F. Wellemeyer, and F. Lorimer
    1962   "How many people have ever lived on earth?" Population Bulletin 18(1).

9,10 Devaney, B.
    1983   "An analysis of variations in U.S. fertility and female labor force participation trends." Demography 20(2):147–62.

13 Diaz-Briquets, S., and L. Perez
    1981   "Cuba: The demography of revolution." Population Bulletin 36(1).

15 Divine, R.
    1957   American Immigration Policy, 1924–1952. New Haven: Yale University Press.

    Dixon, R.
4,10 1971   "Explaining cross-cultural variation in age at marriage and proportion never marrying." Population Studies 25(2):215–34.

9   1976   "The roles of rural women: female seclu-

sion, economic production, and reproductive choice." In R. Ridker (ed.), Population and Development: The Search for Selective Intervention. Baltimore: Johns Hopkins University Press.

    Djerassi, C.
4   1978   "Fertility and contraception in America." Statement prepared for hearings before the U.S. House Select Committee on Population. Washington, D.C.: Government Printing Office.

4   1981   The Politics of Contraception. San Francisco: Freeman.

1   Domschke, E., and D. Goyer
    1986   The Handbook of National Population Censuses, Africa and Asia. Westport: Greenwood Press.

5   Douglas, M.
    1966   "Population control in primitive groups." British Journal of Sociology 17:263–73.

16 Downs, A.
    1982   "The real estate revolution." American Demographics 4(6):20–23.

1   Dublin, L., A. Lotka, and M. Spiegelman
    1949   Length of Life: A Study of the Life Table, revised edition. New York: Ronald Press.

2   Dumond, D.
    1975   "The limitation of human population: a natural history." Science (28 February):713–20.

7   Duncan, R., and C. Perruci
    1976   "Dual occupation families and migration." American Sociological Review 41:252–61.

2   Durand, J.
    1967   "A long-range view of world population growth." Annals of the American Academy of Political and Social Science 369:1–8.

8   Durant, A.
    1984   Personal communication with statistical analyst for the U.S. Immigration and Naturalization Service.

3   Durkheim, E.
    1933   The Division of Labor in Society, translated by George Simpson. Glencoe: Free Press.

10 Dyson, T., and M. Moore
    1983   "On kinship structure, female autonomy, and demographic behavior in India." Population and Development Review 9(1):35–60.

    Easterlin, R. A.
3,5 1968   Population, Labor Force, and Long

3,5   Swings in Economic Growth. New York: National Bureau of Economic Research.

3,5   1978   "What will 1984 be like? Socioeconomic implications of recent twists in age structures." Demography 15(4):397–432.

4   Eaton, J., and A. Mayer
        1954   Man's Capacity to Reproduce. Glencoe: Free Press.

16   Edmondson, B.
        1985   "The market for medical self-care." American Demographics 7(6):34–37.

14   Efron, E.
        1984   The Apocalyptics: Cancer and the Big Lie. New York: Simon & Schuster.

        Ehrlich, P.
13   1968   The Population Bomb. New York: Ballantine Books.

3   1971   The Population Bomb, 2nd edition. New York: Sierra Club/Ballantine Books.

14   Ehrlich, P., and A. Ehrlich
        1972   Population, Resources, Environment, 2nd edition. San Francisco: Freeman.

7   Endacott, G. B.
        1973   A History of Hong Kong. Hong Kong: Oxford University Press.

3   Engels, F.
        1844   "Outlines of a critique of political economy." Reprinted in R. L. Meek, 1953, Marx and Engels on Malthus. London: Lawrence and Wishart.

10   England, P.
        1979   "Women and occupational prestige: a case of vacuous sex equality." Signs 5(2):252–65.

13,   Enke, S.
15   1960   "The economics of government payments to limit population." Economic Development and Cultural Change 8(4), part I:339–48.

        Environmental Fund
14   1976   World Hunger: Too Little Food or Too Many People? Washington, D.C.: Environmental Fund.

14   1981   "The perils of vanishing farmland." The Other Side, No. 23.

6   Epstein, E.
        1965   "The epidemiology of coronary heart disease." Journal of Chronic Diseases 18:735–74.

16   Espenshade, T., and R. Hagemann
        1977   "Economic aspects of enrollment trends." Center for the Study of Population, Florida State University.

15   Evans, D.
        1987   "Economic aspects of Singapore's selec-

3,12   tive family planning policy." Asian and Pacific Population Forum 1(4):1–8.

3,12   Eversley, D.
        1959   Social Theories of Malthus and the Malthusian Debate. Oxford: Clarendon Press.

        Farley, R.
4,9,   1970   Growth of the Black Population. Chicago: Markham.
12

12   1976   "Components of suburban population growth." In B. Schwartz (ed.), The Changing Face of the Suburbs. Chicago: University of Chicago Press.

14   Faulkingham, R., and P. Thorbahn
        1975   "Population dynamics and drought: a village in Niger." Population Studies 29:463–71.

9   Felmlee, D.
        1984   "A dynamic analysis of women's employment exits." Demography 21(2):171–91.

6   Feshbach, M.
        1982   "The Soviet Union: population trends and dilemmas." Population Bulletin 37(3).

11   Fialka, I.
        1981   "Man who helped get Social Security started now strives to save it." Wall Street Journal, 22 September.

16   Finch, J.
        1986   "Biographical spotlight: Joan Finch." Applied Demography 2(2):15.

15   Findley, S.
        1977   Planning for Internal Migration: A Review of Issues and Policies in Developing Countries. U.S. Bureau of the Census Publication ISP-RD-4.

        Firebaugh, G.
12   1979   "Structural determinants of urbanization in Asia and Latin America." American Sociological Review 44(2):199–215.

12   1982   "Population density and fertility in 22 Indian villages." Demography 19(4):481–94.

7,12   Fischer, C.
        1976   The Urban Experience. New York: Harcourt Brace Jovanovich.

11   Fischer, D. H.
        1979   "The politics of aging in America: a short history." Journal of the Institute for Socioeconomic Studies IV(2):51–66.

13   Fishlow, A.
        1965   American Railroads and the Transformation of the Antebellum Economy. Cambridge: Harvard University Press.

7   Fligstein. N.

1981   Going North: Migration of Blacks and Whites From the South, 1900–1950. New York: Academic Press.

8   Foner, A.
     1975   "Age in society: structure and change." American Behavioral Scientist 19(2):144–65.

Food and Agriculture Organization of the United Nations
13   1974   Production Yearbook, 1973. New York: United Nations.
14   1981a   FAO Production Yearbook, 1980. Rome: FAO.
14   1981b   Agriculture: Toward 2000. Rome: FAO.
14   1982a   Production Yearbook, 1981. Rome: FAO.
14   1982b   The State of Food and Agriculture, 1981. Rome: FAO.
14   1983   Yearbook of Fishery Statistics, 1981. Rome: FAO.
14   1984   Potential Population Supporting Capacities of Lands in the Developing World. Rome: FAO.
13   1986a   1985 FAO Production Yearbook, Vol. 39. Rome: FAO.
14   1986b   1985 FAO Trade Yearbook, Vol. 39. Rome: FAO.
14   1986c   The State of Food and Agriculture, 1985. Rome: FAO.

11   Forbes
     1983   "The Forbes Four Hundred." Forbes Magazine 132(9):74.

12   Forstall, R., and M. Gonzalez
     1984   "Twenty questions: what you should know about the new metropolitan areas." American Demographics 6(4):22–31.

6   Fortney, J.
     1987   "The importance of family planning in reducing maternal mortality." Studies in Family Planning 18(2):109.

4   Fortney, J., J. Harper, and M. Potts
     1986   "Oral contraceptives and life expectancy." Studies in Family Planning 17(3):117–25.

12   Foster, G.
     1967   Tzintzuntzan: Mexican Peasants in a Changing World. Boston: Little, Brown.

1   Francese, P.
     1979   "The 1980 Census: the Counting of America." Population Bulletin 34(4).

4   Frank, O.
     1983   "Infertility in sub-Saharan Africa: estimates and implications." Population and Development Review 9(1):137–44.

4   Freedman, R., D. Freedman, and A. Thornton

1980   "Changes in fertility expectations and preferences between 1962 and 1977: their relation to final parity." Demography 17(4):365–78.

9   Freeman, R.
     1976   The Overeducated American. New York: Free Press.

16   Freund, W.
     1982   "The looming impact of population changes." Wall Street Journal, 6 April.

Frey, W.
12   1979   "Central city white flight." American Sociological Review 44(3):425–48.
12   1984   "Life course migration of metropolitan whites and blacks and the structure of demographic change in large central cities." American Sociological Review 49(6):803–27.

2,5   Friedlander, D.
     1983   "Demographic responses and socioeconomic structure: population processes in England and Wales in the nineteenth century." Demography 20(3):249–72.

9   Friedlander, D., and C. Goldscheider
     1984   "Israel's population: the challenge of pluralism." Population Bulletin 39(2).

9   Frisbie, W., and F. Bean
     1978   "Some issues in the demographic study of racial and ethnic groups." In F. Bean and W. Frisbie (eds.), The Demography of Racial and Ethnic Groups. New York: Academic Press.

4   Frisch, R.
     1978   "Population, food intake, and fertility." Science 199:22–30.

16   Frost, D., and M. Deakin
     1983   David Frost's Book of the World's Worst Decisions. New York: Crown.

10   Fuchs, V.
     1983   How We Live. Cambridge: Harvard University Press.

7   Fuguitt, G., and J. Zuiches
     1975   "Residential preferences and population distribution." Demography 12:491–504.

4   Furstenberg, F.
     1976   "The social consequences of teenage parenthood." Family Planning Perspectives 8:148–64.

15   Gadalla, S.
     1978   Is There Hope? Fertility and Family Planning in a Rural Community in Egypt. Chapel Hill: Carolina Population Center.

5   Gadalla, S., J. McCarthy, and O. Campbell
     1985   "How the number of living sons influ-

ences contraceptive use in Manoufia Governorate, Egypt." Studies in Family Planning 16(3):164–69.

12 Galle, O., W. Gove, and J. McPherson
1972 "Population density and pathology: what are the relations for man?" Science 176:23–30.

14 Galloway, P.
1984 "Long term fluctuations in climate and population in the pre-industrial era." Program in Population Research Working Paper No. 14, University of California, Berkeley.

Gallup, G.
15 1976 "What mankind thinks about itself." Reader's Digest 109(654):132–36.
5 1978 "Changes seen in views on family size." San Diego Union, 7 December.

7 Gardner, R.
1981 "Macrolevel influences on the migration decision process." In G. DeJong and R. Gardner (eds.), Migration Decision Making. New York: Pergamon Press.

2 Gendell, M.
1979 "A population crisis in Sweden again?" Intercom 7(3):7–8.

13 Gibbs, R.
1982 "Bumper crops halt imports of corn, rice, beans, wheat." R & D Mexico 1(1):2.

5 Gibson, C.
1976 "The U.S. fertility decline, 1961–1975: the contribution of changes in marital status and marital fertility." Family Planning Perspectives 8:249–52.

11 Gibson, R. M., and C. R. Fisher
1979 "Age differences in health care spending, fiscal year 1977." Social Security Bulletin 42(1).

Gigot, P.
16 1981 "Builders recognizing benefits of meeting elderly's needs." Wall Street Journal, 15 April.
7 1982 "Recession-hit colony worries over prospect China will govern it." Wall Street Journal, 19 November.

3 Glass, D. V. (ed.)
1953 Introduction to Malthus. New York: Wiley.

Glick, P.
9 1975 "A demographer looks at American families." Journal of Marriage and the Family 37(1):15–26.
10 1979a "The Future of the American Family." Current Population Reports, Special Studies, Series P-23, No. 78.

11 1979b "The future marital status and living arrangements of the elderly." The Gerontologist 19(3):301–9.
16 1984 "How American families are changing." American Demographics 6(1):20–25.

9 Glick, P., and R. Parke, Jr.
1965 "New approaches in studying the life cycle of the family." Demography 2:187–202.

9 Goldman, N.
1984 "Changes in widowhood and divorce and expected durations of marriage." Demography 21(3):297–308.

7,9 Goldscheider, C.
1971 Population, Modernization, and Social Structure. Boston: Little, Brown.

9 Goldscheider, C., and W. Mosher
1988 "Religious affiliation and contraceptive usage: changing American patterns, 1955–82." Studies in Family Planning 19(1):48–57.

7,12 Goldstein, S., and A. Goldstein
1981 "The impact of migration on fertility: an 'own children' analysis for Thailand." Population Studies 35(2):265–84.

14 Goliber, T.
1985 Sub-saharan Africa: population pressures on development." Population Bulletin 40(1).

12 Goodman, J., and M. Streitwieser
1982 "Expanding racial differences in city-to-suburb residential mobility." Working Paper No. 1384-09 of the Urban Institute, Washington, D.C.

2 Goodstadt, L.
1982 "China's one-child family: policy and public response." Population and Development Review 8(1):37–58.

6 Gordon, J. (ed.)
1965 Control of Communicable Disease in Man. New York: American Public Health Association.

7,14 Gordon, M.
1975 Agriculture and Population. U.S. Bureau of the Census, Statistical Training Document No. 1. Washington, D.C.: Government Printing Office.

16 Gottschalk, E., Jr.
1981 "Promotions grow few as 'Baby Boom' group eyes managers' jobs." Wall Street Journal, 22 October.

6 Gove, W.
1973 "Sex, marital status, and mortality." American Journal of Sociology 79(1):45–67.

12 Gove, W., and M. Hughes

1983 Overcrowding in the Household: An Analysis of Determinants and Effects. New York: Academic Press.

12 Gove, W., M. Hughes, and O. Galle
1979 "Overcrowding in the home: an empirical investigation of its possible pathological consequences." American Sociological Review 44(1):59–80.

5 Grabill, W., C. Kiser, and P. Whelpton
1958 The Fertility of American Women. New York: Wiley.

11 Grad, S.
1984 "Income of the population 55 and over, 1982." Social Security Administration. Washington, D.C.: Government Printing Office.

11 Graebner, W.
1980 A History of Retirement. New Haven: Yale University Press.

10 Green, P.
1979 "The feminist consciousness." The Sociological Quarterly 20(Summer): 354–74.

Greene, R.
16 1983 "The man behind the Golden Bear." Forbes, 4 July.

Greenhalgh, S.
15 1986 "Shifts in China's population policy 1984–86: views from the central, provincial, and local levels." Population and Development Review 12(3):491–516.

Greep, R., M. Koblinsky, and F. Jaffe
15 1976 Reproduction and Human Welfare: A Challenge to Research. Cambridge: MIT Press.

Griffith, J.
10 1973 "Social pressure on family size intentions." Family Planning Perspectives 5(4):237–42.

Groat, H. T., J. W. Wicks, A. Neal, and G. Hendershot
9 1982 "Working women and childbearing." Data from the National Survey of Family Growth, Series 23, No. 9. Hyattsville, MD: National Center for Health Statistics.

10 Groat, H. T., R. Workman, and A. Neal
1976 "Labor force participation and family formation: a study of working mothers." Demography 13(1):115–26.

10 Grossbard-Schechtman, A.
1985 "Marriage squeezes and the marriage market." In K. Davis and A. Grossbard-Schechtman (eds.), Contemporary Marriage: Comparative Perspectives on a Changing Institution. New York: Russell Sage Foundation.

16 Gruen, N., C. Gruen, and W. Smith
1982 "Demographic changes and their effects on real estate markets in the 1980s." Washington, D.C.: Urban Land Institute.

15 Guenther, R.
1983 "New York community scraps pioneering growth control." Wall Street Journal, 31 August.

10 Gurak, D., and M. Kritz
1982 "Female employment and fertility in the Dominican Republic: a dynamic perspective." American Sociological Review 47(6):810–18.

8,10 Guttentag, M., and P. Secord
1983 Too Many Women? Beverly Hills, CA: Sage.

10 Halaby, C.
1979 "Sexual inequality in the workplace: an employer-specific analysis of pay differences." Social Science Research 8(1):79–104.

6 Halberstein, R.
1973 "Historical-Demographic Analysis of Indian Populations in Tlaxcala, Mexico." Social Biology 20(1):40–50.

12 Hall, E.
1966 The Hidden Dimension. New York: Doubleday.

14 Hammond, A., and T. H. Maugh
1974 "Stratospheric pollution: multiple threats to earth's ozone." Science 186:335–38.

11 Hampson, J.
1983 Old Age: A Study of Aging in Zimbabwe. Gweru, Zimbabwe: Mambo Press.

12 Hance, W.
1970 Population, Migration and Urbanization in Africa. New York: Columbia University Press.

5 Hanley, S., and K. Yamamura
1977 Economic and Demographic Changes in Preindustrial Japan, 1600–1868. Princeton, NJ: Princeton University Press.

13 Hansen, J.
1970 The Population Explosion: How Sociologists View It. New York: Pathfinder Press.

4 Haq, Muhammad
1984 "Age at menarche and the related issue: a pilot study on urban school girls." Family Planning Perspectives 13(6):559–67.

3 Hardin, G.
1968 "The tragedy of the commons." Science 162:1243–48.

14 Harlan, J.
    1976 "The plants and animals that nourish man." Scientific American 235(3):88–97.

6   Hartley, S.
    1972 Population: Quantity Versus Quality. Englewood Cliffs, NJ: Prentice-Hall.

4   Hatcher, R., G. Stewart, F. Guest, R. Finkelstein, and C. Godwin
    1976 Contraceptive Technology, 1976–1977, 8th revised edition. New York: Irvington.

4   Hatcher, R., G. Stewart, F. Stewart, F. Guest, P. Stratton, and A. Wright
    1978 Contraceptive Technology 1978–1979, 9th edition. New York: Irvington.

5   Haupt, A.
    1983 "The shadow of infanticide." Intercom 11(1/2):1.

9   Hauser, R., and P. Featherman
    1974 "Socioeconomic achievements of U.S. men, 1962 to 1972." Science 185:325–31.

12 Hawley, A.
    1972 "Population density and the city." Demography 91:521–30.

10 Hawthorne, G.
    1970 The Sociology of Fertility. New York: Macmillan.

11 Hayflick, L.
    1979 "Progress in cytogerontology." Mechanisms of Aging and Development 9:398–408.

11 Heady, E.
    1976 "The agriculture of the U.S." Scientific American 235(3):106–27.

7   Heaton, T., C. Fredrickson, G. Fuguitt, and J. Zuiches
    1979 "Residential preferences, community satisfaction, and the intention to move." Demography 16(4):565–74.

7   Heer, D.
    1979 "What is the annual net flow of undocumented Mexican immigrants to the United States?" Demography 16(3):417–24.

10 Heer, D., and A. Grossbard-Schechtman
    1981 "The impact of the female marriage squeeze and the contraceptive revolution on sex roles and the Women's Liberation Movement in the United States, 1960 to 1975." Journal of Marriage and the Family 43(1):49–65.

5   Heer, D., and D. Smith
    1969 "Mortality level, desired family size and population increase: further variations on a basic model." Demography 6:141–50.

7   Helal, A.
    1982 "Kuwaiti push against illegal immigrants creates shortage of construction workers." Wall Street Journal, 1 December.

7   Hendrix, L.
    1976 "Kinship, social networks, and integration among Ozark residents and out-migrants." Journal of Marriage and the Family 38:97–104.

14 Hendry, P.
    1988 "Food and population: beyond five billion." Population Bulletin 43(2).

4   Henry, L.
    1961 "Some data on natural fertility." Eugenics Quarterly 8:81–91.

4   Henshaw, S.
    1987 "Induced abortion: a worldwide perspective." International Family Planning Perspectives 13(1):12–16.

4   Henshaw, S., N. Binkin, E. Blaine, and J. Smith
    1985 "A portrait of American women who obtain abortion." Family Planning Perspectives 17(2):90–96.

4   Henshaw, S., J. Forrest, E. Sullivan, and C. Tietze
    1981 Abortion 1977–79: Need and Services in the United States, Each State and Metropolitan Area. New York: The Alan Guttmacher Institute.

16 Henson, J., and P. Zadorozny
    1982 "Future of San Diego—Policy Issues." City of San Diego: San Diego Police Department.

4   Hermann, C., N. Williamson, M. McCann, J. Spieler, B. Janowitz, K. Kennedy, and S. Thapa
    1986 "Periodic abstinence in developing countries: update and policy options." Research Triangle Park, NC: Family Health International.

8   Hernandez, J.
    1974 People, Power and Policy. Palo Alto, CA: National Press Books.

4   Heuser, R.
    1976 Fertility Tables for Birth Cohorts by Color: United States, 1971–73. Rockville, MD: National Center for Health Statistics.

    Hill, A. G.
5   1975 "The demography of the Kuwaiti population of Kuwait." Demography 12(3):537–48.

5   1978 "Fertility trends and differentials in Kuwait." In J. Allman (ed.), Women's Status and Fertility in the Muslim World. New York: Praeger.

3,5   Himes, N.E.
      1976   Medical History of Contraception. New York: Schocken Books.

16   Himonas, J.
      1982   "The changing consumer market." Town Hall Reporter (Los Angeles), October.

13   Hirschman, A.
      1958   The Strategy of Economic Development. New Haven: Yale University Press.

4   Hirschman, C., and M. Butler
      1981   "Trends and differentials in breast feeding: an update." Demography 18(1):39–54.

10   Ho, S.
      1984   "Women's labor force participation in Hong Kong, 1971–1981." Journal of Marriage and the Family 46(2):947–53.

15   Ho, Z.
      1984   "China's battle against a baby boom." The Sunday Mail (Harare, Zimbabwe), 30 September.

12   Hoch, I.
      1976   "City size effects, trends, and policies." Science 193:856–63.

10   Hock, E., M. Gnezda, and S. McBride
      1984   "Mothers of infants: attitudes toward employment and motherhood following birth of the first child." Journal of Marriage and the Family 46(2):425–31.

10   Hoffman, L.
      1975   "The employment of women, education, and fertility." In M. Mednick, S. Tangri, and L. Hoffman (eds.), Women and Achievement. Washington: Hemisphere.

12   Holdrich M.
      1984   "Prospects for metropolitan growth." American Demographics 6(4):33–37.

13   Hollerbach, P.
      1980   "Recent trends in fertility, abortion, and contraception in Cuba." International Family Planning Perspectives 6(3):97–106.

14   Hopkins, R., R. Paarlberg, and M. Wallerstein
      1982   Food in the Global Arena. New York: Holt, Rinehart & Winston.

9   Hout, M.
      1984   "Occupational mobility of black men: 1962 to 1973." American Sociological Review 49(3):308–22.

12   Howell, F., and W. Frese
      1983   "Size of place, residential preferences and the life cycle: how people come to like where they live." American Sociological Review 48(4):569–80.

2   Howell, N.
      1979   Demography of the Dobe Kung. New York: Academic Press.

16   Hughes, C.
      1985   "State data centers: networks of cooperating agencies." News Notes (Committee on Business Demography, Population Association of America) 1(3–4).

14   Hughey, A.
      1983   "Just killing rats isn't sufficient; you need birth control, firm says." Wall Street Journal, 4 August.

4   Hull, J.
      1983   "Researchers trying to develop better birth-control methods." Wall Street Journal, 25 February.

      Huzel, J.
3   1969   "Malthus, the Poor Law, and population in early nineteenth-century England." Economic History Review 22:430–52.

3   1980   "The demographic impact of the old Poor Law: more reflexions on Malthus." Economic History Review 33(3):367–81.

16   Hymowitz, C.
      1983   "Heinz sets out to expand in Africa and Asia, seeking new markets, sources of materials." Wall Street Journal, 20 September.

16   Iacocca, L. (with W. Novak)
      1984   Iacocca: An Autobiography. New York: Bantam Books.

14   Idso, S., R. Jackson, and R. Reginato
      1977   "Remote-sensing of crop yields." Science 196:19–25.

      Intercom
15   1978   "Immigration hot topic in Britain." 6(5):3.

4   1979   "One pregnant woman in every four chooses abortion." 7(5):15.

      International Family Planning Perspectives
4   1981   "Low potassium levels from use of Gossypol linked to paralysis." International Family Planning Perspectives 7(1):24–25.

4   1982   "Oral contraceptives do not increase breast cancer risk, even after more than 11 years of pill use." International Family Planning Perspectives 8(3):107–8.

4   Ireland Central Statistics Office
      1978   Statistical Abstract of Ireland, 1976. Dublin: Stationery Office.

15   Isaacs, S., and R. Cook
      1984   "Laws and policies affecting fertility: a decade of change." Population Reports, Series E, No. 7. Baltimore: Johns Hopkins University Press.

13 Isbister, J.
 1973 "Birth control, income redistribution, and the rate of saving: the case of Mexico." Demography 10:85–94.

11 Ishizuka, K. C.
 1978 The Elder Japanese. San Diego State University: University Center on Aging.

ISR Newsletter (Institute of Social Research, University of Michigan)
9 1979 "Who gets ahead? Family background predicts son's success." Summer.
14 1988 "Farming the sea." Fall/Winter.

12 Jacobs, J.
 1961 The Death and Life of Great American Cities. New York: Random House.

15 Jaffe, F.
 1971 "Toward the reduction of unwanted pregnancy." Science 174:119–27.

4 Jaffe, F., B. Lindheim, and P. Lee
 1981 Abortion Politics: Private Morality and Public Policy. New York: McGraw-Hill.

9 Jain, A.
 1981 "The effect of female education on fertility: a simple explanation." Demography 18(4):577–614.

2,5 Jain, A., and A. Adlakha
 1982 "Preliminary estimates of fertility decline in India during the 1970s." Population and Development Review 8(3):589–606.

9 Janssen, S., and R. Hauser
 1981 "Religion, socialization, and fertility." Demography 18(4):511–28.

7 Jasso, G., and M. Rosenzweig
 1982 "Estimating the emigration rates of legal immigrants using administrative and survey data: the 1971 cohort of immigrants to the United States." Demography 19(3):279–90.

9 Jencks, C., and others
 1972 Inequality: A Reassessment of the Effect of Family and Schooling in America. New York: Basic Books.

Johnson, N.
9 1979 "Minority-group status and the fertility of black Americans, 1970: a new look." American Journal of Sociology 84(6):1386–1400.
9 1982 "Religious differentials in reproduction: the effects of sectarian education." Demography 19(4):495–509.

8 Jones, L.
 1981 Great Expectations: America and the Baby Boom Generation. New York: Ballantine.

7 Jones, S.
 1988 "Hong Kong exodus begins as Chinese takeover nears." Wall Street Journal, 30 March.

4 Kambic, R., M. Kambic, A. Brixius, and S. Miller
 1981 "A thirty-month clinical experience in natural family planning." American Journal of Public Health 71(11):1255–57.

9 Kammeyer, K., N. Yetman, and M. McClendon
 1975 "Race and public policy: family planning services and the distribution of black Americans." Chap. 30 in N. Yetman and C. Steele (eds.), Majority and Minority. Boston: Allyn and Bacon.

1 Kaplan, C., and T. Van Valey
 1980 Census 80: Continuing the Factfinder Tradition. Washington, D.C.: U.S. Bureau of the Census.

14 Karim, M.
 1986 The Green Revolution: An International Bibliography. New York: Greenwood Press.

15 Kaufman, M.
 1986 "Polish birth rate: it's no. 1 in Europe." New York Times, 16 October.

1 Kazemi, F.
 1980 Poverty and Revolution in Iran. New York: New York University Press.

4 Keefe, E. F.
 1962 "Self-observation of the cervix to distinguish days of possible fertility." Bulletin of the Sloane Hospital for Women 8(4):129–36.

Keely, C.
15 1971 "Effects of the Immigration Act of 1965 on selected population characteristics of immigrants to the United States." Demography 8:157–70.
15 1974 "Immigration composition and population policy." Science 185:587–93.
7 1981 Global Refugee Policy: The Case for a Development-Oriented Strategy. New York: The Population Council.

15 Keeny, S. M.
 1970 "Taiwan." Country Profiles. New York: Population Council.

13 Kelley, A.
 1973 "Population growth, the dependency rate, and the pace of economic development." Population Studies 27:405–14.

12 Kelley, A., and J. Williamson
 1984 "Population growth, industrial revolutions, and the urban transition." Population and Development Review 10(3):419–41.

3   Kelly, W., and P. Cutright
     1980 "Modernization and the demographic transition: cross-sectional and longitudinal analyses of a revised model." Sociological Focus 13(4):315–29.

12   Kemper, R.
     1974 "Family and household organization among Tzintzuntzan migrants in Mexico City." In W. Cornelius and F. Trueblood (eds.), Latin American Urban Research, Vol. 4. Beverly Hills, CA: Sage.

12   Kemper, R., and G. Foster
     1975 "Urbanization in Mexico: the view from Tzintzuntzan." In W. Cornelius and F. Trueblood (eds.), Urbanization and Inequality: The Political Economy of Urban and Rural Development in Latin America. Beverly Hills, CA: Sage.

5   Kent, M., and A. Larson
     1982 "Family size preferences: evidence from the World Fertility Surveys." Washington, D.C.: Population Reference Bureau.

7   Keyes, R.
     1973 We, the Lonely People. New York: Harper & Row.

     Keyfitz, N.
13   1965 "Age distribution as a challenge to development." American Journal of Sociology 70:659–68.

2   1966 "How many people have ever lived on the earth?" Demography 3(2):581–82.

8   1968 Introduction to the Mathematics of Population. Reading, MA: Addison-Wesley.

11, 1971 "Migration as a means of population
15   control." Population Studies 25(1):63–72.

3   1972 "Population theory and doctrine: a historical survey." In W. Petersen (ed.), Readings in Population. New York: Macmillan.

A   1977 Applied Mathematical Demography. New York: Wiley.

3,8 1982 "Can knowledge improve forecasts?" Population and Development Review 8(4):729–51.

8   1983 Foreword to N. Bennett (ed.), Sex Selection of Children. New York: Academic Press.

2,5,6 Keyfitz, N., and W. Flieger
     1971 Population: Facts and Methods of Demography. San Francisco: Freeman.

15   Khan, M., and C. Prasad
     1985 "A comparison of 1970 and 1980 survey findings on family planning in India." Studies in Family Planning 16(6):312–20.

5   Khan, M., and I. Sirageldin
     1977 "Son preference and the demand for additional children in Pakistan." Demography 14(4):481–95.

12   Khoo, S.
     1984 "Why Asia's single girls head for the city on the double." Wall Street Journal, 2 July.

15   Khoo, S., and C. Park
     1978 "The effect of family planning programs on fertility decline in four Asian countries." International Family Planning Perspectives and Digest 4(3):67–73.

2   Kilpatrick, J.
     1978 "Population implosion: new twist to old problem." Los Angeles Times, 25 June.

4   Kiser, C., W. Grabill, and A. Campbell
     1968 Trends and Variations in Fertility in the United States. Cambridge: Harvard University Press.

6   Kisker, E., and N. Goldman
     1987 "Perils of single life and benefits of marriage." Social Biology 34(3–4):135.

6   Kitagawa, E., and P. Hauser
     1973 Differential Mortality in the United States: A Study in Socioeconomic Epidemiology. Cambridge: Harvard University Press.

7   Kitano, H.
     1980 Race Relations, 2nd Edition. Englewood Cliffs, NJ: Prentice-Hall.

6   Klebba, A., J. Maurer, and E. Glass
     1974 "Mortality trends for leading causes of death: United States 1950–69." Data from the National Vital Statistics System, Series 20, No. 16. Rockville, MD: National Center for Health Statistics.

10   Kleinman, J., and S. Kessel
     1987 "Racial differences in low birth weight: trends and risk factors." New England Journal of Medicine 317:749.

     Klimas Blanc, A.
9   1982 "A comparison of the mortality of reservation and nonreservation Indians." Paper presented at the annual meeting of the Population Association of America, San Diego.

10   1984 "Nonmarital cohabitation and fertility in the United States and Western Europe." Population Research and Policy Review 3:181–93.

7   Kloppenburg, J.
     1983 "The demand for land." American Demographics 5(1):34–37.

     Knodel, J.
3   1970 "Two and a half centuries of demo-

graphic history in a Bavarian village."
Population Studies 24:353–69.

4   1977   "Breast-feeding   and   population
             growth." Science 198:1111–15.

5   Kobayashi, K.
     1969   "Traditions and transitions in family
             structure in Japan." In National Insti-
             tutes of Health, The Family in Transi-
             tion. Washington, D.C.: Government
             Printing Office.

13   Kocher, J. E.
     1973   Development, Income Distribution, and
             Fertility Decline. New York: Population
             Council.

14   Koenig, R.
     1984   "Proposed use of irradiation stirs de-
             bate." Wall Street Journal, 19 March.

4   Konner, M., and C. Worthman
     1980   "Nursing frequency, gonadal function,
             and birth spacing among Kung hunter-
             gatherers." Science 207:788–91.

7   Kosinski, L., and R. Prothero
     1975   People on the Move: Studies on Internal
             Migration. London: Methuen and Co.

7   Kraly, E.
     1982   "Emigration from the U.S. among the el-
             derly." Paper presented at the annual
             meeting of the Population Association of
             America, San Diego.

6   Kristein, M., C. Arnold, and E. Wynder
     1977   "Health   economics   and   preventive
             care." Science 195:457–62.

15   Krunholz, J.
     1983   "Indonesia pushes plan for moving mil-
             lions off the island of Java." Wall Street
             Journal, 6 September.

     Kuznets, S.
13   1965   Economic Growth of Nations. Cam-
             bridge: Harvard University Press.

13   1972   "Problems in comparing recent growth
             rates for developed and less developed
             countries."   Economic   Development
             and   Cultural   Change   20(2):195–
             209.

     Lapham, R., and W. P. Mauldin
15   1972   "National family planning programs: re-
             view and evaluation." Studies in Family
             Planning 3:29.

15   1984   "Family planning program effort and
             birthrate decline in developing coun-
             tries." International Family Planning
             Perspectives 10(4):109–18.

14   Lappé, F., N. Allen, and D. Kinley
     1982   "Food aid misses most needy." San
             Diego Union, 18 April.

14   Lappé, F., and J. Collins
     1977   Food First. Boston: Houghton Mifflin.

5   Larson, A.
     1981   Patterns of Contraceptive Use Around
             the World. Washington, D.C.: Popula-
             tion Reference Bureau.

6   Laslett, P.
     1971   The World We Have Lost. London:
             Routledge & Kegan Paul.

15   Lavely, W.
     1984   "The rural Chinese fertility transition: a
             report from Shifang Xian, Sichuan."
             Population Studies 38(3):365–84.

     Leasure, J. W.
3   1962   Factors Involved in the Decline of Fertil-
             ity in Spain: 1900–1950. Doctoral dis-
             sertation. Princeton, NJ: Princeton Uni-
             versity.

3,9 1982   "La baisse de la fecondité aux États-Unis
             de 1800 a 1860." Population 3:607–22.

7   Lee, E.
     1966   "A theory of migration." Demography
             3:47–57.

     Lee, R.
2   1972   "Population growth and the beginnings
             of sedentary life among the Kung
             Bushmen." Chap. 14 in Brian Spooner
             (ed.), Population Growth: Anthropologi-
             cal Implications. Cambridge: MIT Press.

3   1976   "Demographic forecasting and the Eas-
             terlin hypothesis." Population and De-
             velopment Review 2:459–68.

13   Leibenstein, H.
     1957   Economic Backwardness and Economic
             Growth. New York: Wiley.

3   Lengyel-Cook, M., and R. Repetto
     1982   "The relevance of the developing coun-
             tries to demographic transition theory:
             further lessons from the Hungarian
             experience."   Population   Studies
             36(1):105–28.

4   Leridon, H.
     1979   "Contraceptive practice in France in
             1978." International Family Planning
             Perspectives 5(1):25–27.

7   Leroux, C.
     1984   "Ellis Island." San Diego Union, 26
             May.

     Lesthaeghe, R.
3   1977   The Decline of Belgian Fertility, 1800–
             1970. Princeton, NJ: Princeton Univer-
             sity Press.

5   1980   "On the social control of human repro-
             duction." Population and Development
             Review 6(4):549–80.

15   Leung, J.
     1983   "Singapore's Lee tells educated women:
             get married and have families." Wall
             Street Journal, 26 August.

16 | Leviton, R.
   1983 "Soyfoods soar on demographic trends." American Demographics 5(3):36–39.

7 | Lichter, D.
   1982 "The migration of dual-worker families: does the wife's job matter?" Social Science Quarterly 63(6):48–57.

12 | Lieberson, S., and D. Carter
   1982 "A model for inferring the voluntary and involuntary causes of residential segregation." Demography 19(4):511–26.

1 | Lightbourne, R., S. Singh, and C. Green
   1982 "The World Fertility Survey: charting global childbearing." Population Bulletin 37(1).

15 | Lin, F., and Q. Zhou
   1981 "Shifang County: Family planning." In Z. Liu et al. (eds.), China's Population: Problems and Prospects. Beijing: New World Press.

Linden, F.
16 | 1983a "Income by degree." American Demographics 5(6):8.
16 | 1983b "Working-women households." American Demographics 5(8):8.

6 | Locke, R.
   1981 "Andrus Center recasts old age for savoring." San Diego Union, 1 February.

4 | London Telegraph
   1979 "Little green pea is Tibetan birth pill." 12 March.

Long, L.
7,A | 1973 "New estimates of migration expectancy in the United States." Journal of the American Statistical Association 68:37–45.
7,12 | 1983 "Population redistribution in the U.S.: Issues for the 1980s." Population Reference Bureau Occasional Papers, Population Trends and Public Policy, No. 3.

7 | Long, L., and C. Boertlein
   1976 "The Geographic Mobility of Americans: An International Comparison." Current Population Reports, Special Studies, Series P-23, No. 64.

7 | Long, L., and D. DeAre
   1982 "Repopulating the countryside: a 1980 census trend." Science 217:1111–16.

12 | Long, L., and D. Spain
   1979 "Racial Succession in Individual Housing Units." Current Population Reports, Special Studies, Series P-23, No. 71.

7 | Louv, R.
   1979 "U.S. magnet lures Mexican migrants." San Diego Union, 25 November: A-1.

4 | Lowe, C., and S. Radius
   1987 "Young adults' contraceptive practices: an investigation of influences." Adolescence 22:291.

16 | Lowenstein, R.
   1982 "Goya Foods Inc., No. 1 in Hispanic market, aims to broaden base." Wall Street Journal, 23 March.

14 | Lowenthal, J.
   1982 "Economic growth vital in fighting hunger." San Diego Union, 11 April.

16 | Lubar, R.
   1982 "Housing's unsheltered future." Fortune, 8 March:84–90.

Lublin, J.
16 | 1982 "More managers are working part-time: some like it, but others have no choice." Wall Street Journal, 2 June.
12 | 1984 "Suburban population ages, causing conflict and radical changes." Wall Street Journal, 1 November.

10 | Lustig, N., and T. Rendon
   1979 "Female employment, occupational status, and socioeconomic characteristics of the family in Mexico." Signs 5(1):143–53.

4 | McCarthy, J. J.
   1977 The sympho-thermal method. Washington, D.C.: Human Life Foundation of America.

14 | McCue, A.
   1982 "Philippines facing ecological disaster as villagers, loggers denude hillsides." Wall Street Journal, 27 April.

4 | McFalls, J.
   1979 "Frustrated fertility: a population paradox." Population Bulletin 34(2).

4 | McFalls, J., and M. McFalls
   1984 Disease and Fertility. New York: Academic Press.

2 | McKeown, T.
   1976 The modern rise of population. London: Edward Arnold.

6 | McKeown, T., and R. Record
   1962 "Reasons for the decline of mortality in England and Wales during the 19th century." Population Studies 16(2):94–122.

16 | Machalaba, D.
   1982 "More magazines aim for affluent readers, but some worry that shakeout is coming." Wall Street Journal, 4 October.

5 | Mackey-Smith, A.
   1984 "Scholastic aptitude test average scores rose 4 points in 1984." Wall Street Journal, 20 September.

16 | Magnuson, E.
   1985 "Symbiosis along 1,936 miles." Time 126(1):54.

4 | Maine, D.

1979 "Does abortion affect later pregnancies?" International Family Planning Perspectives 5(1):22–25.

Malthus, T. R.
3   1798 An Essay on Population. New York: Augustus Kelley, Bookseller; reprinted in 1965.
3,5   1872 An Essay on the Principle of Population, 7th edition. London: Reeves and Turner.

Mamdani, M.
5   1972 The Myths of Population Control. New York: Monthly Review Press.

Mandelbaum, D.
5,10 1974 Human Fertility in India. Berkeley: University of California Press.

Manton, K. G., S. S. Poss, and S. Wing
11   1979 "The black/white mortality crossover: investigation from the perception of the components of aging." The Gerontologist 19(3):291–300.

Marini, M.
9   1984 "Women's educational attainment and parenthood." American Sociological Review 49(4):491–511.

Martin, J.
16   1985 "Virginia's state-local cooperative program for population estimates." News Notes (Committee on Business Demography, Population Association of America) 7:1–2.

Martin, P.
6   1976 "The old men and women of the mountains." Parade, 4 April.

Marx, J.
14   1975 "Air pollution effects on plants." Science 181:731–33.

Masamba, M.
11   1984 Older Persons and Their Families in a Changing Village Society: A Perspective From Zaire. Washington, D.C.: International Federation on Aging.

Masnick, G.
4   1981 "The continuity of birth-expectations data with historical trends in cohort parity distributions: implications for fertility in the 1980s." In G. Hendershot and P. Placek (eds.), Predicting Fertility. Lexington, MA: Lexington Books.

Mason, K., and V. Palan
10   1981 "Female employment and fertility in Peninsular Malaysia: the maternal role incompatibility hypothesis reconsidered." Demography 18(4):549–76.

Mauldin, W. P.
15   1975 "Assessment of national family planning programs in developing countries."

Studies in Family Planning 6(2):30–36.

Maxwell, N.
4   1977 "Medical secrets of the Amazon." America 29(6–7):2–8.

Mayer, J.
14   1976 "The dimensions of human hunger." Scientific American 235(3):40–49.

Mayfield, M.
4   1982 "New contraceptive methods hailed." San Diego Union, 6 October.

Mayhew, B., and R. Levinger
12   1976 "Size and the density of interaction in human aggregates." American Journal of Sociology 82(1):86–109.

Meadows, D.
13   1974 Dynamics of Growth in a Finite World. Cambridge, MA: Wright-Allen Press.

Meadows, D. H., D. L. Meadows, J. Randers, and W. Behrens, III
13   1972 The Limits to Growth. New York: New American Library.

Mehta, R.
5   1975 "White-collar and blue-collar family responses to population growth in India." In M. Franda (ed.), Responses to Population Growth in India. New York: Praeger.

Mehta, S.
10   1982 Revolution and Status of Women in India. New Delhi: Metropolitan.

Meng-Try, E.
7   1981 "Kampuchea: a country adrift." Population and Development Review 7(2):209–28.

Menken, J., J. Trussel, and U. Larsen
4   1986 "Age and infertility." Science 233:1389–94.

Merrick, T.
16   1985 "Teaching applied demography." Paper presented at the annual meeting of the Population Association of America, Boston.

Metchnikoff, E.
6   1908 The Prolongation of Life. New York: Putnam.

Mexico, D. F.
12   1982 Anuario Estadístico de los Estados Unidos Mexicanos, 1980. Mexico: SPP.

Meyers, R.
6   1978 "An investigation of an alleged centenarian." Demography 15(2):235–37.

Midgett, D.
7   1975 "West Indian ethnicity in Great Britain." In H. Safa and B. DuToit (eds.), Migration and Development. The Hague: Mouton.

Mill, J. S.
3   1924   Autobiography. London: Oxford University Press.
3   1848   (1929) Principles of Political Economy. London: Longmans & Green.
12 Miller, J.
    1984   "Annexation: the outer limits of city growth." American Demographics 6(11):30–35.
6   Miller, Marvin
    1979   Suicide After Sixty: The Final Alternative. New York: Springer.
16 Milliken, J.
    1982   Housing: Outlook for the 1980s. New York: Paine Webber–Mitchell Hutchins.
7   Mines, R., and D. Massey
    1982   "A comparison of patterns of U.S.-bound migration in two Mexican sending communities." Paper presented at the annual meeting of the Population Association of America, San Diego.
11 Moment, G.
    1978   "The Ponce De Leon trail today." In S. Dunne et al. (eds.), The Biology of Aging. New York: Plenum Press.
15 Monteith, R., J. Anderson, M. Pineda, R. Santiso, and M. Oberle
    1985   "Contraceptive use and fertility in Guatemala." Studies in Family Planning 16(5):279–88.
14 Morgan, D.
    1976   "American agripower and the future of a hungry world." Saturday Review, 13 November.
    Morrison, P.
15 1974   "Urban growth and decline: San Jose and St. Louis in the 1960s." Science 185:757–62.
16 1980   "How demographers can help legislators." Policy Analysis 6(1):85–98.
7   Morrison, P., and J. Wheeler
    1976   "Rural renaissance in America?" Population Bulletin 31(3).
5,8 Mosher, S.
    1983   "Why are baby girls being killed in China?" Wall Street Journal, 25 July.
    Mosher, W.
4   1982   "Infertility trends among U.S. couples: 1965–1976." Family Planning Perspectives 14(1):22–27.
4   1988   "Fecundity and infertility in the United States." American Journal of Public Health 78(2):181.
4   Mosher, W., and C. Bachrach
    1986   "Contraceptive use: United States, 1982." Data from the National Survey

of Family Growth, Series 23, No. 12. Rockville, MD: National Center for Health Statistics.
    Mosher, W., and G. Hendershot
9   1984a "Religion and fertility: a replication." Demography 21(2):185–92.
9   1984b "Religious affiliation and the fertility of married couples." Journal of Marriage and the Family 46(3):671–77.
16 Mufson, S.
    1985   "Heinz bucks trend in Zimbabwe, considers investments in Africa worthwhile." Wall Street Journal, 2 January.
3   Muhua, C.
    1979   "For the realization of the four modernizations, there must be planned control of population growth." Excerpted in Population and Development Review 5(4):723–30.
12 Mumford, L.
    1968   "The city: focus and function." Pp. 447–54 in D. Sills (ed.), International Encyclopedia of the Social Sciences. New York: Macmillan.
5   Muramatsu, M.
    1971   "Japan." Country Profiles. New York: Population Council.
4   Murphy, J.
    1986   "The month-after pill." Time, 29 December.
5   Nag, M.
    1962   Factors Affecting Human Fertility in Non-Industrial Societies: A Cross-Cultural Study. Yale University Publications in Anthropology, 66. New Haven: Yale University Press.
13 Nagel, J.
    1978   "Mexico's population policy turn-around." Population Bulletin 33(5).
16 Naisbitt, J.
    1982   Megatrends. New York: Warner Books.
11 Nam, C. B., and K. A. Ockay
    1977   "Factors contributing to the mortality crossover pattern." Paper presented at the Twenty-Seventh General Conference of the International Union for the Scientific Study of Population, Mexico.
15 National Academy of Sciences
    1973   In Search of Population Policy. Washington, D.C.: National Academy of Sciences.
    National Center for Health Statistics
6   1975   Vital Statistics of the United States, 1973. Volume II—Mortality, Part B. Hyattsville, MD: NCHS.
6   1976   Vital Statistics of the United States,

4   1972. Volume II—Mortality, Part A. DHEW Publication (HRA) 76–1101. Hyattsville, MD: NCHS.

4   1978a Health—United States: 1978. DHEW Publication (PHS) 78–1232. Hyattsville, MD: NCHS.

11   1978b Vital Statistics of the United States, 1976, Volume II—Section 5, "Life Tables." Hyattsville, MD: NCHS.

5   1979   Monthly Vital Statistics Report 28(7).

16   1980   Health: United States, 1980. Hyattsville, MD: NCHS.

6   1982   Health: United States, 1982. Hyattsville, MD: NCHS.

5   1983   "Births, marriages, divorces, and deaths for 1982." Monthly Vital Statistics Report 31(12).

10   1984a "Advance report of final marriage statistics, 1981." Monthly Vital Statistics Report 32(11).

10   1984b "Trends in teenage childbearing, United States 1970–81." Data from the National Vital Statistics System, Series 21, No. 41. Hyattsville, MD: NCHS.

10   1984c Vital Statistics of the United States, 1979, Vol. III, Marriage and Divorce. Hyattsville, MD: NCHS.

10   1984d Vital Statistics of the United States, 1979, Vol. I, Natality. Hyattsville, MD: NCHS.

11   1984e "Advance report of final mortality statistics, 1982." Monthly Vital Statistics Report, 33(9): Supplement.

6   1987a Vital Statistics of the United States, 1984. Volume II—Mortality, Part A. Hyattsville, MD: NCHS.

16   1987b "Current estimates from the National Health Interview Survey, United States, 1986." Data from the National Health Survey, Series 10, No. 164. Hyattsville, MD: NCHS.

4   1987c "Advance report of final natality statistics, 1985." Monthly Vital Statistics Report 36(4):Supplement.

9   1987d "Advance report of final divorce statistics, 1985." Monthly Vital Statistics Report 36(8):Supplement.

9   1987e "Advance report of final marriage statistics, 1984." Monthly Vital Statistics Report 36(2):Supplement.

6   1988   Health, United States, 1987. Hyattsville, MD: NCHS.

10   National Committee on the Status of Women (India)

      1975   Status of Women in India. New Delhi: The Indian Council of Social Science Research.

National Research Council

1   1978   Counting the People in 1980: An Appraisal of Census Plans. Washington, D.C.: National Academy of Sciences.

14   1982   The Winged Bean: A High-Protein Crop for the Tropics, 2nd Edition. Washington, D.C.: National Research Council.

16   Nelson, H.

      1981   "Geriatric care called poor." Los Angeles Times, 16 July.

Newitt, J.

12   1983   "Big city blues." American Demographics 5(6):26–29.

12   1984   "Where do suburbanites come from?" American Demographics 6(6):24–27.

7   Newman, B.

      1983   "Western Europe hints that foreign workers should go back home." Wall Street Journal, 9 May.

14   Newman, J., and R. Pickett

      1974   "World climates and food supply variations." Science 186:877–81.

14   Newsweek

      1974   "How to ease the hunger pangs." 11 November.

6   1982   "The war against drunk drivers." 13 September.

6   1983a "Good news on estrogen for older women." 28 February.

7   1983b "Nigeria's outcasts: The cruel exodus." 14 February.

14   Nicholls, W. H

      1970   "Development in agrarian economies: the role of agricultural surplus, population pressures, and systems of land tenure." Chap. 10 in C. Wharton (ed.), Subsistence Agriculture and Economic Development. Chicago: Aldine.

3   Nickerson, J.

      1975   Homage to Malthus. Port Washington, NY: National University Publications.

10   Nielsen, J.

      1978   Sex in Society: Perspectives on Stratification. Belmont, CA: Wadsworth.

16   Nordberg, O.

      1983   "Counting on Wall Street." American Demographics 5(8):22–25.

5   Nordland, R.

      1981   "Murders of India's brides over dowries now commonplace." San Diego Tribune, 25 November.

Nortman, D.

15   1974   "Population and family planning programs: a factbook." Reports on Population/Family Planning, No. 2, 6th edition. New York: Population Council.

15   1975   "Population and family planning pro-

grams: a factbook." Reports on Population/Family Planning, No. 2, 7th edition. New York: Population Council.

3   Notestein, F. W.
    1945 "Population—the long view." In T. W. Schultz (ed.), Food for the World. Chicago: University of Chicago Press.

16 Novak, M.
    1979 "The new financial base of American blacks." San Diego Union, 13 September.

    O'Connell, M., and C. Rogers
4,5 1983 "Assessing cohort birth expectations data from the Current Population Survey, 1971–1981." Demography 29(3):369–84.

10 1984 "Out-of-wedlock births, premarital pregnancies and their effect on family formation and dissolution." Family Planning Perspectives 16(4):157–62.

16 Odom, G.
    1981 Personal communication with chairman and chief executive officer of U.S. Home Corporation.

7   Office of Refugee Resettlement
    1987 Refugee Reports 8(12).

13 Ohlin, G.
    1976 "Economic theory confronts population growth." Chap. 1 in Ansley Coale (ed.), Economic Factors in Population Growth. New York: Wiley.

    Omran, A.
2   1973 "The mortality profile." In A. Omran (ed.), Egypt: Population Problems and Prospects. Chapel Hill: Carolina Population Center.

6   1977 "Epidemiologic transition in the United States." Population Bulletin 32(2).

10 Oppenheimer, V. K.
    1967 "The Interaction of Demand and Supply and Its Effect on the Female Labour Force in the U.S." Population Studies 21(3):239–59.

11 Oriol, W.
    1982 Aging in All Nations: A Special Report on the United Nations World Assembly on Aging. Washington, D.C.: National Council on Aging.

9   Orshansky, M.
    1969 "How poverty is measured." Monthly Labor Review 92(2):37–41.

6   Ortiz de Montellano, B.
    1975 "Empirical Aztec medicine." Science 188:215–20.

4   Ory, H.
    1982 "The noncontraceptive health benefits from oral contraceptive use." Interna-

tional Family Planning Perspectives 8(3):93–95.

4   Ory, H., A. Rosenfeld, and L. Landman
    1980 "The pill at 20: an assessment." International Family Planning Perspectives 6(4):125–30.

12 Otten, A.
    1981 "Britons leave cities and public health." Wall Street Journal, 27 August.

7   Packard, V.
    1972 A Nation of Strangers. New York: McKay.

14 Page, T., R. Harris, and S. Epstein
    1976 "Drinking water and cancer mortality in Louisiana." Science 193:55–57.

11 Palmore, E.
    1975 The Honorable Elders. Durham, NC: Duke University Press.

A   Palmore, J., and R. Gardner
    1983 Measuring Mortality, Fertility, and Natural Increase. Honolulu: East-West Population Institute.

    Parks, M.
7   1982a "Hong Kong laws splits babies, illegal mothers." Los Angeles Times, 31 January.

7   1982b "Hong Kong: wealth gap triggers tension." Los Angeles Times, 24 January.

1   Passel, J.
    1976 "Provisional evaluation of the 1970 census count of American Indians." Demography 13:397–409.

1   Passel, J., C. Cowan, and K. Wolter
    1983 "Coverage of the 1980 census." Paper presented at the annual meeting of the Population Association of America, Pittsburgh, Pennsylvania.

1   Passel, J., J. Siegel, and J. Robinson
    1982 "Coverage of the National Population in the 1980 Census by Age, Sex, and Race: Preliminary Estimates by Demographic Analysis." Current Population Reports, Series P-23, No. 115.

15 Paul, E., and H. Pilpel
    1979 "Teenage pregnancy: the law in 1979." Family Planning Perspectives 11(5):297–302.

15 Pebley, A., H. Delgado, and E. Brinemann
    1979 "Fertility desires and child mortality experiences among Guatemalan women." Studies in Family Planning 10(4):129–36.

3   Petersen, W.
    1979 Malthus. Cambridge, MA: Harvard University Press.

4   Petitti, D., and J. Wingerd
    1978 "Use of oral contraceptives, cigarette

smoking, and the risk of subarachnoid hemorrhage." The Lancet 2:234.

11 Pfeiffer, E., and G. Davis
    1974   "Determinants of sexual behavior in middle and old age." In E. Palmore (ed.), Normal Aging II. Durham, NC: Duke University Press.

    Phillips, D. P.
6   1972   "Deathday and birthday: an unexpected connection." In O. Tanur et al. (eds.), Statistics: A Guide to the Unknown. San Francisco: Holden-Day.

6   1974   "The influence of suggestion on suicide." American Sociological Review 39:340–54.

6   1977   "Motor vehicle fatalities increase just after publicized suicide stories." Science 196:1464–65.

6   1978   "Airplane accident fatalities increase just after newspaper stories about murder and suicide." Science 201:748–50.

6   1983   "The impact of mass media violence on U.S. homicides." American Sociological Review 48(4):560–68.

14 Pimentel, D., E. Terhune, R. Dyson-Hudson, S. Rochereau, R. Samis, E. Smith, D. Denman, D. Reifschneider, and M. Shepard
    1976   "Land degradation: effects on food and energy resources." Science 194:149–55.

9   Pohlman, E. (ed.)
    1973   Population: A Clash of Prophets. New York: New American Library.

16 Pol, L.
    1987   Business Demography: A Guide and Reference for Business Planners and Marketers. New York: Quorum Books.

3,14 Poleman, Thomas
      1975   "World food: a perspective." Science 188:510–18.

1   Pollard, A., F. Yusuf, and G. Pollard
    1974   Demographic Technique. Australia: Pergamon Press.

5   Pool, D. I.
    1970   "Ghana: the attitudes of urban males toward family size and family limitation." Studies in Family Planning 60:12–17.

10 Pool, J.
    1972   "A cross-comparative study of aspects of conjugal behavior among women of 3 West African countries." Canadian Journal of African Studies VI(ii):233–59.

15 PopLine (Newsletter of the Population Institute)
    1985   "4-child families could have major impact on Kenya." 7(10):1.

15 Population (UNFPA Newsletter)
    1988   "Smaller families imperative says Kenyan leader." 14(3):1.

    Population Action Council
15 1981   "Family planning leader murdered." Popline 3(9):2.

15 1983a "Urbanization is called dominant problem." 5(3):4.

15 1983b "Chinese official: 'arduous' tasks ahead." Popline 5(9):2–4.

15 1984   "Family planning can reduce infant mortality." Popline 6(3):4.

15 1985   "India seeking two-child family norm by 2000." Popline 7(5):1–2.

16 Population Association of America
    1983   "Activities of demographers in the private sector." Committee on Business Demography (brochure).

    Population Crisis Committee
14 1976   "Food and population." Population, No. 1.

9   1977   "Religious attitudes toward birth control." Population, No. 6.

16 1978   "Third world population growth from a business perspective." Population, No. 8.

6   Population Information Program
    1986   "AIDS—A public health crisis." Population Reports, Series L, No. 6. Johns Hopkins University: Population Information Program.

    Population Reference Bureau
2   1978   "World population: growth on the decline." Inter-Change 7(2).

2   1979a "World population growth in 1979: still soaring." Intercom 7(4).

4   1979b Intercom 7(6,7):2.

13 1981   World Population Data Sheet, 1981.

2,8,
13 1984a World Population Data Sheet, 1984.

15 1984b "Singapore promotes selective sterilization." Population Today 12(11).

1,5 1985a "PAA meets in Boston." Population Today 13(5):2.

2,8,
13 1985b World Population Data Sheet, 1985.

2   1988   World Population Data Sheet, 1988.

13 Portes, A., J. Clark, and M. Lopez
    1982   "Six years later: the process of incorporation of Cuban exiles in the United States." Cuban Studies 11–12 (January):1–24.

16 Posner, B.
    1982   "A report on the states." INC October: 95–100.

15 Poston, D., and B. Gu
    1987   "Socioeconomic development, family planning, and fertility in China." Demography 24(4):531–52.

4,6 Prema, K., and M. Ravindranath
     1982   "The effect of breastfeeding supplements

on the return of fertility." Studies in
Family Planning 13(10):293–96.

16 Prescott, E.
1983 "New men." American Demographics
5(8):16–21.

Preston, S.

6   1970 Older Male Mortality and Cigarette
Smoking. Berkeley: Institute of International Studies, University of California.

6   1976 Mortality Patterns in National Populations: With Special Reference to Recorded Causes of Death. New York: Academic Press.

3   1978 The Effects of Infant and Child Mortality on Fertility. New York: Academic
Press.

11, 1984 "Children and the elderly: divergent
16   paths for America's dependents." Demography 21(4):435–57.

13   1986 "Are the economic consequences of population growth a sound basis for population policy?" In J. Menken (ed.),
World Population and U.S. Policy:
the Choices Ahead. New York:
W. W. Norton & Co.

2,5 Preston, S., and P. Bhat
1984 "New evidence on fertility and mortality
trends in India." Population and Development Review 10(3):481–503.

A   Preston, S., N. Keyfitz, and R. Schoen
1972 Causes of Death: Life Tables for National Populations. New York: Seminar
Press.

10 Preston, S., and J. McDonald
1979 "The incidence of divorce within cohorts
of American marriages contracted since
the Civil War." Demography 16(1):1–
28.

10 Pristag, N.
1984 "Women's work involvement and experience of new motherhood." Journal of
Marriage and the Family 46(2):433–
47.

6   Pumphrey, G.
1940 The Story of Liverpool's Public Service.
London: Hodden & Stoughton.

6   Quinn, T.
1987 "The global epidemiology of the acquired immunodeficiency syndrome." In
B. Silverman and A. Waddell (eds.), Report of the Surgeon General's Workshop
on Children with HIV Infections and
Their Families. Washington, D.C.: Department of Health and Human Services.

5   Rainwater, L.
1960 And the Poor Get Children. Chicago:
Quadrangle Books.

7   Ravenstein, E.

1889 "The laws of migration." Journal of
the Royal Statistical Society 52:241–
301.

9   Reid, J.
1982 "Black Americans in the 1980s." Population Bulletin 37(4).

4   Reining, P., F. Camara, B. Chiñas, R. Fanale, S.
Gojman de Millán, B. Lenkerd, I. Shinolhara,
and I. Tinker
1977 Village Women: Their Changing Lives
and Fertility. Washington, D.C.: American Association for the Advancement of
Science.

3   Repetto, R.
1979 Economic Equality and Fertility in Developing Countries. Baltimore: Johns
Hopkins University Press.

6   Resnick, H.
1974 Teaching Outline in Suicide Studies and
Crisis Intervention. Bowie, MD: Charles
Press.

6   Retherford, R. D.
1975 The Changing Sex Differentials in Mortality. Westport: Greenwood Press.

14 Reutlinger, S., and M. Selowsky
1976 Malnutrition and Nutrition. Baltimore:
Johns Hopkins University Press.

14 Revelle, R.
1984 "The effects of population growth on re-
newable resources." In Population Resources, Environment, and Development, International Conference on
Population, 1984. Department of International Economic and Social Affairs,
Population Studies, No. 90. New York:
United Nations.

13 Reynolds, C.
1970 The Mexican Economy: Twentieth Century Structure and Growth. New Haven:
Yale University Press.

4   Rice, F. J., C. A. Lanctot, and A. C. Garcia-Devesa
1977 "Effectiveness of the sympto-thermal
method of natural family planning." Human Life Foundation of America Newsletter 7(2).

13 Riding, A.
1979 "Food next Mexico challenge." San
Diego Union, 14 January.

15 Ridker, R.
1980 "The no-birth bonus scheme: the use of
savings accounts for family planning in
South India." Population and Development Review 6(1):31–46.

8   Ridley, J., M. Sheps, J. Lingner, and J. Menken
1967 "The effects of changing mortality on
natality." Milbank Memorial Fund
Quarterly 55:77–97.

7   Rieger, J., and J. Beegle

1974   "The integration of rural migrants in new settings." Rural Sociology 39:43–54.

Riley, M. W.

8   1976a "Age strata in social systems." In R. Binstock and E. Shanas, (eds.), Handbook of Aging and the Social Sciences. New York: Van Nostrand Reinhold.

8   1976b "Social gerontology and the age stratification of society." In C. S. Kart and B. Manard (eds.), Aging in America. Port Washington, N.Y.: Alfred.

8   1979   "Aging, social change, and social policy." In M. Riley (ed.), Aging From Birth to Death. Boulder, CO: Westview Press.

9   Rindfuss, R., L. Bumpass, and C. St. John
    1980   "Education and fertility: implications from the roles women occupy." American Sociological Review 45(3):431–47.

12 Ritchey, P., and C. Stokes
    1972   "Residence background, migration, and fertility." Demography 9:217–30.

16 Rives, N., and W. Serow
    1984   Introduction to Applied Demography. Beverly Hills, CA: Sage.

1   Rizek, R.
    1982   "America's diet has changed." San Diego Union, 31 January.

16 Roberts, J.
    1983   "By concentrating on marketing, Stride Rite does well despite slump for shoemakers." Wall Street Journal, 23 February.

4   Roberts, K.
    1978   "The intrauterine device as a health risk." In Fertility and Contraception in America, Hearings before the House Select Committee on Population, Vol. III.

1   Robey, B.
    1983   "Achtung! Here comes the census." American Demographics 5(10):2–4.

13 Robinson, A.
    1982   "A most welcome flood." R & D Mexico 2(7):24–28.

11 Rockstein, M., and M. Sussman
    1979   Biology of Aging. Belmont, CA: Wadsworth.

15 Rose, F.
    1987   "California towns vote to restrict expansion as services lag behind." Wall Street Journal, 27 November.

15 Rosenhause, S.
    1976   "India taking drastic birth control step." Los Angeles Times, 25 September.

9   Rosenhouse-Persson, S., and G. Sabagh
    1983   "Attitudes toward abortion among Catholic Mexican-American women: the

effects of religiosity and education." Demography 20(1):87–98.

6   Rosenwaike, I.
    1979   "A new evaluation of the United States census data on the extreme aged." Demography 16(2):279–88.

7   Rossi, P.
    1955   Why Families Move. New York: Free Press.

7   Rout, L.
    1982   "For most Mexicans, legal entry to U.S. is impossible dream." Wall Street Journal, 4 March.

13 Rowan, C.
    1976   "Population problems illustrated in Mexico." San Diego Union, 9 April.

5,13 Rowe, P.
    1982   "Detailed statistics on the urban and rural population of Mexico: 1950 to 2010." Washington, D.C.: U.S. Bureau of the Census.

2   Rukeyser, L.
    1977   "Population expands at an alarming rate." San Diego Union, 24 November, 1977:A-28.

7,12 Rumbaut, R.
    1985   "Mental health and the refugee experience: a comparative study of Southeast Asian refugees." In T. Owan and T. Nguyen (eds.), Southeast Asian Mental Health: Treatment, Services, Prevention and Research. Washington, D.C.: Government Printing Office.

9,15 Rumbaut, R., and J. Weeks
    1985   "Fertility and adaptation among Indochinese refugees in the United States." Paper presented at the annual meeting of the Psychosocial Workshop, Boston.

4   Russell, A., and N. McWhirter
    1987   1988 Guinness Book of World Records. New York: Bantam Books.

5   Russell, B.
    1951   "New Hopes for a Changing World. New York: Simon and Schuster.

    Russell, C.
16 1983   "The news about Hispanics." American Demographics 5(3):14–27.

16 1984   "The business of demographics." Population Bulletin 39(3).

16 1985   "A high yield investment." American Demographics 7(3):7.

12, 15 Rust, E.
    1975   No Growth: Impacts on Metropolitan Areas. Lexington, MA: Lexington Books.

    Ryder, N.
5   1960   "The cohort as a concept in the study of

8   1964   social change." American Sociological Review 23:843–61.

8   1964   "Notes on the concept of a population." American Journal of Sociology 69(5):447–63.

15   Salaff, J., and A. Wong
1978   "Are disincentives coercive? The view from Singapore." International Family Planning Perspectives and Digest 4(2):50–55.

2   Salas, R.
1978   "World population growth: hopeful signs of a slowdown." The Futurist (October):276–82.

15   Samuel, T.
1966   "The development of India's policy of population control." Milbank Memorial Fund Quarterly 44:49–67.

9   St. John, C.
1982   "Race differences in age at first birth and the pace of subsequent fertility: implications for the minority group hypothesis." Demography 19(3):301–14.

14   Sanchez-Albornoz, N.
1974   The Population of Latin America: A History. Berkeley: University of California Press.

14   Sanderson, F.
1975   "The great food fumble." Science 188:503–18.

5   Sanderson, W.
1979   "Quantitative aspects of marriage, fertility, and family limitation in nineteenth century America: another application of the Coale specifications." Demography 16(3):339–58.

San Diego Union
7   1975   "It's OK to move to Oregon now." 14 December.

7   1976a   "City construction curb upheld by Supreme Court." 24 February.

15   1976b   "Employees told to limit families." 7 September.

15   1976c   "Sterilization strife results in deaths." 28 October.

15   1977a   "China hails birth control gains." 3 March.

13   1977b   "Devaluations leave Mexico monetary situation bleak." 9 January.

6   1977c   "Fiscal pinch threatens homes for aged." 22 January.

4,5   1977d   "Infertility epidemic." Parade Magazine 23 (9 January).

10   1977e   "Women gaining around world." 9 January.

14   1977f   "Bread: more powerful than bullets in global hunger crisis?" 13 March.

2   1978a   "Drop in world population growth startles scientists." 17 February, AA-8.

4   1978b   "Researchers develop fertility forecaster." 2 October.

14   1979a   "EPA to reduce use of lettuce pesticide." 15 January.

7   1979b   "Malaysia repels new refugees." 24 June, A-18.

1   1980a   "Brazil's nose count no easy task." 25 December.

6   1980b   "Study on old age released in China." 10 November.

10   1980c   "Pregnant in Japan." 16 November.

6   1981a   "Oldest U.S. resident buried at 113." 27 January.

2   1981b   "Scientist says 9% of all homo sapiens are now alive." 14 November.

4   1981c   " 'Family planning' turns on green light for sex." 20 February.

6   1981d   "Rules to live by." Quoted in Parade, 20 March.

14   1981e   "New 'food banks' save edibles from dump." 13 February.

16   1981f   "Home buying shift noted." 27 April.

6   1982a   "National minimum drinking age of 21 urged." 24 July.

7   1982b   "Outlaw wreckers plague older, downtrodden cities." 9 July.

6   1982c   "The 'Black Death': Plague claims two New Mexico victims." 19 July.

14   1982d   "China fears continued loss of grain-growing acreage to cash crops, urban areas." 5 February.

1   1983a   "Israel collects detailed information on population of South Lebanon." 14 March.

7   1983b   "Mexico places restrictions on refugee influx." 22 June.

8   1984   "FBI shows 5% drop in serious crimes reported to the police." 28 October.

4   1985a   "5-year contraceptive 'shot' OK'd." 24 February.

14   1985b   "Mexico's crops perish." 11 February.

14   1986   "China kills two billion rats; three billion left." 9 January.

6   1988   "Oldest person dies at age 114." 13 January.

San Francisco Chronicle
2   1974   "World meeting on population crisis." 19 August, p. 8.

4   1976   "The best birth control method?" 22 October.

4   1979   "China has birth control for men." 6 January.

15   Satia, J., and R. Maru
1986   "Incentives and disincentives in the In-

dian Family Welfare Program." Studies in Family Planning 17(3):136–45.

3 Sauvy, A.
   1969 General Theory of Population. New York: Basic Books.

10 Scanzoni, J.
    1975 Sex Roles, Life Styles, and Childbearing. New York: Free Press.

5 Schapera, I.
   1966 Married Life in an African Tribe. Evanston, IL: Northwestern University Press.

8 Schlesinger, S., and J. Sedgwick
   1984 "Can demography explain falling crime?" Wall Street Journal, 14 June.

10 Schneir, M.
    1972 Feminism: The Essential Historical Writings. New York: Random House.

12 Schnore, L., C. Andre, and H. Sharp
    1976 "Black Suburbanization 1930–1970." In B. Schwartz (ed.), The Changing Face of the Suburbs. Chicago: University of Chicago Press.

10 Schoen, R.
    1983 "Measuring the tightness of a marriage squeeze." Demography 20(1):61–78.

A Schoen, R., and V. Nelson
   1974 "Marriage, divorce and mortality: a life table analysis." Demography 11(2):267–90.

14 Schultz, T.
    1974 "The food supply–population growth quandary." In National Academy of Science, Rapid Population Growth. Baltimore: Johns Hopkins University Press.

6 Science
   1974 "What is cancer? What form does it take? How does it kill?" 183 (15 March):1068–69.

6 Scrimshaw, S.
   1978 "Infant mortality and behavior in the regulation of family size." Population and Development Review 4(3):383–403.

11 Segerberg, O.
    1974 The Immortality Factor. New York: Dutton.

7 Seidenbaum, A.
   1976 "Americans still 'moving on.'" Los Angeles Times, 10 December.

5,13 Seiver, D. A.
      1975 "Recent fertility in Mexico: measurement and interpretation." Population Studies 29:341–54.

7 Sell, R., and G. DeJong
   1983 "Deciding whether to move: mobility, wishful thinking and adjustment." Soci-

ology and Social Research 67(2):146–65.

14 Shapley, D.
    1977 "Will fertilizers harm ozone as much as SSTs?" Science 195:658.

9 Shaw, J.
   1984 "Getting married? Check with the IRS first." Wall Street Journal, 31 December.

6 Shedlin, M.
   1988 "IV drug abusing prostitutes: research in AIDS prevention." Paper presented at the 16th Annual Psychosocial Workshop, New Orleans.

5 Shedlin, M., and P. Hollerbach
   1981 "Modern and traditional fertility regulation in a Mexican community: the process of decision-making." Studies in Family Planning 12(6/7):278–296.

7 Sheppard, R.
   1982 "An underdog-eat-underdog world." Time, 14 June.

5 Sheps, M.
   1965 "An analysis of reproductive patterns in an American isolate." Population Studies 19:65–80.

16 Sheraton, M.
    1985 "International pot luck." Time 126(1):98–99.

15 Sherris, J.
    1985 "The impact of family planning programs on fertility." Population Reports, J-29, Population Information Program: Johns Hopkins University Press.

11 Shock, N.
    1974 "Physiological theories of aging." In M. Rockstein (ed.), Theoretical Aspects of Aging. New York: Academic Press.

7 Shryock, H.
   1964 Population Mobility within the United States. Chicago: University of Chicago Press.

1,7 Shryock, H., J. Siegel, and associates
     1973 The Methods and Materials of Demography. U.S. Bureau of the Census. Washington, D.C.: Government Printing Office.

7 Siegel, B.
   1982 "Alien's role: it depends on who is asked." Los Angeles Times, 14 December.

   Siegel, J.
1 1974 "Estimates of coverage of the population by sex, race, and age in the 1970 census." Demography 11:1–23.

11 1979 "Prospective Trends in the Size and Structure of the Elderly Population, Im-

pact of Mortality Trends, and Some Implications." Current Population Reports, Special Studies, Series P-23, No. 78.

1 Siegel, J., and J. Passel
   1979 "Coverage of the Hispanic Population of the United States in the 1970 Census: A Methodological Analysis." Current Population Reports, Series P-23, No. 82.

12 Simmel, G.
   1905 "The metropolis and mental life." In R. Sennet (ed.), Classic Essays on the Culture of Cities. New York: Appleton-Century-Crofts.

5 Simmons, A.
   1974 "Ambivalence toward small families in rural Latin America." Social Biology 21:127–43.

6 Simmons, G., C. Smucker, S. Bernstein, and E. Jensen
   1982 "Post-neonatal mortality in rural India: implications of an economic model." Demography 19(3):371–89.

11 Simmons, L.
   1960 "Aging in preindustrial societies." In C. Tibbetts (ed.), Handbook of Social Gerontology. Chicago: University of Chicago Press.

13 Simon, J.
   1981 The Ultimate Resource. Princeton: Princeton University Press.

14 Singer, P.
   1977 "Reconsidering the famine relief argument." In P. Brown and H. Shue (eds.), Food Policy: The Responsibility of the United States in the Life and Death Choices. New York: Free Press.

13 Sinquefield, J., and B. Sungkono
   1979 "Fertility and family planning trends in Java and Bali." International Family Planning Perspectives 5(2):43–58.

4 Sivin, I., F. Alvarez-Sanchez, S. Diaz, O. McDonald, P. Holma, E. Coutinho, and D. Robertson
   1982 "The NORPLANT contraceptive method: a report on three years of use." Studies in Family Planning 13(8/9):258–61.

2 Smith, D.
   1978 "Mortality and family in the colonial Chesapeake." Journal of Interdisciplinary History 8(3):403–27.

9 Smith, J., and F. Welch
   1981 "No time to be young: the economic prospects for large cohorts in the United States." Population and Development Review 7(1):71–83.

5 Smith, K.
   1951 The Malthusian Controversy, London: Routledge & Kegan Paul.

11, 16 Smith, L.
   1981 "J & J comes a long way from baby." Fortune, 1 June.

12 Smith, P., S. Khoo, and S. Go
   1983 "The migration of women to cities: a comparative perspective." In J. Fawcett, S. Khoo, and P. Smith (eds.), Women in the Cities of Asia: Migration and Urban Adaptation. Boulder, CO: Westview Press.

16 Smith, R.
   1986 "As birth rates rise, so should certain stocks." Wall Street Journal, 12 June.

12 Somer, R.
   1969 Personal Space. Englewood Cliffs, NJ: Prentice-Hall.

15 Soni, V.
   1983 "Thirty years of the Indian family planning program: past performance, future prospects." International Family Planning Perspectives 9(2):35–45.

7 Spaeth, A.
   1983 "With future of Hong Kong uncertain, singles see marriage as escape route." Wall Street Journal, 28 October.

16 Span, P.
   1981 "Advertisers adjust to aging population." San Diego Union, 1 June.

9 Speare, A., M. Speare, and H. Lin
   1973 "Urbanization, non-familial work, education, and fertility in Taiwan." Population Studies 27:323–34.

13 Spengler, J.
   1974 Population Change, Modernization, and Welfare. Englewood Cliffs, NJ: Prentice-Hall.

1 Spiegelman, M.
   1968 Introduction to Demography, revised edition. Cambridge: Harvard University Press.

10 Spitze, G., and J. Spaeth
   1979 "Employment among married female college graduates." Social Science Research 8(2):184–99.

2 Spooner, B. (ed.)
   1972 Population Growth: Anthropological Implications. Cambridge: MIT Press.

15 Srinivasan, K., P. H. Reddy, and K. N. M. Raju
   1978 "From one generation to the next: changes in fertility, family size preferences, and family planning in an Indian state between 1951 and 1975." Studies in Family Planning 9(10–11):258–71.

14 Srivastava, U., E. Heady, K. Rogers, and L. Mayer
    1975 Food Aid and International Economic Growth. Ames: Iowa State University Press.

7   Standefer, J., and A. Drehsler
    1980 "Secession by Hispanics: a reality in year 2000?" San Diego Union, 10 January: A-1.

11 Stanford, E. P.
    1978 The Elder Black. San Diego: San Diego State University, University Center on Aging.

3   Stangeland, C.
    1904 Pre-Malthusian Doctrines of Population. New York: Columbia University Press.

15 Stephenson, G.
    1964 A History of American Immigration. New York: Russell and Russell.

16 Sternlieb, G., and J. Hughes
    1984 "The housing locomotive (and the demographic caboose)." American Demographics 6(3):22–27.

16 Stokes, B.
    1981 "Global housing prospects: the resource constraints." Worldwatch Papers, No. 46. Washington, D.C.: Worldwatch Institute.

9   Stokes, C., and Y-S. Hsieh
    1983 "Female employment and reproductive behavior in Taiwan, 1980." Demography 20(3):313–31.

3   Stolnitz, G. J.
    1964 "The demographic transition: from high to low birth rates and death rates." Chap. 2 in Ronald Freedman (ed.), Population: The Vital Revolution. Garden City: Anchor Books.

    Stolzenberg, R., and L. Waite
10 1977 "Age, fertility expectations and plans for employment." American Sociological Review 42(5):769–83.

9   1984 "Local labor markets, children and labor force participation of wives." Demography 21(2):157–70.

7   Stone, L.
    1975 "On the interaction of mobility dimensions in theory on migration decisions." Canadian Review of Sociology and Anthropology 12:95–100.

7   Strouse, J.
    1980 "Act of desperation." Newsweek, 14 April.

13 Stycos, J.
    1971 Ideology, Faith and Family Planning in Latin America. New York: McGraw-Hill.

3   Sudoplatov, A.
    1978 "The apologetic role of modern bourgeois demography." In Valentey, D. (ed.), The Theory of Population: Essays in Marxist Research. Moscow: Progress Publishers.

14 Sundquist, W. B.
    1977 "The changing structure of U.S. agriculture: implications for world trade." World Development 5(5–7):573–83.

6   Sussman, G.
    1977 "Parisian infants and Norman wet nurses in the early nineteenth century: a statistical study." Journal of Interdisciplinary History 7(4):637–53.

1   Sutherland, I.
    1963 "John Graunt: a tercentenary tribute." Royal Statistical Society Journal, Series A, 126:536–37. Reprinted in K. Kammeyer, 1975. Population: Selected Essays and Research. Chicago: Rand McNally.

10 Swafford, M.
    1978 "Sex differences in Soviet earnings." American Sociological Review 43(5):657–73.

8   Sweet, J.
    1984 "Components of change in the number of households: 1970–1980." Demography 21(2):129–40.

5   Tabah, L.
    1980 "World population trends, a stocktaking." Population and Development Review 6(3):355–90.

3   Ta-k'un, W.
    1960 "A critique of neo-Malthusian theory." Excerpted in Population and Development Review, 1979, 5(4):699–707.

15 Tata, J.
    1987 "Population strategy for India." Populi 14(4):39–45.

9   Tawiah, E.
    1984 "Determinants of cumulative fertility in Ghana." Demography 21(1):1–8.

3   Teitelbaum, M. S.
    1975 "Relevance of demographic transition for developing countries." Science 188:420–25.

3   Thompson, W.
    1929 "Population." American Journal of Sociology 34(6):959–75.

10 Thornton, A., and D. Freedman
    1983 "The changing American family." Population Bulletin 38(4).

15 Tien, H.
    1984 "Induced fertility transition: impact of

population planning and socio-economic change in the People's Republic of China." Population Studies 38(3):385–400.

4 Tietze, C., and S. Lewit
1977 "Legal abortion." Scientific American 236(1):21–27.

10 Tillion, G.
1983 The Republic of Cousins: Women's Oppression in Mediterranean Society. London: Al Saqi Books.

14 Time
1976 "India: war on rats." 31 May.

14 Timmer, C., and W. Falcon
1983 Food Policy Analysis. Baltimore: The Johns Hopkins Press, for the World Bank.

3 Tobias, A.
1979 "The only article on inflation you need to read: we're getting poorer, but we can do something about it." Esquire 92(5):49–55.

12 Tobin, G.
1976 "Suburbanization and the development of motor transportation: transportation technology and the suburbanization process." In B. Schwartz (ed.), The Changing Face of the Suburbs. Chicago: University of Chicago Press.

7,16 Toffler, A.
1970 Future Shock. New York: Bantam Books.

4 Tolor, A., F. Rice, and C. Lanctot
1975 "Personality patterns of American couples practicing the temperature-rhythm method of birth control." Journal of Sex Research 11:117–33.

16 Toman, B.
1982 "Doctors, lawyers feeling the pinch in the hard-hit industrial Midwest." Wall Street Journal, 5 August.

11 Torrey, B., K. Kinsella, and C. Taeuber
1987 "An aging world." U.S. Bureau of the Census, International Population Reports, Series P-95, No. 78.

2 Tsui, A. O., and D. J. Bogue
1978 "Declining world fertility: trends, causes, implications." Population Bulletin 33(4).

5 Turchi, B.
1975 "Microeconomic theories of fertility: a critique." Social Forces 54(1):107–25.

12 Turner, F.
1976 "The rush to the cities in Latin America." Science 192:955–62.

4 Udry, J., and R. Cliquet
1982 "A cross-cultural examination of the relationship between ages at menarche, marriage, and first birth." Demography 19(1):53–64.

United Nations

6 1953 Causes and Consequences of Population Trends. New York: United Nations.

1 1958 Principles and Recommendations for National Population Censuses. Statistical Papers, Series M, No. 27. New York: United Nations.

15 1963 Proceedings of the Asian Population Conference. New York: United Nations.

1 1970 Methods of Measuring Internal Migration. Department of Economic and Social Affairs, Population Studies, No. 47. New York: United Nations.

1 1973a Demographic Yearbook. New York: United Nations.

3 1973b The Determinants and Consequences of Population Trends: New Summary of Findings on Interaction of Demographic, Economic, and Social Factors, Volume I. New York: United Nations.

1,6 1974 Demographic Yearbook. New York: United Nations.

12,13 1975 National Accounts Statistics Yearbook, 1974, Vol. III. New York: United Nations.

13 1976 National Accounts Statistics Yearbook, Volume III. New York: United Nations.

11 1977 Demographic Yearbook, 1976. New York: United Nations.

11 1978a Demographic Yearbook, 1977. New York: United Nations.

13 1978b Yearbook of National Accounts Statistics, 1977, Vol. 2. New York: United Nations.

2 1978c "Population vital statistic report, data available as of 1 October 1978." Statistical Papers, Series A. Vol. 30(4). New York: United Nations.

1,7 1979 Trends and Characteristics of International Migration Since 1950. Department of Economic and Social Affairs, Demographic Studies No. 64. New York: United Nations.

2 1981 World Population Prospects as Assessed in 1980. Population Studies Report No. 78. New York: United Nations.

7 1982a World Population Trends and Policies: 1981 Monitoring Report, Volume I. New York: United Nations.

15 1982b World Population Trends and Policies: 1981 Monitoring Report, Volume II. New York: United Nations.

12	1982c	Estimates and Projections of Urban, Rural and City Populations, 1950–2025: The 1980 Assessment. New York: United Nations.
2	1982d	Model Life Tables for Developing Countries (ST/ESA/SER.A/77). New York: United Nations.
13	1983	Yearbook of National Accounts Statistics, 1981. New York: United Nations.
2	1986	World Population Prospects: Estimates and Projections as Assessed in 1984. New York: United Nations.
13	1987	National Accounts Statistics: Main Aggregates and Detailed Tables, 1985. New York: United Nations.
13	1988	National Accounts Statistics: Analysis of Main Aggregates, 1985. New York: United Nations.

United Nations Fund for Population Activities (UNFPA)

15	1985	"Laos—a push towards larger and healthier families." Population 11(2):1.
13	1987	1986 Report by the Executive Director. New York: United Nations.

4	Universal Press Syndicate

	1982	"Dear Abby," 3 March.

U.S. Bureau of the Census

9	1970	Census of Population. Characteristics of the Population, Part I—Section 2.
7	1972	Current Population Reports, Series P-20, No. 235.
1	1973	Census of Population and Housing: 1970. Estimates of Coverage by Sex, Race, and Age: Demographic Analysis. Washington, D.C.: Government Printing Office.
1	1974	1970 Census of Population. Accuracy of Data for Selected Population Characteristics As Measured by Reinterview. Washington, D.C.: Government Printing Office.
1,7, 15	1975a	1970 Census of Population. Accuracy of Data for Selected Population Characteristics As Measured by the 1970 CPS-Census Match. Washington, D.C.: Government Printing Office.
10	1975b	Current Population Reports, Series P-20, No. 287.
9	1975c	Current Population Reports, Special Studies Series P-23, No. 54.
7,15	1975d	Historical Statistics of the United States. Washington, D.C.: Government Printing Office.
7,9	1976a	Current Population Reports, Series P-20, No. 292.
9	1976b	Current Population Reports, Series P-20, No. 297.

9	1976c	Current Population Reports, Series P-60, No. 101.
5	1977a	Country Demographic Profiles: Sri Lanka.
5	1977b	Country Demographic Profiles: Ghana.
5,15	1978a	Country Demographic Profiles: India.
11	1978b	"Annual housing survey, 1976: United States and regions." Current Housing Reports, Series H-150-76.
11	1978c	"Demographic Aspects of Aging and the Older Population in the United States." Current Population Reports, Special Studies, Series P-23, No. 59 (revised).
15	1978e	Country Demographic Profiles: Republic of China.
1	1979a	1980 Census Update, Supplement to Data User News, Issue No. 9:1–2.
13	1979b	Country Demographic Profiles: Indonesia. Report #15P-DP-18.
7,13	1979c	Country Demographic Profiles: Mexico. Report #ISP-DP-14.
12	1979h	"Social and Economic Characteristics of the Metropolitan and Non-Metropolitan Population: 1970 and 1977." Current Population Reports, Series P-23, No. 75.
2,5,7	1979j	"Illustrative Projections of World Population to the 21st Century." Current Population Reports, Series P-23, No. 79.
12	1979k	"The Journey to Work in the United States, 1975." Current Population Reports, Series P-23, No. 99.
9	1979l	"Estimates of the Population of the United States and Components of Change: 1940 to 1978." Current Population Reports, Series P-25, No. 802.
16	1979n	"Projections of the Number of Households and Families: 1979 to 1995." Current Population Reports, Series P-25, No. 805.
1	1980	"Why do we need the census?" Census '80 Information.
10, 11	1983c	"Population Profile of the United States: 1982." Current Population Reports, Series P-23, No. 130.
9	1983d	"Estimates of the Population of the United States, by Age, Sex, and Race: 1980 to 1982." Current Population Reports, Series P-25, No. 929.
5	1983f	"International Fertility Indicators." Current Population Reports, Series P-20, No. 123.
16	1983g	"Voting and Registration in the Election of November 1982." Current Population Reports, Series P-20, No. 383.
9	1984b	"Educational Attainment in the United States: March 1981 and 1980." Current

Population Reports, Series P-20, No. 390.

9,10, 11 1984d 1980 Census of Population, Vol. I, Detailed Population Characteristics, U.S. Summary. Washington, D.C.: Government Printing Office.

9 1984e "Earnings by Occupation and Education." 1980 Census of Population, Vol. 2, Subject Reports. Washington, D.C.: Government Printing Office.

11 1984h "Demographic and Socioeconomic Aspects of Aging in the United States." Current Population Reports, Series P-23, No. 138.

12 1984i 1980 Census of Population, Subject Reports, "Journey to Work," Section 1. Washington, D.C.: Government Printing Office.

9 1985a "Population Profile of the United States, 1983/84." Current Population Reports, Series P-23, No. 145.

9 1985b "Urban and rural housing characteristics." Current Housing Reports, Series H-150-83, Annual Housing Survey, 1983, Part E.

16 1987a "Money Income of Households, Families, and Persons in the United States: 1985." Current Population Reports, Series P-60, No. 156.

5 1987b "Fertility of American Women: June 1986." Current Population Reports, Series P-20, No. 421.

9 1987c "Money Income and Poverty Status of Families and Persons in the United States: 1986." Advance Data from the March 1987 Current Population Survey. Current Population Reports, Series P-60, No. 157.

11 1987d "Voting and Registration in the Election of November 1986." Current Population Reports, Series P-20, No. 414.

7 1987e "Geographic Mobility: 1985." Current Population Reports, Series P-20, No. 420.

9 1987f "Marital Status and Living Arrangements: March 1986." Current Population Reports, Series P-20, No. 418.

9 1987g "Household Wealth and Asset Ownership: 1984." Data from the Survey of Income and Program Participation. Current Population Reports, Series P-70, No. 7.

7 U.S. Committee for Refugees
1987 World Refugee Survey: 1986 in Review. Washington, D.C.: American Council for Nationalities Services.

1 U.S. Department of Commerce

1986 U.S. Statistical Abstract, 1987. Washington, D.C.: Government Printing Office.

U.S. Department of Justice
8 1971 Crime in the United States, 1970. Washington, D.C.: Federal Bureau of Investigation.

8 1981 Crime in the United States, 1980. Washington, D.C.: Federal Bureau of Investigation.

8 1983 Uniform Crime Reports of the Federal Bureau of Investigation, 1982. Washington, D.C.: Government Printing Office.

8 1986 Uniform Crime Reports, 1986. Washington, D.C.: Government Printing Office.

U.S. Department of Labor
11 1977 Handbook of Labor Statistics, 1977. Washington, D.C.: Government Printing Office.

10 1979 Handbook of Labor Statistics, 1978. Washington, D.C.: Government Printing Office.

16 1982 Occupational Outlook Handbook, 1982–83 Edition. Washington, D.C.: Government Printing Office.

10, 11 1983 Handbook of Labor Statistics. Washington, D.C.: Government Printing Office.

16 1986 Occupational Outlook Handbook, 1986–87 Edition. Washington, D.C.: Government Printing Office.

U.S. Immigration and Naturalization Service
7 1977 1977 Annual Report of the Immigration and Naturalization Service. Washington, D.C.: Government Printing Office.

7 1983 1980 Statistical Yearbook of the Immigration and Naturalization Service. Washington, D.C.: Government Printing Office.

U.S. News and World Report
1 1977 "Our world gets smaller and smaller." 18 July.

5 Urbina, M. (ed.)
1988 Encuesta Nacional Sobre Fecundiad y Salud 1987, Memoria de la Reunion Celebrada el 18 de Febrero de 1988. Mexico: Secretario de Salud, La Direccion General de Planificacion Familiar.

13 Urquidi, V.
1975 Chap. 21 in W. Oltman, On Growth II. New York: Capricorn Books.

13 1987 "Perspectivas sobre la poblacion y el empleo en la frontera norte." Binational Symposium on Population Issues Along the U.S.-Mexico Border, Tijuana, Mexico.

11 Valle, R., and L. Mendoza
1978 The Elder Latino. San Diego: San Diego

State University, University Center on Aging.

13 Van de Walle, E.
1975   "Foundations of the model of doom." Science 189:1077–78.

Van de Walle, E., and J. Knodel

3   1967   "Demographic transition and fertility decline: the European case." In Proceedings of the International Population Conference, Sydney, Australia.

3,5   1980   "Europe's fertility transition: new evidence and lessons for today's developing world." Population Bulletin 34(6).

3 Van de Walle, F.
1980   "Education and the demographic transition in Switzerland." Population and Development Review 6(3):463–72.

15 Van der Wijst, T.
1985   "Transmigration in Indonesia: an evaluation of a population redistribution policy. Population Research and Policy Review 4(1):1–30.

4 Veevers, J. E.
1973   "Voluntary childless wives: an exploratory study." Sociology and Social Research 57(2):356–66.

5 Venieris, Y.
1979   "Dynamic responses of fertility in the U.S.: a stock adjustment model." Presented at the European annual meeting of the Econometric Society, Athens.

15 Vicker, R.
1982   "Ecology-minded Oregon, in need of jobs, makes industry feel a bit more welcome." Wall Street Journal, 15 July.

1,2,5 Visaria, P., and L. Visaria
1981   "India's population: second and growing." Population Bulletin 36(4).

11 Viscusi, W. K.
1979   Welfare of the Elderly: An Economic Analysis and Policy Prescription. New York: Wiley.

14 Wade, N.
1974   "Green revolution (II): problems of adopting a western technology." Science 186:1186–92.

10 Waite, L., and R. Stolzenberg
1976   "Intended childbearing and labor force participation of young women: insights from nonrecursive models." American Sociological Review 41(2):235–51.

Wall Street Journal

5   1981a   "College entrance-test scores." 29 September.

16   1981b   "The books that businessmen are reading." 25 June.

15   1981c   "Soviets seek to boost birthrate with bonuses." 4 June.

6,9   1982   "Death on the road." 14 April.

16   1983a   "Financial services aimed at homosexuals thrive in some places." 10 February.

16   1983b   "CBS sets its eye on potentially huge Chinese TV market." 1 June.

15   1984a   "The people peril." 20 July.

16   1984b   "R. J. Reynolds unit, China sign a pact for cigarette plant." 30 May.

15   1985a   "Norway moves to boost birthrate." 16 January.

16   1985b   "Beatrice Co. agrees to venture in China." 19 March.

16   1985c   "New-wave perks help keep baby-boomer executives happy." 23 April.

16   1985d   "Sneaker-maker Nike eyes China's two billion feet." 11 December.

16   1987   "Chrysler Corp. to enter Chinese market with major sale of engine equipment." 21 July.

16   1988   "Market watch." 26 January.

Walsh, D.

16   1983a   "Banking on demographics." American Demographics 5(6):40–41.

16   1983b   "The grapes of growth." American Demographics 5(5):32–35.

8,15 1984   "Consider college towns." American Demographics 6(4):16–21.

16   1985a   "Rating the test markets." American Demographics 7(5):38–43.

16   1985b   "Huguley Hospital advertises fitness." American Demographics 7(6):16.

16 Walsh, D., and A. Lloyd
1984   "Personnel planning's new agenda." American Demographics 6(9):35–37.

Walsh, J.

13   1974   "U.N. conference: topping any agenda is the question of development." Science 185:1144.

14   1975   "U.S. agribusiness and agricultural trends." Science 188:531–34.

5 Ware, H.
1975   "The limits of acceptable family size in western Nigeria." Journal of Biosocial Science 7:273–96.

7 Warren, R., and J. Passel
1987   "A count of the uncountable: estimates of undocumented aliens counted in the 1980 United States census." Demography 24(3):375.

9 Washburn, W.
1984   "Queuing up for quotas via the census." Wall Street Journal, 26 July.

12 Weber, A.
1899   The Growth of Cities in the Nineteenth Century. New York: Columbia University Press.

16 Weber, A.

1982 "Nobody has 'stolen' American productivity." San Diego Union, 21 November.

Weeks, J.

12 1970 "Urban and rural natural increase in Chile." Milbank Memorial Fund Quarterly 48(1):71–89.

6,10 1976 Teenage Marriages: A Demographic Analysis. Studies in Population and Urban Demography: No. 2. Westport: Greenwood Press.

2 1978 Population: Introduction to Concepts and Issues, 1st Edition. Belmont, CA: Wadsworth.

11 1979 "Retirement homes: economic realities and implications for ethnic minority elders." In E. Percil Stanford (ed.), Retirement: Concepts and Realities of Ethnic Minority Elders. San Diego: San Diego State University, University Center on Aging.

9 1981 Population: Introduction to Concepts and Issues, 2nd Edition. Belmont, CA: Wadsworth.

4 1982 "An evaluation of the use-effectiveness of fertility awareness methods of family planning." Journal of Biosocial Science 14(1):32–38.

8 1984 Aging: Concepts and Social Issues. Belmont, CA: Wadsworth.

7 Weeks, J., and J. Spielberg
1979 "The ethnodemography of midwestern Mexican Americans." In S. West and J. Macklin (eds.), The Chicano Experience. Boulder, CO: Westview Press.

11 Weg, R.
1975 "Changing physiology of aging: normal and pathological." In D. Woodruff and J. Birreu (eds.), Aging: Scientific Perspectives and Social Issues. New York: Van Nostrand.

10 Weinrich, A.
1979 Women and Racial Discrimination in Rhodesia. New York: United Nations.

9 Weisbord, R.
1973 "Birth control and the black American: a matter of genocide?" Demography 10:571–90.

12 Weller, R., J. Mascisco, and G. Martine
1971 "Relative importance of the components of urban growth in Latin America." Demography 8(2):225–32.

2 Wells, R.
1971 "Family size and fertility control in eighteenth-century America: a study of Quaker families." Population Studies 25(1):73–82.

2 1982 Revolutions in Americans' Lives. Westport: Greenwood Press.

1 1985 Uncle Sam's Family: Issues in and Perspective on American Demographic History. Albany: State University of New York Press.

10 Wells, T.
1984 "Starting too soon." Popline 6(6):8.

2 Westing, A.
1981 "A note on how many humans have ever lived." BioScience 31(7):523–24.

Westoff, C.

9,10 1976a "The decline of unplanned births in the United States." Science 191:38–41.

4,9 1976b "Trends in contraceptive practice: 1965–1973." Family Planning Perspectives 8:54–58.

10 1978a "Some speculations on the future of marriage and fertility." Family Planning Perspectives 10(2):79–83.

10 1978b "Marriage and fertility in the developed countries." Scientific American 239(6):51–57.

9 Westoff, C., and E. Jones
1979 "The end of 'Catholic' fertility." Demography 16(2):209–17.

8 Westoff, C., and R. Rindfuss
1974 "Sex preselection in the United States: some implications." Science 184:633–36.

4 Westoff, C., and N. Ryder
1977 "The predictive validity of reproductive intentions." Demography 14(4):431–54.

4,15 Westoff, L., and C. Westoff
1971 From Now To Zero. Boston: Little, Brown.

15 Widjojo, N.
1970 Population Trends in Indonesia. Ithaca: Cornell University Press.

4 Wiest, W.
1982 "Hormonal contraception for men: acceptability and effects on sexuality." Studies in Family Planning 13(11):328–42.

6 Wigglesworth, A.
1983 "Mortality is linked to birth rates." Popline 5(6):7–8.

6 Wilder, M.
1976 "Differentials in health characteristics by marital status, United States, 1971–1972." Series 10, Data from the National Health Survey, No. 104, DHEW publication No. (HRA) 76–1531.

7 Williams, J.
1981 "The non-changing determinants of non-metropolitan migration." Rural Sociology 46(2):183–202.

Williams, J., and A. Sofranko

7   1979   "Motivations for the immigration component of population turnaround in nonmetropolitan areas." Demography 16(2):239–56.

7   1981   "Why people move." American Demographics 3(7):30–31.

Williamson, N.

8   1976   Sons or Daughters: A Cross-Cultural Survey of Parental Preferences. Beverly Hills, CA: Sage.

8   1983   "Parental sex preferences and sex selection." In N. Bennett (ed.), Sex Selection of Children. New York: Academic Press.

9   Wilson, W.

1978   The Declining Significance of Race. Chicago: University of Chicago Press.

16   Winans, R.

1983   "Investment advisor sees a 'Golden Age' ahead for economy, based on demographic trends." Wall Street Journal, 18 May.

11   Wing, S., K. Manton, E. Stallard, C. Hames, and H. Tyroler

1985   "The black/white mortality crossover: investigation in a community-based study." Journal of Gerontology 40(1):78–84.

12   Wirth, L.

1938   "Urbanism as a way of life." American Journal of Sociology 44:3–24.

16   Witt, B.

1983   "Having a baby? You might be able to save some money in Las Vegas." Wall Street Journal, 13 July.

Wittwer, S. H.

14   1975   "Food production, technology and the resource base." Science 188:579–84.

14   1977   "Assuring our food supply—technology, resources and policy." World Development 5(5–7):487–95.

7   Wolin, M.

1982   "Americans turn down many jobs vacated by ouster of aliens." Wall Street Journal, 6 December.

7   Woodrow, K.

1988   "Measuring net immigration to the United States—the emigrant population and recent emigration flows." Paper presented at the annual meeting of the Population Association of America, New Orleans.

World Bank

13, 1974   Population Policies and Economic Devel-
15   opment. Baltimore: Johns Hopkins University Press.

13, 1984a   World Development Report, 1984. New
15   York: Oxford University Press.

14   1984b   Toward Sustained Development in Sub-Saharan Africa. Washington, D.C.: World Bank.

15   1986   Population Growth and Policies in Sub-Saharan Africa. Washington, D.C.: World Bank.

13   1987   World Development Report, 1987. London: Oxford University Press.

Wortman, S.

14   1976   "Food and agriculture." Scientific American 23(3):30–39.

Wrigley, E. A.

1   1966   An Introduction to English Historical Demography. New York: Basic Books.

2   1969   Population and History. New York: World University Library.

5   1974   Population and History. New York: McGraw-Hill.

4   Yaukey, D.

1961   Fertility Differences in a Modernizing Country. Princeton, NJ: Princeton University Press.

12   Youssef, N.

1971   "Social structure and the female labor force: the case of women workers in Muslim Middle Eastern countries." Demography 8:427–39.

5   Zajonc, R.

1976   "Family configuration and intelligence." Science 192:227–36.

12   Zarate, A., and A. de Zarate

1975   "On the reconciliation of research findings of migrant–nonmigrant fertility differentials in urban areas." International Migration Review 9(2):115–56.

4,10 Zelnick, M., and J. Kantner

1980   "Sexual activity, contraceptive use and pregnancy among metropolitan area teenagers: 1971–1979. Family Planning Perspectives 12(5):230–37.

10   Zelnick, M., and F. Shah

1983   "First intercourse among young Americans." Family Planning Perspectives 15(2):64–69.

6   Zinsser, H.

1935   Rats, Lice and History. Boston: Little, Brown.

12   Zlaff, V.

1973   "Ethnic segregation in urban Israel." Demography 10(2):161–84.

12   Zuiches, J., and G. Fuguitt

1971   "Residential preferences: implications for population redistribution in nonmetropolitan areas." Mimeographed paper prepared for the U.S. Commission on Population Growth and the American Future.

INDEX